ELSEVIER'S
DICTIONARY OF
COMPUTER
GRAPHICS

ELSEVIER'S DICTIONARY OF COMPUTER GRAPHICS

in

English, German, French and Russian

compiled by

P. MANOILOV, G. MANOILOV and B. DELIJSKA
Sofia, Bulgaria

2000
ELSEVIER
Amsterdam – Lausanne – New York – Oxford – Shannon – Singapore – Tokyo

ELSEVIER SCIENCE B.V.
Sara Burgerhartstraat 25
P.O. Box 211, 1000 AE Amsterdam, The Netherlands

First edition 2000

Library of Congress Cataloging-in-Publication Data

Manoilov, P. (Peter), 1951-
  Elsevier's dictionary of computer graphics in English, German, French, and Russian /
compiled by P. Manoilov, G. Manoilov, and B. Delijska.-- 1st ed.
    p. cm.
  Includes bibliographical references.
  ISBN 0-444-50027-8 (alk. paper)
    1. Computer graphics--Dictionaries--Polyglot. 2. Dictionaries, Polyglot. I. Manoilov,
G. II. Deliiska, Boriana. III. Title.

  T385 .M35 2000
  006.6'03--dc21

                                                              00-060990

ISBN: 0-444-50027-8

♾ The paper used in this publication meets the requirements of ANSI/NISO Z39.48-1992 (Permanence of Paper).
Printed in The Netherlands.

PREFACE

The dictionary contains 10,540 terms with more than 2,600 cross-references that are commonly used in the theory and practice of computer graphics. We have included terms from all areas, related to a) the theory of computer graphics – descriptive geometry, projective geometry, topology, fractal geometry, color science; and b) the practice of computer graphics – computer-aided design (CAD) systems, technical drawing, computer art, computer animation, business graphics, scientific visualization, virtual reality, graphical programming, image processing, graphical computer devices.

Besides the commonly used terms in the above-mentioned areas, the dictionary also includes terms that are currently coming into use, especially in the areas of computer-aided design systems, computer art, computer animation, virtual reality, graphical programming. These terms were extracted from Internet sites and from current publications of journals in the respective languages.

The dictionary consists of two parts. In the first part, the *Basic Table*, the English terms are listed alphabetically and numbered consecutively. The English term is followed by its German, French and Russian equivalents. The synonyms of the English terms are also given as cross-references to the main entries, in their proper alphabetical order. The second part, *the Indexes,* contains separate alphabetical indexes of the German, French and Russian terms. The reference number(s) with each term stands for the number of the English term(s) in the basic table.

The authors hope that *Elsevier's Dictionary of Computer Graphics* will be a valuable tool for engineers, scientists, artists, students and for everyone who takes interest in computer graphics.

Dr. P. Manoilov
G. Manoilov
Dr. B. Delijska

BIBLIOGRAPHY

ed. J. Arvo, *Graphic gems* (Cornel University Academic Press, Ithaca, New York, 1991)

K. Becker, M. Dorfler, *Systèmes dynamiques et fractals* (Teknea, Toulouse-Barcelone-Marseille, 1991)

P. Croy, *Grafik, Form + Technik* (Muster-Schmidt Verlag, Göttingen, 1990)

G. Eisenreich, R. Sube, *Technik-Wörterbuch, Mathematik, Englisch-Deutsch-Französisch-Russisch* (VEB Verlag Technik, Berlin, 1982)

P. Haberäcker, *Digitale Bildverarbeitung* (Carl Hanser Verlag, München-Wien, 1989)

F. S. Hill Jr., *Computer Graphics* (Macmillan Publishing Company, New York, 1990)

D. Jackèl, *Grafik-Computer, Grundlagen, Architekturen und Konzepte computergrafischer Sichtsysteme* (Springer Verlag, Berlin, 1992)

W. J. Koschnick, *Standard Dictionary of Advertising Mass Media and Marketing* (Walter de Gruyter, New York, 1983)

K. Peeva, B. Delijska, *Elsevier's Dictionary of Computer Science and Mathematics* (Elsevier, Amsterdam, 1995)

K. Peeva, H.–J. Vogel, R. Lozanov, P. Peeva, *Elsevier's Dictionary of Mathematics* (Elsevier, Amsterdam, 2000)

Ph. Quéau, *Le virtuel* (Edition Champ Vallon, 1993)

St. Schiffermüller, *CorelDRAW 6–7–8* (Micro Application, Paris, 1998)

ред. М. Белоцерковский, *Машинная графика и вычислительная геометрия в задачах машиностроения* (АН СССР, Москва, 1989)

Т. Боув, Ч. Родс, *Настольная издательская система PAGEMAKER для персонального компьютера* (Финансы и статистика, Москва, 1991)

Д. Грайс, *Графические средства персонального компьютера* (Мир, Москва, 1989)

EXPLANATION OF SPECIAL SIGNS

1. The italics *d*, *f* and *r* in the basic table stand respectively for the German, French and Russian equivalents of the English terms.

2. The gender of nouns is indicated as follows:

f	feminine	*fpl*	feminine plural
m	masculine	*mpl*	masculine plural
n	neuter	*npl*	neuter plural

3. The symbol *v* designates a verb.

4. Synonyms and abbreviations are separated by semicolons.

5. The abbreviation (US) means American usage; (UK) means United Kingdom use.

6. Two kinds of brackets are used:

   [ ] the information can be either included or left out;

   ( ) the information does not form an integral part of the expression, but helps to clarify it.

Basic Table

A

1 abbreviated; abridged; reduced
d gekürzt; abgekürzt
f abrégé; écourté
r сокращенный; укороченный

2 abbreviation
d Kürzung *f*; Abkürzung *f*
f abrègement *m*; abréviation *f*; abréviature *f*
r сокращение *n*; аббревиатура *f*

3 aberration
d Aberration *f*
f aberration *f*
r аберрация *f*; отклонение *n*

4 aberration centre
d Aberrationszentrum *n*
f centre *m* d'aberration
r центр *m* аберрации

5 abort
d Abbruch *m*
f rupture *f*
r прерывание *n*; прекращение *n*

* **abridged → 1**

6 abridged notation
d abgekürzte Bezeichnung *f*
f notation *f* abrégée
r сокращенное обозначение *n*

7 abridged view
d abgekürzte Ansicht *f*
f vue *f* abrégée
r сокращенный вид *m*

8 abscissa
d Abszisse *f*
f abscisse *f*
r абсцисса *f*

9 abscissa of a point; X-coordinate of a point
d Abszisse *f* eines Punktes; X-Koordinate *f* eines Punktes
f abscisse *f* d'un point; première coordonnée *f* d'un point
r абсцисса *f* точки; Х-координата *f* точки; первая координата *f* точки

10 absence
d Fehlen *n*
f absence *f*

r отсутствие *n*

11 absence of correlation
d Unkorreliertheit *f*
f absence *f* de corrélation
r отсутствие *n* корреляции

12 absolute
d absolut
f absolu
r абсолютный

13 absolute altitude; absolute elevation; absolute height
d absolute Höhe *f*
f altitude *f* absolue
r абсолютная высота *f*

14 absolute coordinates
d absolute Koordinaten *fpl*
f coordonnées *fpl* absolues
r абсолютные координаты *fpl*

15 absolute cylindrical coordinates
d absolute zylindrische Koordinaten *fpl*
f coordonnées *fpl* cylindriques absolues
r абсолютные цилиндрические координаты *fpl*

* **absolute elevation → 13**

* **absolute height → 13**

16 absolute maximum; global maximum
d absolutes Maximum *n*; globales Maximum
f maximum *m* absolu; maximum global
r абсолютный максимум *m*; глобальный максимум

17 absolute minimum; global minimum
d absolutes Minimum *n*; globales Minimum
f minimum *m* absolu; minimum global
r абсолютный минимум *m*; глобальный минимум

18 absolute motion
d absolute Bewegung *f*; wahre Bewegung
f mouvement *m* absolu
r абсолютное движение *n*; истинное движение

19 absolute sensitivity
d Absolutempfindlichkeit *f*
f sensibilité *f* absolue
r абсолютная чувствительность *f*

20 absolute time scale
d absolute Zeitskala *f*
f échelle *f* absolue de temps
r абсолютная шкала *f* времени

21 absolute value
d Absolutwert *m*; absolute Größe *f*
f valeur *f* absolue
r абсолютная величина *f*; абсолютное значение *n*

22 absolute vector
d absoluter Vektor *m*
f vecteur *m* absolu
r абсолютный вектор *m*

23 absolute XY coordinates
d absolute XY-Koordinaten *fpl*
f coordonnées *fpl* XY absolues
r абсолютные XY координаты *fpl*

* **absorbability** → 33

* **absorbent** → 24

24 absorbing; absorbent
d absorbierend
f absorbant
r поглощающий; абсорбирующий

25 absorbing colors
d absorbierende Farben *fpl*
f couleurs *fpl* absorbantes
r поглощающие цвета *mpl*

26 absorbing filter; absorption filter
d Absorptionsfilter *m*; absorbierender Filter *m*
f filtre *m* absorbant; filtre d'absorption
r поглощающий фильтр *m*

27 absorbing layer
d absorbierende Schicht *f*
f couche *f* d'absorption; couche absorbante
r поглощающий слой *m*

* **absorptance** → 31

28 absorption
d Absorption *f*
f absorption *f*
r поглощение *n*

29 absorption analysis; spectral absorption analysis
d Absorptions[spektral]analyse *f*
f analyse *f* [spectrale] absorptive
r абсорбционный [спектральный] анализ *m*

30 absorption band
d Absorptionsband *n*
f bande *f* d'absorption
r полоса *f* поглощения

31 absorption coefficient; absorptance
d Absorptionskoeffizient *m*;

Absorptionsgrad *m*; Absorptionsfaktor *m*
f coefficient *m* d'absorption; facteur *m* d'absorption; absorptance *f*
r коэффициент *m* поглощения; степень *f* поглощения

* **absorption filter** → 26

32 absorption spectrum
d Absorptionsspektrum *n*
f spectre *m* d'absorption
r спектр *m* поглощения

33 absorptivity; absorbability
d Absorptionsvermögen *n*; Absorptionsfähigkeit *f*; Absorbierbarkeit *f*
f absorptivité *f*; absorbabilité *f*
r поглощающая способность *f*; абсорбируемость *f*; поглощаемость *f*; абсорбционная способность

34 abstract *adj*
d abstrakt
f abstrait
r абстрактный

35 abstract *v*
d abstrahieren
f abstraire
r абстрагировать

36 abstract functional structure
d abstrakte funktionale Struktur *f*
f structure *f* abstraite fonctionnelle
r абстрактная функциональная структура *f*

37 abstraction
d Abstraktion *f*
f abstraction *f*
r абстракция *f*

38 abstract space
d abstrakter Raum *m*
f espace *m* abstrait
r абстрактное пространство *n*

39 abundant; redundant; excessive
d reichlich; überflüssig; unmäßig
f abondant; redondant
r избыточный

40 accelerate *v*
d beschleunigen
f accélérer
r ускорять

41 accelerated graphics port; AGP
d beschleunigter Grafikport *m*; AGP
f port *m* graphique accéléré; AGP
r ускоренный графический порт *m*

42 accelerated motion
d beschleunigte Bewegung *f*
f mouvement *m* accéléré
r ускоренное движение *n*

43 accelerate *v* fills
d Füllungen beschleunigen
f accélérer des remplissages
r ускорять заливки; ускорять закрашивания

44 accelerate *v* objects
d Objekte beschleunigen
f accélérer des objets
r ускорять объекты

45 acceleration
d Beschleunigung *f*; Akzeleration *f*
f accélération *f*
r ускорение *n*; разгон *m*

46 acceleration slider
d Beschleunigungsschieber *m*
f glisseur *m* d'accélération
r ползунок *m* ускорения

* **accelerator → 48**

47 accelerator
d Beschleuniger *m*
f accélérateur *m*
r ускоритель *m*

48 accelerator [key]
d Beschleunigungstaste *f*
f clé *m* accélérateur
r быстрая клавиша *f*

49 accent
d Akzent *m*; Gravis *m*
f accent *m*
r акцент *m*; акцент *m*; ударение *n*

50 accentuate *v*; emphasize *v*
d betonen; hervorheben
f accentuer
r выделять

51 accept *v*
d annehmen; akzeptieren
f accepter
r воспринимать; принимать

52 acceptability
d Annehmbarkeit *f*
f acceptabilité *f*
r приемлемость *f*

53 acceptor
d Akzeptor *m*
f accepteur *m*; acheteur *m*

r акцептор *m*; приемник *m*

54 access
d Zugang *m*; Zugriff *m*
f accès *m*
r доступ *m*

55 accessibility; reachability; attainability
d Erreichbarkeit *f*; Zugänglichkeit *f*
f accessibilité *f*
r достижимость *f*; доступность *f*

56 accessible boundary point
d erreichbarer Randpunkt *m*
f point *m* frontière accessible
r достижимая граничная точка *f*

57 accessible point
d erreichbarer Punkt *m*
f point *m* accessible
r достижимая точка *f*

58 accessible space
d erreichbarer Raum *m*
f espace *m* accessible
r достижимое пространство *n*

59 accessible vertex
d erreichbarer Knoten *m*
f sommet *m* accessible
r достижимая вершина *f*

60 access level
d Zugriff-Pegel *m*
f niveau *m* d'accès
r уровень *m* доступа

61 accessory
d Zubehör *n*
f accessoire *m*
r аксессуар *m*; реквизит *m*;
     принадлежность *f*

62 accessory analytical plane
d akzessorische analytische Ebene *f*
f plan *m* analytique accessoire
r присоединенная аналитическая
     плоскость *f*

63 accessory point
d akzessorischer Punkt *m*
f point *m* accessoire
r присоединенная точка *f*

* **accidental → 7728**

64 accommodate *v*
d anpassen
f accommoder
r аккомодировать; приспасабливать

65 **accommodation**
d Unterbringung *f*; Akkommodation *f*
f accommodation *f*
r аккомодация *f*; приспосабливание *n*

66 **accommodation of lens**
d Linsenakkommodation *f*
f accommodation *f* de lentille
r аккомодация *f* линзы

* **accordance** → 2018

67 **account**
d Rechnung *f*
f compte *m*; décompte *m*
r расчет *m*; смета *f*

68 **accumulate** *v*
d akkumulieren; ansammeln; anhäufen
f accumuler
r аккумулировать; накапливать

69 **accumulated error; stored error; cumulative error**
d akkumulierter Fehler *m*; kumulativer Fehler
f erreur *f* [ac]cumulée
r накопленная ошибка *f*

70 **accumulation point**
d Häufungspunkt *m*
f point *m* d'accumulation
r точка *f* накопления

71 **accuracy; exactness; exactitude; precision; fidelity**
d Genauigkeit *f*; Exaktheit *f*; Präzision *f*; Treue *f*
f exactitude *f*; précision *f*; fidélité *f*
r точность *f*; верность *f*

* **accuracy grade** → 78

72 **accuracy of drawing; drawing accuracy; accuracy of tracing; accuracy of plotting**
d Zeichengenauigkeit *f*; Plottengenauigkeit *f*
f précision *f* du traçage; précision de tracement
r точность *f* вычерчивания; точность черчения

73 **accuracy of elevation**
d Höhengenauigkeit *f*
f précision *f* altimétrique
r точность *f* высотных точек

74 **accuracy of map**
d Kartengenauigkeit *f*
f précision *f* de la carte
r точность *f* карты

75 **accuracy of measurement; measurement**

accuracy; precision of measurement; measurement precision
d Messgenauigkeit *f*
f précision *f* de la mesure; exactitude *f* de la mesure
r точность *f* измерения

* **accuracy of plotting** → 72

76 **accuracy of position; planimetric accuracy**
d Lagegenauigkeit *f*
f précision *f* planimétrique
r точность *f* позиции; точность планового положения

77 **accuracy of survey**
d Genauigkeit *f* der Aufnahme
f précision *f* de levé
r точность *f* съемки

* **accuracy of tracing** → 72

78 **accuracy rating; accuracy grade**
d Genauigkeitsgrenze *f*; Genauigkeitsgrad *m*; Genauigkeitsklasse *f*
f degré *m* de précision; classe *f* d'exactitude; classe de précision
r степень *f* точности; класс *m* точности

79 **accuracy requirement**
d Genauigkeitsanspruch *m*
f nécessité *f* de précision
r требование *n* к точности

* **achromate** → 81, 84

80 **achromate eyepiece**
d achromatisches Okular *n*
f oculaire *m* achromatique
r ахроматический окуляр *m*

81 **achromatic; achromate**
d achromatisch; farblos
f achromatique; incolore
r ахроматический; бесцветный

82 **achromatic color**
d achromatische Farbe *f*
f couleur *f* acromatique; plage *f* de gris
r ахроматический цвет *m*

83 **achromaticity**
d Farblosigkeit *f*
f achromaticité *f*
r ахроматичность *f*; бесцветность *f*

84 **achromatic lens; achromatic objective; achromate**
d achromatische Linse *f*; Achromat *m*

f lentille *f* achromatique; achromat *m*
r ахроматическая линза *f*; ахромат *m*

85 achromatic light
d achromatisches Licht *n*
f lumière *f* achromatique
r ахроматический свет *m*

* **achromatic objective** → 84

86 achromatic prism
d achromatisches Prisma *n*
f prisme *m* achromatique
r ахроматическая призма *f*

87 achromatism
d Achromatismus *m*
f achromatisme *m*
r ахроматизм *m*

88 achromatism of magnification
d Achromatismus *m* der Vergrößerung
f achromatisme *m* de grossissement
r ахроматизм *m* увеличения

* **acnodal point** → 89

89 acnode; acnodal point; isolated point
d isolierter Punkt *m*
f acnòde *m*; point *m* acnodal; point isolé
r изолированная точка *f*

90 acoustic; sound; phonic; tone; audio
d akustisch; Ton-; Laut-; Schall-
f acoustique; sonore; son
r акустический; звуковой; тональный; аудио-

91 acoustic tablet
d akustisches Tablett *n*
f tablette *f* acoustique
r акустический планшет *m*

* **acoustooptic** → 92

92 acoustooptic[al]
d akustooptisch
f acousto-optique
r акустооптический

93 acoustooptical effect
d akustooptischer Effekt *m*
f effet *m* acousto-optique
r акустооптический эффект *m*

94 actinic
d aktinisch
f actinique
r актинический

95 actinic focus
d aktinischer Fokus *m*
f foyer *m* actinique
r актинический фокус *m*

96 actinic light
d aktinisches Licht *n*
f lumière *f* actinique
r актинический свет *m*

97 actinism
d Aktinismus *m*
f actinisme *m*
r актинизм *m*; актиничность *f*

98 action
d Aktion *f*; Wirkung *f*
f action *f*
r действие *n*; воздействие *n*

99 action choice
d Aktionsauswahl *f*
f option *f* d'action; commande *f* immédiate
r выбор *m* действия

100 action redoing
d Aktionswiederherstellung *f*
f rétablissement *m* d'action
r переделывание *n* действия

101 activate *v*
d aktivieren; einschalten; anregen
f activer; agir
r активи[зи]ровать; воздействовать

102 activated layer
d aktivierte Schicht *f*
f plan *m* activé
r активизированный слой *m*

103 activation
d Aktivierung *f*; Einschaltung *f*
f activation *f*
r актив[из]ация *f*; возбуждение *n*

104 active
d aktiv; wirksam
f actif
r активный; действенный

105 active dimension style
d aktiver Dimensionsstil *m*
f style *m* de cotation actif; style de cote actif
r активный стиль *m* измерения; активный стиль размерности

106 active document
d aktives Dokument *n*
f document *m* actif
r активный документ *m*

107 active edge
   d aktive Kante *f*
   f arête *f* active
   r активное ребро *n*

108 active layer; current layer
   d aktive Schicht *f*
   f plan *m* actif; plan courant
   r активный слой *m*; рабочий слой

109 active layer property
   d Eigenschaft *f* der aktiven Schicht
   f propriété *f* de plan actif
   r свойство *n* активного слоя

110 active line
   d Aktivlinie *f*
   f ligne *f* active
   r активная линия *f*

111 active linetype
   d aktiver Linientyp *m*
   f type *m* de ligne actif
   r активный тип *m* линии

112 active matrix
   d Aktivmatrix *f*
   f matrice *f* active
   r активная матрица *f*

113 active-matrix color screen
   d Aktivmatrix-Farbbildschirm *m*
   f écran *m* couleur à matrice active
   r цветной экран *m* на активной матрице

114 active object
   d aktives Objekt *n*
   f objet *m* actif
   r активный объект *m*

115 active profile
   d aktives Profil *n*
   f profil *m* actif
   r активный профиль *m*

116 active region
   d aktive Region *f*
   f région *f* active
   r активный регион *m*

117 active selection
   d aktive Auswahl *f*
   f sélection *f* active
   r активный выбор *m*

118 active selection set
   d aktiver Auswahlsatz *m*
   f ensemble *m* de sélection actif
   r активная совокупность *f* выбора

119 active sensor
   d aktiver Sensor *m*
   f senseur *m* actif
   r активный сенсор *m*

120 active space
   d aktiver Raum *m*
   f espace *m* actif
   r активное пространство *n*

121 active status
   d aktiver Status *m*
   f état *m* actif
   r активное состояние *n*

122 active style
   d aktiver Stil *m*
   f style *m* actif
   r активный стиль *m*

123 active text style
   d aktiver Textstil *m*
   f style *m* de texte actif
   r активный текстовой стиль *m*

124 active UCS
   d aktives Benutzerkoordinatensystem *n*
   f système *m* de coordonnées utilisateur actif
   r активная пользовательская система *f* координат

125 active viewpoint
   d aktiver Aug[en]punkt *m*
   f point *m* de vue actif
   r активная точка *f* зрения

126 active viewport
   d aktives Ansichtsfenster *n*
   f clôture *f* active
   r активная область *f* просмотра; активное окно *n* просмотра

127 active window
   d aktives Fenster *n*
   f fenêtre *f* active
   r активное окно *n*

128 ActiveX automation
   d ActiveX-Automation *f*
   f automation *f* ActiveX
   r ActiveX автоматизация *f*

129 ActiveX event
   d ActiveX-Ereignis *n*
   f événement *m* ActiveX
   r ActiveX событие *n*

130 activity
   d Aktivität *f*

f activité *f*
r активность *f*

* **actor** → 9432

* **actual** *adj* → 2346

131 act *v* **without fixed points**
d fixpunktfrei operieren
f opérer sans points fixes
r действовать без неподвижных точек

132 acuity
d Schärfe *f*
f acuité *f*
r острота *f*

* **acute** → 135

133 acute
d spitz; scharf
f aigu
r острый

134 acute angle
d spitzer Winkel *m*
f angle *m* aigu
r острый угол *m*

135 acute[-angled]
d spitzwinklig
f acutangle
r остроугольный

136 acute bisectrix
d spitze Bisektrix *f*
f bissectrice *f* aigue
r остроугольная биссектриса *f*

137 acute triangle
d spitzwinkliges Dreieck *n*
f triangle *m* acutangle
r остроугольный треугольник *m*

138 acyclic; circuit-free; loopfree
d azyklisch; kreisfrei; zyklusfrei; schlingenfrei; schleifenfrei
f acyclique; sans circuits; sans cycles; sans boucles
r ациклический; ацикличный; без циклов

139 acyclic graph; circuit-free graph; graph without loops
d azyklischer Graph *m*; kreisfreier Graph; zyklusfreier Graph; Graph ohne Schleifen
f graphe *m* acyclique; graphe sans circuits; graphe sans cycles; graphe sans boucles
r ациклический граф *m*; граф без циклов; граф без контуров; граф без петель

140 adapt *v*
d anpassen
f adapter
r адаптировать; приспосабливать

141 adaptable; adaptive
d anpassungsfähig; adaptiv
f adaptable; adaptatif
r адаптивный; совместимый

142 adaptation
d Anpassung *f*
f adaptation *f*
r адаптация *f*

* **adaptive** → 141

143 adaptive filter
d adaptiver Filter *m*
f filtre *m* adaptatif
r адаптивный фильтр *m*

144 adaptive image restoration
d adaptiver Bildwiederaufbau *m*
f restauration *f* d'image adaptative
r адаптивное восстановление *n* изображения

* **adaptive meshing** → 7711

145 adaptive unsharp filter
d adaptiver unscharfer Filter *m*
f filtre *m* non distinct adaptatif
r адаптивный нерезкий фильтр *m*

146 add *v*
d addieren; hinzufügen
f additionner; sommer; ajouter
r складывать; суммировать; прибавлять; добавить; добавлять

147 add *v* **frame**
d Frame hinzufügen
f ajouter un cadre
r добавить кадр

* **add-in** → 150

148 add-in manager
d Add-In-Manager *m*
f gestionnaire *m* additionnel
r добавляемый менажер *m*

149 addition; summation; summing
d Addition *f*; Summierung *f*
f sommation *f*; addition *f*
r сложение *n*; суммирование *n*

150 additional; additive; add-in
d additiv; erweitert; zusätzlich; nachträglich; Add-In-

    f additionnel; additif
    r дополнительный; аддитивный; добавляемый; расширяемый

   * **additive** → 150

151 additive blend
    d additive Überblendung *f*
    f dégradé *m* additif
    r аддитивное переливание *n*

152 additive chromatic system; additive color system
    d additives Farbsystem *n*; Normalfarbsystem *n*
    f système *m* chromatique additif
    r аддитивная хроматическая система *f*; система аддитивного синтеза цветов

153 additive color mixing
    d additive Farbmischung *f*
    f mélange *m* de couleurs additif
    r аддитивное смешивание *n* цветов

154 additive color model
    d additives Farbmodell *n*
    f modèle *m* de couleur additif
    r аддитивная цветовая модель *f*

155 additive colors; additive primaries
    d additiv vermischte Primärfarben *fpl*; additiv vermischte Farben *fpl*
    f couleurs *fpl* obtenues par synthèse additive
    r аддитивно смешиваемые цвета *mpl*; аддитивные первичные цвета

   * **additive color system** → 152

156 additive mask
    d additive Maske *f*
    f masque *f* additive
    r аддитивная маска *f*

157 additive mask mode
    d Modus *m* der additiven Maske
    f mode *m* de masque additive
    r режим *m* аддитивной маски

158 additive noise level
    (in the images)
    d additiver Geräuschpegel *m*
    f niveau *m* de bruit additif
    r уровень *m* аддитивной помехи

   * **additive primaries** → 155

159 additive rotation
    d additive Drehung *f*; zusätzliche Rotation *f*
    f rotation *f* additive
    r аддитивное вращение *n*

160 additivity
    d Additivität *f*
    f additivité *f*
    r аддитивность *f*

161 additivity of luminance
    d Luminanzadditivität *f*
    f additivité *f* de luminance
    r аддитивность *f* светового излучения

162 add *v* noise
    d Rauschen hinzufügen
    f ajouter un bruit
    r добавить шум

163 add *v* perspective
    d Perspektive hinzufügen
    f ajouter une perspective
    r добавить перспективу

164 add *v* preset
    d Voreinstellung hinzufügen
    f ajouter une présélection
    r добавлять предварительную установку

165 address
    d Adresse *f*
    f adresse *f*
    r адрес *m*

166 address *v*
    d adressieren
    f adresser
    r адресовать

167 addressability
    d Adressbereich *m*
    f adressabilité *f*; possibilité *f* d'adressage; capacité *f* d'adressage
    r адресуемость *f*

168 addressable coursor; addressing coursor
    d adressierbarer Kursor *m*
    f curseur *m* adressable
    r адресуемый курсор *m*

169 addressable point
    d adressierbarer Punkt *m*
    f point *m* adressable; position *f* adressable
    r адресуемая позиция *f*

   * **addressing coursor** → 168

170 address *v* point
    d Punkt adressieren
    f adresser un point
    r адресовать точку

171 add *v* transparency
    d Transparenz hinzufügen

f ajouter une transparence
r добавлять прозрачности

172 adhere *v*
d haften
f adhérer
r прилипнуть; прилипать; примыкать;
   прилегать

* adherence → 176

173 adherent
d adhärent
f adhérent
r примыкающий; прилегающий;
   присоединенный

174 adherent point; point of adherence
d Adhärenzpunkt *m*
f point *m* adhérent; point d'adhérence
r точка *f* слипания

175 adherent vortex
d gebundener Wirbel *m*
f tourbillon *m* asservi
r присоединенный вихрь *m*

176 adhesion; adherence; sticking
d Adhäsion *f*; Festhalten *f*; Anheften *n*
f adhésion *f*; adhérence *f*
r прилипание *n*; примыкание *n*; слипание *n*

177 adjacency
d Adjazenz *f*; Angrenzende *n*
f adjacence *f*
r прилегание *n*; смежность *f*

178 adjacent; juxtaposed
d adjazent; anliegend; benachbart
f adjacent; juxtaposé
r смежный; соседний; прилежащий;
   вспомагательный

179 adjacent angle
d anliegender Winkel *m*; Nebenwinkel *m*
f angle *m* adjacent
r соседний угол *m*; смежный угол;
   прилежащий угол

* adjacent angles → 189

180 adjacent arcs
d adjazente Bögen *mpl*
f arcs *mpl* adjacents
r смежные дуги *fpl*

181 adjacent edge
d adjazente Kante *f*; benachbarte Kante
f arête *f* adjacente
r смежное ребро *n*

182 adjacent elements
d adjazente Elemente *npl*
f éléments *mpl* adjacents
r смежные элементы *mpl*

183 adjacent face
d adjazente Fläche *f*; benachbarte Fläche
f face *f* adjacente
r смежная грань *f*; смежная сторона *f*

184 adjacent facets
d angrenzende Facetten *fpl*; nachfolgende
   Facetten; anliegende Facetten
f facettes *fpl* adjacentes
r смежные фацеты *mpl*

185 adjacent leg of a right triangle
d anliegende Kathete *f*
f côté *m* adjacent de l'angle droit
r прилежащий катет *m*

186 adjacent picture
d Nachbarbild *n*
f image *f* voisine
r смежное изображение *n*

187 adjacent rows
d nebeneinanderstehende Zeilen *fpl*
f lignes *fpl* adjacentes
r смежные строки *fpl*; соседние строки

188 adjacent side
d anliegende Seite *f*
f côté *m* adjacent
r прилежащая сторона *f*

189 adjacent [supplementary] angles
d Nebenwinkel *mpl*
f angles *mpl* adjacents supplémentaires
r смежные углы *mpl*

190 adjacent vertices
d adjazente Knoten[punkte] *mpl*; benachbarte
   Knoten[punkte]
f sommets *mpl* adjacents
r смежные вершины *fpl*

191 adjoin *v*
d adjungieren; angrenzen an
f [ad]joindre
r присоединять

192 adjoint; adjugate
d adjungiert
f adjoint
r сопряженный; присоединенный

193 adjoint graph
d adjungierter Graph *m*

f graphe *m* adjoint
r сопряженный граф *m*; присоединенный граф

* **adjugate** → 192

194 adjunction
d Adjunktion *f*
f adjonction *f*
r сопряжение *n*; присоединение *n*

195 adjust *v*; **regulate** *v*; **tune** *v*
d justieren; einstellen; abstimmen
f ajuster; régler
r регулировать; настраивать; юстировать

196 adjustable cell
d einstellbare Zelle *f*
f cellule *f* ajustable
r регулируемая клетка *f*; настраиваемая клетка

* **adjusting** → 197

197 adjustment; adjusting; alignment
d Einstellung *f*; Justierung *f*
f ajustement *m*; ajustage *m*; mise *f* au point
r настраивание *n*; настройка *f*; юстировка *f*

198 adjustment of polygonal traverse
d Ausgleichung *f* des Polygonzugs
f compensation *f* de cheminement polygonal
r уравнивание *n* полигонального хода

199 administration
d Verwaltung *f*; Administration *f*
f administration *f*
r администрация *f*; администрирование *n*

200 admissibility; permissibility
d Zulässigkeit *f*
f admissibilité *f*
r допустимость *f*

201 admissible; feasible; permissible; allowable; allowed
d zulässig
f admissible; permis; autorisé; tolérable
r допустимый; приемлемый; разрешенный

202 admissible coloration
d zulässige Färbung *f*
f coloriage *m* admissible
r допустимая раскраска *f*

203 admissible deformation
d zulässige Deformation *f*
f déformation *f* admissible
r допустимая деформация *f*

204 admissible error
d zulässiger Fehler *m*
f erreur *f* admissible
r допустимая погрешность *f*

205 admissible value; permissible value
d zulässiger Wert *m*
f valeur *f* admissible
r допустимое значение *n*

206 advanced
d erweitert; modern
f avancé
r продвинутый; развитый; прогрессивный; современный

207 advanced filter
d erweiterter Filter *m*
f filtre *m* avancé
r продвинутый фильтр *m*

208 advanced modeling extension; AME
d erweiterte Modellierungsentwicklung *f*
f extension *f* avancée de modélisation
r развитое расширение *n* моделирования

209 advanced settings
d erweiterte Einrichtungen *fpl*
f paramètres *mpl* avancés
r продвинутые установки *fpl* [параметров]

210 advanced setup wizard
d Assistent *m* der erweiterten Einrichtung
f assistant *m* d'établissement avancé
r советник *m* продвинутой установки

211 aerial camera; aerocamera
d Luftbildkamera *f*; Fliegerkamera *f*
f chambre *f* aérienne
r аэрофотокамера *f*

212 aerial camera lens
d Luftaufnahmeobjektiv *n*; Luftbildobjektiv *n*
f objectif *m* de la chambre aérienne
r объектив *m* аэрофотокамеры

213 aerial perspective; air perspective
d Luftperspektive *f*
f perspective *f* aérienne
r воздушная перспектива *f*

214 aerial view
d Luftansicht *f*; Luftbild *n*
f vue *f* aérienne
r вид *m* с воздуха

215 aerial view window
d Luftansichtsfenster *n*
f fenêtre *f* de vue aérienne
r окно *n* вида с воздуха

*   **aerocamera** → 211

216   aesthetics
  d   Ästhetik *f*
  f   esthétique *f*
  r   эстетика *f*

*   **affiche** → 7356

217   affine
  d   affin
  f   affin
  r   аффинный

218   affine combination
  d   affine Kombination *f*
  f   combinaison *f* affine
  r   аффинная комбинация *f*

219   affine coordinates
  d   affine Koordinaten *fpl*
  f   coordonnées *fpl* affines
  r   аффинные координаты *fpl*

220   affine geometry
  d   affine Geometrie *f*
  f   géométrie *f* affine
  r   аффинная геометрия *f*

221   affine invariant
  d   affine Invariante *f*
  f   invariant *m* affin
  r   аффинный инвариант *m*

222   affine isometry
  d   affine Isometrie *f*
  f   isométrie *f* affine
  r   аффинная изометрия *f*

*   **affine map** → 223

223   affine map[ping]
  d   affine Abbildung *f*
  f   application *f* affine
  r   аффинное отображение *n*

224   affine plane
  d   affine Ebene *f*
  f   plan *m* affin
  r   аффинная плоскость *f*

225   affine plotter
  d   Affin-Plotter *m*
  f   traceur *m* affin; traceur permettant le dessin
       en perspective à partir d'une projection
       horizontale
  r   аффинный графопостроитель *m*

*   **affine relation** → 6984

226   affine rendering
  d   affines Rendering *n*
  f   rendu *m* affin
  r   аффинное тонирование *n*; аффинный
       рендеринг *m*

227   affine rotation
  d   affine Drehung *f*
  f   rotation *f* affine
  r   аффинное вращение *n*; аффинный
       поворот *m*

228   affine space
  d   affiner Raum *m*
  f   espace *m* affin
  r   аффинное пространство *n*

229   affine transformation
  d   affine Transformation *f*; affine Umformung *f*
  f   transformation *f* affine
  r   аффинное преобразование *n*

230   affinity
  d   Affinität *f*
  f   affinité *f*
  r   аффинность *f*

231   after-image
  d   Nach[ab]bild *n*; Nachabbildung *f*
  f   post-image *f*; image consécutive
  r   остаточное изображение *n*;
       последовательный образ *m*; последующий
       образ

232   agate
  d   Pariser Schrift *m*; Agate *n*
  f   agate *f*
  r   полиграфический агат *m*

233   agate algorithm
  d   Agate-Algorithmus *m*
  f   algorithme *m* agate
  r   агат-алгоритм *m*

234   agenda slide
  d   Agenda-Diapositiv *n*
  f   diapositive *f* d'agenda
  r   плановый слайд *m*

235   agent; robot; bot
  d   Agent *m*; Bot *m*; Roboter *m*
  f   agent *m*; bot *m*; robot *m*; logiciel *m*
       automatique
  r   агент *m*

236   aggregate
  d   Aggregat *n*
  f   agrégat *m*
  r   агрегат *m*; совокупность *f*; комплект *m*

237 **aggregate function**
  d Aggregat-Funktion *f*
  f fonction *f* d'agrégation
  r агрегатная функция *f*

238 **aggregation**
  d Aggregation *f*; Gesamtheit *f*
  f agrégation *f*
  r агрегация *f*; совокупность *f*

  * **AGP → 41**

239 **AGP configuration**
  d AGP-Konfiguration *f*
  f configuration *f* AGP
  r конфигурация *f* AGP

  * **AI → 587**

240 **aid**
  d Mittel *n*
  f aide *f*
  r [вспомагательное] средство *n*

241 **aiming**
  d Zielen *n*; Zielung *f*
  f visée *f*
  r визирование *n*

242 **aiming angle**
  d Zielwinkel *m*
  f angle *m* de visée
  r угол *m* визирования

243 **aiming axis; aiming line; axis of sight; sighting line**
  d Zielachse *f*; Visierachse *f*; Ziellinie *f*
  f axe *m* de visée; ligne *f* de visée; droite *f* de visée
  r линия *f* визирования; визирная ось *f*; визирная линия

244 **aiming circle; aiming field**
  d Zielkreis *m*; Pickbereich *m*
  f champ *m* de visée
  r поле *m* прицеливания

245 **aiming direction; sighting direction**
  d Zielrichtung *f*
  f direction *f* de visée; direction de regard
  r направление *n* визирования

  * **aiming field → 244**

246 **aiming level**
  d Zielhöhe *f*
  f niveau *m* de visée
  r уровень *m* визирования

  * **aiming line → 243**

247 **aiming mark; sighting mark**
  d Zieltafel *f*; Visiermarke *f*
  f repère *m* de visée; index *m* de visée; voyant *m*
  r прицел *m* визирования; марка *f* визирования

248 **aim[ing] point; target point**
  d Zielpunkt *m*
  f point *m* de visée; point de cible
  r целевая точка *f*; точка визирования

249 **aiming symbol**
  d Leitsymbol *n*; Zielsymbol *n*
  f symbole *m* de guidage; symbole de positionnement; symbole de visée
  r направляющий символ *m*; символ прицеливания

  * **aim point → 248**

250 **airbrush; spraycan**
  d Airbrush *n*
  f aérographe *m*
  r пульверизатор *n*; распылитель *m*; краскодувка *f*; краскопульт *m*; аэрограф *m*

251 **airbrush effect**
  d Airbrush-Effekt *m*
  f effet *m* d'aérographe
  r эффект *m* краскодувки

252 **airbrush tool**
  d Airbrush-Hilfsmittel *n*
  f outil *m* aérographe
  r инструмент *m* распыления

  * **air perspective → 213**

  * **AI system → 588**

  * **alarm → 253**

253 **alarm [signal]**
  d Alarmsignal *n*; Alarm *m*
  f alarme *f*; signal *m* d'alarme
  r сигнал *m* предупреждения

  * **aleatory → 7728**

254 **alert box**
  d Alert-Kasten *m*
  f boîte *f* d'alerte
  r ящик *m* предупреждения; ящик извещения

255 **algebraic topology**
  d algebraische Topologie *f*
  f topologie *f* algébrique
  r алгебраическая топология *f*

256 **algorithm**
  d Algorithmus *m*

f algorithme *m*
r алгоритм *m*

257 algorithmic animation
   d algorithmische Animation *f*
   f animation *f* algorithmique
   r алгоритмическая анимация *f*

* **alias → 262**

258 aliased line; aliasing line
   d nichtglatte Linie *f*; Aliasing-Linie *f*
   f ligne *f* crénelée
   r неровная линия *f*; ступенчатая линия

259 aliasing; desmoothing; stairstepping
   (undesired visual effect by occasion of
   definition of bitmap image)
   d Aliasing *n*; Desmoothing *n*
   f crénelage *m*; repliement *m*
   r неровность *f*; ступенчатость *f*

260 aliasing effect
   d Aliasing-Effekt *m*
   f effet *m* de crénelage
   r эффект *m* ступенчатости; эффект
   неровности

* **aliasing line → 258**

261 aliasing noise
   d Aliasing-Rauschen *n*
   f distorsion *f* de repliement
   r искажение *n* из-за неровности

262 alias [name]
   d Aliasname *m*; Pseudonym *n*;
   Parallelbezeichnung *f*
   f alias *m*; pseudonyme *m*; pseudo *m*; nom *m*
   alternatif
   r псевдоимя *n*; альтернативное имя *n*;
   псевдоним *m*

263 align *v*; justify *v*; equalize *v*
   d ausrichten; abgleichen
   f aligner; égaliser; mettre au point
   r выравнивать; подравнять; равнять;
   приравнивать; уравнивать

264 align *v* and distribute *v* layers
   d ausrichten und verteilen von Schichten
   f aligner et distribuer des plans
   r подравнять и упорядочить слои

* **aligned *adj* → 5091**

265 aligned bundle; coherent bundle
   d geordnetes Bündel *n*; kohärentes Bündel
   f faisceau *m* aligné; faisceau rangé
   r когерентный пучок *m*

* **aligned dimension → 266**

**266 aligned [linear] dimension; oblique
   dimension; slanted dimension**
   d schräge Dimension *f*
   f cote *f* linéaire alignée; cotation *f* [linéaire]
   alignée; dimension *f* oblique
   r наклонная размерность *f*

267 aligner
   d Justiergerät *n*; Fluchtgerät *n*
   f dispositif *m* d'alignement; aligneur *m*
   r эталонный прибор *m*; устройство *n* точной
   регулировки

* **aligner → 268**

268 aligner [bar]
   d Justierschiene *f*
   f barre *f* d'alignement
   r выравнивающая лента *f*

* **aligning → 269**

* **alignment → 197**

**269 alignment; aligning; equalization;
   justifying; justification**
   d Ausrichtung *f*; Ausgleichen *n*; Ausgleich *m*;
   Abgleich *m*
   f alignement *m*; égalisation *f*; justification *f*
   r выравнивание *n*; налаживание *n*

270 alignment chart; nomogram
   d Nomogramm *n*
   f nomogramme *m*
   r номограмма *f*

271 align *v* text to baseline
   d den Text an der Schriftlinie ausrichten
   f aligner le texte à la ligne de base
   r подравнять текст к базовой линии

* **align *v* text to frame → 3826**

* **align *v* text to object → 3827**

272 align *v* to grid
   d an dem Gitter ausrichten
   f aligner sur la grille
   r подравнять к сетке

* **A-list → 617**

273 all-color; full-color
   d Vollfarb-
   f de toutes couleurs; à plein couleur
   r полноцветный

274 all-color copier
   d Vollfarb-Kopierer *m*

f copieur *m* à pleine couleur
r полноцветное копирующее устройство *n*

275 all-color mode
d Vollfarb-Modus *m*
f mode *m* de toutes couleurs
r полноцветный режим *m*

276 all-color page
d Vollfarbseite *f*
f page *f* de toutes couleurs
r полноцветная страница *f*

277 all-color printer
d Vollfarb-Drucker *m*
f imprimante *f* de toutes couleurs
r полноцветный принтер *m*

278 all-color scanner
d Vollfarb-Scanner *m*
f scanner *m* de toutes couleurs
r полноцветный сканер *m*

* **all-digital display → 2770**

279 alley
(the space between images or columns)
d Gasse *f*; Pfad *m*; Zwischenraum *m* zwischen
Bildern oder Spalten
f ruelle *f*, venelle *f*
r дорожка *f*; коридор *m*; аллея *f*

* **allocate → 2978**

280 allocation
d Zuordnung *f*; Zuweisung *f*
f allocation *f*
r размещение *n*; распределение *n*

281 allocation of gray values
d Grauwertverteilung *f*
f allocation *f* de valeurs de gris
r распределение *n* оттенков серого;
размещение *n* кодов серого

282 allocation point
d Zuordnungspunkt *m*
f point *m* d'allocation
r точка *f* распределения

* **allowable → 201**

* **allowance → 6973**

* **allowed → 201**

283 all-pass filter; universal filter
d Allpassfilter *m*
f filtre *m* passe-tout
r универсальный фильтр *m*

284 all-point addressable; APA
d volladressierbar
f à points [tous] adressables; adressable en tous
points
r полноадресуемый

285 all-point addressable area
d volladressierbares Gebiet *n*
f zone *f* adressable en tous points
r полноадресуемая область *f*

286 all selection
d volle Auswahl *f*
f sélection *f* totale
r полный выбор *m*; полный отбор *m*

287 alphabet
d Alphabet *n*
f alphabet *m*
r алфавит *m*

* **alphabetical character → 5511**

288 alpha blending
d Alpha-Überblendung *f*; Alpha-Blending *n*
f mélange *m* alpha
r альфа смешение *n* (механизм управления
прозрачностью)

289 alpha-channel; mask channel
(a temporary storage area for masks)
d Alphakanal *m*
f canal *m* alpha
r альфа-канал *m*

290 alphageometric graphics
d alphageometrische Grafik *f*
f graphique *m* alphagéométrique
r буквенно-геометрическая графика *f*

291 alpha-layer
d Alpha-Schicht *f*
f couche *f* alpha
r альфа-слой *m*

292 alphamosaic graphics
d alphamosaische Grafik *f*
f graphique *m* alphamosaïque
r буквенно-мозаичная графика *f*

293 alteration; altering; modification
d Änderung *f*; Veränderung *f*; Alteration *f*;
Modifizierung *f*
f altération *f*; modification *f*
r изменение *n*; модифицирование *n*

* **altering → 293**

* **alternate → 300**

294 alternate *v*
d alternieren; [ab]wechseln
f alterner
r переменять; обменивать[ся]; менять; сменить

295 alternate angles
d Wechselwinkel *mpl*
f angles *mpl* alternes
r накрест лежащие углы *mpl*

296 alternate exterior angles; exterior alternate angles
d äußere Wechselwinkel *mpl*
f angles *mpl* alternes externes
r внешние накрест лежащие углы *mpl*

297 alternate interior angles; interior alternate angles
d innere Wechselwinkel *mpl*
f angles *mpl* alternes internes
r внутренние накрест лежащие углы *mpl*

298 alternate *v* **scale**
d Maßstab wechseln
f alterner l'échelle
r сменить шкалу

299 alternate *v* **unit**
d Einheit wechseln
f alterner l'unité
r переменять [мерную] единицу

300 alternating; alternate; alternative
d alternierend; abwechselnd
f alterné; alternatif
r альтернирующий; чередующийся; альтернативный; обходный

301 alternation
d Alternation *f*
f alternance *f*
r чередование *n*; альтернирование *n*; смена *f*

* **alternative → 300**

302 alternative font file
d Datei *f* der alternierenden Schrift
f fichier *m* de police alternative
r файл *m* с альтернативным шрифтом

* **alternative routing → 8087**

303 altitude; height
d Höhe *f*; Aufriss *m*
f hauteur *f*; altitude *f*
r высота *f*; возвышение *n*; профиль *m*

304 altitude of a cone
d Kegelhöhe *f*

f hauteur *f* d'un cône
r высота *f* конуса

305 altitude of a cylinder
d Höhe *f* eines Zylinders
f hauteur *f* d'un cylindre
r высота *f* цилиндра

* **altitude of a face → 8773**

306 altitude of a pyramid
d Höhe *f* einer Pyramide
f hauteur *f* d'une pyramide
r высота *f* пирамиды

307 altitude of a triangle
d Höhe *f* eines Dreiecks
f hauteur *f* d'un triangle
r высота *f* треугольника

308 always on top
d immer im Vordergrund
f toujours visible
r всегда впереди

* **ambience → 3475**

309 ambient; environmental
d Umgebungs-; Raum-
f ambiant
r окружающий; внешний

310 ambient color
d Umgebungsfarbe *f*
f couleur *f* ambiante
r окружающий цвет *m*

311 ambient light; environment light
d Umgebungslicht *n*
f lumière *f* ambiante; lumière d'ambiance
r окружающий свет *m*

312 ambiguity; vagueness
d Mehrdeutigkeit *f*; Vagheit *f*; Ambiguität *f*
f ambiguïté *f*
r неясность *f*; неоднозначность *f*

313 ambiguous; vague
d ambig; mehrdeutig; vag[e]; unbestimmt
f ambigu; vague
r неоднозначный; двусмысленный; неясный; многозначный

314 ambiguous coordinate transformation
d mehrdeutige Koordinatentransformation *f*
f transformation *f* de coordonnées ambiguë
r неоднозначное преобразование *n* координат

* **AME → 208**

315 American standard code of information interchange; ASCII
d amerikanischer Standardcode *m* zum Informationsaustausch
f code *m* standard pour échange d'information
r американский стандартный код *m* обмена информации

316 amount
d Betrag *m*; Gehalt *m*; Aufwand *m*
f montant *m*; teneur *f*
r количество *n*; сумма *f*

317 amount of calculation; volume of computation
d Rechenaufwand *m*
f volume *m* de calcul
r объем *m* вычисления

318 amount of information
d Informationsgehalt *m*
f quantité *f* d'information
r количество *n* информации; объем *m* информации

319 ampersand
(&)
d Ampersand *m*; Und-Zeichen *n*
f ampersand *m*
r амперсанд *m*

320 amplification
d Verstärkung *f*
f amplification *f*
r усиление *n*

321 amplitude
d Amplitude *f*
f amplitude *f*
r амплитуда *f*

322 amusing font
d unterhaltende Schrift *f*
f police *f* amusante
r забавный шрифт *m*

323 anaglyph
d Anaglyphe *f*; Anaglyphenbild *n*
f anaglyphe *m*
r анаглиф *m*

* **analog** → 326, 327

324 analog display; analog monitor
d Analogbidschirm *m*
f afficheur *m* analogique
r аналоговый дисплей *m*

* **analog monitor** → 324

325 analog plotter
d Analogplotter *m*
f traceur *m* analogique
r аналоговый графопостроитель *m*

326 analog[ue] *adj*
d analog
f analogue; analogique
r аналогический; аналоговый

327 analog[ue]
d Analog *n*
f analogue *m*
r аналог *m*

328 analog video
d Analogvideo *n*
f vidéo *m* analogique
r аналоговое видео *n*

329 analogy
d Analogie *f*
f analogie *f*
r аналогия *f*; сходство *n*

* **analyse** *v* → 346

330 analyser; analyzer
d Analysator *m*
f analyseur *m*
r анализатор *m*

331 analysis
d Analysis *f*; Analyse *f*
f analyse *f*
r анализ *m*

332 analysis of data; data analysis
d Datenanalyse *f*
f analyse *f* des données
r анализ *m* данных

* **analytic** → 333

333 analytic[al]
d analytisch
f analytique
r аналитический

334 analytical arc
d analytisches Kurvenstück *n*
f arc *m* [de courbe] analytique
r аналитическая дуга *f*; аналитический отрезок *m* кривой

335 analytical curve
d analytische Kurve *f*
f courbe *f* analytique
r аналитическая кривая *f*

336 analytical expression
d analytischer Ausdruck *m*
f expression *f* analytique
r аналитическое выражение *n*

337 analytical form
d analytische Form *f*
f forme *f* analytique
r аналитическая форма *f*

338 analytically representable function
d analytisch darstellbare Funktion *f*
f fonction *f* représentable analytiquement
r функция *f*, представимая аналитически

339 analytical method
d analytische Methode *f*; analytisches
   Verfahren *n*
f méthode *f* analytique
r аналитический метод *m*

* **analytical plane → 1424**

340 analytical solution
d analytische Lösung *f*
f solution *f* analytique
r аналитическое решение *n*

341 analytical surface
d analytische Fläche *f*
f surface *f* analytique
r аналитическая поверхность *f*

**342 analytic function; holomorphic function;
   regular function**
d analytische Funktion *f*; holomorphe Funktion;
   reguläre Funktion
f fonction *f* analytique; fonction holomorphe;
   fonction régulière
r аналитическая функция *f*; голоморфная
   функция; регулярная функция

343 analytic geometry
d analytische Geometrie *f*
f géométrie *f* analytique
r аналитическая геометрия *f*

344 analytic geometry of the plane
d analytische Geometrie *f* der Ebene
f géométrie *f* analytique du plan; géométrie
   analytique plane
r аналитическая геометрия *f* плоскости

345 analytic geometry of the space
d analytische Geometrie *f* des Raums
f géométrie *f* analytique de l'espace
r аналитическая геометрия *f* пространства

346 analyze *v*; analyse *v*
d analysieren

f analyser
r анализировать

* **analyzer → 330**

347 anamorphic image
d anamorphisches Bild *n*
f image *f* anamorphique
r анаморфное изображение *n*

* **anamorphic lens → 8659**

348 anamorphosis
d Anamorphosis *f*
f anamorphose *f*
r анаморфоз *m*; анаморфирование *n*

349 anastigmatic lens
d anastigmatisches Objektiv *n*
f objectif *m* anastigmatique
r анастигматический объектив *m*

350 anastigmatism
d Anastigmatismus *m*; Anastigmasie *f*
f anastigmatisme *m*
r анастигматизм *m*

351 ancestor node
d vorhergehender Knoten *m*
f nœud *m* ancêtre
r узел-предок *m*

352 anchor
d Anker *m*
f ancre *f*; signet *m*; pointeur *m* de lien
r якорь *m*; опора *f*

353 anchorage
d Verankerung *f*
f accrochage *m*; ancrage *m*
r закрепление *n*; анкераж *m*

354 anchorage zone
d Verankerungszone *f*
f zone *f* d'accrochage
r зона *f* закрепления

355 anchor point
d Ankerpunkt *m*
f point *m* d'ancrage
r якорная точка *f*; точка закрепления

* **anchor ring → 9781**

356 angle
d Winkel *m*
f angle *m*
r угол *m*

* **angle at a circumference → 5107**

357 **angle at the center; central angle**
 d Zentralwinkel *m*; Mittelpunktswinkel *m*
 f angle *m* au centre; angle central
 r центральный угол *m*

358 **angle between a chord and a tangent**
 (of a circle)
 d Sehnentangentenwinkel *m*;
 Tangentensehnenwinkel *m*
 f angle *m* entre corde et tangente; angle entre
 sécante et tangente
 r угол *m* между касательной (к окружности)
 и хордой (из точки касания)

359 **angle between a line and a plane**
 d Winkel *m* zwischen einer Gerade und einer
 Ebene
 f angle *m* d'une droite et d'un plan
 r угол *m* между прямой и плоскостью

360 **angle between two curves**
 d Winkel *m* zwischen zwei Kurven
 f angle *m* de deux courbes
 r угол *m* между двумя кривыми

361 **angle between two cutting planes**
 d Winkel *m* zwischen zwei Schnittebenen
 f angle *m* de deux plans sécants
 r угол *m* между двумя пересекающимися
 плоскостями

 * **angle between two lines → 365**

362 **angle between two plane curves**
 d Winkel *m* zwischen zwei ebenen Kurven
 f angle *m* de deux courbes planes
 r угол *m* между двумя кривыми на
 плоскости; угол между двумя плоскими
 кривыми

363 **angle between two planes**
 d Winkel *m* zwischen zwei Ebenen
 f angle *m* de deux plans; angle d'un couple de
 plans
 r угол *m* между двумя плоскостями

364 **angle between two skew lines**
 d Winkel *m* zwischen zwei windschiefen
 Geraden
 f angle *m* entre deux droites gauches
 r угол *m* между двумя скрещивающимися
 прямыми

365 **angle between two [straight] lines**
 d Winkel *m* zwischen zwei Geraden
 f angle *m* de deux droites; angle d'un couple de
 droites
 r угол *m* между двумя прямыми

366 **angle between two vectors**
 d Winkel *m* zwischen zwei Vektoren
 f angle *m* de deux vecteurs
 r угол *m* между двумя векторами

 * **angle-bisector → 948**

367 **angle brackets; chevrons**
 (< >)
 d spitze Klammern *fpl*; Winkelklammern *fpl*
 f parenthèses *fpl* anguleuses; chevrons *mpl*;
 équerres *fpl*
 r угловые скобки *fpl*

368 **angled arrow**
 d wink[e]liger Pfeil *m*
 f flèche *f* angulaire
 r угловатая стрелка *f*; изогнутая стрелка

369 **angle direction**
 d Winkelrichtung *f*
 f direction *f* d'angle
 r направление *n* отсчета углов

370 **angled text**
 d wink[e]liger Text *m*
 f texte *m* angulaire
 r угловой текст *m*

371 **angle geometry**
 d Winkelgeometrie *f*
 f géométrie *f* d'angle
 r геометрия *f* угла

 * **angle measure → 5871**

372 **angle of aperture; aperture angle**
 d Öffnungswinkel *m*
 f angle *m* d'ouverture
 r апертурный угол *m*; угол захвата

373 **angle of contingence**
 d Berührungswinkel *m*; Kontingenzwinkel *m*
 f angle *m* de contingence
 r угол *m* смежности; угол [сопри]касания

374 **angle of convergence; convergence angle;**
 parallactic angle; angular parallax
 d Konvergenzwinkel *m*; parallaktischer
 Winkel *m*
 f angle *m* parallactique; angle de convergence;
 parallaxe *m* oculaire
 r угол *m* сходимости; параллактический
 угол

375 **angle of coverage; angle of field**
 d Bildwinkel *m*; Gesichtswinkel *m*
 f angle *m* de champ [visuel]
 r угол *m* поля зрения

 * **angle of departure → 378**

376 angle of depression; depression angle
d Absenkungswinkel *m*; Depressionswinkel *m*
f angle *m* de dépression
r угол *m* понижения; угол склонения (светила)

377 angle of deviation; deflection angle
d Ablenk[ungs]winkel *m*
f angle *m* de déflexion; angle de déviation
r угол *m* отклонения

378 angle of elevation; elevation; angle of departure
d Erhebungswinkel *m*; Elevationswinkel *m*
f angle *m* d'élévation; angle de hauteur
r угол *m* возвышения; вертикальный угол

* **angle of field → 375**

379 angle of gradient; gradient angle
d Gradient[en]winkel *m*
f angle *m* de gradient
r угол *m* градиента

380 angle of incidence; incidence angle; angle of inclination; inclination angle; angle of slope; angle of tilt; tilt angle; slant angle
d Einfallswinkel *m*; Neigungswinkel *m*; Inklinationswinkel *m*; Kippungswinkel *m*; Böschungswinkel *m*
f angle *m* d'incidence; angle d'inclinaison; angle de déclivité; angle de talus
r угол *m* уклона; угол наклона; угол ската; угол откоса

* **angle of inclination → 380**

* **angle of intersection → 2311**

381 angle of perspective
d Perspektivwinkel *m*
f angle *m* de perspective
r угол *m* перспективы

382 angle of precession
d Präzessionswinkel *m*
f angle *m* de précession
r угол *m* прецессии

383 angle of reflection; reflecting angle
d Reflexionswinkel *m*
f angle *m* de réflexion
r угол *m* отражения

384 angle of refraction; refraction angle; refracting angle
d Brechungswinkel *m*; Refraktionswinkel *m*
f angle *m* de réfraction
r угол *m* переломления

385 angle of rotation; rotation angle
d Drehungswinkel *m*; Drehwinkel *m*
f angle *m* de rotation
r угол *m* вращения; угол поворота

* **angle of second curvature → 387**

* **angle of slope → 380**

386 angle of the hatch pattern
d Schraffurmuster-Winkel *m*
f angle *m* de modèle de la hachure
r угол *m* наклона шаблона штриховки

* **angle of tilt → 380**

387 angle of torsion; angle of second curvature
d Windungswinkel *m*; Torsionswinkel *m*
f angle *m* de torsion; angle de deuxième courbure
r угол *m* кручения; угол второй кривизны

388 angle of twist; twist angle; spiral angle; helix angle
d Verdreh[ungs]winkel *m*
f angle *m* de vrillage; angle [d'hélice] de la goujure
r изогнутый угол *m*

389 angle of view; viewing angle; visual angle
d Blickwinkel *m*; Sehwinkel *m*; Betrachtungswinkel *m*
f angle *m* visuel; angle de visionnement
r угол *m* зрения; угол взгляда

* **anglepreserving projection → 2039**

390 angle smoothing
d Winkelglättung *f*
f lissage *m* d'angle
r сглаживание *n* угла

* **angle vertex → 10151**

391 angular
d winkelig; Winkel-
f angulaire
r угловой; угловатый

392 angular bias
d Winkelverzerrung *f*; Winkelverschiebung *f*; Winkelversetzung *f*
f écart *m* angulaire
r угловое смещение *n*

393 angular coefficient
(of a straight line)
d Richtungskoeffizient *m*; Steigungskoeffizient *m*; Richtungsfaktor *m*; Richtungszahl *f*

f coefficient *m* de direction; coefficient angulaire
r коэффициент *m* наклона; угловой коэффициент

394 angular degree; arc degree
d Winkelgrad *m*; Bogengrad *m*; Altgrad *m*
f degré *m* angulaire
r угловой градус *m*; старый градус; дуговой градус

* **angular diameter → 473**

395 angular dimension
d Winkeldimension *f*; anguläre Dimension *f*
f dimension *f* angulaire; cote *f* angulaire
r угловой размер *m*; угловая размерность *f*

396 angular dimension line
d Winkeldimensionslinie *f*
f ligne *f* de cotation angulaire; ligne de cote angulaire
r угловая размерная линия *f*

397 angular distance; latitude
d Winkelabstand *m*; Winkeldistanz *f*; Winkelentfernung *f*
f distance *f* angulaire; latitude *f*
r угловое расстояние *n*; широта *f*

* **angular field → 3737**

* **angular field of vision → 3737**

* **angular measure → 5871**

* **angular measurement → 4257**

398 angular metric
d Winkelmetrik *f*
f métrique *f* angulaire
r угловая метрика *f*

* **angular parallax → 374**

399 angular point; corner point; salient point
(of a curve)
d Eckpunkt *m*; Knickpunkt *m*; Knickstelle *f*
f point *m* anguleux
r угловая точка *f*; точка излома

400 angular point coordinates
d Eckpunktkoordinaten *fpl*
f coordonnées *fpl* d'un point anguleux
r координаты *fpl* угловой точки

401 angular second; sexagesimal second; second
(of angle or arc)
d Winkelsekunde *f*; Bogensekunde *f*; Sekunde *f*

f seconde *f* [angulaire]; seconde de l'angle; seconde d'arc; seconde sexagésimale
r [угловая] секунда *f*

402 angular unit
d Winkeleinheit *f*
f unité *f* angulaire
r угловая единица *f*

403 animated bump map
d animiertes Bump-Map *n*
f texture *f* relief animée; bump-map *m* animé
r анимированное рельефное текстурирование *n*

404 animated caption
d Trickuntertitel *m*
f caption *f* animée
r анимированная надпись *f*

405 animated cartoon
d Trickfilm *m*
f film *m* d'animation
r мультипликация *f*

406 animated characters
d animierte Zeichen *npl*
f caractères *mpl* animés
r оживленные символы *mpl*

407 animated column diagram
d animiertes Säulendiagramm *n*
f diagramme *m* à barres animé
r оживленная прямоугольная диаграмма *f*

* **animated digital video → 4063**

408 animated drawing
d Trickzeichnung *f*
f dessin *m* animé
r оживленный рисунок *m*; анимированный рисунок

* **animated GIF → 409**

409 animated GIF [image]
d animiertes GIF-Bild *n*
f image *f* GIF animée
r анимированный GIF рисунок *m*

410 animated graphics
d animierte Grafik *f*
f graphique *m* animé
r оживленная графика *f*

* **animated image → 6081**

411 animated slide
d animiertes Diapositiv *n*

f diapositive *f* animée
r анимированный слайд *m*

* **animated stereo** → 6083

412 animated texture
d animierte Textur *f*
f texture *f* animée
r анимированная текстура *f*

413 animated title
d Tricktitel *m*
f titre *m* animé
r анимированный титул *m*

414 animated video; motion video
d animiertes Video *n*
f vidéo *m* animé
r оживленное видео *n*; анимированное видео

415 animation
d Animation *f*
f animation *f*
r анимация *f*; оживление *n*

416 animation facility; animation option
d Animationsmöglichkeit *f*
f possibilité *f* d'animation
r возможность *f* анимирования

417 animation file
d Animationsdatei *f*
f fichier *m* d'animation
r анимационный файл *m*

418 animation frame
(a single image)
d Animationsaufnahme *f*
f cadre *m* d'animation
r анимационный кадр *m*

* **animation option** → 416

419 animation scene
d Animationsszene *f*
f scène *f* d'animation; scène animée
r анимационная сцена *f*

420 animation scene manager
d Manager *m* der Animationsszene
f gestionnaire *m* de scènes animées
r менажер *m* анимационных сцен

421 animation sequence
d Animationsfolge *f*
f séquence *f* d'animations
r анимационная последовательность *f*

422 animation software

d Animation-Software *f*; Programmierhilfen *fpl* für Animation
f logiciel *m* d'animation
r программное обеспечение *n* анимации

423 anisotrope; anisotropic; nonisotropic
d anisotrop; nichtisotrop
f anisotrope; non isotrope
r анизотропный; неизотропный

424 anisotrope texture memory
d anisotroper Texturspeicher *m*
f mémoire *f* de textures anisotropes
r память *f* анизотропных текстур

* **anisotropic** → 423

425 anisotropic filtering
d anisotrope Filtrierung *f*
f filtrage *m* anisotrope
r анизотропное фильтрирование *n*; анизотропная фильтрация *f*

426 anisotropic line; nonisotropic line
d anisotrope Gerade *f*; nichtisotrope Gerade
f droite *f* anisotrope; droite non isotrope
r анизотропная прямая *f*; неизотропная прямая

427 anisotropic plane; nonisotropic plane
d anisotrope Ebene *f*; nichtisotrope Ebene
f plan *m* anisotrope; plan nonisotrope
r анизотропная плоскость *f*; неизотропная плоскость

428 anisotropic reflectance
d anisotrope Reflektanz *f*
f réflectance *f* anisotrope
r анизотропная отражательная способность *f*

429 anisotropy
d Anisotropie *f*
f anisotropie *f*
r анизотропия *f*

430 anisotropy coefficient
d Anisotropiekoeffizient *m*
f coefficient *m* d'anisotropie
r коэффициент *m* анизотропии

431 anisotropy inspection
(of digital images)
d Inspektion *f* der Anisotropie
f inspection *f* d'anisotropie
r проверка *f* анизотропии

* **annex** → 483

432 annotation
d Annotation *f*

f annotation *f*
r аннотация *f*

433 announcement; notification
d Annonce *f*; Ankündigung *f*; Durchsage *f*;
Ansage *f*; Meldung *f*; Zuschreiben *n*
f annonce *f*; notification *f*
r объявление *n*; известие *n*; уведомление *n*

434 annular; ring[-shaped]; loop
d Ring-; ringförmig
f annulaire; en anneau
r кольцевой; кольцеобразный

435 annular domain; ring domain
d Ringgebiet *n*
f domaine *m* annulaire
r кольцевая область *f*

436 annular surface
d ringförmige Fläche *f*
f surface *f* annulaire
r кольцеобразная поверхность *f*

* **annulus** → 1505

437 anonymous
d anonym
f anonyme
r анонимный

438 anonymous block; unnamed block
d anonymer Block *m*
f bloc *m* anonyme
r анонимный блок *m*; безыменный блок

439 antialiased circle
d glätteter Kreis *m*
f cercle *m* anticrénelé
r сглаженный круг *m*

440 antialiased circle generation
d Generierung des glätteten Kreises
f génération *f* de cercle anticrénelé
r генерирование *n* сглаженного круга

441 antialiased line
d glättete Linie *f*
f ligne *f* anticrénelée; ligne d'anticrénelage
r сглаженная линия *f*

442 antialiased text
d glätteter Text *m*
f texte *m* anticrénelé
r сглаженный текст *m*

443 antialiased wireframe
d glätteter Drahtrahmen *m*
f structure *f* filaire anticrénelée
r сглаженный каркас *m*

444 antialiasing; dejagging
(of a curve)
d Kantenglättungsverfahren *n*; Antialiasing *n*
f anticrénelage *m*; lissage *m*
r сглаживание *n* [границ кривых, наклонных
линий и шрифтов]; плавное изменение *n*;
уменьшение *n* ступенчатости;
антиалиасинг *m*

445 antialiasing circuit
d Antialiasing-Schaltung *f*
f circuit *m* d'anticrénelage
r схема *f* компенсации спектральных
наложений

**446 anti-blur mask; blur mask; unsharp[ed]
mask**
d Unscharfmaske *f*
f masque *f* anti-buée; masque non distincte
r маска *f* расплывания; нечеткая маска;
нерезкая маска

**447 anticlockwise; counterclockwise;
sinistrorse; sinistrorsum** *adj*
d dem Uhrzeigersinn entgegen; entgegengesetzt
zum Uhrzeigersinn; linksgängig;
linksgewunden; linkswendig
f contre sens des aiguilles de la montre; en sens
antihoraire; sinistrorsum
r против часовой стрелки

448 anticlockwise direction
d dem Uhrzeigersinn entgegengesetzte
Richtung *f*
f direction *f* en sens antihoraire
r направление *n* против часовой стрелки

* **anticlockwise rotation** → 2273

* **antiglare** → 454

449 antiglare filter; glare filter
d Antireflexfilter *m*
f filtre *m* d'anti-éblouissement
r антибликовый фильтр *m*

450 antiglare panel
d Entspiegelungstafel *f*
f panneau *m* antireflet
r бликоподавляющая панель *f*

451 antinode
d Antiknoten[punkt] *m*
f antinœud *m*
r антиузел *m*

452 antiparallel
d antiparallel
f antiparallèle
r антипараллельный

453 antiparallel lines
  d antiparallele Geraden *fpl*
  f lignes *fpl* antiparallèles
  r антипараллельные прямые *fpl*

* **antipodal** → 2711

* **antipodal point** → 2712

454 antireflecting; antiglare
  d Antireflex-
  f antireflet; antiréfléchissant; antiréflexif
  r противоотражающий; неотражающий;
    бликоподавляющий

**455 antireflecting coated layer; antireflection
    coating**
  d Antireflexbelag *m*
  f couche *f* antiréflexive; revêtement *m*
    antiréfléchissant
  r противоотражающий слой *m*;
    противоотражающее покрытие *n*

456 antireflection
  d Antireflexion *f*
  f antiréflexion *f*
  r противоотражение *n*

* **antireflection coating** → 455

457 antisymmetric; skew-symmetric
  d antisymmetrisch; schiefsymmetrisch
  f antisymétrique
  r антисимметрический; антисимметричный;
    кососимметрический

458 antisymmetry
  d Antisymmetrie *f*
  f antisymétrie *f*
  r антисимметрия *f*

* **APA** → 284

459 APA display
  d volladressierbares Display *n*; Display mit
    voller Punktadressierung
  f écran *m* à points [tous] adressables
  r полноадресуемый экран *m*

460 APA graphics
  d volladressierbare Grafik *f*
  f graphique *m* adressable en tous points
  r полноадресуемая графика *f*

461 aperture
  d Apertur *f*; Öffnung *f*; Maskenöffnung *f*;
    Bildpunktblende *f*
  f ouverture *f*; aperture *f*; embouchure *f*
  r апертура *f*; отверстие *n*; скважина *f*;
    открытие *n*

* **aperture angle** → 372

462 aperture box
  d Apertur-Kasten *m*
  f boîte *f* d'aperture
  r ящик *m* апертуры

463 aperture distortion
  d Apertur-Verzerrung *f*
  f distorsion *f* d'aperture
  r искажение *n* апертуры

464 aperture illumination
  d Apertur-Illumination *f*
  f illumination *f* d'aperture
  r высвечивание *n* апертуры

465 aperture imaging
  d Apertur-Abbildung *f*
  f imagination *f* d'ouverture
  r изображение *n* апертуры

466 aperture mask
  d Apertur-Maske *f*; Lochmaske *f*
  f masque *f* d'aperture
  r апертурная маска *f*

**467 aperture of lens; objective aperture;
    objective opening**
  d Objektivöffnung *f*
  f ouverture *f* de l'objectif
  r отверстие *n* объектива; открытие *n*
    объектива

* **aperture stop** → 2717

* **apex** → 10144

468 apex angle of a cone
  d Öffnungswinkel *m* eines Kegels
  f angle *m* d'ouverture d'un cône
  r угол *m* раствора при вершине конуса

* **apex angles** → 10156

* **apex of a cone** → 10149

* **apex of a curve** → 10150

**469 apostrophe; quotation mark
    (')**
  d Apostroph *m*; Hochkomma *n*;
    Auslassungszeichen *n*
  f apostrophe *m*
  r апостроф *m*; кавычка *f*

470 apparent; seeming; illusory
  d Schein-; scheinbar; illusorisch
  f apparent; illusoire
  r кажущийся; иллюзорный; фиктивный

471 **apparent contrast**
  d scheinbarer Kontrast *m*
  f contraste *m* apparent
  r кажущийся контраст *m*

472 **apparent coordinates**
  d scheinbare Koordinaten *fpl*
  f coordonnées *fpl* apparentes
  r кажущиеся координаты *fpl*; фиктивные
  координаты

473 **apparent diameter; angular diameter**
  (of a star)
  d scheinbarer Durchmesser *m*
  f diamètre *m* apparent; diamètre angulaire
  r видимый диаметр *m*; угловой диаметр

474 **apparent field**
  d scheinbares Feld *n*
  f champ *m* apparent
  r мнимое поле *n*

475 **apparent intersection**
  d scheinbarer Durchschnitt *m*
  f intersection *f* apparente
  r кажущееся пересечение *n*; фиктивное
  пересечение

476 **apparent luminance**
  d sichtbare Luminanz *f*
  f luminance *f* apparente
  r видимая яркость *f*

477 **apparent motion**
  d scheinbare Bewegung *f*
  f mouvement *m* apparent
  r кажущееся движение *n*

478 **apparent relief**
  d scheinbares Relief *n*
  f relief *m* apparent
  r кажущийся рельеф *m*; фиктивный рельеф

479 **apparent symmetry**
  d Scheinsymmetrie *f*
  f symétrie *f* apparente
  r кажущаяся симметрия *f*; мнимая
  симметрия

480 **appearance**
  d Erscheinen *n*; Veröffentlichung *f*
  f apparence *f*; allure *f*; spectacle *m*
  r появление *n*; внешнее представление *n*

481 **Appel's algorithm**
  d Appel-Algorithmus *m*
  f algorithme *m* d'Appel
  r алгоритм *m* Аппеля

482 **append** *v*

  d anhängen; beifügen
  f attacher; ajouter
  r добавлять; присоединять

483 **appendix; annex**
  d Anhang *m*
  f appendice *m*; annexe *f*
  r приложение *n*; дополнение *n*

484 **applicability**
  d Anwendbarkeit *f*
  f applicabilité *f*
  r приложимость *f*; применимость *f*

485 **applicable**
  d anwendbar
  f applicable
  r приложимый; применимый

  * **application** → 491

486 **application; employment**
  d Anwendung *f*; Verwendung *f*
  f application *f*
  r применение *n*; использование *n*;
  приложение *n*

487 **application icon**
  d Anwendungssymbol *n*
  f icône *f* d'application
  r значок *m* приложения; значок прикладной
  программы

488 **application name**
  d Anwendungsname *m*
  f nom *m* d'application
  r имя *n* приложения

489 **application object**
  d Anwendungsobjekt *n*
  f objet *m* application
  r объект *m* приложения

490 **application screen; application window**
  d Anwendungsfenster *n*
  f écran *m* d'application
  r экран *m* приложения

491 **application [software]**
  d Anwendungssoftware *f*; Anwendung *f*;
  Applikation *f*; Aufgabe *f*
  f logiciel *m* appliqué; progiciel *m*
  r приложное программное обеспечение *n*;
  приложение *n*

  * **application window** → 490

492 **applied optics**
  d angewandte Optik *f*

f optique *f* appliquée
r прикладная оптика *f*

493 apply *v*
   d anwenden; aufbringen; anlegen
   f appliquer; employer
   r наносить; применять; приложить;
      прикладывать

494 apply *v* **option**
   d Option anwenden
   f appliquer une option
   r применять опцию

   * **appraisal** → 3537

495 approach
   d Vorgehen *n*; Herangehen *n*
   f approche *f*
   r подход *m*; приближение *n*

496 approach *v*
   d nähern
   f approcher; tendre
   r приближать[ся]

497 appropriate color profile
   d geeignetes Farbprofil *n*
   f profil *m* de couleur approprié
   r подходящий цветовой профиль *m*

498 approximability
   d Approximierbarkeit *f*
   f approximabilité *f*
   r аппроксимируемость *f*

499 approximable
   d approximierbar
   f approchable; approximable
   r аппроксимируемый

500 approximate
   d angenähert; Näherungs-; approximativ
   f approché; approximatif
   r приближенный

501 approximate *v*; **half-adjust** *v*
   d annähern
   f approximer
   r аппроксимировать

**502 approximate calculation; approximate
      computation**
   d Näherungsrechnung *f*; approximative
      Berechnung *f*
   f calcul *m* approché
   r приближенное вычисление *n*

   * **approximate computation** → 502

503 approximate coordinate
   d Näherungskoordinate *f*
   f coordonnée *f* approchée
   r приближенная координата *f*

504 approximated curve
   d angenäherte Kurve *f*
   f courbe *f* approximative
   r аппроксимированная кривая *f*

505 approximate estimation
   d angenäherte Abschätzung *f*
   f estimation *f* approchée
   r приближенная оценка *f*

506 approximate measurement
   d Grobmessung *f*; Näherungsmessung *f*
   f mesure *f* approximative
   r грубое измерение *n*; приближенное
      измерение

   * **approximate method** → 5934

507 approximate *v* **primitives**
   d Primitivelemente annähern
   f approximer des primitives
   r аппроксимировать примитивы

508 approximate solution
   d Näherungslösung *f*; approximative Lösung *f*
   f solution *f* approchée
   r приближенное решение *n*

509 approximate value
   d Näherungswert *m*; angenäherter Wert *m*
   f valeur *f* approchée; valeur approximative
   r приближенное значение *n*;
      аппроксимирующее значение

   * **approximating function** → 514

510 approximation
   d Approximation *f*; Annäherung *f*; Näherung *f*
   f approximation *f*
   r аппроксимация *f*; приближение *n*

511 approximation algorithms
   d Approximationsalgorithmus *mpl*
   f algorithmes *mpl* d'approximation
   r алгоритмы *mpl* аппроксимации

512 approximation by functions
   d Approximation *f* mittels Funktionen;
      Approximation durch Funktionen
   f approximation *f* par fonctions
   r аппроксимация *f* посредством функций;
      аппроксимация функциями

**513 approximation error; error of
      approximation**
   d Approximationsfehler *m*; Näherungsfehler *m*

  f erreur *f* d'approximation
  r ошибка *f* аппроксимации; ошибка
   приближения; погрешность *f*
   приближения; погрешность
   аппроксимации

514 approximation function; approximating function
  d Näherungsfunktion *f*;
   Approximationsfunktion *f*; approximierende
   Funktion *f*
  f fonction *f* d'approximation; fonction
   approximative
  r аппроксимирующая функция *f*

  * **approximation method → 5934**

515 approximation problem
  d Approximationsproblem *n*
  f problème *m* d'approximation
  r задача *f* аппроксимации

516 approximation theory
  d Approximationstheorie *f*
  f théorie *f* d'approximation
  r теория *f* приближений; теория
   аппроксимации

  * **aquarelle → 10387**

  * **Arabic digit → 517**

  * **Arabic figure → 517**

517 Arabic numeral; Arabic digit; Arabic figure
  d arabische Ziffer *f*; arabische Zahl *f*
  f chiffre *m* arabe
  r арабская цифра *f*

  * **arbitrary → 7728**

518 arbitrary axis
  d willkürliche Achse *f*
  f axe *m* arbitraire
  r произвольная ось *f*

519 arbitrary data
  d willkürliche Daten *npl*
  f données *fpl* arbitraires
  r произвольные данные *npl*

520 arbitrary origin
  d willkürlich gewählter Nullpunkt *m*
  f origine *f* arbitraire
  r произвольное начало *n*

521 arc
  d Bogen *m*
  f arc *m*

  r дуга *f*; кривизна *f*

  * **arc aligned text → 9548**

  * **arc-connected → 542**

  * **arc degree → 394**

  * **arc endpoint → 3431**

522 arc entity
  d Bogeneinheit *f*
  f entité *f* arc
  r примитив *m* дуга

523 Archimedian solids
  d Archimedische Körper *mpl*
  f solides *mpl* d'Archimède
  r тела *npl* Архимеда

524 Archimedian spiral
  d Archimedische Spirale *f*
  f spirale *f* d'Archimède
  r спираль *f* Архимеда

525 architectural design
  d architektonische Zeichnung *f*
  f dessin *m* architectural
  r архитектурный чертеж *m*

526 architectural format
  d architektonisches Format *n*
  f format *m* architectural
  r архитектурный формат *m*

527 architectural ornament
  d architektonisches Ornament *n*
  f ornement *m* architectural
  r архитектурный орнамент *m*

528 architectural units
  d architektonische Einheiten *fpl*
  f unités *fpl* architecturales
  r архитектурные единицы *fpl*

529 architecture
  d Architektur *f*
  f architecture *f*
  r архитектура *f*

530 archive; history
  d Archiv *n*
  f archives *fpl*; historique *m*
  r архив *m*; предистория *f*; хронология *f*

531 archiving; filing
  d Archivierung *f*
  f archivage *m*
  r архивное хранение *n*; архивирование *n*

532 arc-length; length of an arc
  d Bogenlänge *f*
  f longueur *f* d'un arc
  r длина *f* дуги

533 arc light source
  d Bogenlichtquelle *f*
  f source *f* d'éclairage à l'arc; source lumineuse
      à l'arc
  r дуговой световой источник *m*

534 arc measures
  d Bogenmaße *npl*
  f mesures *fpl* d'arc
  r размерности *fpl* дуги

535 arc-node topology
  d Bogen-Knoten-Topologie *f*
  f topologie *f* arc-nœud
  r топология *f* дуг и узлов

536 arc of a circle; circular arc
  d Kreisbogen *m*
  f arc *m* circulaire; arc de cercle
  r дуга *f* окружности

537 arc rectification
  d Rektifikation *f* des Bogens
  f rectification *f* d'un arc
  r выпрямление *n* дуги

538 arc segment
  d Bogensegment *n*
  f segment *m* d'arc
  r сегмент *m* дуги

539 arc smoothness
  d Bogenglätte *f*
  f égalité *f* d'arc
  r гладкость *f* дуги

540 arc spot
  d Bogen[brenn]fleck *m*
  f spot *m* de l'arc; point *m* lumineux de l'arc
  r [фокальное] пятно *n* дуги

541 arcwise
  d bogenweise
  f par arcs
  r дугообразно

542 arc[wise]-connected
  d bogenverknüpft; bogenweise
      zusammenhängend
  f connexé par arcs
  r дугообразно связный; жордановосвязный

543 arcwise connectivity
  d bogenweiser Zusammenhang *m*
  f connexité *f* par arcs

  r связность *f* с помощью дуг; дуговидная
      связность

544 area
      (as a surface)
  d Fläche *f*; Inhalt *m*
  f aire *f*
  r площадь *f*

  * **area → 7972, 10518**

545 area-based zooming
  d Fläche-basiertes Zoomen *n*
  f zoom *m* axé sur la superficie
  r масштабирование *n* взгляда, базированное
      на площади

**546 area chart; area graph; area diagram;
      surface chart; surface graph**
  d Flächendiagramm *n*
  f diagramme *m* en aires; diagramme
      surfacique; graphique *m* de surface
  r диаграмма *f* с областями; площадная
      диаграмма

547 area decomposition
  d Gebietszerlegung *f*
  f décomposition *f* de zone
  r разбиение *n* области

548 area desaturating
  d Gebietsentsättigung *f*
  f désaturation *f* de zone
  r ненасыщение *n* области

  * **area diagram → 546**

  * **area fill → 7974**

  * **area graph → 546**

549 areal; areolar
  d Sektor-; Flächen-; areolar
  f d'aire; aréolaire
  r секторный; ареальный; ареоларный

  * **areal element → 3345**

550 area of a circle
  d Kreisfläche *f*; Kreisinhalt *m*
  f aire *f* du cercle
  r площадь *f* круга

551 area of a sphere
  d Kugeloberfläche *f*
  f aire *f* de sphère
  r поверхность *f* шара; поверхность сферы;
      площадь *f* поверхности шара

552 area of a surface; surface area
  d Flächeninhalt *m*

f aire *f* de surface
r площадь *f* поверхности

553 area of a surface of revolution; area of a surface of rotation
d Mantelfläche *f* eines Drehkörpers;
Oberfläche *f* eines Rotationskörpers
f aire *f* d'une surface de révolution
r площадь *f* поверхности [тела] вращения

* **area of a surface of rotation → 553**

* **area of influence → 10519**

* **area patch → 9374**

554 area saturating
d Gebiet[s]sättigung *f*
f saturation *f* d'aire
r насыщение *n* области

555 area selection
d Gebiet[s]auswahl *f*
f sélection *f* de surface
r выбор *m* поверхности

* **areolar → 549**

556 Argend diagram
d Argend-Diagramm *n*
f diagramme *m* d'Argend
r диаграмма *f* Аргенда

557 argument
d Argument *n*
f argument *m*
r аргумент *m*

558 argument of a function; independent variable of a function
d Argument *n* einer Funktion; unabhängige Variable *f* einer Funktion
f argument *m* d'une fonction; variable *f* indépendante d'une fonction
r аргумент *m* функции; независимая переменная *f* функции

* **arithmetic → 449**

559 arithmetic[al]
d arithmetisch
f arithmétique
r арифметический

560 arithmetic[al] expression
d arithmetischer Ausdruck *m*
f expression *f* arithmétique
r арифметическое выражение *n*

561 arithmetic blending

d arithmetische Überblendung *f*
f dégradé *m* arithmétique
r арифметическое переливание *n*; арифметическое смешение *n*

* **arithmetic expression → 560**

* **arm → 4493**

* **arm of an angle → 8665**

562 arrange *v*
d anordnen
f arranger
r размещать; расставлять; раскладывать; располагать

563 arrange *v* all
d alles anordnen
f arranger tout
r размещать все

564 arrangement
d Anordnung *f*; Arrangement *n*
f arrangement *m*; disposition *f*; agencement *m*
r размещение *n*; расположение *n*; расстановка *f*

* **array → 5847**

565 array
d Feld *n*
f tableau *m*; champ *m*
r массив *m*

566 array element
d Feldelement *n*; Systemelement *n*
f élément *m* de tableau; élément de champ
r элемент *m* массива

567 array operation; array processing
d Feldoperation *f*; Feldverarbeitung *f*
f opération *f* sur un tableau; traitement *m* de champ
r операция *f* над массивом; обработка *f* массива

568 array pitch
d Pitch *m* eines Felds
f pas *m* de grille d'un champ
r шаг *m* сетки массива

* **array processing → 567**

569 arrow
d Zählpfeil *m*; Pfeil *m*
f flèche *f*
r стрелка *f*; стрелочка *f*

570 arrow angle
d Pfeilwinkel *m*

f angle *m* de flèche
r угол *m* стрелки

571 arrow block
  d Pfeilblock *m*
  f bloc *m* de flèches
  r блок *m* стрелок

572 arrow block name
  d Pfeilblockname *m*
  f nom *m* de bloc de flèches
  r имя *n* блока стрелок

573 arrow button
  d Pfeilknopf *m*
  f bouton *m* fleché
  r кнопка *f* стрелки

574 arrow graph
  d Pfeildiagramm *n*; gerichtetes
    Liniendiagramm *n*
  f diagramme *m* fléché
  r стрелочная диаграмма *f*

575 arrowhead
  d Pfeilspitze *f*
  f pic *m* de flèche
  r верх *m* стрелки; конец *m* линии

576 arrowhead forms; arrowhead styles
  d Pfeilspitzen-Formen *fpl*
  f formes *fpl* de pic de flèche
  r формы *fpl* концов стрелки

577 arrowhead outline
  d Pfeilspitzen-Umriss *m*
  f bordure *f* de pic de flèche
  r очертание *n* конца стрелки

578 arrowhead selector
  d Pfeilspitzen-Auswahlfeld *n*
  f sélecteur *m* de pic de flèche
  r селектор *m* конца стрелки

* **arrowhead styles → 576**

579 arrow key
  d Pfeiltaste *f*
  f touche *f* de flèche; touche avec flèche
  r клавиша *f* стрелки

580 arrow pointer
  d Zeigerpfeil *m*
  f pointeur *m* flèche
  r указатель *m* в виде стрелки

581 arrow-shaped; sagittal
  d Pfeil-; pfeilförmig
  f sagittal; en forme de flèche
  r стрельчатый; стрелообразный

582 article
  d Artikel *m*
  f article *m*
  r статья *f*; параграф *m*; предмет *m*

583 articulation
  d Verständlichkeit *f*; Gliederung *f*
  f articulation *f*
  r артикуляция *f*; расчленение *n*;
    членораздельность *f*; разборчивость *f*

* **artifacts → 4941**

584 artificial
  d künstlich
  f artificiel
  r искусственный

585 artificial computer-generated world
  d durch Computer generierte künstliche Welt *f*
  f monde *m* artificiel, généré par ordinateur
  r искусственный мир *m*, генерированный
    компьютером

586 artificial form
  d Kunstform *f*
  f forme *f* artificielle
  r искусственная форма *f*

**587 artificial intelligence; AI; machine
intelligence**
  d künstliche Intelligenz *f*; KI;
    Maschinenintelligenz *f*
  f intelligence *f* artificielle; IA
  r искусственный интеллект *m*; ИИ

588 artificial intelligence system; AI system
  d System *n* der künstlichen Intelligenz
  f système *m* d'intelligence artificielle; système
    d'IA
  r система *f* искусственного интеллекта

589 artificial light
  d künstliches Licht *n*
  f lumière *f* artificielle
  r искусственный свет *m*

590 artificial reality
  d künstliche Realität *f*
  f réalité *f* artificielle
  r искусственная реальность *f*

* **artificial vision → 5741**

591 artistic effect
  d künstlerischer Effekt *m*
  f effet *m* artistique
  r художественный эффект *m*

592 artistic filter
  d künstlerischer Filter *m*

f filtre *m* artistique
r фильтр *m* художественных эффектов

593 artistic text
d künstlerischer Text *m*
f texte *m* artistique
r художественный текст *m*

594 artwork
d Zeichenvorlage *f*; topologische Vorlage *f*
f schéma *m* topologique
r топологическая схема *f*

595 ascending; bottom-up; increasing
d aufsteigend; hochsteigend; ansteigend; wachsend; zunehmend
f ascendant; montant; levant; de bas en haut; croissant
r возрастающий; восходящий

596 ascending branch; rising branch
(of a curve)
d aufsteigender Ast *m*; ansteigender Ast
f branche *f* ascendante
r восходящая ветвь *f*

597 ascending order
d aufsteigende Anordnung *f*
f ordre *m* ascendant
r возрастающий порядок *m*

598 ascending ordering
d aufsteigende Ordnung *f*
f ordonnancement *m* ascendant
r упорядочение *n* по возрастанию

* **ASCII** → 315

599 aspatial data
d nichträumliche Daten *npl*
f données *fpl* non spatiaux
r непространственные данные *npl*

600 aspect
d Aspekt *m*
f aspect *m*
r вид *m*

601 aspect of primitive
d Aspekt *m* des Primitivelements
f aspect *m* de primitive
r вид *m* примитива

602 aspect ratio
d Seitenverhältnis *n*
f rapport *m* largeur/hauteur; rapport caractéristique; rapport d'aspect
r отношение *n* широта/высота; характеристическое отношение

603 aspheric
d asphärisch
f asphérique
r асферический

604 aspheric lens
d asphärische Linse *f*
f lentille *f* asphérique
r асферическая линза *f*

605 assemble *v*
d zusammensetzen; assemblieren; komponieren
f assembler
r собирать; компоновать; ассемблировать

606 assertion box
d Behauptungskasten *m*; Versicherungskasten *m*; Beteuerungsbox *f*
f pavé *m* d'organigramme
r ящик *m* утверждения

* **assessment** → 3537

607 assign *v*
d zuordnen; zuweisen
f assigner; attribuer
r назначать; присваивать

608 assignation; assignment; assigning
d Zuordnung *f*; Zuweisung *f*; Festsetzung *f*
f assignation *f*; affectation *f*; attribution *f*
r присваивание *n*; приписывание *n*; назначение *n*

609 assigned value
d zugeordneter Wert *m*
f valeur *f* assignée
r присваиваемое значение *n*

* **assigning** → 608

* **assignment** → 608

610 assignment sign
d Wertzuweisungszeichen *n*
f signe *m* d'assignation; signe d'affectation
r знак *m* присваивания

611 assign *v* **to layer**
d einer Schicht zuweisen
f assigner vers un plan
r присваивать слою

612 associate *v*; **join** *v*
d anschließen; vereinigen; verbinden
f associer; joindre
r ассоциировать; [при]соединять

613 associated elements
d assoziierte Elemente *npl*

f éléments *mpl* associés
r ассоциированные элементы *mpl*

614 associated function
d assoziierte Funktion *f*
f fonction *f* associée
r присоединенная функция *f*

615 associated objects
d vereinigte Objekte *npl*
f objets *mpl* associés
r присоединенные объекты *mpl*

616 association
d Assoziation *f*
f association *f*
r связывание *n*; ассоциация *f*

617 association list; A-list
d Assoziationsliste *f*
f liste *f* d'associations
r список *m* ассоциаций

618 associative
d assoziativ
f associatif
r ассоциативный

619 associative dimension
d assoziative Dimension *f*
f cotation *f* associative
r ассоциативная размерность *f*

620 associative hatch
d assoziative Schraffur *f*
f hachure *f* associative
r ассоциативная штриховка *f*

621 associative hatch property
d Eigenschaft *f* der assoziativen Schraffur
f propriété *f* d'hachure associative
r свойство *n* ассоциативной штриховки

622 associative hatch selection
d Auswahl *f* der assoziativen Schraffur
f sélection *f* d'hachure associative
r выбор *m* ассоциативной штриховки

623 associativity
d Assoziativität *f*
f associativité *f*
r ассоциативность *f*

* **assume** *v* → 9346

* **assumed** → 4957

* **astable** → 5132

624 asterisk

d Asterisk *n*
f astérisque *m*
r звездочка *f*

* **asterisk-shaped polygon** → 9155

625 astigmatism
d Astigmatismus *m*
f astigmatisme *m*
r астигматизм *m*

626 astroid; tetracuspid; hypocycloid of four cusps
d Astroide *f*; Sternkurve *f*
f astroïde *m*; as *m* carreau
r астроида *f*

* **asymmetric** → 627

627 asymmetric[al]; skew *adj*
d asymmetrisch; schief; schräg
f asymétrique; oblique; gauche
r асимметричный; косой; перекошенный

628 asymmetric filter
d asymmetrischer Filter *m*
f filtre *m* asymétrique
r асимметрический фильтр *m*

629 asymmetry; skewness
d Asymmetrie *f*; Schiefheit *f*
f dissymétrie *f*; asymétrie *f*; obliquité *f*
r скошенность *f*; асимметрия *f*; несимметрия *f*

630 asymptote
d Asymptote *f*
f asymptote *f*
r асимптота *f*

631 asymptotic
d asymptotisch
f asymptotique
r асимптотический

632 asymptotic analysis
d asymptotische Analyse *f*
f analyse *f* asymptotique
r асимптотический анализ *m*

633 atmospheric effects
d atmosphärische Effekte *mpl*
f effets *mpl* atmosphériques
r атмосферные эффекты *mpl*

634 attach *v*
d anschließen; anbringen; befestigen
f attacher; fixer
r [при]соединять; закреплять; пристраивать

635 **attach *v* an option**
  d eine Option anschließen
  f attacher une option
  r присоединять опцию

636 **attached drawing**
  d angeschlossene Zeichnung *f*
  f dessin *m* attaché
  r присоединенный чертеж *m*

  * **attaching → 637**

637 **attachment; attaching; fastening**
  d Anschluss *m*; Befestigung *f*
  f attachement *m*; fixage *m*; fixation *f*
  r присоединение *n*; закрепление *n*;
      скрепление *n*

  * **attachment point → 9668**

638 **attach *v* to the layer**
  d an die Schicht anschließen
  f attacher au plan
  r присоединять к слою

639 **attack**
  d Sturm *m*
  f attaque *f*
  r атака *f*; пробой *m*

  * **attainability → 55**

640 **attempt; experiment; trial**
  d Versuch *m*; Probe *f*; Experiment *n*
  f épreuve *f*; expérience *f*; essai *m*
  r попытка *f*; опыт *m*; эксперимент *m*; проба *f*

  * **attendance → 5761**

641 **attenuation; damping; falloff; drop-off**
  d Dämpfung *f*; Abblendung *f*
  f atténuation *f*; amortissement *m*;
      affaiblissement *m*
  r затухание *n*; гашение *n*; успокоение *n*;
      ослабление *n*

642 **attenuation of light**
  d Lichtabblendung *f*
  f atténuation *f* de la lumière
  r ослабление *n* света; затухание *n* света

643 **attenuation of point light**
  d Lichtquellenabblendung *f*
  f atténuation *f* de la lumière point
  r затухание *n* точечного источника света

  * **attraction power → 644**

644 **attractiveness; attraction power**
  d Attraktivität *f*; Anziehungskraft *f*

  f attractivité *f*; pouvoir *m* d'attraction;
      puissance *f* d'attraction
  r привлекательность *f*; притягательная
      сила *f*

645 **attractor**
  d Attraktor *m*
  f attracteur *m*
  r аттрактор *m*

646 **attribute**
  d Attribut *n*
  f attribut *m*
  r атрибут *m*

647 **attribute attaching**
  d Attributsbefestigung *f*
  f attachement *m* d'attribut
  r присоединение *n* атрибута

648 **attribute class**
  d Attributsklasse *f*
  f classe *f* d'attribut
  r класс *m* атрибута

649 **attribute data**
  d Attributdaten *npl*
  f données *fpl* d'attribut
  r атрибутные данные *npl*

650 **attribute definition**
  d Attribut-Definition *f*
  f définition *f* d'attribut
  r атрибутная дефиниция *f*

651 **attribute information**
  d Attribut-Information *f*
  f information *f* d'attribut
  r атрибутная информация *f*

652 **attribute object**
  d Attribut-Objekt *n*
  f objet *m* attribut
  r объект *m* типа атрибута

653 **attribute option**
  d Attribut-Option *f*
  f option *f* d'attribut
  r опция *f* атрибута

654 **attribute prompt**
  d Attributsanzeige *f*
  f consigne *f* d'attribut
  r подсказка *f* атрибута

655 **attribute reference**
  d Attributsverweis *m*
  f référence *f* d'attribut
  r ссылка *f* атрибута

656 attribute table
 d Attributstabelle *f*
 f table *f* d'attributs
 r таблица *f* атрибутов

657 attribute tag
 d Attributsetikett *n*
 f étiquette *f* d'attribut
 r тег *m* атрибута; атрибутный тег

658 attribute tag field
 d Feld *n* des Attributsetiketts
 f champ *m* d'étiquette d'attribut
 r поле *n* атрибутного тега

659 attribute value
 d Attributswert *m*
 f valeur *f* d'attribut
 r значение *n* атрибута

 * **audio → 90**

660 audio stereo casque
 d Audio-Stereo-Helm *m*
 f casque *f* audio stéréo
 r аудиостереонаушник *m*

 * **audiovideo → 662**

661 audiovideo interleaving; AVI
 d Audio-Video-Abwechslung *f*
 f entrelacement *m* d'audio et vidéo
 r чередование *n* аудио и видео

662 audiovisual; audiovideo
 d audiovisuell
 f audiovisuel; audiovidéo
 r аудиовизуальный

663 audiovisual library
 d audiovisuelle Bibliothek *f*
 f bibliothèque *f* audiovisuelle
 r библиотека *f* аудиовизуальных файлов

664 audiovisual presentation
 d audiovisuelle Präsentation *f*
 f présentation *f* audiovisuelle
 r аудиовизуальное представление *n*

665 audiovisual program; videogram
 d audiovisuelles Programm *n*; Videogramm *n*
 f programme *m* audiovisuel; vidéogramme *m*
 r аудиовизуальная программа *f*;
   видеограмма *f*

 * **audit *v* → 1450**

666 auditing; revision
 d Revision *f*; Prüfung *f*; Kontrollierung *f*

 f contrôle *m*; vérification *f*; révision *f*
 r ревизия *f*; проверка *f*; контроль *m*

667 audit report
 d Auflagenprüfungsbericht *m*;
   Auflagenkontrolle *f*; Prüfungsbericht *m*
 f rapport *m* d'audit; rapport de révision; rapport
   d'enquête; rapport d'évaluation; apport *m* de
   contrôle
 r отчет *m* ревизии

668 augment *v*
 d vermehren; zunehmen; zugeben
 f augmenter
 r увеличивать[ся]; усиливать

**669 augmentation; augmenting; magnification;
   magnifying**
 d Vergrößerung *f*; Zunahme *f*; Augmentation *f*
 f augmentation *f*; croissance *f*; grossissement *m*
 r увеличение *n*

670 augmented reality
 d vergrößerte Realität *f*
 f réalité *f* augmentée
 r расширенная реальность *f*

 * **augmenting → 669**

671 authorization
 d Berechtigungszuweisung *f*
 f autorisation *f*
 r санкция *f*; предоставление *n* права доступа

672 authorization code
 d Berechtigungszuweisungscode *m*
 f code *m* d'autorisation
 r код *m* санкции; код регистрирования

 * **auto-adapting → 8480**

 * **auto-aligning *adj* → 8482**

673 autobackup
 d automatisches Backup *n*
 f archivage *m* automatique
 r автоматическое архивирование *n*

 * **auto-checking → 8485**

674 autocorrelation
 d Autokorrelation *f*
 f autocorrélation *f*
 r автокорреляция *f*

675 autocovariance
 d Autokovarianz *f*
 f autocovariance *f*
 r автоматическая ковариантность *f*

676 **autodimension**
  d automatische Dimension *f*
  f cote *f* automatique
  r автоматическое измерение *n*

677 **autofocus; self-focus**
  d Selbstfokus *m*
  f autofocus *m*
  r автоматический фокус *m*

678 **autofocusing; self-focusing**
  d Selbstfokussierung *f*
  f autofocalisation *f*; mise *f* au point
    automatique
  r самофокусирование *n*; автоматическое
    фокусирование

679 **autofocusing; self-focusing** *adj*
  d selbstfokussierend
  f autofocalisant
  r самофокусирующийся

  * **autoformat** → 680

680 **autoformat[ing]**
  d Selbstformatierung *f*
  f formatage *m* automatique
  r автоматическое форматирование *n*

681 **auto-inflating**
  d automatische Vergrößerung *f*
  f haussement *m* automatique
  r автоматическое надувание *n*;
    автоматическое вздувание *n*

682 **auto-join**
  d automatische Teilnahme *f*; automatische
    Verbindung *f*
  f union *f* automatique
  r автоматическое соединение *n*

683 **automapping**
  d automatisches Mapping *n*
  f automappage *m*; automapping *m*
  r автоматическое отображение *n*

684 **automated cartography**
  d automatische Kartografie *f*
  f cartographie *f* automatisée
  r автоматизированная картография *f*

685 **automated digitizing**
  d automatische Digitalisierung *f*
  f digitalisation *f* automatique
  r автоматическое дигитализирование *n*

686 **automated feature extraction**
  (of a human face)
  d automatische Gesichtszug-Extraktion *f*
  f extraction *f* automatique des traits du visage

  r автоматическое выделение *n* черт лица

687 **automated feature recognition**
  (of a human face)
  d automatische Gesichtszug-Erkennung *f*
  f reconnaissance *f* automatique des traits du
    visage
  r автоматическое распознавание *n* черт лица

688 **automatic; self-acting**
  d automatisch; selbstwirkend; selbsttätig
  f automatique
  r автоматический; самодействующий

689 **automatic chroma control; automatic
    chrominance control; automatic color gain
    control**
  d automatische Farbtonregelung *f*;
    Farbkontrastautomatik *f*
  f contrôle *m* automatique de chrominance
  r автоматическое управление *n* цветовой
    интенсивности

  * **automatic chrominance control** → 689

  * **automatic color gain control** → 689

690 **automatic contrast**
  d automatischer Kontrast *m*
  f contraste *m* automatique
  r автоматический контраст *m*

691 **automatic contrast control**
  d automatische Kontrastregelung *f*
  f réglage *m* automatique du contraste
  r автоматическая регулировка *f*
    контрастности

692 **automatic extension line**
  (of dimension)
  d automatische Hilfslinie *f*
  f ligne *f* d'extension automatique
  r автоматическая вспомагательная линия *f*

693 **automatic face reconstruction**
  d automatische Gesichtsrekonstruktion *f*
  f reconstruction *f* automatique de visage;
    reconstruction automatique de face
  r автоматическая реконструкция *f* лица

694 **automatic framing; autositing**
  d automatische Rahmung *f*
  f cadrage *m* automatique; autocadrage *m*
  r автоматическое кадрирование *n*

695 **automatic graph design**
  d automatisches Design *n* des Graphs
  f dessin *m* automatique de graphe
  r автоматический дизайн *m* графа

696 automatic group selection
d automatische Auswahl *f* der Gruppe
f sélection *f* de groupe automatique
r автоматический выбор *m* группы

697 automatic pen capping
d automatisches Stift-Deckung *f*
f rebouchage *m* automatique de plume
r автоматическое перекрытие *n* пера

698 automatic reduction; auto-reduction
d automatische Verkleinerung *f*
f réduction *f* automatique; auto-réduction *f*
r автоматическое уменьшение *n*

699 automatic regeneration
d automatische Regenerierung *f*
f régénération *f* automatique
r автоматическое регенерирование *n*

700 automatic selection
d automatische Auswahl *f*
f sélection *f* automatique
r автоматическая выборка *f*

* **automatic shadow function** → 701

701 automatic shadow[ing] function
d automatische Schattenfunktion *f*
f fonction *f* d'ombrage automatique
r функция *f* автоматического затенения

702 automatic stacking
d automatische Stapelung *f*
f empilage *m* automatique
r автоматическая запись *f* в стек

* **automation** → 703

703 automati[zati]on
d Automati[sati]on *f*; Automatisierung *f*
f automati[sati]on *f*
r автоматизация *f*

704 automatize *v*
d automatisieren
f automatiser
r автоматизировать

* **autonomous** → 6457

705 autonomous system
d autonomes System *n*
f système *m* autonome
r автономная система *f*

706 autonomy
d Autonomie *f*
f autonomie *f*
r автономия *f*

707 auto-panning
d automatisches Schwenken *n*
f panoramique *m* automatique
r автоматическое панорамирование *n*

708 autoplot
d automatisches Plotten *n*; automatische grafische Darstellung *f*
f tracé *m* automatique
r автоматическое вычерчивание *n*

709 auto-reduce *v*
d autoreduzieren
f auto-réduire
r автоматически уменьшать

* **auto-reduction** → 698

710 autoscroll
d automatisches Rollen *n*
f défilement *m* automatique
r автопрокрутка *f*

711 autosimilarity
d automatische Ähnlichkeit *f*
f autosimilarité *f*
r автоматическое подобие *n*

* **autositing** → 694

712 auto-smoothing
d Auto-Glättung *f*
f auto-lissage *m*
r автоматическое сглаживание *n*

713 autosnap
d Autofang *m*
f autocrénelage *m*; accrochage *m* automatique
r автоматическое привязывание *n* к объекту; автоматическая объектная привязка *f*

714 autosnap marker
d Autofang-Marker *m*
f marquer *m* d'accrochage automatique
r маркер *m* автоматической привязки

715 autosnap setting
d Autofang-Einrichtung *f*
f établissement *m* d'accrochage automatique
r установление *n* автоматического привязывания

* **autospool** → 716

716 autospool[ing]
d Autospulung *f*
f autospoulage *m*
r автоматический спулинг *m*

717 auto-spreading
d automatische Spreizung *f*; automatische

Ausdehnung *f*
f grossissement *m* automatique
r автоматическое растягивание *n*

* **auto-testing** → 8485

718 **autotrace**
   d Autospur *f*
   f trace *f* automatique
   r автотрассировка *f*

* **autotracing** → 719

719 **autotrac[k]ing**
   d Auto-Tracing *n*
   f poursuite *f* automatique
   r автоматическое прослеживание *n*

720 **autotype; halftone block**
   d Autotypie *f*
   f autotypie *f*
   r автотипия *f*; факсимильный отпечаток *m*

721 **autowrap**
   d Auto-Umhüllung *f*; Auto-Umbruch *m*
   f auto-habillage *m*
   r автоматическое окутывание *n*;
      автоматическое завертывание *n*

722 **auxiliary**
   d Hilfs-
   f auxiliaire
   r вспомагательный

723 **auxiliary alphabet**
   d Hilfsalphabet *n*
   f alphabet *m* auxiliaire
   r вспомагательный алфавит *m*

724 **auxiliary cone; cone of slope**
   d Böschungskegel *m*
   f cône *m* de talus
   r конус *m* откоса

725 **auxiliary construction**
   d Hilfskonstruktion *f*
   f construction *f* auxiliaire
   r вспомагательное построение *n*

726 **auxiliary function**
   d Hilfsfunktion *f*
   f fonction *f* auxiliaire
   r вспомагательная функция *f*

727 **auxiliary line**
   d Hilfslinie *f*
   f ligne *f* auxiliaire
   r вспомагательная линия *f*

728 **auxiliary view**

d Hilfsansicht *f*
f vue *f* auxiliaire
r вспомагательный вид *m*

729 **availability**
   d Verfügbarkeit *f*
   f disponibilité *f*
   r готовность *f*; наличность *f*

730 **available data**
   d verfügbare Daten *npl*
   f données *fpl* accessibles
   r доступные данные *npl*

* **available time** → 3330

* **avatar** → 7812

731 **avatar's owner**
   d Avatar-Besitzer *m*
   f propriétaire *m* d'avatar
   r собственник *m* аватара

* **average** → 5862, 5866

732 **average calculating speed**
   d mittlere Rechengeschwindigkeit *f*
   f vitesse *f* moyenne de calcul
   r средняя скорость *f* вычисления

733 **average error; mean error**
   d mittlerer Fehler *m*; durchschnittlicher Fehler
   f erreur *f* moyenne
   r средняя ошибка *f*; средняя погрешность *f*

* **average value** → 5866

734 **averaging**
   d Mittel[wert]bildung *f*; Mittelung *f*
   f prise *f* en moyenne
   r усреднение *n*

735 **averaging method**
   d Mittelungsverfahren *n*; Mittelungsmethode *f*
   f méthode *f* du centrage; méthode des
      moyennes
   r метод *m* усреднения; способ *m* усреднения

* **AVI** → 661

736 **AVI file format**
   d AVI-Dateiformat *n*
   f format *m* de fichier AVI
   r формат *m* файла AVI

737 **axial**
   d axial
   f axial
   r осевой; аксиальный

738 axial beam; axial ray; principal ray
  d Axialstrahl m; Hauptstrahl m
  f rayon m axial; rayon principal
  r осевой луч m; аксиальный луч; главный
     луч

739 axial collineation
  d axiale Kollineation f
  f collinéation f axiale
  r аксиальная коллинеация f

740 axial complex
  d Achsenkomplex m
  f complexe m axial; complexe des axes
  r осевой комплекс m

741 axial compression
  d axiale Kompression f
  f compression f axiale
  r осевое сжатие n

742 axial coordinates
  d Achsenkoordinaten fpl
  f coordonnées fpl axiales
  r осевые координаты fpl; аксиальные
     координаты

743 axial elongation; axial strain
  d axiale Verlängerung f; Axialdehung f
  f [r]allongement m axial
  r осевое удлинение n; осевое растяжение n

744 axial error
  d Achsenfehler m
  f erreur f des axes; erreur axiale
  r осевая ошибка f

  * **axially symmetric → 745**

745 axially symmetric[al]
  d achs[en]symmetrisch
  f à symétrie axiale
  r осесимметричный

746 axially symmetric table
  d achsensymmetrische Tabelle f
  f table f à symétrie axiale
  r осесимметричная таблица f

747 axial misalignment; misalignment
  d Achsenversetzung f; Ausrichtungsfehler m;
     Fluchtungsfehler m
  f défaut m d'alignement axial; désaccord m
  r несовпадение n с осью; несоосность f;
     нецентрированность f

748 axial point
  d Axialpunkt m
  f point m axial
  r осевая точка m

749 axial ratio
  d Axialverhältnis n; Achsenverhältnis n
  f rapport m axial; rapport des axes
  r осевое соотношение n; отношение n осей

  * **axial ray → 738**

750 axial rotation
  d Axialdrehung f
  f rotation f autour d'un axe; rotation axiale
  r осевая ротация f

  * **axial strain → 743**

751 axial symmetry
  d Axialsymmetrie f; Achsensymmetrie f
  f symétrie f axiale
  r осевая симметрия f

  * **axioms of incidence in projective geometry
     → 7542**

752 axis
  d Achse f
  f axe m
  r ось f

  * **axis direction → 2870**

  * **axis endpoint → 3432**

**753 axis of a Cartesian coordinate system; axis
     of a Cartesian frame**
  d Koordinatenachse f eines kartesischen
     Koordinatensystems
  f axe m d'un repère cartésien
  r координатная ось f в декартовой системе
     координат

  * **axis of a Cartesian frame → 753**

  * **axis of a conic → 754**

754 axis of a conic [section]
  d Achse f eines Kegels; Achse eines
     Kegelschnitts
  f axe m d'une conique
  r ось f конического сечения; ось кривой
     второго порядка

755 axis of affinity
  d Affinitätsachse f
  f axe m d'affinité
  r ось f аффинного преобразования; ось
     аффинности

**756 axis of a frame; axis of reference; reference
     axis**
  d Bezugsachse f

f axe *m* d'un repère; axe de référence
r ось *f* отсчета; ось относимости

757 axis of an ellipse
d Achse *f* einer Ellipse
f axe *m* d'une ellipse
r ось *f* эллипса

758 axis of a parabola
d Parabelachse *f*
f axe *m* d'une parabole
r ось *f* параболы

759 axis of a pencil of planes
d Achse *f* eines Ebenenbündels
f axe *m* d'une gerbe de plans
r ось *f* связки плоскостей

* **axis of bundle of planes** → 770

* **axis of bundle of spheres** → 771

* **axis of collineation** → 766

760 axis of contraction; axis of shortening
d Schrumpfungsachse *f*
f axe *m* de contraction
r ось *f* сжатия

761 axis of coordinates; coordinate axis
d Koordinatenachse *f*
f axe *m* de coordonnées
r ось *f* координат; координатная ось

762 axis of curvature; curvature axis; bend axis
d Krümmungsachse *f*
f axe *m* de courbure
r ось *f* кривизны; ось изгиба

763 axis of deformation
d Deformationsachse *f*
f axe *m* de déformation
r ось *f* деформации

764 axis of helical displacement
d Achse *f* der spiralförmigen Verschiebung
f axe *m* de déplacement hélicoïdal; axe de vissage
r ось *f* спирального смещения

* **axis of homology** → 766

765 axis of inclination
d Neigungsachse *f*
f axe *m* d'inclinaison
r ось *f* наклона

766 axis of perspective; axis of perspectivity; axis of collineation; axis of homology

d Achse *f* der Perspektive; Perspektivitätsachse *f*; Kollineationsachse *f*; Homologieachse *f*
f axe *m* de perspectivité; axe perspectif; axe d'homologie
r ось *f* перспективы; ось гомологии

* **axis of perspectivity** → 766

767 axis of projection; projection axis; ground line
d Projektionsachse *f*
f axe *m* de projection
r ось *f* проекции; ось проектирования

768 axis of real affine space
d Achse *f* des realen affinen Raums
f axe *m* d'un espace affin réel
r ось *f* реального аффинного пространства

* **axis of reference** → 756

* **axis of revolution** → 769

769 axis of rotation; rotational axis; axis of revolution; pivot axis
d Dreh[ungs]achse *f*; Rotationsachse *f*; Stehachse *f*
f axe *m* de rotation; axe de révolution
r ось *f* вращения; ось поворота; поворотная ось

770 axis of sheaf of planes; axis of bundle of planes
d Ebenenbündelachse *f*
f axe *m* d'un faisceau de plans
r ось *f* пучка плоскостей

771 axis of sheaf of spheres; axis of bundle of spheres
d Achse *f* einer Garbe von Sphären; Achse eines Sphärenbündels
f axe *m* d'un faisceau de sphères
r ось *f* связки сфер

* **axis of shortening** → 760

* **axis of sight** → 243

772 axis of symmetry
d Symmetrieachse *f*; Spiegelungsachse *f*
f axe *m* de symétrie
r ось *f* симметрии

773 axis of the celestial sphere
d Himmelsachse *f*; Weltachse *f*
f axe *m* du monde; axe de la sphère céleste
r ось *f* мира; ось небесной сферы

774 axis of the eye
d Augachse *f*

f axe *m* de l'œil
r ось *f* глаза

775 axis traverse
d Achsenhub *m*
f déplacement *m* de l'axe
r осевой ход *m*

776 axis tripod
d Stativ *n*
f trépied *m*; tripode *m*
r штатив *m*; тренога *f*

777 axonometric drawing
d axonometrische Zeichnung *f*
f dessin *m* axonométrique
r аксонометрический чертеж *m*

778 axonometric image
d axonometrisches Bild *n*
f image *f* axonométrique
r аксонометрическое изображение *n*

* **axonometric mapping** → 779

**779 axonometric projection; axonometric
       mapping**
d axonometrische Projektion *f*
f projection *f* axonométrique
r аксонометрическая проекция *f*

780 axonometry
d Axonometrie *f*
f axonométrie *f*
r аксонометрия *f*

781 azimuth
d Azimut *m/n*
f azimut *m*
r азимут *m*

782 azimuthal angle
d Azimutalwinkel *m*
f angle *m* azimutal
r азимутальный угол *m*

783 azimuthal correction
d azimutales Eindrehen *n*
f rotation *f* en azimut
r азимутальная поправка *f*

* **azimuthal orthomorphic projection** →
    9199

784 azimuthal projection
d Azimutalprojektion *f*
f projection *f* azimutale
r азимутальная проекция *f*

B

785 back clipping plane
d hintere Schnittebene *f*
f plan *m* de [dé]coupage arrière; plan d'écrêtage arrière
r задняя отсекающая плоскость *f*

* **back direction** → 6529

786 backdrop
(of a scene)
d Hintergrund[vorgang] *m*; Kulisse *f*
f arrière-plan *m* (sur une scène)
r фон *m*; фоновая плоскость *f*

787 back edge
d Hinterkante *f*; Hinterrand *m*
f arête *f* arrière
r заднее ребро *n*

788 backface
d Hinterfläche *f*; Rückseite *f*
f face *f* arrière
r задняя поверхность *f*; задняя сторона *f*

* **backface elimination** → 791

789 backface option
d Hinterflächen-Option *f*
f option *f* de face arrière
r опция *f* задней поверхности

790 backface polygons eliminating
d Eliminierung *f* der Rückseite-Polygone
f élimination *f* de polygones de face arrière
r уничтожение *n* полигонов задней поверхности

791 backface removal; backface elimination; backfacing
d Hinterflächenentfernung *f*; Rückseitenpflücken *n*; Backfacing *n*
f élimination *f* de face arrière
r устранение *n* задней поверхности

792 backface selection
d Rückseitenauswahl *f*
f sélection *f* de face arrière
r выбор *m* задней поверхности

* **backfacing** → 791

793 backflow
d Rückdurchfluss *m*
f écoulement *m* inverse
r противоток *m*; обратный поток *m*

* **background** → 9172

794 background; foil
d Hintergrund *m*; Untergrund *m*
f fond *m*; arrière-plan *m*; plan *m* d'arrière
r фон *m*; задний план *m*

795 background color
d Hintergrundfarbe *f*; Grundfarbe *f*
f couleur *f* de fond; couleur d'arrière-plan
r цвет *m* фона

* **background display image** → 9172

796 background frames
d Hintergrundsaufnahmen *fpl*
f cadres *mpl* d'arrière-plan; cadres de fond
r фоновые кадры *mpl*

797 background gray
d Hintergrundgrau-Farbe *f*
f gris *m* d'arrière plan
r серый цвет *m* фона

798 background hatch saturation
d Sättigung *f* der Hintergrundschraffur
f saturation *f* de hachure de fond
r насыщенность *f* штриховки фона

799 background image
d Hintergrundbild *n*
f image *f* de fond
r фоновое изображение *n*

800 background light; backlight
d Hintergrundlicht *n*; Gegenlicht *n*
f lumière *f* de fond; lumière en contre-jour; lumière de derrière
r фоновый свет *m*

801 background lighting; backlighting; opposite lighting
d Hintergrundbeleuchtung *f*; Gegenlicht *n*; Rückenbeleuchtung *f*
f rétro-éclairage *m*; éclairage *m* par l'arrière; luminance *f* d'arrière-plan
r фоновое освещение *n*; заднее высвечивание *n*; противоположное освещение

802 background object
d Hintergrundobjekt *n*
f objet *m* de fond
r фоновый объект *m*

803 background pattern
d Hintergrundmuster *n*

f motif *m* de fond; modèle *m* de fond
r модель *f* фона

* **background projection** → 7839

* **background space** → 2172

804 **background subtraction**
d Subtrahieren *n* des Hintergrunds
f soustraction *f* d'arrière-plan
r вычитание *n* фона

* **backlight** → 800

* **backlighting** → 801

805 **back mirroring**
d Rückspiegelung *f*
f réflexion *f* spéculaire en arrière
r обратное зеркальное отражение *n*

806 **backplane**
d Rückwandplatine *f*
f plan *m* arrière
r задняя плоскость *f*

* **backscatter** → 807

807 **backscatter[ing]**
d Rückstreuung *f*
f rétrodiffusion *f*; diffusion *f* en arrière
r обратное рассеяние *n*

808 **backslash**
(\ )
d Backslash *n*; umgekehrter Schrägstrich *m*;
inverser Schrägstrich
f barre *f* oblique inverse; barre de haut en bas
r обратная косая черта *f*

809 **backspace; backspacing**
d Rückwärtsschritt *m*; Rücksetzen *n* um eine
Position
f espace[ment] *m* [d']arrière; rappel *m* [arrière];
retour *m* à une position
r обратное перемещение *n*; возврат *m* на
одну позицию

810 **backspace key**
d Rückwärtsschritt-Taste *f*
f touche *f* d'espacement arrière
r клавиша *f* для возврата на одну позицию

* **backspacing** → 809

811 **backup**
d Sicherung *f*; Reserve *f*; Backup *n*
f réserve *f*; archivage *m*; sauvegarde *f*
r резерв *m*; архив *m*

812 **backup copy**
d Sicherungskopie *f*; Backup-Kopie *f*
f copie *f* de réserve; copie d'archives
r резервная копия *f*; архивная копия

813 **backup file**
d Sicher[stell]ungsdatei *f*
f fichier *m* doubleur; fichier de secours
r дублирующий файл *m*; архивный файл

* **back view** → 7840

814 **balance; equilibrium**
d Gleichgewicht *n*; Balance *f*
f balance *f*; équilibre *m*
r равновесие *n*; баланс *m*

815 **balance filter**
d Balancefilter *m*
f filtre *m* d'équilibre
r фильтр *m* калибровки

816 **balancing**
d Auswuchtung *f*; Auswuchten *n*
f équilibrage *m*
r балансирование *n*; уравновешивание *n*

* **ball** → 819

817 **ballistic curve**
d ballistische Kurve *f*
f courbe *f* balistique
r баллистическая кривая *f*

* **ball lens** → 9044

818 **balloon; bubble**
d Ballon *m*; Sprechblase *f*; Blase *f*
f ballon *m*; bulle *f*
r кружок *m*; шар *m*; пузырек *m*

819 **ball [terminal]; teardrop**
d Kugel *f*
f boule *f*
r шар *m*; каплевидный элемент *m*

820 **band**
d Band *n*
f bande *f*
r полоса *f*

821 **band; bar; strip[e]**
d Streifen *m*; Leiste *f*
f barre *f*; ruban *m*; feuillet *m*
r лента *f*

822 **banding**
(defect of halftone screens or screen tints
output by laser printers or imagesetters)
d Bandeinpassen *n*; Siebkettung *f*

f effet *m* de bande; étirement *m*

r нанесение *n* полос; обозначение *n* полосами

823 band-pass filter
d Bandpassfilter *m*
f filtre *m* passe-bande
r полосовой фильтр *m*

* **band plotter** → 879

824 bank
(of data)
d Bank *f*
f banque *f*
r банк *m*

825 banner
(large headline, usually across the full width of a page)
d Banner *n*; Balkenüberschrift *f*; Werbeband *n*; Spruchband *n*
f bandeau *m*; bannière *m*
r баннер *m*; фантик *m*; заголовок *m*; шапка *f*; титул *m*; объявление *n*; реклама *f*

826 banner block
d Bannerblock *m*
f bloc *m* de bannière
r блок *m* баннера

* **bar** → 821, 9245

827 bar chart; column graph; bar diagram; bar graph; column diagram; histogram
d Streifendiagramm *n*; Staffelbild *n*; Balkendiagramm *n*; Histogramm *n*
f diagramme *m* à colonnes; diagramme à tuyaux d'orgue; histogramme *m*
r столбиковая диаграмма *f*; столбчатая диаграмма; диаграмма в виде столбцов; гистограмма *f*

828 bar code
d Barcode *m*; Strichcode *m*; Balkencode *m*
f code *m* à barre
r штрих-код *m*

* **bar diagram** → 827

* **bar graph** → 827

829 bar menu
d Menüzeile *f*
f menu *m* barre
r лента-меню *f*

830 Bartlet window
d Bartlet-Fenster *n*
f fenêtre *f* de Bartlet

r окно *n* Бартлета

831 barycentric coordinates
d baryzentrische Koordinaten *fpl*
f coordonnées *fpl* barycentriques
r барицентрические координаты *fpl*

* **base** → 857

832 base; basis
d Basis *f*; Grund *m*
f base *f*
r база *f*; базис *m*; основа *f*

* **base characteristics** → 852

833 base colors; basic colors
d Grundfarben *fpl*
f couleurs *fpl* de base
r базовые цвета *mpl*; основные цвета

834 base coordinate system
d Basiskoordinatensystem *n*
f système *m* de coordonnées de base
r система *f* базисных координат

* **base curve** → 2861

* **based map** → 850

835 base edge
d Grundkante *f*; Basiskante *f*
f arête *f* de base
r ребро *n* основания

836 base entities
d Grundeinheiten *fpl*
f entités *fpl* de base
r базисные примитивы *mpl*

837 base for calibration; comparison base
d Eichbasis *f*; Vergleichsbasis *f*; Kontrollbasis *f*
f base *f* d'étalonnage
r эталонный базис *m*; контрольный базис

838 base grip
d basischer Griff *m*; gemeiner Griff; Basisgriff *m*
f poignée *f* de base
r базисный захват *m*; опорный захват; базовый захват

839 base layer
d Basisschicht *f*
f plan *m* de base
r базовый слой *m*

840 baseline
d Basislinie *f*; Grundlinie *f*
f ligne *f* de base
r базовая линия *f*

841 baseline dimension
  d Grundliniendimension *f*
  f cotation *f* en ligne de base
  r измерение *n* с базовой линии

842 baseline shift
  d Grundlinienverschiebung *f*
  f décalage *m* de ligne base
  r смещение *n* базовой линии

843 base map; basic map
  d Grundkarte *f*
  f carte *f* de base
  r основная карта *f*; первичная карта

844 base menu
  d Grundmenü *n*
  f menu *m* de base
  r базовое меню *n*

845 base of a cone
  d Basis *f* eines Kegels
  f base *f* d'un cône
  r основание *n* конуса

846 base of a triangle
  d Grundseite *f* eines Dreiecks
  f base *f* d'un triangle
  r основание *n* треугольника

847 base pattern
  d Grundmotiv *n*
  f motif *m* de base
  r основной мотив *m*

848 base point
  d Basispunkt *m*
  f point *m* de base; point fondamental
  r базисная точка *f*; базовая точка

849 base point of rotation
  d Basisdrehpunkt *m*
  f point *m* de base de rotation
  r базовая точка *f* поворота

  * **base point-preserving map → 850**

850 base point-preserving map[ping]; based map
  d grundpunkterhaltende Abbildung *f*; basispunkttreue Abbildung; punktierte Abbildung
  f application *f* pointée
  r пунктированное отображение *n*; отображение, сохраняющее отмеченные точки

851 base projection
  d Basisprojektion *f*
  f projection *f* de la base

  r базисная проекция *f*

852 base properties; base characteristics
  d Grundeigenschaften *fpl*
  f propriétés *fpl* de base
  r основные свойства *npl*; основные характеристики *fpl*

853 base stencils
  d Basismatrizen *fpl*
  f stencils *mpl* de base
  r базовые шаблоны *mpl*

854 base structure
  d Grundstruktur *f*
  f structure *f* de base
  r базовая структура *f*

855 base surface
  (of a frustum)
  d Grundfläche *f*
  f surface *f* de base
  r поверхность *f* основания

856 base table
  d Basistabelle *f*
  f table *f* de base
  r базовая таблица *f*

  * **base vector → 864**

857 basic; base; fundamental
  d Basis-; fundamental; Grund-; grundsätzlich
  f de base; basique; fondamental
  r основной; базисный; фундаментальный

858 basic blend
  d Basis-Überblendung *f*
  f dégradé *m* de base
  r базовое переливание *n*

  * **basic colors → 833**

859 basic component
  d Basiskomponente *f*; Grundbaustein *m*
  f composante *f* basique
  r базисный компонент *m*; основной градивный элемент *m*

860 basic dimension
  d Basisdimension *f*
  f dimension *f* basique
  r базовое измерение *n*

  * **basic map → 843**

861 basic representation
  d Basisdarstellung *f*
  f représentation *f* de base
  r базисное представление *n*

862 basic spatial unit
d räumliche Basiseinheit *f*
f unité *f* spatiale de base
r основная пространственная единица *f*

863 basic symbol
d Grundzeichen *n*; Grundsymbol *n*
f symbole *m* de base; symbole fondamental
r базисный символ *m*; основной знак *m*

864 basic vector; base vector
d Basisvektor *m*
f vecteur *m* de base
r базисный вектор *m*

* **basis** → 832

865 batch
d Batch *m*; Stapel *m*; Schub *m*
f lot *m*; train *m*; pile *f*
r пакет *m*; группа *f*

* **batching** → 867

866 batch plotting
d Batchplotten *n*; Stapelplotten *n*
f tracé *m* par lots
r пакетное вычерчивание *n*

867 batch processing; batching
d Batch-Verarbeitung *f*; Stapelverarbeitung *f*; blockweise Verarbeitung *f*
f traitement *m* en groupes; traitement échelonné; traitement par lots
r пакетная обработка *f*; групповая обработка

* **bay** → 868

868 bay [plane]
d Strahl[er]ebene *f*
f plan *m* de rayonnement
r плоскость *f* излучения

869 beam; ray
d Strahl *m*
f rayon *m*; faisceau *m*; jet *m*
r луч *m*; пучок *m* [лучей]

870 beam angle; hotspot cone angle
(the brightness part of a light beam)
d Strahlenwinkel *m*
f angle *m* de faisceau
r угол *m* пучка

871 beam convergence
d Strahl[en]konvergenz *f*
f convergence *f* des faisceaux
r сходимость *f* лучей

872 beam coupling

d Strahlenkopplung *f*
f couplage *m* de faisceaux
r связь *f* лучей

873 beam focusing
d Strahlfokussierung *f*; Strahlbündelung *f*
f focalisation *f* de faisceau; focalisation des rayons
r фокусировка *f* пучка

* **beam object** → 7789

* **beam pen** → 5554

874 beam position
d Strahlposition *f*
f position *f* de rayon
r позиция *f* луча

* **bearing angle** → 2865

* **bearing point** → 2873

* **before-image** → 7383

* **begin** *v* → 6631

* **begin** → 6632

875 behavioral controller
d Verhaltenscontroller *m*
f contrôleur *m* de comportement
r контроллер *m* поведения

876 behavioral simulation
d Verhaltenssimulierung *f*
f simulation *f* comportementale
r поведенческая симуляция *f*

877 believability
d Glaubwürdigkeit *f*
f véracité *f*; véridicité *f*; droiture *f*
r достоверность *f*; правдоподобие *n*

878 believable approximation
d glaubwürdige Approximation *f*
f approximation *f* vraisemblable
r правдоподобная аппроксимация *f*

* **belt-bed plotter** → 3190

879 belted plotter; band plotter
d Bandplotter *m*
f traceur *m* à bande
r ленточный графопостроитель *m*

* **Beltrami mapping** → 4157

* **Beltrami's mapping** → 4157

880 bend *v*
  d biegen
  f cintrer
  r гнуть; сгибать; изгибать

* **bend** → 882

* **bend axis** → 762

881 bend direction
  d Krümmungsrichtung *f*
  f direction *f* de courbure
  r направление *n* изгиба

* **bending of light** → 6544

* **bending radius** → 7715

882 bend[ing]; sweep; courbure
  d Biegung *f*; Knick *m*; Krümmung *f*
  f coude *m*; courbure *f*; flexion *f*
  r изгиб *m*; излом *m*; кривизна *f*

883 bend point of a curve
  d Extrempunkt *m* einer Kurve
  f point *m* extrême d'une courbe
  r экстремальная точка *f* кривой

* **bend radius** → 7715

884 bent optical axis
  d gekrümmte optische Achse *f*
  f axe *m* optique courbé
  r искривленная оптическая ось *f*

885 Bernstein polynomials
  d Bernstein-Polynome *npl*
  f polynômes *mpl* de Bernstein
  r полиномы *mpl* Бернштейна

886 best-fit trends
  d Richtungen *fpl* der besten Übereinstimmung
  f tendances *fpl* de meilleur ajustement
  r наилучше аппроксимированные
    тренды *mpl*; наилучше прилегаемые
    тренды

887 beta-spline; B-spline
  d Beta-Spline *m*; B-Spline *m*
  f bêta-spline *m*; B-spline *m*
  r В-сплайн *m*

* **betweening** → 6036

* **bevel** → 1395

888 bevel angle
  d Abschrägungswinkel *m*
  f angle *m* de biseau; angle de biseautage
  r угол *m* фаски

889 bevel depth
  d Abschrägungstiefe *f*
  f profondeur *f* de biseau
  r глубина *f* откоса; глубина *f* фаски

890 beveled
  d abgeschrägt
  f chanfreiné; biseauté
  r скошенный

891 beveled boundary
  d abgeschrägte Grenze *f*
  f bord *m* biseauté
  r скошенная граница *f*

892 beveled corners; blunted corners
  d abgeschrägte Ecken *fpl*
  f angles *mpl* biseautés
  r скошенные углы *mpl*

893 beveled edges
  d abgeschrägte Kanten *fpl*
  f arêtes *fpl* chanfreinés
  r скошенные ребра *npl*

894 beveled extrusion
  d abgeschrägte Extrusion *f*
  f extrusion *f* biseautée
  r скошенная экструзия *f*

895 beveled surfaces
  d abgeschrägte Flächen *fpl*
  f surfaces *fpl* biseautées
  r скошенные поверхности *fpl*

* **beveling** → 1396

* **bevelling** → 1396

896 Bézier approximation
  d Bézier-Approximation *f*
  f approximation *f* Bézier
  r аппроксимация *f* Безье

897 Bézier curve
  d Bézier-Kurve *f*
  f courbe *f* de Bézier
  r кривая *f* Безье

898 Bézier patch
  d Bézier-Stück *n*
  f surface *f* paramétrique de Bézier
  r фрагмент *m* Безье

899 Bézier polygon
  d Bézier-Vieleck *n*
  f polygone *m* de Bézier
  r многоугольник *m* Безье

900 Bézier surfaces
  d Bézier-Flächen *fpl*

f surfaces *fpl* [polynomiales] de Bézier
r поверхности *fpl* Безье

901 Bézier tool
  d Hilfsmittel *n* "Bézier"
  f outil *m* "Bézier"
  r инструмент *m* Безье

  * **bias** → 902

902 bias[ing]
  d Verschiebung *f*
  f biais *m*
  r смещение *n*; перекос *m*

903 bichromatic; dichromatic
  d bichromatisch
  f bichromatique
  r двухцветный

904 bichromatic graph
  d bichromatischer Graph *m*
  f graphe *m* bichromatique
  r двухцветный граф *m*

  * **bichromy** → 2722

  * **bicolor pattern** → 9954

905 biconcave; doubly concave; concavo-concave
  d bikonkav
  f biconcave; concavo-concave
  r двояковогнутый

906 bicone; double cone
  d Doppelkegel *m*; Doppelkonus *m*
  f bicône *m*; double cône *m*
  r двойной конус *m*; полный конус

907 biconical
  d bikonisch; Doppelkonus-
  f biconique
  r биконический; двухконусный

908 bicubic patch
  d bikubisches Flächenstück *n*
  f surface *f* paramétrique bicubique
  r бикубический кусок *m*

909 bicubic surface
  d bikubische Fläche *f*
  f surface *f* bicubique
  r бикубическая поверхность *f*

  * **bidimensional** → 9956

910 bidirectional; bothway; two-directional; two-way
  d bidirektional; Zweirichtungs-;

doppelgerichtet; Zweiweg-
f bidirectionnel
r двунаправленный; в двух направлениях

911 bidirectional asymmetry
  d bidirektionale Asymmetrie *f*
  f asymétrie *f* bidirectionnelle
  r двунаправленная асимметрия *f*

912 bidirectional linear object
  d bidirektionales lineares Objekt *n*
  f objet *m* linéaire bidirectionnel
  r двунаправленный линейный объект *m*

  * **bidirectional reflectance function** → 913

913 bidirectional reflectance [distribution] function; BRDF
  d Funktion *f* [der Verteilung] der bidirektionalen Reflektanz
  f fonction *f* [de distribution] de réflectance bidirectionnelle
  r функция *f* [распределения] двунаправленного отражения

914 bifocal lens
  d Bifokallinse *f*
  f lentille *f* bifocale
  r бифокальная линза *f*

915 big black arrow
  d großer Schwarzpfeil *m*
  f grosse flèche *f* noire
  r большая черная стрелка *f*

916 big font
  d große Schrift *f*
  f police *f* grosse
  r крупный шрифт *m*

917 bilateral; two-sided; double-side[d]
  d bilateral; doppelseitig
  f bilatéral; bilatère
  r двусторонний

  * **bilateral surface** → 9959

918 bilevel grid
  d Zweipegel-Gitter *n*
  f grille *f* à deux niveaux
  r двууровневая сетка *f*; двухэтажная сетка

919 bilinear filtering
  d bilineare Filtrierung *f*; bilineares Filtering *n*
  f filtrage *m* bilinéaire
  r билинейное фильтрирование *n*; билинейная фильтрация *f*

920 bilinear interpolation
  d bilineare Interpolation *f*

 f interpolation *f* bilinéaire
 r билинейная интерполяция *f*

921 bilinear patch
 d bilineares Oberflächenstück *n*
 f surface *f* paramétrique bilinéaire
 r билинейный кусок *m*; билинейный
  фрагмент *m*

922 bilinear pixel interpolation
 d bilineare Pixel-Interpolation *f*
 f interpolation *f* bilinéaire des pixels
 r билинейная интерполяция *f* пикселов

923 bimodal
 d bimodal
 f bimodal
 r бимодальный

924 bimodality
 d Bimodalität *f*
 f bimodalité *f*
 r бимодальность *f*

925 bimodality checking
 d Bimodalitätsprüfung *f*
 f vérification *f* de bimodalité
 r проверка *f* бимодальности

926 binary DXF file format
 d binäres DXF-Dateiformat *n*
 f format *m* binaire DXF de fichier
 r формат *m* файла DXF

927 binary file
 d binäre Datei *f*
 f fichier *m* binaire
 r двоичный файл *m*

 * **binary image** → 930

928 binary image output
 d Binärbildausgabe *f*
 f sortie *f* d'image binaire
 r выход *m* бинарного изображения

929 binary outline picture
 d Binärumriss-Bild *n*
 f image *f* de contour binaire
 r бинарное изображение *n* контура

930 binary picture; binary image
 d Binärbild *n*
 f image *f* binaire
 r бинарное изображение *n*

 * **bind** → 5655

931 bind *v*; **link** *v*; **connect** *v*
 d binden; verbinden; verknüpfen

 f joindre; lier
 r связывать; соединять

932 binded straight lines
 d gebundene Geraden *fpl*
 f droites *fpl* reliées
 r связанные прямые *fpl*

 * **binding** → 5655

933 bind option
 d Bindungs-Option *f*
 f option *f* d'attachement
 r опция *f* привязки

934 binocular; bi-ocular
 d binokular
 f binoculaire
 r биокулярный

935 binocular parallax
 d binokulare Parallaxe *f*
 f parallaxe *f* binoculaire
 r биокулярный параллакс *m*

936 binoculars; double eye-glass; field glass
 d Binokel *n*; Doppelfernrohr *n*
 f binocle *m*; jumelles *fpl*
 r бинокль *m*; бинокуляр *m*

937 binocular stereo
 d Binokularstereo *n*
 f stéréo *m* binoculaire
 r биокулярное стерео *n*

938 binocular vision
 d binokulares Sehen *n*
 f vision *f* binoculaire
 r биокулярное зрение *n*

 * **bi-ocular** → 934

939 biometric identification systems
 d biometrische Identifizierungssysteme *npl*
 f systèmes *mpl* d'identification biométriques
 r биометрические идентификационные
  системы *fpl*

940 biosensor
 d Biosensor *m*
 f biosenseur *m*
 r биосенсор *m*

941 bipartite graph
 d zweiteiliger Graph *m*
 f graphe *m* biparti[te]
 r двудольный граф *m*

942 bipolar cell
 d Bipolarzelle *f*

f cellule *f* bipolaire
r биполярная клетка *f*

943 bipolar coordinates
d Bipolarkoordinaten *fpl*
f coordonnées *fpl* bipolaire
r биполярные координаты *fpl*

944 bird's eye perspective; bird's eye view; military perspective
d Vogelperspektive *f*; Militärperspektive *f*
f vue *f* à vol d'oiseau; perspective *f* militaire
r перспектива *f* с птичьего полета; вид *m* с птичьего полета; военная перспектива

* **bird's eye view** → **944**

* **birefringence** → **3091**

945 birefringent
d doppelbrechend
f biréfringent
r двоякопреломляющий

* **bisecting** *adj* → **5888**

946 bisecting plane
d Halbierungsebene *f*; winkelhalbierende Ebene *f*
f plan *m* bissecteur; bissecteur *m*
r бисекторная плоскость *f*; бисектральная плоскость

947 bisection
d Bisektion *f*; Halbierung *f*; Zweiteilung *f*
f bissection *f*
r деление *n* пополам; деление на две равные части

* **bisector** → **948**

948 bisectrix; [angle-]bisector
d Bisektrix *f*; Winkelhalbierende *f*
f bissectrice *f*
r биссектриса *f* [угла]

949 bit
d Bit *n*
f bit *m*
r бит *m*

950 bitangent curves
d sich in zwei Punkten berührende Kurven *fpl*
f courbes *fpl* bitangentes
r дважды касательные кривые *fpl*

951 bitangent of a plane curve
d Doppeltangente *f* einer ebenen Kurve
f bitangente *f* d'une courbe plane
r общая касательная *f* в двух различных точках; двойная касательная плоской кривой

* **bit-angle** → **5739**

952 bit blit; BLT
(a family of algorithms for moving an copying of bit arrays between main and display memory)
d Transfer *m* der Bitblöcke
f transfert *m* de blocs de bits
r перекачка *f* битовых блоков

953 bit chain; bit string
d Bitkette *f*
f chaîne *f* de bits
r битовая строка *f*; цепочка *f* битов

* **1-bit color mode** → **6469**

954 bit depth
(of color images)
d Bittiefe *f*
f profondeur *f* en bits
r битова глубина *f*; глубина в битах

* **bitmap** → **7762**

955 bitmap autotrace function
d Bitmap-Autotrace-Funktion *f*
f fonction *f* de trace automatique du bitmap
r функция *f* автотрассировки растрового отображения

956 bitmap background
d Bitmap-Hintergrund *m*
f arrière-plan *m* bitmap; fond *m* bitmap
r растровый фон *m*

957 bitmap-based program
d Bitmap-basiertes Programm *n*
f programme *m* orienté bitmap
r программа *f*, базированная на растровых изображениях

958 bitmap color mask
d Bitmap-Farbmaske *f*
f masque *f* couleur bitmap
r растровая цветовая маска *f*

959 bitmap copy
d Bitmap-Kopie *f*
f copie *f* bitmap
r растровая копия *f*

* **bitmap display** → **966**

960 bitmap file
d Bitmap-Datei *f*

   f fichier *m* bitmap
   r файл *m* растровой графики; файл
   растрового изображения; файл текстуры

961 bitmap font
   d Bitmap-Schrift *f*
   f police *f* bitmap
   r растровый шрифт *m*

962 bitmap format
   d Bitmap-Format *n*
   f format *m* bitmap; format image-point
   r формат *m* растрового отображения

   * **bitmap graphics** → 7759

   * **bitmap image** → 7762

963 bitmap importing
   d Bitmap-Importieren *n*
   f importation *f* d'image pixélisée
   r внесение *n* растрового отображения;
   импортирование *n* растрового
   изображения

964 bitmap mode
   d Bitmap-Modus *m*
   f mode *m* bitmap
   r режим *m* растрового отображения

   * **bitmap object** → 7769

965 bitmap pattern
   d Bitmap-Muster *n*
   f motif *m* bitmap
   r растровый узор *m*; растровый рисунок *m*

966 bitmap[ped] display; bitmap[ped] screen
   d Bitmap-Bildschirm *m*; Bitmap-Display *n*
   f écran *m* bitmap; écran [graphique] par points;
   écran pixel; écran pixélisé
   r растровый экран *m*

   * **bitmapped graphics** → 7759

   * **bitmapped screen** → 966

967 bitmap print
   d Bitmap-Druck *m*
   f impression *f* bitmap
   r растровая печать *f*; печать точками

968 bitmap resolution
   d Bitmap-Auflösungsvermögen *n*
   f résolution *f* bitmap
   r разрешающая способность *f* растровой
   графики

969 bitmap rotator
   d Bitmap-Rotator *m*

   f rotateur *m* bitmap
   r растровый вращатель *m*

   * **bitmap screen** → 966

970 bitmap selecting
   d Bitmap-Selektion *f*
   f sélection *f* de bitmap
   r выбор *m* растрового отображения

971 bitmap size
   d Bitmap-Größe *f*
   f taille *f* de bitmap
   r размер *m* растрового изображения

972 bitmaps tracing
   d Bitmap-Tracing *n*
   f traçage *m* de bitmaps
   r трассировка *f* растровых изображений

973 bitonal
   d bitonal
   f bitonal
   r в двух тональностях

974 bitonal image
   d bitonales Bild *n*
   f image *f* bitonale
   r изображение *n* в двух тональностях

975 bitplane; color plane
   d Bitebene *f*; Farbebene *f*
   f plan *m* binaire
   r битовая плоскость *f*; цветовая плоскость

976 bitplanes filter
   d Bitebenen-Filter *m*
   f filtre *m* de planes binaires
   r фильтр *m* битовых плоскостей

977 bitrate
   d Bitrate *f*
   f débit *m* binaire
   r скорость *f* передачи битов

   * **bits by pixel** → 978

978 bits per pixel; bits by pixel
   d Bits *npl* pro Pixel; Pixel-Bit-Tiefe *f*
   f bits *mpl* par pixel
   r число *n* битов на пиксел

   * **bit string** → 953

979 bivariate distribution; 2D distribution
   d bivariate Verteilung *f*; 2D-Verteilung *f*
   f distribution *f* à deux variables;
   distribution 2D
   r двумерное распределение *n*

980 black-and-white bitmap
  d Schwarzweiß-Bitmap *n*
  f bitmap *m* noir et blanc
  r черно-белое растровое изображение *n*

981 black-and-white color mode
  d Schwarzweiß-Farbmodus *m*
  f mode *m* couleur noir et blanc
  r режим *m* черно-белого изображения

982 black-and-white display
  d Schwarzweiß-Bildschirm *m*
  f écran *m* noir et blanc
  r черно-белый экран *m*

983 black-and-white image
  d Schwarzweiß-Bild *n*
  f image *f* noire et blanche
  r черно-белое изображение *n*

984 black-and-white printer
  d Schwarzweißdrucker *m*
  f imprimante *f* noir et blanche
  r черно-белый принтер *m*

  * **black-and-white scan → 985**

985 black-and-white scan[ning]
  d Schwarzweiß-Scannen *n*
  f échantillonnage *m* en noir et blanc
  r черно-белое сканирование *n*

986 blackering; blacking; darkening
  d Schwärzung *f*
  f noircissement *m*
  r почернение *n*

  * **blacking → 986**

987 black level
  d Schwarzniveau *n*
  f niveau *m* de noir
  r уровень *m* черного

988 black point
  d Schwarzpunkt *m*
  f point *m* de noir
  r точка *f* черного

989 black screen
  (of death)
  d schwarzer Bildschirm *m*; Schwarzscreen *n*
  f écran *m* noir
  r черный экран *m*

  * **blank → 8917**

990 blank; idle; vacant; empty; void
  d leer; frei; unbenutzt; unbesetzt
  f blanc; vide; vacant; vierge; inutile; libre
  r пустой; незанятый; свободный; холостой;
  бездействующий

  * **blank character → 4794, 8917**

991 blanking
  d unsichtbar Machen *n*; Abschalten *n*
  f extinction *f*; occultation *f*
  r гашение *n*

992 blank space
  d Leerstelle *f*; Zwischenraum *m*; Lücke *f*
  f espace *m* vide; blanc *m*; vide *m*; hiatus *m*
  r пустое пространство *n*; промежуток *m*;
  интервал *m*

993 bleach *v*
  d bleichen; abschwächen
  f blanchir; délaver
  r обесцвечивать; отбеливать

994 bleaching
  d Bleichung *f*; Abschwächung *f*
  f blanchissement *m*; blanchissage *m*
  r отбеливание *n*

  * **bleed → 996**

995 bleed control
  d Schnittrand-Kontrolle *f*
  f contrôle *m* de débordement
  r контроль *m* обреза

996 bleed[ing]
  (printing that extends to the edge of a sheet or
  page after trimming)
  d Schnittrand *m*; Beschnitt *m*; Anschnitt *m*;
  Anschneiden *n*
  f débordement *m*; étalement *m*
  r иллюстрация *f* в обрез; иллюстрация на
  всю страницу

997 bleed limit
  d Beschnitt-Grenze *f*
  f limite *f* de débordement
  r граница *f* обреза

998 blend *v*
  (of colors)
  d überblenden
  f dégrader
  r переливать; незаметно переходить из
  оттенка в оттенок

  * **blend *v* → 5989**

  * **blend → 1004, 5995**

999 blend angle
  d Überblendungswinkel *m*

f angle *m* de dégradé
r угол *m* переливания

1000 blend attributes
  d Überblendungsattribute *npl*
  f attributs *mpl* de dégradé
  r атрибуты *mpl* переливания; атрибуты
      смешивания

1001 blend components
  d Überblendungskomponenten *fpl*
  f composants *mpl* de dégradé
  r компоненты *mpl* переливания

1002 blend direction
  d Überblendungsrichtung *f*
  f direction *f* de dégradé
  r направление *n* переливания; направление
      перехода одного цвета в другой

1003 blend effect
  d Überblendungseffekt *m*
  f effet *m* de dégradé
  r эффект *m* переливания

1004 blend[ing]
  d Überblendung *f*; Überblenden *n*
  f dégradé *m*; dégradation *f*
  r переливание *n*; переход *m* от одного цвета
      в другой

  * **blending → 5995**

1005 blending function
  d Misch[ungs]funktion *f*
  f fonction *f* de mélange
  r функция *f* смешения

1006 blending level
  d Mischungsniveau *n*
  f niveau *m* de mélange
  r уровень *m* смешения

1007 blending objects
  d Überblendungsobjekte *npl*
  f objets *mpl* de dégradé
  r объекты *mpl* переливания

1008 blending on a path
  d Überblendung *f* entlang einer Strecke
  f dégradé *m* sur un tracé; dégradé au long d'un
      tracé
  r переливание *n* вокруг трассы

1009 blending rate
  d Überblendungskoeffizient *m*;
      Überblendungsrate *f*
  f vitesse *f* de dégradé
  r коэффициент *m* переливания

1010 blending region
  d Misch[ungs]bereich *m*
  f région *f* de mélange
  r регион *m* смешения

1011 blend mode
  d Mischungsmodus *m*
  f mode *m* de mélange
  r режим *m* смешивания

1012 blend reversing
  d Überblendungsumkehrung *f*
  f renversement *m* de dégradé
  r реверсирование *n* переливания

1013 blend rollup
  d Überblendungs-Rollup *n*
  f déroulement *m* séquentiel ascendant de
      dégradé
  r свертывание *n* переливания

1014 blend selecting
  d Überblendungsauswahl *f*
  f sélection *f* de dégradé
  r выбор *m* переливания

  * **blind → 2717**

1015 blind angle; dead angle
  d [sicht]toter Winkel *m*
  f angle *m* mort
  r мертвый угол *m*

  * **blind emboss → 1016**

1016 blind emboss[ing]
  d erhabene Blindprägung *f*; erhabene
      Blindpressung *f*
  f mise *f* en relief
  r рельефное тиснение *n*; бескрасочное
      тиснение; блинт *m*

1017 blind spot; friar
  d [sicht]toter Raum *m*
  f espace *m* mort
  r мертвая зона *f*; непропечатка *f*

  * **blinking → 3845**

1018 blinking bar
  d blinkender Strich *m*
  f barre *f* clignotante
  r мерцающая черта *f*

1019 blinking cursor
  d blinkender Kursor *m*
  f curseur *m* clignotant
  r мерцающий курсор *m*

1020 blinking rectangle
  d blinkendes Rechteck *n*

f rectangle *m* clignotant
r мерцающий прямоугольник *m*

1021 blip
(on the screen)
d Echozeichen *n*; Leuchtzeichen *n*; Blip *n*
f marque *f* de recherche; pavé *m* optique
r отметка *f*; метка *f*

1022 blitter
(a processor in the graphics board)
d Blitter *n*
f processeur *m* graphique
r блитер *m*; модуль *m* блитирования

1023 block
d Block *m*
f bloc *m*
r блок *m*

1024 block *v*; **lock** *v*
d blockieren; sperren
f bloquer
r блокировать

1025 block adjustment
d Blockausgleich *m*; Blockausgleichung *f*
f compensation *f* en bloc
r уравнивание *n* блока

1026 block attribute
d Blockattribut *n*
f attribut *m* de bloc
r атрибут *m* блока

1027 block attribute variable
d Variable *f* des Blockattributs
f variable *f* d'attribut de bloc
r переменная *f* блокового атрибута

1028 block-by-block mode
(of description of geometric objects)
d Block-zu-Block-Modus *m*
f mode *m* bloc par bloc
r поблочный режим *m*

1029 block collection object
d Blocksammlungsobjekt *n*
f objet *m* collection de blocs
r объект *m* типа коллекции блоков

1030 block color
d Blockfarbe *f*
f couleur *f* de bloc
r цвет *m* блока

1031 block definition
d Blockdefinition *f*
f définition *f* de bloc
r дефиниция *f* блока

* **block diagram** → 3878

1032 block entity
d Blockeinheit *f*
f entité *f* bloc
r примитив *m* блок

* **block graphics** → 6040

1033 blocking
d Blockierung *f*
f blocage *m*; partage *m* en blocs
r разбиение *n* на блоки

* **blocking** → 5685

1034 block insertion
d Blockeinfügung *f*
f insertion *f* de bloc
r вставка *f* блока

1035 block leader
d Block-Leiter *m*
f directeur *m* de bloc
r заголовок *m* блока

1036 block name
d Blockname *m*
f nom *m* de bloc
r имя *n* блока

1037 block number
d Blocknummer *f*
f numéro *m* de bloc
r номер *m* блока

1038 block object
d Block-Objekt *n*
f objet *m* bloc
r объект *m* типа блока

1039 block reference
d Blockverweis *m*
f référence *f* de bloc
r блоковая ссылка *f*

* **block rotation** → 8206

* **block scheme** → 3878

1040 block size
d Blocklänge *f*
f taille *f* de bloc
r размер *m* блока

1041 block table
d Blocktabelle *f*
f table *f* de blocs
r таблица *f* блоков

* **bloom** → 1042

1042 bloom[ing]
(of an image)
d Ausblühen *n*; Aufblasen *n* des Leuchtflecks;
Bildweichheit *f*
f éblouissement *m*; efflorescence *f*;
hyperluminosité *f* du spot
r помутнение *n*; расплывание *n*; ореол *m*

* **BLT** → 952

1043 blue filter
d Blaufilter *m*
f filtre *m* bleu
r синий фильтр *m*

1044 blueprint
d Blaupause *f*; Lichtpause *f*
f croquis *m*; avant-projet *m*; schéma *m*
directeur
r синька *f*; однокрасочная проба *f*;
светокопия *f*

1045 blue screen
(of death)
d blauer Bildschirm *m*; Blue-Screen *n*
f écran *m* bleu
r синий экран *m*

1046 blue trace arrows
d blaue Tracing-Pfeile *mpl*
f flèches *fpl* bleu de traçage
r синие стрелки *f* трассировки

* **blunted corners** → 892

1047 blur *v*
d trüben; verwischen; verschwimmen;
schmitzen
f embrumer
r размывать; расплывать; помутнять;
потемнять

* **blur** → 1051, 1052

1048 blur *v*
d doppel drucken; verdoppeln
f double imprimer
r раздвоенно печатать

1049 blur effect
d Unscharfeffekt *m*
f effet *m* d'embrumer; effet d'embuer; effet flou
r эффект *m* помутнения; эффект размывания

1050 blur filter
d Unscharffilter *m*
f filtre *m* à embrumer
r фильтр *m* размывания

1051 blur[ing]
d Unschärfe *f*; Schmitz *m*
f flou *m*; adoucissement *m*
r размывание *n* [границ]; нерезкость *f*;
помутнение *n*

1052 blur[ing]
d Doppeldruck *m*; vermischter Druck *m*
f impression *f* double
r двойная печать *f*

* **blur mask** → 446

* **blurred** → 4088

1053 blurred image
d Unscharfbild *n*
f image *f* floue
r расплывчатое изображение *n*; неясное
изображение

* **body** → 8873

1054 body animation
d Körperanimation *f*
f animation *f* de corps
r анимация *f* тела

1055 body characteristics
d Körpermerkmale *npl*
f caractéristiques *fpl* de corps
r характеристики *fpl* тела

1056 body entity; solid entity
d Körpereinheit *f*
f entité *f* corps
r примитив *m* тело

1057 body-fixed coordinate system
d körperfestes Koordinatensystem *n*
f système *m* de coordonnées lié au corps
r система *f* координат, связанная с телом

1058 body mesh
d Körpermasche *f*
f maille *f* du corps
r телесная сетка *f*

1059 body model
d Körpermodell *n*
f modèle *m* de corps
r телесная модель *f*

1060 body object
d Körperobjekt *n*
f objet *m* corps
r объект *m* типа тела

* **body of revolution** → 8893

1061 boilerplate
d Standardtextbibliotek *f*
f bibliothèque *f* de textes standardisés
r библиотека *f* стандартных текстов

* bold → 1064

1062 bold
d Fett-; fett; halbfett
f gras
r жирный; полужирный; толстый; получерный

1063 bold character
d Fettzeichen *n*
f caractère *m* gras
r получерный символ *m*; жирный символ

1064 bold [face]; bold typeface
d Fettschrifttyp *m*
f type *m* de caractères gras
r получерный тип *m* шрифта

1065 bold format
d Fettformat *n*
f format *m* gras
r жирный формат *m*

* bold typeface → 1064

1066 bond *v*
d befestigen
f bondériser; coupler
r скреплять; сцеплять

1067 bonus tools
d Extrahilfsmittel *npl*; Gratishilfsmittel *npl*; unbezahlte Hilfsmittel *npl*
f outils *mpl* extra
r бонус-инструменты *mpl*; премиальные инструменты

1068 booklet
d Broschüre *f*
f fascicule *m*
r свиток *m*; брошюра *f*

1069 bookmark
d Lesezeichen *n*; Bookmark *n*
f favori *m*; signet *m*; onglet *m*; marque-page *f*; carnet *m* d'adresses
r закладка *f*

1070 Boolean; logic[al]
d Boolesch; logisch
f booléen; logique
r булев; логический

1071 Boolean method
d Boolesche Methode *f*

f méthode *f* booléenne
r булев мутод *m*

1072 Boolean modeling
d Boolesche Modellierung *f*
f modélisation *f* booléenne
r булево моделирование *n*

1073 Boolean operation; logic[al] operation
d Boolesche Operation *f*; logische Operation
f opération *f* booléenne; opération logique
r булева операция *f*; логическая операция

1074 border
d Kante *f*; Rahmen *m*
f bordure *f*; bord *m*
r рамка *f*; полоса *f*; кайма *f*

1075 border color
d Rahmenfarbe *f*
f couleur *f* de bordure
r цвет *m* рамки

* bordering → 2140

1076 border of a map
d Kartenrahmen *m*; Kartenrand *m*
f filet *m* de cadre; filet à border
r рамка *f* листа карты

1077 border style
d Rahmenstil *m*
f style *m* de bordure
r стиль *m* окаймления

* bot → 235

* bothway → 910

1078 bottom extent
d Extent *m* nach unten
f étendue *f* du bas
r расширение *n* книзу

1079 bottom left corner
d Ecke *f* unten links
f coin *m* à gauche inférieur
r нижний левый угол *m*

1080 bottom margin
d untere Grenze *f*
f marge *f* du bas; marge inférieure
r нижняя граница *f*

1081 bottom node
d unterer Knoten *m*
f nœud *m* du bas; nœud inférieur
r нижний узел *m*

1082 bottom of page
d Fuß *m* der Seite; unterer Rand *m* der Seite

f fond *m* de page
r нижняя граница *f* страницы; конец *m* страницы; основание *n* страницы; низ *f* страницы

1083 bottom right corner
d Ecke unten rechts
f coin *m* à l'endroit inférieur
r нижний правый угол *m*

1084 bottom surface
d untere Fläche *f*
f surface *f* du bas; surface inférieure
r нижняя поверхность *f*

* **bottom-up → 595**

1085 bottom-up movement
d aufsteigende Bewegung *f*
f mouvement *m* de bas en haut
r восходящее движение *n*

1086 bottom view
d untere Ansicht *f*
f vue *f* du bas
r нижний вид *m*; вид снизу

1087 bottom window border
d unterer Fensterrand *m*
f bordure *f* inférieure de la fenêtre
r нижняя кайма *f* окна

* **bound** *v* → 2092

1088 bound; boundary; frontier; limit; margin
d Grenze *f*; Rand *m*; Schranke *f*; Limit *n*
f borne *f*; frontière *f*; limite *f*
r граница *f*; край *m*; предел *m*; лимит *m*

* **boundary → 1088**

1089 boundary; frontier *adj*
d Grenz-; Rand-
f limite
r граничный; краевой

1090 boundary arc
d Randbogen *m*
f arc *m* de frontière
r дуга *f* границы; граничная дуга

1091 boundary behaviour
d Randverhalten *n*
f comportement *m* à la frontière
r поведение *n* на границе

1092 boundary cell
d Randzelle *f*
f cellule *f* frontière
r граничная клетка *f*; граничная ячейка *f*

1093 boundary condition
d Randbedingung *f*
f condition *f* aux limites; condition de limite
r граничное условие *n*

1094 boundary correspondence
d Ränderzuordnung *f*
f correspondance *f* des frontières
r соответствие *n* границ; соотнесенность *f* границ

1095 boundary curve
d Randkurve *f*
f courbe *f* frontière
r граничная кривая *f*

1096 boundary edge; bounding edge
d Randkante *f*
f arête *f* frontière; côte *f* frontière
r граничное ребро *n*

1097 boundary extraction
d Grenzextraktion *f*
f extraction *f* de frontière
r извлечение *n* границы

1098 boundary field
d Grenzfeld *n*
f champ *m* frontière
r граничное поле *n*

1099 boundary form
d Randform *f*
f forme *f* frontière
r граничная форма *f*

1100 boundary hatch
d Grenzschraffur *f*
f hachure *f* frontière
r граничная штриховка *f*

1101 boundary layer
d Grenzschicht *f*
f couche *f* frontière
r граничный слой *m*

1102 boundary line
d Grenzlinie *f*
f ligne *f* frontière
r граничная линия *f*

1103 boundary name table
d Tabelle *f* der Grenznamen
f table *f* de noms de limites
r таблица *f* граничных имен

1104 boundary object
d Randobjekt *n*
f objet *m* limite
r объект *m* типа границы

1105 **boundary of a domain**
  d Rand *m* eines Bereichs; Rand eines Gebiets
  f frontière *f* d'un domaine
  r граница *f* области

1106 **boundary of a surface**
  d Rand *m* einer Fläche
  f bord *m* d'une surface
  r граница *f* поверхности

1107 **boundary point; frontier point**
  d Randpunkt *m*; Grenzpunkt *m*
  f point *m* frontière; point limite
  r граничная точка *f*; краевая точка

1108 **boundary set**
  d Randsatz *m*
  f ensemble *m* de frontières
  r множество *n* граней

  * **boundary trim** → 1109

1109 **boundary trim[ming]**
  d Grenzzuschneidung *f*; Grenzbeschneiden *n*
  f coupure *f* de limite
  r обрезание *n* границы

1110 **bounded; limited; restricted**
  d beschränkt; begrenzt
  f borné; limité
  r ограниченный

1111 **bounded box; bounding box; bounding rectangle**
  d begrenztes Kästchen *n*; begrenztes Rechteck *n*
  f boîte *f* délimitée; case *f* délimitée
  r ограничающий ящик *m*; граничный прямоугольник *m*

1112 **bounded domain**
  d beschränkter Bereich *m*; beschränktes Gebiet *n*
  f domaine *m* borné
  r ограниченная область *f*

  * **bounded map** → 1113

1113 **bounded map[ping]**
  d beschränkte Abbildung *f*
  f application *f* bornée
  r ограниченное отображение *n*

1114 **bounded space**
  d beschränkter Raum *m*
  f espace *m* borné
  r ограниченное пространство *n*

  * **bounding box** → 1111

  * **bounding edge** → 1096

  * **bounding rectangle** → 1111

1115 **bounding sphere**
  d Begrenzungskugel *f*
  f sphère *f* délimitée
  r ограничивающая сфера *f*

1116 **bounding surface**
  d Grenzfläche *f*; Randfläche *f*
  f surface *f* frontière
  r граничная поверхность *f*

1117 **boundless; unbounded; unlimited**
  d unbeschränkt
  f non borné; non limité
  r неограниченный

  * **bowl** → 6695

1118 **box**
  d Kasten *m*; Kästchen *n*; Box *f*
  f boîtier *m*; boîte *f*; box *m*; case *f*
  r ящик *m*; коробка *f*

1119 **box** *v*
  d einrahmen; in Kasten setzen; einpacken
  f boxer
  r класть в ящик; помещать в коробку

  * **box** → 6820

1120 **boxing**
  d Setzung *f* in Kasten
  f découpage *m* en boîtes
  r упаковка *f* в ящик

  * **box plot** → 3878

1121 **bracketing**
  d Einklammern *n*
  f mise *f* entre crochets
  r заключение *n* в скобки

1122 **brackets**
  (a sign)
  d Klammern *fpl*
  f crochets *mpl*
  r скобки *fpl*

1123 **branch**
  d Zweig *m*; Abzweig *m*; Ast *m*
  f branche *f*
  r ветвь *f*; переход *m*

1124 **branching; ramification**
  d Verzweigung *f*; Verzweigen *n*
  f [em]branchement *m*; ramification *f*
  r ветвление *n*; разветвление *n*

* **branching node** → 1125

1125 branching vertex; branching node
d Verzweigungsknoten *m*
f sommet *m* de branchement
r узел *m* [раз]ветвления

1126 branch of a curve
d Kurvenzweig *m*; Kurvenast *m*
f branche *f* de la courbe
r ветвь *f* кривой

1127 branch of a tree
d Zweig *m* eines Baums
f branche *f* d'un arbre
r ветвь *f* дерева

* **BRDF** → 913

1128 breadth; width
d Breite *f*
f largeur *f*
r ширина *f*; широта *f*

* **break** → 1130

1129 break *v*; interrupt *v*
d unterbrechen
f interrompre
r прерывать; обрывать

1130 break[ing]; interruption
d Unterbrechung *f*; Interrupt *m*
f interruption *f*; coupure *f*
r прерывание *n*; обрывание *n*

1131 break lines
d Unterbrechungslinien *fpl*; Bruchlinien *fpl*
f lignes *fpl* d'interruption
r линии *fpl* прерывания

1132 breakpoint
d Unterbrechungsstelle *f*; Haltepunkt *m*;
   Bedarfsschaltepunkt *m*
f point *m* d'interruption; point d'arrêt
r точка *f* прерывания; точка останова

1133 Bresenham's algorithm
d Bresenham-Algorithmus *m*
f algorithme *m* de Bresenham
r алгоритм *m* Брезенгама

1134 Bresenham's circles
d Bresenham-Kreise *mpl*
f cercles *mpl* de Bresenham
r круги *mpl* Брезенгама

* **brighten** → 1135

1135 brighten[ing]; dual brightness

d Blankschleifen *n*; Aufhellung *f*; Auswittern *n*
f surbrillance *f*; brillantage *m*;
   éclaircissement *m*
r озарение *n*; прояснение *n*

1136 brighten lens
d Helligkeitslinse *f*
f lentille *f* de surbrillance
r линза *f* прояснения

* **brightness** → 5551

1137 brightness; brilliance; lustre; luster (US)
d Klarheit *f*; Glanz *m*
f clarté *f*; brillance *f*; lustre *m*
r блеск *m*; глянец *m*

1138 brightness contrast
d Helligkeitskontrast *m*
f contraste *m* de brillance
r контраст *m* яркости

1139 brightness control
d Helligkeitsregelung *f*
f commande *f* de brillance
r управление *n* яркости

1140 brightness filter
d Helligkeitsfilter *m*
f filtre *m* de brillance
r фильтр *m* яркости

1141 brightness meter
d Helligkeitsmeter *n*
f mètre *m* de brillance
r измеритель *m* яркости

* **brightness mode** → 1145

1142 brightness of the image; image brightness
d Bildhelligkeit *f*
f brillance *f* de l'image
r яркость *f* изображения

1143 brightness relief
d Helligkeitsrelief *n*
f relief *m* par contraste de luminosité
r рельеф *m* яркости

1144 brightness resolution
d Auflösung *f* der Helligkeit
f résolution *f* de brillance
r разрешение *n* яркости

1145 brightness [setup] mode
d Helligkeit-Einrichtungsmodus *m*
f mode *m* [d'établissement] de brillance
r режим *m* [установления] освещенности

1146 brightness slider
d Helligkeitsschieber *m*

f glisseur *m* de brillance
r ползунок *m* яркости

1147 brightness value; light value
   d Helligkeitswert *m*
   f valeur *f* de brillance
   r величина *f* яркости

   * **brilliance** → 1137

1148 Brillouin zones
   d Brillouin-Zonen *fpl*
   f zones *fpl* de Brillouin
   r зоны *fpl* Бриллюэна

1149 bring *v*; fetch *v*
   d bringen; einbringen; einreichen; holen
   f ramener; apporter
   r приносить; доставлять; приводить;
      довести

1150 bring *v* to back; move *v* to back
   d zurücksetzen; zurückrücken
   f apporter à l'arrière-plan
   r двинуть назад

1151 bring *v* to focus
   d scharfabbilden
   f focaliser
   r фокусировать

1152 bring *v* to front; move *v* to front
   d vorrücken
   f ramener à l'avant-plan
   r двинуть вперед

1153 bring *v* to top
   d nach oben aufheben
   f ramener au dessus
   r выдвигать кверху

1154 broken
   d gebrochen; kaputt
   f brisé
   r сломанный

1155 broken edge
   d gebrochene Kante *f*
   f arête *f* brisée
   r сломанное ребро *n*

1156 broken graph
   d gebrochener Graph *m*
   f graphique *m* à ligne brisée
   r сломанный граф *m*

1157 broken line
   d gebrochene Linie *f*
   f ligne *f* brisée
   r сломанная линия *f*

1158 broken pencil icon
   d Symbol *n* "gebrochener Stift"
   f icône *f* en forme de crayon brisé
   r значок *m* "сломанный карандаш"

1159 browse *v*
   d ansehen; durchsuchen
   f parcourir; feuilleter
   r пересмотреть; просматривать;
      разглядывать; пролистать

1160 browse dialog box
   d Browser-Dialogbox *f*
   f boîte *f* de dialogue de revue
   r диалоговый ящик *m* просмотра

1161 browser; viewer; navigator
   d Browser *m*; Suchprogramm *n*; Navigator *m*
   f logiciel *m* de visualisation; visionneur *m*;
      visionneuse *f*; module *m* de revue;
      butineur *m*; navigateur *m*
   r программа *f* просмотра; визуализатор *m*;
      браузер *m*; бродилка *f*; вьювер *m*;
      навигатор *m*

1162 browser-based application
   d Browser-basierte Anwendung *f*
   f application *f* basée à butineur
   r приложение *n*, основанное браузером

1163 browser window
   d Browser-Fenster *n*
   f fenêtre *f* du butineur
   r окно *n* браузера

1164 browse *v* scrapbook
   d Skizzenbuch durchsuchen
   f parcourir un classeur
   r просматривать альбом

1165 browsing
   d Browsing *n*; Durchsicht *f*
   f revue *f*; survol *m*; feuilletage *m*
   r просмотр *m*; пролистание *n*

1166 browsing window
   d Vorschaufenster *n*
   f fenêtre *f* de survol
   r окно *n* рассмотрения

   * **brush** → 6743

1167 brushes library
   d Pinselbibliothek *f*
   f bibliothèque *f* de brosses
   r библиотека *f* кистей

1168 brush nib
   d Pinselspitze *f*

    f bec *m* de brosse
    r кончик *m* кисти

1169 brush size
    d Pinselgröße *f*
    f taille *f* de brosse
    r размер *m* кисти

1170 brush stroke
    d Pinselstrich *m*
    f trait *m* de brosse; frappe *f* de balai
    r мазок *m* щеткой; штрих *m* кисти; взмах *m* щеткой

1171 brush texture
    d Pinseltextur *f*
    f texture *f* de brosse
    r текстура *f* с помощью кисти

    * **brush tool** → 6745

    * **brush tool options** → 1172

1172 brush tool settings; brush tool options
    d Pinsel-Hilfsmittel-Einrichtungen *fpl*
    f paramètres *mpl* d'outil de brosse; options *fpl* d'outil de brosse
    r параметры *mpl* инструмента "кисть"

1173 brush type
    d Pinseltyp *m*
    f type *m* de brosse
    r тип *m* кисти

    * **B-spline** → 887

1174 B-spline surface
    d B-Spline-Fläche *f*
    f surface *f* B-spline
    r В-сплайновая поверхность *f*

    * **bubble** → 818

1175 bubble chart
    d Blasenschaubild *n*
    f diagramme *m* à bulles; graphique *m* à bulles
    r пузырьковая диаграмма *f*

    * **bubble-jet printer** → 5087

    * **buck** → 5809

1176 buffering
    d Pufferung *f*
    f tamponnage *m*
    r буферирование *n*; буферизация *f*

1177 buffer zone
    d Pufferzone *f*
    f zone *f* tampon

    r буферная зона *f*

1178 bug patch; soft patch; patch (in a software)
    d Flicken *n*; Direktkorrektur *f*
    f correctif *m*; rapiècement *m*; patch *m*
    r заплата *f*; патч *m*; вставка *f*

1179 builder
    d Bilder *m*
    f bâtisseur *m*
    r построитель *m*; компоновщик *m*; создатель *m*

    * **built-in** → 6186

1180 built-in formulas
    d eingebaute Formeln *fpl*
    f formules *fpl* incorporées
    r встроенные формулы *fpl*

1181 built-in function
    d eingebaute Funktion *f*
    f fonction *f* incorporée; fonction intégrée
    r встроенная функция *f*

1182 built-in table formats
    d eingebaute Tafelformate *npl*
    f formats *mpl* de tables incorporés
    r встроенные табличные форматы *mpl*

1183 built-in templates
    d eingebaute Schablonen *fpl*
    f maquettes *fpl* incorporées
    r встроенные шаблоны *mpl*; встроенные макеты *mpl*

    * **bulge** → 1187

    * **bullet** → 1185

1184 bullet position
    d Blickfangpunktstelle *f*
    f position *f* de balle
    r позиция *f* пульки

1185 bullet [sign]
    d Blickfangpunkt *m*
    f balle *f*; puce *f*; gros point *m*
    r жирная точка *f*; пулька *f*; маркер *m*

1186 bullet size
    d Blickfangpunktgröße *f*
    f taille *f* de balle
    r размер *m* пульки

1187 bump; bulge
    d Beule *f*; Wulst *m*
    f bosse *f*; boursouflure *f*; renflement *m*;

inégalité *f*; gibbosité *f*
 r неровность *f*; выпуклость *f*

1188 bump map
 d Bump-Map *n*
 f texture *f* relief; bump-map *m*
 r рельефная текстура *f*

1189 bump-map image
 d Bump-Map-Bild *n*
 f image *f* de texture relief
 r изображение *n* рельефной текстурой

1190 bump-mapped normal; bump normal
 d Bump-Map-Normale *f*
 f normale *f* à une texture relief
 r нормаль *f* рельефной текстуры

1191 bump-mapping
 d Bump-Mapping *n*
 f mise *f* à une texture relief; bump-mapping *m*
 r рельефное текстурирование *n*;
   отображение *n* неровностей поверхности

1192 bump-mapping processor
 d Bump-Mapping-Prozessor *m*
 f processeur *m* de bump-mapping
 r процессор *m* рельефного текстурирования

1193 bump-mapping surface
 d Bump-Mapping-Fläche *f*
 f surface *f* de texture relief
 r рельефно текстурированная поверхность *f*

* **bump normal** → 1190

* **bunch** → 6926

* **bundle** → 6926

* **bundle of circles** → 6927

1194 bundle of complexes; sheaf of complexes
 d Komplexbündel *n*
 f étoile *f* de complexes; gerbe *f* de complexes
 r связка *f* комплексов

1195 bundle of curves; sheaf of curves
 d Kurvenbündel *n*
 f gerbe *f* de courbes
 r связка *f* кривых

1196 bundle of lines; bundle of rays; pencil of lines; pencil of rays; sheaf of lines; star of rays
 d Geradenbündel *n*; Strahlenbündel *n*; Strahlenbüschel *n*
 f gerbe *f* de droites; pinceau *m* de droites; étoile *f* de rayons
 r связка *f* прямых; связка лучей; пучок *m*

прямых

* **bundle of planes** → 6932

* **bundle of rays** → 1196

1197 bundle of spheres; sheaf of spheres; star of spheres; pencil of spheres
 d Sphärenbündel *n*; Garbe *f* von Sphären
 f réseau *m* de sphères; étoile *f* de sphères
 r связка *f* сфер; пучок *m* сфер

1198 bus
 d Bus *m*; Schiene *f*
 f bus *m*; barre *f*
 r шина *f*

1199 business graphics; management graphics; presentation graphics
 d Geschäftsgrafik *f*, Präsentationsgrafik *f*
 f graphique *m* de gestion; graphique d'affaires; graphique de [re]présentation
 r деловая графика *f*; представительная графика

1200 business logo; logo[type]; emblem
 d Logo *n*; Firmenlogo *n*; Emblem *n*
 f sigle *f*; mire *f*; logo *m*
 r фирменный знак *m*

* **butt** → 2643

* **button** → 5364

1201 button; knob
 d Schaltfläche *f*; Knopf *m*
 f bouton *m*; case *f* de commande
 r кнопка *f*; бутон *m*

* **button bar** → 1202

1202 button bar [menu]; button menu
 d Tastenmenü *n*; Knopfmenü *n*; Schaltflächeleiste *f*
 f barre *f* d'onglets
 r лента[-меню] *f* кнопок; кнопочное меню *n*

1203 button editor
 d Knopfeditor *m*
 f éditeur *m* par boutons
 r кнопочный редактор *m*

1204 button icon
 d Tastenikone *f*
 f icône *f* de bouton
 r икона *f* кнопки

* **button menu** → 1202

1205 button property
 d Knopfeigenschaft *f*

f propriété *f* de bouton
r свойство *n* кнопки

1206 Butz's algorithm
d Butz-Algorithmus *m*
f algorithme *m* de Butz
r алгоритм *m* Бутца

1207 by block
d wie ein Block *m*
f par bloc
r как блок

* **by coordinates → 2238**

1208 by layer
d wie eine Schicht *f*
f par couche; par plan
r как слой

1209 byte
d Byte *n*
f octet *m*
r байт *m*

C

* **CAD** → 1971

1210 cadastral mapping
d Katasterkartografie *f*
f cartographie *f* cadastrale
r кадастральная картография *f*

* **cadastral plan** → 6611

* **cadastral survey** → 6611

1211 cadastre
d Kataster *m/n*
f cadastre *m*
r кадастр *m*

1212 CAD project
d CAD-Projekt *n*
f projet *m* CAO
r САПР-проект *m*

1213 cadre; frame
d Frame *n*; Zeitfenster *n*; einzelnes Videobild *n*
f cadre *m* [d'image vidéo]
r кадр *m*

1214 calculate *v*; **compute** *v*; **reckon** *v*
d ausrechnen; berechnen; rechnen
f calculer; compter
r вычислять; рассчитывать; подсчитывать

1215 calculating rule; computing rule
d Rechenregel *f*; Berechnungsregel *f*; Rechenvorschrift *f*
f règle *f* de calcul
r правило *n* вычисления

1216 calculation; computation; computing
d Berechnung *f*; Rechnen *n*
f calcul *m*; comptage *m*
r вычисление *n*; исчисление *n*; [ра]счет *m*

1217 calendar
d Kalender *m*
f calendrier *m*
r календарь *m*

1218 calibrate *v*; **gauge** *v*; **graduate** *v*
d eichen; kalibrieren
f calibrer; étalonner; jauger; graduer
r калибровать; эталонировать; градуировать; тарировать

1219 calibrated focal length; calibrated principal distance
d kalibrierte Fokallänge *f*
f distance *f* focale calibrée
r калиброванное фокусное расстояние *n*

1220 calibrated mode
(of a tablet)
d kalibrierter Modus *m*
f mode *m* calibré
r калиброванный режим *m*

* **calibrated principal distance** → 1219

* **calibrating** → 1221

1221 calibration; calibrating
d Eichung *f*; Kalibrierung *f*
f calibrage *m*; étalonnage *m*; tarage *m*
r калибровка *f*

1222 calibration bar
d Kalibrierungsbalken *m*
f barre *f* de calibrage; barre d'étalonnage
r лента *f* калибровки; лента эталонирования

* **call** → 1231

1223 call *v*; **invoke** *v*
d aufrufen; rufen
f appeler
r вызывать; обращаться

1224 called drawing
d aufgerufene Zeichnung *f*
f dessin *m* appelé
r вызываемый рисунок *m*; вызываемый чертеж *m*

1225 calligraphic
d kalligrafisch
f calligraphique
r каллиграфический

1226 calligraphic border
d kalligrafischer Umriss *m*
f bordure *f* calligraphique
r каллиграфическая кайма *f*

1227 calligraphic display
d Liniengrafikgerät *n*; kalligrafisches Display *n*
f affichage *m* à balayage cavalier
r векторный дисплей *m*

1228 calligraphic outline
d kalligrafische Kontur *f*
f contour *m* calligraphique
r каллиграфический контур *m*

1229 calligraphic straight line
d kalligrafische Gerade *f*

f ligne *f* droite calligraphique; droite *f* calligraphique
r каллиграфическая прямая *f*

1230 calligraphy
  d Kalligrafie *f*; Schönschreibekunst *f*
  f calligraphie *f*
  r каллиграфия *f*

1231 call[ing]
  d Aufruf *m*; Ruf *m*
  f appel *m*
  r вызов *m*; обращение *n*

1232 calling program
  d Aufrufprogramm *n*
  f programme *m* appelant
  r вызывающая программа *f*

*   **callout → 1277**

1233 callout line
  d Bezeichnungslinie *f*; Referenzlinie *f*
  f ligne *f* de légende
  r строка *f* надписи

1234 camera
  d Kamera *f*
  f caméra *f*
  r камера *f*; фотографический аппарат *m*

1235 camera adjusting
  d Kameraeinstellung *f*
  f régulation *f* de caméra; ajustage *m* de caméra
  r настраивание *n* камеры

1236 camera angle
  d Bildwinkel *m* der Kamera
  f angle *m* de champ de la caméra; angle de caméra
  r угол *m* изображения камеры

1237 camera axis
  d Kameraachse *f*
  f axe *m* de la caméra
  r ось *f* камеры

1238 camera block
  d Kamerablock *m*
  f bloc *m* de caméra
  r блок *m* камеры

1239 camera calibration
  d Kamerakalibration *f*
  f calibrage *m* de caméra
  r эталонирование *n* камеры; калибровка *f* камеры

1240 camera calibration algorithm
  d Kamerakalibrationsalgorithmus *m*

f algorithme *m* de calibrage de caméra
r алгоритм *m* эталонирования камеры

1241 camera-captured image
  d durch Kamera gesammeltes Bild *n*
  f image *f* captée par caméra
  r изображение *n*, захваченное камерой

1242 camera cone; frustum of vision
  d Kamerakegel *m*; Sehkegelstumpf *m*
  f cône *m* de caméra
  r конус *m* камеры; зрительный усеченный конус

1243 camera control; camera managing
  d Kamerasteuerung *f*
  f contrôle *m* de caméra; gestion *f* de caméra
  r управление *n* камеры

1244 camera cue
  d Aufnahmelichtmarke *f*
  f repère *m* de caméra
  r индикатор *m* камеры; маркер *m* камеры

1245 camera direction
  d Kamerarichtung *f*
  f orientation *f* de caméra
  r направление *n* камеры

1246 camera lens
  d Kameraobjektiv *n*; Kameralinse *f*
  f lentille *f* de caméra; objectif *m* de caméra
  r камерная линза *f*

1247 camera location; camera position
  d Kameraposition *f*
  f localisation *f* de caméra; position *f* de caméra
  r позиция *f* камеры

*   **camera managing → 1243**

1248 camera model
  d Kameramodell *n*
  f modèle *m* de caméra
  r модель *f* камеры

1249 camera node
  d Kameraknoten[punkt] *m*
  f nœud *m* de caméra
  r узел *m* камеры

1250 camera pan
  d Kamerarichtungsanpassung *f*
  f panoramique *f* de caméra
  r панорамирование *n* камерой

1251 camera point
  d Kamerapunkt *m*
  f point *m* de caméra
  r точка *f* камеры

* camera position → 1247

1252 **camera positioning**
 d Kamerapositionierung *f*
 f positionnement *m* de la caméra
 r позиционирование *n* камеры

1253 **camera-ready copy**
 d für eine Fotografie fertige Kopie *f*
 f copie *f* prête à photo
 r оригинал-макет *m*

1254 **camera rotating**
 d Kameradrehung *f*
 f rotation *f* de la caméra
 r вращение *n* камеры

1255 **camera sliding**
 d Kameragleitung *f*
 f glissement *m* de caméra
 r скольжение *n* камеры

1256 **camera tool**
 d Kamerahilfsmittel *n*
 f outil *m* "caméra"
 r инструмент *m* "камера"

1257 **camera view**
 d Kameraansicht *f*; Kamerablick *m*
 f vue *f* de la caméra
 r взгляд *m* с камеры; вид *m* из камеры

1258 **camera viewpoint**
 d Aug[en]punkt *m* der Kamera
 f point *m* de vue de la caméra
 r точка *f* зрения камеры

1259 **camera walking**
 d Kamerafahrt *f*
 f mouvement *m* de caméra
 r движение *n* камеры

* camera zoom → 1260

1260 **camera zoom[ing]**
 d Kamera-Zoomen *n*
 f zoom *m* de caméra
 r зумирование *n* камеры; масштабирование *n* взгляда с камеры

* cancel → 1265

1261 **cancel** *v*; **reset** *v*
 d abbrechen; ausstreichen; ungültig machen
 f casser; rejeter; supprimer; annuler
 r отменять; прекращать; уничтожать

* cancelable → 1263

* cancelable element → 1264

1262 **cancel button**
 d Taste *f* "Abbrechen"
 f bouton *m* d'annulation
 r кнопка *f* отмены; кнопка прекращения

* canceling → 1265

1263 **cancel[l]able**
 d kürzbar
 f simplifiable; réductible
 r сократимый

1264 **cancel[l]able element**
 d kürzbares Element *n*
 f élément *m* simplifiable
 r сократимый элемент *m*

1265 **cancel[lation]; canceling**
 d Annullierung *f*; Abbruch *m*
 f annulation *f*; élimination *f*
 r уничтожение *n*; прекращение *n*

1266 **canvas**
 d Leinwand *f*
 f canevas *m*
 r полотно *n*; картина *f*; канва *f*; холст *m*

1267 **canvas filter**
 d Wandfilter *m*
 f filtre *m* canevas
 r фильтр *m* холста

1268 **canvas texture**
 d Wand-Textur *f*
 f texture *f* canevas
 r текстура *f* холста

1269 **cap**
 d Kappe *f*
 f capot *m*; capote *f*; capuchon *m*
 r крышка *f*; шапка *f*; предел *m*

* cap → 1273, 1289, 8685

1270 **capability**
 d Leistungsfähigkeit *f*; Kapazität *f*
 f capacité *f*; habileté *f*
 r возможность *f*; способность *f*

1271 **cap height**
 d Kappenhöhe *f*
 f hauteur *f* de couvercle
 r высота *f* крышки

1272 **capitalization**
 (of text)
 d Großschreibung *f*; Kapitalisierung *f*
 f mise *f* en lettres majuscules
 r выделение *n* заглавными буквами

    *   **capital letter** → 10070

1273 cap[ping]
    d Verstopfung *f*; Deckung *f*
    f rebouchage *m*; operculage *m*; surpassement *m*
    r перекрытие *n*; запирание *n*

1274 capsulate *v*
    d kapseln
    f capsuler
    r капсулировать

1275 capsulation; encapsulation
    d Kapselung *f*; Verkapselung *f*
    f [en]capsulage *m*; enrobage *m*
    r капсулирование *n*; герметизация *f*;
       инкапсуляция *f*

1276 capsule; shell; casing
    d Kapsel *f*
    f capsule *f*; étui *m*
    r капсюль *m*; мембрана *f*

1277 caption; callout; image signature
    (identifying or descriptive text accompanying
    a photograph, illustration or another visual
    element)
    d Bildunterschrift *f*; Bilduntertitel *m*;
       Bildtext *m*; Bildüberschrift *f*; Referenz *f*
    f signature *f* d'image; caption *f*; référence *f*
    r надпись *f*; метка-идентификатор *m*;
       выноска *f*

1278 caption property
    d Legendeneigenschaft *f*
    f propriété *f* de légende
    r характеристика *f* легенды

1279 capture; grabbing; lock-on
    d Sammlung *f*; Sammeln *n*; Erfassung *f*;
       Fangen *n*
    f capture *f*; captage *m*
    r захват *m*; улавливание *n*

1280 capture *v*; **grip** *v*
    (of a dynamic image)
    d erfassen; sammeln
    f capter; saisir; empoigner
    r ловить; хватать; собирать; захватывать;
       улавливать

1281 capture area
    d Sammlungsbereich *m*
    f domaine *m* de capture
    r область *f* захвата; область улавливания

1282 capture device; capturer
    d Sammler *m*
    f capteur *m*
    r уловитель *m*

1283 captured image
    d gesammeltes Bild *n*
    f image *f* captée
    r захваченное изображение *n*

1284 capture process
    d Sammlungsprozess *m*
    f processus *m* de capture
    r процесс *m* захвата

    *   **capturer** → 1282

1285 cardinal interpolation
    d Kardinalinterpolation *f*
    f interpolation *f* cardinale
    r кардинальная интерполяция *f*

1286 cardinal point; Gauss point
    d Kardinalpunkt *m*
    f point *m* cardinal
    r кардинальная точка *f*

1287 cardinal spline
    d Kardinalspline *m*
    f spline *m* cardinale
    r кардинальный сплайн *m*

1288 cardioid
    d Kardioide *f*; Herzlinie *f*
    f cardioïde *f*
    r кардиоида *f*

    *   **caret** → 1289

**1289 caret [character]; circumflex [accent]; hat;
    cap; cover; top**
    (^)
    d Hut *m*; Dach *n*
    f signe *m* d'insertion; accent *m* circonflexe
    r знак *m* вставки; крышка *f*

1290 carrier; support
    d Träger *m*; Carrier *m*
    f porteur *m*; support *m*
    r носитель *m*

**1291 carrier chrominance signal; chrominance
    signal; chroma signal**
    d Farbartsignal *n*; Chrominanzsignal *n*;
       Farbwertsignal *n*
    f signal *m* de support de chrominance
    r несущий сигнал *m* цветовой
       интенсивности

    *   **carry-in** *v* → 3446

1292 Cartesian
    d kartesisch; Cartesisch-
    f cartésien
    r декартов

1293 Cartesian coordinate system
 d kartesisches Koordinatensystem *n*
 f système *m* de coordonnées cartésiennes
 r декартова система *f* координат

1294 cartographical drawing; map drawing
 d kartografische Zeichnung *f*; Kartenzeichnen *n*
 f dessin *m* cartographique
 r картографический чертеж *m*

 * **cartographical grid** → 5789

1295 cartographical projection; map projection
 d kartografische Projektion *f*;
   Kartenprojektion *f*
 f projection *f* cartographique
 r картографическая проекция *f*

1296 cartographical symbol
 d kartografisches Symbol *n*; Kartenzeichen *n*;
   Signatur *f*
 f symbole *m* cartographique
 r картографическое обозначение *n*;
   картографический условный знак *m*

1297 cartography; mapmaking; mapping
 d Kartografie *f*
 f cartographie *f*
 r картография *f*

1298 cartometry
 d Kartometrie *f*
 f cartométrie *f*
 r картометрия *f*

1299 cascade *adj*
 d überlappend
 f cascade
 r каскадный

1300 cascade; stage
 d Kaskade *f*; Stufe *f*; Staffel *f*
 f cascade *f*; étage *m*
 r каскад *m*; ступень *f*

1301 cascade list
 d überlappende Liste *f*
 f liste *f* en cascade
 r каскадный список *m*

 * **cascade noise factor** → 1302

1302 cascade noise figure; cascade noise factor
 d Kaskaden-Rauschzahl *f*
 f facteur *m* de bruit en cascade
 r каскадный коэффициент *m* искажения

1303 cascading choice
 d überlappende Auswahl *f*
 f option *f* en cascade

 r каскадный выбор *m*

1304 cascading menu
 d überlappendes Menü *n*
 f menu *m* [en] cascade
 r каскадное меню *n*; меню каскада

 * **cascading sheets** → 1305

1305 cascading[-style] sheets
 d überlappende Blätter *npl*
 f feuilles *fpl* en cascade
 r каскадно расположенные листы *mpl*

1306 cascading windows
 d Fensterskaskade *f*; Kaskadenanordnung *f* der
   Fenster; überlappende Fenster *npl*
 f fenêtres *fpl* en cascade
 r каскадно разположенные окна *npl*; окна
   каскадом

1307 case
 d Fach *n*; Register *n*
 f case *f*; registre *m*
 r регистр *m*

1308 case sensitivity
 d Register-Empfindlichkeit *f*
 f sensitivité *f* au case
 r учет *m* регистра (клавиатуры)

 * **casing** → 1276

 * **cast** → 1309

1309 cast[ing]; coercion
   (of the datatypes)
 d Abguss *m*; Guss *m*; Druckguss *m*
 f transtypage *m*
 r приведение *n*

 * **catalog** → 2880

1310 catalog of images; picture catalog
 d Bilderkatalog *m*; Bilderverzeichnis *n*
 f catalogue *m* d'images
 r каталог *m* изображений

 * **catalogue** → 2880

1311 category
 d Kategorie *f*
 f catégorie *f*
 r категория *f*

 * **catenary** → 1312

1312 catenary [curve]
 d Kettenkurve *f*; Kettenlinie *f*

f caténaire *f*; courbe *f* de la chaînette; chaînette *f*
r цепная линия *f*

* **catenary surface → 1313**

* **catenation → 1392**

1313 catenoid; catenary surface
d Kettenfläche *f*; Katenoid *n*
f caténoïde *f*
r катеноид *m*

1314 caustic
d Kaustik *f*
f caustique *f*
r каустическая поверхность *f*; каустика *f*

1315 caustic curve
d Kaustikkurve *f*
f courbe *f* caustique
r каустическая кривая *f*

1316 caustic effects
d Kaustikeffekte *mpl*
f effets *mpl* caustiques
r эффекты *mpl* отраженного или преломленного водой или кристаллом света

1317 caustic illumination
d Kaustikbeleuchtung *f*
f illumination *f* caustique
r каустическая иллюминация *f*

1318 cavity
d Hohlraum *m*
f cavité *f*
r полость *f*

1319 Cayley geometry
d Cayley-Geometrie *f*
f géométrie *f* de Cayley
r геометрия *f* Кэйли

* **CD → 6545**

1320 celestial equator
d Himmelsäquator *m*
f équateur *m* céleste
r небесный экватор *m*

1321 celestial sphere
d Himmelskugel *f*
f sphère *f* céleste
r небесная сфера *f*

1322 cell
d Zelle *f*
f cellule *f*; alvéole *f*

r ячейка *f*; клетка *f*

1323 cell
(of a table)
d Zelle *f*
f cellule *f*; élément *m*
r элемент *m*; клетка *f*

* **cell array → 1337**

1324 cell border
d Zellrahmen *m*
f bordure *f* de cellule
r рамка *f* клетки; кайма *f* клетки

1325 cell boundary
d Zellenrand *m*
f bord *m* de la cellule; frontière *f* de la cellule
r граница *f* ячейки

1326 cell color
d Zellenfarbe *f*
f couleur *f* de cellule
r цвет *m* клетки

1327 cell content
d Zelleninhalt *m*
f contenu *m* de cellule
r содержание *n* клетки

1328 cell filling
d Zellenfüllung *f*
f remplissage *m* de cellule
r заливка *f* клетки; закрашивание *n* клетки

1329 cell formatting
d Zellenformatierung *f*
f formatage *m* de cellule
r форматирование *n* клетки

1330 cell merging
d Zellenverschmelzung *f*
f fusionnement *m* de cellules
r слияние *n* клеток

1331 cell name
d Zellenname *m*
f nom *m* de cellule
r имя *n* клетки

1332 cell reference
d Zellenverweis *m*
f référence *m* à la cellule
r ссылка *f* к клетке

1333 cell rotating
d Zellendrehung *f*
f rotation *f* de cellule
r вращение *n* клетки; поворот *m* клетки

1334 cell size
d Zellengröße f
f grandeur f de cellule
r размер m ячейки

1335 cell splitting
d Zellenaufteilung f
f séparation f de cellules
r разделение n клеток; расщепление n клеток

1336 cell types
(tetrahedra, pyramids, prisms and hexahedra)
d Zellentypen mpl
f types mpl cellulaires
r клеточные типы mpl

1337 cell[ular] array
d reguläre Zellenanordnung f; Zellenfeld n
f champ m de cellules; matrice f cellulaire
r регулярная структура f ячеек; матрица f с регулярной структурой

1338 cellular texture
d zellulare Textur f
f texture f cellulaire
r клеточная текстура f

1339 cell unlock
d Zellenentsperrung f
f déverrouillage m d'une cellule
r разблокирование n клетки

1340 cell width
d Zellenbreite f
f largeur f de cellule
r ширина f клетки

1341 census block
d Zensus-Block m; Vollerhebungsblock m
f bloc m de recensement
r учетный блок m; блок полного набора характеристик

1342 center; centre
d Zentrum n
f centre m
r центр m

1343 center v a drawing
d Zeichnung zentrieren
f centrer un dessin
r центрировать рисунок

1344 center alignment
d zentrierte Ausrichtung f
f alignement m de centre
r выравнивание n центра

1345 centered
d zentriert
f centré
r центрированный

1346 centered wallpaper
d zentriertes Hintergrundbild n
f fond m d'écran centré
r центрированный экранный фон m

1347 cent[e]ring
d Zentrierung f
f centrage m
r центрирование n

1348 centerline
d zentrale Leitung f; Mittellinie f; Mittelachse f
f ligne f centrale; ligne de centre; médiane f de cercle
r центральная линия f; линия центра

1349 center mark
d Mittelmarke f
f marque f centrale
r маркер m центра

1350 center of a ball; center of a sphere
d Mittelpunkt m einer Kugel; Kugelmittelpunkt m; Zentrum n einer Kugel
f centre m d'une boule
r центр m шара; центр сферы

1351 center of a circle; center of a circumference
d Kreismittelpunkt m; Mittelpunkt m eines Kreises
f centre m d'un cercle
r центр m круга; центр окружности

* **center of a circumference** → 1351

* **center of a conic** → 1352

1352 center of a conic [section]
d Kegelschnittzentrum n
f centre m d'une conique
r центр m кривой второго порядка; центр коники

1353 center of a hyperbola
d Mittelpunkt m einer Hyperbel
f centre m d'une hyperbole
r центр m гиперболы

1354 center of an ellipse
d Mittelpunkt m einer Ellipse; Zentrum n einer Ellipse
f centre m d'une ellipse
r центр m эллипса

1355 center of an ellipsoid
d Mittelpunkt m eines Ellipsoids

f centre *m* d'un ellipsoïde
r центр *m* эллипсоида

1356 center of a pencil
    d Träger *m* eines Bündels; Träger eines
       Büschels; Grundpunkt *m* eines Büschels
    f centre *m* d'un faisceau
    r центр *m* пучка

**1357 center of a pencil of lines; vertex of a sheaf
    of lines**
    d Scheitel *m* eines Geradenbüschels; Träger *m*
       eines Geradenbündels; Grundpunkt *m*
    f centre *m* d'un faisceau de droites; sommet *m*
       d'un pinceau de droites; support *m*
    r центр *m* пучка прямых; носитель *m* связки
       прямых

**1358 center of a pencil of planes; vertex of a
    bundle of planes**
    d Scheitel *m* eines Ebenenbündels;
       Grundpunkt *m*; Träger *m*
    f centre *m* d'une gerbe de plans; sommet *m* d'un
       pinceau de plans; support *m*
    r центр *m* связки плоскостей; носитель *m*
       связки плоскостей

1359 center of a regular polygon
    d Mittelpunkt *m* eines regulären Polygons
    f centre *m* d'un polygone régulier
    r центр *m* правильного многоугольника

    * **center of a sphere** → 1350

1360 center of a star
    d Mittelpunkt *m* eines Sterns; Sternzentrum *n*
    f centre *m* d'une étoile
    r центр *m* звезды

1361 center of curvature
    d Krümmungsmittelpunkt *m*;
       Krümmungszentrum *n*
    f centre *m* de courbure
    r центр *m* кривизны; центр закругления

1362 center of gravity
    d Schwerpunkt *m*
    f centre *m* de la gravité
    r центр *m* тяжести

    * **center of homology** → 1364

1363 center of mass; mass center
    d Massenmittelpunkt *m*
    f centre *m* de masse
    r центр *m* массы; центр инерции

**1364 center of perspective; center of
    perspectivity; center of projection; center
    of homology**

    d Zentrum *n* der Perspektive;
       Projektionszentrum *n*; Mittelpunkt *m* der
       Kollineation; Homologiezentrum *n*
    f centre *m* de perspective; centre perspectif;
       centre de projection; centre de collinéation;
       centre d'homologie
    r центр *m* перспективы; центр проекции;
       центр проектирования; центр гомологии

    * **center of perspectivity** → 1364

1365 center of picture
    d Bildmittelpunkt *m*; Abbildungsmittelpunkt *m*
    f centre *m* de l'image; point *m* central de
       l'image
    r центр *m* изображения

1366 center of principal curvature
    d Hauptkrümmungsmittelpunkt *m*
    f centre *m* de courbure principale
    r центр *m* главной кривизны

    * **center of projection** → 1364

1367 center of rotation; pivot center
    d Rotationszentrum *n*
    f centre *m* de rotation
    r центр *m* вращения

1368 center of symmetry
    d Symmetriezentrum *n*
    f centre *m* de symétrie
    r центр *m* симметрии

1369 center of viewpoint
    d Aug[en]punkt-Zentrum *n*
    f centre *m* de point de vue
    r центр *m* точки зрения

1370 center of vorticity
    d Wirbeltopf *m*
    f centre *m* de tourbillonnement
    r центр *m* завихрения

1371 center point; central point
    d Mittelpunkt *m*
    f point *m* central
    r центральная точка *f*; точка центра

**1372 center-to-center distance; center-to-center
    spacing**
    d Mittel[punkts]abstand *m*
    f distance *f* entre les centres
    r расстояние *n* между центрами

    * **center-to-center spacing** → 1372

1373 centigrade
    d Neuminute *f*; Zentesimalminute *f*

f centigrade *m*; minute *f* centésimale

r сотая доля *f* градуса; градусовая минута *f*

1374 central
d zentral; Zentral-; Mittel-
f central
r центральный

* **central angle** → 357

1375 central angle of a regular polygon
d Zentralwinkel *m* eines regulären Polygons
f angle *m* central d'un polygone régulier
r центральный угол *m* правильного многоугольника

1376 central axis
d Zentralachse *f*
f axe *m* central
r центральная ось *f*

1377 central axonometry
d zentrale Axonometrie *f*; Zentralaxonometrie *f*
f axonométrie *f* centrale
r центральная аксонометрия *f*

* **central collineation** → 6998

* **central conic** → 1378

1378 central conic [section]; conic of centres
d zentraler Kegelschnitt *m*; Mittelpunktskegelschnitt *m*
f conique *f* des centres; section *f* conique à centre
r центральное коническое сечение *n*; коническое сечение центров

1379 central curve
d Mittelpunktskurve *f*
f courbe *f* à centre
r центральная кривая *f*

1380 central element
d zentrales Element *n*
f élément *m* central
r центральный элемент *m*

1381 centrally symmetric
d zentralsymmetrisch
f à symétrie centrale
r центральносимметричный

1382 central perspective
d Zentralperspektive *f*
f perspective *f* centrale
r центральная перспектива *f*

* **central point** → 1371

1383 central projection; conic[al] projection; perspective projection; perspective mapping; perspective
d Zentralprojektion *f*; Kegelprojektion *f*; perspektivische Projektion *f*; Perspektive *f*; Perspektivität *f*
f projection *f* centrale; projection conique; projection perspective; perspective *f*
r центральная проекция *f*; коническая проекция; перспективная проекция; перспектива *f*

1384 central section
d Mittelpunktsschnitt *m*
f section *f* centrale
r центральное сечение *n*

1385 central surface
d Mittelpunktfläche *f*; zentrale Fläche *f*
f surface *f* centrale
r центральная поверхность *f*

1386 central symmetry
d Zentralsymmetrie *f*
f symétrie *f* centrale
r центральная симметрия *f*

* **centre** → 1342

* **centre line** → 5626

* **centre of the escribed circle** → 3559

* **centre of the escribed sphere** → 3560

1387 centricity
d Zentrizität *f*
f centricité *f*
r центричность *f*

* **centring** → 1347

1388 centrode; poid; polhode
d Zentrode *f*; Mittelpunktsbahn *f*; Polhodie *f*
f centrode *f*; polhodie *f*
r центроида *f*; полодия *f*; полоида *f*

1389 centroid
d Zentroid *n*
f centroïde *m*
r центроид *m*

1390 chain
d Kette *f*; Folge *f*; Kettenzug *m*
f chaîne *f*
r цепь *f*; простой список *m*; цепочка *f*

1391 chain dimensioning; continued dimensioning
d weitere Dimensionierung *f*; weitere

Bemaßung *f*
f cotation *f* continue; dimensionnement *m* continu
r цепное задание *n* размеров

* **chain-dot screen** → 3377

* **chained fade** → 2304

1392 **chaining; catenation**
d Kettung *f*; Verkettung *f*
f chaînage *m*; enchaînement *m*
r цепное связывание *n*; сцепление *n*

1393 **chain of triangles**
d Dreieckskette *f*
f chaîne *f* de triangles
r цепь *f* треугольников; ряд *m* треугольников

1394 **chain structure**
d Kettenstruktur *f*
f structure *f* en chaîne
r цепная структура *f*

1395 **chamfer; bevel; feather**
d Schräge *f*
f biseau *m*; chanfrein *m*
r фаска *f*; откос *m*

* **chamfered edge** → 3715

* **chamfered joint** → 3716

1396 **chamfering; bevel[l]ing**
d Abschrägung *f*; Stemmung *f*
f biseautage *m*; chanfreinage *m*
r скошение *n*

1397 **change** *v*
d ändern; wechseln
f changer
r [из]менять

1398 **change**
d Änderung *f*
f change[ment] *m*
r перемена *f*; изменение *n*

1399 **change** *v* **icon**
d Ikone wechseln
f changer une icône
r заменять икону

1400 **change of coordinate system**
d Übergang *m* von einem Koordinatensystem zu einem anderen
f changement *m* de système de coordonnées
r замена *f* координатной системы

1401 **change of frame; frame change**
d Bezugssystemwechsel *m*; Wechsel *m* des Bezugssystems
f changement *m* de repère
r замена *f* репера

1402 **change of scale**
d Maßstabsänderung *f*
f changement *m* d'échelle
r изменение *n* масштаба

1403 **change** *v* **source**
d Quelle wechseln
f changer une source
r заменять источник

1404 **change** *v* **view**
d Ansicht wechseln
f changer de présentation
r заменять вид

1405 **channel**
d Kanal *m*
f canal *m*
r канал *m*

1406 **chaos**
d Chaos *n*
f chaos *m*
r хаос

1407 **chaotic zones**
d chaotische Zonen *fpl*
f zones *fpl* chaotiques
r хаотические зоны *fpl*

1408 **chapter**
d Kapitel *n*
f chapitre *m*
r глава *f*; секция *f*; раздел *m*

* **char** → 1409

1409 **character; char; symbol**
d Zeichen *n*; Symbol *n*
f caractère *m*; symbole *m*
r знак *m*; символ *m*

1410 **character attribute**
d Zeichenattribut *n*
f attribut *m* de caractère
r атрибут *m* знака

1411 **character bar; symbol bar**
d Symbolleiste *f*
f barre *f* de caractères
r лента *f* символов

1412 **character cell; dot matrix field**
d Position *f* des Symbols

f position *f* de caractère
r знакоместо *n*; символьная ячейка *f*

1413 character code
d Zeichencode *m*
f code *m* de caractère
r код *m* символа

* **character contour** → **1430**

* **character design** → **1414**

1414 character design[ing]
d Zeichen-Design *n*
f dessin *m* de caractère
r символьный дизайн *m*

1415 character fade-in
d Zeichenaufblendung *f*
f apparition *f* graduelle de caractères
r постепенное возникновение *n* символов

1416 character fade-out
d Zeichenabblendung *f*
f disparition *f* graduelle de caractères
r постепенное исчезновение *n* символов

1417 character font; symbol font; type font; font; type [style]
d Zeichenschriftart *f*; Schrift[art] *f*; Font *n*
f police *f* [de caractères]; fonte *f*; style *m* de types
r шрифт *m*; литера *f*; комплект *m* шрифта; гарнитура *f* [шрифта]

1418 character formatting
d Zeichenformatierung *f*
f formatage *m* de caractère
r форматирование *n* символа

1419 character generator
d Zeichengenerator *m*
f générateur *m* de caractères
r генератор *m* символов

* **character graphics** → **7622**

1420 character-height unit
d Einheit *f* der Zeichenhöhe
f unité *f* de hauteur de caractère
r единица *f* высоты символа

* **characteristic** → **1422**

1421 characteristic
d Charakteristik *f*
f caractéristique *f*
r характеристика *f*; особенность *f*; свойство *n*

1422 characteristic [curve]; response [curve]
d charakteristische Kurve *f*; Charakteristik *f*; Kennlinie *f*
f courbe *f* caractéristique; caractéristique *f*
r характеристическая кривая *f*; характеристика *f*

* **characteristic group** → **1423**

1423 characteristic group [of points]
d charakteristische Punktgruppe *f*; charakteristische Gruppe *f*
f groupe *m* [de points] caractéristique
r характеристическая группа *f* [точек]

1424 characteristic plane; analytical plane; synectic plane
d charakteristische Ebene *f*; analytische Ebene; synektische Ebene
f plan *m* caractéristique; plan analytique; plan synectique
r характеристическая плоскость *f*; аналитическая плоскость; синэктическая плоскость

1425 characteristic polynomial
d charakteristisches Polynom *n*
f polynôme *m* caractéristique
r характеристический полином *m*

1426 characteristic population
d charakteristische Population *f*
f population *f* caractéristique
r характеристическая популяция *f*

1427 characteristic vector; eigenvector
d charakteristischer Vektor *m*; Eigenvektor *m*
f vecteur *m* caractéristique; vecteur propre
r характеристический вектор *m*; собственный вектор

1428 character map; symbol table
d Zeichentabelle *f*; Symboltabelle *f*
f table *f* de caractères; table de symboles
r таблица *f* символов

1429 character matching
d Character-Anpassung *f*; Character-Abgleich *m*
f adaptation *f* des caractères
r согласование *n* символов

1430 character outline; character contour; character shape
d Zeichenumriss *m*; Zeichenkontur *f*
f contour *m* du caractère; forme *f* du caractère
r контур *m* знака; очертание *n* символа; форма *f* символа

* **character pitch** → **7446**

1431　character properties
　d　Symboleigenschaften *fpl*
　f　propriétés *fpl* des caractères
　r　свойства *npl* символов; признаки *mpl* символов

1432　character set
　d　Zeichensatz *m*; Zeichenvorrat *m*
　f　jeu *m* de caractères; répertoire *m* de caractères
　r　набор *m* знаков; набор символов

　*　**character shape** → **1430**

1433　character size
　d　Symbolgröße *f*
　f　taille *f* de caractère
　r　размер *m* символа

1434　character spacing; inter-character space
　d　Zeichenabstand *m*; Abstand *m* zwischen Zeichen; Zeichenlücke *f*
　f　espace *m* entre caractères
　r　расстояние *n* между знаками; интервал *m* между знаками

1435　character subscript
　d　tiefgestelltes Zeichen *n*
　f　indice *m* inférieur de caractère
　r　символ *m* нижний индекс; нижний индекс *m* символа

1436　character superscript
　d　hochgestelltes Zeichen *n*
　f　indice *m* supérieur de caractère
　r　символ *m* верхний индекс; верхний индекс *m* символа

1437　character-to-background contrast
　d　Zeichen-Hintergrundkontrast *m*
　f　contraste *m* caractère-fond
　r　контраст *m* знак-фон

1438　character weight
　d　Zeichengewicht *n*
　f　poids *m* de caractère
　r　толщина *f* символа; вес *m* символа

　*　**charge** → **5673**

　*　**chart** → **3129, 5782**

1439　chart; diagram; graph[ic]; plot
　d　Diagramm *n*; Schaubild *n*; Kurvenblatt *n*; Kurvenbild *n*; Grafik *f*
　f　diagramme *m*; graphique *m*; courbe *f* représentative
　r　диаграмма *f*; схема *f*; график *m*; лист *m* кривых

1440　chart area

**　**
　d　Diagrammgebiet *n*
　f　domaine *m* de diagramme
　r　область *f* диаграммы

1441　chart axes
　d　Diagrammachsen *fpl*
　f　axes *mpl* de diagramme
　r　оси *fpl* диаграммы

1442　chart border
　d　Diagrammrahmen *m*
　f　bordure *f* de diagramme
　r　рамка *f* диаграммы

1443　chart component
　d　Diagrammkomponente *f*
　f　composante *f* de diagramme
　r　элемент *m* диаграммы

1444　chart field
　d　Diagrammfeld *n*
　f　champ *m* de diagramme
　r　поле *n* диаграммы

　*　**charting** → **1445**

1445　chart plotting; charting
　d　Diagrammplotten *n*; Diagrammaufzeichnung *f*
　f　tracement *m* de diagramme; tracement de graphique
　r　вычерчивание *n* диаграммы

1446　chart sheet
　d　Diagrammblatt *n*
　f　feuille *f* de diagramme
　r　лист *m* диаграммы

1447　chart template
　d　Diagrammschablone *f*
　f　modèle *m* de diagramme
　r　шаблон *m* диаграммы

1448　chart type
　d　Diagrammtyp *m*
　f　type *m* de diagramme
　r　тип *m* диаграммы

1449　chart wizard
　d　Diagramm-Assistent *m*
　f　assistant *m* de diagrammes
　r　советчик *m* построения диаграммы

1450　check *v*; test *v*; verify *v*; audit *v*
　d　überprüfen; [nach]prüfen; verifizieren
　f　essayer; examiner; vérifier
　r　проверять; испытывать

1451　checkbox
　d　Kontrollkasten *m*; Kontrollkästchen *n*

f case *f* à cocher; cocher *m*; boîte *f* d'essai; case d'option
r тестовый ящик *m*; поле *n* для галочки; графа *f* для галочки; флажок *m*; переключатель *m*; триггерная кнопка *f*

1452 check mark
d Häkchen *n*
f coche *f*
r отметка *f*; галочка *f*

1453 chessboard distance
d Schachbrettdistanz *f*
f distance *f* d'échiquier
r шахматное расстояние *n*

1454 chessboard pattern
d Schachbrett-Motiv *n*
f motif *m* en échiquier
r шахматный узор *m*; рисунок *m* в клетку

* **chevrons** → **367**

* **chiffre** → **2756**

1455 child color
d abgeleitete Farbe *f*; untergeordnete Farbe
f couleur *f* fille
r дочерный цвет *m*; потомственный цвет

1456 child dimension style
d untergeordneter Dimensionsstil *m*
f style *m* de cote fils
r потомственный стиль *m* размерности

1457 child object
d untergeordnetes Objekt *n*
f objet *m* fils
r потомственный объект *m*

1458 chip
d optisches Mikrobild *n*
f micro-image *f* optique
r оптическое микроизображение *n*

1459 chip
d Chip *m*
f puce *f*
r чип *m*

1460 chip designer
d Chip-Designer *m*
f concepteur *m* de puces
r проектировщик *m* чипов

* **choice** → **8460**

* **choice device** → **8478**

1461 choice of coordinates

d Zeigerwahl *f*
f choix *m* des coordonnées
r выбор *m* координат

1462 choice of style; style selection
d Stilwahl *f*
f sélection *f* de style
r выбор *m* стиля

* **choose** *v* → **8451**

1463 chord
d Sehne *f*; Bisekante *f*; Doppelsekante *f*
f corde *f*
r хорда *f*

1464 chordal distance; spherical distance
d chordaler Abstand *m*; Kugelabstand *m*
f distance *f* cordale; distance sphérique
r хордальное расстояние *n*; сферическое расстояние

* **chord direction** → **2871**

1465 chord length
d Sehnenlänge *f*
f longueur *f* de corde
r длина *f* хорды

1466 chord of a circle
d Kreissehne *f*
f corde *f* d'un cercle
r хорда *f* окружности

* **chord through a focus of a conic** → **3893**

* **chroma** → **1478**

1467 chroma amplifier
d Farbartverstärker *m*
f amplificateur *m* de chrominance
r усилитель *m* интенсивности цвета

1468 chroma-keying; keying
(the process of mixing two video sequences, e.g. live video with synthetic animation)
d Einblendung *f*; Stanzen *n*
f chroma-incrustation *f*; incrustation *f*
r цветовая рирпроекция *f*

1469 chroma-mapping; gamut mapping
d Chroma-Mapping *n*; Gamut-Mapping *n*
f chroma-mappage *m*
r хроматическое отображение *n*; хроматическое наложение *n*

* **chroma signal** → **1291**

1470 chromatic
d chromatisch

f chromatique
r цветной; хроматический

1471 chromatic aberration
d chromatische Aberration *f*;
Farb[en]abweichung *f*
f aberration *f* chromatique
r хроматическая аберрация *f*

* **chromatic decomposition** → 8993

1472 chromatic dispersion
d chromatische Dispersion *f*; Farbdispersion *f*
f dispersion *f* chromatique
r хроматическая дисперсия *f*

1473 chromatic distortion
d chromatische Distorsion *f*
f distorsion *f* chromatique
r хроматическое искажение *n*

1474 chromaticity; chromaticness
d Farbart *f*; Farbvalenz *f*; Chromazität *f*
f chromaticité *f*
r цветность *f*, хроматизм *m*

1475 chromaticity coordinate
d Farbkoordinate *f*
f coordonnée *f* de chromaticité
r координата *f* цветности

* **chromaticity diagram** → 1713

* **chromaticity triangle** → 1857

* **chromaticity value** → 1860

* **chromaticness** → 1474

1476 chromatic number
d chromatische Zahl *f*
f nombre *m* chromatique
r хроматическое число *n*

* **chromatic space** → 1840

* **chromatic system** → 1847

1477 chromatic wheel; color wheel; color circle
d Farbkreis *m*
f roue *f* chromatique; roue de couleurs
r хроматическое колесо *n*

1478 chrominance; chroma
(portion of a video signal which corresponds
to color values and includes information
about hue and saturation)
d Chrominanz *f*; Farbqualität *f*;
Farb[en]einheit *f*; Chroma *n*
f chrominance *f*; chroma *m*

r интенсивность *f* цвета; цветовая
плотность *f*

* **chrominance signal** → 1291

1479 cicero
(= 12 didots)
d Cicero *n*
f cicero *m*
r цицеро *m*

* **cipher** → 2756

1480 circle
d Kreis *m*
f cercle *m*
r окружность *f*; круг *m*

* **circle diameter** → 2702

1481 circle entity
d Kreiseinheit *f*
f entité *f* cercle
r примитив *m* окружность

* **circle graph** → 7071

* **circle mask** → 1499

1482 circle object
d Kreisobjekt *n*
f objet *m* cercle
r объект *m* типа окружности

1483 circle of contact
d Berührungskreis *m*
f cercle *m* de contact
r окружность *f* касания

1484 circle of curvature; osculating circle
d Krümmungskreis *m*; Oskulationskreis *m*;
Schmiegungskreis *m*
f cercle *m* de courbure; cercle oscillateur
r круг *m* кривизны; соприкасающаяся
окружность *f*; окружность кривизны

1485 circle of diffusion
d Zerstreuungskreis *m*
f tache *f* de diffusion
r круг *m* рассеивания

1486 circle property
d Kreiseigenschaft *f*
f propriété *f* de cercle
r свойство *n* окружности

1487 circle rectification
d Rektifikation *f* des Kreises
f rectification *f* de cercle
r спрямление *n* окружности

* circle segment → 8448

1488 circle smoothness
    d Kreisglätte *f*
    f égalité *f* de cercle
    r гладкость *f* окружности

* circuit-free → 138

* circuit-free graph → 139

1489 circular
    d Kreis-
    f circulaire
    r кольцевой; циклический; циркулярный; круговой

* circular arc → 536

1490 circular arrow
    d Kreispfeil *m*
    f flèche *f* circulaire
    r круговая стрелка *f*

1491 circular blend
    d Kreisüberblendung *f*
    f dégradé *m* circulaire
    r циклическое переливание *n*

1492 circular body; circular solid
    d Kreiskörper *m*
    f corps *m* circulaire
    r круговое тело *n*

1493 circular cell
    d Kreiszelle *f*
    f cellule *f* circulaire
    r круговая клетка *f*

* circular chart → 7071

1494 circular cone
    d Kreiskegel *m*
    f cône *m* circulaire
    r круговой конус *m*

1495 circular curve
    d zirkulare Kurve *f*; Kreiskurve *f*
    f courbe *f* circulaire
    r циркулярная кривая *f*

1496 circular cylinder
    d Kreiszylinder *m*
    f cylindre *m* circulaire
    r круговой цилиндр *m*

1497 circular domain
    d Kreisbereich *m*; Kreisgebiet *n*
    f domaine *m* circulaire
    r круговая область *f*

* circular-free → 5291

* circular function → 9900

* circular helix → 4560

1498 circularity
    d Rundheit *f*
    f circularité *f*
    r цикличность *f*

1499 circular mask; circle mask
    d Rundmaske *f*
    f masque *f* circulaire
    r круговая маска *f*

* circular measure → 7701

* circular measure of an angle → 5873

* circular motion → 1500

1500 circular movement; circular motion
    d Kreisbewegung *f*; kreisförmige Bewegung *f*
    f mouvement *m* circulaire
    r круговое движение *n*; циклическое движение

1501 circular nomogram
    d Kreisnomogramm *n*; Kreistafel *f*
    f nomogramme *m* circulaire
    r круговая номограмма *f*

* circular points of infinity → 2425

1502 circular profile
    d Kreisprofil *n*
    f profil *m* circulaire
    r круговой профиль *m*

1503 circular reference
    d Kreisreferenz *f*; Kreisbezug *m*
    f référence *f* circulaire
    r циклическая ссылка *f*

1504 circular region
    d Rundregion *f*
    f région *f* circulaire
    r круговой регион *m*

1505 circular ring; annulus; donut
    d [ebener] Kreisring *m*
    f couronne *f* [circulaire]; anneau *m* [circulaire]
    r [плоское] круговое кольцо *n*

1506 circular screen; round screen; round dots
    d Kreisraster *m*
    f trame *f* circulaire
    r [концентрично-]круглый растр *m*

    * **circular sector** → 8441

1507 circular selection
  d Kreisauwahl *f*
  f sélection *f* circulaire
  r циклическая выборка *f*

1508 circular shift; cycle shift; cyclic shift;
      end-around shift; ring shift
  d zyklische Verschiebung *f*; Ringschiften *n*
  f décalage *m* circulaire; déplacement *m*
    cyclique
  r циклический сдвиг *m*; кольцевой сдвиг

    * **circular solid** → 1492

1509 circular visual selector
  d rundes visuelles Auswahlfeld *n*
  f sélecteur *m* visuel circulaire
  r круговой визуальный селектор *m*

1510 circular whirl
  d zirkularer Wirbel *m*; Kreiswirbel *m*
  f tourbillon *m* circulaire
  r круговой вихрь *m*; циркулярный вихрь

1511 circulate *v*; **rotate** *v*; **revolve** *v*
  d umlaufen; rotieren; drehen
  f circuler
  r циркулировать; вращать[ся]

1512 circulation
  d Zirkulation *f*; Kreislauf *m*
  f circulation *f*
  r циркуляция *f*; периодическое повторение *n*

    * **circules** → 2425

    * **circules of a plane** → 2425

    * **circumcenter** → 1513

1513 circumcentre; circumcenter
  d Mittelpunkt *m* des Umkreises;
    Umkreismittelpunkt *m*
  f centre *m* du cercle circonscrit
  r центр *m* описанной окружности

1514 circumcircle; circumscribed circle
  d Umkreis *m*; umbeschriebener Kreis *m*
  f cercle *m* circonscrit; circonférence *f*
    circonscrite
  r описанная окружность *f*

1515 circumference
    (of a circle)
  d Zirkumferenz *f*; Kreisperipherie *f*
  f circonférence *f*; périphérie *f* de cercle
  r периферия *f* круга; окружность *f*

    * **circumflex** → 1289

    * **circumflex accent** → 1289

    * **circumradius** → 7719, 7720

1516 circumscribe *v*
  d umschreiben
  f circonscrire
  r описывать

1517 circumscribed
  d umschrieben
  f circonscrit
  r описанный

    * **circumscribed circle** → 1514

1518 circumscribed cone
  d umschriebener Kegel *m*
  f cône *m* circonscrit
  r описанный конус *m*

1519 circumscribed cylinder
  d umschriebener Zylinder *m*
  f cylindre *m* circonscrit
  r описанный цилиндр *m*

1520 circumscribed figure
  d umschriebene Figur *f*
  f figure *f* circonscrite
  r описанная фигура *f*

1521 circumscribed polygon
  d Tangentenvieleck *n*
  f polygone *m* circonscrit
  r описанный многоугольник *m*

1522 circumscribed quadrangle
  d umschriebenes Viereck *n*
  f quadrilatère *m* circonscrit
  r описанный четырехугольник *m*

1523 circumscribed sphere; circumsphere
  d umschriebene Kugel *f*
  f sphère *f* circonscrite
  r описанная сфера *f*

1524 circumscribed triangle
  d umschriebenes Dreieck *n*
  f triangle *m* circonscrit
  r описанный треугольник *m*

    * **circumsphere** → 1523

1525 circumvention; encirclement
  d Umgehung *f*; Umlauf *m*
  f contournement *m*; détour *m*
  r обход *m*; мода *f* покрытия; мода оболочки

1526 **circumvolution**
  d Umkreisung *f*
  f circonvolution *f*; circumduction *f*
  r изгиб *m*; извилина *f*; навивание *n*

1527 **cissoid**
  d Zissoide *f*; Cissoide *f*
  f cissoïde *f*
  r циссоида *f*

1528 **cissoidal curve**
  d zissoidale Kurve *f*
  f courbe *f* cissoïde
  r циссоидальная кривая *f*

1529 **clarity**
  d Deutlichkeit *f*; Anschaulichkeit *f*
  f clarté *f*; lisibilité *f*
  r ясность *f*; наглядность *f*

1530 **class**
  d Klasse *f*
  f classe *f*
  r класс *m*

1531 **classification; grading**
  d Klassifizierung *f*; Klassifikation *f*
  f classification *f*; classement *m*
  r классификация *f*; распределение *n*;
    классирование *n*

1532 **classifier**
  d Klassifikator *m*; Klassifizierer *m*
  f class[ificat]eur *m*
  r классификатор *m*

1533 **classify** *v*
  d klassifizieren; klassieren
  f classifier; classer
  r классифицировать

  * **clean** *v* → **1536**

  * **clean** → **1535**

  * **clean data** → **10095**

1534 **cleaner**
  d Reinigungseinrichtung *f*; Reiniger *m*
  f nettoyeur *m*; épurateur *m*
  r устройство *n* очистки

1535 **clean[ing]; clear[ing]; clearance;
    purification; purging**
  d Reinigung *f*
  f nettoyage *m*; purification *f*
  r очищение *n*; очистка *f*

  * **clear** → **1535**

1536 **clear** *v*; **clean** *v*; **discard** *v*; **remove** *v*
  d löschen; reinigen
  f balayer; effacer
  r очищать; стирать; удалить

1537 **clear** *v* **all**
  d alles löschen
  f effacer tout
  r стирать все

  * **clearance** → **1535**

1538 **clear** *v* **effect**
  d Effekt löschen
  f effacer un effet
  r очищать эффект; стирать эффект

  * **clearing** → **1535**

1539 **clear method**
  d Löschungsmethode *f*
  f méthode *f* d'effaçage
  r метод *m* очищения

1540 **clear** *v* **screen**
  d Bildschirm löschen
  f effacer d'écran
  r очищать экран

1541 **cliché**
  d Klischee *n*
  f cliché *m*
  r клише *n*

1542 **click**
  d Klick *m*; Klicken *n*
  f clic *m*; click *m*
  r клик *m*; щелчок *m*; нажатие *n* кнопки

  * **clickable area** → **4718**

  * **clickable image** → **1543**

1543 **clickable image [map]; image map; hot
    image; interactive graphics**
  d klickbare Imagemap *f*
  f image *f* réactive; image cliquable; carte *f*
    sensible; carte-image *f*; carte imagée
  r адресуемое изображение *n*

1544 **click** *v* **and drag** *v*
  d klicken und ziehen
  f cliquer et glisser
  r нажать [кнопку] и переместить

  * **click-to-type focus** → **3576**

1545 **client; customer**
  d Kunde *m*

f client *m*
r клиент *m*; заказчик *m*

1546 client application
d Kundenanwendung *f*
f application *f* d'acheteur; application d'acquéreur
r заказное приложение *n*

* **client installation** → 2397

1547 clip
d Clip *m*; Teil *m* in einem grafischen Dokument
f clip *m*; agrafe *f*
r клип *m*; вырезка *f*; фрагмент *m*

1548 clip *v*
d schneiden; zerschneiden; kappen
f découper
r срезать; отсекать

1549 clip algorithm
d Schneidalgorithmus *m*
f algorithme *m* de découpage
r алгоритм *m* отсекания

1550 clipart
(ready-made images)
d Clipart *f*
f clipart *m*; graphique *m* prédessiné
r иллюстративная вставка *f*; графический фрагмент *m*; аппликация *f*

1551 clipart collection
d Clipart-Sammlung *f*
f collection *f* de cliparts
r коллекция *f* вырезок

1552 clipart scrapbook
d Clipart-Skizzenbuch *n*
f classeur *m* de cliparts
r альбом *m* вырезок

1553 clipboard
d Einfügungspuffer *m*
f presse-papiers *m*
r буфер *m* обмена

1554 clipdepth
d Schnitttiefe *f*
f profondeur *f* de coupe
r глубина *f* среза

1555 clip gallery
d Clipgalerie *f*
f galerie *f* de clips
r галерея *f* картинок

1556 clipped noise
d begrenztes Rauschen *n*

f bruit *m* coupé
r ограниченный шум *m*

1557 clipper
d Begrenzerschaltung *f*
f écrêteur *m*
r инструмент *m* отсекания

1558 clipping; scissoring; cutting
d Ausschnitt *m*; Schneiden *n*; Kappen *n*; Klippen *n*
f [dé]coupage *m*; écrêtage *m*; détourage *m*
r отсечение *n*; усечение *n*; срезание *n*; отсекание *n*

1559 clipping boundaries
d Schnittgrenzen *fpl*
f limites *fpl* de découpage
r границы *fpl* отсекания

1560 clipping hole
d Schneideloch *n*
f trou *m* de découpage
r отсекающее отверстие *n*

1561 clipping mode
d Schnittmodus *m*
f mode *m* de découpage
r режим *m* отсекания

1562 clipping path
d Schnittstrecke *f*
f tracé *m* de découpage
r отсекающая трасса *f*

1563 clipping planes
d Schnittebenen *fpl*
f plans *mpl* de découpage
r отсекающие плоскости *fpl*

1564 clip[ping] rectangle
d Schnittrechteck *n*
f rectangle *m* de découpage
r отсекающий прямоугольник *m*

1565 clipping region
d Schnittbereich *m*
f région *f* de découpage
r отсекающий регион *m*

* **clip polygon** → 7276

* **clip rectangle** → 1564

1566 clockwise
d im Uhrzeigersinn
f en sens des aiguilles d'une montre; en sens horaire
r по часовой стрелке

* **clockwise blend** → 1567

1567 clockwise blend[ing]
  d Überblendung *f* im Uhrzeigersinn
  f dégradé *m* en sens horaire
  r переливание *n* по часовой стрелке

1568 clockwise path button
  d Schaltfläche *f* der Strecke im Uhrzeigersinn
  f bouton *m* de tracé horaire
  r кнопка *f* трассы по часовой стрелке

1569 clockwise rotation
  d Drehung *f* nach rechts; Rotation *f* im
       Uhrzeigersinn; Rechtsdrehung *f*
  f rotation *f* en sens horaire
  r вращение *n* по часовой стрелке

1570 clone *v*
  d klonen
  f cloner
  r клонировать

1571 clone; cloning
  d Klonen *n*
  f clone *m*; clonage *m*
  r клонирование *n*

1572 clone frame
  d Klonen-Frame *n*
  f cadre-imitation *m*
  r кадр-имитация *f*

* **clone tool** → 1573

* **cloning** → 1571

1573 cloning tool; clone tool
  d Klonen-Hilfsmittel *n*
  f outil *m* de clonage
  r инструмент *m* клонирования

1574 close *v*
  d abschließen; schließen
  f fermer
  r замыкать; закрывать

1575 close coupling; tight coupling
  d Kurzkupplung *f*
  f attelage *m* serré
  r сильная связь *f*

1576 closed
  d geschlossen; abgeschlossen
  f fermé; clos
  r замкнутый; закрытый

* **closed area** → 1582

1577 closed ball

  d abgeschlossene Kugel *f*
  f boule *f* fermée
  r замкнутая сфера *f*; замкнутый шар *m*

* **closed contour** → 1588

1578 closed cross
  d geschlossenes Kreuz *n*
  f croix *m* fermé
  r замкнутый крест *m*

1579 closed cross intersections
  d geschlossene Querdurchschnitte *mpl*
  f intersections *fpl* en croix fermées
  r замкнутые перекрестные пересечения *npl*

1580 closed curve
  d geschlossene Kurve *f*
  f courbe *f* fermée
  r замкнутая кривая *f*

* **closed cycle** → 1586

1581 closed disk
  d abgeschlossener Kreis *m*
  f disque *m* fermé
  r замкнутый круг *m*

1582 closed domain; closed area
  d abgeschlossener Bereich *m*; abgeschlossenes
       Gebiet *n*
  f domaine *m* fermé; zone *f* fermée
  r замкнутая область *f*

1583 closed field
  d abgeschlossener Körper *m*
  f corps *m* clos
  r замкнутое поле *n*

1584 closed form; closed shape
  d geschlossene Form *f*
  f forme *f* fermée
  r замкнутая форма *f*

1585 closed geometric object
  d geschlossenes geometrisches Objekt *n*
  f objet *m* géométrique fermé
  r замкнутый геометрический объект *m*

1586 closed loop; loop; closed cycle
  d geschlossene Schleife *f*; Schleife *f*; Schlinge *f*;
       geschlossener Wirkungskreis *m*
  f boucle *f* [fermée]; cycle *m* fermé; lacet *m*
  r замкнутый цикл *m*; шлейф *m*; петля *f*

1587 closed object
  d geschlossenes Objekt *n*
  f objet *m* fermé
  r замкнутый объект *m*

1588 closed outline; closed contour
d geschlossene Kontur *f*
f contour *m* fermé
r замкнутый контур *m*

1589 closed path
d geschlossene Strecke *f*; geschlossener Weg *m*
f tracé *m* fermé; chemin *m* fermé
r замкнутая дорожка *f*; замкнутая трасса *f*

1590 closed plane
d abgeschlossene Ebene *f*
f plan *m* fermé
r замкнутая плоскость *f*

1591 closed polygon
d geschlossenes Polygon *n*
f polygone *m* fermé
r замкнутый полигон *m*

1592 closed polyline
d geschlossene Polylinie *f*
f polyligne *f* fermée
r замкнутая полилиния *f*

1593 closed region
d abgeschlossene Region *f*
f région *f* fermée
r замкнутый регион *m*

* **closed shape** → 1584

1594 closed spherical layer
d abgeschlossene Kugelschicht *f*
f couronne *f* sphérique fermée
r замкнутый сферический слой *m*; замкнутый шаровой слой

1595 closed spline
d abgeschlossener Spline *m*
f spline *m* fermé
r замкнутый сплайн *m*

1596 closed structure
d geschlossene Struktur *f*
f structure *f* fermée
r замкнутая структура *f*

1597 closed surface
d geschlossene Fläche *f*
f surface *f* fermée
r замкнутая поверхность *f*

1598 closed tee intersection
(intersection of multilines at T-form)
d geschlossener T-Form-Durchschnitt *m*
f intersection *f* en T fermée
r замкнутое Т-образное пересечение *n*

1599 closed texture

d geschlossene Textur *f*; feste Textur
f texture *f* fermée
r замкнутая текстура *f*

1600 close scanning
d Feinabtastung *f*
f balayage *m* à haute définition
r точное сканирование *n*

1601 close-up view
d Nahaufnahme *f*
f vue *f* [de plan] rapprochée
r крупномасштабный вид *m*; вид крупным планом

1602 closure
d Abschluss *m*; Abschließung *f*; Hülle *f*; Fermeture *n*
f fermeture *f*; clôture *f*
r замыкание *n*; закрытие *n*

1603 cloth animation
d Kleidungsanimation *f*
f animation *f* de vêtement
r анимация *f* одежды

1604 clothing design
d Kleidungsdesign *n*
f conception *f* de vêtement; dessin *m* de vêtement
r проектирование *n* одежды

1605 cloth simulator
d Stoffsimulator *m*
f simulateur *m* de vêtement
r симулятор *m* ткани

* **cloverleaf** → 9873

1606 cluster; subassembly
(group of tiles)
d Cluster *m*
f grappe *f*; bouquet *m*; cluster *m*; batterie *f* [de dérouleurs]
r кластер *m*; блок *m*

1607 cluster analysis
d Cluster-Analyse *f*
f analyse *f* cluster
r кластерный анализ *m*

* **clustered nodes** → 1608

* **clustered radiosity** → 1609

* **clustered structure** → 1610

1608 cluster[iz]ed nodes
d gruppierte Knoten *mpl*

f nœuds *m* en grappes
r сгруппированные узлы *mpl*

1609 cluster[iz]ed radiosity
   d gruppiertes Radiosity *n*
   f radiosité *f* en grappes
   r сгрупированное диффузное отражение *n*

1610 cluster[iz]ed structure
   d gruppierte Struktur *f*
   f structure *f* en grappes
   r кластерная структура *f*

1611 cluster point
   d Cluster-Punkt *m*
   f point *m* de grappe
   r кластерная точка *f*

   * **CLUT** → 1780

   * **CMM** → 1784

   * **CMY** → 2418

1612 CMY color
   d CMY-Farbe *f*
   f couleur *f* CMY
   r цвет *m* CMY

1613 CMY color mode
   d CMY-Farbmodus *m*
   f mode *m* couleur CMY
   r цветной режим *m* CMY

1614 CMY color model
   d CMY-Farbmodell *n*
   f modèle *m* de couleur CMY; système *m* de trichromie CMY
   r цветная модель *f* CMY

1615 CMY color value
   d CMY-Farbwert *m*
   f valeur *f* de couleur CMY
   r код *m* цвета CMY

1616 CMY device
   d CMY-Gerät *n*
   f dispositif *m* CMY
   r устройство *n* CMY

   * **CMYK** → 2419

1617 CMYK color
   d CMYK-Farbe *f*
   f couleur *f* CMYK
   r цвет *m* CMYK

1618 CMYK color format
   d CMYK-Farbformat *n*
   f format *m* de couleur CMYK

   r цветной формат *m* CMYK

1619 CMYK color mode
   d CMYK-Farbmodus *m*
   f mode *m* couleur CMYK
   r режим *m* цвета CMYK

1620 CMYK color model
   d CMYK-Farbmodell *n*
   f modèle *m* de couleur CMYK; système *m* de quadrichromie CMYK
   r цветовая модель *f* CMYK

1621 CMYK color space
   d CMYK-Farbraum *m*
   f espace *m* couleur CMYK
   r цветовое пространство *n* CMYK

1622 CMYK color value
   d CMYK-Farbwert *m*
   f valeur *f* de couleur CMYK
   r код *m* цвета CMYK

1623 CMYK complementary color
   d CMYK-Komplementärfarbe *f*
   f couleur *f* complémentaire CMYK
   r дополнительный цвет *m* CMYK

1624 CMYK image
   d CMYK-Bild *n*
   f image *f* CMYK
   r изображение *n* CMYK

1625 CMYK output device
   d CMYK-Ausgabegerät *n*
   f dispositif *m* de sortie CMYK
   r выходное устройство *n* CMYK

1626 CMYK printer
   d CMYK-Drucker *m*
   f imprimante *f* CMYK
   r принтер *m* CMYK

1627 CMYK printing process
   d CMYK-Druckprozess *m*
   f processus *m* d'impression CMYK
   r процесс *m* печатания CMYK

1628 CMYK system
   d CMYK-System *n*
   f système *m* CMYK
   r система *f* CMYK

1629 CMY printer
   d CMY-Drucker *m*
   f imprimante *f* CMY
   r принтер *m* CMY

1630 coarse scanning
   d Grobabtastung *f*

f balayage *m* approximatif
r грубое сканирование *n*

1631 cocyclic points
d konzyklische Punkte *mpl*; Punkte auf einer Kreislinie
f points *mpl* cocycliques
r точки *fpl*, лежащие на одной окружности

1632 code
d Code *m*; Kode *m*
f code *m*
r код *m*

1633 code character
d Codezeichen *n*
f caractère *m* de code; signe *m* de code; symbole *m* de code
r кодовый знак *m*

1634 code chart; code list
d Codeschema *n*; Codeliste *f*
f schéma *m* de code; liste *f* de code
r кодовая таблица *f*

* **coded** → 3415

1635 coded aperture imaging
d codierte Apertur-Abbildung *f*
f imagination *f* d'ouverture codée
r кодированное изображение *n* отверстия

1636 coded binary file
d codierte Binärdatei *f*
f fichier *m* binaire codé
r кодированный двоичный файл *m*

1637 coded image
d codiertes Bild *n*
f image *f* codée
r закодированное изображение *n*

1638 coded image data
d Daten *npl* des codierten Bilds
f données *fpl* d'image codées
r данные *npl* для кодированного изображения

* **code list** → 1634

1639 code page
d Codeseite *f*
f page *f* code
r кодовая страница *f*

1640 coding; encoding
d Codieren *n*; Verschlüsseln *n*; Codierung *f*
f codage *m*; codification *f*
r кодирование *n*

1641 coefficient; factor; rate
d Koeffizient *m*; Faktor *m*
f coefficient *m*; facteur *m*
r коэффициент *m*; фактор *m*

1642 coefficient domain
d Koeffizientenbereich *m*
f domaine *m* des coefficients
r область *f* коэффициентов

* **coefficient of asymmetry** → 1650

1643 coefficient of contrast; contrast factor; contrast ratio
d Kontrastkoeffizient *m*; Kontrastverhältnis *n*
f facteur *m* de contraste
r коэффициент *m* контрастности

1644 coefficient of dilatation; dilatation coefficient; dilatation factor
d Dilatationskoeffizient *m*
f coefficient *m* de dilatation
r коэффициент *m* растяжения

1645 coefficient of distortion; distortion coefficient
d Verzerrungsfaktor *m*
f coefficient *m* de distorsion
r коэффициент *m* искажения

1646 coefficient of magnification; magnification factor
d Vergrößerungsfaktor *m*; Vergrößerungskoeffizient *m*
f coefficient *m* d'agrandissement; coefficient de grossissement
r коэффициент *m* увеличения

1647 coefficient of proportionality; proportionality factor; factor of proportionality
d Proportionalitätsfaktor *m*; Proportionalitätszahl *f*
f coefficient *m* de proportionnalité; facteur *m* de proportionnalité
r коэффициент *m* пропорциональности; множитель *m* пропорциональности

1648 coefficient of reduction; reduction factor
d Reduktionskoeffizient *m*; Verkleinerungskoeffizient *m*; Verkürzungsfaktor *m*
f coefficient *m* de réduction
r коэффициент *m* уменьшения

1649 coefficient of refraction
d Refraktionskoeffizient *m*
f coefficient *m* de réfraction
r коэффициент *m* рефракции

1650 **coefficient of skewness; coefficient of asymmetry**
  d Koeffizient *m* der Asymmetrie
  f coefficient *m* d'asymétrie
  r коэффициент *m* асимметрии; показатель *m* асимметрии

1651 **coefficient of torsion; torsion coefficient**
  d Torsionskoeffizient *m*; Torsionszahl *f*
  f coefficient *m* de torsion
  r коэффициент *m* кручения

  * **coercion** → 1309

1652 **cognitive modeling**
  d kognitive Modellierung *f*
  f modelage *m* cognitif
  r познавательное моделирование *n*; когнитивное моделирование

1653 **coherence; coherency**
  d Kohärenz *f*
  f cohérence *f*
  r связанность *f*; согласованность *f*; когерентность *f*

  * **coherency** → 1653

  * **coherent bundle** → 265

1654 **coherent light**
  d Kohärenzlicht *n*
  f lumière *f* cohérente
  r когерентный свет *m*

1655 **coherent light source**
  d Kohärenzlichtquelle *f*
  f source *f* d'éclairage cohérente
  r когерентный источник *m* света

1656 **cohesion**
  d Kohäsion *f*; Zusammenhalt *m*
  f cohésion *f*
  r сцепление *n*

  * **coiled** → 8837

1657 **coincide *v*; match *v***
  d koinzidieren; übereinstimmen
  f coïncider
  r совпадать

1658 **coincidence; matching**
  d Koinzidenz *f*
  f coïncidence *f*
  r совпадение *n*

1659 **coincidence curve**
  d Koinzidenzkurve *f*
  f courbe *f* de coïncidence

  r прилегающая кривая *f*

1660 **coincidence point**
  d Koinzidenzpunkt *m*
  f point *m* de coïncidence
  r точка *f* совпадения

1661 **coincidence surface**
  d Koinzidenzfläche *f*
  f surface *f* de coïncidence
  r прилегающая поверхность *f*

1662 **coincident**
  d koinzidierend; übereinstimmend
  f coïncident
  r совпадающий

1663 **coincident faces**
  d Koinzidenzflächen *fpl*
  f faces *fpl* coïncidentes
  r совпадающие грани *fpl*

1664 **coincident figures**
  d übereinstimmende Figuren *fpl*
  f figures *fpl* coïncidentes
  r совпадающие фигуры *fpl*

1665 **coincident planes; coinciding planes**
  d übereinstimmende Ebenen *fpl*
  f plans *mpl* confondus; plans coïncidents
  r совпадающие плоскости *fpl*

  * **coinciding planes** → 1665

1666 **cold colors**
  d kalte Farben *fpl*
  f couleurs *fpl* froides
  r холодные цвета *mpl*

  * **collaborative virtual environment;** → 2984

1667 **collage**
  d Ankleben *n*; Kleben *n*; Ansetzen *n*
  f collage *m*
  r коллаж *m*

  * **collapse *v* to a point** → 8660

1668 **collate *v***
  d vergleichen und sortieren
  f collationner
  r сопоставлять и упорядочивать

1669 **collating sequence**
  d Sortierfolge *f*; Mischfolge *f*
  f séquence *f* de collation
  r последовательность *f* объединения; сортирующая последовательность

1670 **collection**
  d Kollektion *f*; Sammlung *f*

f collection *f*
r коллекция *f*; совокупность *f*; набор *m*;
комплект *m*

* **collection of groups** → 4455

* **collector**→ 1671

1671 **collector [lens]**
d Kollimationslinse *f*
f lentille *f* collectrice; collecteur *m*
r коллекторная линза *f*; коллектор *m*

1672 **collimated**
d kollimiert; gebündelt
f collimaté
r коллимированный; коллимационный

1673 **collimated beam; focused beam**
d kollimierter Strahl; gebündelter Strahl *m*
f faisceau *m* collimaté; faisceau focalisé;
faisceau concentré
r направленный луч *m*; коллимированный
луч

1674 **collimated imagery**
d kollimierte Abbildung *f*
f visionnique *m* collimaté
r коллимированные изображения *npl*

1675 **collimated light**
d kollimiertes Licht *n*; Parallellicht *n*
f lumière *f* collimatée
r коллимированный свет *m*

1676 **collimated light beam**
d Parallelstrahlenbündel *n*
f faisceau *m* de lumière collimaté
r коллимированный пучок *m* света

1677 **collimated point source**
d kollimierte Punktquelle *f*
f source *f* ponctuelle collimatée
r коллимированный точечный источник *m*

1678 **collimating point**
d Bildmarke *f*
f repère *m* de cliché; repère d'image
r координатная метка *f*; наблюдаемая точка *f*

1679 **collimation**
d Kollimation *f*
f collimation *f*
r коллимация *f*

1680 **collimation axis; collimation line**
d Kollimationsachse *f*
f axe *m* de collimation; ligne *f* de collimation
r коллимационная ось *f*

* **collimation line** → 1680

1681 **collimator**
d Kollimator *m*
f collimateur *m*; canalis[at]eur *m*
r коллиматор *m*

1682 **collinear**
d kollinear
f colinéaire
r коллинеарный

1683 **collinear image points**
d kollineare Bildpunkte *mpl*
f points *mpl* d'image colinéaires
r коллинеарные точки *fpl* изображения

1684 **collinearity**
d Kollinearität *f*
f colinéarité *f*
r коллинеарность *f*

1685 **collinear lines**
d kollineare Geraden *fpl*
f droites *fpl* colinéaires
r коллинеарные прямые *fpl*

1686 **collinear points**
d kollineare Punkte *mpl*
f points *mpl* alignés; points colinéaires
r точки *fpl*, лежащие на одной прямой;
коллинеарные точки

1687 **collinear vectors; parallel vectors**
d kollineare Vektoren *mpl*; parallele Vektoren
f vecteurs *mpl* colinéaires; vecteurs parallèles
r коллинеарные векторы *mpl*; параллельные
векторы

1688 **collineation**
d Kollineation *f*
f collinéation *f*
r коллинеация *f*; коллинеарное
соответствие *n*; гомография *f*

* **collineatory transformation** → 7577

1689 **collision**
d Kollision *f*; Konfliktsituation *f*
f collision *f*; situation *f* de conflit; conflit *m*
r столкновение *n*; коллизия *f*; конфликт *m*;
конфликтная ситуация *f*

1690 **collision-based model**
d Kollision-basiertes Modell *n*
f modèle *m* orienté aux collisions
r модель *f*, базированная на коллизии

1691 **collision detection system**
d Kollisionsdetektionssystem *n*

    f système *m* de détection de collisions
    r система *f* обнаруживания коллизий

1692 colon
    (:)
    d Doppelpunkt *m*
    f caractère *m* deux points
    r двоеточие *n*

1693 color
    d Farbe *f*
    f couleur *f*
    r цвет *m*

    * **4-color → 3957**

1694 color adjustment
    d Farbeinstellung *f*
    f ajustement *m* de couleur
    r наладка *f* цвета

1695 color approximation
    d Farbapproximation *f*
    f approximation *f* des couleurs
    r аппроксимация *f* цветов

1696 color area
    (on bitmap image)
    d Farbfläche *f*
    f zone *f* de couleur
    r цветовая зона *f*

1697 color artwork
    d Farbzeichnenvorlage *f*
    f schéma *m* topologique en couleurs
    r цветная топологическая схема *f*

    * **coloration → 1774**

1698 color attributes; color components
    d Farbattribute *npl*
    f attributs *mpl* de couleur
    r атрибуты *mpl* цвета

1699 color balance filter
    d Farbbalancefilter *m*
    f filtre *m* d'équilibre des couleurs
    r фильтр *m* калибровки цветов

1700 color bar
    d Farbstreifen *m*
    f barre *f* de couleurs; matrice *f* de couleurs
    r цветовая лента *f*

1701 color bar code
    d farbiger Balkencode *m*
    f code *m* à barre des couleurs
    r цветной штрих-код *m*

1702 color bitmap

    d Farbbitmap *n*
    f bitmap *m* couleur
    r цветное растровое отображение *n*

    * **color blend → 1703**

1703 color blend[ing]
    d Farbüberblendung *f*
    f dégradé *m* en couleurs
    r переливание *n* цветов

1704 color blending system
    d Farbüberblendungssystem *n*
    f système *m* de dégradé en couleurs
    r система *f* переливания цветов

1705 color body
    d Farbkörper *m*
    f corps *m* en couleurs
    r цветное тело *n*

1706 color box
    d Farbkasten *m*
    f boîte *f* en couleurs
    r цветовой ящик *m*

1707 color brightness; color lightness
    d Farbhelligkeit *f*
    f brillance *f* de couleur; luminosité *f* de couleur
    r яркость *f* цвета; цветовая яркость

    * **color build → 1726**

1708 color builder
    d Farbbilder *m*
    f bâtisseur *m* de couleurs
    r построитель *m* цветов

1709 color calibration
    d Farbkalibrierung *f*; Farbbalance *f*
    f calibrage *m* de couleurs; équilibre *m* des couleurs; réglage *m* du blanc
    r эталонирование *n* цветов; калибровка *f* цветов

1710 color calibration bar
    d Streifen *m* der Farbkalibrierung
    f barre *f* de calibrage en couleurs
    r лента *f* эталонирования цветов

    * **color cast → 9695**

1711 color center
    d Farbzentrum *n*
    f centre *m* coloré
    r центр *m* окраски

1712 color channel; color pathway
    d Farbkanal *m*

   f canal *m* couleur; voie *f* perceptive pour les
      couleurs
   r цветовой канал *m*

1713 color chart; chromaticity diagram
   d Farbtafel *f*; Farbdiagramm *n*
   f carte *f* de couleurs; diagramme *m* de
      chromaticité
   r шкала *f* цветового охвата; цветной тест *m*;
      диаграмма *f* цветности

   * **color choosing** → 1824

   * **color circle** → 1477

1714 color clipping
   d Farbschneiden *n*
   f écrêtage *m* de la couleur
   r цветовое отсекание *n*

   * **color coder** → 1748

1715 color coding
   d Farbcodierung *f*
   f codage *m* de couleurs
   r кодирование *n* цветов

1716 color communication system
   d Farbkommunikationssystem *n*
   f système *m* de communication couleur
   r система *f* цветовой коммуникации

1717 color comparator
   d Farbkomparator *m*
   f comparateur *m* de couleurs
   r компаратор *m* цветов

1718 color complement
   d Farbkomplement *n*
   f complément *m* de couleur
   r дополнение *n* цвета

   * **color components** → 1698

1719 color composite
   d Farbkomposit *n*
   f composante *f* de couleur
   r составляющая *f* цвета

1720 color contrast
   d Farbkontrast *m*
   f contraste *m* de couleurs
   r цветовой контраст *m*

1721 color conversion
   d Farbkonvertierung *f*; Farbkonversion *f*
   f conversion *f* de couleur
   r превращение *n* цвета

1722 color conversion filter

   d Farbkonvertierungsfilter *m*;
      Farbkonversionsfilter *m*
   f filtre *m* de conversion de la couleur
   r фильтр *m* превращения цвета

1723 color copier
   d Farbkopierer *m*
   f copieur *m* en couleurs; copieur couleur
   r цветное копирующее устройство *n*

1724 color copy
   d Farbkopie *f*
   f copie *f* en couleurs; copie couleur
   r цветная копия *f*

1725 color correction
   d Farbkorrektion *f*; Farbkorrektur *f*
   f correction *f* de couleur
   r коррекция *f* цвета

1726 color creation; color build
      (overlap two or more screen tints to create a
      new color)
   d Farbkreation *f*; Farbbildung *f*
   f création *f* d'une couleur
   r образование *n* цвета; создание *n* цвета

1727 color cube
   d Farbwürfel *m*
   f cube *m* couleur
   r цветной куб *m*

1728 color cycling
   d zyklischer Wechsel *m* der Farben;
      Farbzyklus *m*
   f bouclage *m* de couleurs
   r циклическая смена *f* цветов

1729 color data
   d Farbdaten *npl*
   f données *fpl* de couleur
   r цветовые данные *npl*

1730 color definition
   d Farbdefinition *f*
   f définition *f* de couleur
   r дефиниция *f* цвета

1731 color degree
   d Farbgrad *m*
   f degré *m* de couleur
   r градус *m* цвета

1732 color deleting
   d Farblöschen *n*
   f effaçage *m* de couleur
   r стирание *n* цвета

1733 color density
   d Farbdichte *f*

    f densité *f* de couleur
    r плотность *f* цвета

1734 color depth; pixel depth
    (number of bits of color information per pixel)
    d Farbtiefe *f*; Pixeltiefe *f*
    f profondeur *f* de couleur
    r глубина *f* цвета; разрядность *f* атрибутов пиксела

1735 color descriptor
    d Farbdeskriptor *m*
    f descripteur *m* de couleur
    r описатель *m* цвета

1736 color descriptor table
    d Farbdeskriptortabelle *f*
    f table *f* de descripteurs de couleurs
    r таблица *f* описателей цветов

1737 color dialog box
    d Farbdialogbox *f*
    f boîte *f* de dialogue de couleurs
    r диалоговый ящик *m* цветов

1738 color diffraction
    d Farbbeugung *f*; Farbdiffraktion *f*
    f diffraction *f* de couleur
    r дифракция *f* цвета

1739 color display; color monitor; color screen
    d Farbdisplay *n*; Farbbildschirm *m*; Farbmonitor *m*
    f écran *m* en couleurs; écran couleur; afficheur *m* en couleurs
    r цветной дисплей *m*; монитор *m* цветного изображения

1740 color dithering
    d Farb-Dithering *n*; Farbrastern *n*
    f juxtaposition *f* de couleurs
    r псевдосмешение *n* цветов; размывание *n* цветов

1741 color docking
    d Farbankern *n*
    f amarrage *m* de couleurs
    r стыковка *f* цветов

1742 colored
    d farbig
    f coloré
    r цветной; закрашенный

1743 color editing
    d Farbbearbeitung *f*
    f édition *f* de couleur
    r редактирование *n* цвета

1744 colored light
    d farbiges Licht *n*
    f lumière *f* colorée
    r цветной свет *m*

1745 colored rectangle
    d farbiges Rechteck *n*
    f rectangle *m* coloré
    r закрашенный прямоугольник *m*

1746 colored sphere
    d farbige Kugel *f*
    f sphère *f* colorée
    r закрашенная сфера *f*

1747 colored tile
    d farbige Musterkachel *f*
    f mosaïque *f* colorée
    r закрашенный мозаичный шаблон *m*

1748 color [en]coder
    d Farbcoder *m*
    f codeur *m* des couleurs
    r шифратор *m* цветов

1749 color expansion
    d Farbenerweiterung *f*
    f expansion *f* de couleurs
    r расширение *n* цветов

1750 color fidelity
    d Farbtreue *f*
    f fidélité *f* de couleur
    r цветовая точность *f*

1751 color film
    d Farbfilm *m*
    f film *m* en couleurs
    r цветная пленка *f*; цветной фильм *m*

1752 color filter
    d Farbfilter *m*; farbiger Filter *m*
    f filtre *m* de couleurs
    r цветной фильтр *m*

1753 color format
    d Farbformat *n*
    f format *m* de couleur
    r формат *m* цвета

    * **color gamma** → 7740

    * **color gamut** → 7740

1754 color gradation
    d Farbgradation *f*; Farbabstufung *f*; Farbabtönung *f*
    f gradation *f* de couleurs
    r цветовая градация *f*

1755 color gradient
  d Farbgradient *m*
  f gradient *m* de couleur
  r градиент *m* цвета

1756 color gradient bar
  d Farbgradientstreifen *m*
  f barre *f* de gradients de couleur
  r цветная градиентная лента *f*

1757 color graphics
  d Farbgrafik *f*
  f graphique *m* en couleurs
  r цветная графика *f*

1758 color halftone
  d Farbhalbton *m*
  f demi-teinte *f* en couleurs
  r цветной полутон *m*

1759 color harmony
  d Farbharmonie *f*
  f harmonie *f* de couleurs
  r цветовая гармония *f*

1760 color hiding; color masking
  d Farbversteckung *f*
  f masquage *m* de couleurs
  r скрытие *n* цвета; маскирование *n* цвета

1761 color hue; color tint; color tonality; color shade; color ton
  d Farbton *m*; Farbnuance *f*; Hue *n*
  f teinte *f* [couleur]; nuance *f* [couleur]; tonalité *f* chromatique; ton *m*
  r краска *f*; оттенок *m* цвета; цветовой оттенок; цветной тон *m*

1762 color hue filter
  d Farbtonfilter *m*
  f filtre *m* de teinte couleur
  r фильтр *m* цветового оттенка

1763 color image recorder
  d Farbbildrecorder *m*
  f enregistreur *m* d'images en couleurs
  r регистрирующее устройство *n* цветных изображений

1764 colorimeter
  d Kolorimeter *n*
  f colorimètre *m*
  r колориметр *m*

1765 colorimetric
  d kolorimetrisch
  f colorimétrique
  r колориметрический

1766 colorimetric balance

  d kolorimetrisches Gleichgewicht *n*
  f équilibrage *m* colorimétrique
  r колориметрический баланс *m*

1767 colorimetric model
  d kolorimetrisches Modell *n*
  f modèle *m* colorimétrique
  r колориметрическая модель *f*

1768 colorimetric system
  d kolorimetrisches System *n*
  f système *m* colorimétrique
  r колориметрическая система *f*

1769 colorimetry
  d Kolorimetrie *f*
  f colorimétrie *f*
  r колориметрия *f*

1770 color index
  d Farbindex *m*
  f indice *m* couleur
  r цветной индекс *m*

  * coloring → 1774

1771 coloring problem; problem of coloration
  d Färbungsproblem *n*
  f problème *m* de coloriage
  r задача *f* раскраски; задача о раскрашивании

1772 color intensity
  d Farbintensität *f*
  f intensité *f* de couleur; intensité chromatique
  r интенсивность *f* цвета

  * color invert → 1773

1773 color invert[ing]
  d Farbinvertierung *f*
  f inversion *f* de couleur
  r инвертирование *n* цвета

1774 color[iz]ation; coloring
  d Färbung *f*; Kolorierung *f*
  f coloriage *m*; coloration *f*
  r раскраска *f*; раскрашивание *n*

1775 color killer
  d Colorkiller *m*; Farbsperre *f*
  f extincteur *m* de couleur
  r подавитель *m* цвета; выключатель *m* цвета

1776 color laser printer
  d Farblaserdrucker *m*
  f imprimante *f* laser couleur
  r цветной лазерный принтер *m*

  * color lightness → 1707

* **color lookup table** → 1780

1777 color management; color processing
d Farbverwaltung *f*
f traitement *m* de couleur
r обработка *f* цвета

1778 color management software
d Farbverwaltungssoftware *f*
f logiciel *m* de traitement de couleurs
r программное обеспечение *n* для управления цветов

1779 color manager
d Farben-Manager *m*
f gestionnaire *m* de couleurs
r менажер *m* цветов

1780 color map; color [lookup] table; CLUT
d Farbkarte *f*
f table *f* de couleurs; table des fausses couleurs
r [справочная] таблица *f* цветов; таблица цветности

1781 color mapping
d Farbabbildung *f*
f mappage *m* couleur
r отображение *n* цвета; наложение *n* цвета

1782 color mask
d Farbmaske *f*
f masque *f* en couleurs
r цветная маска *f*

* **color masking** → 1760

* **color match** → 1783

1783 color match[ing]
d Farbanpassung *f*; Farbabstimmung *f*
f correspondance *f* de couleurs
r соответствие *n* цветов; сочетание *n* цветов

1784 color matching method; CMM
d Farbanpassungsmethode *f*
f méthode *f* de correspondance de couleurs
r алгоритм *m* цветовых сочетаний

1785 color matching system
d Farbanpassungssystem *n*; Farbabstimmungssystem *n*
f système *m* de correspondance de couleurs
r система *f* соответствия цветов; система цветовых преобразований

1786 color mixer
d Farbmischer *m*
f mélangeur *m* de couleurs
r цветовой смеситель *m*

1787 color mixing
d Farbmischung *f*
f mixage *m* de couleurs; mélange *m* de couleurs
r смешивание *n* цветов

1788 color mixing system
d Farbmischsystem *n*
f système *m* de mélange de couleurs
r система *f* смешивания цветов

1789 color mode
d Farbmodus *m*
f mode *m* en couleurs
r цветной режим *m*

1790 color model
d Farbmodell *n*
f modèle *m* en couleurs
r цветовая модель *f*

* **color monitor** → 1739

1791 color moving
d Farbverlauf *m*
f déplacement *m* de couleur
r смещение *n* цвета

1792 color name
d Farbname *m*
f nom *m* de couleur
r имя *n* цвета

1793 color negative
d Farbnegativ *n*
f négatif *m* couleur
r цветной негатив *m*

1794 color number
d Farbnummer *f*
f numéro *m* de couleur
r номер *m* цвета

1795 color palette
d Farbpalette *f*
f palette *f* des couleurs
r цветовая палитра *f*

1796 color palette adapting
d Farbpalettenanpassung *f*
f adaptation *f* de palette de couleurs
r адаптирование *n* цветовой палитры

* **color pathway** → 1712

1797 color pattern
d Farbmuster *n*
f motif *m* en couleurs
r цветной узор *m*

1798 color pen
d Farbstift *m*
f plume *m* couleur
r цветное перо *n*

* **color photo** → 1799

1799 color photo[graph]
d Farbfoto *n*
f photo *f* en couleurs; photo couleur
r цветная фотография *f*; цветной снимок *m*

1800 color picker
d Farbenauswahl-Schaltfläche *f*
f bouton *m* de sélection de couleur
r бутон *m* выбора цвета; цветоподборщик *m*

* **color plane** → 975

* **color plotter** → 6086

1801 color preview
d Farbvorschau *f*
f aperçu *m* d'avance des couleurs
r предварительный просмотр *m* цветов

1802 color primitive
d Farbprimitiv *n*
f primitive *f* couleur
r цветной примитив *m*

1803 color printer
d Farbdrucker *m*
f imprimante *f* en couleurs; imprimante couleur
r цветной принтер *m*

* **color print** → 1803

1804 color print[ing]
d Farbendruck *m*
f impression *f* en couleurs; impression couleur;
impression polychrome
r цветная печать *f*; многокрасочная печать

* **4-color printing process** → 3958

* **color processing** → 1777

1805 color profile
d Farbprofil *n*
f profil *m* couleur
r цветовой профиль *m*

1806 color profile tuning
d Farbprofil-Einstellung *f*
f ajustage *m* de profil couleur
r настраивание *n* цветового профиля

1807 color profile wizard
d Farbprofil-Assistent *m*

f assistant *m* de profil couleur
r советчик *m* о цветовом профиле

1808 color proof; color sample
d Farbprobe *f*
f preuve *f* couleur
r цветовая проба *f*

1809 color purity
d Farbreinheit *f*
f pureté *f* des couleurs
r цветовая чистота *f*

* **color range** → 7740

1810 color reference frame
d Farbbezugssystem *n*
f repère *m* de couleurs
r система *f* отсчета цветов

1811 color refinements
d Verfeinerungen *fpl* der Farben
f raffinages *mpl* de couleurs
r улучшения *npl* цветов

1812 color renaming
d Farbumbenennung *f*
f changement *m* de nom de couleur
r переименование *n* цвета

1813 color rendering
d Farbrendering *n*; Farbwiedergabe *f*
f rendu *m* en couleurs; rendu couleur
r цветное тонирование *n*; цветный
рендеринг *m*

1814 color replacer
d Farb-Austauscher *m*
f substitueur *m* de couleur
r заменитель *m* цвета

1815 color replacer tool
d Farbersetzungshilfsmittel *n*
f outil *m* de substitution de couleurs
r инструмент *m* замещения цветов

1816 color replacing
d Farbersetzung *f*
f substitution *f* de couleur
r замещение *n* цвета

1817 color reproduction method
d Farbenreproduktionsmethode *f*
f méthode *f* de reproduction de couleurs
r метод *m* воспроизведения цветов

1818 color resizing
d Farb-Größenänderung *f*
f redimensionnement *m* de couleurs
r переоразмерение *n* цветов

    *   **color sample** → 1808

1819 color saturation
    d Farbsättigung *f*; Farbenintensität *f*
    f saturation *f* de couleur
    r насыщение *n* цвета; насыщенность *f* цвета

    *   **colors boundary** → 1838

1820 color scale
    d Farbskala *f*
    f échelle *f* de couleurs
    r шкала *f* цветов

1821 color scanner
    d Farbscanner *m*
    f scanner *m* en couleurs; scanner couleur
    r цветной сканер *m*

1822 color scheme
    d Farbschema *f*
    f schéma *m* de couleurs
    r комбинация *f* взаимодополняющихся цветов [для элементов экрана]

    *   **color screen** → 1739

1823 color scrolling
    d Farbbildlauf *m*
    f défilement *m* de couleurs
    r прокручивание *n* цветов

1824 color selection; color choosing
    d Farbselektion *f*; Farbauswahl *f*
    f sélection *f* de couleur
    r выбор *m* цвета

1825 color selection area
    d Farbauswahlbereich *m*
    f zone *f* de sélection de couleur
    r область *f* выбора цвета

1826 color selector
    d Farbselektor *m*; Farbwähler *m*
    f sélecteur *m* de couleurs
    r селектор *m* цветов; отборщик *m* цветов

1827 color-sensitive
    d farbempfindlich
    f sensible aux couleurs
    r цветочувствительный

1828 color-sensitive mask
    d farbempfindliche Maske *f*
    f masque *f* sensible aux couleurs
    r цветочувствительная маска *f*

1829 color sensitivity
    d Farbempfindlichkeit *f*
    f sensibilité *f* chromatique
    r цветовая чувствительность *f*; цветочувствительность *f*

1830 color-separated image
    d Farbanteilbild *n*
    f image *f* à couleurs séparées
    r цветоотдельное изображение *n*

1831 color separation
    d Farbteilung *f*; Farbauszug *m*; Farbentrennung *f*
    f séparation *f* des couleurs; sélection *f* des couleurs
    r разделение *n* цветов; цветоотделение *n*; цветоделение *n*

1832 color separation equipment
    d Farbauszug-Ausrüstung *f*
    f équipement *m* de séparation en couleurs
    r цветоотделительное оборудование *n*

    *   **color shade** → 1761

1833 color shading
    d Farbschattierung *f*
    f ombrage *m* couleur
    r цветовое оттенение *n*

1834 color simulation
    d Farbensimulierung *f*
    f simulation *f* de couleurs
    r симуляция *f* цветов

1835 color slide
    d Farbdiapositiv *n*
    f diapositive *f* en couleurs
    r цветной диапозитив *m*; цветной слайд *m*

1836 color slider
    d Farbschieber *m*
    f glisseur *m* de couleurs
    r ползунок *m* цветов

1837 color slider bar
    d Streifen *m* des Farbschiebers
    f barre *f* de glisseur de couleurs
    r лента *f* ползунка цветов

1838 colors limit; colors boundary
    d Grenze *f* der Farbe; Farbengrenze *f*
    f limite *f* des couleurs
    r граница *f* цветов

1839 color sorting
    d Farbsortierung *f*
    f triage *m* des couleurs
    r сортирование *n* цветов

1840 color space; chromatic space
    d Farbraum *m*

f espace *m* de couleurs; espace chromatique
r пространство *n* цветов; цветовое пространство; хроматическое пространство

1841 color space boundaries
d Begrenzungen *fpl* des Farbraums
f limites *fpl* de l'espace chromatique
r границы *fpl* хроматического пространства

1842 color space model
d Farbraummodell *n*
f modèle *m* d'espace chromatique
r модель *f* цветового пространства

1843 color spectrum
d Farbenspektrum *n*
f spectre *m* de couleurs
r спектр *m* цветов; хроматический спектр

1844 color spot
d Farbfleck *m*
f tache *f* couleur
r цветное пятно *n*

1845 color statistics
d Farbenstatistik *f*
f statistique *f* de couleurs
r статистика *f* цветов

1846 color style
d Farbstil *m*
f style *m* de couleur
r цветной стиль *m*

1847 color system; chromatic system
d Farbsystem *n*
f système *m* de couleurs
r цветовая система *f*

* **color table → 1780**

1848 color target
d Farbziel *n*
f cible *f* en couleurs
r цветная цель *f*

1849 color temperature
d Farbtemperatur *f*
f température *f* de couleur
r температура *f* цвета

1850 color texture
d Farbtextur *f*
f texture *f* colorée
r цветная текстура *f*

1851 color-texture camera
d Farbtextur-Kamera *f*
f caméra *f* de texture colorée

r камера *f* цветной текстуры

* **color tint → 1761**

1852 color tolerance
d Farbtoleranz *f*
f tolérance *f* de couleur
r допуск *m* цвета

* **color ton → 1761**

* **color tonality → 1761**

1853 color transform effect
d Farbänderungseffekt *m*
f effet *m* de transformation de couleurs
r эффект *m* преобразования цветов

1854 color transform filter
d Farbänderungsfilter *m*
f filtre *m* de transformation de couleurs
r фильтр *m* преобразования цветов

1855 color transparency
d Farbtransparenz *f*
f transparence *f* de couleur
r прозрачность *f* цвета

1856 color trapping
d Farbtrap *m*
f captage *m* de couleur
r улавливание *n* цвета

1857 color triangle; chromaticity triangle
d Farbdreieck *n*
f triangle *m* de chromaticité
r треугольник *m* цветности

1858 color triplet
d Farbtripel *n*
f triplet *m* couleur
r цветовая тройка *f*; цветовой триплет *m*

1859 color utility
d Farb-Dienstprogramm *n*
f utilité *f* de couleur
r утилит *m* обработки цветов

1860 color value; chromaticity value
d Farbwert *m*
f valeur *f* de couleur; valeur de chromaticité
r значение *n* цветности; код *m* цвета

1861 color variation
d Farbvariation *f*
f variation *f* de couleur
r вариация *f* цвета

1862 color vision
d Farbenwahrnehmung *f*

f vision *f* en couleurs
r цветное зрение *n*

* **color wheel** → 1477

1863 column
d Spalte *f*
f colonne *f*
r колонка *f*; столбец *m*; графа *f*

* **column diagram** → 827

* **column graph** → 827

1864 column heading; column title
d Spaltentitel *m*
f en-tête *f* de colonne; titre *m* de colonne
r колонтитул *m*; заголовок *m* колонки

1865 column image
d Spaltenbild *n*
f image *f* de colonne
r изображение *n* колонки

1866 column number
(of a rectangular array of geometrical objects)
d Spaltenzahl *f*
f nombre *m* de colonnes
r число *n* колонок

1867 column offset
d Spaltenabstand *m*
f décalage *m* de colonne
r смещение *n* колонки

1868 column pattern
d Spaltenmuster *n*
f motif *m* de colonne
r рисунок *m* колонки

* **column title** → 1864

1869 column width
d Spaltenbreite *f*
f largeur *f* de colonne
r ширина *f* колонки

1870 combination
d Kombination *f*
f combinaison *f*
r комбинация *f*; сочетание *n*

1871 combination charts; combined charts
d kombinierte Diagramme *npl*
f diagrammes *mpl* combinés
r комбинированные диаграммы *fpl*

1872 combine *v*
d kombinieren
f combiner

r комбинировать

* **combined charts** → 1871

1873 combined form
d kombinierte Form *f*
f forme *f* combinée
r комбинированная форма *f*

1874 combined objects; grouped objects
d kombinierte Objekte *npl*
f objets *mpl* combinés
r комбинированные объекты *mpl*

1875 combined path; grouped path
d kombinierte Strecke *f*
f tracé *m* combiné
r комбинированная дорожка *f*

1876 combo box
d Kombinationsfeld *n*
f zone *f* de liste déroulante
r комбинированное окно *n*

1877 command; instruction
d Befehl *m*; Instruktion *f*; Kommando *n*
f commande *f*; instruction *f*
r команда *f*; инструкция *f*

1878 command alias
d Aliasname *m* des Befehls
f pseudonyme *m* de commande
r псевдоимя *n* команды

1879 command button
d Befehlsschaltfläche *f*
f bouton *m* de commande
r кнопка *f* команды

1880 command key
d Befehlstaste *f*
f clé *f* de commande
r клавиша *f* команды

1881 command line
d Befehlszeile *f*
f ligne *f* de commande
r командная строка *f*

1882 command line history
d Befehlszeilenchronologie *f*
f historique *m* de la ligne de commande
r хронология *f* командной строки

1883 command line history window
d Fenster *n* der Befehlszeilenchronologie
f fenêtre *f* d'historique de la ligne de commande
r окно *n* хронологии командной строки

* **command line switch** → 1884

1884 command line switch[ing]
d Durchschaltung *f* der Befehlszeile
f commutation *f* de la ligne de commande
r переключение *n* командной строки

1885 command mode
d Befehlsmodus *m*
f mode *m* de commande
r командный режим *m*

1886 command prefix
d Befehlspräfix *n*
f préfixe *m* de commande
r префикс *m* команды

1887 command prompt
d Befehlsanzeige *f*
f invite *f* de commande
r подсказка *f* команды

1888 command script; script
d Skript *n*
f script *m*
r скрипт *m*

1889 command window
d Befehlsfenster *n*
f fenêtre *f* de commande
r окно *n* команды

1890 command word; verb
d Befehlswort *m*
f mot *m* de commande
r слово *n* команды

1891 common
d gemeinsam
f commun
r общий

1892 common impression
d Gesamteindruck *m*
f impression *f* générale
r общее впечатление *n*

1893 common object
d Gemeinsamobjekt *n*
f objet *m* commun
r общий объект *m*

1894 common perpendicular
d gemeinsames Lot *n*
f perpendiculaire *f* commune
r общий перпендикуляр *m*

1895 common perpendicular of two skew lines
d gemeinsames Lot *n* zweier windschiefer
Geraden

f perpendiculaire *f* commune à deux droites
gauches
r общий перпендикуляр *m* между двумя
скрещивающимися прямыми; общий
перпендикуляр двух скрещивающихся
прямых

1896 commutative
d kommutativ
f commutatif
r коммутативный

1897 commutative diagram
d kommutatives Diagramm *n*
f diagramme *m* commutatif
r коммутативная диаграмма *f*

1898 compact
d kompakt
f compact
r компактный

* **compact disk** → 6545

* **compaction** → 1959

1899 compactness
d Kompaktheit *f*
f compacité *f*
r компактность *f*

1900 compact presentation
d kompakte Darstellung *f*
f présentation *f* compacte
r компактное представление *n*; сжатое
представление

1901 compare *v*
d vergleichen
f comparer
r сравнивать

1902 comparison
d Vergleich *m*
f comparaison *f*
r сравнение *n*

* **comparison base** → 837

1903 compass
d Bussole *f*; Kompaß *m*
f boussole *f*
r буссоль *f*; компас *m*

1904 compass circle
d Bussolenkreis *m*
f cercle-boussole *m*
r круг *m* буссоли

1905 compass needle
d Bussolennadel *f*; Kompaßnadel *f*

f aiguille f de boussole
r буссольная стрелка f; игла f компаса

1906 compatibility
d Verträglichkeit f; Kompatibilität f
f compatibilité f
r совместимость f; совместность f

1907 compensating computation
d Ausgleichrechnung f
f calcul m de compensation
r уравнительное вычисление n; вычисление при уравнивании

1908 compensating eyepiece
d Ausgleichokular n
f oculaire m de compensation
r компенсирующий окуляр m

1909 compensating filter; equalize filter
d Ausgleichsfilter m
f filtre m de compensation; filtre compensateur
r компенсирующий фильтр m; компенсационный фильтр; выравнивающий фильтр

1910 compensation
d Kompensation f; Ausgleich m
f compensation f
r уравнивание n; компенсация f

1911 compile v
d kompilieren
f compiler
r компилировать

1912 complement
d Komplement n; Ergänzung f
f complément m
r дополнение n

1913 complementary
d komplementär; Komplement[är]-; ergänzend; Ergänzungs-
f complémentaire
r дополнительный

1914 complementary angle
d Komplementwinkel m
f angle m complémentaire
r дополнительный угол m

1915 complementary arc
d Komplementärbogen m
f arc m complémentaire
r дополнительная дуга f

1916 complementary color; secondary color
d Komplementärfarbe f
f couleur f complémentaire

r дополнительный цвет m

* complementary triangle → 5883

1917 complete
d vollständig
f complet
r полный; завершенный

1918 complete v
d fertigstellen
f achever
r дополнять

1919 completeness
d Vollständigkeit f
f complétude f
r полнота f

1920 completeness condition
d Vollständigkeitsbedingung f
f condition f de complétude
r условие n полноты

1921 complete quadrangle
d vollständiges Viereck n
f quadrangle m complet
r полный четырехвершинник m

1922 complete quadrilateral
d vollständiges Vierseit n
f quadrilatère m complet
r полный четырехсторонник m

1923 complete surface; total surface area
d vollständige Oberfläche f; Flächeninhalt m der vollständigen Oberfläche
f aire f totale
r полная поверхность f; площадь f полной поверхности

1924 complete survey
d Gesamtaufnahme f
f levé m d'ensemble
r суммарная съемка f; обзорная съемка

1925 completing the square
d Ergänzung f zum vollständigen Quadrat
f complément m au carré total
r дополнение n до полного квадрата

1926 complex adj
d komplex
f complexe
r комплексный; сложный; составной

1927 complex boundaries
d Komplexgrenzen fpl
f limites fpl complexes
r сложные границы fpl

1928 complex clipping
  d Komplexschneiden *n*
  f écrêtage *m* complexe
  r комплексное отсекание *n*

1929 complexity
  d Komplexität *f*
  f complexité *f*
  r сложность *f*

1930 complexity of an object
  d Komplexität *f* eines Objektes
  f complexité *f* d'un objet
  r сложность *f* объекта

1931 complex lens
  d komplexe Linse *f*
  f lentille *f* complexe
  r составная линза *f*

1932 complex linetype
  d komplexer Linientyp *m*
  f type *m* de ligne complexe
  r составной тип *m* линии; комплексный тип линии

1933 complex mask
  d komplexe Maske *f*
  f masque *f* complexe
  r составная маска *f*

1934 complex object; composite object; compound object
  d Komplexobjekt *n*
  f objet *m* complexe; objet composé
  r составной объект *m*; комплексный объект

1935 complex polygon
  d Komplexpolygon *n*
  f polygone *m* complexe
  r составной полигон *m*

1936 complex solid; composite solid
  d Komplexkörper *m*; zusammengesetzter Körper *m*
  f solide *m* complexe; solide composé
  r составное тело *n*; комплексное тело

1937 complex surface
  d Komplexfläche *f*
  f surface *f* complexe
  r сложная поверхность *f*; комплексная поверхность

1938 component
  d Komponente *f*; Bauelement *n*; Baustein *m*
  f composant *m*; composante *f*
  r компонент *m*; компонента *f*; [схемный] элемент *m*; составляющая *f*

1939 component of a vector
  d Vektorkomponente *f*
  f composante *f* d'un vecteur
  r компонента *f* вектора

1940 compose *v*; set *v*
  d zusammenstellen; anfertigen
  f composer; instaurer
  r составлять; формировать

1941 composed image; composite image
  d zusammengesetztes Bild *n*
  f image *f* composée
  r составное изображение *n*

1942 composite; compound
  d zusammengesetzt; Komposit-
  f composé; composite
  r составной; сложный

1943 composite channel
  d kombinierter Kanal *m*
  f canal *m* composite
  r составной канал *m*

1944 composite color image
  d zusammengesetztes Farbbild *n*
  f image *f* couleur composite
  r составное цветное изображение *n*; сложное цветное изображение

  * composite image → 1941

1945 composite lighting simulation
  d Simulation *f* der kombinierten Beleuchtung
  f simulation *f* d'éclairage composite
  r симуляция *f* комбинированного освещения

  * composite object → 1934

1946 composite printer
  d Komposit-Drucker *m*
  f imprimante *f* composite
  r комбинированный принтер *m*

1947 composite regions
  d zusammengesetzte Regionen *fpl*
  f régions *fpl* composées
  r составные регионы *mpl*

  * composite solid → 1936

1948 composite texture
  d zusammengesetzte Textur *f*
  f texture *f* composite
  r составная текстура *f*; комбинированная текстура

1949 composite tolerances
  d zusammengesetzte Toleranzen *fpl*

f tolérances *fpl* composites
r комбинированные допуски *mpl*

1950 composite topology
d zusammengesetzte Topologie *f*
f topologie *f* composite
r составная топология *f*

1951 composite video signal
d zusammengesetztes Videosignal *n*;
Komposit-Videosignal *n*
f signal *m* vidéo composite
r составной видеосигнал *m*

1952 composition
d Komposition *f*
f composition *f*
r состав *m*; композиция *f*

* **compound** → **1942**

1953 compound bar chart
d zusammengesetztes Streifendiagramm *n*
f diagramme *m* à barres composé
r составная столбиковая диаграмма *f*

1954 compound blend
d zusammengesetzte Überblendung *f*
f dégradé *m* composé
r составное переливание *n*

1955 compound document
d zusammengesetztes Dokument *n*
f document *m* composé
r составной документ *m*

* **compound object** → **1934**

1956 compress *v*
d komprimieren; verdichten
f comprimer
r сжать; уплотнять; компрессировать

1957 compressed digital video
d komprimiertes Digitalvideo *n*
f vidéo *m* numérique compressé
r уплотненное цифровое видео *n*

1958 compressibility
d Kompressibilität *f*; Zusammendrückbarkeit *f*
f compressibilité *f*
r сжимаемость *f*

1959 compression; compaction; condensation
d Kompression *f*; Komprimierung *f*
f compression *f*; compaction *f*
r сжатие *n*; уплотнение *n*; компрессия *f*

1960 compression algorithm
d Kompressionsalgorithmus *m*

f algorithme *m* de compression
r алгоритм *m* сжатия; алгоритм компрессирования

1961 compression coefficient; compression ratio
(of image coding)
d Kompressionsverhältnis *n*;
Kompressionsfaktor *m*
f coefficient *m* de compression; taux *m* de compression
r коэффициент *m* компрессии; коэффициент сжатия

1962 compression option
d Kompressionsoption *f*
f option *f* de compression
r опция *f* уплотнения

* **compression ratio** → **1961**

* **computation** → **1216**

1963 computational
d Rechen-
f computationnel
r вычислительный

1964 computational geometry
d Rechengeometrie *f*
f géométrie *f* computationnelle
r вычислительная геометрия *f*

1965 computation of areas
d Flächenberechnung *f*
f calcul *m* des aires
r вычисление *n* площадей

1966 computation of coordinates; coordinate calculation
d Koordinatenberechnung *f*
f calcul *m* des coordonnées
r вычисление *n* координат

1967 computation of heights
d Höhenberechnung *f*
f calcul *m* des altitudes
r вычисление *n* высот

* **compute** *v* → **1214**

1968 computed image
d errechnetes Bild *n*
f image *f* calculée
r вычисленное изображение *n*

1969 computer
d Computer *m*; Rechner *m*
f ordinateur *m*
r компьютер *m*

1970 computer[-aided] animation
  d computerunterstützte Animation *f*
  f animatique *f*; dessin *m* animé par ordinateur
  r анимация *f* с помощью компьютера;
       компьютерная анимация

1971 computer-aided design; CAD
  d computerunterstütztes Design *n*; CAD
  f conception *f* assistée par ordinateur; CAO
  r проектирование *n* с помощью компьютера;
       система автоматизации проектирования;
       САПР

  * **computer-aided drafting** → 1972

**1972 computer-aided drawing; computer-aided
       drafting**
  d computerunterstütztes Zeichnen *n*
  f dessin *m* assisté par ordinateur; DAO
  r черчение *n* с помощью компьютера

1973 computer-aided geometric design
  d computerunterstütztes Geometriedesign *n*
  f conception *f* géométrique assistée par
       ordinateur
  r геометрическое проектирование *n* с
       помощью компьютера

1974 computer-aided graphic arts
  d computerunterstützte Grafikkunst *f*
  f arts *mpl* graphiques assistés par ordinateur
  r рисование *n* с помощью компьютера

  * **computer animation** → 1970

1975 computer-generated characters
  d durch Computer generierte Zeichen *npl*
  f caractères *mpl* générés par ordinateur
  r символы *mpl*, генерированные
       компьютером

1976 computer-generated color
  d durch Computer generierte Farbe *f*
  f couleur *f* générée par ordinateur
  r цвет *m*, генерированный компьютером

1977 computer-generated diffraction pattern
  d durch Computer generiertes
       Diffraktionsbild *n*
  f image *f* de diffraction générée par ordinateur
  r дифракционная картина *f*,
       генерированная компьютером

1978 computer-generated hologram
  d durch Computer generiertes Hologramm *n*
  f hologramme *m* généré par ordinateur
  r голограмма *f*, генерированная
       компьютером

1979 computer-generated image; synthetic

image
  d durch Computer generiertes Bild *n*
  f image *f* générée par ordinateur; image
       synthétique; image de synthèse
  r изображение *n*, генерированное
       компьютером

1980 computer-generated imagery
  d durch Computer generierte Abbildung *f*
  f imagerie *f* générée par ordinateur
  r изображения *npl*, генерированные
       компьютером

1981 computer graphics; infography
  d Computergrafik *f*; Rechnergrafik *f*
  f infographie *f*; graphique *m* d'ordinateur
  r компьютерная графика *f*; машинная
       графика

1982 computer graphics metafile
  d Computergrafik-Metadatei *f*
  f métafichier *m* d'infographie
  r графический метафайл *m*

**1983 computer graphics workstation; graphics
       workstation**
  d grafische Arbeitsstation *f*
  f station *f* de travail graphique
  r графическая рабочая станция *f*

**1984 computer illustration program; illustration
       program; paint program**
  d Malprogramm *n*
  f programme *m* d'illustrations
  r программа *f* для иллюстраций

1985 computer simulation
  d Computersimulation *f*
  f simulation *f* [assistée] par ordinateur
  r компьютерное моделирование *n*

1986 computer tomography; CT
  d Computertomografie *f*
  f tomographie *f* par ordinateur
  r компьютерная томография *f*

1987 computer vision
  d Computersehen *n*
  f vision *f* d'ordinateur
  r компьютерное зрение *n*

  * **computing** → 1216

  * **computing rule** → 1215

1988 concatenate *v*
  d verketten; ketten
  f concaténer
  r конкатенировать

1989 concatenation
  d Konkatenation *f*
  f concaténation *f*
  r конкатенация *f*

1990 concave
  d konkav
  f concave
  r вогнутый

1991 concave angle
  d konkaver Winkel *m*; hohler Winkel
  f angle *m* concave
  r вогнутый угол *m*

1992 concave-convex
  d konkav-konvex
  f concave-convexe
  r вогнуто-выпуклый

* **concave curve** → 1994

1993 concave domain
  d konkaver Bereich *m*; konkaves Gebiet *n*
  f domaine *m* concave
  r вогнутая область *f*

1994 concave [down] curve
  d konkave Kurve *f*
  f courbe *f* concave
  r вогнутая [книзу] кривая *f*; выпуклая [кверху] кривая

* **concave down** → 1995

1995 concave down[ward]; convex up[ward]
  d nach unten konkav; nach oben konvex
  f concave vers le bas; convexe vers le haut
  r вогнутый вниз; выпуклый вверх

1996 concave grating
  d konkaves Gitter *n*
  f réseau *m* concave
  r вогнутая решетка *f*

1997 concave lens
  d konkave Linse *f*
  f lentille *f* concave
  r вогнутая линза *f*

1998 concave normal
  d konkave Normale *f*
  f normale *f* concave
  r вогнутая нормаль *f*

1999 concave objects
  (by collision simulation)
  d konkave Objekte *npl*
  f objets *mpl* concaves
  r вогнутые объекты *mpl*

2000 concave polygon
  d konkaves Vieleck *n*; konkaves Polygon *n*
  f polygone *m* concave
  r вогнутый многоугольник *m*

2001 concave polyhedron
  d konkaves Polyeder *n*
  f polyèdre *m* concave
  r вогнутый многогранник *m*

2002 concave surface
  d konkave Fläche *f*
  f surface *f* concave
  r вогнутая поверхность *f*

* **concave up** → 2003

2003 concave up[ward]; convex down[ward]
  d nach oben konkav; nach unten konvex
  f concave vers le haut; convexe vers le bas
  r вогнутый вверх; выпуклый вниз

2004 concave vertex
  d konkaver Knoten *m*
  f sommet *m* concave
  r вогнутая вершина *f*

2005 concavity
  d Konkavität *f*
  f concavité *f*
  r вогнутость *f*

2006 concavity downward; convexity upward
  d Konkavität *f* nach unten; Konvexität *f* nach oben
  f concavité *f* dirigée vers le bas; convexité *f* dirigée vers le haut
  r вогнутость *f* вниз; выпуклость *f* вверх

2007 concavity upward; convexity downward
  d Konkavität *f* nach oben; Konvexität *f* nach unten
  f concavité *f* dirigée vers le haut; convexité *f* dirigée vers le bas
  r вогнутость *f* вверх; выпуклость *f* вниз

* **concavo-concave** → 905

2008 concentration
  d Konzentration *f*
  f concentration *f*
  r концентрация *f*; сосредоточение *n*

2009 concentric
  d konzentrisch
  f concentrique
  r концентрический

2010 concentric blend
  d konzentrische Überblendung *f*

f dégradé *m* concentrique
r концентрическое переливание *n*

2011 concentric circles
d konzentrische Kreise *mpl*
f cercles *mpl* concentriques
r концентрические окружности *fpl*

2012 concentric conics
d konzentrische Kegelschnitte *mpl*
f coniques *fpl* concentriques
r концентрические конические сечения *npl*

2013 concentric isometric circles
d konzentrische isometrische Kreise *mpl*
f cercles *mpl* isométriques concentriques
r концентрические изометрические окружности *fpl*

2014 concentricity
d Konzentrizität *f*
f concentricité *f*
r концентричность *f*

2015 concentric spheres
d konzentrische Kugeln *fpl*
f sphères *fpl* concentriques
r концентрические сферы *fpl*

2016 conceptual model
d Konzeptualmodell *n*
f modèle *m* conceptuel
r концептуальная модель *f*

2017 conchoid
d Konchoide *f*; Muschelkurve *f*; Muschellinie *f*
f conchoïde *f*
r конхоида *f*

2018 concordance; accordance
d Übereinstimmung *f*
f concordance *f*
r согласованность *f*; согласование *n*

2019 concurrency
d Konkurrenz *f*
f concurrence *f*
r совпадение *n*

2020 concurrent; copunctual
d durch einen gemeinsamen Punkt; mit einem gemeinsamen Punkt
f concourant; de concours
r имеющий общую точку; проходящий через ту же точку

2021 concurrent; simultaneous
d gleichzeitig; simultan
f concurrent; simultané
r одновременный; совместный

2022 concurrent lines; intersecting lines
d sich schneidende Geraden *fpl*
f droites *fpl* concourantes; droites sécantes
r прямые *fpl*, пересекающиеся в общей точке; прямые, проходящие через одну точку; пересекающиеся прямые

2023 concurrent planes; copunctual planes
d Ebenen *fpl* durch einen gemeinsamen Punkt
f plans *mpl* concourants
r плоскости *fpl*, имеющие только одну общую точку; плоскости, принадлежащие на одной связке

* **condensation → 1959**

2024 condition
d Kondition *f*; Bedingung *f*
f condition *f*
r условие *n*

2025 conditional format
d konditionales Format *n*
f format *m* conditionnel
r условный формат *m*

2026 condition for parallelism
d Parallelitätsbedingung *f*
f condition *f* de parallélisme
r условие *n* параллельности

2027 cone
d Kegel *m*; Konus *m*
f cône *m*
r конус *m*

2028 cone angle
d Konuswinkel *m*; Kegelwinkel *m*
f angle *m* de cône
r угол *m* конуса

* **cone of light → 6930**

2029 cone of revolution
d Rotationskegel *m*
f cône *m* de révolution
r конус *m* вращения

* **cone of slope → 724**

2030 cone-sphere intersection
d Kegel-Kugel-Durchschnitt *m*
f intersection *f* entre cône et sphère
r взаимное пресечение *n* конуса и сферы

2031 cone tracing
d Kegel-Trassieren *n*
f traçage *m* conique
r трассировка *f* конусом; коническая трассировка

2032 configuration
  d Konfiguration *f*
  f configuration *f*
  r конфигурация *f*

2033 configuration file
  d Konfigurationsdatei *f*
  f fichier *m* de configuration
  r конфигурационный файл *m*

2034 configuration variable
  d Konfigurationsvariable *f*
  f variable *f* de configuration
  r переменная *f* конфигурации

2035 configure *v*
  d konfigurieren; ausformen
  f configurer
  r конфигурировать; образовывать

2036 confirm *v*; **validate** *v*
  d bestätigen
  f confirmer; valider
  r подтверждать

2037 confocal
  d konfokal
  f homofocal
  r софокусный; конфокальный

2038 confocal conics
  d konfokale Kegelschnitte *mpl*
  f coniques *fpl* homofocales
  r конфокальные конические сечения *npl*

**2039 conformal projection; equal-angle
  projection; anglepreserving projection;
  orthomorphic projection**
  d konforme Projektion *f*; winkeltreue
    Abbildung *f*; orthomorphe Projektion
  f projection *f* conforme; projection équiangle;
    projection orthomorphique
  r конформная проекция *f*; равноугольная
    проекция; ортоморфная проекция

2040 congruence
  d Kongruenz *f*
  f congruence *f*
  r сходство *n*; соответствие *n*;
    конгруэнтность *f*

2041 congruence of lines
  d Kongruenz *f* der Linien
  f congruence *f* de lignes
  r конгруэнтность *f* линий

2042 congruent
  d kongruent
  f congruent; congru
  r конгруэнтный; сравнимый

2043 congruent angles
  d kongruente Winkel *mpl*
  f angles *mpl* congru[ent]s
  r конгруэнтные углы *mpl*; равные углы;
    равновеликие углы

2044 congruent figures; equivalent figures
  d kongruente Figuren *fpl*
  f figures *fpl* congruentes; figures équivalentes;
    figures égaux
  r конгруэнтные фигуры *fpl*; равные фигуры;
    одинаковые фигуры

2045 congruent polygons
  d kongruente Polygone *npl*
  f polygones *mpl* congruents
  r равные многоугольники *mpl*

2046 congruent segments
  d längengleiche Strecken *fpl*
  f segments *mpl* congruents
  r равные отрезки *mpl*

2047 congruent transformation
  d kongruente Transformation *f*;
    Kongruenztransformation *f*
  f transformation *f* congruente
  r конгруэнтное преобразование *n*

2048 congruent triangles
  d kongruente Dreiecke *npl*
  f triangles *mpl* égaux
  r конгруэнтные треугольники *mpl*; равные
    треугольники

  *   conic → 2053

2049 conical
  d konisch
  f conique
  r конический

2050 conical fill
  d konische Füllung *f*
  f remplissage *m* conique
  r коническое заполнение *n*

2051 conical lens
  d konische Linse *f*
  f lentille *f* conique
  r коническая линза *f*

  *   **conical projection** → 1383

2052 conical surface
  d Kegelfläche *f*
  f surface *f* conique
  r коническая поверхность *f*

  *   **conic of centres** → 1378

* conic projection → 1383

2053 conic [section]; curve of second degree;
     quadric curve
  d Kegelschnitt m; Kurve f zweiter Ordnung
  f conique f, courbe f de deuxième ordre
  r коническое сечение n; коника f; кривая f
    второго порядка

* conic section in projective geometry →
  7545

2054 conjoint
  d gemeinsam
  f conjoint
  r общий; объединенный; соединенный

2055 conjoint boundary
  d Gemeinsamgrenze f
  f limite f conjointe; limite unie
  r общая граница f

2056 conjugacy
  d Konjugiertsein n; Konjugium n
  f propriété f d'être conjugué
  r сопряженность f

2057 conjugate
  d konjugiert
  f conjugué
  r сопряженный

2058 conjugate circles
  d konjugierte Kreise mpl
  f cercles mpl conjugués
  r сопряженные окружности fpl

2059 conjugate diameters of a conic
  d konjugierte Durchmesser npl eines
    Kegelschnitts
  f diamètres mpl d'une conique conjugués
  r сопряженные диаметры mpl коники

2060 conjugate focus
  d konjugierter Fokus m
  f foyer m conjugué
  r сопряженный фокус m

* conjugate hyperbolae → 2061

2061 conjugate hyperbolas; conjugate
     hyperbolae
  d konjugierte Hyperbeln fpl
  f hyperboles fpl conjuguées
  r сопряженные гиперболы fpl

2062 conjugate lines
     (of a conic)
  d konjugierte Geraden fpl
  f droites fpl conjuguées

  r сопряженные прямые fpl

* conjugate net → 2063

2063 conjugate net [of curves]
  d konjugiertes Netz n; konjugiertes
    Kurvennetz n
  f réseau m [de courbes] conjugué
  r сопряженная сеть f [кривых]

2064 conjugate points
  d konjugierte Punkte mpl; zugehörige Punkte;
    homologe Punkte
  f points mpl conjugués
  r сопряженные точки fpl

2065 conjugation
  d Konjugation f
  f conjugaison f
  r сопряжение n

* connect v → 931

2066 connected
  d verbunden; zusammenhängend
  f connexe; connecté
  r связной; связанный

2067 connected curve
  d zusammenhängende Kurve f
  f courbe f connexe
  r связная кривая f

2068 connected graph
  d zusammenhängender Graph m; verbundener
    Graph
  f graphe m connexe
  r связный граф m

* connectedness → 2075

2069 connected space
  d zusammenhängender Raum m
  f espace m connexe
  r связное пространство n

2070 connected status
  d verbundener Status m
  f état m connecté
  r связанное состояние n

2071 connected surface
  d zusammenhängende Fläche f
  f surface f connexe
  r связная поверхность f

2072 connected vertices
  d verbundene Knotenpunkte mpl
  f sommets mpl connectés
  r связанные вершины fpl; соединенные
    вершины

2073 connecting curve
- *d* Übergangskurve *f*; Übergangsbogen *m*
- *f* courbe *f* de raccordement
- *r* переходная кривая *f*; соединительная кривая

2074 connection
- *d* Konnektion *f*; Anschluss *m*
- *f* connexion *f*; raccordement *m*
- *r* [при]соединение *n*; связывание *n*; включение *n*; подключение *n*

2075 connectivity; connectedness
- *d* Konnektivität *f*; Zusammenhang *m*
- *f* connecivité *f*; connexité *f*
- *r* связываемость *f*; связность *f*

2076 connector line
- *d* Verbindungslinie *f*
- *f* ligne *f* de connexion
- *r* линия *f* связи

2077 connect *v* to environment
- *d* zur Umgebung verbinden
- *f* raccorder vers l'environnement
- *r* связывать со средой

2078 connect *v* to printer
- *d* zum Drucker verbinden
- *f* raccorder à l'imprimante
- *r* подключать к принтеру

2079 conoid
- *d* Konoid *n*
- *f* conoïde *m*
- *r* коноид *m*

2080 conoidal cone
- *d* Konoidkegel *m*
- *f* cône *m* conoïde
- *r* коноидальный конус *m*

2081 consequence
- *d* Folgerung *f*; Konsequenz *f*
- *f* conséquence *f*
- *r* следствие *n*

* **consequent → 9299**

2082 consistency
- *d* Konsistenz *f*; Widerspruchsfreiheit *f*
- *f* consistance *f*
- *r* согласованность *f*; непротиворечивость *f*

2083 consistency check
- *d* Konsistenzüberprüfung *f*; Konsistenzkontrolle *f*
- *f* contrôle *m* de consistance
- *r* проверка *f* на совместимость

2084 consistent
- *d* konsistent; verträglich; vereinbar; widerspruchsfrei
- *f* consistant
- *r* совместимый; совместный

2085 consolidation
- *d* Konsolidierung *f*; Verfestigung *f*
- *f* consolidation *f*
- *r* консолидация *f*; слияние *n*; укрупнение *n*

2086 constant *adj*
- *d* konstant
- *f* constant
- *r* постоянный; константный

* **constant → 2090**

2087 constant curvature
- *d* konstante Krümmung *f*
- *f* courbure *f* constante
- *r* постоянная кривизна *f*

* **constant map → 2088**

2088 constant map[ping]
- *d* konstante Abbildung *f*
- *f* application *f* constante
- *r* постоянное отображение *n*

2089 constant of refraction
- *d* Refraktionskonstante *f*
- *f* constante *f* de la réfraction
- *r* постоянная *f* рефракции

* **constant shading → 3856**

2090 constant [value]
- *d* Konstante *f*; konstanter Wert *m*
- *f* constante *f*; valeur *f* constante
- *r* константа *f*; постоянная *f*; постоянное значение *n*

2091 constellation
(group of stars in a certain pattern)
- *d* Konstellation *f*; Sternbild *n*
- *f* constellation *f*; groupe *m* de nombres étoilés du même type
- *r* созвездие *n*

2092 constrain *v*; restrain *v*; restrict *v*; bound *v*
- *d* begrenzen; einschränken
- *f* limiter; réserver
- *r* ограничивать

* **constraint → 8111**

2093 constraint angle
- *d* Beschränkungswinkel *m*
- *f* angle *m* contraint
- *r* ограничивающий угол *m*

2094 constraint axis
 d Beschränkungsachse f
 f axe m contraint
 r ограничивающая ось f

2095 constraint cursor movement
 d Beschränkungsweg m des Cursors
 f mouvement m de curseur contraint
 r ограниченное движение n курсора

2096 constraint plane
 d Beschränkungsebene f
 f plan m contraint
 r ограничивающая плоскость f

2097 construction
 d Konstruktion f
 f construction f
 r конструкция f

2098 construction algorithm
 d Konstruktionsalgorithmus m
 f algorithme m de construction
 r алгоритм m конструкции

2099 construction line
 d Konstruktionslinie f
 f ligne f de construction
 r конструктивная линия f

2100 construction plane
  (local 2D coordinate system defined
  relatively to absolute 3D coordinate system)
 d Konstruktionsebene f
 f plan m de construction
 r конструктивная плоскость f

2101 construction problem
 d Konstruktionsaufgabe f
 f problème m de construction
 r задача f на построение

2102 constructive geometry
 d konstruktive Geometrie f
 f géométrie f constructive
 r конструктивная геометрия f

 * **constructive line → 5053**

2103 constructive solid geometry; CSG
  (geometry of combined solids)
 d konstruktive Körpergeometrie f
 f géométrie f de solides constructive
 r конструктивная блочная геометрия f

 * **consumer → 10081**

 * **contact → 9468**

2104 contact element

 d Berührungselement n; Kontaktelement n
 f élément m de contact
 r элемент m касания

2105 container
 d Container m; Behälter m
 f conteneur m; container m; contenant m;
  réceptacle m
 r контейнер m; сосуд m

2106 container object
 d Container-Objekt n
 f objet m contenant
 r объект m типа контейнера

2107 content
 d Inhalt m
 f contenu m
 r содержание n; вместимость f

2108 contention
 d Kontention f
 f contention f
 r состязание n; соревнование n

2109 context
 d Kontext m
 f contexte m
 r контекст m

 * **context help → 2110**

 * **context menu → 2111**

2110 context[-sensitive] help
 d Kontexthilfe f
 f aide f contextuelle
 r контекстная помощь f

2111 context[-sensitive] menu
 d Kontextmenü n
 f menu m contextuel
 r контекстное меню n; сокращенное меню

2112 contiguity
 d Benachbartheit f; Benachbartsein n
 f contiguïté f
 r смежность f

2113 continuation; prolongation
 d Fortsetzung f
 f continuation f; prolongement m
 r продолжение n

 * **continued dimensioning → 1391**

2114 continuity
 d Kontinuität f
 f continuité f
 r непрерывность f

2115 **continuity level**
  d Stetigkeitsniveau *n*
  f degré *m* de continuité
  r уровень *m* непрерывности

2116 **continuous**
  d stetig; kontinuierlich; Dauer-
  f continu; continuel
  r продолжительный; непрерывный

2117 **continuous boundary**
  d stetiger Rand *m*
  f bord *m* continu; frontière *f* continue
  r непрерывная граница *f*

2118 **continuous contour**
  d stetiger Umriss *m*
  f contour *m* continu
  r непрерывный контур *m*

2119 **continuous curve**
  d stetige Kurve *f*
  f courbe *f* continue
  r непрерывная кривая *f*

2120 **continuous database**
  d kontinuierliche Datenbasis *f*
  f base *f* de données continue
  r непрерывная база *f* данных

2121 **continuous geometrical objects**
  d kontinuierliche geometrische Objekte *npl*
  f objets *mpl* géométriques continus
  r непрерывные геометрические объекты *mpl*

2122 **continuous linetype**
  d kontinuierlicher Linientyp *m*
  f type *m* de ligne continu
  r непрерывный тип *m* линии

2123 **continuous mapping**
  d kontinuierliche Abbildung *f*
  f application *f* continue
  r непрерывное отображение *n*

2124 **continuous spectrum**
  d kontinuierliches Spektrum *n*
  f spectre *m* continu
  r непрерывный спектр *m*

2125 **continuous tone; contone; full tone**
  d kontinuierlicher Ton *m*
  f tonalité *f* continue; ton *m* continu
  r непрерывный оттенок *m*; безрастровый тон *m*

  * **continuous-tone colors** → 4074

2126 **continuous-tone image; contone image**
      (all photographs and illustrations having a range of shades)
  d Bild *n* mit kontinuierlichem Ton; Contone *n*
  f image *f* en dégradé; image à tonalité continue; image à ton continu
  r псевдополутоновое изображение *n*; безрастровое изображение; многотоновое изображение

2127 **continuous zooming**
  d kontinuierliches Zoomen *n*
  f zoom *m* continu
  r непрерывное масштабирование *n*

  * **contone** → 2125

2128 **contone chip**
  d Contone-Chip *m*
  f chip *m* d'image en ton continu
  r микросхема *f* формирования безрастрового изображения

  * **contone image** → 2126

  * **contour** → 5517

2129 **contour; outline**
  d Kontur *f*; Umriss *m*
  f contour *m*
  r контур *m*; очертание *n*

2130 **contour adjustment**
  d Umrisseinstellung *f*
  f ajustement *m* de contour
  r настраивание *n* контура

2131 **contour analysis**
  d Analyse *f* der Kontur
  f analyse *f* des contours
  r анализ *m* контуров

  * **contour attributes** → 6681

  * **contour characteristics** → 6684

2132 **contour color; outline color**
  d Konturfarbe *f*
  f couleur *f* de contour
  r цвет *m* контура

2133 **contoured map**
  d Höhen[schicht]linienkarte *f*; Schicht[en]linienkarte *f*
  f carte *f* en courbes [de niveau]
  r карта *f* с горизонталями; контурная карта

2134 **contoured object**
  d konturiertes Objekt *n*
  f objet *m* en contour
  r окаймленный объект *m*

* contour elevation → 5517

2135 contour extraction
   d Konturextraktion f
   f extraction f de contour
   r выделение n контура

2136 contour form
   d Konturform f
   f forme f de contour
   r форма f контура

2137 contour group
   d Konturgruppe f
   f groupe m de contours
   r группа f контуров

2138 contour image
   d Konturbild n
   f image f en contour
   r контурное изображение n

2139 contour information
   d Konturinformation f
   f information f de contour
   r контурная информация f

2140 contouring; outlining; bordering
   d Umrisszeichnung f; Berandung f;
      Einfassung f; Ränderung f
   f mise f en contour; bordurage m
   r вычерчивание n контуров;
      оконтуривание n; окаймление n;
      обрамление n; окантовка f

2141 contour line
   d Konturlinie f
   f ligne f de contour; trait m de contour
   r контурная линия f

2142 contour number; contour value
   d Höhen[schicht]linienzahl f
   f cote f de courbe
   r цифровая отметка f горизонтали

2143 contour representation
   d Umrissdarstellung f
   f représentation f de contour
   r представление n контура

2144 contour segmentation
   d Kontur-Segmentierung f
   f segmentation f de contour
   r сегментирование n контура

2145 contour selection
   d Umriss-Auswahl f
   f sélection f de contour
   r выбор m контура

2146 contour settings
   d Kontureinrichtungen fpl
   f établissements mpl de contour
   r установление n параметров контура

2147 contour surface
   d Konturfläche f
   f surface f de contour
   r поверхность f контура

* contour tool → 6686

* contour value → 2142

2148 contracted
   d verengt; zusammenzogen; kontrahiert
   f contracté
   r свернутый; сжатый

* contracted → 2364

* contracted cycloid → 2365

* contracted epicycloid → 2366

2149 contracted graph
   d kontrahierter Graph m
   f graphe m contracté
   r сжатый граф m

* contracted hypocycloid → 2367

* contraction → 8658

2150 contrast
   d Kontrast m
   f contraste m
   r контраст m

2151 contrast altering; contrast change
   d Kontrast-Änderung f
   f changement m de contraste
   r изменение n контраста; изменение
      контрастности

* contrast change → 2151

2152 contrast control
   d Kontrastregelung f
   f contrôle m de contraste
   r управление n контрастом

2153 contrast correction
   d Kontrastkorrektur f
   f correction f de contraste
   r исправление n контраста; коррекция f
      контраста

* contrast factor → 1643

2154 contrast filter
   d Kontrastfilter *m*
   f filtre *m* de contraste
   r фильтр *m* контраста

2155 contrast image; hard image
   d Kontrastbild *n*
   f image *f* contraste
   r контрастное изображение *n*

   * **contrast range** → **2611**

   * **contrast ratio** → **1643**

2156 contrasts accentuation
   (of an image)
   d Kontrastversteilerung *f*
   f accentuation *f* des contrastes
   r усиление *n* контрастов

2157 contrast slider
   d Kontrastschieber *m*
   f glisseur *m* de contraste
   r ползунок *m* контраста

2158 contrast threshold
   d Kontrastschwelle *f*
   f seuil *m* de contraste
   r порог *m* контраста

2159 contrast transfer function
   d Kontrastübertragungsfunktion *f*
   f fonction *f* de transfert de contraste
   r переходная функция *f* контраста

2160 control *v*
   d kontrollieren
   f contrôler
   r контролировать

2161 control
   d Kontrolle *f*; Steuerung *f*
   f contrôle *m*; commande *f*
   r управление *n*

   * **control ball** → **8184**

2162 control character
   d Steuerzeichen *n*
   f caractère *m* de contrôle
   r управляющий символ *m*

2163 control code
   d Steuercode *m*
   f code *m* de commande
   r управляющий код *m*

2164 control curve
   d Regelungskurve *f*
   f courbe *f* de contrôle
   r контрольная кривая *f*

2165 controller
   d Controller *m*
   f contrôleur *m*
   r контроллер *m*

2166 control object
   d Steuerobjekt *n*; Kontrollobjekt *n*
   f objet *m* de contrôle
   r управляющий объект *m*; контрольный
      объект

2167 control panel
   d Kontrollfeld *n*
   f panneau *m* de configuration; tableau *m* de
      commande
   r управляющая панель *f*; окно *n* настройки
      компьютера

2168 control point
   d Festpunkt *m*; Steuerpunkt *m*; Passpunkt *m*
   f point *m* de contrôle; point d'appui
   r контрольная точка *f*; тестовая точка;
      опорная точка

2169 control points alignment
   d Ausrichtung *f* der Festpunkte
   f alignement *m* de points de contrôle
   r выравнивание *n* контрольных точек

2170 control points arrangement
   d Anordnung *f* der Festpunkte
   f arrangement *m* de points d'appui
   r расположение *n* опорных точек

2171 control polygon
   d Steuerpolygon *n*
   f polygone *m* de contrôle
   r контрольный многоугольник *m*

2172 control space; background space
   d Steuerraum *m*
   f espace *m* de contrôle
   r опорное пространство *n*

2173 control string
   d Steuerkette *f*
   f chaîne *f* de contrôle
   r контрольная цепочка *f*

2174 control vertex
   d Steuerknoten *m*
   f sommet *m* de contrôle
   r контрольная вершина *f*

2175 convention
   d Vereinbarung *f*
   f convention *f*
   r соглашение *n*

2176 convergence
  d Konvergenz f
  f convergence f
  r сходимость f

  * convergence angle → 374

2177 convergence correction
  d Konvergenzkorrektur f
  f correction f de convergence
  r коррекция f сходимости

2178 convergence of a filter
  d Konvergenz f des Filters
  f convergence f d'un filtre
  r сходимость f фильтра

  * convergent lens → 2180

2179 convergent surface
  d konvergente Fläche f
  f surface f convergente
  r конвергентная поверхность f

**2180 converging lens; convergent lens; convex
      lens**
  d Konvergenzlinse f; Sammellinse f; konvexe
    Linse f
  f lentille f convergente; lentille convexe
  r фокусирующая линза f; конвергентная
    линза

  * conversational mode → 2698

2181 conversion; converting
  d Konvertierung f; Umformung f
  f conversion f
  r преобразование n; превращение n;
    конверсия f

**2182 conversion of coordinates; coordinate
      transformation**
  d Koordinatentransformation f;
    Koordinatenumformung f
  f transformation f de coordonnées; conversion f
    de coordonnées
  r преобразование m координат;
    координатная трансформация f

2183 convert v
  d konvertieren; umwandeln; verwandeln
  f convertir
  r преобразовывать; превращать

2184 converter
  d Konverter m; Umwandler m; Wandler m
  f convertisseur m; traducteur m
  r конвертер m; преобразователь m

  * converting → 2181

2185 convert v to a bitmap
  d in ein Bitmap konvertieren
  f convertir en image bitmap
  r преобразовывать в растровое изображение

2186 convert v to black-and-white
  d in Schwarzweiß konvertieren
  f convertir en noir et blanc
  r преобразовывать в черно-белый

2187 convert v to curve
  d in Kurven konvertieren
  f convertir en courbe
  r преобразовывать в кривую

2188 convert v to duotone
  d in Zweiton konveretieren
  f convertir en deux tons
  r преобразовывать в два цвета

2189 convert v to grayscale
  d in Graustufen konvertieren
  f convertir en niveau de gris
  r преобразовывать в шкалу полутонов;
    преобразовывать в оттенки серого цвета

2190 convex
  d konvex
  f convexe
  r выпуклый

2191 convex angle
  d konvexer Winkel m
  f angle m convexe
  r выпуклый угол m

2192 convex arc
  d konvexer Bogen m
  f arc m convexe
  r конвексная дуга f; выпуклая дуга

2193 convex body
  d konvexer Körper m
  f corps m convexe
  r выпуклое тело n

2194 convex closure
  d konvexe Abschließung f
  f fermeture f convexe
  r выпуклая замкнутость f

2195 convex combination
  d konvexe Kombination f
  f combinaison f convexe
  r выпуклая комбинация f

2196 convex cone
  d konvexer Kegel m
  f cône m convexe
  r выпуклый конус m

2197 convex cup curve
d von unten konvexe Kurve *f*
f courbe *f* convexe vers le bas
r выпуклая вниз кривая *f*

2198 convex curve
d konvexe Kurve *f*
f courbe *f* convexe
r выпуклая кривая *f*

2199 convex domain; convex region
d konvexer Bereich *m*; konvexes Gebiet *n*
f domaine *m* convexe
r выпуклая область *f*

* **convex down** → 2003

* **convex downward** → 2003

2200 convex envelope; convex hull
d konvexe Hülle *f*
f enveloppe *f* convexe
r выпуклая оболочка *f*

* **convex hull** → 2200

2201 convex hull algorithms
d Algorithmen *mpl* der konvexen Hüllen
f algorithmes *mpl* d'enveloppes convexes
r алгоритмы *mpl* выпуклых оболочек

2202 convexity
d Konvexität *f*
f convexité *f*
r выпуклость *f*

* **convexity downward** → 2007

* **convexity upward** → 2006

2203 convex layers
d konvexe Schichten *fpl*
f couches *f* convexes
r выпуклые слои *mpl*

* **convex lens** → 2180

2204 convex normal
d konvexe Normale *f*
f normale *f* convexe
r выпуклая нормаль *f*

2205 convex polygon
d konvexes Polygon *n*; konvexes Vieleck *n*
f polygone *m* convexe
r выпуклый многоугольник *m*

2206 convex polyhedron
d konvexes Polyeder *n*
f polyèdre *m* convexe

r выпуклый многогранник *m*

* **convex region** → 2199

* **convex up** → 1995

* **convex upward** → 1995

2207 convolution
d Konvolution *f*
f convolution *f*
r свертка *f*; свертывание *n*

2208 convolution kernel
d Konvolutionskern *m*
f noyau *m* de convolution
r ядро *n* свертывания

2209 convolution operation
d Faltungsoperation *f*
f opération *f* de convolution
r операция *f* свертки

2210 convolution processor
d Faltungsprozessor *m*
f processeur *m* de convolution
r процессор *m* свертки

2211 convolve *v*
d zusammenrollen
f plier; envelopper
r скручиваться; свертывать[ся]; сплетать[ся]

2212 Coons' patch
d Coons-Oberflächenstück *n*
f surface *f* paramétrique de Coons
r кусок *m* Куна

2213 Coons' surface
d Coons-Oberfläche *f*
f surface *f* de Coons
r поверхность *f* Куна

2214 coordinate
d Koordinate *f*
f coordonnée *f*
r координата *f*

* **coordinate axis** → 761

* **coordinate calculation** → 1966

2215 coordinate direction
d Koordinatenrichtung *f*
f direction *f* de coordonnée
r направление *n* координаты

2216 coordinate display
d Koordinatendisplay *n*

f affichage *m* de coordonnées
r координатый дисплей *m*

2217 coordinate filter; point filter
d Koordinatenfilter *m*
f filtre *m* de coordonnées; filtre de points
r координатный фильтр *m*

* **coordinate fountain** → 6633

2218 coordinate-free
d koordinatenlos
f sans coordonnées
r бескоординатный

2219 coordinate function
d Koordinatenfunktion *f*
f fonction *f* coordonnée
r координатная функция *f*

2220 coordinate generator
d Koordinatengenerator *m*
f générateur *m* de coordonnées
r генератор *m* координат

2221 coordinate geometry
d Koordinatengeometrie *f*
f géométrie *f* coordonnée
r координатная геометрия *f*

2222 coordinate graphics; line graphics
d Koordinatengrafik *f*; Liniengrafik *f*
f infographie *f* par coordonnées; graphique *m* coordonné
r координатная графика *f*; линейная графика

2223 coordinate grid; network of coordinates
d Koordinatennetz *n*; Koordinatengitter *n*
f réseau *m* de quadrillage de coordonnées
r сетка *f* координат

2224 coordinate indexing
d Koordinatenindexierung *f*
f indexation *f* coordonnée
r координатное индексирование *n*

2225 coordinate line
d Koordinatenlinie *f*
f ligne *f* de coordonnées
r координатная линия *f*

2226 coordinate measurement
d Koordinatenmessung *f*
f mesure *f* des coordonnées
r измерение *n* координат

2227 coordinate method
d Koordinatenmethode *f*
f méthode *f* des coordonnées
r метод *m* координат

* **coordinate origin** → 6633

2228 coordinate plane
d Koordinatenebene *f*
f plan *m* de coordonnées
r координатная плоскость *f*

2229 coordinate representation
d Koordinatendarstellung *f*; koordinatenmäßige Darstellung *f*
f représentation *f* en coordonnées; présentation *f* à coordonnées
r координатное представление *n*

2230 coordinates in space; spatial coordinates
d räumliche Koordinaten *fpl*; Raumkoordinaten *fpl*
f coordonnées *fpl* spatiaux
r пространственные координаты *fpl*; координаты в пространстве

* **coordinates in the plane** → 7135

2231 coordinate smoothing
(points are placed in their neighbors' center of mass)
d Koordinaten-Glättung *f*
f lissage *m* de coordonnées
r сглаживание *n* координат

2232 coordinates of a point
d Koordinaten *fpl* eines Punkts
f coordonnées *fpl* d'un point
r координаты *fpl* точки

2233 coordinates of a vector
d Koordinaten *fpl* eines Vektors; Vektorkoordinaten *fpl*
f coordonnées *fpl* d'un vecteur
r координаты *fpl* вектора

* **coordinate source** → 6633

2234 coordinate system
d Koordinatensystem *n*
f système *m* de coordonnées; repère *m*
r координатная система *f*; система координат

* **coordinate system rotating** → 8205

* **coordinate system transformation** → 9822

2235 coordinate table
d Koordinatentabelle *f*
f table *f* des coordonnées
r таблица *f* координат

* **coordinate transformation** → 2182

* coordinate translation → 9830

2236 coordinate triangle
  d Koordinatendreieck n
  f triangle m de coordonnées
  r координатный треугольник m

2237 coordinate value
  d Koordinatenwert m
  f valeur f de coordonnée
  r стойность f координаты

2238 coordinatewise; by coordinates
  d koordinatenweise
  f par coordonnées
  r покоординатно

2239 coplanar
  d komplanar
  f coplanaire
  r компланарный

2240 coplanar lines
  d komplanare Geraden fpl
  f droites fpl coplanaires
  r компланарные прямые fpl

2241 coplanar regions
  d komplanare Regionen fpl
  f régions fpl coplanaires
  r компланарные регионы mpl

2242 coplanar vectors
  d komplanare Vektoren mpl
  f vecteurs mpl coplanaires
  r компланарные векторы mpl

2243 copolar figures
  d copolare Figuren fpl
  f figures fpl polaires réciproques
  r взаимно полярные фигуры fpl

* copunctual → 2020

* copunctual planes → 2023

* copy → 2246

2244 copy v
  d kopieren
  f copier
  r копировать

2245 copy; manifold
  d Kopie f; Exemplar n
  f copie f; exemplaire m
  r копия f; экземпляр m

2246 copy[ing]
  d Kopieren n; Vervielfältigen n

f copiage m
r копирование n

2247 copyright
  d Autorrecht n; Urheberrecht n; Copyright n
  f droit m d'auteur; droit d'exploitation; copyright m
  r авторское право n; копирайт m

2248 copyright symbol
  (©)
  d Copyrightzeichen n
  f symbole m de droit d'exploitation; symbole de copyright
  r знак m авторского права

2249 copy special
  d Spezialkopie f
  f copie f spéciale
  r специальная копия f

2250 copy v to layer
  d in Schicht kopieren
  f copier dans le plan
  r копировать в слой

2251 core
  d Kern m
  f cœur m; âme f
  r сердцевина f; сердечник m

2252 corner
  d Ecke f; Winkel m
  f coin m; corner m
  r угол m

2253 corner condition
  d Eck[en]bedingung f
  f condition f aux coins
  r условие n на вершине; условие на угле

2254 corner handle
  d Eckgriff m
  f poignée f angulaire
  r захват m угла

2255 corner joint
  d Ecken-Verbindung f
  f union f angulaire
  r угловое соединение n; угловое сочленение n

* corner point → 399

2256 corner point angle
  d Eckpunktwinkel m
  f angle m de point anguleux
  r угол m угловой точки

2257 corner threshold
  d Eckschwelle f

f seuil *m* angulaire
r угловой порог *m*

2258 **correct** *v*
d korrigieren
f corriger
r корректировать; исправлять

2259 **correcting filter**
d Korrekturfilter *m*
f filtre *m* de correction
r исправляющий фильтр *m*

2260 **correction**
d Korrektur *f*
f correction *f*
r поправка *f*; коррекция *f*; исправление *n*

2261 **correctness**
d Richtigkeit *f*; Korrektheit *f*
f exactitude *f*; justesse *f*
r правильность *f*

2262 **correlation**
d Korrelation *f*
f corrélation *f*
r корреляция *f*; взаимная зависимость *f*

2263 **correlation in projective geometry**
d Korrelation *f* in der projektiven Geometrie
f corrélation *f* en géométrie projective
r корреляция *f* в проективной геометрии

2264 **correlative equation**
d Korrelationsgleichung *f*
f équation *f* corrélative
r уравнение *n* корреляции

2265 **correspond** *v*
d entsprechen
f correspondre
r соответствовать

2266 **correspondence; matching**
d Korrespondenz *f*; Entsprechung *f*;
Übereinstimmung *f*
f correspondance *f*
r соответствие *n*

2267 **corresponding angles**
d entsprechende Winkel *mpl*
f angles *mpl* correspondants
r соответственные углы *mpl*

2268 **corresponding views**
d entsprechende Ansichten *fpl*
f vues *fpl* en correspondance
r соответствующие представления *npl*

2269 **corrupt** *v*; **damage** *v*; **destroy** *v*

d zerstören; beschädigen
f endommager; corrompre
r разрушать; повреждать; портить

* **coted height** → 7235

* **coted line** → 5647

* **coted projection** → 9739

2270 **coterminal angles**
d koterminale Winkel *mpl*
f angles *mpl* à côtés coïncidents
r углы *mpl* с совпадающими сторонами

* **count** → 9467

* **counterclockwise** → 447

* **counterclockwise blend** → 2271

2271 **counterclockwise blend[ing]**
d Überblendung *f* gegen den Uhrzeigersinn
f dégradé *m* anti-horaire
r переливание *n* против часовой стрелки

2272 **counterclockwise path button**
d Schaltfläche *f* der zum Uhrzeigersinn
entgegensetzten Strecke
f bouton *m* de tracé anti-horaire
r кнопка *f* дорожки против часовой стрелки

2273 **counterclockwise rotation; anticlockwise
rotation**
d Umlauf *m* entgegen dem Uhrzeigersinn; dem
Uhrzeigersinn entgegengesetzte Drehung *f*
f rotation *f* sinistrorsum; rotation dans le sens
contraire des aiguilles d'une montre; rotation
dans le sens positif; rotation en sens
antihoraire
r вращение *n* против часовой стрелки

2274 **coup; stroke; impact**
d Anschlag *m*
f coup *m*; frappe *f*; impact *m*
r удар *m*; нажатие *n*

* **couple** → 6753

2275 **coupled boundary set**
d verkoppelter Randsatz *m*; gekoppelter
Randsatz
f ensemble *m* de frontières liées
r связное множество *n* граней

2276 **coupled projection**
d Doppelprojektion *f*
f projection *f* double
r двойная проекция *f*

* courbure → 882

2277 covariance
 d Kovarianz *f*
 f covariance *f*
 r ковариантность *f*

2278 covariance matrix
 d Kovarianzmatrix *f*
 f matrice *f* de covariance
 r матрица *f* ковариантности

2279 covariant
 d kovariant
 f covariant
 r ковариантный

2280 covariant coordinates
 d kovariante Koordinaten *fpl*
 f coordonnées *fpl* covariantes
 r ковариантные координаты *fpl*

* cover → 1289

2281 coverage
 d Überdeckung *f*
 f couverture *f*
 r покрытие *n*

2282 coverage extent
 d Überdeckungsextent *m*
 f étendue *f* de couverture
 r расширение *n* покрытия

2283 coverage units
 d Überdeckungseinheiten *fpl*
 f unités *fpl* de couverture
 r единицы *fpl* покрытия

* covering of the plane with tiles → 9681

* cover ring → 2717

* covert → 4596

2284 create *v*
 d bilden; erstellen; entwerfen
 f créer
 r создать; создавать

2285 create arrow command
 d Pfeil-Kreationsbefehl *m*
 f commande *f* de création de flèche
 r команда *f* создания стрелки

2286 create *v* **pattern**
 d Muster entwerfen
 f créer un modèle; créer un motif
 r проектировать модель; создать мотив

2287 create pattern command
 d Muster-Kreationsbefehl *m*
 f commande *f* de création de motif
 r команда *f* создания рисунка

2288 creation; formation
 d Erstellung *f*; Formierung *f*; Kreation *f*
 f création *f*; formation *f*
 r образовывание *n*; создание *n*;
 формирование *n*

2289 creator
 d Gründer *m*
 f créateur *m*
 r создатель *m*

2290 crest line
 d Kammweg *m*; Rückenlinie *f*
 f ligne *f* de faîte
 r линия *f* гребня; гребневая линия

2291 crispness
 (of a texture)
 d Knusprigkeit *f*
 f croustillance *f*
 r жесткость *f*; твердость *f*; резкость *f*

2292 crooked image
 d geschwungenes Bild *n*
 f image *f* coudée; image cintrée
 r изогнутое изображение *n*

* crop → 9912

* crop *v* → 9910

2293 crop mark; cut mark
 (line near the edges of an image indicating
 portions to be reproduced)
 d Schneidemarke *f*
 f repère *m* de coupe; repère de cadrage
 r маркер *m* кадрирования; маркер отсекания

* cropped effect → 2529

* cropping → 4000, 9912

2294 cropping area
 d Beschneid[en]bereich *m*
 f zone *f* de coupage
 r область *f* отсекания; вырезанная область

2295 cropping the screen in rendering
 d Bildschirm-Beschneiden beim Rendering
 f découpage *m* d'écran en temps de rendu
 r отсекание *n* экрана при тонировании

2296 crop tool
 d Beschneiden-Hilfsmittel *n*

f outil *m* de découpage
r инструмент *m* отсекания

2297 cross
   d Kreuz *n*
   f croix *m*
   r крест *m*

   * **cross** → 9860

2298 crossbar
   d Querstrich *m*
   f barre *f* [transversale]
   r поперечная черта *f*; соединительный штрих *m*

2299 crossbar selector
   d Koordinatenselektor *m*
   f sélecteur *m* crossbar; sélecteur coordonné
   r координатный селектор *m*

2300 cross-cap; handle of the second kind
   d Kreuzhaube *f*; Henkel *m* zweiter Art
   f bonnet *m* croisé; anse *f* de deuxième espèce
   r скрещенный колпак *m*; "перехлестнутый чепец" *m*; ручка *f* второго рода

2301 cross color interference
   d gegenseitige Farbstörung *f*
   f interférence *f* de couleurs qui se chevauchement; brouillage *m* de couleurs réciproque
   r взаимная интерференция *f* цветов; перекрестная интерференция цветов

2302 cross-correlation
   d Querkorrelation *f*; Kreuzkorrelation *f*
   f corrélation *f* croisée; corrélation avec retards; corrélation avec décalage
   r перекрестное соотношение *n*; взаимная корреляция *f*

   * **cross-cut** → 2317

   * **cross-dissolve** → 2304

2303 crossed arrows
   d gekreuzte Pfeile *mpl*
   f flèches *fpl* croisées
   r скрещенные стрелки *fpl*

2304 cross-fade; chained fade; cross-dissolve
   d Ketten-Überblendung *f*
   f fondu *m* enchaîné
   r цепное замирание *n*

2305 crosshair
   d Fadenkreuz *n*
   f réticule *m* en croix; croisée *f* des fils; fils *mpl* croisés

r крест *m* нитей; сетка *f* нитей; перекрестие *n*

   * **cross-haired cursor** → 2306

2306 crosshair pointer; cross-haired cursor; puck
   d Fadenkreuz-Zeiger *m*
   f pointeur *m* en croix; pointeur en fils croisés
   r указатель *m* прицела

2307 crosshair size
   d Fadenkreuz-Größe *f*
   f taille *f* de fils croisés
   r размер *m* креста нитей

2308 cross hatching
   d Kreuzschraffen *n*
   f hachure *f* croisée
   r перекрестное штрихование *n*

2309 cross-hatch pattern
   d Kreuzschraffen-Muster *n*
   f modèle *m* de hachure croisée
   r модель *f* перекрестной штриховки

   * **crossing** → 5246

2310 crossing; traverse
   d Kreuzung *f*
   f croisement *m*
   r скрещение *n*

2311 crossing angle; angle of intersection; intersection angle
   d Schnittwinkel *m*
   f angle *m* d'intersection; angle de croisement
   r угол *m* пересечения

2312 crossing point
   d Kreuz[ungs]punkt *m*
   f point *m* de croisement; point d'incidence
   r точка *f* скрещения

2313 crossing polygons
   d Schnittpolygone *npl*
   f polygones *mpl* croisés
   r пересекающиеся многоугольники *mpl*

2314 crossing windows
   d Schnittfenster *npl*
   f fenêtres *fpl* croisées
   r пересекающиеся окна *npl*

   * **cross interlacing** → 5203

2315 cross intersection
   d Querdurchschnitt *m*
   f intersection *f* transversale
   r поперечное пересечение *n*

* crosslike → 2325

* cross-plane → 2316

* cross-plane of projection → 2316

* cross-point → 5252

* cross-profile → 2317

2316 cross projection plane; cross-plane [of projection]
d Kreuzrissebene f
f plan m de projection en profil
r плоскость f профильной проекции

2317 cross-section; cross-cut; cross-profile; transverse profile
d Querschnitt m; Querprofil n
f section f transversale; profil m en travers; profil transversal
r поперечное сечение n; поперечный разрез m; поперечный профиль m

2318 cross-sectional contour
d Querschnittkontur f
f contour m transversal
r поперечный контур m

2319 cross-sectional modeling
d Querschnittmodellierung f
f modélisation f à partir de sections [transversales]
r моделирование n поперечными сечениями

2320 cross-section plane
d Querschnittebene f
f plan m de section transversale; plan en coupe
r плоскость f поперечного сечения

2321 cross shading
d Kreuzschattierung f
f ombrage m croisé
r перекрестное оттенение n

* cross-shaped adj → 2325

2322 cross size
d Querausmaß n
f taille f transversale
r поперечный размер m

2323 crosswise
d kreuzweise
f croisement; à travers
r накрест

2324 cross zigzag pattern
d Querzickzack-Muster n
f image f zigzag à travers
r поперечное зигзагообразное изображение n

* cruciform → 2326

2325 cruciform; crosslike; cross-shaped adj
d kreuzförmig
f en forme de croix; cruciforme
r крестообразный; крестовидный

2326 cruciform [curve]
d Kreuzkurve f
f courbe f cruciforme
r крестообразная кривая f; крестовидная кривая

* crude approximation → 8213

2327 crumble v
d abbröckeln; zerbröckeln
f froisser
r крошить; раздроблять; толочь; растирать; распадать[ся]

* CSG → 2103

* CT → 1986

2328 cube
d Würfel m
f cube m
r куб m

* cubic → 2331

2329 cubic
d kubisch
f cubique
r кубический

2330 cubic convolution
d kubische Faltung f; kubische Konvolution f
f convolution f cubique
r кубическое свертывание n

2331 cubic [curve]
d kubische Kurve f
f courbe f cubique
r кубическая кривая f

2332 cubic environment mapping
d kubische Abbildung f der Umgebung
f mappage m d'environnement cubique
r кубическое картирование n окружения

2333 cubic map
d kubische Karte f
f carte f cubique
r кубическая карта f; кубическая таблица f

2334 **cubic spline**
 d kubischer Spline *m*
 f spline *m* cubique
 r кубический сплайн *m*

2335 **cubic tetrahedron**
 d kubisches Tetraeder *n*
 f tétraèdre *m* cubique
 r кубический тетраэдр *m*

2336 **cubic texturing**
 d kubische Texturierung *f*
 f texturation *f* cubique
 r кубическое текстурирование *n*

2337 **cubic triangle**
 d kubisches Dreieck *n*
 f triangle *m* cubique
 r кубический треугольник *m*

 * **cuboid** → 7865

2338 **cue; reference mark**
    (on the screen)
 d Strichmarke *f*; Cue *n*
 f caractère *m* indicateur; repère *m*
 r индикаторный знак *m*; репер *m*; знак
    сноски

 * **cue** → 10320

2339 **culling; dropping**
 d Pflücken *n*
 f écartement *m*
 r отстранение *n*; игнорирование *n*;
    отбрасывание *n*

2340 **culling strategies**
 d Pflückstrategien *fpl*
 f stratégies *fpl* d'écartement
 r стратегии *fpl* отбрасывания

 * **cumulative error** → 69

 * **cup** → 8688

2341 **curl; rotor; vector rotation**
 d Rotor *m*; vektorielle Rotation *f*; Wirbel *m*
 f curl *m*; tourbillon *m*; vecteur *m* rotationnel;
    rotationnel *m*
 r вихрь *m*; ротор *m*; завиток *m*

 * **curl of discontinuity** → 2316

2342 **curl of discontinuity [at a surface]; surface
    curl**
 d Flächenrotor *m*; Flächenwirbel *m*
 f rotationnel *m* de surface; rotationnel de
    discontinuité
 r вихрь *m* разрыва [на поверхности];

поверхностный ротор *m*

2343 **curl** *v* **page**
 d Seite aufrollen
 f coiffer une page; friser une page
 r завить страницу

 * **curly** → 8218

2344 **curly braces**
 d geschweifte Klammern *fpl*
 f accolades *fpl*
 r фигурные скобки *fpl*

 * **currency sign** → 2345

2345 **currency symbol; currency sign**
 d Währungssymbol *n*
 f symbole *m* de monnaie; symbole monétaire;
    signe *m* de monnaie
 r валютный символ *m*; символ валюты

2346 **current; actual** *adj*
 d laufend; gegenwärtig; aktuell
 f courant; en cours; actuel
 r текущий; рабочий

 * **current coordinates** → 8249

2347 **current direction**
 d laufende Richtung *f*
 f direction *f* courante
 r текущее направление *n*

 * **current layer** → 108

2348 **current object**
 d aktuelles Objekt *n*
 f objet *m* courant
 r текущий объект *m*; рабочий объект

2349 **current object area**
 d Gebiet *n* des aktuellen Objekts
 f zone *f* d'objet courant
 r зона *f* текущего объекта

2350 **current object scale factor**
 d Skalenfaktor *m* des aktuellen Objekts
 f facteur *m* d'échelle d'objet courant
 r коэффициент *m* масштабирования
    рабочего объекта

2351 **current page; working page**
 d Arbeitsseite *f*
 f page *f* en cours; page de travail
 r рабочая страница *f*

2352 **current position**
 d aktuelle Position *f*

f position *f* courante
r текущая позиция *f*

2353 current window; working window
  d aktuelles Fenster *n*; Arbeitsfenster *n*
  f fenêtre *f* courante; fenêtre de travail
  r текущее окно *n*; рабочее окно

2354 cursor
  d Cursor *m*; Kursor *m*; Schreibmarke *f*;
     Lichtmarke *f*
  f curseur *m*
  r курсор *m*

2355 cursor arrow
  d Cursorpfeil *m*
  f flèche *f* du curseur
  r стрелочка *f* указателя курсора

2356 cursor blinking
  d Cursorblinken *n*
  f clignotement *m* de curseur
  r мерцание *n* курсора

  *   **cursor indicator → 2358**

2357 cursor key
  d Cursor[positionier]taste *f*; Cursorsteuertaste *f*
  f touche *f* de curseur
  r клавиша *f* [движения] курсора

2358 cursor mark; cursor indicator
  d Cursorindikator *m*
  f indicateur *m* de curseur
  r индикатор *m* курсора

2359 cursor menu
  d Cursormenü *n*
  f menu *m* de curseur
  r меню *n* курсора

2360 cursor movement
  d Cursorweg *m*
  f mouvement *m* de curseur
  r движение *n* курсора

2361 cursor position
  d Cursorposition *f*
  f position *f* de curseur
  r позиция *f* курсора

2362 cursor size
  d Cursorgröße *f*
  f taille *f* de curseur
  r размер *m* курсора

2363 cursor state
  d Cursorstatus *m*
  f état *m* de curseur
  r состояние *n* курсора

2364 curtate; shortened; short-cut; contracted
  d verkürzt
  f raccourci
  r укороченный; сжатый

2365 curtate cycloid; contracted cycloid
  d verkürzte Zykloide *f*
  f cycloïde *f* raccourcie
  r укороченная циклоида *f*

2366 curtate epicycloid; contracted epicycloid
  d verkürzte Epizykloide *f*
  f épicycloïde *f* raccourcie
  r укороченная эпициклоида *f*

**2367 curtate hypocycloid; contracted
       hypocycloid**
  d verkürzte Hypozykloide *f*
  f hypocycloïde *f* raccourcie
  r укороченная гипоциклоида *f*

  *   **curvature axis → 762**

2368 curvature form
  d Krümmungsform *f*
  f forme *f* de courbure
  r форма *f* кривизны

2369 curvature of a curve
  d Kurvenkrümmung *f*
  f courbure *f* d'une courbe
  r кривизна *f* кривой

  *   **curvature radius → 7715**

2370 curvature vector
  d Krümmungsvektor *m*
  f vecteur *m* de courbure
  r вектор *m* кривизны

2371 curve
  d Kurve *f*
  f courbe *f*
  r кривая *f*

2372 curve arc
  d Kurvenbogen *m*
  f arc *m* d'une courbe
  r дуга *f* кривой

2373 curve complexity
  d Komplexität der Kurve
  f complexité *f* de la courbe
  r сложность *f* кривой

2374 curved surface
  d Kurvenfläche *f*
  f surface *f* courbée
  r изогнутая поверхность *f*

2375 curve-fit polyline
  d Polylinie *f* mit Form der Kurve
  f polyligne *f* lissée en courbe
  r полилиния *f*, сглаженная кривой

2376 curve fitting
  d Kurvenanpassung *f*; Fitten *n* der Kurve;
    Kurvenausgleich *m*
  f ajustement *m* d'une courbe; ajustement de la
    courbe; lissage *m* d'une courbe
  r вычерчивание *n* кривой [по точкам];
    сглаживание *n* кривой; выравнивание *n*
    кривой

2377 curve generator
  d Kurvengenerator *m*
  f générateur *m* de courbes
  r генератор *m* кривых

  *   **curve in space** → **8919**

2378 curve object
  d Kurvenobjekt *n*
  f objet *m* courbe
  r объект *m* типа кривой

**2379 curve of intersection; intersection curve;
     intersection line; line of intersection**
  d Schnittkurve *f*; Schnittlinie *f*
  f courbe *f* d'intersection; ligne *f* d'intersection
  r кривая *f* пересечения; линия *f* пересечения

  *   **curve of second degree** → **2053**

2380 curve of Sierpinski
  d Sierpinski-Kurve *f*
  f courbe *f* de Sierpinski
  r кривая *f* Серпиньского

2381 curve segment
  d Kurvensegment *n*; Kurvenabschnitt *m*
  f segment *m* d'une courbe
  r сегмент *f* кривой

2382 curve shape
  d Kurvenform *f*
  f forme *f* d'une courbe
  r форма *f* кривой

2383 curve splitting
  d Kurvenaufteilung *f*
  f scission *f* de la courbe
  r расщепление *n* кривой

2384 curvilinear
  d krummlinig
  f curviligne; curvilinéaire
  r криволинейный

2385 curvilinear arc
  d krummliniger Bogen *m*
  f arc *m* curviligne
  r криволинейная дуга *f*

2386 curvilinear coordinates
  d krummlinige Koordinaten *fpl*
  f coordonnées *fpl* curvilignes
  r криволинейные координаты *fpl*

2387 curvilinear figure
  d krummlinige Figur *f*
  f figure *f* curviligne
  r криволинейная фигура *f*

  *   **cusp** → **2388**

2388 cusp [node]; peak point
  d Scheitelpunkt *m*; Zacke *f*
  f point *m* de rebroussement; cuspide *m*; point
    de crête
  r острый выступ *m*; точка *f* перегиба
    [кривой]; пиковая точка

2389 custom chart format
  d angepaßtes Diagrammformat *n*
  f format *m* de diagramme personnalisé
  r заказной формат *m* диаграммы

2390 custom child object
  d angepaßtes untergeordnetes Objekt *n*
  f objet *m* fils personnalisé
  r заказной потомственный объект *m*

2391 custom color
  d angepaßte Farbe *f*
  f couleur *f* personnalisée
  r заказной цвет *m*

2392 custom color map
  d angepaßte Farbkarte *f*
  f carte *f* couleur personnalisée
  r заказная цветная таблица *f*

2393 custom color palette
  d angepaßte Farbpalette *f*
  f palette *f* de couleurs personnalisées
  r заказная палитра *f* цветов

2394 custom component
  d angepaßte Komponente *f*
  f composante *f* personnalisée
  r заказной компонент *m*

2395 custom dialog box
  d angepaßte Dialogbox *f*
  f boîte *f* de dialogue personnalisée
  r заказной диалоговый ящик *m*

2396 custom dictionary
  d angepaßtes Wörterbuch *n*

f dictionnaire *m* personnalisé
r заказной словарь *m*

* **customer** → 1545

2397 custom installation; client installation
d angepaßte Anlage *f*
f installation *f* personnalisée
r заказная установка *f*

2398 customization; customizing
d Personalisierung *f*; kundenspezifische
   Produktgestaltung *f*
f personnalisation *f*; production *f* à la demande
r разработка *f* заказного варианта

2399 customize *v*
d kundenspezifisch herstellen
f produire à la demande
r изготовлять по заказу

2400 customized file
d kundenspezifische Datei *f*
f fichier *m* personnalisé
r заказной файл *m*

* **customizing** → 2398

2401 custom label
d angepaßtes Etikett *n*
f étiquette *f* d'utilisateur
r пользовательская метка *f*

2402 custom menu
d angepaßtes Menü *n*
f menu *m* personnalisé
r заказное меню *n*

2403 custom nib
(of a pen of an arrow)
d angepaßte Spitze *f*
f bec *m* personnalisé
r заказной кончик *m*

2404 custom object
d angepaßtes Objekt *n*
f objet *m* personnalisé
r заказной объект *m*

2405 custom palette
d angepaßte Palette *f*
f palette *f* personnalisée
r заказная палитра *f*

2406 custom pattern
d angepaßtes Muster *n*
f motif *m* personnalisé; modèle *m* personnalisé
r заказной мотив *m*; заказной рисунок *m*

2407 custom toolbar

d angepaßter Hilfsmittelstreifen *m*
f barre *f* d'outils personnalisé
r заказная панель *f* инструментов

2408 cut *v*
d ausschneiden
f [dé]couper
r вырезать

* **cut** → 8430

2409 cut *v* **all**
d alles ausschneiden
f [dé]couper tout
r удалять все

* **cut mark** → 2293

* **cut plane** → 7146

2410 cut point
d Schnittpunkt *m*
f point *m* de section
r точка *f* сечения

2411 cut set
d Schnittmenge *f*
f ensemble *m* de sections
r множество *n* сечений

* **cutting** → 1558

2412 cutting *adj*
d schneidend; Schnitt-
f sécant; coupant
r секущий; пересекающий

2413 cutting angle
d Schnittwinkel *m*; Schneidwinkel *m*
f angle *m* de coup; angle sécant
r угол *m* засечки; угол среза

2414 cutting edge
d Schnittkante *f*; Schneidkante *f*
f arête *f* de coupe; bord *m* coupant; tranchant *m*
r секущее ребро *n*

2415 cutting edge geometry
d Schneidkantengeometrie *f*
f géométrie *f* d'arête de coupe
r геометрия *f* секущего ребра

* **cutting object** → 8432

* **cutting plane** → 7146

2416 cutting planes; intersecting planes
d sich schneidende Ebenen *fpl*
f plans *mpl* sécants; plans coupants
r пересекающиеся плоскости *fpl*

*   **CVE** → 2984

2417 cyan filter
  d Cyan-Filter *m*
  f filtre *m* cyan
  r зеленовато-голубой фильтр *m*;
      циан-фильтр *m*

2418 cyan, magenta and yellow; CMY
  d Cyan, Magenta und Gelb
  f cyan, magenta et jaune
  r зеленовато-голубой, фиолетовый и
      желтый

2419 cyan, magenta, yellow and black; CMYK
  d Cyan, Magenta, Gelb und Schwarz
  f cyan, magenta, jaune et noir
  r зеленовато-голубой, фиолетовый, желтый
      и черный; голубой, пурпурный, желтый,
      черный

2420 cyberart
  d Cyberart *f*
  f cyberart *m*
  r компьютерное произведение *n* искусства

*   **cyber glove** → 2481

2421 cyberspace
  d Cyberspace *m*; künstlicher Raum *m*
  f cyberespace *m*
  r киберпространство *n*

2422 cyberworld
  d künstliche Welt *f*
  f cybermonde *m*
  r кибермир *m*

2423 cycle; loop
  d Zyklus *m*
  f cycle *m*
  r цикл *m*

*   **cycle shift** → 1508

2424 cyclic
  d zyklisch
  f cyclique
  r циклический

*   **cyclic plane** → 2426

**2425 cyclic points; circular points of infinity;
      focoids; circules [of a plane]**
  d [absolute] Kreispunkte *mpl*; unendlichferne
      Kreispunkte; imaginäre Kreispunkte; absolute
      Punkte *mpl*
  f points *mpl* cycliques imaginaires; points
      ombilicaux du plan; ombilics *mpl*
  r циклические точки *fpl*; бесконечные

мнимые круговые точки; бесконечно
удаленные точки

2426 cyclic [projective] plane
  d zyklische Ebene *f*
  f plan *m* cyclique
  r циклическая плоскость *f*

2427 cyclic quadrilateral
  d zyklisches Vierseit *n*
  f quadrilatère *m* cyclique
  r циклический четырехсторонник *m*

*   **cyclic shift** → 1508

2428 cycling
  d zyklische Wiederholung *f*
  f bouclage *m*
  r циклирование *n*

2429 cycloid
  d Zykloide *f*; Radlinie *f*; Radkurve *f*;
      Rollkurve *f*
  f cycloïde *f*
  r циклоида *f*

2430 cycloidal curve
  d zykloidale Kurve *f*
  f courbe *f* cycloïdale
  r циклоидальная кривая *f*

2431 cylinder
  d Zylinder *m*
  f cylindre *m*
  r цилиндр *m*

2432 cylinder of revolution
  d Drehzylinder *m*
  f cylindre *m* de révolution
  r цилиндр *m* вращения

2433 cylindrical
  d zylindrisch
  f cylindrique
  r цилиндрический

2434 cylindrical coordinates
  d zylindrische Koordinaten *fpl*;
      Zylinderkoordinaten *fpl*
  f coordonnées *fpl* cylindriques
  r цилиндрические координаты *fpl*

2435 cylindrical coordinate system
  d zylindrisches Koordinatensystem *n*
  f système *m* de coordonnées cylindriques
  r цилиндрическая система *f* координат

2436 cylindrical equal-area projection
  d flächentreue Zylinderprojektion *f*

    f projection *f* cylindrique équivalente;
      projection isocylindrique
    r цилиндрическая равновеликая проекция *f*

   * **cylindrical helix** → **4560**

2437 cylindrical information space
    d zylindrischer Informationsraum *m*
    f espace *m* d'information cylindrique
    r цилиндрическое информационное
      пространство *n*

2438 cylindrical lens
    d Zylinderlinse *f*
    f lentille *f* cylindrique
    r цилиндрическая линза *f*

2439 cylindrical projection
    d Zylinderprojektion *f*, Zylinderabbildung *f*
    f projection *f* cylindrique
    r цилиндрическая проекция *f*

2440 cylindrical surface
    d Zylinderfläche *f*
    f surface *f* cylindrique
    r цилиндрическая поверхность *f*

2441 cylindrical tropism
    d Zylindertropismus *m*
    f tropisme *m* cylindrique
    r цилиндрический тропизм *m*

2442 cylindroid
    d Zylindroid *n*
    f cylindroïde *m*
    r цилиндроид *m*

2443 Cyrus-Beck clipping
    d Cyrus-Beck-Schneiden *n*
    f découpage *m* de Cyrus-Beck
    r отсекание *n* Сайруса-Бека

D

* **2D** → 9956

* **3D** → 9649

2444 dab
  d Farbballen *m*
  f tache *f* de couleur
  r шлепок *m*; мазок *m*; пятно *n* [краски]

2445 dab *v*
  d abklatschen
  f tacher; marquer de taches
  r делать легкие мазки

* **DAC** → 2757

2446 2D acceleration
  d 2D-Beschleunigung *f*
  f accélération *f* 2D
  r 2D ускорение *n*

2447 3D acceleration
  d 3D-Beschleunigung *f*
  f accélération *f* 3D
  r 3D ускорение *n*

2448 3D accelerator
  d 3D-Beschleuniger *m*
  f accélérateur *m* 3D
  r 3D акселератор *m*

* **damage** *v* → 2269

2449 damage; deterioration
  d Schaden *m*; Beschädigung *f*; Verletzen *n*;
     Zerstörung *f*
  f dommage *m*; détérioration *f*; destruction *f*
  r порча *f*; повреждение *n*; разрушение *n*;
     износ *m*

2450 damaged area
  d beschädigte Zone *f*
  f zone *f* détériorée
  r поврежденная зона *f*

* **damping** → 641

2451 dangling edge
  d hängende Randkante *f*
  f arête *f* pendante
  r висячий край *m*; висячее ребро *n*

2452 dangling vertex

  d hängender Knoten[punkt] *m*
  f sommet *m* pendant
  r висячая вершина *f*

2453 3D animated characters
  d animierte 3D-Zeichen *npl*
  f caractères *mpl* animés en 3D
  r трехмерные оживленные символы *mpl*

2454 2D animation
  d 2D-Animation *f*
  f animation *f* 2D
  r 2D анимация *f*

2455 3D architectural design
  d architektonisches 3D-Design *n*
  f conception *f* architecturale en 3D
  r трехмерное архитектурное
     проектирование *n*

2456 3D architectural model
  d architektonisches 3D-Modell *n*
  f modèle *m* architectural 3D
  r трехмерная архитектурная модель *f*

2457 3D area chart
  d 3D-Flächendiagramm *n*
  f diagramme *m* en aires 3D
  r трехмерная площадная диаграмма *f*

* **dark** *adj* → 6437

* **dark area** → 2459

2458 dark color
  d dunkle Farbe *f*
  f couleur *f* sombre
  r мрачный цвет *m*

* **darkening** → 986

* **darkening grade** → 4271

2459 dark zone; dark area
  d dunkler Bereich *m*
  f zone *f* sombre
  r темная зона *f*

2460 2D array
  d 2D-Datenfeld *n*
  f tableau *m* 2D
  r двумерный массив *m*; 2D массив

2461 3D array
  d 3D-Datenfeld *n*
  f tableau *m* 3D
  r трехмерный массив *m*; 3D массив

2462 3D artifacts
  d 3D-Artefakte *npl*

f artéfacts *m* 3D
r 3D артефакты *mpl*; трехмерные ложные изображения *npl*

* **dash → 9245**

2463 dash-dot line; dot-dash line
d strichpunktierte Linie *f*; Strichpunktlinie *f*
f ligne *f* en trait-point; ligne de point-tiret
r штрих-пунктирная линия *f*

2464 dashed line
d Strichlinie *f*
f ligne *f* en trait
r штрих-линия *f*

2465 dashed region
d strichmarkierte Region *f*
f région *f* en trait
r заштрихованный регион *m*

2466 dash marking; stroke marking
d Strichmarkierung *f*
f marquage *m* en trait
r штриховое маркирование *n*

2467 data
d Daten *npl*
f données *fpl*
r данные *npl*

2468 data access
d Datenzugriff *m*
f accès *m* aux données
r выборка *f* данных; доступ *m* к данным

2469 data acquisition; data collection; data capture
d Datenerfassung *f*; Messwerterfassung *f*
f acquisition *f* de données; saisie *f* de données; collection *f* de données
r сбор *m* данных; совокупность *f* данных

* **data analysis → 332**

2470 data array
d Datenfeld *n*
f tableau *m* de données
r массив *m* данных

2471 database
d Datenbasis *f*
f base *f* de données
r база *f* данных

2472 database object
d Datenbasis-Objekt *n*
f objet *m* base de données
r объект *m* типа базы данных

2473 database table
d Datenbasis-Tabelle *f*
f tableau *m* de base de données
r таблица *f* базы данных

* **data capture → 2469**

* **data collection → 2469**

2474 data consolidation
d Datenkonsolidierung *f*
f consolidation *f* de données
r консолидация *f* данных

* **data element → 2484**

2475 data entry; data input
d Dateneingabe *f*
f entrée *f* de données
r ввод *m* данных

2476 data-entry field; entry field
d Dateneingabefeld *n*
f zone *f* de saisie; zone d'entrée
r поле *n* ввода данных

2477 data exchange
d Datenaustausch *m*
f échange *m* de données
r обмен *m* данными

2478 data extrapolation
d Datenextrapolation *f*
f extrapolation *f* de données
r экстраполяция *f* данных

2479 data file
d Datendatei *f*
f fichier *m* de données
r файл *m* данных

2480 data format
d Datenformat *n*
f format *m* de données
r формат *m* данных

2481 data glove; sensor glove; wired glove; cyber glove
d Datenhandschuh *m*
f gant *m* sensitif; gant de données
r электронная перчатка *f*; сенсорная перчатка

2482 data importing
d Datenimport *m*
f importation *f* de données
r внесение *n* данных

* **data input → 2475**

2483 data integrity
  d Datenintegrität *f*
  f intégrité *f* des données
  r целостность *f* данных

2484 data item; data element; datum
  d Dateneinzelheit *f*; Datenelement *n*;
     Datengrundeinheit *f*; Angabe *f*; Datum *n*
  f détail *m* de données; élément *m* de données;
     donnée *f*; datum *m*
  r элемент *m* данных; данная величина *f*;
     данное *n*

2485 data management
  d Datenverwaltung *f*
  f gestion *f* de données
  r управление *n* данными

  * **data out → 2486**

2486 data out[put]
  d Datenausgabe *f*
  f sortie *f* de données; émission *f* de données;
     extraction *f* de données
  r вывод *m* данных

  * **data pooling → 7319**

2487 data reduction
  d Datenreduktion *f*
  f réduction *f* de données
  r преобразование *n* данных

  * **data structure → 5061**

2488 data type
  d Datentyp *m*
  f type *m* de données
  r тип *m* данных

  * **datum → 2484**

2489 datum
  d Datum *n*; Null *f*; Bezugsgröße *f*
  f datum *m*; référence *f* de base
  r начало *n* отсчета; нуль *m*

2490 datum axis
  d Datumsachse *f*
  f axe *m* datum
  r отсчетная ось *f*

2491 datum dimension
  d Datumsdimension *f*
  f cotation *f* de référence
  r исходный размер *m*

2492 datum identifier
  d Datumsidentifikator *m*
  f identificateur *m* de référence

  r идентификатор *m* отсчета

2493 datum-level
  d Datumspegel *m*; Bezugshorizont *m*
  f niveau *m* de référence
  r условный уровень *m*; нуль *m* высоты

  * **datum line → 5466**

  * **datum mark → 7220**

  * **datum plane → 7144**

  * **datum point → 7220**

2494 dazzle *v*
  d blenden
  f diaphragmer
  r диафрагмировать

  * **dazzle → 4224**

2495 2D bitmap
  d 2D-Bitmap *n*
  f bitmap *m* 2D
  r двумерное растровое изображение *n*

2496 2D bitmap special effects
  d 2D-Bitmap-Spezialeffekte *mpl*
  f effets *mpl* de bitmap 2D spéciaux
  r специальные эффекты *mpl* двумерного
     растрового изображения

2497 3D bitmap special effects
  d 3D-Bitmap-Spezialeffekte *mpl*
  f effets *mpl* de bitmap 3D spéciaux
  r специальные эффекты *mpl* трехмерного
     растрового изображения

2498 3D blocks
  d 3D-Blöcke *mpl*
  f blocs *mpl* 3D
  r 3D блоки *mpl*

2499 3D box
  d 3D-Kasten *m*
  f boîtier *m* 3D; boîte *f* 3D
  r 3D ящик *m*

  * **DC → 2661**

2500 2D Cartesian coordinates; XY coordinates
  d 2D-kartesische Koordinaten *fpl*
  f coordonnées *fpl* cartésiennes à deux
     dimensions
  r двумерные декартовы координаты *fpl*

**2501 3D Cartesian coordinates; XYZ
     coordinates**
  d 3D-kartesische Koordinaten *fpl*

f coordonnées *fpl* cartésiennes
tridimensionnelles
r трехмерные декартовы координаты *fpl*

* **3D character** → 3215

2502 3D chart
 d 3D-Diagramm *n*
 f diagramme *m* 3D
 r 3D диаграмма *f*

* **DCL** → 2696

2503 3D code system
 d 3D-Codesystem *n*
 f système *m* de code 3D
 r трехмерная система *f* кодирования

2504 3D computing
 d 3D-Rechnen *n*
 f calcul *m* 3D
 r трехмерное исчисление *n*

2505 2D convex hull; planar convex hull
 d flache konvexe Hülle *f*
 f enveloppe *f* convexe plane
 r плоская выпукла оболочка *f*

2506 3D convex hull
 d 3D-konvexe Hülle *f*
 f enveloppe *f* convexe 3D
 r трехмерная выпуклая оболочка *f*

2507 2D coordinates
 d 2D-Koordinaten *fpl*
 f coordonnées *fpl* en deux dimensions;
 coordonnées 2D
 r 2D координаты *fpl*; двумерные
 координаты

2508 3D coordinates
 d 3D-Koordinaten *fpl*
 f coordonnées *fpl* tridimensionnelles;
 coordonnées 3D
 r 3D координаты *fpl*; трехмерные
 координаты

2509 3D corner
 d 3D-Ecke *f*
 f coin *m* 3D
 r 3D угол *m*

2510 2D cosine pattern
 d 2D-Kosinus-Muster *n*
 f modèle *m* 2D cosinusoïdal
 r двумерный косинусоидальный шаблон *m*

2511 2D cross-correlation
 d 2D-Querkorrelation *f*
 f corrélation *f* croisée à deux dimensions

r двумерное перекрестное соотношение *n*

* **DCS** → 2639, 2662, 2925

2512 3D data capture device
 d 3D Daten-Sammelgerät *n*
 f dispositif *m* de capture de données 3D
 r устройство *n* захвата трехмерных данных

* **DDC** → 2926

2513 3D depth
 d 3D-Tiefe *f*
 f profondeur *f* 3D
 r 3D глубина *f*

2514 3D digital image
 d digitales 3D-Bild *n*
 f image *f* numérique 3D
 r трехмерное цифровое изображение *n*

2515 3D digitizing
 d 3D-Diskretisierung *f*
 f digitalisation *f* 3D
 r 3D дигитализирование *n*

2516 3D digitizing techniques
 d 3D-Diskretisierungstechnik *f*
 f technique *f* de digitalisation 3D
 r метод *m* трехмерного дигитализирования

2517 3D distance
 d 3D-Abstand *m*
 f distance *f* 3D
 r 3D расстояние *n*

2518 3D distortion
 d 3D-Verzerrung *f*
 f distorsion *f* 3D
 r 3D искажение *n*

* **2D distribution** → 979

2519 2D drawing
 d 2D-Zeichnung *f*
 f dessin *m* 2D
 r 2D чертеж *m*; 2D рисунок *m*

2520 3D drawing
 d 3D-Zeichnung *f*
 f dessin *m* 3D
 r 3D чертеж *m*; 3D рисунок *m*

2521 3D dynamic view
 d dynamische 3D-Ansicht *f*
 f vue *f* dynamique 3D
 r трехмерный динамический вид *m*

* **dead angle** → 1015

2522 **dead reckoning; DR**
  d Koppelnavigation f; Besteckrechnung f
  f navigation f à l'estime
  r расчет m траектории движения;
      счисление n пути

2523 **dead reckoning model; DRM**
  d Koppelnavigationsmodell n
  f modèle m de navigation à l'estime
  r модель f счисления пути

2524 **dead reckoning position**
  d Koppelort m; geschätztes Besteck
  f point m estimé [simple]
  r точка f счисления пути

2525 **debugging**
  d Debugging n; Fehlerverfolgung f und
      Fehlerbeseitigung f
  f mise f au point; débugage m; dépannage m
  r отладка f; наладка f; устранение n ошибок;
      устранение неисправностей

2526 **decagon**
  d Dekagon n; Zehneck n
  f décagone m
  r десятиугольник m

2527 **decahedron**
  d Dekaeder n; Zehnflächner m
  f décaèdre m
  r декаэдр m; десятигранник m

2528 **decal**
  d Abziehbild n; Decal n
  f décalcomanie f
  r переводная картинка f

2529 **decal effect; cropped effect**
  d Decal-Effekt m; Abzieheffekt m
  f effet m de décalcomanie
  r эффект m переводной картинки

2530 **decameter**
  d Dekameter n/m
  f décamètre m.
  r декаметр m

2531 **decimal**
  d dezimal
  f décimal
  r десятичный

2532 **decimal dimension**
  d dezimale Dimension f
  f dimension f décimale
  r десятичный размер m

  * **decimeter** → 2533

2533 **decimetre; decimeter; dm**
  d Dezimeter n
  f décimètre m
  r дециметр m

2534 **decision; solution; resolution**
  d Lösung f; Entscheidung f
  f décision f; solution f; résolution f
  r решение n

  * **declarator** → 2625

2535 **decoherence**
  d Entfrittung f
  f décohérence f
  r декогерирование n; отстранение n
      слипания

2536 **decompose** v
  d zerlegen; zergliedern; [auf]spalten
  f décomposer; développer
  r разложить; разлагать

2537 **decomposition**
  d Dekomposition f; Zerlegung f
  f décomposition f
  r разложение n; декомпозиция f

2538 **decompression**
      (of an image)
  d Dekompression f
  f décompression f
  r декомпрессия f

2539 **deconcentration**
  d Dekonzentration f
  f déconcentration f
  r деконцентрация f

2540 **decorrelation**
  d Dekorrelation f
  f décorrélation f
  r декорреляция f

2541 **decremental direction**
  d Dekrementalrichtung f
  f direction f de décrément
  r направление n уменьшения

2542 **2D edge**
  d 2D-Kante f
  f arête f 2D
  r 2D ребро n

2543 **3D edge**
  d 3D-Kante f
  f arête f 3D
  r 3D ребро n

2544 **2D edge detect effect**
  d 2D-Kantenerkennungseffekt m

f effet *m* de détection d'arêtes 2D
r эффект *m* обнаруживания двумерных
ребер

2545 3D editing
d 3D-Bearbeitung *f*
f édition *f* 3D
r 3D редактирование *n*

* **deepness** → 2617

2546 default
d Standard-
f sous-entendu; standard
r подразумеваемый; стандартный

2547 default colors
d Standardfarben *fpl*
f couleurs *fpl* par défaut
r стандартные цвета *mpl*; цвета по
умолчанию

2548 default declaration
d Standarddeklaration *f*;
Standardvereinbarung *f*
f déclaration *f* par défaut; convention *f* standard
r стандартное описание *n*; объявление *n* по
умолчанию

2549 default fill
d Standardfüllung *f*
f remplissage *m* standard; remplissage par
défaut
r стандартное заполнение *n*; закрашивание *n*
по умолчанию

* **default graphics** → 9141

2550 default graphic style
d Standardgrafikstil *m*
f style *m* graphique par défaut
r стандартный графический стиль *m*

2551 default layer
d Standardschicht *f*
f plan *m* par défaut
r стандартный слой *m*; слой по умолчанию

2552 default option
d Standardoption *f*; Option *f* im Normalfall
f option *f* par défaut; option standard
r выбор *m* по умолчанию; стандартный
выбор

2553 default outline
d Standardkontur *f*
f contour *m* par défaut
r стандартный контур *m*

2554 default palette

d Standardpalette *f*
f palette *f* par défaut; palette standard
r стандартная палитра *f*; аппаратная палитра

2555 default printer
d Standarddrucker *m*
f imprimante *f* par défaut
r принтер *m* по умолчанию

2556 default setting
d Standardeinrichtung *f*
f établissement *m* standard; établissement par
défaut
r стандартная установка *f*

2557 defect; fault
d Defekt *m*; Mangel *m*
f défaut *m*; défectuosité *f*; faute *f*; défaillance *f*
r дефект *m*; неисправность *f*

2558 define *v*; **determine** *v*
d definieren; bestimmen
f définir; déterminer
r определять; дефинировать

2559 defined; definite; determined
d definiert; bestimmt; determiniert; erklärt;
festlegend
f défini; déterminé
r определенный; дефинированный

2560 defined blocks
d definierte Blöcke *mpl*
f blocs *mpl* définis
r дефинированные блоки *mpl*

* **definite** → 2559

2561 definition
d Definition *f*
f définition *f*
r определение *n*; дефиниция *f*

* **definition** → 8635

* **definition chart** → 8107

2562 definition of projection
d Abbildungsschärfe *f*
f définition *f* de projection
r четкость *f* проекции

2563 deflected beam
d abgelenkter Strahl *m*
f faisceau *m* dévié
r отклоненный луч *m*

2564 deflected normal vector
d abgelenkter Normalenvektor *m*

f vecteur *m* dévié de la normale
r отклоненный вектор *m* нормали

2565 deflection
   d Deflektion *f*; Ausschlag *m*
   f déflexion *f*
   r отклонение *n*; дефлексия *f*

   * **deflection angle → 377**

2566 deflector
   d Deflektor *m*; Ablenker *m*
   f déflecteur *m*
   r дефлектор *m*

2567 defocused image
   d defokussiertes Bild *n*
   f image *f* défocalisée
   r дефокусированное изображение *n*

2568 defocusing
   d Defokussierung *f*
   f défocalisation *f*
   r дефокусировка *f*; расфокусировка *f*

2569 deformation
   d Deformation *f*; Deformierung *f*
   f déformation *f*
   r деформация *f*

2570 deformation function
   d Deformationsfunktion *f*
   f fonction *f* de déformation
   r функция *f* деформации

2571 deformation lattice
   d Deformationsgitter *n*
   f treillis *m* de déformation
   r деформационная сетка *f*

2572 deformation of image
   d Bildverzerrung *f*; Bilddeformation *f*
   f déformation *f* de l'image
   r искажение *n* изображения

   * **deform *v* continuously to a point → 8660**

2573 defragmentation
   d Defragmentation *f*
   f defragmentation *f*
   r дефрагментирование *n*

2574 degeneracy; degeneration
   d Ausartung *f*; Entartung *f*
   f dégénérescence *f*; dégénération *f*
   r вырождение *n*

   * **degenerate → 8743**

2575 degenerate circle
   d ausgearteter Kreis *m*

f cercle *m* dégénéré
r вырожденный круг *m*; вырожденная окружность *f*

   * **degenerate conic → 2576**

2576 degenerate conic [section]; singular conic [section]
   d ausgearteter Kegelschnitt *m*; singulärer Kegelschnitt; entarteter Kegelschnitt
   f conique *f* dégénérée; conique singulière
   r вырожденное коническое сечение *n*

2577 degenerate mapping
   d ausgeartete Abbildung *f*
   f application *f* dégénérée
   r вырожденное отображение *n*

   * **degeneration → 2574**

2578 degradation
   d Degradation *f*
   f dégradation *f*
   r ухудшение *n*; снижение *n*; деградация *f*

   * **degree → 4268**

2579 degree; order
   d Grad *m*; Potenz *f*
   f degré *m*; ordre *m*
   r порядок *m*; степень *f*

2580 degree of a curve; order of a curve
   d Grad *m* einer Kurve
   f degré *m* d'une courbe; ordre *m* d'une courbe
   r порядок *m* кривой

2581 degree of approximation
   d Annäherungsgrad *m*; Approximationsgrad *m*
   f degré *m* d'approximation
   r степень *f* аппроксимации; степень приближения

2582 degree of a surface; order of a surface
   d Grad *m* einer Fläche
   f ordre *m* d'une surface
   r порядок *m* поверхности

2583 degree of attenuation
   d Dämpfungsgrad *m*
   f taux *m* d'atténuation
   r степень *f* ослабления

2584 degree of freedom
   d Freiheitsgrad *m*
   f degré *m* de liberté
   r степень *f* свободы

2585 degree of reflection
   d Reflexionsgrad *m*

f degré *m* de réflexion
r степень *f* отражения

2586 degree sign
(°)
d Gradzeichen *n*
f signe *m* de degré
r символ *m* градуса

* **dejagging** → 444

2587 Delaunay area
d Delaunay-Zone *f*
f zone *f* de Delaunay
r зона *f* Делоне

2588 Delaunay triangle
d Delaunay-Dreieck *n*
f triangle *m* de Delaunay
r треугольник *m* Делоне

2589 Delaunay triangulation
d Delaunay-Triangulation *f*
f triangulation *f* de Delaunay
r триангуляция *f* Делоне

2590 delay; lag[ging]
d Verzögerung *f*; Nacheilung *f*
f retard[ement] *m*; délai *m*
r запаздывание *n*; замедление *n*; задержка *f*

* **delete** *v* → 3356

2591 delete key; Del key
d Löschtaste *f*
f touche *f* d'effacement
r клавиша *f* стирания; клавиша Del

2592 delete option
d Löschoption *f*
f option *f* d'effacement
r опция *f* стирания

2593 delete *v* **page**
d Seite löschen
f effacer une page
r стирать страницу

* **deleting** → 2594

* **deletion** → 3519

2594 deletion; deleting
d Streichen *n*
f écartement *m*; effacement *m*
r вычеркивание *n*; исключение *n*; удаление *n*; стирание *n*

2595 delimiter; limiter
d Begrenzer *m*

f [dé]limiteur *m*; séparateur *m*
r разделитель *m*; ограничитель *m*

* **delimiter sign** → 8538

2596 delink *v*
d entketten
f déchaîner; détacher
r разрывать; разъединять

* **Del key** → 2591

2597 delta frame
(containing only the data that has actually changed since the last frame)
d Delta-Bild *n*
f cadre *m* delta
r дельта-кадр *m*

2598 deltoid; kite
(convex quadrilateral with two distinct pairs of equal adjacent sides)
d Deltoid *m*
f deltoïde *m*
r дельтоид *m*

* **DEM** → 2771

* **demand** → 8083, 8084

2599 3D emboss effect; 3D relief effect
d 3D-Reliefeffekt *m*
f effet *m* de relief 3D
r эффект *m* 3D рельефа

* **demo** → 2602

2600 demo mode
d Demomodus *m*
f mode *m* démo
r демо-режим *m*

2601 demonstration
d Demonstration *f*
f démonstration *f*
r демонстрация *f*

* **demo package** → 2602

2602 demosoftware; demoware; demo package; demo
d Demonstrationspaket *n*
f logiciel *m* de démonstration; démo *m*
r демонстрационный пакет *m*; демо

* **demoware** → 2602

2603 denote *v*; **notch** *v*
d kennzeichnen; bezeichnen
f désigner; signifier; noter
r означать; обозначать

2604 dense
d dicht
f dense
r плотный; компактный

2605 densitometer
d Densitometer *n*; Dichtemesser *m*
f densitomètre *m*
r измеритель *m* плотности; денситометр *m*

2606 densitometer scale
d Dichtemesserskala *f*
f échelle *f* de densitomètre; échelle densimétrique
r шкала *f* денситометра

2607 densitometric curve; density curve
d Schwärzungskurve *f*
f courbe *f* densimétrique; courbe de densité; courbe de noircissement
r кривая *f* зачернения

2608 densitometry
d Densitometrie *f*; Dichtemessung *f*
f densimétrie *f*
r денситометрия *f*

2609 density
d Dichte *f*; Dichtheit *f*; Dichtigkeit *f*
f densité *f*
r плотность *f*; густота *f*

* **density curve** → 2607

2610 density of points
d Punktdichte *f*
f densité *f* des points
r плотность *f* точек

2611 density range; contrast range
d Dichteumfang *m*; Densitätsumfang *m*; Kontrastumfang *m*
f amplitude *f* de densité; amplitude de noircissement; amplitude de contraste; écart *m* de densité
r диапазон *m* [оптических] плотностей

2612 dents
(the opposites of bumps in texture)
d Beulen *fpl*
f bosselures *fpl*
r вдавленные места *npl*; взбоины *fpl*

2613 depend *v*
d abhängen
f dépendre
r зависеть

2614 dependence
d Abhängigkeit *f*

f dépendance *f*
r зависимость *f*

2615 dependent symbols
d abhängige Zeichen *npl*
f symboles *mpl* dépendants
r зависимые символы *mpl*

2616 depot
d Ablage *f*
f dépôt *m*
r склад *m*; устройство *n* хранения

* **depression** → 5722

* **depression angle** → 376

2617 depth; deepness
d Tiefe *f*
f profondeur *f*
r глубина *f*

* **depth buffer** → 10509

2618 depth of focus
d Schärfentiefe *f*
f profondeur *f* de foyer
r глубина *f* резкости (изображения)

2619 derived map
d abgeleitete Karte *f*
f carte *f* dérivée
r производная карта *f*; извлеченная карта

2620 desaturation
d Entsättigung *f*
f désaturation *f*
r ненасыщеность *f*

2621 descendant node
d absteigender Knoten *m*
f nœud *m* descendant
r узел-потомок *m*

2622 descender
(portion of a lowercase letter falling below its baseline)
d Unterlänge *f*
f jambage *m*
r нижний выносной элемент *m*; свисающий элемент

2623 description
d Deskription *f*; Beschreibung *f*
f description *f*
r описание *n*; дескрипция *f*

2624 descriptive geometry
d deskriptive Geometrie *f*; darstellende Geometrie

f géométrie *f* descriptive
r дескриптивная геометрия *f*

2625 descriptor; declarator
d Deskriptor *m*; Vereinbarungszeichen *n*
f descripteur *m*
r дескриптор *m*; описатель *m*

2626 deselect *v*
d abwählen
f désélectionner
r отменять выбор; снимать выделение (на экране)

* **deselecting** → 2627

2627 deselection; deselecting
d Abwählung *f*
f désélection *f*
r отмена *f* отбора

* **design** → 2631, 3132

* **design** *v* → 6742

2628 design; project; plan
d Entwurf *m*; Projekt *m*; Design *n*; Plan *m*; Bauplan *m*
f projet *m*; plan *m*
r проект *m*; дизайн *m*; план *m*

2629 design *v*; **project** *v*
d entwerfen; anlegen; konstruieren
f concevoir; projeter
r проектировать

2630 designation
d Bestimmung *f*
f désignation *f*
r назначение *n*; предназначение *n*

* **designation** → 6311

* **designer** → 3162

2631 design[ing]
d Projektierung *f*
f conception *f*; établissement *m* d'un projet
r проектирование *n*

* **design limits** → 3151

2632 design software
d Konstruktionssoftware *f*
f logiciel *m* de conception
r программное обеспечение *n* для проектирования

2633 design tool
d Designhilfsmittel *n*

f outil *m* de conception
r инструмент *m* проектирования

2634 design vector
(interpolation between states of data structure, especially for exploration of intervening states in realtime)
d Design-Vektor *m*
f vecteur *m* de dessin
r вектор *m* проекта; вектор проектирования; тестовый вектор

2635 deskew *v*
d entzerren
f écarter les déformations
r выравнивать; исправлять [деформации]

2636 deskew command
d Entzerrungsbefehl *m*
f commande *f* d'écartement de déformations
r команда *f* исправления деформаций

2637 desktop *adj*
d Desktop-; Tisch-
f tabulaire; bureautique; à plat
r настольный

2638 desktop
d Desktop *n*
f appareil *m* du bureau
r рабочий стол *m* (метафорическое представление на экране)

2639 desktop color separation; DCS
d Desktop-Farbeinteilung *f*
f séparation *f* de couleurs bureautique
r настольное разделение *n* цветов

2640 desktop device
d Desktop-Gerät *n*
f dispositif *m* bureautique
r настольное устройство *n*

2641 desktop scanner
d Tischabtaster *m*; Tischscanner *m*; Desktopscanner *m*
f scanner *m* tabulaire; scanner de table
r настольный сканер *m*

2642 desktop system
d Tischsystem *n*
f système *m* bureautique
r настольная система *f*

* **desmoothing** → 259

2643 destination; butt; goal
d Verwendungszweck *m*; Ziel *n*; Goal *n*
f destination *f*; but *m*; objectif *m*
r назначение *n*; место *n* назначения; цель *f*; предназначение *n*

2644 destination application
    d Zielanwendung *f*
    f application *f* de destination
    r целевое приложение *n*

2645 destination location
    d Zielstellung *f*
    f location *f* de destination
    r позиция *f* назначения

    * **destroy** *v* → **2269**

    * **detach** *v* → **2892**

2646 detachment
    d Trennung *f*; Abtrennung *f*
    f détachement *m*
    r разъединение *n*; разделение *n*

2647 detach option
    d Trennungsoption *f*
    f option *f* de détachement
    r опция *f* разъединения

2648 detail
    d Detail *n*; Einzelheit *f*
    f détail *m*
    r деталь *f*; подробность *f*

2649 detail drawing
    d Detailzeichnung *f*; Teilzeichnung *f*
    f esquisse *f* détaillée; croquis *m* détaillé
    r подробная схема *f*

2650 detail management algorithm
    d Algorithmus *m* der Detailbearbeitung
    f algorithme *m* de traitement de détails
    r алгоритм *m* обработки деталей

2651 detail textures
    d detaillierte Texturen *fpl*
    f textures *fpl* détaillées
    r подробные текстуры *fpl*

2652 detectable element; detectable segment
    d erkennbares Element *n*; erkennbares
        Segment *n*
    f élément *m* détectable; segment *m* détectable
    r обнаруживаемый элемент *m*

    * **detectable segment** → **2652**

2653 detect *v* edges
    d Kante erkennen
    f détecter les arêtes
    r обнаруживать ребра

2654 detection of collinear image points
    d Erkennung *f* kollinearer Bildpunkte
    f détection *f* de points colinéaires d'image
    r обнаруживание *n* коллинеарных точек
        изображения

    * **deterioration** → **2449**

    * **determine** *v* → **2558**

    * **determined** → **2559**

2655 developable tangent surface
    d abwickelbare Tangentenfläche *f*
    f surface *f* tangentielle développable
    r развертывающаяся касательная
        поверхность *f*

2656 development; extension
    d Entwicklung *f*; Abwicklung *f*
    f développement *m*; élaboration *f*
    r развитие *n*; разложение *n*; разработка *f*;
        развертка *f*

2657 deviation
    d Ablenkung *f*; Abweichung *f*; Deviation *f*
    f déviation *f*
    r девиация *f*; отклонение *n*

2658 deviation tolerance
    d Ablenkungstoleranz *f*
    f tolérance *f* de déviation
    r допуск *m* отклонения

2659 device
    d Gerät *n*
    f dispositif *m*; appareil *m*
    r устройство *n*

2660 device coordinate buffer
    d Gerätekoordinatenspeicher *m*
    f tampon *m* de coordonnées d'appareil
    r буфер *m* координат устройства

2661 device coordinates; DC
    d Gerätekoordinaten *fpl*
    f coordonnées *fpl* d'appareil
    r координаты *fpl* устройства

2662 device coordinate system; DCS
    d Gerätekoordinatensystem *n*
    f système *m* de coordonnées d'appareil
    r координатная система *f* устройства

2663 device driver
    d Gerätetreiber *m*
    f driver *m* de dispositif; pilote *m* de dispositif
    r драйвер *m* устройства

2664 device-independent bitmap
    d geräteunabhängiges Bitmap *n*
    f bitmap *m* indépendant de dispositif
    r растровое отображение *n*, независимое от
        устройства

2665 **device space**
d Gerätekoordinatenraum *m*
f espace *m* d'appareil; espace périphérique
r пространство *n* устройства

2666 **dextrorse; dextrorsum**
d rechtsgängig; rechtsgewunden; rechtswendig
f dextrorsum; de la gauche vers la droite; droit
r слева направо; завитый вправо; правый (о винтовой линии); с правой резьбой

2667 **dextrorse curve; dextrorsum curve; right-handed curve**
d rechtsgewundene Kurve *f*; rechtsgängige Kurve
f courbe *f* dextrorsum
r кривая *f* правого вращения

2668 **dextrorse helix; right-hand[ed] helix**
d rechtsgängige Schraubenlinie *f*
f hélice *f* rétrograde; hélice dextrorsum
r винтовая линия *f* правого вращения; завитая вправо винтовая линия

2669 **dextrorse screw; right[-handed] screw**
d Rechtsschraube *f*
f vis *f* dextrorsum; vis à droite
r правый винт *m*

* **dextrorsum → 2666**

* **dextrorsum curve → 2667**

2670 **3D face**
d 3D-Fläche *f*
f face *f* 3D
r 3D грань *f*

2671 **3D face modeling**
d 3D-Flächenmodellierung *f*
f modelage *m* de face 3D
r моделирование *n* 3D грани

2672 **2D figure; 2D shape; plane figure**
d 2D-Figur *f*
f figure *f* 2D; figure plane
r 2D фигура *f*; планарная фигура

* **3D figure → 3198**

2673 **2D filter**
d 2D-Filter *m*
f filtre *m* 2D
r 2D фильтр *m*

2674 **3D filter**
d 3D-Filter *m*
f filtre *m* 3D
r 3D фильтр *m*

2675 **2D geometry**
d 2D-Geometrie *f*
f géométrie *f* 2D
r 2D геометрия *f*

2676 **3D geometry**
d 3D-Geometrie *f*
f géométrie *f* 3D
r 3D геометрия *f*

2677 **3D geometry processor**
d 3D-Geometrie-Prozessor *m*
f processeur *m* de géométrie 3D
r процессор *m* 3D геометрии

2678 **3D glasses**
d 3D-Brille *f*
f lunettes *fpl* 3D
r 3D очки *npl*

* **3D graphic card → 2682**

2679 **3D graphics**
d dreidimensionale Grafik *f*; 3D-Grafik *f*
f infographie *f* tridimensionnelle; graphique *m* à trois dimensions; graphique 3D
r 3D графика *f*

2680 **3D graphics animation**
d 3D-Grafik-Animation *f*
f animation *f* de graphique 3D
r анимация *f* 3D графики

2681 **3D graphics benchmark program**
d 3D-Grafikbenchmark-Programm *n*
f test *m* d'évaluation de graphique 3D; programme *m* d'évaluation de graphique 3D
r эталонный тест *m* 3D графики

2682 **3D graphic[s] card**
d 3D-Grafikkarte *f*
f carte *f* graphique 3D
r карта *f* 3D графики

2683 **3D hardware**
d 3D-Hardware *f*
f matériel *m* 3D
r аппаратные средства *npl* трехмерной графики

2684 **3D head motion**
d 3D-Kopf-Bewegung *f*
f mouvement *m* de tête 3D
r трехмерное движение *n* головы

2685 **3D homogeneous clipping**
d homogenes 3D-Schneiden *n*
f découpage *m* 3D homogène
r трехмерное однородное отсекание *n*

2686 **3D homogeneous coordinates**
  d homogene 3D-Koordinaten *fpl*
  f coordonnées *fpl* 3D homogènes
  r трехмерные гомогенные координаты *fpl*

  * **diagonal** → 2690

2687 **diagonal** *adj*
  d diagonal
  f diagonal
  r диагональный

2688 **diagonal artifacts**
  d diagonale Artefakte *npl*
  f artéfacts *mpl* diagonaux
  r диагональные артефакты *mpl*

2689 **diagonal border**
  d diagonale Kante *f*
  f bordure *f* diagonale
  r диагональная кайма *f*

2690 **diagonal [line]**
  d Diagonale *f*
  f diagonale *f*
  r диагональ *f*

2691 **diagonal of the face**
  d Flächendiagonale *f*
  f diagonale *f* de la face
  r диагональ *f* грани

2692 **diagonal point**
  d Diagonalpunkt *m*
  f point *m* diagonal
  r диагональная точка *f*

2693 **diagonal view**
  d Schrägansicht *f*
  f vue *f* diagonale
  r диагональное представление *n*;
      диагональный вид *m*

  * **diagram** → 1439

  * **diagrammatic** → 2694

2694 **diagrammatic[al]**
  d Diagramm-; schematisch
  f schématique
  r диаграммный

  * **diagrammatic representation** → 4355

  * **dialog** → 2699

2695 **dialog box**
  d Dialogbox *f*; Dialogfeld *n*
  f boîte *f* de dialogue; case-dialogue *f*
  r диалоговый ящик *m*

2696 **dialog control language; DCL**
  d Sprache *f* der Dialogregelung
  f langage *m* de réglage de dialogue
  r диалоговый язык *m* управления

2697 **dialog field**
  d Dialogfeld *n*
  f champ *m* de dialogue
  r диалоговое поле *n*

2698 **dialog mode; conversational mode;
      interactive mode**
  d Dialogbetrieb *m*; Dialogarbeitsweise *f*
  f mode *m* à dialogue; mode interactif
  r диалоговый режим *m*; интерактивный
      режим

2699 **dialog[ue]**
  d Dialog *m*
  f dialogue *m*
  r диалог *m*

2700 **diameter**
  d Durchmesser *m*; Diameter *n/m*
  f diamètre *m*
  r диаметр *m*

2701 **diameter dimensions**
  d Diameter-Dimensionen *fpl*
  f dimensions *fpl* diamétraux
  r диаметральные измерения *npl*

  * **diameter of a ball** → 2707

2702 **diameter of a circle; circle diameter;
      diameter of a circumference**
  d Kreisdurchmesser *m*; Durchmesser *m* eines
      Kreises
  f diamètre *m* d'un cercle
  r диаметр *m* круга; диаметр окружности

  * **diameter of a circumference** → 2702

  * **diameter of a conic** → 2703

2703 **diameter of a conic [section]**
  d Durchmesser *m* eines Kegelschnitts
  f diamètre *m* d'une conique; diamètre d'une
      courbe du second degré
  r диаметр *m* кривой второго порядка;
      диаметр линии второго порядка

2704 **diameter of a hyperbola**
  d Durchmesser *m* einer Hyperbel
  f diamètre *m* d'une hyperbole
  r диаметр *m* гиперболы

2705 **diameter of an ellipse**
  d Durchmesser *m* einer Ellipse

 f diamètre *m* d'une ellipse
 r диаметр *m* эллипса

2706 diameter of a parabola
 d Durchmesser *m* einer Parabel
 f diamètre *m* d'une parabole
 r диаметр *m* параболы

2707 diameter of a sphere; diameter of a ball
 d Durchmesser *m* einer Kugel
 f diamètre *m* d'une sphère; diamètre d'une boule
 r диаметр *m* сферы; диаметр шара

2708 diameter symbol
 d Diameter-Symbol *n*
 f symbole *m* de diamètre
 r символ *m* диаметра

2709 diametral plane
 d Diametralebene *f*; Durchmesserebene *f*
 f plan *m* diamétral
 r диаметральная плоскость *f*

2710 diametrically
 d diametral
 f diamétralement
 r диаметрально

 * **diametrically opposed** → 2711

2711 diametrically opposite; diametrically opposed; antipodal
 d antipodär
 f diamétralement opposé; antipodal
 r диаметрально противоположный; антиподальный

2712 diametrically opposite point; antipodal point
 d diametraler Gegenpunkt *m*; Diametralpunkt *m*
 f point *m* diamétralement opposé
 r диаметрально противоположная точка *f*

2713 diamond; rhomb[us]; lozenge
 d Rhombus *m*; Raute *f*
 f losange *m*; rhombe *m*
 r ромб *m*

2714 diamond-shaped
 d rhomboidal; rautenförmig; rhombisch
 f rhomboïdal; en losange
 r ромбовидный

2715 diamond-shaped artifacts
 d rhomboidale Artefakte *npl*
 f artéfacts *mpl* en losange; artéfacts rhomboïdaux
 r ромбовидные артефакты *mpl*

2716 diamond-shaped dot
 d rhomboidaler Punkt *m*
 f point *m* rhomboïdal
 r ромбовидная точка *f*

2717 diaphragm; cover ring; aperture stop; blind
 d Blende *f*; Membrane *f*
 f diaphragme *m*
 r диафрагма *f*

2718 diaphragm aperture
 d Blendenöffnung *f*
 f ouverture *f* du diaphragme
 r открытие *n* диафрагмы

 * **diapositive** → 8781

2719 dichroic
 d dichroisch; zweifarbig
 f dichroïque
 r дихроичный

2720 dichroic filter
 d dichroischer Filter *m*
 f filtre *m* dichroïque
 r дихроичный фильтр *m*

2721 dichroic mirror
 d dichroischer Spiegel *m*
 f miroir *m* dichroïque
 r дихроичное зеркало *n*

 * **dichroism** → 2722

 * **dichromatic** → 903

2722 dichro[mat]ism; bichromy
 d Dichroismus *m*; Zweifarbigkeit *f*
 f dichroïsme *m*; pléochroïsme *m*; bichromie *f*
 r дихроизм *m*; плеохроизм *m*; двухцветность *f*

 * **didot** → 2723

2723 didot [point]; French point
 (=1,07 US points or 0,376 mm)
 d Didot-Punkt *m*
 f point *m* didot; point typographique; point français
 r пункт *m* Дидо; французский пункт; типографическая точка *f*

2724 difference
 d Differenz *f*
 f différence *f*
 r разность *f*

2725 difference in shade
 d Tönungsunterschied *m*

f différence *f* de tonalité
r разность *f* оттенка

2726 differential geometry
  d Differentialgeometrie *f*
  f géométrie *f* différentielle
  r дифференциальная геометрия *f*

2727 differential image
  d Differentialbild *n*
  f image *f* différentielle
  r дифференциальное изображение *n*

2728 differential linearity
  d Differentiallinearität *f*
  f linéarité *f* différentielle
  r дифференциальная линейность *f*

2729 differential non-linearity
  d differentiale Nichtlinearität *f*
  f non-linéarité *f* différentielle
  r дифференциальная нелинейность *f*

2730 differential scaling
  d Differentialskalierung *f*
  f mise *f* à l'échelle différentielle
  r дифференциальное масштабирование *n*

2731 diffraction
  d Diffraktion *f*; Beugung *f*
  f diffraction *f*
  r дифракция *f*

2732 diffraction angle
  d Beugungswinkel *m*
  f angle *m* de diffraction
  r угол *m* дифракции

2733 diffraction filter
  d Diffraktionsfilter *m*
  f filtre *m* de diffraction
  r дифракционный фильтр *m*

2734 diffraction grating
  d Beugungsgitter *n*; optischer Raster *m*;
     fotoelektrisches Strichgitter *n*
  f réseau *m* de diffraction
  r дифракционная решетка *f*

2735 diffraction pattern
  d Beugungsmuster *n*; Diffraktionsbild *n*
  f figure *f* de diffraction
  r дифракционная картина *f*

2736 diffraction region
  d Beugungsbereich *m*
  f zone *f* de diffraction
  r дифракционная зона *f*

2737 diffraction spectrum

d Beugungsspektrum *n*
  f spectre *m* de diffraction
  r дифракционный спектр *m*

2738 diffuse *v*; **scatter** *v*
  d diffundieren; streuen; zerstreuen; ausstreuen
  f diffuser; disséminer; disperser
  r рассеивать; разбрасывать

2739 diffuse color
  d diffuse Farbe *f*
  f couleur *f* diffuse
  r диффузный цвет *m*

2740 diffuse-cutting filter; diffusing filter
  d Diffusionsfilter *m*
  f filtre *m* de diffusion
  r фильтр *m* рассеивания

2741 diffused light; diffuse light; scattered light
  d diffuses Licht *n*; gestreutes Licht
  f lumière *f* diffuse
  r рассеянный свет *m*; диффузный свет

2742 diffuse illumination; diffuse lighting
  d diffuse Beleuchtung *f*
  f illumination *f* diffuse; éclairage *m* diffus
  r диффузная иллюминация *f*; диффузное
     освещение *n*

*   diffuse light → 2741

*   diffuse lighting → 2742

2743 diffuse lighting function
  d diffuse Beleuchtungsfunktion *f*
  f fonction *f* d'éclairage diffus
  r функция *f* диффузной иллюминации

2744 diffuse lighting table
  d diffuse Beleuchtungstafel *f*
  f table *f* d'éclairage diffus
  r таблица *f* диффузной иллюминации

*   diffusely reflected light → 2747

2745 diffuser
  d Diffusor *m*
  f diffuseur *m*
  r распылитель *m*; диффузор *m*

2746 diffuse reflection
  d diffuse Reflexion *f*
  f réflexion *f* diffuse
  r диффузное отражение *n*; рассеянное
     отражение

**2747 diffuse reflective light; diffusely reflected
     light**
  d diffuses Reflexlicht *n*

f lumière *f* réfléchissante diffuse
r диффузный рефлективный свет *m*

2748 diffuse shading
  d diffuse Schattierung *f*
  f ombrage *m* diffuse
  r диффузное оттенение *n*

2749 diffusing cone
  (of spotlight)
  d Diffundierungskegel *m*
  f pyramide *f* diffusante
  r рассеивающий конус *m*

  * **diffusing filter** → 2740

2750 diffusing screen
  d Diffundierungsbildschirm *m*; Streuschirm *m*;
     Bildschirm *m* von diffusem Licht
  f écran *m* de dispersion
  r диффузный экран *m*

2751 diffusion
  d Diffusion *f*
  f diffusion *f*
  r диффузия *f*; рассеяние *n*

2752 diffusion coefficient; scattering coefficient
  d Diffusionskoeffizient *m*;
     Streu[ungs]koeffizient *m*;
     Streu[ungs]faktor *m*
  f coefficient *m* de diffusion
  r коэффициент *m* диффузии; коэффициент
     рассеяния

2753 diffusion coefficient of the surface
  d Diffusionskoeffizient *m* der Fläche
  f coefficient *m* de diffusion de la surface
  r диффузный коэффициент *m* поверхности

2754 diffusion length
  d Diffusionslänge *f*
  f longueur *f* de diffusion
  r диффузионная длина *f*

2755 diffusion zone
  d Diffusionszone *f*
  f zone *f* de diffusion; zone diffusée
  r диффузионная зона *f*

2756 digit; chiffre; cipher; figure
  d Ziffer *f*
  f chiffre *m*; digit *m*
  r цифра *f*

  * **digital** → 6329

2757 digital-analog converter; DAC
  d Digital-Analog-Konverter *m*; D/A-
     Umwandler; DAC

f convertisseur *m* numérique-analogique
r цифрово-аналоговый преобразователь *m*;
   ЦАП

2758 digital animation
  d Digitalanimation *f*
  f animation *f* numérique
  r цифровая анимация *f*

2759 digital camera
  d Digitalkamera *f*
  f caméra *f* numérique
  r цифровая камера *f*

2760 digital cinematography
  d digitale Kinematografie *f*
  f cinématographie *f* numérique
  r цифровая кинематография *f*

2761 digital circuit
  d digitale Schaltung *f*
  f circuit *m* numérique
  r цифровая схема *f*

2762 digital color
  d Digitalfarbe *f*
  f couleur *f* numérique
  r цифровой цвет *m*

2763 digital color camera
  d Digitalfarbkamera *f*
  f caméra *m* numérique en couleurs
  r цифровая цветная камера *f*

2764 digital color copying
  d digitales Farbkopieren *n*
  f copiage *m* numérique en couleurs
  r цифровое цветное копирование *n*

2765 digital color image
  d Digitalfarbbild *n*
  f image *f* numérique en couleurs
  r цифровое цветовое изображение *n*

2766 digital copier
  d digitaler Farbkopierer *m*
  f copieur *m* numérique
  r цифровое копировальное устройство *n*

2767 digital data; numerical data
  d digitale Daten *npl*
  f données *fpl* digitaux; données numériques
  r цифровые данные *npl*

2768 digital description of the model
  d digitale Beschreibung *f* des Modells
  f description *f* numérique de la maquette
  r цифровое описание *n* модели

2769 digital design
  d digitaler Entwurf *m*

f projet *m* digital
r цифровое проектирование *n*

2770 **digital display; numeric[al] display; all-digital display**
d digitales Display *n*; numerisches Display; Digitalmonitor *m*
f écran *m* digital; afficheur *m* numérique
r цифровой дисплей *m*; цифровой экран *m*

2771 **digital elevation model; DEM**
d digitales Höhenlinienmodell *n*
f modèle *m* altimétrique digital; modèle d'élévation numérique
r цифровая модель *f* высотных точек

2772 **digital filter**
d Digitalfilter *m*
f filtre *m* numérique
r цифровой фильтр *m*

2773 **digital filtering**
d digitale Filtrierung *f*
f filtrage *m* numérique
r цифровое фильтрирование *n*

2774 **digital filter simulation**
d Simulierung *f* des Digitalfilters
f simulation *f* de filtre numérique
r симулирование *n* цифрового фильтра

2775 **digital focus**
d Digitalfokus *m*
f foyer *m* numérique
r цифровой фокус *m*

*   **digital format** → 6337

2776 **digital halftoning; digital rasterization**
d digitale Halbtönung *f*
f création *f* de grisé numérique
r цифровое формирование *n* полутонового изображения

2777 **digital image; numeric[al] image**
d digitales Bild *n*; digitales Abbild *n*
f image *f* numérique
r цифровое изображение *n*

2778 **digital image copyright**
d Digitalbild-Copyright *n*
f copyright *m* d'image numérique
r авторское право *n* цифрового изображения; копирайт *m* цифрового изображения

2779 **digital image processing**
d digitale Bildverarbeitung *f*
f traitement *m* d'images numériques
r обработка *f* цифровых изображений

2780 **digital image synthesis**
d Digitalbild-Synthese *f*
f synthèse *f* d'image numérique
r синтез *m* цифрового изображения

2781 **digital imaging**
d digitale Abbildung *f*
f imagination *f* numérique; technique *f* de numérisation d'images
r цифровое изображение *n*

*   **digitalization** → 2901

2782 **digit[al]ize** *v*
d digitalisieren
f numériser; digitaliser
r дигитализировать; преобразовывать в цифровую форму

2783 **digital model**
d numerisches Modell *n*
f modèle *m* numérique; modèle digital
r цифровая модель *f*; дигитальная модель

2784 **digital photography; digitized photography**
d numerisches Foto *n*; digitalisierte Fotografie *f*; digitales Foto
f photo[graphie] *f* numérique; photo[graphie] numérisée
r цифровой снимок *m*; дискретизированная фотография *f*; оцифрованной снимок

2785 **digital photo memory**
d numerischer Fotospeicher *m*
f photothèque *m* numérique
r цифровая фотооптическая память *f*

2786 **digital photomontage**
d numerische Fotomontage *f*
f photomontage *m* numérique
r цифровой фотомонтаж *m*

2787 **digital plotter**
d numerischer Kurvenschreiber *m*
f traceur *m* numérique
r цифровой графопостроитель *m*

2788 **digital probe**
d digitale Probe *f*
f sonde *f* numérique
r цифровой зонд *m*

*   **digital rasterization** → 2776

2789 **digital space**
d digitaler Raum *m*
f espace *m* numérique
r цифровое пространство *n*

2790 digital special effects
  d digitale Specialeffekte *mpl*
  f effets *mpl* spéciaux numériques
  r цифровые специальные эффекты *mpl*

2791 digital surface
  d Digitalfläche *f*
  f surface *f* numérique
  r цифровая поверхность *f*

2792 digital template
  d Digitalmaske *f*
  f masque *f* numérique
  r цифровая маска *f*

2793 digital terrain model
  d digitales Geländemodell *n*
  f modèle *m* du terrain nimérique
  r цифровая модель *f* местности

2794 digital topography
  d digitale Topografie *f*
  f topographie *f* numérique
  r цифровая топография *f*

2795 digital video
  d numerisches Video *n*; Digitalvideo *n*
  f vidéo *m* numérique
  r цифровое видео *n*

2796 digital video compression
  d Digitalvideo-Kompression *f*
  f compression *f* de vidéo numérique
  r уплотнение *n* цифрового видео

2797 digital watermark; digmark
  d digitales Wasserzeichen *n*
  f filigrane *m* numérique; filigrane électronique
  r цифровой водяной знак *m*

2798 digital X-ray imaging
  d digitale Röntgenstrahlen-Abbildung *f*
  f imagination *f* numérique de rayons X
  r цифровое отображение *n* X-лучей

2799 digital zoom
  d digitales Zoomen *n*
  f zoom *m* numérique
  r цифровое динамическое масштабирование *n*

  * **digitization** → 2901

  * **digitize** → 2782

2800 digitized device; digitizer; quantifier
  d Digitalgeber *m*; Digitalisierer *m*; Digitizer *m*; digitalisierendes Gerät *n*
  f dispositif *m* digitalisé; digitaliseur *m*; capteur *m* digital; numériseur *m*
  r устройство *n* оцифровки; дигитайзер *m*

2801 digitized image
  d digitalisiertes Bild *n*
  f image *f* numérisée
  r оцифрованное изображение *n*; изображение, преобразованное в цифровую форму

  * **digitized photography** → 2784

  * **digitizer** → 2800

2802 digitizer configuration
  d Digitizer-Konfiguration *f*
  f configuration *f* de digitaliseur
  r конфигурация *f* дигитайзера

2803 digitizer driver
  d Digitizer-Treiber *m*
  f driver *m* de digitaliseur
  r драйвер *m* дигитайзера

2804 digitizer tablet; digitizing tablet; tablet
  d Tablett *n*; Täfelchen *n*
  f tablette *f* [à numériser]; planchette *f*
  r планшет *m*; блокнот *m*

2805 digitizer template
  d Digitalisierer-Schablone *f*
  f modèle *m* de numériseur
  r шаблон *m* дигитайзера

  * **digitizing** → 2901

  * **digitizing tablet** → 2804

  * **digmark** → 2797

2806 digmark line
  d Linie *f* des digitalen Wasserzeichens
  f ligne *f* de filigrane numérique
  r линия *f* цифрового водяного знака

2807 digmark placement
  d Position *f* des digitalen Wasserzeichens
  f position *f* de filigrane numérique
  r местоположение *n* цифрового водяного знака

2808 digmark text
  d Text *m* des digitalen Wasserzeichens
  f texte *m* de filigrane numérique
  r текст *m* цифрового водяного знака

2809 digraph
  d Digraph *m*
  f digramme *m*
  r диграф *m*; диграмма *f*; составная буква *f*

2810 dihedral
  d diedral; zweiflächig
  f diédral
  r диэдрический; двугранный

2811 dihedral angle; face angle
  d Diederecke *f*; Flächenwinkel *m*; Zweiflach *n*
  f angle *m* dièdre
  r двугранный угол *m*; двугранник *m*; плоский угол [при вершине] многогранника

2812 dihedron
  d Dieder *n*
  f dièdre *m*
  r диэдр *m*

2813 dilatation
  d Dilatation *f*
  f dilatation *f*
  r растяжение *n*; дилатация *f*

  * **dilatation coefficient** → 1644

  * **dilatation factor** → 1644

2814 2D image
  d 2D-Bild *n*; zweidimensionales Bild *n*
  f image *f* 2D; image à deux dimensions
  r 2D изображение *n*; двумерное изображение

2815 3D image
  d 3D-Bild *n*; dreidimensionales Bild *n*
  f image *f* 3D; image à trois dimensions
  r 3D изображение *n*; трехмерное изображение

2816 3D image analysis
  d 3D-Bildanalyse *f*
  f analyse *f* d'image 3D
  r анализ *m* 3D изображения

2817 3D image synthesis
  d 3D-Bildsynthese *f*
  f synthèse *f* d'image 3D
  r синтез *m* 3D изображения

  * **dimension** → 2825

2818 dimension
  d Ausmaß *n*; Vermaß *n*
  f dimension *f*; cote *f*
  r размер *m*; величина *f*

2819 dimensionality
  d Dimensionalität *f*
  f dimensionnalité *f*
  r размерность *f*

2820 dimension arrow
  d Dimensionspfeil *m*
  f flèche *f* de cotation
  r размерная стрелка *f*

2821 dimension commands
  d Dimensionsbefehle *mpl*
  f commandes *fpl* de cotation
  r команды *fpl* измерения

2822 dimension entity
  d Dimensionseinheit *f*
  f entité *f* à coter
  r примитив *m* размер

2823 dimension format
  d Dimensionsformat *n*
  f format *m* de dimension
  r формат *m* размера

2824 dimension geometry
  d Dimensionsgeometrie *f*
  f géométrie *f* de cotation
  r геометрия *f* измерения

2825 dimension[ing]
  d Dimensionierung *f*; Bemaßung *f*
  f cotation *f*; dimensionnement *m*
  r определение *n* размеров; проставление *n* размеров; задание *n* размеров

2826 dimensioning mode
  d Dimensionierungsmodus *m*
  f mode *m* de dimensionnement
  r режим *m* задания размеров

2827 dimensioning symbol
  d Dimensionierungssymbol *n*
  f symbole *m* de dimensionnement
  r символ *m* измерения

2828 dimensioning system
  d Dimensionierungssystem *n*
  f système *m* de dimensionnement
  r система *f* задания размеров

2829 dimensionless
  d dimensionslos
  f sans dimension
  r безразмерный

2830 dimension line
  d Dimensionslinie *f*; Maßlinie *f*
  f ligne *f* de cotation; ligne de cote; trait *m* de cote; ligne de dimension
  r размерная линия *f*

2831 dimension line arc
  d Bogen *m* der Dimensionslinie

f arc *f* de ligne de dimension
r дуга *f* размерной линии

2832 dimension menu
d Dimensionsmenü *n*
f menu *m* de dimension
r меню *n* измерения

2833 dimension property
d Dimensionseigenschaft *f*
f propriété *f* de dimension
r свойство *n* измерения

2834 dimension scale
d Dimensionsskala *f*
f échelle *f* de dimension
r шкала *f* измерения

2835 dimension style
d Dimensionsstil *m*
f style *m* de cotation; style de cote
r измерительный стиль *m*; стиль размерности

2836 dimension style families
d Dimensionsstil-Familien *fpl*
f familles *fpl* de styles de cote
r семьи *fpl* измерительных стилей

2837 dimension style name
d Dimensionsstil-Name *m*
f nom *m* de style de cote
r имя *n* измерительного стиля

2838 dimension style overriding
d Aufhebung *f* des Dimensionsstils
f annulation *f* de style de cote
r отмена *f* измерительного стиля

2839 dimension text
d Dimensionstext *m*
f texte *m* de cote; texte de cotation
r размерный текст *m*

2840 dimension tool
d Dimensionshilfsmittel *n*
f outil *m* de cote; outil de cotation; outil de dimension
r инструмент *m* проставления размеров

2841 dimension toolbar
d Dimensionshilfsmittelstreifen *m*
f barre *f* d'outils de cotation
r инструментальная панель *f* измерения

2842 dimension unit
d Dimensionseinheit *f*
f unité *f* de dimension; unité de cote
r единица *f* размерности

2843 dimension value
d Dimensionswert *m*
f valeur *f* de la cote
r значение *n* размера

2844 dimension variables
d Dimensionsvariablen *fpl*
f variables *fpl* de cotation
r размерные переменные *fpl*

2845 dimetric projection
d dimetrische Projektion *f*
f projection *f* dimétrique
r диметрическая проекция *f*

2846 dimetric skew axonometry; frontal axonometry
d dimetrische Axonometrie *f*; Frontalperspektive *f*
f axonométrie *f* dimétrique; axonométrie frontale
r диметрия *f*; фронтальная аксонометрия *f*

2847 dingbat
(typographic symbol, such as a bullet, used for emphasis or decoration)
d Schnörkel *m*; Ornament *n*
f symbole *m* décoratif
r дингбат *m*; графический значок *m*; декоративный значок

2848 3D interactive view
d interaktive 3D-Ansicht *f*
f vue *f* 3D interactive
r трехмерный диалоговый вид *m*

* **diopt** → **2849**

2849 diopt[er]
d Diopter *n*
f dioptre *m*
r диоптр *m*

* **dip angle** → **3693**

2850 direct
d direkt
f direct
r прямой; непосредственный

* **direct blend** → **2851**

2851 direct blend[ing]
d direkte Überblendung *f*
f dégradé *m* direct
r прямое переливание *n*

* **direct cone** → **8159**

* **directed** → **6619**

2852 **directed acyclic graph**
 d azyklischer gerichteter Graph *m*
 f graphe *m* orienté acyclique
 r ациклический ориентированный граф *m*

2853 **directed angle; oriented angle**
 d orientierter Winkel *m*
 f angle *m* orienté
 r ориентированный угол *m*; направленный
   угол

2854 **directed edge**
 d gerichtete Kante *f*
 f arête *f* orientée
 r ориентированное ребро *n*

2855 **directed graph; oriented graph; orgraph**
 d gerichteter Graph *m*; orientierter Graph
 f graphe *m* dirigé; graphe orienté
 r направленный граф *m*; ориентированный
   граф; орграф *m*

2856 **directed light; directional light; oriented
   light**
 d gerichtetes Licht *n*
 f lumière *f* orientée; lumière dirigée
 r направленный свет *m*

2857 **directed line; oriented line**
 d gerichtete Gerade *f*; orientierte Gerade
 f droite *f* orientée
 r ориентированная прямая *f*

2858 **direct glare**
 d Direktblendung *f*
 f reflet *m* direct
 r прямой блик *m*

2859 **direct illumination**
 d direkte Illumination *f*
 f illumination *f* directe
 r направленная иллюминация *f*

2860 **direct image**
 d direktes Bild *n*
 f image *f* directe
 r прямое изображение *n*

2861 **directing curve; direction curve; base
   curve**
 d Leitkurve *f*; Richtungskurve *f*
 f courbe *f* directrice
 r направляющая [кривая] *f*

2862 **direction; sense; way**
 d Richtung *f*
 f direction *f*; sens *m*
 r направление *n*

2863 **directional; directive**

d leitend; führend; Richtungs-
 f directionnel; directif; directeur
 r направляющий; управляющий

* **directional light** → 2856

2864 **directional sharpen filter**
 d leitender Schärfefilter *m*
 f filtre *m* distinct directionnel
 r направляющий резкий фильтр *m*

2865 **direction angle; bearing angle**
 d Richtungswinkel *m*
 f angle *m* directeur
 r направляющий угол *m*

2866 **direction angles of a line**
 d Richtungswinkel *mpl* einer Geraden
 f angles *mpl* directeurs d'une droite
 r направляющие углы *mpl* прямой

2867 **direction chain**
 d Richtungskette *f*
 f chaîne *f* de direction
 r цепочка *f* направления

2868 **direction code**
 d Richtungscode *m*
 f code *m* de direction
 r код *m* направления

* **direction curve** → 2861

2869 **direction keys**
 d Richtungstasten *fpl*
 f touches *fpl* de direction
 r клавиши *fpl* направления

2870 **direction of axis; axis direction**
 d Achsenrichtung *f*; Richtung *f* der Achse
 f direction *f* d'axe
 r направление *n* оси

2871 **direction of chord; chord direction**
 d Sehnenrichtung *f*
 f direction *f* de corde
 r направление *n* хорды

2872 **direction of incidence; incident direction**
 d Einfallsrichtung *f*
 f direction *f* d'incidence
 r направление *n* падения

2873 **direction point; bearing point**
 d Richt[ungs]punkt *m*
 f point *m* visé; point de direction
 r ориентировочная точка *f*; точка
   направления наблюдения

2874 **directions measurement**
 d Richtungsmessung *f*

   f mesure *f* des directions
   r измерение *n* направлений

2875 direction vector
   d Richtungsvektor *m*
   f vecteur *m* directeur
   r направляющий вектор *m*

   * **directive** → 2863

   * **direct light** → 2876

2876 direct light[ing]
   d direkte Beleuchtung *f*; direktes Licht *n*
   f éclairage *m* direct
   r прямое освещение *n*

2877 director cone
   (of a ruled surface)
   d Richt[ungs]kegel *m*; Leitkegel *m*
   f cône *m* directeur
   r направляющий конус *m*

2878 director plane
   d Leitebene *f*
   f plan *m* directeur
   r направляющая плоскость *f*

2879 director surface
   d Leitfläche *f*
   f surface *f* directrice
   r направляющая поверхность *f*

2880 directory; catalog[ue]
   d Directory *n*; Katalog *m*; Ordner *m*
   f catalogue *m*; répertoire *m*; directoire *f*
   r справочник *m*; каталог *m*

2881 directrix
   d Direktrix *f*
   f directrice *f*; ligne *f* directrice
   r директриса *f*

2882 directrix of a cone
   d Leitkurve *f* eines Kegels
   f directrice *f* d'un cône
   r направляющая *f* конуса

2883 directrix of a conic surface
   d Leitkurve *f* einer Kegelfläche
   f directrice *f* d'une surface conique
   r направляющая *f* конической поверхности

2884 directrix of a cylinder
   d Leitkurve *f* eines Zylinders
   f directrice *f* d'un cylindre
   r направляющая *f* цилиндра

2885 directrix of a cylindrical surface
   d Leitkurve *f* einer Zylinderfläche

   f directrice *f* d'une surface cylindrique
   r направляющая *f* цилиндрической
   поверхности

2886 directrix of a surface of revolution
   d Leitkurve *f* einer Rotationsfläche; Leitkurve
   einer Dreh[ungs]fläche
   f directrice *f* d'une surface de révolution;
   génératrice *f* d'une surface de révolution
   r направляющая *f* поверхности вращения;
   образующая *f* поверхности вращения

2887 direct scanning
   d Direktabtastung *f*
   f balayage *m* direct
   r прямое сканирование *n*

2888 direct screen focusing
   d direkte Bildschirmfokussierung *f*
   f focalisation *f* d'écran directe
   r прямое фокусирование *n* экрана

2889 direct sunlight
   d Tageslichteinfall *m*
   f éclairage *m* naturel direct
   r прямой солнечный свет *m*

2890 direct viewing
   d direkte Visualisierung *f*
   f visionnement *m* direct
   r прямая визуализация *f*

   * **DIS** → 2980

   * **disable** *v* → 5071

   * **disable** → 5072

   * **disarm** *v* → 5071

   * **disc** → 2906

   * **discard** *v* → 1536, 7996

2891 discarded line
   d ausrangierte Linie *f*
   f ligne *f* désaffectée
   r отброшенная линия *f*

   * **discharge** → 10034

2892 disconnect *v*; **detach** *v*; **disjoint** *v*
   d trennen; abtrennen
   f déconnecter; disjoindre
   r разъединять; размыкать; прерывать;
   отделять

2893 discontinuity
   d Unstetigkeit *f*; Diskontinuität *f*;
   Sprunghaftigkeit *f*

f discontinuité *f*
r разрыв *m*; разрывность *f*; прерывность *f*

2894 discontinuous
d unstetig; sprunghaft
f discontinu
r разрывный

2895 discrete
d diskret
f discret
r дискретный

2896 discrete curves
d diskrete Kurven *fpl*
f courbes *fpl* discrètes
r дискретные кривые *fpl*

2897 discrete distribution
d diskrete Verteilung *f*
f distribution *f* discrète
r дискретное распределение *n*

2898 discrete Laplacian filter
d diskreter Laplace-Filter *m*
f filtre *m* laplacien discret
r дискретный фильтр *m* Лапласа

2899 discrete reflection
d diskrete Reflexion *f*
f réflexion *f* discrète
r дискретное отражение *n*

2900 discrete space
d diskreter Raum *m*
f espace *m* discret
r дискретное пространство *n*

2901 discretization; digit[al]ization; digitizing; quantization; quantizing
d Diskretisierung *f*; Quantisierung *f*; Quantelung *f*
f discrétisation *f*; digitalisation *f*; numérisation *f*; quantification *f*
r дискретизация *f*; дискретизирование *n*; дигитализирование *n*; оцифровка *f*; квантование *n*; преобразование *n* в цифровую форму

2902 discriminating; discriminative; discriminatory
d ausscheidend; unterscheidend
f discriminant; sélectif
r отличительный; дискриминирующий; избирательный

* **discriminative → 2902**

* **discriminatory → 2902**

* **disjoint** *v* → **2892**

2903 disjoint
d disjunkt; elementefremd; durchschnittsfremd
f disjoint
r непересекающийся; без общих элементов; без общих точек

2904 disjoint circles
d disjunkte Kreise *mpl*; durchschnittsfremde Kreise
f cercles *mpl* disjoints
r непересекающиеся окружности *fpl*

2905 disjoint domains
d disjunkte Gebiete *npl*
f domaines *mpl* disjoints
r непересекающиеся области *fpl*; области без общих точек

2906 disk; disc
d Platte *f*; Speicherplatte *f*
f disque *m*
r диск *m*

2907 disparity
d Disparität *f*; Ungleichheit *f*; Verschiedenheit *f*
f disparité *f*
r несоответствие *n*; несоразмерность *f*; неравенство *n*

2908 dispersion; scattering
d Dispersion *f*; Streuung *f*
f dispersion *f*
r дисперсия *f*; рассеивание *n*; разброс *m*

* **dispersion diagram → 8329**

2909 dispersion equation
d Dispersionsgleichung *f*
f équation *f* de dispersion
r дисперсионное уравнение *n*

2910 dispersion spectra variation
d Änderungen *fpl* der Dispersionsspektra
f variations *fpl* des spectres de dispersion
r изменение *n* дисперсионных спектров

2911 dispersion spectrum
d Dispersionsspektrum *n*
f spectre *m* de dispersion
r дисперсионный спектр *m*

2912 dispersive
d streuend; dispersiv; dispergierend
f dispersif
r рассеивающий; диспергированный

2913 dispersive fading
d dispersiver Schwund *m*

f fading *m* dispersif
r рассеивающий фединг *m*

2914 **displace *v* filter**
   d Filter verschieben
   f déplacer un filtre; décaler un filtre
   r перемещать фильтр

   * **displacement** → 8643

   * **displacement map** → 2915

2915 **displacement map[ping]**
   d Verschiebungsabbildung *f*
   f application *f* de déplacement
   r отображение *n* смещения

   * **displacement operator** → 9833

2916 **displacement point**
   d Verschiebungspunkt *m*
   f point *m* de déplacement
   r точка *f* смещения

2917 **displacement value**
   d Verschiebungswert *m*
   f valeur *f* de déplacement
   r значение *n* смещения

   * **display** → 2927, 2932, 5035

2918 **displayable attribute**
   d Darstellungsattribut *n*
   f attribut *m* affichable
   r воспроизводимый атрибут *m*

   * **display area** → 2946

2919 **display attribute**
   d Displayattribut *n*
   f attribut *m* graphique; attribut visuel
   r атрибут *m* дисплея

2920 **display buffer; screen buffer**
   d Bildschirmpuffer *m*
   f tampon *m* d'afficheur
   r буфер *m* дисплея

   * **display card** → 10208

2921 **display command; display instruction**
   d Darstellungsbefehl *m*
   f commande *f* d'affichage; instruction *f* graphique
   r команда *f* визуализации

2922 **display configuration**
   d Displaykonfiguration *f*
   f configuration *f* d'afficheur
   r конфигурация *f* дисплея

2923 **display console**
   d grafischer Arbeitsplatz *m*
   f console *f* de visualisation
   r графический терминал *m*

2924 **display-control function**
   d Darstellungssteuerungsfunktion *f*
   f fonction *f* de contrôle d'affichage
   r функция *f* управления представлением

2925 **display coordinate system; DCS**
   d Bildschirm-Koordinatensystem *n*
   f système *m* de coordonnées d'afficheur
   r координатная система *f* дисплея; экранная координатная система

2926 **display data channel; DDC**
   d Kanal *m* der Darstellungsdaten
   f canal *m* de données d'afficheur
   r канал *m* дисплейных данных

2927 **display [device]; monitor**
   d Monitor *m*; Display *n*; Bildschirmgerät *n*; Anzeigegerät *n*
   f visuel *m*; visu *m*; afficheur *m*; display *m*; moniteur *m*
   r дисплей *m*; устройство *n* визуального изображения; монитор *m*; контрольное устройство

2928 **display driver; screen driver**
   d Bildschirmtreiber *m*
   f pilote *m* d'écran; pilote d'affichage; pilote d'afficheur
   r драйвер *m* дисплея; экранный драйвер

2929 **display element**
   d Darstellungselement *n*
   f élément *m* d'affichage
   r элемент *m* изображения

2930 **display group; display segment**
   d Anzeige-Segment *n*
   f groupe *m* graphique
   r сегмент *m* изображения

2931 **display image**
   d Bildschirmbild *n*
   f image *f* d'afficheur
   r дисплейное изображение *n*

2932 **display[ing]**
   d Bildschirm-Darstellung *f*
   f affichage *m*
   r изображение *n* на экране; визуализация *f*

   * **display instruction** → 2921

2933 **display line**
   d Darstellungslinie *f*

f ligne *f* d'affichage
r линия *f* на экране дисплея

2934 display mode
d Darstellungsmodus *m*; Anzeigebetriebsart *f*
f mode *m* d'affichage
r режим *m* изображения на экране

2935 display optimization tool
d Hilfsmittel *n* der Bildschirmoptimierung
f outil *m* d'optimisation de l'affichage
r инструмент *m* оптимизации дисплея

2936 display option
d Bildschirm-Option *f*
f option *f* d'afficheur
r опция *f* дисплея

2937 display order
d Darstellungsordnung *f*
f ordre *m* d'affichage
r порядок *m* изображения

2938 display position
d Position *f* auf dem Bildschirm
f position *f* d'affichage
r позиция *f* на экране дисплея

2939 display preferences
d Bildschirmpräferenz *f*
f préférences *fpl* d'affichage
r предпочтительные параметры *mpl* дисплея

2940 display process
d Display-Prozess *m*
f processus *m* d'affichage
r процесс *m* изображения

2941 display processor
d Displayprozessor *m*
f processeur *m* d'afficheur
r дисплейный процессор *m*

2942 display properties
d Bildschirmeigenschaften *fpl*
f propriétés *fpl* d'afficheur
r характеристики *fpl* дисплея

2943 display quality
d Darstellungsqualität *f*
f qualité *f* d'affichage
r качество *n* изображения на экране

* **display segment** → **2930**

2944 display space
d Darstellungsbereich *m*
f espace *m* d'affichage
r пространство *n* изображения

2945 display standard
d Darstelungsstandard *m*
f standard *m* d'affichage
r стандарт *m* изображения

2946 display surface; display area
d Darstellungsfläche *f*; Sichtfläche *f*
f surface *f* d'affichage
r носитель *m* изображения

2947 display technique; display technology
d Darstellungtechnik *f*; Anzeigetechnik *f*;
   Anzeigeverfahren *n*
f technique *f* d'affichage; procédé *m* d'affichage
r техника *f* индикации; техника
   изображения

* **display technology** → **2947**

2948 display update
d Bildschirmaktualisierung *f*
f mise *f* à jour d'afficheur
r регенерирование *n* дисплея; обновление *n*
   дисплея

2949 display variable
d Bildschirmvariable *f*
f variable *f* d'afficheur
r дисплейная переменная *f*

* **display view** → **8389**

2950 display window
d Schaufenster *n* des Bildschirms
f fenêtre *f* d'affichage
r окно *n* дисплея

* **dissemination** → **2951**

2951 dissipation; dissemination
d Dissipation *f*; Zerstreuung *f*
f dissipation *f*; dissémination *f*
r рассеяние *n*; диссипация *f*

* **dissociate** *v* → **3578**

2952 dissolve
   (of frames)
d Überblendung *f*
f fondu *m*
r наплыв *m*; плавная смена *f* изображений

2953 dissolve *v*
d überblenden; ineinander übergehen lassen
f dissoudre
r растворять[ся]; разлагать[ся]

* **distance** → **3654**

2954 distance
d Abstand *m*; Entfernung *f*; Distanz *f*

f distance *f*
r расстояние *n*

2955 **distance between a point and line**
d Abstand *m* zwischen Punkt und Gerade;
Abstand Punkt-Gerade; Abstand eines
Punktes von einer Geraden
f distance *f* d'un point à une droite
r расстояние *n* от точки до прямой

2956 **distance between a point and a plane**
d Abstand *m* zwischen Punkt und Ebene;
Abstand Punkt-Ebene
f distance *f* d'un point à un plan
r расстояние *n* от точки до плоскости

2957 **distance between two points**
d Abstand *m* zwischen zwei Punkten
f distance *f* entre deux points
r расстояние *n* между двумя точками

2958 **distance between two skew lines**
d Abstand *m* zwischen zwei windschiefen
Geraden
f distance *f* entre deux droites gauches
r расстояние *n* между двумя
скрещивающимися прямыми

2959 **distance circle**
d Distanzkreis *m*
f cercle *m* de distance
r окружность *f* расстояния

2960 **distance constant**
d Abstandskonstante *f*
f constante *f* de distance
r постоянная *f* расстояния

2961 **distance equation**
d Abstandsgleichung *f*; Streckengleichung *f*
f équation *f* des distances
r уравнение *n* расстояний

2962 **distance function**
d Abstandsfunktion *f*; Distanzfunktion *f*
f fonction *f* de distance
r функция *f* расстояния

* **distance in central projection** → 3654

2963 **distance in the mean**
d Abstand *m* im Mittel
f distance *f* en moyenne
r расстояние *n* в среднем

2964 **distance option**
d Abstandsoption *f*
f option *f* de distance
r выбор *m* расстояния

2965 **distant light**
d Fernlicht *n*
f lumière *f* distante
r дистанционный свет *m*

2966 **distant objects**
d entferne Objekte *npl*
f objets *mpl* distants
r дистанционные объекти *mpl*

2967 **distant virtual environment**
d ferne Virtualumgebung *f*
f environnement *m* virtuel à distance
r дистанционное виртуальное окружение *n*

2968 **distinct**
d verschieden; unterschiedlich
f distinct[if]; distingué; différent
r отчетливый; различимый; отличный

2969 **distinctive feature**
d charakteristisches Merkmal *n*;
Unterscheidungsmerkmal *n*
f caractéristique *f* particulière; caractéristique
distinctive
r отличительный признак *m*

2970 **distorted**
d verzerrt
f tordu
r искаженный

2971 **distorted image**
d verzerrtes Bild *n*
f image *f* tordue
r искаженное изображение *n*

2972 **distorted scene**
d verzerrte Szene *f*
f scène *f* tordue
r искаженная сцена *f*

2973 **distortion**
d Distorsion *f*; Verzerrung *f*
f distorsion *f*
r искажение *n*; дисторсия *f*

2974 **distortion angle**
d Verzerrungswinkel *m*
f angle *m* de distorsion
r угол *m* искажения

* **distortion coefficient** → 1645

2975 **distortion correction**
d Verzerrungskorrektur *f*
f correction *f* de distorsion
r коррекция *f* дисторсии

2976 **distortion curve**
d Verzerrungskurve *f*

f courbe *f* de distorsion
r кривая *f* дисторсии

2977 distortion degree
d Verzerrungsstufe *f*
f degré *m* de distorsion
r степень *f* искажения

2978 distribute *v*; **allocate** *v*
d verteilen
f distribuer
r распределять

2979 distributed
d verteilt
f distribué; réparti
r распределенный; дистрибутивный

2980 distributed interactive simulation; DIS
d verteilte interaktive Simulierung *f*
f simulation *f* interactive distribuée
r распределенная интерактивная
    симуляция *f*

2981 distributed objects
d verteilte Objekte *npl*
f objets *mpl* distribués
r распределенные объекты *mpl*

2982 distributed simulation
d verteilte Simulierung *f*
f simulation *f* distribuée
r распределенная симуляция *f*

2983 distributed viewer
d verteiltes Suchprogramm *n*
f visionneur *m* distribué
r распределенный вьювер *m*

2984 distributed virtual environment;
    collaborative virtual environment; CVE
d verteilte Virtualumgebung *f*
f environnement *m* virtuel distribué
r распределенное виртуальное
    пространство *n*

2985 distribution
d Verteilung *f*
f distribution *f*; répartition *f*
r распределение *n*

2986 distribution density
d Verteilungsdichte *f*
f densité *f* de la distribution
r густота *f* распределения

2987 distribution of definition
d Schärfenverteilung *f*
f répartition *f* de la netteté
r распределение *n* резкости

* **dither** → 2990

2988 dither *v*
d rastern
f juxtaposer; approximer les couleurs;
    interpoler les couleurs
r размывать; псевдосмешивать;
    имитировать полутона

2989 dithered color
d gerasterte Farbe *f*
f couleur *f* juxtaposée; couleur approximative;
    couleur interpolée
r аппроксимированный цвет *m*; размытый
    цвет

2990 dither[ing]
    (representing a color by mixing dots of
    closely related colors)
d Dithering *n*; Rastern *n*
f juxtaposition *f*; tramage *m*
r [псевдо]смешение *n*; имитация *f*
    полутонов; размывание *n*; размытие *n*;
    сжатие *n* палитры

2991 dither matrix
d Dithermatrix *f*
f matrice *f* de juxtaposition
r матрица *f* псевдосмешения; матрица
    имитации полутонов

2992 divergence
d Divergenz *f*
f divergence *f*
r расходимость *f*

2993 divergent; diverging
d divergierend
f divergent
r расходящийся; рассеивающий

2994 divergent beam; diverging beam
d divergierender Strahl *m*
f faisceau *m* divergent
r расходящийся луч *m*

2995 divergent lens; diverging lens
d Zerstreuungslinse *f*
f lentille *f* divergente
r рассеивающая линза *f*

2996 divergent light; diverging light
d divergierendes Licht *n*
f lumière *f* divergente
r расходящийся свет *m*

* **diverging** → 2993

* **diverging beam** → 2994

* **diverging lens** → 2995

* **diverging light** → 2996

2997 **diversion**
  d Umleitung *f*
  f diversion *f*
  r отклонение *n*

2998 **diversion indicator**
  d Umleitungskennung *f*
  f indicateur *m* de diversion
  r указатель *m* отклонения

2999 **diversity**
  d Diversity *n*; Unterschied *m*;
    Verschiedenartigkeit *f*
  f diversité *f*
  r разнообразие *n*; различие *n*; разность *f*

3000 **divide** *v*
  d dividieren
  f diviser
  r делить

* **divided screen** → 9090

3001 **divide option**
  d Teilungsoption *f*
  f option *f* à diviser
  r опция *f* деления

3002 **division**
  (as an operation)
  d Division *f*; Teilung *f*
  f division *f*; partage *m*
  r деление *n*

3003 **division**
  (as a section)
  d Teil *m*
  f division *f*
  r раздел *m*

3004 **division of the circle**
  d Kreisteilung *f*
  f division *f* du cercle
  r деление *n* круга; деление окружности

* **divorced image** → 3084

* **DLL** → 3254

3005 **3D localization**
  d 3D-Lokalisierung *f*
  f localisation *f* 3D
  r 3D местоположение *n*

* **dm** → 2533

3006 **3D macrostructure**
  d 3D-Makrostruktur *f*
  f macrostructure *f* 3D
  r 3D макроструктура *f*

3007 **2D manifold**
  d 2D-Kopie *f*
  f copie *f* 2D
  r 2D копия *f*

3008 **2D map**
  d 2D-Karte *f*
  f carte *f* 2D
  r 2D карта *f*

3009 **3D map**
  d 3D-Karte *f*
  f carte *f* 3D
  r 3D карта *f*

3010 **3D mesh**
  d 3D-Masche *f*
  f maille *f* 3D
  r 3D сетка *f*; 3D решетка *f*

3011 **3D mesh objects**
  d 3D-Maschenobjekte *npl*
  f objets *mpl* maillés 3D
  r трехмерные решетчатые объекты *mpl*

3012 **2D 1/2 model**
  d 2,5D-Modell *n*
  f modèle *m* 2D 1/2; modèle 2,5D
  r 2,5D модель *f*

3013 **3D model**
  d 3D-Modell *n*
  f modèle *m* 3D
  r 3D модель *f*

* **3D modeler** → 3017

3014 **3D model exporting**
  d 3D-Modell-Exportieren *n*
  f exportation *f* de modèle 3D
  r экспортирование *n* 3D модели

3015 **3D model importing**
  d 3D-Modell-Importieren *n*
  f importation *f* de modèle 3D
  r импортирование *n* 3D модели

3016 **3D modeling**
  d 3D-Modellierung *f*
  f modelage *m* 3D
  r 3D моделирование *n*

3017 **3D modeling program; 3D modeler**
  d 3D-Modellierungsprogramm *n*;
    3D-Modellierer *m*

f programme *m* de modelage 3D;
modélisateur *m* 3D
r программа *f* для 3D моделирования

3018 3D model manipulating
d 3D-Modell-Manipulieren *n*
f manipulation *f* de modèle 3D
r обработка *f* 3D модели

3019 3D model space
d 3D-Modellraum *m*
f espace *m* de modèle 3D
r трехмерное модельное пространство *n*

3020 3D mouse
d 3D-Maus *f*
f souris *f* 3D
r 3D мышь *f*

3021 3D noise
d 3D-Geräusch *n*
f bruit *m* 3D
r 3D искажение *n*; 3D шум *m*

3022 2D object
d 2D-Objekt *n*
f objet *m* 2D
r 2D объект *m*

3023 3D object
d 3D-Objekt *n*
f objet *m* 3D
r 3D объект *m*

3024 dock *v*
d andocken
f amarrer
r стыковать

3025 dockable template
d andockbare Schablone *f*
f modèle *m* amarré
r присоединенный шаблон *m*;
"перетаскиваемый" шаблон

3026 dockable toolbar; docked toolbar
d andockbarer Hilfsmittelstreifen *m*
f barre *f* d'outils amarrée
r присоединенная инструментальная
панель *f*

*   **docked toolbar** → **3026**

3027 docked visible line
d angedockte sichtbare Linie *f*
f ligne *f* visible amarrée
r присоединенная видимая линия *f*

*   **docker** → **3028**

3028 docker [window]
d Andock-Fenster *n*
f fenêtre *f* fixe
r фиксированное окно *n*

3029 docking
d Verankern *n*
f amarrage *m*
r стыковка *f*

3030 document
d Dokument *n*; Beleg *m*
f document *m*
r документ *m*

3031 documentation
d Dokumentation *f*
f documentation *f*
r документация *f*

3032 documentation navigating
d Dokumentationsnavigation *f*
f navigation *f* de documentation
r навигация *f* по документу

3033 document components
d Bestandteile *mpl* des Dokuments
f composantes *fpl* de document
r компоненты *mpl* документа

3034 document icon
d Dokumentsymbol *n*
f icône *f* de document
r значок *m* документа

3035 document image analysis
d Dokumentbild-Analyse *f*
f analyse *f* d'image de document
r анализ *m* изображения документа

3036 document imaging
d Dokument-Abbildung *f*
f imagination *f* de document; présentation *f* de
document en image
r изображение *n* документа

3037 document object
d Dokument-Objekt *n*
f objet *m* document
r объект *m* типа документа

3038 document setting
d Dokument-Einrichtung *f*
f établissement *m* de document
r установление *n* параметров документа

3039 document structure
d Struktur *f* des Dokuments
f structure *f* de document
r структура *f* документа

* **document view** → 3040

3040 document view[ing]
  d Dokumentansicht *f*
  f visualisation *f* de document
  r визуализация *f* документа

3041 document window
  d Dokumentfenster *n*
  f fenêtre *f* de document
  r окно *n* документа

3042 dodecagon
  d Dodekagon *n*; Zwölfeck *n*
  f dodécagone *m*
  r двенадцатиугольник *m*

3043 dodecahedron
  d Dodekaeder *n*; Zwölfflächner *m*
  f dodécaèdre *m*
  r двенадцатигранник *m*; додекаэдр *m*

3044 2D offset effect
  d 2D-Offset-Effekt *m*; 2D-Abstand-Effekt *m*
  f effet *m* de décalage 2D
  r эффект *m* 2D смещения

3045 dogleg routing
  d abknickende Leitweglenkung *f*
  f acheminement *m* par polylignes
  r трассировка *f* ломаными линиями

3046 dolly-shot; trucking shot
  d Aufnahme *f* vom Kamerawagen aus;
     Fahraufnahme *f*; Kamerawagenaufnahme *f*
  f cadre *m* enregistré par caméra en mouvement
  r кадр *m*, снятый с движения

3047 domain
  d Domäne *f*
  f domaine *m*
  r домен *m*; область *f*

3048 dome
  d Kuppel *f*
  f voûte *f*
  r купол *m*; свод *m*

* **donut** → 1505

3049 3D operation
  d 3D-Operation *f*
  f opération *f* 3D
  r 3D операция *f*

3050 Doppler effect
  d Doppler-Effekt *m*
  f effet *m* Doppler-Fizeau
  r эффект *m* Деплера

3051 dot
  d Punkt *m*; Punktmarke *f*
  f marque *f* ponctuelle; index *m* ponctuel;
     point *m*
  r точка *f*

* **dot** → 8366

3052 dot *v*; **punctuate** *v*; **point** *v*
  d punktieren
  f pointiller; pointer
  r пунктировать; ставить точку; означать
     точками

3053 dot and line background pattern
  d punktiertes und lineares
     Hintergrundmuster *n*
  f motif *m* de fond d'arrière en lignes et points
  r точечно-линейная модель *f* фона

3054 dot area
  d Rasterpunktfläche *f*
  f aire *f* de point de trame
  r площадь *f* растрового элемента; площадь
     растровой точки

3055 dot chaining
  d Rasterpunktverkettung *f*
  f chaînage *m* de points de trame
  r сцепление *n* растровых точек;
     перекрытие *n* двух соседних растровых
     точек

* **dot-chaining screen** → 3377

3056 dot chart
  d Punktdiagramm *n*
  f diagramme *m* à points; graphique *m* par
     points
  r точечная диаграмма *f*

3057 dot counter
  (in display)
  d Punkt-Zähler *m*
  f compteur *m* de points
  r счетчик *m* точек

* **dot-dash line** → 2463

**3058 dot-for-dot reproduction; pointwise
     reproduction**
  d punktweise Reproduktion *f*
  f reproduction *f* point par point
  r поточечное воспроизведение *n*

3059 dot gain; dot spread
  d Punktverbreiterung *f*
  f grossissement *m* du point
  r расплывание *m* растровой точки;
     увеличение *n* размера растровой точки

3060 dot generator
(in a plotter)
 d Punktgenerator *m*
 f générateur *m* de points
 r генератор *m* точек

3061 dot grid
 d Punktgitter *n*
 f grille *f* à points
 r точечная решетка *f*

3062 dot interlace scanning
 d Bildpunkt-verschachtelte Abtastung *f*
 f échantillonnage *m* point par point entrelacé
 r поточное презрядовое сканирование *n*

3063 dot mask
 d Punktmaske *f*
 f masque *f* en points
 r точечная маска *f*

3064 dot matrix
 d Punktmatrix *f*
 f matrice *f* de points
 r точечная матрица *f*

3065 dot-matrix character
 d Punktmatrixzeichen *n*; Punktrasterzeichen *n*
 f caractère *m* dans une matrice de points
 r точечный символ *m*

3066 dot-matrix character generator
 d Raster-Zeichengenerator *m*
 f générateur *m* de caractères par points
 r генератор *m* точечных символов

 * **dot matrix field** → 1412

 * **dot pitch** → 8367

 * **dots** → 3364

3067 dot-scanning method
 d Punktscannen-Verfahren *n*
 f méthode *f* d'échantillonnage par points
 r точечный метод *m* сканирования

3068 dot shape
 d Rasterpunktform *f*; Punktform *f*
 f forme *f* de point de trame
 r форма *f* растровой точки

3069 dots per inch; dpi
 d Punkte *mpl* pro Zoll
 f points *mpl* au pouce
 r точек *fpl* на дюйм

 * **dot spread** → 3059

3070 dotted

 d punktiert; gepunktet
 f ponctuel
 r точечный; пунктирный

3071 dotted curve
 d punktierte Kurve *f*
 f courbe *f* en pointillé
 r пунктирная кривая *f*

3072 dotted frame
 d punktierter Rahmen *m*
 f cadre *m* en pointillé
 r пунктирная рамка *f*; пунктирный кадр *m*

3073 dotted line; dotted rule
 d punktierte Linie *f*
 f ligne *f* pointillée; pointillé *m*
 r пунктирная линия *f*; точечная линия; пунктир *m*

3074 dotted pair
 d punktiertes Paar *n*
 f paire *f* en pointillé
 r точечная пара *f*; простейшее точечное выражение *n*

 * **dotted rule** → 3073

3075 dotting
 d Punktierung *f*
 f pointillage *m*
 r пунктирование *n*

3076 double
 d doppelt; Doppel-; zweifach
 f double
 r двойной; сдвоенный; удвоенный

3077 double angle
 d Doppelwinkel *m*
 f angle *m* double
 r двойной угол *m*

3078 double arrow
 d Doppelpfeil *m*
 f double flèche *f*
 r двойная стрелка *f*

3079 double buffering
 d Doppelpufferung *f*
 f tamponnage *m* double
 r двойное буферирование *n*; двойная буферизация *f*

3080 double click
 d Doppelklick *m*
 f double clic *m*
 r двойной клик *m*; двойной щелчок *m*; двойное нажатие *n* кнопки

* **double cone** → 906

3081 double curve
d Doppelkurve f
f courbe f double
r двойная кривая f

* **double eye-glass** → 936

3082 double hatch
d Doppelschraffur f
f hachure f double
r двойная штриховка f

3083 double-hatched
d doppelt schraffiert
f à hachure double
r двойно-штрихованный

3084 double image; divorced image; double picture
d Doppelbild n
f image f double; image dédoublée
r двойное изображение n

3085 double knot
d Doppelknoten m
f nœud m double
r двойной узел m

3086 double line
d Doppellinie f; Doppelgerade f
f ligne f double; droite f double
r двойная линия f; двойная прямая f

3087 double loop
d Doppelschleife f
f double lacet m
r двойная петля f

3088 double modulation
d Doppelmodulation f
f modulation f double
r двойная модуляция f

* **double picture** → 3084

3089 double picture plotter
d Stereoauswertegerät n
f appareil m de restitution stéréoscopique
r стереообрабатывающий графопостроитель m

* **double plane** → 3838

* **double point** → 3840

3090 double quotes; quotation marks; quote marks; quotes
(")
d Anführungsstriche pl

f guillemets mpl
r кавычки fpl

3091 double refraction; birefringence
d Doppelbrechung f
f réfraction f double; biréfringence f
r двойное лучепреломление n

3092 double seizure
d Doppelbelegung f
f engagement m double
r двойное занятие n

* **double-side** → 917

* **double-sided** → 917

3093 double tangent
d Doppeltangente f
f tangente f double
r двойная касательная f

3094 double underline v
d doppelt unterstrichen
f souligner double
r двойно подчеркивать

3095 doubling; duplication; replication
d Duplikation f; Verdoppelung f; Duplizierung f
f duplication f
r удвоение n; дублирование n

* **doubly concave** → 905

3096 downloadable images
d heruntergeladene Bilder npl
f images fpl téléchargeables
r разгружаемые изображения npl

* **download** → 3097

3097 download[ing]
d Herunterladen n
f téléchargement m; déchargement m
r разгрузка f

3098 down scroll arrow
d Bildlaufpfeil m abwärts
f flèche f de défilement ver le bas
r стрелка f прокрутки вниз

3099 3D page curl effect
d 3D-Seiteaufroll-Effekt m
f effet m de roulage de page 3D
r эффект m трехмерного завитка страницы

3100 2D patch; planar patch
d 2D-Oberflächenstück n

f surface *f* paramétrique 2D; surface
paramétrique plane
r плоский кусок *m*; плоский фрагмент *m*

3101 3D patch
d 3D-Oberflächenstück *n*
f surface *f* paramétrique 3D
r трехмерный кусок *m*; 3D фрагмент *m*

3102 3D perspective effect
d 3D-Perspektive-Effekt *m*
f effet *m* de perspective 3D
r эффект *m* трехмерной перспективы

* dpi → 3069

3103 3D pie chart
d dreidimensionales Sektordiagramm *n*
f diagramme *m* sectionné tridimensionnel
r трехмерная секторная диаграмма *f*

3104 2D pixelate effect
d 2D-Mosaik-Effekt *m*
f effet *m* pixélisé 2D
r двумерный мозаичный эффект *m*

3105 2D point
d 2D-Punkt *m*
f point *m* 2D
r 2D точка *f*

3106 3D point
d 3D-Punkt *m*
f point *m* 3D
r 3D точка *f*

3107 3D point-by-point scan
d 3D-Punkt-zu-Punkt-Scannen *n*
f balayage *m* 3D point à point
r трехмерное поточечное сканирование *n*

3108 2D polar coordinates
d 2D-Polarkoordinaten *fpl*
f coordonnées *fpl* polaires à deux dimensions
r двумерные полярные координаты *fpl*

3109 3D polar shape
d 3D-Polarfigur *f*
f forme *f* polaire 3D
r трехмерная полярная фигура *f*

3110 3D polygon
d 3D-Polygon *n*
f polygone *m* 3D
r 3D многоугольник *m*

3111 3D polygon mesh
d 3D-Polygonmasche *f*
f maillage *m* par polygones 3D
r трехмерная многоугольная сеть *f*

3112 2D polyline
d 2D-Polylinie *f*
f polyligne *f* 2D
r 2D полилиния *f*

3113 3D polyline
d 3D-Polylinie *f*
f polyligne *f* 3D
r 3D полилиния *f*

3114 3D procedural texture
d prozedurale 3D-Textur *f*
f texture *f* procédurale 3D
r трехмерная процедурная текстура *f*

3115 3D projection
d 3D Projektion *f*
f projection *f* 3D
r 3D проекция *f*

3116 3D pseudo-manifold
d 3D-Pseudo-Kopie *f*
f pseudo-copie *f* 3D
r 3D псевдо-копия *f*

3117 3D psychedelic effect
d psychedelischer 3D-Effekt *m*
f effet *m* psychédélique 3D
r трехмерный флюоресцирующий эффект *m*

* DR → 2522

* draft → 3129, 8212, 8214

* drafting → 3132

3118 drafting paper
d Zeichnungspapier *n*
f papier *m* de dessin
r чертежная бумага *f*

3119 drafting standard
d Zeichnungsstandard *m*
f standard *m* de conception
r стандарт *m* черчения

3120 drafting technique
d Zeichnungstechnik *f*
f technique *f* de conception
r чертежная техника *f*

3121 draft view
d Entwurfsansicht *f*
f vue *f* d'ébauche
r схематический вид *m*; схематическое
представление *n*

* drag → 3126

3122 drag *v*; **draw** *v*
d ziehen; führen

f glisser; traîner; déposer
r переместить; таскать; увлекать

3123 drag and drop
d Ziehen *n* und Loslassen *n*; Z&L
f glissement *m* et relâchement *m*
r перемещение *n* и опускание *n*; таскание *n* и опускание

3124 drag-and-drop insertion of objects
d Einfügung *f* der Objekte durch Ziehen und Loslassen
f insertion *f* d'objets par glissement et relâchement
r вставка *f* объектов перемещением и опусканием

3125 dragged object
d gezogenes Objekt *n*
f objet *m* entraîné; objet lissé
r перемещаемый объект *m*

3126 drag[ging]
d Ziehen *n*; Nachziehen *n*
f [en]traînement *m*; traînage *m*; glissement *m*
r перемещение *n*; таскание *n*; буксировка *f*

3127 3D random-point generation
d Generierung *f* der dreidimensionalen zufälligen Punkte
f génération *f* de points tridimensionnels aléatoires
r генерирование *n* трехмерных случайных точек

3128 drape fills
d Gewebefüllungen *fpl*
f remplissages *mpl* en drapeaux
r закрашивания *npl* складками

* **draught** → 8214

* **draw** → 3131

* **draw** *v* → 3122

3129 draw *v*; **chart** *v*; **draft** *v*; **trace** *v*
d zeichnen
f tracer; tirer; étirer; dessiner
r чертить

3130 drawer
d Zeichner *m*; Entwerfer *m*
f tiroir *m*
r выдвижной ящик *m*; выдвижная доска *f*

3131 draw[ing]
d Zeichnung *f*
f dessin *m*
r чертеж *m*; рисунок *m*

3132 drawing; design; drafting
d Zeichnung *f*; Zeichnen *n*
f tracement *m*; étirage *m*
r черчение *n*

* **drawing accuracy** → 72

3133 drawing aids
d Zeichnensmittel *npl*
f aides *fpl* de tracement
r чертежные [вспомогательные] средства *npl*

3134 drawing area
d Zeichnensbereich *m*
f espace *m* de dessin
r чертежное поле *n*; плоскость *f* построения

3135 drawing browser
d Zeichnungsbrowser *m*
f butineur *m* de dessins
r браузер *m* чертежей

3136 drawing callout
d Zeichnungslegende *f*
f légende *f* de dessin
r чертежная легенда *f*

3137 drawing charcoal
d Zeichenkohle *f*
f charbon *m* de dessin
r уголь *m* для рисования

* **drawing clipping** → 3139

3138 drawing color
d Zeichenfarbe *f*
f couleur *f* de dessin
r цвет *m* черчения

3139 drawing cutting; drawing clipping
d Zeichnungsschnitt *m*
f découpage *m* de dessin
r выделение *n* чертежа; отсекание *n* чертежа

3140 drawing database
d Zeichnungsdatenbasis *f*
f base *f* de données de dessin
r база *f* данных чертежа

3141 drawing direction
d Zeichnungsrichtung *f*
f direction *f* de dessin
r направление *n* черчения

3142 drawing environment
d Zeichnungsumgebung *f*
f environnement *m* de dessin
r среда *f* проектирования

3143 drawing extent
d Zeichnungsumfang *m*

f étendue *f* de dessin
r охват *m* рисунка

* **drawing file** → 7168

3144 drawing file format
d Zeichnungsdatei-Format *n*
f format *m* de fichier de dessin
r формат *m* чертежного файла

3145 drawing formatting
d Zeichnungsformatierung *f*
f formatage *m* de dessin
r форматирование *n* рисунка

3146 drawing geometry
d Zeichnen-Geometrie *f*
f géométrie *f* de dessin
r чертежная геометрия *f*

3147 drawing image
d Zeichnen-Bild *n*
f image *f* de dessin
r изображение *n* чертежа

3148 drawing integrity
d Zeichnungsintegrität *f*
f intégrité *f* d'un dessin
r целостность *f* чертежа

3149 drawing interchange binary file format; DXB file format
d DXB-Dateiformat *n*
f format *m* de fichier DXB
r файловый формат *m* DXB

3150 drawing interchange format; DXF
d Zeichnungsaustausch-Format *n*; DXF-Format *n*
f format *m* DXF
r формат *m* DXF

3151 drawing limits; design limits
d Zeichengrenzen *fpl*
f limites *fpl* de dessin; contours *mpl* de dessin
r границы *fpl* черчения

3152 drawing mode
d Zeichenmodus *m*
f mode *m* de tracement
r режим *m* черчения

3153 drawing object
d Zeichenobjekt *n*
f objet *m* de dessin
r чертежный объект *m*

3154 drawing order
d Zeichenordnung *f*
f ordre *m* de tracement

r порядок *m* черчения

3155 drawing page
d Zeichenseite *f*
f page *f* de dessin
r страница *f* рисунка

3156 drawing parameter
d Zeichensparameter *m*
f paramètre *m* de dessin
r чертежный параметр *m*

3157 drawing pen
d Zeichenfeder *f*
f plume *f* à dessin
r чертежное перо *n*

3158 drawing processor
d Zeichnungsprozessor *m*; Drawing-Prozessor *m*
f processeur *m* de dessin
r чертежный процессор *m*

3159 drawing prototype; prototype drawing
d Zeichnungsprototyp *m*
f dessin *m* prototype; dessin de base
r чертеж-прототип *m*

3160 drawing rate
d Zeichenschnelligkeit *f*
f vitesse *f* de tracement
r скорость *f* черчения

* **drawing scale** → 8296

3161 drawing settings
d Zeichnungseinrichtungen *fpl*
f paramètres *mpl* de dessin
r установление *n* параметров чертежа

* **drawing size** → 7176

3162 drawing software; graphics designer; designer
(software for design and illustration)
d Zeichensoftware *f*; Grafik-Designer *m*
f logiciel *m* de dessin; dessineur *m*; concepteur *m*
r программное обеспечение *n* проектирования; графический проектировщик *m*

* **drawing standard** → 9139

3163 drawing status
d Zeichnungsstatus *m*
f état *m* de dessin
r состояние *n* чертежа

3164 drawing style
d Zeichnungsstil *m*

  f style *m* de tracement
  r чертежный стиль *m*; стиль черчения

3165 drawing time
  d Zeichnungszeit *f*
  f temps *m* de tracement
  r время *n* черчения

3166 drawing tool
  d Zeichnungshilfsmittel *n*
  f outil *m* de tracement; outil tracé; outil de dessin
  r чертежный инструмент *m*

3167 drawing units; plot units
  d Zeichnungseinheiten *fpl*; Plottmaßeinheiten *fpl*
  f unités *fpl* de dessin; unités de traçage
  r чертежные единицы *fpl*

3168 drawing utility
  d Zeichnungsdienstprogramm *n*
  f utilité *f* de dessin
  r чертежный утилит *m*

3169 drawing web format; DWF
  d DWF-Format *n*
  f format *m* DWF
  r формат *m* DWF

3170 drawing window
  d Zeichenfenster *n*
  f fenêtre *f* de tracement
  r чертежное окно *n*; чертежный экран *m*

3171 draw menu
  d Zeichenmenü *n*
  f menu *m* de tracement
  r меню *n* черчения

3172 draw toolbar
  d Zeichnungshilfsmittelstreifen *m*
  f barre *f* d'outils de tracement
  r инструментальная лента *f* черчения

3173 3D region
  d 3D-Region *f*
  f région *f* 3D
  r 3D регион *m*

  * **3D relief effect** → 2599

3174 drift
  d Abdrift *f*
  f dérive *f*
  r дрейф *m*

3175 drift angle
  d Abdriftwinkel *m*
  f angle *m* de dérive

  r угол *m* сноса; угол дрейфа

3176 driver
  (a program)
  d Driver *m*; Treiber *m*
  f driver *m*; pilote *m*; programme *m* de gestion
  r драйвер *m*

  * **DRM** → 2523

3177 drop *v*
  d loslassen; auslassen
  f lâcher
  r спускать; отпускать; опускать

  * **drop cap** → 3185

3178 drop-down
  d Dropdown-
  f déroulant
  r выпадающий; ниспадающий; раскрывающийся

3179 drop-down box
  d Dropdown-Feld *n*
  f boîte *f* déroulante
  r ниспадающее окно *n*; выпадающее окно

3180 drop-down combo box
  d Dropdown-Kombinationsfeld *n*
  f zone *f* de liste déroulante fixe
  r раскрывающееся комбинированное окно *n*

3181 drop-down list box
  d Dropdown-Listenfeld *n*
  f zone *f* de liste déroulante modifiable; boîte *f* de liste déroulante modifiable
  r раскрывающееся окно *n* списка

  * **dropdown menu** → 7633

  * **drop-off** → 641

  * **drop *v* off** → 3695

3182 drop-off angle
  d Winkel *m* des Abweichungsfalls
  f gradient *m* de décroissance de déviation
  r угол *m* затухания

3183 dropped edge
  d gebogener Rand *m*
  f bord *m* de coupe déformé
  r выпадающий край *m*

3184 dropped frames
  d herausgefallene Bilder *npl*
  f cadres *mpl* perdus
  r потерянные кадры *mpl*

* **dropping → 2339**

3185 dropping capital; drop cap
  d Initial *n*; verrutschter Buchstabe *m*
  f lettrine *f*
  r буквица *f*; большая стилизованная первая
      буква *f*

3186 drop shadow; flat shadow
      (screen tint or rule touching an illustration,
      box or type to give a 3D effect)
  d hinterlegter Schatten *m*
  f ombre *f* portée; ombre plate
  r падающая тень *f*; плоская тень

3187 3D rotate effect
  d 3D-Drehungseffekt *m*
  f effet *m* de rotation 3D
  r эффект *m* трехмерного поворота

3188 3D rotate filter
  d 3D-Drehungsfilter *m*
  f filtre *m* de rotation 3D
  r фильтр *m* трехмерного поворота

3189 3D rotation
  d 3D-Rotation *f*
  f rotation *f* 3D
  r 3D вращение *n*; 3D поворот *m*

3190 drum plotter; belt-bed plotter
  d Trommelplotter *m*; Walzenplotter *m*;
      Walzenschreiber *m*
  f traceur *m* à rouleau; traceur à tambour
  r барабанный графопостроитель *m*;
      рулонный графопостроитель

3191 drum scanner
  d Trommelscanner *m*
  f scanner *m* à tambour
  r барабанный сканер *m*

3192 3D scanner
  d 3D-Scanner *m*
  f scanner *m* 3D
  r 3D сканер *m*

* **3D scatter diagrams → 3193**

3193 3D scatter plots; 3D scatter diagrams
  d 3D-Dispersionspunktediagramme *npl*;
      3D-Punktwolken *fpl*
  f graphiques *mpl* de dispersion 3D
  r трехмерные диаграммы *fpl* разброса

3194 3D scene
  d 3D-Szene *f*
  f scène *f* 3D
  r 3D сцена *f*

3195 3D scene acquisition
  d 3D-Szenenerfassung *f*
  f acquisition *f* de scènes 3D
  r сбор *m* 3D сцен; накопление *n* 3D сцен

3196 3D scene model
  d 3D-Szenenmodell *n*
  f modèle *m* de scènes 3D
  r модель *f* 3D сцен

3197 3D seismic survey
  d seismische 3D-Aufnahme *f*
  f levé *m* sismique en 3D
  r трехмерная сейсмическая съемка *f*

* **2D shape → 2672**

3198 3D shape; 3D figure
  d 3D-Figur *f*
  f figure *f* 3D
  r 3D фигура *f*

3199 3D sharpen effect
  d 3D-Schärfeeffekt *m*
  f effet *m* de netteté 3D
  r 3D-эффект *m* резкости

3200 3D software
  d 3D-Software *f*
  f logiciel *m* 3D
  r трехмерное программное обеспечение *n*

3201 2D solid
  d 2D-Körper *m*
  f solide *m* 2D
  r 2D тело *n*

3202 3D solid
  d 3D-Körper *m*
  f solide *m* 3D
  r 3D тело *n*

3203 2D solid line
  d 2D-Vollinie *f*
  f ligne *f* solide à deux dimensions
  r двумерная плотная линия *f*

3204 3D solid model; solid model
  d 3D-Festkörper-Modell *n*
  f modèle *m* solide
  r [трехмерная] твердотелая модель *f*

3205 3D solid projection
  d 3D-Festkörper-Projektion *f*
  f projection *f* de solide 3D
  r проекция *f* трехмерного тела

3206 3D solid shape
  d 3D-Körperform *f*

f forme *f* solide 3D
r трехмерная монолитная форма *f*

3207 2D space
   d 2D-Raum *m*
   f espace *m* 2D
   r 2D пространство *n*

3208 3D space
   d 3D-Raum *m*
   f espace *m* 3D
   r 3D пространство *n*

   * **3D spiral → 4560**

3209 3D spline
   d 3D-Spline *m*
   f spline *m* 3D
   r 3D сплайн *m*

3210 3D spreadsheet
   d 3D-Rechenblatt *n*
   f tableur *m* 3D
   r 3D электронная таблица *f*

3211 3D stereographic image
   d 3D stereografisches Bild *n*
   f image *f* stéréographique 3D
   r трехмерное стереографическое
      изображение *n*

3212 3D stereo noise filter
   d 3D-Stereo-Gerausch-Filter *m*
   f filtre *m* de bruit stéréo 3D
   r фильтр *m* трехмерного стерео-искажения

3213 3D style
   d 3D-Stil *m*
   f style *m* 3D
   r 3D стиль *m*

3214 3D surface digitizing
   d 3D-Flächendigitalisierung *f*
   f numérisation *f* de surfaces 3D
   r дигитализирование *n* 3D поверхностей

3215 3D symbol; 3D character
   d 3D-Symbol *n*
   f symbole *m* 3D
   r 3D символ *m*

3216 2D template
   d 2D-Schablone *f*
   f modèle *m* 2D
   r 2D шаблон *m*

3217 3D text
   d 3D-Text *m*
   f texte *m* 3D
   r 3D текст *m*

3218 3D text positioning
   d 3D-Text-Positionieren *n*
   f positionnement *m* de texte 3D
   r позиционирование *n* трехмерного текста

3219 dual
   d dual
   f dual
   r дуальный; двойственный

   * **dual brightness → 1135**

3220 duality; reciprocity; reciprocation
   d Dualität *f*; Reziprozität *f*
   f dualité *f*; réciprocité *f*
   r двойственность *f*; взаимность *f*

   * **duality principle → 7441**

3221 duality relation
   d Dualitätsrelation *f*; Dualitätsbeziehung *f*
   f relation *f* de dualité
   r соотношение *n* двойственности

3222 dual projective line
   d duale projektive Gerade *f*
   f droite *f* projective duale
   r дуальная проективная прямая *f*;
      двойственная проективная прямая

3223 dual screen
   (DOS screen and high-resolution graphics
   screen appearing on two separate monitors)
   d Zwei-Schirm *m*
   f écran *m* dual
   r дуальный экран *m*

3224 dull
   d matt; stumpf
   f mat
   r матовый

3225 dull color
   d matte Farbe *f*
   f couleur *f* mate
   r матовый цвет *m*

3226 dummy; fictive; pseudo-
   d blind; Schein-; Leer-; fiktiv; Pseudo-
   f fictif; pseudo-; formel; factice; muet
   r фиктивный; псевдо-; холостой

   * **dummy character → 4794**

3227 duotone
   (two inks)
   d Zweiton *m*; Doppeltonfarbe *f*
   f ton *m* double
   r двухцветный тон *m*

3228 duotone editing
d   Zweitonbearbeitung *f*
f   édition *f* de ton double
r   редактирование *n* двухцветного тона

3229 duotone mode
d   Zweitonmodus *m*
f   mode *m* de ton double
r   режим *m* двутонового представления [изображения]

3230 duplicate *v*
d   verdoppeln; duplizieren
f   doubler; dupliquer
r   дублировать

3231 duplicate; redundant replica
d   Duplikat *n*; Doppel *n*; Zweitexemplar *n*
f   duplicata *m*; réplique *f*
r   дубликат *m*

3232 duplicated object
d   dupliziertes Objekt *n*
f   objet *m* dupliqué
r   дублированный объект *m*

* **duplication → 3095**

* **duplication fill → 3233**

3233 duplication fill[ing]
d   duplizierte Füllung *f*
f   remplissage *m* double
r   удвоенное заполнение *n*

3234 duration
d   Dauer *f*
f   durée *f*
r   продолжительность *f*

* **duty factor → 8923**

3235 3D vector rate
d   3D-Vektorrate *f*
f   taux *m* vectoriel 3D
r   трехмерное векторное отношение *n*

3236 3D video-communication
d   3D-Videokommunikation *f*
f   communication *f* vidéo 3D
r   3D видеокоммуникация *f*

3237 3D videogame
d   3D-Videospiel *n*
f   jeu *m* vidéo 3D
r   3D видеоигра *f*

3238 2D view
d   2D-Ansicht *f*; 2D-Ausblick *m*
f   vue *f* 2D

r   2D представление *n*

3239 3D view
d   3D-Ansicht *f*; 3D-Ausblick *m*
f   vue *f* 3D
r   3D представление *n*

3240 3D viewer
d   3D-Suchprogramm *n*; dreidimensionales Suchprogramm *n*
f   visionneur *m* 3D
r   3D вьювер *m*

3241 3D viewing processor
d   3D-Viewing-Prozessor *m*
f   processeur *m* de visualisation 3D
r   процессор *m* трехмерной визуализации

3242 3D viewpoint
d   3D-Aug[en]punkt *m*
f   point *m* de vue 3D
r   трехмерная точка *f* зрения

3243 2D virtual world
d   2D-Virtualwelt *f*
f   monde *m* virtuel 2D
r   двумерный виртуальный мир *m*

3244 3D virtual world
d   3D-Virtualwelt *f*
f   monde *m* virtuel 3D
r   трехмерный виртуальный мир *m*

3245 2D vision system
d   2D-Sehsystem *n*
f   système *m* de vision 2D
r   двумерная система *f* зрения

3246 3D visualization
d   3D-Visualisierung *f*
f   visualisation *f* 3D
r   3D визуализация *f*

3247 3D voxel data
d   3D-Voxeldaten *npl*
f   données *fpl* de pixels 3D
r   3D данные *npl* об элементах объема

3248 2D wet paint effect
d   2D-Nässe-Farbeneffekt *m*
f   effet *m* de peinture humide 2D
r   2D эффект *m* непросохшей краски

* **DWF → 3169**

3249 DWF file
d   DWF-Datei *n*
f   fichier *m* DWF
r   файл *m* DWF

3250 3D wireframe model
 d 3D-Drahtrahmenmodell *n*
 f modèle *m* 3D fil de fer; modèle 3D filaire
 r трехмерная каркасная модель *f*

3251 3D world
 d 3D-Welt *f*
 f monde *m* 3D
 r 3D мир *m*

 * **DXB file format** → 3149

 * **DXF** → 3150

 * **dye** → 9695

3252 dyed agate
 d gefärbtes Agate *n*
 f agate *f* teintée
 r затененный агат *m*

3253 dynamic
 d dynamisch
 f dynamique
 r динамический

3254 dynamically linked library; DLL
 d dynamisch verknüpfte Programmbibliothek *f*;
      DLL
 f bibliothèque *f* chaînée dynamiquement
 r динамически связанная библиотека *f*

3255 dynamic dimension line
 d dynamische Dimensionslinie *f*
 f ligne *f* de cotation dynamique
 r динамическая размерная линия *f*

 * **dynamic display image** → 3934

3256 dynamic dragging
 d dynamisches Ziehen *n*
 f entraînement *m* dynamique
 r динамическое перемещение *n*

3257 dynamic drape
 d dynamisches Drapieren *n*
 f drapage *m* dynamique
 r динамическая складка *f*

 * **dynamic image** → 3934

3258 dynamic lighting
 d dynamische Beleuchtung *f*
 f éclairage *m* dynamique
 r динамическое освещение *n*

3259 dynamic link
 d dynamische Verknüpfung *f*
 f liaison *f* dynamique
 r динамическая связь *f*

3260 dynamic model
 d dynamisches Modell *n*
 f modèle *m* dynamique
 r динамическая модель *f*

3261 dynamic object rendering
 d dynamisches Objekt-Rendering *n*
 f rendu *m* d'objet dynamique
 r динамическое тонирование *n* объекта

3262 dynamic option
 d dynamische Option *f*
 f option *f* dynamique
 r динамический выбор *m*

3263 dynamic range
      (of tones)
 d dynamischer Bereich *m*
 f rangée *f* dynamique
 r динамический диапазон *m*

3264 dynamics
 d Dynamik *f*
 f dynamique *f*
 r динамика *f*

3265 dynamic simulation
 d dynamische Simulation *f*
 f simulation *f* dynamique
 r динамическая симуляция *f*

3266 dynamic spectral width
 d dynamische Spektralbreite *f*
 f largeur *f* spectrale dynamique
 r динамическая ширина *f* спектра

3267 dynamic threshold
 d dynamischer Schwellwert *m*
 f seuil *m* dynamique
 r динамический порог *m*

3268 dynamic time warping
 d dynamische Zeitkrümmung *f*
 f gauchissement *m* de temps dynamique
 r динамическое искажение *n* времени

3269 dynamic view
 d dynamische Ansicht *f*
 f vue *f* dynamique
 r динамический вид *m*

3270 dynamic visual filtering
 d dynamische visuelle Filtrierung *f*
 f filtrage *m* visuel dynamique
 r динамическое визуальное
      фильтрирование *n*

3271 dynamic zooming
 d dynamisches Zoomen *n*
 f zoom *m* dynamique
 r динамическое масштабирование *n*

E

3272 eastern light
d Ostlicht *n*
f orientale lumière *f*
r восточный свет *m*

3273 eccentricity
d Exzentrizität *f*
f excentricité *f*
r эксцентрицитет *m*; эксцентричность *f*

3274 eccentricity of ellipsoid
d Exzentrizität *f* des Ellipsoids
f excentricité *f* d'ellipsoïde
r эксцентрицитет *m* эллипсоида

3275 eccentric position
d exzentrische Lage *f*
f position *f* excentrique
r эксцентрическая позиция *f*

3276 echo
d Echo *n*
f écho *m*
r эхо *n*

3277 echo image
d Echobild *n*
f écho-image *f*
r эхо-изображение *n*

* **ECS → 3455**

3278 edge
d Rand *m*; Schranke *f*
f tranche *f*, côte *f*, bord *m*
r граница *f* [поверхностей]; грань *f*; край *m*; кромка *f*

3279 edge
(of a graph)
d Kante *f*
f côte *f*; arête *f*
r ребро *n*

3280 edge-based algorithm
d Kantenalgorithmus *m*
f algorithme *m* à base d'arêtes
r алгоритм *m*, основанный на реберном представлении

3281 edge-based triangle subdivision
d kantenbasierte Dreieckunterteilung *f*
f subdivision *f* de triangle à base d'arêtes
r треугольное подразделение *n*, основанное на реберном представлении

3282 edge comparison
d Randvergleich *m*
f comparaison *f* de côtes
r сравнение *n* краев

3283 edge-defined surface mesh
d durch Kanten definierte Flächenmasche *f*
f maille *f* surfacique à base d'arêtes
r сеточная поверхность *f*, дефинированная ребрами

3284 edge detail
d Kantendetail *n*
f détail *m* d'arête
r элемент *m* ребра

* **edge detect → 3285**

* **edge detect filter → 3286**

3285 edge detect[ion]
d Randerkennung *f*
f détection *f* des côtes
r обнаружение *n* краев; выделение *n* краев

3286 edge detect[ion] filter
d Randerkennungsfilter *m*
f filtre *m* de détection des côtes
r фильтр *m* обнаружения краев

3287 edge effect
d Randeffekt *m*
f effet *m* de côte
r краевой эффект *m*

3288 edge extraction
d Kantenextraktion *f*
f extraction *f* d'arêtes
r извлечение *n* ребер

* **edge fog → 3289**

3289 edge fog[ging]; marginal veil
d Randschleier *m*
f voile *m* marginal
r краевая вуаль *f*

3290 edge line
d Randlinie *f*
f ligne *f* de côte
r краевая линия *f*

3291 edge matching
d Kantenübereinstimmung *f*
f coïncidence *f* d'arêtes
r соответствие *n* ребер; совпадение *n* ребер

3292 **edge number**
  d Kantenzahl *f*
  f nombre *m* d'arêtes
  r число *n* ребер

3293 **edge of a dihedral angle**
  d Schnittgerade *f* zweier Halbebenen
  f arête *f* d'un dièdre
  r ребро *n* двугранного угла

3294 **edge of a network**
  d Kante *f* eines Netzwerkes; Rand *m* eines Netzwerkes
  f arête *f* d'un réseau
  r ребро *n* сети

3295 **edge of a polyhedron**
  d Kante *f* eines Polyeders
  f arête *f* d'un polyèdre
  r ребро *n* многогранника

3296 **edge processor**
  d Kantenprozessor *m*; Edge-Prozessor *m*
  f processeur *m* [de traitement] de côtes; processeur d'arêtes
  r процессор *m* обработки краев; процессор обработки ребер

3297 **edge shading**
  d Randabschattung *f*
  f ombrage *m* d'arêtes
  r затенение *n* ребер; затенение краев

  * **edge sharpness** → 3299

3298 **edge surface**
  d Kantenfläche *f*
  f surface *f* d'arête
  r реберная поверхность *f*; граненая поверхность

3299 **edge[-to-edge] sharpness**
  d Kantenschärfe *f*
  f contraste *m* marginal
  r резкость *f* контуров

3300 **edge tokens**
  d Randmarken *fpl*
  f étiquettes *fpl* des côtes
  r метки *fpl* краев; метки ребер

3301 **edge visibility**
  d Kantensichtbarkeit *f*
  f visibilité *f* d'arête
  r видимость *f* ребра

  * **edit** → 3306

3302 **edit** *v*
  d bearbeiten
  f éditer
  r редактировать

3303 **editable image**
  d Bearbeitungsbild *n*
  f image *f* éditable
  r редактируемое изображение *n*

3304 **edit** *v* **arrowhead**
  d Pfeilspitze bearbeiten
  f éditer un pic de flèche
  r редактировать конец стрелки

3305 **edit** *v* **bitmap**
  d Bitmap bearbeiten
  f éditer un bitmap
  r редактировать растровое изображение

3306 **edit[ing]**
  d Bearbeitung *f*; Aufbereitung *f*; Editieren *n*
  f mise *f* en forme; édition *f*; rédaction *f*
  r редактирование *n*

3307 **editing commands**
  d Bearbeitungsbefehle *mpl*
  f commandes *fpl* d'édition
  r команды *fpl* редактирования

3308 **editing function**
  d Editierfunktion *f*
  f fonction *f* d'édition
  r функция *f* редактирования

3309 **editing program; editor**
  d Bearbeitungsprogramm *n*; Editierprogramm *n*; Editor *m*
  f programme *m* d'édition; éditeur *m*
  r редактирующая программа *f*; редактор *m*

3310 **editing time**
  d Editierzeit *f*
  f temps *m* d'édition
  r время *n* редактирования

3311 **edit menu**
  d Bearbeitungsmenü *n*
  f menu *m* d'édition
  r меню *n* редактирования

3312 **edit mode**
  d Bearbeitungsbetrieb *m*
  f mode *m* d'édition
  r режим *m* редактирования

  * **editor** → 3309

3313 **edit** *v* **tiling of pattern**
  d Musterkachelung bearbeiten
  f éditer un pavage
  r редактировать мозаичное размещение шаблона

3314 effect
  d Effekt *m*
  f effet *m*
  r эффект *m*; результат *m*; воздействие *n*

3315 effect application
  d Effekt-Anwendung *f*
  f application *f* d'effet
  r применение *n* эффекта

3316 effective; efficient
  d effektiv; effizient
  f effectif; efficace
  r эффективный

3317 effective area
  d Nutzfläche *f*
  f aire *f* utile
  r рабочая площадь *f*

3318 effective mass
  d effektive Masse *f*
  f masse *f* effective; masse apparente
  r эффективная масса *f*

3319 effector
  d Effektor *m*
  f effecteur *m*
  r эффектор *m*; спецификатор *m*

3320 effect tool
  d Effekt-Hilfsmittel *n*
  f outil *m* d'effets
  r инструмент *m* [визуальных] эффектов

3321 effect tool picker
  d Auswahl-Schaltfläche *f* des Effekt-Hilfsmittels
  f dispositif *m* de désignation d'effets; bouton *m* de sélection d'effets
  r указатель *m* инструмента эффектов; подборщик *m* эффектов

3322 efficiency
  d Effektivität *f*; Effizienz *f*; Wirkungsgrad *m*
  f efficacité *f*; efficience *f*
  r эффективность *f*

* **efficient → 3316**

3323 egg-box lens
  d Linse *f* mit gekreuzten Platten
  f lentille *f* multicellulaire
  r многоклеточная линза *f*

* **eiconal → 3328**

3324 eiconal approximation
  d Eikonalnäherung *f*
  f approximation *f* eiconale

  r эйкональное приближение *n*

3325 eiconal equation
  d Eikonalgleichung *f*
  f équation *f* eiconale
  r эйкональное уравнение *n*

3326 eigenvalue
  d Eigenwert *m*
  f valeur *f* propre
  r собственное значение *n*

* **eigenvector → 1427**

3327 eight curve
  d Achter *m*; Achterkurve *f*
  f huit *m*
  r восьмерка *f*

3328 eikonal; eiconal; geodesic distance
  d Eikonal *n*; geodätischer Abstand *m*; geodätische Entfernung *f*
  f [e]iconale *f*; distance *f* géodésique
  r эйконал *m*; геодезическое расстояние *n*; оптическая длина *f* пути

3329 eject *v*
  d ausstoßen; vorschieben
  f éjecter
  r выдавать; выбрасывать

3330 elapsed time; uptime; available time
  d verwendete Zeit *f*; Benutzungszeit *f*
  f temps *m* écoulé; temps de fonctionnement
  r время *n* работы; полное время (работы системы)

3331 elapsed timer
  d Benutzungszeitzähler *m*
  f minuterie *f* à mesurer la durée totale de fonctionnement
  r часы *pl* использованного времени; счетчик *m* использованного времени

3332 elastic
  d elastisch
  f élastique
  r упругий; эластический

3333 elastic deformation
  d elastische Verformung *f*
  f déformation *f* élastique
  r упругая деформация *f*

3334 elastic objects
  d elastische Objekte *npl*
  f objets *mpl* élastiques
  r эластические объекты *mpl*

3335 electronic beam
  d Elektronenstrahl *m*

   f rayon *m* électronique
   r электронный луч *m*

3336 electronic color
   d elektronische Farbe *f*
   f couleur *f* électronique
   r электронный цвет *m*

3337 electronic color management
   d elektronische Farbverwaltung *f*
   f traitement *m* de couleur électronique
   r управление *n* электронного цвета

3338 electronic game
   d elektronisches Spiel *n*
   f jeu *m* électronique
   r электронная игра *f*

   * **electronic pen** → 5554

3339 electronic retouching
   d elektronische Retusche *f*
   f retouche *f* électronique
   r электронная ретушь *f*

3340 electronic spreadsheet; spreadsheet [program]
   d Tabellenkalkulationsprogramm *n*; Rechenblatt *n*; Journalbogen *m*; Tabellenkalkulation *f*
   f feuille *f* de calcul électronique; programme *m* tableur; tableur *m*
   r электронная таблица *f*; программа *f* табличных вычислений

3341 electrophotographic printer
   d elektrofotografischer Drucker *m*
   f imprimante *f* électrophotographique
   r электрофотографическое печатающее устройство *n*

   * **electrophotography** → 10489

3342 electrostatic plotter
   d elektrostatischer Plotter *m*
   f traceur *m* électrostatique
   r электростатический графопостроитель *m*

   * **electrothermic printer** → 9636

3343 element
   d Element *n*
   f élément *m*
   r элемент *m*

3344 elementary logical connections
   d elementare logische Verknüpfungen *fpl*
   f connexions *fpl* logiques élémentaires
   r основные логические операции *fpl*

   * **elementary vortex** → 3350

   * **element by element** → 3351

   * **element cursor** → 8462

3345 element of area; areal element; surface element
   d Flächenelement *n*; Oberflächenelement *n*
   f élément *m* d'aire; élément de surface
   r элемент *m* площади; элемент поверхности

3346 element of a set; member of a set
   d Element *n* einer Menge
   f élément *m* d'un ensemble
   r элемент *m* множества

3347 element of infinity; infinite element; ideal element; improper element
   d unendlichfernes Element *n*; ideales Element; Fernelement *n*
   f élément *m* de l'infini; élément idéal; élément impropre
   r бесконечно удаленный элемент *m*; несобственный элемент

3348 element of mass
   d Massenelement *n*
   f élément *m* de masse
   r элемент *m* массы

3349 element of volume; volume element; voxel; volume pixel
   d Volumenelement *n*; Raumelement *n*; Voxel *n*
   f élément *m* de volume; pixel *m* 3D
   r элемент *m* объема

3350 element of vortex; vortex element; elementary vortex
   d Wirbelelement *n*; Elementarwirbel *m*
   f élément *m* [de] tourbillon
   r элемент *m* вихря; вихревой элемент

3351 element-wise; element by element
   d elementweise
   f élément par élément; par éléments
   r поэлементно

3352 elevate *v*; lift *v*
   d erheben; abheben; hochheben
   f élever; lever; hausser
   r возвышать; поднимать; приподнимать

3353 elevated
   d erhöht
   f élevé
   r [при]поднятый; воздвигнутый; возведенный

3354 elevation
   d Elevation *f*

f élévation *f*
r возвышение *n*

* **elevation** → 378

3355 elevation mode
d Elevationsmodus *m*
f mode *m* d'élévation
r режим *m* возвышения

* **elevator** → 8399

3356 eliminate *v*; **delete** *v*; **reset** *v*
d eliminieren; beseitigen; ausschließen
f éliminer; détruire
r уничтожать; вычеркивать; исключать

3357 elimination
d Elimination *f*; Beseitigung *f*
f élimination *f*
r исключение *n*; элиминация *f*;
   элиминирование *n*

3358 elimination algorithm
d Eliminationsalgorithmus *m*
f algorithme *m* d'élimination
r алгоритм *m* исключения

3359 ellipse
d Ellipse *f*
f ellipse *f*
r эллипс *m*

3360 ellipse axes
d Achsen *fpl* der Ellipse
f axes *mpl* d'une ellipse
r оси *fpl* эллипса

3361 ellipse endpoints
d Endpunkte *mpl* der Ellipse
f points *mpl* d'ellipse finals
r краевые точки *fpl* эллипсы

3362 ellipse radius ratio
d Radiusverhältnis *n* der Ellipse
f rapport *m* des rayons d'ellipse
r соотношение *n* радиусов эллипса

3363 ellipse smoothness
d Ellipsenglätte *f*
f égalité *f* d'ellipse
r гладкость *f* эллипса

3364 ellipsis; dots
   (wild-card character)
d Auslassungspunkte *mpl*;
   Fortführungspunkte *mpl*
f points *mpl* de suspension
r эллипсис *m*; многоточие *n*

3365 ellipsoid
d Ellipsoid *n*
f ellipsoïde *m*
r эллипсоид *m*

* **ellipsoidal** → 3367

3366 ellipsoid of revolution
d Drehungsellipsoid *n*
f ellipsoïde *m* de révolution
r эллипсоид *m* вращения

* **elliptic** → 3367

3367 elliptic[al]; ellipsoidal
d elliptisch
f elliptique; ellipsoïdal
r эллиптический

3368 elliptic[al] arc
d elliptischer Bogen *m*
f arc *m* elliptique
r эллиптическая дуга *f*

3369 elliptic[al] area
d elliptische Zone *f*
f zone *f* elliptique
r эллиптическая зона *f*

3370 elliptic[al] cone
d elliptischer Kegel *m*
f cône *m* elliptique
r эллиптический конус *m*

3371 elliptic[al] coordinates
d elliptische Koordinaten *fpl*
f coordonnées *fpl* elliptiques
r эллиптические координаты *fpl*

3372 elliptic[al] cross-section
d elliptischer Querschnitt *m*
f section *f* transversale elliptique
r эллиптическое поперечное сечение *n*

3373 elliptic[al] curve
d elliptische Kurve *f*
f courbe *f* elliptique
r эллиптическая кривая *f*

3374 elliptic[al] cycloid
d Elliptozykloide *f*
f cycloïde *f* elliptique
r эллиптическая циклоида *f*

3375 elliptic[al] cylinder
d elliptischer Zylinder *m*
f cylindre *m* elliptique
r эллиптический цилиндр *m*

3376 elliptic[al] dot
d elliptischer Rasterpunkt *m*;

elliptischer Punkt *m*
f point *m* de trame elliptique
r растровая точка *f* эллиптической формы

3377 elliptic[al] dot screen; dot-chaining screen; chain-dot screen
d Kettenpunktraster *m*
f trame *f* à points elliptiques; trame à points en chaîne
r растр *m* с эллиптическими цепеобразными элементами

3378 elliptic[al] mask
d elliptische Maske *f*
f masque *f* elliptique
r эллиптическая маска *f*

3379 elliptic[al] paraboloid
d elliptisches Paraboloid *n*
f paraboloïde *m* elliptique
r эллиптический параболоид *m*

3380 elliptic[al] torus
d elliptischer Torus *m*
f tore *m* elliptique
r эллиптический тор *m*

* **elliptic arc** → **3368**

* **elliptic area** → **3369**

* **elliptic cone** → **3370**

* **elliptic coordinates** → **3371**

* **elliptic cross-section** → **3372**

* **elliptic curve** → **3373**

* **elliptic cycloid** → **3374**

* **elliptic cylinder** → **3375**

* **elliptic dot** → **3376**

* **elliptic dot screen** → **3377**

3381 ellipticity
d Elliptizität *f*
f ellipticité *f*
r эллиптичность *f*

* **elliptic mask** → **3378**

* **elliptic paraboloid** → **3379**

* **elliptic torus** → **3380**

* **elongate** *v* → **7591**

* **elongated** → **7584**

3382 elongation; prolongation; lengthening
d Verlängerung *f*; Längsdehnung *f*
f allongement *m*; élongation *f*
r удлинение *n*

3383 embedded chart
d eingebettetes Diagramm *n*
f diagramme *m* incorporé
r встроенная диаграмма *f*

3384 embedded objects
d eingebettete Objekte *npl*
f objets *mpl* encastrés
r встроенные объекты *mpl*

3385 embedded sensor
d eingebetteter Sensor *m*
f senseur *m* encastré
r встроенный сенсор *m*

3386 embedded window
d eingebettetes Fenster *n*
f fenêtre *f* encastrée
r вложенное окно *n*

* **embedding** → **6189**

3387 embedding mapping
d Einbettungsabbildung *f*
f application *f* d'encastrement
r отображение *n* вложения

* **emblem** → **1200**

3388 emboss *v*
d prägen
f gaufrer; bosseler; estamper
r выдавливать выпуклый рисунок; чеканить; гофрировать; лепить рельеф; украшать рельефом

3389 emboss[ed] effect; relief effect
d Reliefeffekt *m*
f effet *m* relief
r эффект *m* рельефа

3390 embossed surface; surface in relief
d Relieffläche *f*
f surface *f* en relief
r рельефная поверхность *f*

* **emboss effect** → **3389**

3391 emboss filter
d Relieffilter *m*
f filtre *m* de relief
r фильтр *m* рельефа

3392 emergent light
d ausfallendes Licht *n*
f lumière *f* émergente
r эмергентный свет *m*

3393 emission
d Emission *f*
f émission *f*
r эмиссия *f*; излучение *n*

* **emission angle** → 3394

3394 emission [beam] angle; radiation angle
d Emissionswinkel *m*; Strahlungswinkel *m*
f angle *m* d'émission; angle d'éjection; angle de rayonnement
r угол *m* излучения

3395 emission limit
d Emissionsgrenze *f*
f limite *f* d'émission
r граница *f* излучения

* **emission line** → 9003

* **emissive** → 7705

3396 emissive display
d Bildschirm *m* mit Emission
f afficheur *m* à émission
r дисплей *m* с излучением

3397 emissivity
d Emissionsvermögen *n*; Emissionsfähigkeit *f*; Strahlungsvermögen *n*
f émissivité *f*; pouvoir *m* d'émission
r эмиссионная способность *f*; способность излучения

3398 emitting; radiant
d strahlend
f rayonnant
r излучающий

3399 emitting aperture
d Austrittsöffnung *f*
f ouverture *f* émissive
r излучающее отверстие *n*

* **emitting area** → 3401

3400 emitting diameter
d Strahlungsflächendurchmesser *m*
f diamètre *m* d'émission
r диаметр *m* излучающей поверхности

3401 emitting surface; emitting area
d Emissionfläche *f*; strahlende Fläche *f*; Strahlungsfläche *f*
f zone *f* émissive

r излучающая область *f*; зона *f* излучения

* **emoticon** → 8806

* **emphasis** → 4635

* **emphasize** *v* → 50, 4630, 9983

3402 empirical
d Erfahrungs-; empirisch
f empirique
r эмпирический; опытный

3403 empirical data
d empirische Daten *npl*
f données *fpl* empiriques
r эмпирические данные *npl*

* **employment** → 486

* **empty** → 990

3404 empty cell
d leere Zelle *f*
f cellule *f* vide
r пустая клетка *f*

3405 emulation
d Emulation *f*
f émulation *f*
r эмуляция *f*

3406 emulator
d Emulator *m*
f émulateur *m*
r эмулятор *m*

3407 emulsion
d Emulsion *f*
f émulsion *f*
r эмульсия *f*

3408 enable *v*
d wirksam machen; freigeben
f permettre; autoriser; résoudre
r разрешать; позволять

3409 encapsulate *v*
d einkapseln; verkapseln
f [en]capsuler
r герметизировать

3410 encapsulated PostScript; EPS
d eingekapselter PostScript *m*
f PostScript *m* encapsulé
r капсулированный язык *m* описания страниц

3411 encapsulated Postscript file; EPS file
d EPS-Datei *f*

f fichier *m* EPS
r файл *m* EPS

3412 encapsulated type
(of data)
d eingekapselter Typ *m*
f type *m* encapsulé
r скрытый тип *m*

* **encapsulation** → 1275

3413 encasement; package
d Gehäuse *n*; Verpackung *f*
f boîtier *m*; revêtement *m*; emballage *m*
r корпус *m*; упаковка *f*

* **encirclement** → 1525

3414 enclose *v*; **include** *v*
d umschließen; einschließen; einkapseln
f enclore; inclure; contenir
r включать в себя; охватывать; заключать

* **enclosure** → 3726

3415 encoded; coded
d codiert
f codé
r кодированный

* **encoding** → 1640

3416 encryption
d Zeichenverschlüsselung *f*
f cryptage *m*; chiffrage *m*; chiffrement *m*; cryptoopération *f*
r шифрование *n*

* **end** → 3797

3417 end
d Ende *n*
f fin *f*; bout *m*
r конец *m*

3418 end-aligned
d endbündig
f aligné sur la fin
r выравненный в конце

3419 end angle
d Endwinkel *m*
f angle *m* final
r конечный угол *m*

* **end-around shift** → 1508

3420 end coordinates
d Endkoordinaten *fpl*
f coordonnées *fpl* finales

r конечные координаты *fpl*

* **endecagon** → 4569

* **endecahedron** → 4571

3421 end face
d Endfläche *f*
f face *f* d'extrémité
r выходной торец *m*

3422 ending color
d Endfarbe *f*
f couleur *f* de fin
r цвет *m* окончания

3423 ending width
d Endbreite *f*
f largeur *f* de fin
r ширина *f* окончания

3424 End key
d End-Taste *f*
f touche *f* End
r клавиша *f* End

* **endless** → 5051

* **end mark** → 3425

3425 end mark[er]; end tag
d Endmarke *f*; Endsteuerzeichen *n*
f marque *f* de fin; marqueur *m* de fin
r метка *f* конца; маркер *m* конца

* **end node** → 3430

3426 end object; terminal object; final object
d Endobjekt *n*
f objet *m* final
r конечный объект *n*; концевой объект

3427 end page
d letzte Seite *f*
f page *f* finale
r конечная страница *f*

3428 endpoint; terminal point
d Endpunkt *m*
f point *m* final; extrémité *f*
r конечная точка *f*

3429 endpoint marker
d Endpunkt-Marker *m*
f marqueur *m* de point final
r маркер *m* конечной точки

3430 endpoint node; end node
d Endpunkt-Knoten *m*

f nœud *m* d'extrémité; nœud périphérique
r периферный узел *m*; конечный узел

3431 endpoint of arc; arc endpoint
  d Endpunkt *m* des Bodens
  f point *m* d'arc final
  r конечная точка *f* дуги

3432 endpoint of axis; axis endpoint
  d Endpunkt *m* der Achse
  f point *m* d'axe final
  r конечная точка *f* оси

3433 end sequence
  d begrenzte Folge *f*
  f séquence *f* finale
  r конечная последовательность *f*

  * **end tag → 3425**

  * **endurance → 9230**

  * **end vertex → 9527**

3434 end view
  d endgültige Ansicht *f*
  f vue *f* de derrière
  r конечный вид *m*

  * **engine → 5740**

3435 engineering analysis
  d technische Analyse *f*
  f analyse *f* technique
  r технический анализ *m*

3436 engineering data; operating data
  d technische Daten *npl*
  f données *fpl* techniques
  r технические данные *npl*

3437 engineering design
  d technischer Entwurf *m*
  f projet *m* technique; conception *f* technique
  r технический проект *m*

3438 engineering [design] graphics
  d Ingenieurgrafik *f*
  f graphique *m* technique
  r инженерная графика *f*

3439 engineering drawing and graphics technology
  d Ingenieurzeichnung- und Grafik-Technologie *f*
  f technologie *f* de dessin et graphique technique
  r технология *f* черчения и инженерной графики

  * **engineering graphics → 3438**

3440 engrave *v*
  d gravieren
  f graver
  r гравировать

3441 engraved effect
  d eingravierter Effekt *m*
  f effet *m* engravé
  r эффект *m* гравирования

3442 enhanced view
  d erweiterte Ansicht *f*
  f vue *f* améliorée
  r расширенное представление *n*

3443 enhancement; improvement
  d Verbesserung *f*; Anreicherung *f*
  f enrichissement *m*; amélioration *f*
  r улучшение *n*; обогащение *n*

3444 enhancement of the contrast
  d Verbesserung *f* des Kontrastes
  f amélioration *f* du contraste
  r улучшение *n* контраста

  * **enlarge *v* → 7591**

3445 enlarged scale
  d verlängerter Maßstab *m*
  f échelle *f* élargie
  r увеличенный масштаб *m*

  * **enlargement → 3574**

  * **enquiry → 8083**

  * **ensemble → 8557**

3446 enter *v*; introduce *v*; carry-in *v*
  d einführen
  f entrer; introduire
  r входить; вводить

3447 Enter key
  d Enter-Taste *f*
  f touche *f* Enter; touche de validation
  r клавиша *f* ввода; клавиша Enter

3448 enterprise
  d Problembereich *m*; Unternehmen *n*
  f entreprise *f*
  r предметная область *f*; предприятие *n*

3449 enterprise level
  (of data)
  d Enterprise-Ebene *f*; Fachebene *f*
  f niveau *m* d'entreprise
  r предметный уровень *m*

3450 entire; integral *adj*
  d ganz; Voll-
  f entier
  r целый; полный

3451 entire part
  d ganzer Teil *m*
  f partie *f* entière
  r целая часть *f*

3452 entity
  d Entität *f*; Wesen *n*
  f entité *f*
  r сущность *f*; категория *f*; целость *f*

3453 entity
  (transformed graphic primitive with assigned
  nongeometric properties)
  d Einheit *f*
  f entité *f* [géométrique]
  r [геометрический] примитив *m*

3454 entity class
  d Einheitsklasse *f*
  f classe *f* d'entité
  r класс *m* примитива

3455 entity coordinate system; ECS
  d Koordinatensystem *n* der Einheit
  f système *m* de coordonnées d'entité
  r координатная система *f* примитива

3456 entity deformation
  d Einheitsdeformation *f*
  f déformation *f* d'entité
  r искажение *n* примитива

3457 entity name
  d Einheitsname *m*
  f nom *m* d'entité
  r имя *n* примитива

3458 entity-relationship model
  d Einheitsbeziehungsmodell *n*
  f modèle *m* de relations entre entités
  r модель *f* взаимосвязи примитивов

3459 entity selection set
  d Einheit-Auswahlsatz *m*
  f ensemble *m* de sélection d'entités
  r коллекция *f* отбора примитивов

3460 entity sort order
  d Ordnung *f* der Einheitssortierung
  f ordre *m* de triage d'entités
  r порядок *m* сортировки примитивов

3461 entity transformation
  d Einheitstransformation *f*
  f transformation *f* d'entité

  r преобразование *n* примитива

3462 entity type
  d Einheitstyp *m*
  f type *m* d'entité
  r тип *m* примитива

* entrance → 3463

* entry → 5098

3463 entry; entrance
  d Eintritt *m*; Einführung *f*
  f entrée *f*
  r вхождение *n*; введение *n*

* entry field → 2476

3464 entry node
  (of a graph)
  d Eingabeknoten *m*
  f nœud *m* entrant
  r входящий узел *m*

3465 enumeration
  d Aufzählung *f*; Abzählung *f*
  f énumération *f*
  r перечисление *n*; пересчет *m*

3466 enumeration data
  d Zählungsdaten *npl*
  f données *fpl* énumérées
  r перечисленные данные *npl*

* envelope → 3474, 3468

3467 envelope; shell; sheet; hull
  d Hülle *f*
  f enveloppe *f*
  r оболочка *f*

3468 envelope [curve]
  d Hüllkurve *f*
  f courbe *f* enveloppe; enveloppe *f*;
  enveloppante *f*
  r огибающая [кривая] *f*

3469 envelope of a family of lines
  d Einhüllende *f* einer Geradenschar
  f enveloppe *f* d'une famille de droites
  r огибающая *f* семейства прямых

3470 envelope of a family of plane curves
  d Einhüllende *f* einer ebenen Kurvenschar;
  Enveloppe *f* einer ebenen Kurvenschar
  f enveloppe *f* d'une famille de courbes planes
  r огибающая *f* семейства плоских кривых

3471 envelope of a family of surfaces
  d Einhüllende *f* einer Flächenschar

f enveloppe *f* d'une famille de surfaces
r огибающая *f* семейства поверхностей

3472 envelope style
d Hüllenstil *m*
f style *m* des enveloppes
r стиль *m* оболочек

3473 envelope tool
d Hilfsmittel *n* "Hülle"
f outil *m* "enveloppe"
r инструмент *m* "оболочка"

3474 enveloping surface; envelope
d Hüllfläche *f*, Enveloppenfläche *f*, Enveloppe *f*
f surface *f* enveloppe; enveloppe *f*
r огибающая [поверхность] *f*

3475 environment; ambience
d Umgebung *f*; Einkreisung *f*
f environnement *m*; ambiance *f*
r среда *f*; окружение *n*; окрестность *f*

* **environmental → 309**

3476 environmental design
d Umgebungsdesign *n*
f dessin *m* de l'environnement
r проектирование *n* окружения;
проектирование окрестности

3477 environment description
d Umgebungsbeschreibung *f*
f description *f* d'environnement
r описание *n* окружения

3478 environment image
d Umgebungsbild *n*
f image *f* d'environnement
r изображение *n* окрестности

* **environment light → 311**

3479 environment mapping
d Umgebungsabbildung *f*
f application *f* d'environnement
r отображение *n* окрестности; проекция *f*
окрестности

3480 environment name
d Umgebungsname *m*
f nom *m* d'environnement
r имя *n* окружения

3481 environment setting
d Umgebungseinrichtung *f*
f établissement *m* d'environnement
r установление *n* окружения

3482 epicycloid

d Epizykloide *f*
f épicycloïde *f*
r эпициклоида *f*

3483 epitrochoid
d Epitrochoide *f*
f épitrochoïde *f*
r эпитрохоида *f*

* **EPS → 3410**

* **EPS file → 3411**

3484 epsilon-sphere; spherical neighborhood of radius
d sphärische Umgebung *f* des Radius
f voisinage *m* sphérique de rayon
r сферическая окрестность *f* радиуса

3485 equal
d gleich
f égal
r равный; одинаковый

* **equal-angle projection → 2039**

* **equal-area projection → 3515**

3486 equality
d Gleichheit *f*
f égalité *f*
r равенство *n*

* **equalization → 269**

* **equalize *v* → 263**

* **equalize filter → 3487**

3487 equal objects
d gleiche Objekte *npl*
f objets *mpl* égaux
r одинаковые объекты *mpl*

* **equal sign → 3489**

3488 equal-size shapes
d Formen *fpl* mit gleicher Größe
f formes *fpl* à tailles égales
r фигуры *fpl* одинакового размера

3489 equal symbol; equal sign
(=)
d Gleichheitszeichen *n*
f signe *m* d'égalité; signe égal
r знак *m* равенства

3490 equation
d Gleichung *f*

f équation *f*
r уравнение *n*

* **equation in a polar coordinate system →**
  7242

3491 equation of a plane
d Gleichung *f* der Ebene; Ebenengleichung *f*
f équation *f* d'un plan
r уравнение *n* плоскости

3492 equation of a straight line
d Gleichung *f* der Geraden; Geradengleichung *f*
f équation *f* d'une droite
r уравнение *n* прямой

3493 equator
d Äquator *m*
f équateur *m*
r экватор *m*

3494 equatorial plane
d Äquatorebene *f*
f plan *m* équatorial; plan de l'équateur
r экваториальная плоскость *f*; плоскость экватора

3495 equatorial system
d Äquatorsystem *n*
f système *m* équatorial
r экваториальная система *f*

3496 equiangular
d gleichwinklig
f équiangle; équiangulaire
r равноугольный

* **equiangular hyperbola → 3501**

* **equiangular spiral → 5691**

3497 equidistant
d abstandstreu
f équidistant
r равнопромежуточный

3498 equidistant projection
d abstandstreue Projektion *f*
f projection *f* équidistante
r равнопромежуточная проекция *f*

3499 equilateral
d gleichseitig
f équilatéral; équilatère
r равносторонний; равнобочный

3500 equilateral cone
d gleichseitiger Kegel *m*
f cône *m* équilatère
r равносторонний конус *m*

3501 equilateral hyperbola; rectangular hyperbola; equiangular hyperbola
d gleichseitige Hyperbel *f*
f hyperbole *f* équilatère
r равносторонняя гипербола *f*; равнобочная гипербола

3502 equilateral polygon; regular polygon
d regelmäßiges Polygon *n*
f polygone *m* équilatère; polygone régulier
r равносторонний многоугольник *m*; правильный многоугольник

3503 equilateral triangle; regular triangle
d gleichseitiges Dreieck *n*; regelmäßiges Dreieck
f triangle *m* équilatéral; triangle régulier
r равносторонний треугольник *m*; правильный треугольник

* **equilibrium → 814**

3504 equilibrium point
d Gleichgewichtspunkt *m*
f point *m* d'équilibre
r точка *f* равновесия; точка покоя

3505 equipment; facility
d Ausrüstung *f*; Ausstattung *f*; Apparatur *f*; Einrichtung *f*
f équipement *m*; appareillage *m*
r оборудование *n*; аппаратура *f*; сооружения *npl*

3506 equipotential
d äquipotential
f équipotentiel
r эквипотенциальный; равномощный

3507 equipotent[ial] line; potential line
d Äquipotentiallinie *f*; Potentiallinie *f*; Niveaulinie *f*
f ligne *f* équipotentielle; ligne de potentiel constant
r эквипотенциальная линия *f*

3508 equipotent[ial] surface; potential surface; level surface
d Äquipotentialfläche *f*; Potentialfläche *f*; Niveaufläche *f*
f surface *f* équipotentielle; surface de niveau
r эквипотенциальная поверхность *f*; равномощная поверхность

* **equipotent line → 3507**

* **equipotent surface → 3508**

3509 equitangential curve
d Äquitangentialkurve *f*

f courbe *f* équitangentielle
r равнокасательная кривая *f*

3510 equivalence
d Äquivalenz *f*
f équivalence *f*
r эквивалентность *f*

3511 equivalent
d äquivalent; gleichwertig; gleichbedeutend
f équivalent
r эквивалентный; равнозначный

3512 equivalent elements
d äquivalente Elemente *npl*
f éléments *mpl* équivalents
r эквивалентные элементы *mpl*

* **equivalent figures** → **2044**

3513 equivalent forms
d äquivalente Formen *fpl*
f formes *fpl* équivalentes
r эквивалентные формы *fpl*

3514 equivalent knots
d äquivalente Knoten *mpl*
f nœuds *mpl* équivalents
r эквивалентные узлы *mpl*

3515 equivalent projection; equal-area projection
d äquivalente Projektion *f*; flächen[ge]treue Projektion
f projection *f* équivalente
r равновеликая проекция *f*

3516 equivalent representation
d äquivalente Darstellung *f*
f représentation *f* équivalente
r эквивалентное представление *n*

3517 erased object
d ausradiertes Objekt *n*
f objet *m* effacé
r стертый объект *m*

3518 eraser tool
d Hilfsmittel *n* "Radierer"
f outil *m* "gomme"; outil effaceur
r инструмент *m* "резинка для стирания"; стирающий инструмент

3519 erasing; erasure; deletion
d Löschung *f*; Löschen *n*; Radieren *n*
f effacement *m*; effaçage *m*
r стирание *n*

* **erasure** → **3519**

3520 erect *v* **a perpendicular to a line at a point**
d die Senkrechte auf einer Geraden in einem Punkt errichten
f élever une perpendiculaire sur une droite en un point
r восставить перпендикуляр к прямой в точке

3521 erect image; upright image
d aufrecht[stehend]es Bild *n*
f image *f* droite; image à l'endroit
r выпрямленное изображение *n*

3522 erroneous
d fehlerhaft; falsch; irrig
f erroné
r ошибочный

3523 error
d Fehler *m*
f erreur *f*
r ошибка *f*; погрешность *f*

3524 error diffusion
d Fehlerdiffusion *f*
f diffusion *f* d'erreurs
r рассеивание *n* ошибок

3525 error-diffusion dithering
d Fehlerdiffusionsdithering *n*
f juxtaposition *f* de diffusion d'erreurs
r размывание *n* распространения ошибок

3526 error handling
d Fehlerbehandlung *f*
f management *m* d'erreurs
r обработка *f* ошибок

3527 error message
d Fehlermeldung *f*
f message *m* d'erreur
r сообщение *n* об ошибке

* **error of approximation** → **513**

* **error of observation** → **6440**

* **ESC** → **3529**

3528 escape
d Escape *n*; Umschalten *n*; Umschaltung *f*; Codewechsel *m*
f échappement *m*; changement *m* de code
r переключение *n*; смена *f* кода

3529 escape character; ESC
d Escape-Zeichen *n*; Umschalt[ungs]zeichen *n*; Code-Umschaltzeichen *n*

f caractère *m* d'échappement; caractère d'extraction; caractère de changement de code

r знак *m* перехода; символ *m* выхода; знак смены регистра

3530 ESC key
d Escape-Taste *f*; ESC-Taste *f*
f touche *f* Echap
r клавиша *f* Esc

3531 escribed angle
d Tangentenwinkel *m*
f angle *m* exinscrit
r вневписанный угол *m*; описанный угол

3532 escribed circle; excircle
d Ankreis *m*; angeschriebener Kreis *m*
f cercle *m* exinscrit
r вневписанная окружность *f*

* **escribed circle of a triangle** → 3567

* **escribed sphere** → 3592

* **essential** → 8684

* **essentially singular point** → 3534

3533 essential point
d wesentlicher Punkt *m*
f point *m* essentiel
r существенная точка *f*

3534 essential singularity; significant singularity; essentially singular point
d wesentliche Singularität *f*; wesentlich singulärer Punkt *m*
f singularité *f* essentielle; singularité signifiante; point *m* singulier essentiel
r существенная особенность *f*; существенно особая точка *f*; существенная особая точка

3535 essential supremum; essup
d wesentliches Supremum *n*
f supremum *m* essentiel
r существенная верхняя грань *f*

* **essup** → 3535

* **establishment** → 8561

3536 estimate *v*; evaluate *v*
d schätzen; auswerten; bewerten
f estimer; évaluer
r оценивать

* **estimating function** → 3539

3537 estimation; assessment; evaluation; valuation; appraisal
d Abschätzung *f*; Schätzung *f*; Bewertung *f*;

Auswertung *f*
f estimation *f*; appréciation *f*; évaluation *f*
r оценка *f*; оценивание *n*

3538 estimation problem
d Schätzungsproblem *n*; Estimationsaufgabe *f*
f problème *m* d'estimation
r задача *f* оценивания

3539 estimator; estimating function
d Schätzfunktion *f*
f estimateur *m*; fonction *f* d'estimation
r функция *f* оценки

3540 Euclidean distance
d Euklidische Distanz *f*
f distance *f* euclidienne
r евклидово расстояние

3541 Euclidean geometry
d Euklidische Geometrie *f*
f géométrie *f* euclidienne
r евклидова геометрия *f*

3542 Euclidean metric
d Euklidische Metrik *f*
f métrique *f* euclidienne
r евклидова метрика *f*

3543 Euclidean plane
d Euklidische Ebene *f*
f plan *m* euclidien
r евклидова плоскость *f*

3544 Euclidean space
d Euklidischer Raum *m*
f espace *m* euclidien
r евклидово пространство *n*

3545 Euler angle
d Euler-Winkel *m*
f angle *m* d'Euler
r угол *m* Эйлера

3546 Euler number
d Euler-Zahl *f*
f nombre *m* d'Euler
r число *n* Эйлера

3547 Euler operations
d Euler-Operationen *fpl*
f opérations *fpl* d'Euler
r операции *fpl* Эйлера

3548 Euler operator
d Euler-Operator *m*
f opérateur *m* d'Euler
r оператор *m* Эйлера

* **evaluate *v*** → 3536

* evaluation → 3537

3549 **event**
d Ereignis *n*; Vorgang *m*
f événement *m*
r событие *n*

3550 **evolute**
d Evolute *f*
f développée *f*
r эволюта *f*

3551 **evolute of a plane curve**
d Evolute *f* einer ebenen Kurve
f développée *f* d'une courbe plane
r эволюта *f* плоской кривой

3552 **evolvent; involute**
d Evolvente *f*; Involute *f*
f développante *f*; involute *f*
r эвольвента *f*; инволюта *f*

* **evolvent of a curve** → 3553

3553 **evolvent of a [plane] curve; involute of a [plane] curve**
d Evolvente *f* einer [ebenen] Kurve; Involute *f* einer [ebenen] Kurve
f développante *f* d'une courbe [plane]; involute *f* d'une courbe [plane]
r эвольвента *f* [плоской] кривой; инволюта *f* [плоской] кривой

3554 **evolvent of the circle**
d Evolvente *f* des Kreises; Kreisevolvente *f*
f développante *f* du cercle
r эвольвента *f* окружности

3555 **exact**
d exakt; genau
f exact; précis
r точный

* **exactitude** → 71

* **exactness** → 71

3556 **example**
d Beispiel *n*; Exempel *n*
f exemple *m*
r пример *m*

3557 **exceed** *v*
d überschreiten
f dépasser
r превышать

3558 **exceeding**
d Überschreitung *f*
f dépassement *m*

r превышение *n*

3559 **excentre; centre of the escribed circle**
d Mittelpunkt *m* des Ankreises; Ankreismittelpunkt *m*
f centre *m* du cercle exinscrit
r центр *m* вневписанной окружности

3560 **excentre; centre of the escribed sphere**
d Mittelpunkt *m* der Ankugel; Ankugelmittelpunkt *m*
f centre *m* de la sphère exinscrite
r центр *m* внекасательной сферы

3561 **exception; exclusion**
d Ausnahme *f*; Exzeption *f*; Exklusion *f*
f exception *f*; exclusion *f*
r исключение *n*

3562 **exceptional condition**
d Ausnahmebedingung *f*
f condition *f* exceptionnelle
r исключительное условие *n*

3563 **exceptional point**
d Ausnahmepunkt *m*; Ausnahmestelle *f*
f point *m* exceptionnel
r исключительная точка *f*

3564 **excess**
d Überschuss *m*; Exzess *m*
f excès *m*
r избыток *m*

* **excessive** → 39

3565 **exchange; interchange**
d Austausch *m*; Umtausch *m*; Wechsel *m*; Auswechs[e]lung *f*
f échange *m*
r [взаимо]обмен *m*; размен *m*; перестановка *f*; замена *f*

3566 **exchangeability; interchangeability**
d Austauschbarkeit *f*; Auswechselbarkeit *f*
f échangeabilité *f*; interchangeabilité *f*
r [взаимо]заменяемость *f*

* **excircle** → 3532, 3567

3567 **excircle [of a triangle]; escribed circle of a triangle**
d Ankreis *m* eines Dreiecks; angeschriebener Kreis *m* eines Dreiecks
f cercle *m* exinscrit d'un triangle
r вневписанная окружность *f* треугольника

* **exclusion** → 3561

3568 **execute** *v*
d ausführen

f exécuter
r выполнять

3569 execution
    d Ausführung *f*; Ablauf *m*
    f exécution *f*
    r исполнение *n*; выполнение *n*

3570 exit; output; quit
    d Ausgang *m*; Austritt *m*
    f sortie *f*
    r выход *m*

3571 exit angle; output angle
    d Austritt[s]winkel *m*
    f angle *m* de sortie; angle d'émergence
    r угол *m* выхода

3572 exit node
    (of a graph)
    d Ausgangsknoten *m*
    f nœud *m* sortant
    r исходящий узел *m*

    * **expand** *v* → **3593**

3573 expandable; extensible
    d erweiterbar
    f expansible; extensible
    r расширяемый

3574 expansion; extension; enlargement
    d Erweiterung *f*; Expandierung *f*; Dehnung *f*;
       Extension *f*
    f expansion *f*; extension *f*; élargissement *m*
    r расширение *n*

    * **experiment** → **640**

3575 explicit
    d explizit
    f explicite
    r явный

3576 explicit focus; click-to-type focus
    d expliziter Fokus *m*
    f cible *f* explicite
    r явный фокус *m*

3577 explicit representation
    d explizite Darstellung *f*
    f représentation *f* explicite
    r явное представление *n*

3578 explode *v*; **dissociate** *v*
    d explodieren; zerlegen; auflösen
    f dissocier; éclater
    r разъединять; развязывать; разбивать

3579 exploded block

d zerlegter Block *m*
f bloc *m* décomposé
r развязанный блок *m*; расчлененный блок

3580 exploded hatch
    d zerlegte Schraffur *f*
    f hachure *f* décomposée
    r развязанная штриховка *f*; разорванная
       штриховка

3581 exploded text
    d zerlegter Text *m*
    f texte *m* décomposé
    r развязанный текст *m*; расчлененный текст

3582 exploded view
    d Explosionszeichnung *f*; auseinandergezogene
       Darstellung *f*
    f vue *f* décomposée; vue éclatée
    r покомпонентное представление *n*
       (изображения); расчлененное
       представление

3583 exploding
    (of a block of geometrical objects or images)
    d Explodieren *n*; Zerlegung *f*; Dekomposition *f*
    f décomposition *f*; dissolution *f*; dissociation *f*
    r разъединение *n*; развязывание *n*

    * **exploration** → **8320**

    * **exploring** → **8320**

3584 exponential
    d exponential
    f exponentiel
    r экспоненциальный; показательный

3585 exponential curve
    d Exponentialkurve *f*
    f courbe *f* exponentielle
    r экспоненциальная кривая *f*

3586 exponential growth trend
    d Tendenz *f* der exponentialen Entwicklung
    f tendance *f* croissante exponentielle
    r экспоненциально растущий тренд *m*

    * **export** → **3589**

3587 export *v*
    d exportieren
    f exporter
    r экспортировать

    * **exportation** → **3589**

3588 export *v* **bitmap**
    d Bitmap exportieren

f exporter un bitmap
r экспортировать растровое отображение

3589 export[ing]; exportation
d Versand *m*; Export *m*
f exportation *f*
r экспортирование *n*; износ *m*; отправка *f*;
отсылка *f*

3590 exposure
d Belichtung *f*
f exposition *f*
r экспонирование *n*

*   **expunge** *v* → 9236

*   **exradius** → 7721, 7722

3591 expression
d Ausdruck *m*
f expression *f*
r выражение *n*

3592 exsphere; escribed sphere
d Ankugel *f*
f sphère *f* exinscrite
r вневписанная сфера *f*; внекасательная
сфера

3593 extend *v*; **expand** *v*
d erweitern; ausdehnen
f étendre; élargir; agrandir
r расширять

*   **extended** → 7584

3594 extended apparent intersection
d erweiterter sichtbarer Durchschnitt *m*
f intersection *f* apparente étendue
r расширенное видимое пересечение *n*

*   **extended cycloid** → 7585

*   **extended epicycloid** → 7587

*   **extended hypocycloid** → 7588

3595 extended intersection
d erweiterter Durchschnitt *m*
f intersection *f* étendue
r расширенное пересечение *n*

3596 extended light source
d erweiterte Lichtquelle *f*
f source *f* d'éclairage étendue
r расширенный световой источник *m*

3597 extended line
d erweiterte Gerade *f*; abgeschlossene Gerade
f droite *f* achevée

r расширенная прямая *f*; прямая,
пополненная бесконечными точками

3598 extended-time scale; slow-time scale
d gedehnte Zeitskala *f*
f échelle *f* de temps étendu; échelle de temps
ralenti
r расширенный масштаб *m* времени

3599 extended trim
d erweiterte Zuschneidung *f*
f tronque *f* étendue
r расширенная обрезка *f*

*   **extensible** → 3573

*   **extension** → 2656, 3574

3600 extension line
(of a dimension)
d Hilfslinie *f*
f ligne *f* d'extension
r вспомогательная линия *f*

3601 extent
d Extent *m*
f étendue *f*; zone *f* d'étendue
r экстент *m*; зона *f* расширения;
расширение *n*

**3602 exterior; external; outer; outside;
outward** *adj*
d Außen-; äußer
f extérieur; externe
r внешний; наружный

3603 exterior; outside
d Äußere *n*; Außenseite *f*
f extérieur *m*
r внешняя часть *f*; внешность *f*; наружная
часть

*   **exterior alternate angles** → 296

3604 exterior angle
d Außenwinkel *m*
f angle *m* extérieur; angle externe
r внешний угол *m*

3605 exterior angle of a circle
d Sekantenwinkel *m*
f angle *m* extérieur d'un cercle
r угол *m* с вершиной вне круга

3606 exterior angle of a triangle
d Außenwinkel *m* des Dreiecks
f angle *m* extérieur d'un triangle
r внешний угол *m* треугольника

3607 exterior bisector; exterior bisectrix
d äußere Winkelhalbierende *f*;

Außenwinkelhalbierende *f*
f bissectrice *f* extérieure
r биссектриса *f* внешнего угла

* **exterior bisectrix** → 3607

3608 exterior clipping
d äußeres Schneiden *n*
f découpage *m* extérieure
r внешнее отсекание *n*

3609 exterior domain
d Außengebiet *n*
f domaine *m* extérieur
r внешняя область *f*

3610 exterior grid
d äußeres Gitter *n*
f grille *f* extérieure
r внешняя сетка *f*

3611 exterior node
d äußerer Knoten *m*
f nœud *m* extérieur
r внешний узел *m*

3612 exterior opposite angles
d äußere entgegengesetzt liegende Winkel *mpl*;
äußere entgegengesetzte Winkel
f angles *mpl* coexternes; angles extérieurs du
même côté de la sécante
r внешние односторонние углы *mpl*

3613 exterior point
d äußerer Punkt *m*
f point *m* extérieur
r внешняя точка *f*

* **external** → 3602

3614 external cavity
d äußerer Hohlraum *m*
f cavité *f* extérieure
r внешняя полость *f*; внешний объем *m*

3615 external command
d äußerer Befehl *m*
f commande *f* externe
r внешняя команда *f*

3616 external contour
d äußere Kontur *f*
f contour *m* externe
r внешний контур *m*

3617 external curvature; extrinsic curvature
d äußere Krümmung *f*
f courbure *f* externe
r внешняя кривизна *f*

3618 external data
d äußere Daten *npl*
f données *fpl* externes
r внешние данные *npl*

3619 external database
d äußere Datenbasis *f*
f base *f* de données externe
r внешняя база *f* данных

3620 external database toolbar
d Hilfsmittelstreifen *m* der äußeren Datenbasis
f barre *f* d'outils de base de données externe
r инструментальная лента *f* внешней базы
данных

3621 external data identification
(in CAD and GIS)
d Identifikation *f* der äußeren Daten
f identification *f* de données externes
r обозначение *n* внешних данных

3622 external document
d äußeres Dokument *n*
f document *m* externe
r внешний документ *m*

3623 external query
d Außenabfrage *f*
f interrogation *f* externe
r внешний запрос *m*

3624 external reference
d Außenreferenz *f*
f référence *f* externe
r внешняя ссылка *f*

3625 external reference file
d Außenreferenz-Datei *f*
f fichier *m* de références externes
r файл *m* внешних ссылок

3626 external tangent
d äußere Tangente *f*
f tangente *f* extérieure
r внешняя касательная *f*

3627 external viewer
d Außensuchprogramm *n*
f visionneur *m* externe
r внешняя программа *f* просмотра; внешний
вьювер *m*

3628 extract *v*; **fetch** *v*
d extrahieren; ausziehen; schleppen
f extraire
r извлекать; выделять

3629 extract *v* **attribute information**
d Attribut-Information schleppen

f extraire une information d'attributs
r извлекать атрибутную информацию

3630 extraction
  d Extraktion *f*; Auszug *m*
  f extraction *f*
  r извлечение *n*; выделение *n*

3631 extract *v* content
  d Inhaltsverzeichnis schleppen
  f extraire un contenu
  r извлекать содержание

3632 extra-light *adj*
  d überhell
  f très clair; extra-clair; extra-lumineux
  r сверхсветлый

3633 extrapolate *v*
  d extrapolieren
  f extrapoler
  r экстраполировать

3634 extrapolation
  d Extrapolieren *n*; Extrapolierung *f*;
    Extrapolation *f*
  f extrapolation *f*
  r экстраполяция *f*; экстраполирование *n*

3635 extremal
  d Extremale *f*
  f extrémale *f*
  r экстремаль *f*

3636 extremal; extreme; limit *adj*
  d extremal
  f extrême; extrémal
  r экстремальный; предельный

3637 extremal element
  d Extremalelement *n*
  f élément *m* extrémal
  r экстремальный элемент *m*

  * **extremal point → 3639**

  * **extreme → 3636**

3638 extreme graphics
  d extreme Grafik *f*
  f graphique *m* extrême
  r экстремальная графика *f*; критическая
    графика

3639 extremum point; extremal point
  d Extrem[al]punkt *m*; Extremalstelle *f*
  f point *m* extrémal
  r экстремальная точка *f*; точка экстремума

  * **extrinsic curvature → 3617**

3640 extrude *v*
  d extrudieren
  f mettre en relief; étendre
  r экструдировать

3641 extruded object
  d extrudiertes Objekt *n*
  f objet *m* extrudé; objet en relief
  r экструдированный объект *m*

3642 extruded solid
  d extrudierter Körper *m*
  f solide *m* extrudé; solide en relief
  r экструдированное тело *n*

3643 extruded surface
  d extrudierte Fläche *f*
  f surface *f* extrudée
  r экструдированная поверхность *f*

3644 extruded text
  d extrudierter Text *m*
  f texte *m* extrudé
  r экструдированный текст *m*

3645 extruder
  d Extruder *m*
  f extrudeuse *f*
  r экструдер *m*

3646 extrusion
  d Extrusion *f*; Extrudierung *f*
  f extrusion *f*
  r экструзия *f*

3647 extrusion depth
  d Extrudierungstiefe *f*
  f profondeur *f* d'extrusion
  r глубина *f* экструзии

3648 extrusion effect
  d Extrudierungseffekt *m*
  f effet *m* d'extrusion
  r эффект *m* экструзии

3649 extrusion thickness
  d Extrudierungsdicke *f*
  f épaisseur *f* d'extrusion
  r толщина *f* экструзии

3650 eye
  d Auge *n*; Öse *f*; Ohr *n*
  f œil *m*; oreille *f*
  r очко *n*; глазок *m*; ушко *n*; петля *f*

3651 eyeball
  d Augapfel *m*
  f globe *f* oculaire
  r глазное яблоко *n*

3652 eye-chart
  d Augendiagramm *n*
  f diagramme *m* de l'œil
  r глаз-диаграмма *f*; оптометрическая
   таблица *f*; индикаторная диаграмма *f*

3653 eye direction
  d Sehrichtung *f*; Blickrichtung *f*
  f direction *f* de l'œil
  r зрительное направление *n*

**3654 eye distance; distance [in central
   projection]**
  d Sehabstand *m*; Sehdistanz *f*
  f distance *f* de l'œil
  r зрительное расстояние *n*

3655 eyedropper
  d Pipette *f*
  f pipette *f*
  r пипетка *f*

3656 eyedropper tool
  d Hilfsmittel *n* "Pipette"
  f outil *m* "pipette"
  r инструмент *m* "пипетка"

  * **eye glass → 3657**

  * **eye icon → 3659**

3657 eyepiece; eye glass
  d Okular *n*
  f oculaire *m*
  r окуляр *m*

  * **eye position → 7225**

3658 eye tracking
  d Verfolgung *f* mit Augen
  f poursuite *f* d'œil
  r прослеживание *n* глазами

3659 eye-type icon; eye icon
  d Augentyp-Symbol *n*; Augensymbol *n*
  f icône *f* en forme d'œil
  r икона *f* глаз

F

3660 **face**
(of human)
d Gesicht *n*
f visage *m*
r лицо *n*

3661 **face** *v*
d verkleiden
f surfacer
r покрывать; облицовать

* **face** → **4033**

* **face angle** → **2811**

* **face geometry** → **3682**

3662 **face metaphor**
d Gesicht-Metapher *f*
f métaphore *f* d'un visage
r лицевая метафора *f*

3663 **face normal**
d Flächennormale *f*
f normale *f* à la face
r нормаль *f* к грани

3664 **face of a polyhedral angle**
d Seitenfläche *f* des Raumwinkels
f face *f* d'un angle polyèdre
r грань *f* многогранного угла

3665 **face recognition**
d Gesichterkennung *f*
f reconnaissance *f* de visage
r распознавание *n* лица

3666 **face recognition software**
d Gesichterkennungssoftware *f*
f logiciel *m* de reconnaissance de visage
r программное обеспечение *n* распознавания
лица

* **facet** → **3676**

3667 **facet analysis**
d Facettenanalyse *f*
f analyse *f* par facettes
r фацетный анализ *m*

3668 **facet[ed] shading**
d Facettenschattierung *f*; facettierte
Schattierung *f*

f ombrage *m* de facettes
r затушевывание *n* граней; фацетированное
затенение *n*

3669 **faceted surfaces**
d facettierte Fläche *f*
f surfaces *fpl* à facettes
r фацетные поверхности *fpl*

3670 **face template**
d Gesichtsschablone *f*
f modèle *m* de visage
r лицевой шаблон *m*

3671 **faceting**
d Facettierung *f*
f mise *f* à facettes
r фацетирование *n*

3672 **facet normal**
d Facettennormale *f*
f normale *f* à une facette
r нормаль *f* к фацету

* **facet shading** → **3668**

3673 **facet size**
d Facettengröße *f*
f taille *f* de facette
r размер *m* фацета

3674 **facet sorting**
d Facettensortierung *f*
f triage *m* des facettes
r сортирование *n* фацетов

3675 **facet synthesis**
d Facettensynthese *f*
f synthèse *f* de facettes
r синтез *m* фацетов

3676 **facet[te]**
(planar element in a mesh)
d Facette *f*
f facette *f*
r фацет *m*; грань *f*

3677 **facial**
d Gesichts-
f facial
r лицевой

3678 **facial analysis**
d Gesichtsanalyse *f*
f analyse *f* faciale
r анализ *m* лица

3679 **facial animation**
d Gesichtsanimation *f*

f animation *f* faciale
r оживление *n* лица

3680 facial deformation
d Gesichtsdeformation *f*
f déformation *f* faciale
r лицевая деформация *f*

3681 facial expression recognition
d Erkennung *f* des Gesichtsausdrucks
f reconnaissance *f* d'expression de la face
r распознавание *n* выражения лица

3682 facial geometry; face geometry
d Gesichtsgeometrie *f*
f géométrie *f* faciale
r лицевая геометрия *f*

3683 facial image morphing
d Morphing *n* des Gesichtsbildes
f morphage *m* d'image faciale
r морфинг *m* изображения лица;
метаморфоза *f* изображения лица

* **facility** → 3505

3684 facing
d Verkleidung *f*
f surfaçage *m*
r наружное покрытие *n*; внешний слой *m*;
облицовка *f*; кант *m*; отделка *f*

* **factor** → 1641, 6128

* **factor of proportionality** → 1647

3685 fade; fading
(of an image)
d Fading *n*; Schwund *m*
f fading *m*; décroissance *f*
r замирание *n*; затухание *n*; фединг *m*

3686 fade-in
(of an image)
d Aufblendung *f*
f apparition *f* graduelle; apparition progressive
r постепенное возникновение *n*

3687 fade *v* out
d ausblenden; abblenden
f disparaître graduellement
r постепенно исчезать

3688 fade-out; going to black
(of an image)
d Ausblendung *f*; Abblendung *f*; Abblende *f*;
Verdunkelung *f*
f disparition *f* graduelle; disparition progressive
r постепенное исчезновение *n*

3689 fade-out rate
d Ausblend[ungs]geschwindigkeit *f*
f vitesse *f* de disparition graduelle
r скорость *f* постепенного исчезновения

3690 fader
d Aufblendregler *m*; Ausblendregler *m*
f équilibreur *m* [avant-arrière]
r регулятор *m* яркости изображения

* **fading** → 3685

3691 fading effect
d Fading-Effekt *m*
f effet *m* de fading
r эффект *m* затухания

**3692 faithful representation; true
representation**
d getreue Darstellung *f*
f représentation *f* fidèle
r точное представление *n*

3693 fall angle; dip angle
d Fallwinkel *m*
f angle *m* de pente
r угол *m* падения

3694 fall line; steepest line; line of steepest slope
d Fallinie *f*
f ligne *f* de pente
r линия *f* падения

3695 fall *v* off; drop *v* off
d abfallen; sinken; herunterfallen
f diminuer; atténuer; baisser; réduire
r спадать; отпадать; уменьшаться;
ослабевать; отваливаться

* **falloff** → 641

3696 falloff angle
d abfallender Winkel *m*
f angle *m* d'atténuation
r угол *m* спада

3697 falloff cone angle; field angle
(defines the full cone of the light)
d abfallender Kegelwinkel *m*
f angle *m* conique d'atténuation
r конический угол *m* спада

* **fall scale** → 4283

* **false code** → 4796

3698 false color
d Falschfarbe *f*; False-Color *n*
f fausse couleur *f*
r фальшивый цвет *m*

3699 false light
  d falsches Licht *n*
  f fausse lumière *f*
  r фальшивый свет *m*

3700 false perspective; pseudo-perspective
  d Pseudoperspektive *f*
  f pseudo-perspective *f*
  r псевдо-перспектива *f*

3701 family of curves; group of curves; system of curves
  d Kurvenschar *f*; Kurvensystem *n*
  f famille *f* de courbes
  r семейство *n* кривых [линий]; фамилия *f* кривых

3702 family of generators; generating set
  d erzeugende Menge *f*; Generatormenge *f*
  f ensemble *m* de générateurs
  r семейство *n* образующих

3703 family of lines
  d Linienfamilie *f*
  f famille *f* de lignes
  r семейство *n* линий

3704 family of planes
  d Ebenenschar *f*; Ebenenfamilie *f*
  f famille *f* de plans
  r семейство *n* плоскостей

3705 family of shapes
  d Formenfamilie *f*
  f famille *f* de formes
  r семейство *n* фигур

3706 family of surfaces
  d Flächenschar *f*; Flächenfamilie *f*
  f famille *f* de surfaces
  r семейство *n* поверхностей

  * fancy → 3707

3707 fantasy; fancy
  d Phantasie *f*
  f fantaisie *f*
  r фантазия *f*; галлюцинация *f*

3708 fashion and cosmetic graphics
  d Mode- und Kosmetik-Grafik *f*
  f graphique *m* de cosmétique et de mode
  r графика *f* моды и козметики

3709 fast anamorphic image scaling
  d schnelle Skalierung *f* des anamorphischen Bilds
  f mise *f* rapide en échelle d'image anamorphique
  r быстрое масштабирование *m* искаженного изображения

3710 fast animation
  d schnelle Animation *f*
  f animation *f* rapide
  r быстрая анимация *f*

  * fastening → 637

3711 fast mode
  d schneller Modus *m*
  f mode *m* rapide
  r быстрый режим *m*

3712 fast zoom
  d schnelles Zoomen *n*
  f zoom *m* rapide
  r быстрое изменение *n* масштаба

  * fault → 2557

3713 fault threshold
  d Fehlerschwelle *f*; Fehlerschwellwert *m*
  f seuil *m* de défauts
  r порог *m* ошибок

3714 favorite fill
  d bevorzugte Füllung *f*
  f remplissage *m* favori
  r фаворитное закрашивание *n*

  * feasible → 201

  * feather → 1395

3715 feathered edge; winged edge; chamfered edge
  d gefiederte Kante *f*
  f arête *f* en biseau; arête allégée
  r скошенное ребро *n*

3716 feathered joint; chamfered joint
  d Ausziehstoss *m*; Schienenauszugsvorrichtung *f*
  f joint *m* [de rail] en biseau
  r скошенное соединение *n*

3717 feathering effect
  (of the shadow)
  d Verlaufseffekt *m*
  f effet *m* d'écume
  r эффект *m* пены

3718 feathering properties
  (of the shadow)
  d Verlaufseigenschaften *fpl*
  f propriétés *fpl* d'écume
  r свойства *npl* пены

  * feature → 4854, 9735

3719 **feature; property**
  d Merkmal *n*; Eigenschaft *f*; Feature *n*
  f propriété *f*; particularité *f*; signe *m*; moyen *m*
  r признак *m*; свойство *n*; особенность *f*

3720 **feature legend**
  (for pen parameters)
  d Merkmal-Legende *f*
  f légende *f* des signes
  r легенда *f* признаков

  * **feature map** → 8015

3721 **feature space**
  d Merkmalsraum *m*
  f espace *m* de signes
  r пространство *n* признаков

3722 **feature vector**
  d Relief-Vektor *m*
  f vecteur *m* de relief
  r вектор *m* рельефа

3723 **feature VGA connector; VGA output connector**
  (for connecting expansion boards to a graphics board using a flat cable)
  d VGA-Ausgangsstecker *m*
  f connecteur *m* de sortie VGA
  r выходной соединитель *m* VGA

3724 **feed** *v*
  d zuführen; vorschieben
  f avancer; acheminer; alimenter; entraîner
  r подавать; продвигать

3725 **feedback**
  d Rückführung *f*; Rückkopplung *f*
  f ré[tro]action *f*; rétrocouplage *m*; action *f* de retour
  r обратная связь *f*

  * **FE mesh** → 3808

3726 **fence; enclosure**
  d Grenzschichtzaun *m*; Zaun *m*
  f cloison *f*; clôture *f*; barrière *f*
  r ограждение *n*; ограда *f*; заграждающая метка *f*

3727 **fence line**
  d Zaunlinie *f*
  f ligne *f* de cloison
  r заграждающая линия *f*

3728 **fence object**
  d Zaunobjekt *n*
  f objet *m* cloison
  r заграждающий объект *m*

3729 **fence selection**
  d Zaunauswahl *f*
  f sélection *f* de cloison
  r выбор *m* ограждения

  * **fenestration** → 10432

3730 **ferroelectric LCD**
  d ferroelektrisches Flüssigkristalldisplay *n*
  f afficheur *m* à cristaux liquides ferro-électriques; afficheur CLF
  r дисплей *m* на ферроэлектрических жидких кристаллах

  * **fetch** *v* → 1149, 3628

  * **fictive** → 3226

3731 **fictive camera**
  d fiktive Kamera *f*
  f caméra *f* fictive
  r фиктивная камера *f*

  * **fidelity** → 71

3732 **fidelity criterion**
  d Genauigkeitskriterium *n*
  f critère *m* de fidélité
  r критерий *m* точности

3733 **field**
  d Feld *n*
  f champ *m*
  r поле *n*

  * **field angle** → 3697

3734 **field depth**
  d Feldtiefe *f*
  f profondeur *f* de champ
  r глубина *f* поля

  * **field glass** → 936

3735 **field length**
  d Feldlänge *f*
  f longueur *f* de champ
  r длина *f* поля

3736 **field navigation**
  d Feldnavigation *f*
  f navigation *f* entre zone
  r передвижение *n* в зоне

3737 **field of view; field of vision; FOV; visual field; angular field [of vision]**
  d Sehfeld *n*; Gesichtsfeld *n*; Blickfeld *n*
  f champ *m* [angulaire] visuel; champ de vision
  r поле *n* зрения

* **field of vision** → 3737

3738 field prompt
  d Feldanzeige *f*
  f invite *f* de zone; indicatif *m* de zone
  r подсказка *f* поля

3739 field radiance
  d Feldstrahldichte *f*
  f radiance *f* de champ
  r полевая яркость *f* излучения

3740 field-radiance function
  d Feldstrahldichte-Funktion *f*
  f fonction *f* de radiance de champ
  r функция *f* полевой яркости излучения

3741 field-radiance operator
  d Feldstrahldichte-Operator *m*
  f opérateur *m* de radiance de champ
  r оператор *m* полевой яркости излучения

* **FIF** → 3970

3742 figurative
  d figurativ
  f figuratif
  r фигуративный; фигуральный; образный; символьный

* **figure** → 2756, 3939

* **figures in central perspective** → 6990

* **figures in central projection** → 6990

3743 file
  d Datei *f*; File *n*
  f fichier *m*
  r файл *m*

3744 file compression
  d Dateikompression *f*
  f compression *f* de fichier
  r сжатие *n* файла

3745 file conversion
  d Dateikonvertierung *f*
  f transformation *f* de fichier
  r конверсия *f* файла

3746 file descriptor
  d Dateideskriptor *m*
  f descripteur *m* de fichier
  r описатель *m* файла

3747 file format
  d Dateiformat *n*
  f format *m* de fichier
  r формат *m* файла

3748 file format converter
  d Dateiformat-Umwandler *m*
  f convertisseur *m* de format de fichier
  r преобразователь *m* формата файлов

3749 file format for background images
  d Dateiformat *n* der Hintergrundbilder
  f format *m* de fichier d'images de fond
  r файловый формат *m* фоновых изображений

3750 file format for environment images
  d Dateiformat *n* der Umgebungsbilder
  f format *m* de fichier d'images d'environnement
  r файловый формат *m* изображений окрестности

3751 file format for exporting
  d Dateiformat *n* des Exportierens
  f format *m* de fichier pour exportation
  r файловый формат *m* экспортирования

3752 file format for extract attribute data
  d Dateiformat *n* der Attributdaten-Extraktion
  f format *m* de fichier d'extraction des données d'attributs
  r файловый формат *m* извлечения атрибутных данных

3753 file format for import
  d Format *n* der importierenden Datei
  f format *m* de fichier d'importation
  r формат *m* импортного файла

3754 file preview
  d Dateivorschau *f*
  f prévisualisation *f* de fichier
  r предварительный просмотр *m* файла

3755 file type
  d Dateityp *m*
  f type *m* de fichier
  r тип *m* файла

* **filing** → 531

3756 fill *v*
  d füllen; ausfüllen
  f remplir; garnir
  r заполнять

* **fill** *v* → 6741

* **fill** → 3767

* **fill character** → 3763

3757 fill color
  d Füll[ungs]farbe *f*

f couleur *f* de remplissage
r цвет *m* заполнения

3758 fill command
d Füll[ungs]befehl *m*
f commande *f* de remplissage
r команда *f* заполнения

3759 filled
d gefüllt
f rempli
r заполненный; закрашенный

3760 filled area
d gefüllter Bereich *m*
f domaine *m* rempli
r заполненая зона *f*; закрашенная область *f*

3761 filled ellipse
d gefüllte Ellipse *f*
f ellipse *f* remplie
r закрашенный эллипс *m*

3762 filled ring
d gefüllter Ring *m*
f anneau *m* rempli
r закрашенное кольцо *n*

3763 filler; fill character
d Füllungszeichen *n*
f caractère *m* de remplissage
r символ-заполнитель *m*

* **fillet** → 3764

3764 fillet[ing]
d Abrundung *m*; Runden *n*; Rundung *f*
f filetage *m*
r округление *n*

3765 filleting test
d Abrundungstest *m*
f essai *m* de filetage
r проверка *f* округления

3766 fillet radius
d Abrundungsradius *m*
f rayon *m* de filetage
r радиус *m* округления

3767 fill[ing]
d Füllung *f*; Auffüllen *n*; Füllen *n*
f remplissage *m*; garnissage *m*
r закрашивание *n*; заливка *f*

3768 filling adjustment
d Füllungseinstellung *f*
f ajustement *m* de remplissage
r настройка *f* закрашивания; налаживание *n* заливки

3769 filling attributes
d Füllungsattribute *npl*
f attributs *mpl* de remplissage
r атрибуты *mpl* закрашивания; атрибуты заливки

3770 filling by drag
d Füllung *f* durch Ziehen
f remplissage *m* par entraînement
r закрашивание *n* перемещением; заливка *f* волочением

* **filling factor** → 8923

3771 filling label
d Füllungsetikett *n*
f étiquette *f* de remplissage
r метка *f* закрашивания; метка заливки

3772 filling properties
d Füllungseigenschaften *fpl*
f propriétés *fpl* de remplissage
r свойства *npl* закрашивания; свойства заливки

3773 fill[ing] type
d Füllungstyp *m*
f type *m* de remplissage
r тип *m* закрашивания; тип заливки

* **fill light** → 3774

3774 fill light [source]
d Füllungslichtquelle *n*
f lumière *f* d'appoint
r источник *m* света закрашивания

3775 fill mode
d Füllungsmodus *m*
f mode *m* de remplissage
r режим *m* закрашивания; режим заливки

3776 fill pattern
d Füllungsmuster *n*
f motif *m* de remplissage
r закраска *f*

3777 fill preview
d Füllungsvorschau *f*
f prévisualisation *f* de remplissage
r предварительный просмотр *m* закрашивания

3778 fill rate
d Füllungsrate *f*
f vitesse *f* de remplissage
r скорость *f* заливки (текстурами); филрейт *m*

3779 fill style
d Füllungsstil *m*

f style *m* de remplissage
r стиль *m* закрашивания; стиль заливки

3780 fill tool
d Füllungshilfsmittel *n*; Hilfsmittel *n* "Füllung"
f outil *m* "remplissage"
r инструмент *m* "закрашивание"

* **fill transform → 3781**

3781 fill transform[ing]
d Transformation *f* der Füllung
f transformation *f* de remplissage
r трансформация *f* заполнения

* **fill type → 3773**

3782 film
d Film *m*
f film *m*
r фильм *m*; пленка *f*

3783 film clip
d Filmausschnitt *m*; Filmsequenz *f*
f clip *m* filmé; séquence *f* filmée
r фильмовый клип *m*

* **film recorder → 7027**

3784 film scanner
d Filmscanner *m*
f scanner *m* de pellicule
r пленочной сканер *m*

3785 filter
d Filter *m*; Sieb *n*
f filtre *m*
r фильтр *m*

3786 filter cell
d Filterstufe *f*
f cellule *f* de filtre
r клетка *f* фильтра

* **filter coefficient → 3790**

3787 filter color
d Filterfarbe *f*
f couleur *f* de filtre
r цвет *m* фильтра

3788 filter combination
d Filterkombination *f*
f combinaison *f* de filtres
r комбинация *f* фильтров

3789 filter command
d Filterbefehl *m*
f commande *f* de filtrage
r команда *f* фильтрирования

3790 filter factor; filter coefficient
d Filterfaktor *m*
f coefficient *m* de filtrage
r коэффициент *m* фильтрирования

3791 filtering; filtration
d Filterung *f*; Filtrierung *f*; Filtering *n*
f filtrage *m*; filtration *f*
r фильтрация *f*; фильтрирование *n*

3792 filtering operator
d Filtrierungsoperator *m*
f opérateur *m* de filtrage
r оператор *m* фильтрирования

3793 filtering selection set
d Filtrierungsauswahlsatz *m*
f ensemble *m* de sélection de filtrage
r фильтрирующая совокупность *f* выбора

3794 filter law
d Filtersatz *m*
f loi *f* de filtrage
r правило *n* фильтрирования

3795 filter list
d Filterliste *f*
f liste *f* de filtres
r список *m* фильтров

3796 filter test
d Filtertest *m*
f essai *m* de filtre
r проверка *f* фильтра

* **filtration → 3791**

3797 final; end; finite
d endlich; finit
f fini; final
r конечный; концевой; финитный

* **final object → 3426**

3798 find *v*
d finden; suchen
f trouver; découvrir; [re]chercher
r найти; искать

3799 finder
d Sucher *m*; Finder *m*
f viseur *m*; chercheur *m*
r визир *m*; видоискатель *m*

3800 finding
d Erforschung *f*
f localisation *f*
r отыскание *n*

3801 fine grain
d Feinkorn *n*

f grain *m* fin
r мелкозернистость *f*

3802 fine sheaf
  d feine Garbe *f*
  f faisceau *m* fin
  r тонкий пучок *m*

3803 finger
  d Finger *m*
  f doigt *m*; finger *m*
  r палец *m*; гриф *m*

3804 fingerprint
  d Fingerabdruck *m*
  f empreinte *f* digitale
  r отпечаток *m* пальца

3805 fingerprint identification
  d Fingerabdruck-Identifikation *f*
  f identification *f* d'empreintes digitales
  r идентификация *f* отпечатка пальца

  * **finishing** → 9529

  * **finite** → 3797

3806 finite element
  d endliches Element *n*; finites Element
  f élément *m* fini
  r конечный элемент *m*

3807 finite-element analysis
  d Analyse *f* der finiten Elemente
  f analyse *f* d'éléments finis
  r анализ *m* конечных элементов

3808 finite-element mesh; FE mesh
  d Masche *f* der finiten Elemente
  f maille *f* d'éléments finis
  r сетка *f* конечных элементов

3809 finite-element modeling
  d Modellierung *f* der finiten Elemente
  f modélisation *f* d'éléments fins
  r моделирование *n* конечных элементов

3810 finite path
  d endlicher Weg *m*
  f chemin *m* fini
  r конечный путь *m*

3811 first color fill picker
  d Auswahl-Schaltfläche *f* der ersten
     Füll[ungs]farbe
  f dispositif *m* de désignation de la première
     couleur de remplissage
  r бутон *m* выбора первого цвета заполнения

  * **first distance** → 3812

**3812 first distance [from one of planes of
     projection]**
  d erster Tafelabstand *m*
  f distance *f* première
  r расстояние *n* от горизонтальной плоскости

  * **first focus** → 4036

3813 first normal form
  d erste Normalform *f*
  f première forme *f* normale
  r первая нормальная форма *f*

  * **first plane of projection** → 4702

3814 first principal plane
     (in two-plane projection)
  d erste Hauptebene *f*
  f premier plan *m* principal
  r первая главная плоскость *f*

  * **first projection** → 4703

  * **first trace** → 3815

**3815 first trace [line]; horizontal trace [line] of a
     plane**
  d horizontale Spurlinie *f* [einer Ebene]; erste
     Spurlinie; erste Spur *f*
  f première trace *f*; trace horizontale d'un plan
  r горизонтальный след *m* плоскости; след в
     горизонтальной плоскости проекции

  * **first trace point** → 3812

3816 first trace point [of a line]
  d erster Spurpunkt *m* [der Linie]
  f premier point *m* de trace [de ligne]
  r первый след *m* [прямой]; горизонтальный
     след [прямой]

3817 fish eye lens
  d Fischaugenobjektiv *n*
  f lentille *f* d'œil de poisson
  r объектив *m* типа "рыбий глаз"

3818 fish-tank effect
  d Aquarium-Effekt *m*
  f effet *m* d'aquarium
  r эффект *m* аквариума

  * **fit** → 3829

3819 fit *v*
  d fitten; anpassen
  f ajuster; accoler
  r подходить; точно соответствовать;
     прилаживать; налаживать

3820 fit *v* **data**
 d Daten anpassen
 f ajuster des données
 r налаживать данные

3821 fit *v* **options**
 d Optionen anpassen
 f ajuster des options
 r налаживать опции

3822 fit *v* **points**
 d Punkte ausrichten
 f ajuster des points
 r настраивать точки; аппроксимировать точки

3823 fitted curve
 d ausgleichende Kurve *f*
 f courbe *f* ajustée
 r выравненная кривая *f*; сглаженная кривая

3824 fitted points
 d ausgerichtete Punkte *mpl*
 f points *mpl* ajustés; points lissés
 r сглаженные точки *fpl*

3825 fit *v* **text**
 d Text anpassen; Text ausrichten
 f accoler du texte
 r налаживать текст

3826 fit *v* **text to frame; align** *v* **text to frame**
 d den Text an einen Rahmen ausrichten
 f accoler du texte à l'encadré
 r налаживать текст к рамке

3827 fit *v* **text to object; align** *v* **text to object**
 d den Text an ein Objekt ausrichten
 f accoler du texte sur un objet
 r налаживать текст к объекту

3828 fit *v* **text to path**
 d den Text an eine Strecke anpassen
 f accoler du texte au tracé
 r налаживать текст к дорожке

3829 fit[ting]
 d Anpassung *f*; Passung *f*; Fitten *n*; Ausrichtung *f*
 f ajustement *m*; ajustage *m*; raccord *m*; calage *m*
 r наладка *f*; подгонка *f*; пригонка *f*; припасовка *f*

3830 fitting of artwork
 d Anpassung *f* der topologischen Vorlage
 f ajustement *m* de schéma topologique
 r наладка *f* топологической схемы

3831 fit tolerance

 d Anpassungstoleranz *f*
 f tolérance *f* d'ajustage
 r допуск *m* налаживания

3832 fixed
 d fixiert; fest; Fix-; Fest-; feststehend
 f fixe
 r фиксированный; неподвижный; закрепленный

3833 fixed colors
 d feste Farben *fpl*
 f couleurs *fpl* fixes
 r фиксированные цвета *mpl*

3834 fixed coordinate system
 d feststehendes Koordinatensystem *n*
 f système *m* de coordonnées stationnaire
 r фиксированная система *f* координат

3835 fixed frequency monitor
 (analog monitor which can only sync to a very narrow range of scan frequencies)
 d Festfrequenz-Monitor *m*
 f moniteur *m* à fréquence fixe
 r монитор *m* фикисированной частоты

 * **fixed image** → 9172

 * **fixed line** → 3836

3836 fixed line [of an involution]
 d Fixgerade *f* [einer Involution]
 f droite *f* fixe [d'une involution]
 r неподвижная прямая *f* [инволюции]

3837 fixed palette
 d feste Palette *f*
 f palette *f* fixe
 r фиксированная палитра *f*

 * **fixed plane** → 3838

3838 fixed plane [of an involution]; double plane
 d Fixebene *f* [einer Involution]; Doppelebene *f*
 f plan *m* fixe [d'une involution]; plan double
 r неподвижная плоскость *f* [инволюции]; двойная плоскость

3839 fixed point
 (of a mapping)
 d Fixpunkt *m*; fester Punkt *m*
 f point *m* fixe
 r фиксированная точка *f*; неподвижная точка

3840 fixed point of an involution; double point; self-corresponding point
 d Fixpunkt *m* einer Involution; Doppelpunkt *m*

f point *m* fixe d'une involution; point double
r неподвижная точка *f* инволюции; двойная точка

3841 fixed ratio
  d festes Verhältnis *n*
  f rapport *m* fixe; taux *m* fixe
  r постоянное отношение *n*

  * **fixed threshold** → 9177

3842 fixed width
  d feste Breite *f*
  f largeur *f* fixe
  r фиксированная ширина *f*

  * **flabby sheaf** → 8333

3843 flag; sentinel
  d Kennzeichen *n*; Zustandsmarke *f*; Flag *n*
  f repérage *m*; drapeau *m*; flag *m*
  r флаг *m*; признак *m* состояния

  * **flagging** → 5811

3844 flare
  d Reflektionslicht *n*; Überstrahlung *f*; Flackerfeuer *n*
  f feu *m* de détresse; fusée *f* lumineuse; fusée éclairante
  r вспыхивание *n*; вспышка *f*

3845 flashing; flicker[ing]; blinking
  d Flackern *n*; Blinken *n*; Flimmerung *f*
  f clignotement *m*; papillotement *m*; scintillement *m*
  r мигание *n*; мерцание *n*

  * **flat** → 7127

  * **flat angle** → 9214

3846 flatbed plotter
  d Tischplotter *m*
  f table *f* traçante à plat; traceur *m* à plat
  r планшетный графопостроитель *m*; плоский графопостроитель

3847 flatbed scanner
  d Flachbettscanner *m*
  f scanner *m* à plat
  r плоский сканер *m*; планшетный сканер

3848 flat buttons
  (onto toolbar)
  d Schaltflächen *fpl*
  f boutons *mpl* plats; onglets *mpl*
  r иконки *fpl* бутонов

  * **flat curve** → 7136

3849 flat curve generation
  d Generierung *f* der flachen Kurve
  f génération *f* de courbe plane
  r генерирование *n* плоской кривой

  * **flat display** → 3855

3850 flat drop-off
  d flacher Abfall *m*; platter Abfall
  f descente *f* plate
  r плоский наклон *m*

3851 flat LCD
  d flaches Flüssigkristalldisplay *n*
  f afficheur *m* à cristaux liquides plat
  r плоский жидкокристаллический дисплей *m*

3852 flatness
  d Flachheit *f*; Ebenheit *f*; Plattheit *f*
  f planéité *f*
  r гладкость *f*; приплюснутость *f*; плоскость *f*

3853 flat rendering
  d flaches Rendering *n*
  f rendu *m* plat
  r плоскостное тонирование *n*; плоскостный рендеринг *m*

3854 flat ring
  d flacher Ring *m*
  f anneau *m* plat
  r плоское кольцо *n*

3855 flat screen; flat display
  d flacher Bildschirm *m*; Flachbildschirm *m*
  f écran *m* plat; écran en plan
  r плоский экран *m*

3856 flat shading; constant shading
  d Flachschattierung *f*
  f ombrage *m* plat; ombrage constant
  r плоскостное оттенение *n*; плоское затенение *n*

  * **flat shadow** → 3186

3857 flat slab
  d Flachplatte *f*; Flachpalette *f*
  f brame *m* plat; dalle *f* plane
  r плоская плита *f*; плоская пластина *f*

3858 flat spot
  d flacher Fleck *m*
  f tache *f* plate
  r плоское пятно *n*

3859 flatten *v*
  d abflachen

f aplanir
r выравнивать

* **flattened** → 6408

3860 flattening
d Abplattung *f*; Richten *n*
f aplatissement *m*; dressage *m*
r выравнивание *n*

3861 flaws
d Mängel *mpl*; Fehler *mpl*; Risse *mpl*;
Sprünge *mpl*
f défauts *mpl*
r недостатки *mpl*; трещины *fpl*; щели *fpl*

* **flex** → 5056

3862 flexibility
d Flexibilität *f*; Elastizität *f*
f flexibilité *f*
r гибкость *f*; упругость *f*

3863 flexible
d flexibel; biegsam
f flexible
r гибкий; огибаемый

* **flex point** → 7218

* **flicker** → 3845

* **flickering** → 3845

3864 flicker noise
d Flimmer-Geräusch *n*
f bruit *m* de scintillement
r искажение *n* мерцания

* **flip** → 3865

* **flip image** → 8124

3865 flip[ping]
d Ausflippen *m*
f retournement *m*; rabattement *m*
r переворачивание *n*

3866 floating
d fließend; schwimmend
f flottant
r плавающий

* **floating bar** → 3872

3867 floating menu
d fließendes Menü *n*
f menu *m* flottant
r плавающее меню *n*

3868 floating objects
d fließende Objekte *npl*
f objets *mpl* flottants
r плавающие объекты *mpl*

* **floating-point depth buffer** → 3869

**3869 floating-point Z buffer; floating-point
depth buffer**
d Gleitkomma-Z-Puffer *m*
f Z-buffer *m* à virgule flottante
r буфер *m* глубины с плавающей запятой

3870 floating rule
(usually between columns, whose ends do not
touch other rules)
d fließende Linie *f*
f règle *f* flottante
r плавающая линейка *f*

3871 floating selection
d fließende Selektion *f*
f sélection *f* flottante
r плавающий выбор *m*

3872 floating toolbar; floating bar
d fließender Werkzeugstreifen *m*
f barre *f* [d'outils] flottante
r плавающая инструментальная лента *f*;
плавающая панель *f* инструментов

3873 floating viewport
d fließendes Ansichtsfenster *n*
f clôture *f* flottante
r плавающая область *f* просмотра;
плавающее окно *n* просмотра

3874 flood fill
d Flutfüllung *f*
f remplissage *m* par inondation
r закрашивание *n* заливанием

3875 flood-fill algorithm
d Flutfüllungsalgorithmus *m*
f algorithme *m* de remplissage par inondation
r алгоритм *m* закрашивания заливанием

* **floodlight** → 3876

3876 floodlight[ing]
d Flutlicht-Beleuchtung *f*; Flutlicht *n*
f éclairage *m* par projecteur; éclairage par
projection
r прожекторное освещение *n*

3877 flow; flux; stream
d Fluss *m*; Strom *m*; Strömung *f*
f flux *m*; flot *m*
r поток *m*

3878 flowchart; flow diagram; block diagram; block scheme; box plot
- *d* Flussdiagramm *n*; Ablaufdiagramm *n*; Ablaufschema *n*; Blockdiagramm *n*; Block[schalt]bild *n*; Blockschema *n*; Boxplot *n*
- *f* diagramme *m* de flux; diagramme de blocs; schéma-bloc *m*
- *r* блок-схема *f*; схема *f* последовательности; диаграмма *f* последовательности

* **flow diagram** → 3878

3879 flow graph
- *d* Flussgraph *m*
- *f* graphe *m* de flux
- *r* потоковый граф *m*; граф поток

3880 flowing
- *d* fließend; zufließend
- *f* courant; fluant; en écoulement
- *r* текущий; гладкий; плавный; мягкий

3881 flow line; stream line; line of stream
- *d* Flusslinie *f*; Stromlinie *f*; Ablauflinie *f*
- *f* ligne *f* de flux; ligne d'évolution; ligne d'écoulement; ligne de liaison
- *r* линия *f* потока; линия тока [векторного поля]; линия связи

3882 flow visualization
- *d* Flussvisualisierung *f*
- *f* visualisation *f* d'écoulement
- *r* поточная визуализация *f*

3883 Floyd-Steinberg error propagation
- *d* Floyd-Steinberg-Fehlerverbreitung *f*
- *f* propagation *f* d'erreur de Floyd-Steinberg
- *r* распространение *n* ошибки Флойда-Стейнберга

3884 Floyd-Steinberg filter
- *d* Floyd-Steinberg-Filter *m*
- *f* filtre *m* de Floyd-Steinberg
- *r* фильтр *m* Флойда-Стейнберга

* **flux** → 3877

3885 flyback; retrace
- *d* Rücklauf *m*
- *f* retour *m* du spot; retour de balayage
- *r* обратный ход *m* [луча]

3886 flying simulation
- *d* Flugsimulation *f*
- *f* simulation *f* au vol
- *r* плавающая симуляция *f*

* **flying-spot scan** → 3887

3887 flying-spot scan[ning]
- *d* Flying-Spot-Abtastung *f*
- *f* balayage *m* au vol; balayage point par point
- *r* сканирование *n* бегущего пятна

* **flyout** → 3888

3888 flyout [icon]
   (a set of icons nested under a single icon)
- *d* Flyout *n*
- *f* volet *m*
- *r* множество *n* икон, объединенных в одну

* **FMP** → 3923

3889 FMP file
- *d* FMP-Datei *f*
- *f* fichier *m* FMP
- *r* файл *m* FMP

3890 focal
- *d* fokal
- *f* focal
- *r* фокусный; фокальный

3891 focal axis
- *d* Fokalachse *f*
- *f* axe *m* focal
- *r* фокальная ось *f*

3892 focal axis of a conic
- *d* Fokalachse *f* eines Kegelschnitts
- *f* axe *m* focal d'une conique
- *r* фокальная ось *f* конического сечения

3893 focal chord of a conic; chord through a focus of a conic
- *d* Sehne *f* durch einen Brennpunkt einer Kurve zweiter Ordnung
- *f* corde *f* focale d'une conique; corde passante par un foyer d'une conique
- *r* фокальная хорда *f* конического сечения; хорда, проходящая через фокус кривой второго порядка

3894 focal circle
- *d* Fokalkreis *m*
- *f* cercle *m* focal
- *r* фокальная окружность *f*

3895 focal conic
- *d* Fokalkegelschnitt *m*
- *f* conique *f* focale
- *r* фокальное коническое сечение *n*

3896 focal curve
- *d* Fokalkurve *f*
- *f* courbe *f* focale
- *r* фокальная кривая *f*

* **focal distance** → 3898

3897 focal ellipse
d Fokalellipse *f*
f ellipse *f* focale
r фокальный эллипс *m*

* **focalization** → 3908

3898 focal length; focal distance
d fokale Länge *f*; Brennweite *f*;
Schärfeebenenabstand *m*
f longueur *f* focale; distance *f* focale; focale *f*
r фокусное расстояние *n*

3899 focal line
d Fokallinie *f*; Brennlinie *f*
f ligne *f* focale
r фокальная линия *f*

3900 focal parameter; semi-focal chord
(of a conic section)
d Fokalparameter *m*; Halbparameter *m*
f paramètre *m* focal
r фокальный параметр *m*

3901 focal plane
d Fokalebene *f*; Brennebene *f*
f plan *m* focal
r фокальная плоскость *f*

3902 focal point; focus
d Brennpunkt *m*; Fokus *m*
f foyer *m*; point *m* focal
r фокальная точка *f*; фокус *m*

3903 focal property
d Brennpunktseigenschaft *f*; Fokaleigenschaft *f*
f propriété *f* focale
r фокальное свойство *n*

3904 focal radius
d Brennstrahl *m*
f rayon *m* focal
r фокальный радиус *m*

3905 focal spot
d Fokalfleck *m*
f tache *f* focale
r фокальное пятно *n*

3906 focal surface
d Fokalfläche *f*; Brennfläche *f*
f surface *f* focale
r фокальная поверхность *f*

* **focoids** → 2425

* **focus** → 3902

* **focused beam** → 1673

3907 focus emphasis
d Fokus-Hervorhebung *f*
f mise *f* en évidence du foyer
r выделение *n* фокуса

3908 focusing; focalization
d Fokussierung *f*
f focalisation *f*
r фокусировка *f*; фокусирование *n*

3909 focus of a hyperbola
d Brennpunkt *m* einer Hyperbel
f foyer *m* d'une hyperbole
r фокус *m* гиперболы

3910 focus of an ellipse
d Brennpunkt *m* einer Ellipse
f foyer *m* d'une ellipse
r фокус *m* эллипса

3911 focus of a parabola
d Brennpunkt *m* einer Parabel
f foyer *m* d'une parabole
r фокус *m* параболы

3912 fog
d Schleier *m*; Nebel *m*
f voile *m*; brouillard *m*
r вуаль *f*; туман *m*

3913 fog background
d Schleierhintergrund *m*
f fond *m* de voile
r фон *m* вуали

3914 fog effect
(in 3D image)
d Nebeleffekt *m*
f effet *m* de voile; effet de brouillard
r эффект *m* вуали

3915 fog filter
d Fog-Filter *m*; Schleierfilter *m*
f filtre *m* de voile
r фильтр *m* вуали

3916 foil
d Metallfolie *f*
f lame *f*; fleuret *m*; feuille *f* mince
r фольга *f*; станиоль *m*

* **foil** → 794

3917 foil blur
d Hintergrundunschärfe *f*
f flou *m* de fond
r расплывание *n* фона

* **fold** → 3919

3918 folder
 d Heftmappe *f*; Mappe *f*
 f dossier *m*
 r фольдер *m*; программная группа *f*; папка *f*

3919 fold[ing]
 d Faltung *f*
 f plissement *m*; pliage *m*; pliement *m*
 r сгибание *n*; огибание *n*

3920 fold line
 d gefaltete Linie *f*
 f ligne *f* de plissement
 r линия *f* сгибания; линия свертки

3921 folio
  (a page number)
 d Folie *f*; Folio *n*
 f folio *m*
 r колонцифра *f*

* **font** → 1417

* **font map** → 3922

3922 font map[ping]
 d Schriftabbildung *f*
 f image *f* de police
 r отображение *n* шрифта

3923 font mapping table; FMP
 d Schrift-Abbildungstabelle *f*
 f table *f* d'application de polices
 r таблица *f* отображения шрифтов

3924 font name
 d Schriftname *m*
 f nom *m* de la police
 r имя *n* шрифта

3925 font options
 d Schriftoptionen *fpl*
 f options *fpl* de police
 r опции *fpl* шрифта

3926 font size
 d Schrifthöhe *f*; Schriftgröße *f*; Schriftgrad *m*
 f taille *f* de police
 r кегль *m*; размер *m* шрифта

* **font style** → 9963

* **font with a fixed pitch** → 6034

3927 footer
 d Fußzeile *f*; Fußnote *f*
 f note *f* en bas de page
 r нижний колонтитул *m*

3928 foot of a perpendicular
 d Lotfußpunkt *m*; Fußpunkt *m*
 f pied *m* d'une perpendiculaire
 r основание *n* перпендикуляра

* **forbidden code** → 4796

3929 force *v*
 d zwingen; erzwingen
 f forcer
 r принудительно задавать; вынуждать

3930 forecasting; prediction; prognosis
 d Vorhersage *f*; Prognostizierung *f*; Prediktion *f*
 f prédiction *f*; prévision *f*
 r предсказание *n*; прогнозирование *n*

3931 forecasting simulation
 d Prediktionssimulierung *f*
 f simulation *f* de prévision
 r симуляция *f* предсказания

3932 foreground
 d Vordergrund *m*
 f premier plan *m*; avant plan
 r передний план *m*

3933 foreground color
 d Vordergrundfarbe *f*
 f couleur *f* de premier plan; couleur de front
 r цвет *m* переднего плана; цвет символов

3934 foreground [display] image; dynamic [display] image
 d Vordergrundbild *n*; dynamisches Bild *n*
 f image *f* principale; image de premier plan
 r основное изображение *n*; накладываемое изображение

3935 foreground gray
 d Vordergrundgrau-Farbe *f*
 f gris *m* de premier plan; gris d'avant plan
 r серый цвет *m* переднего плана

* **foreground image** → 3934

* **foreshortening** → 7900

3936 forest
 d Wald *m*; Forst *m*
 f forêt *f*
 r лес *m*

3937 fork
 d Gabel *f*
 f fourche *f*; aiguillage *m*
 r [раз]вилка *f*

3938 form
 d Formblatt *n*

   f formulaire *m*
   r формуляр *m*; бланк *m*

3939 form; figure; shape
   d Form *f*; Figur *f*; Gestalt *f*
   f forme *f*; figure *f*
   r форма *f*; фигура *f*

3940 formal
   d formal
   f formel
   r формальный

3941 formalism
   d Formalismus *m*
   f formalisme *m*
   r формализм *m*

3942 formalization
   d Formalisierung *f*
   f formalisation *f*
   r формализация *f*

3943 formal system
   d formales System *n*
   f système *m* formel
   r формальная система *f*

3944 format
   d Format *n*
   f format *m*
   r формат *m*

   * **format effector** → 5459

3945 format file
   d Formatdatei *f*
   f fichier *m* de formats
   r файл *m* форматов

3946 format for animation files
   d Format *n* der Animationsdateien
   f format *m* de fichiers d'animation
   r формат *m* анимационных файлов

   * **formation** → 2288

3947 formatting
   d Formatieren *n*; Formatierung *f*
   f formatage *m*
   r форматирование *n*; задание *n* формата

   * **former** → 8615

3948 form flash
   d Formulareinblendung *f*
   f impression *f* d'un formulaire
   r накладывание *n* бланка; проецирование *n* бланка

3949 form tolerance
   d Formtoleranz *f*

   f tolérance *f* de forme
   r допуск *m* формы

   * **forward node** → 4038

3950 forward shot; forward sight; forward vision
   d Vorwärtsstrahl *m*; Vorblick *m*
   f visée *f* [en] avant; visée directe; coup *m* avant
   r визирование *n* вперед

   * **forward sight** → 3950

   * **forward slash** → 8775

   * **forward vision** → 3950

3951 foundations
   (of a theory)
   d Grundlagen *pl*
   f fondements *mpl*
   r основы *fpl*

3952 foundations of geometry
   d Grundlagen *fpl* der Geometrie
   f fondements *mpl* de la géométrie
   r основы *fpl* геометрии

   * **fountain fill** → 3953

3953 fountain fill[ing]
   d Verlaufsfüllung *f*
   f remplissage *m* par dégradé
   r закрашивание *n* с источника; фонтанное закрашивание

3954 fountain pen
   d Füllfederhalter *m*; Federhalter *m*; Füller *m*
   f stylo *m*
   r авторучка *f*

3955 fountain step
   d Verlaufsschritt *m*
   f pas *m* de fontaine
   r шаг *m* источника

3956 fountain transparency
   d Verlauftransparenz *f*
   f transparence *f* de fontaine
   r прозрачность *f* источника

3957 four-color; 4-color; quadrichromatic; quadricolor
   d vierfarbig; Vierfarben-; Vierfarb-
   f en quatre couleurs; quadrichromatique
   r четырехцветный

3958 four-color print[ing] process; 4-color print[ing] process; quadricolor print process
   d Vierfarbendruckverfahren *n*;

Vierfarbendruck *m*;
4-Farben-Druckprozess *m*
f processus *m* d'impression en quatre couleurs
r процесс *m* четырехцветной печати;
четырехцветное печатание *n*

* **four-color print process** → 3958

**3959 four-color problem; problem of coloring
maps in four colors**
d Vierfarbenproblem *n*
f problème *m* du coloriage des cartes; problème
des quatre couleurs
r задача *f* о четырех красках

3960 Fourier images
d Fourier-Bilder *npl*
f images *fpl* de Fourier
r изображения *npl* Фурье

3961 Fourier polygons
d Fourier-Polygone *npl*
f polygones *mpl* de Fourier
r многоугольники *mpl* Фурье

3962 Fourier spectrum
d Fourierspektrum *n*
f spectre *m* de Fourier
r спектр *m* Фурье

* **FOV** → 3737

* **fps** → 3997

3963 fractal
d Fractal *n*
f fractale *f*
r фрактал *m*

3964 fractal attractor
d fractaler Attraktor *m*
f attracteur *m* fractal
r фрактальный аттрактор *m*

3965 fractal compression
d Kompression *f* des Fractals
f compression *f* de fractale
r сжатие *n* фрактала

3966 fractal curve
d fractale Kurve *f*
f courbe *f* fractale
r фрактальная кривая *f*

3967 fractal dimension
d Fractaldimension *f*
f dimension *f* de fractale
r размер *m* фрактала

3968 fractal formula
d Fractalformel *f*
f formule *f* de fractale
r формула *f* фрактала; фрактальная формула

3969 fractal image; fractal pattern
d fractales Bild *n*
f image *f* fractale
r фрактальное изображение *n*

3970 fractal image format; FIF
d Fractalbildformat *n*
f format *m* d'image fractale
r формат *m* фрактального изображения

3971 fractal imaging
d Fractalabbildung *f*
f imagination *f* fractale
r фрактальное изображение *n*

3972 fractal microscope
d Fractal-Mikroskop *n*
f microscope *m* fractal
r фрактальный микроскоп *m*

3973 fractal modeling
d Fractalmodellierung *f*
f modelage *m* de fractale
r фрактальное моделирование *n*

* **fractal pattern** → 3969

3974 fractal surface
d fractale Fläche *f*; fractale Oberfläche *f*
f surface *f* fractale
r фрактальная поверхность *f*

3975 fractal trees
d Fractalbäume *mpl*
f arbres *mpl* fractals
r фрактальные деревья *npl*

3976 fragment
d Fragment *n*
f fragment *m*
r фрагмент *m*

3977 fragmentation
d Fragmentierung *f*; Zerstückelung *f*
f fragmentation *f*
r фрагментирование *n*

* **frame** → 1213, 3988

3978 frame
(of data)
d Frame *n*; Datenübertragungsblock *m*;
DÜ-Block *m*; Datenblockrahmen *m*
f trame *f*; frame *m*; bloc *m* de données
r фрейм *m*; блок *m* данных

3979 frame
(limits of design page)
d Rahmen *m*
f cadre *m*
r рамка *f*

* **frame animation** → 3983

3980 frame-based image segmentation
d Frame-basierte Bildsegmentierung *f*
f segmentation *f* d'image orientée trame
r фреймовое сегментирование *n* изображения

3981 frame-based language
d Frame-basierte Sprache *f*
f langage *m* orienté trame
r фреймовый язык *m*

3982 frame buffer; frame store; frame memory; image buffer
d Rahmenpuffer *m*; Frame-Buffer *m*
f tampon *m* d'image; zone *f* de mémoire d'image; mémoire *f* d'image
r дисплейный буфер *m*; кадровый буфер

3983 frame[-by-frame] animation
d Bild-zu-Bild-Animation *f*
f animation *f* image par image
r [по]кадровая анимация *f*

* **frame change** → 1401

3984 frame color
d Frame-Farbe *f*
f couleur *f* de cadre
r цвет *m* кадра

3985 frame [data] format
d Rahmen[daten]format *n*; Datenblockformat *n*
f format *m* de bloc [de données]
r формат *m* фрейма; формат блока [данных]

3986 framed text
d geschulterter Text *m*
f texte *m* encadré
r текст *m* в рамке

* **frame format** → 3985

* **frame grabbing** → 4821

3987 frame line
d Rahmenlinie *f*
f ligne *f* de cadre
r линия *f* рамки

* **frame memory** –› 3982

3988 frame of reference; reference frame; frame
(a motionless body to which moving bodies are attached)
d Bezugsrahmen *m*; Basisrahmen *m*
f repère *m*
r репер *m*

3989 frame procedure
d Rahmenprozedur *f*
f procédure *f* d'images
r фреймовая процедура *f*

3990 frame processing
d Rahmenverarbeitung *f*
f traitement *m* de trame
r обработка *f* фрейма

3991 frame projection rate
d Bild[er]projektionsgeschwindigkeit *f*
f vitesse *f* de projection de cadres
r скорость *f* проектирования кадров

3992 framer
d Gestalter *m*
f système *m* de cadrage; encadreur *m*
r система *f* кадрирования

3993 frame rate
d Bild[er]geschwindigkeit *f*
f fréquence *f* de cadres
r скорость *f* кадров

3994 frame rate analysis
d Analyse *f* der Bild[er]geschwindigkeit
f analyse *f* de vitesse des cadres
r анализ *m* скорости кадров

3995 frame reject
d Bildausschuss *m*
f rejet *m* de cadre
r режекция *f* кадра

3996 frame size
(in pixels)
d Rahmengröße *f*; Frame-Größe *f*
f taille *f* de cadre
r размер *m* кадра

3997 frames per second; fps
d Bilder *npl* pro Sekunde
f cadres *mpl* par seconde
r кадры *mpl* в секунду

* **frame start** → 9162

* **frame store** → 3982

* **frame switch** → 3998

3998 frame switch[ing]
d Bild[er]-Durchschaltung *f*

   f commutation *f* de cadres
   r переключение *n* кадров

3999 framework of control points
   d Festpunktnetz *n*
   f réseau *m* de points de contrôle; réseau de
      points d'appui
   r сеть *f* опорных точек

4000 framing; cropping
   d Framing *n*; Umrahmung *f*; Einrahmung *f*;
      Rahmung *f*
   f tramage *m*; cadrage *m*
   r формирование *n* кадра; кадрирование *n*;
      кадрировка *f*

4001 free curve
   d freie Kurve *f*
   f courbe *f* [de forme] libre
   r кривая *f* произвольной формы

4002 free-curve generator
   d Freikurvengenerator *m*
   f générateur *m* de courbes libres
   r генератор *m* произвольных кривых

4003 free-form area
   d Zone *f* in freier Form
   f zone *f* de forme libre
   r зона *f* произвольной формы

4004 free-form deformation
   d Deformation *f* in freier Form
   f déformation *f* de forme libre
   r деформация *f* произвольной формы

   * **free-form line → 4009**

4005 free-form polygon mesh
   d Polygonmasche *f* in freier Form
   f maillage *m* par polygones à formes libres
   r многоугольная сеть *f* произвольной формы

4006 freeforms
   d Freiformen *fpl*
   f formes *fpl* libres
   r произвольные формы *fpl*

4007 freehand area
   d Freihandbereich *m*
   f zone *f* à main levée
   r область *f* ручного рисования

   * **freehand curve → 4009**

4008 freehand drawing
   d Freihandzeichen *n*
   f dessin *m* à main levée
   r ручное рисование *n*; рисование
      свободной рукой

4009 freehand line; free-form line; freehand
     curve
   d Freihandlinie *f*
   f ligne *f* à main levée; courbe *f* à main levée
   r линия *f*, нарисованная свободной рукой

4010 freehand sketching
   d Freihandskizzen *n*
   f ébauchage *m* à la main levée
   r ручное набрасывание *n*; ручное
      рисование *n* эскизов; свободное рисование

4011 freehand tool
   d Freihandwerkzeug *m*;
      Hilfsmittel *n* "Freihand"
   f outil *m* à main levée
   r инструмент *m* ручного рисования

4012 freehand tracking
   d Freihandverfolgung *f*; Freihand-Tracking *n*
   f poursuite *f* à main levée
   r свободное прослеживание *n*

4013 free node
   d freier Knoten *m*
   f nœud *m* libre
   r свободный узел *m*

4014 freeplotting
   d freies Plotten *n*
   f traçage *m* libre; tracement *m* libre
   r свободное вычерчивание *n*

4015 free surface
   d freie Fläche *f*
   f surface *f* libre
   r свободная поверхность *f*

4016 free transform tool
   d Hilfsmittel *n* "freie Umwandlung"
   f outil *m* "transformation libre"
   r инструмент *m* произвольной
      трансформации

4017 freeze *v*
   d einfrieren; gefrieren
   f figer; geler; congeler
   r замораживать

4018 freeze frame; frozen frame
   d Freeze-Frame *n*
   f cadre *m* figé; cadre fixe
   r замороженный кадр *m*; фиксированный
      кадр

4019 freeze image; frozen image
   d gefrorenes Bild *n*; stehendes Bild
   f image *f* gelée; image figée
   r замороженное изображение *n*

4020 freeze mode
d fixierter Modus *m*
f mode *m* fixe
r фиксированный режим *m*

4021 freeze status
(of a layer)
d gefrorener Status *m*
f état *m* [con]gelé; état figé
r замороженное состояние *n*

4022 freezing
d Gefrierung *f*
f congélation *f*
r замораживание *n*

4023 freezing of layer
d Schichtgefrierung *f*
f congélation *f* du plan
r замораживание *n* слоя

* **French point** → 2723

* **Frenet frame** → 6084

4024 frequency
(number of samples per second in a sound or video file)
d Frequenz *f*
f fréquence *f*
r частота *f*

* **freshen** *v* **up** → 7964

* **friar** → 1017

4025 frieze
d Fries *m*
f frise *f*
r фриз *m*; лента *f* с повтаряющимся мотивом

4026 frontal
d frontal
f frontal
r фронтальный; передний

* **frontal axonometry** → 2846

4027 frontal outline
d Frontalkontur *f*
f contour *m* frontal
r передний контур *m*

4028 frontal projection
d Frontalprojektion *f*
f projection *f* frontale
r фронтальная проекция *f*

4029 front clipping plane; hither plane; near plane
d frontale Schnittebene *f*

f plan *m* frontal de coupe; plan avant [de découpage]
r фронтальная отсекающая плоскость *f*

4030 front color
d vordere Farbe *f*
f couleur *f* frontal
r передний цвет *m*

4031 front edge
d Vorderkante *f*
f arête *f* en avant; arête frontale
r переднее ребро *n*

4032 front elevation
d vordere Elevation *f*
f élévation *f* frontale
r фронтальное возвышение *n*

4033 front face; face
d Frontseite *f*; Vorderseite *f*; Vorderfläche *f*
f face *f* [frontale]
r лицевая сторона *f*; лицевая поверхность *f*; [передняя] грань *f*; фасад *m*; лицо *n*

4034 front focal length
d vordere Brennweite *f*
f longueur *f* focale antérieure; longueur focale d'objet
r фокальное расстояние *n* в пространстве объекта

4035 front focal plane; object focal plane
d vordere Brennebene *f*; Objektbrennebene *f*
f plan *m* focal antérieur; plan focal d'objet
r фокальная плоскость *f* [в пространстве] объекта

4036 front focal point; front focus; first focus
d vorderer Brennpunkt *m*
f foyer *m* antérieur; foyer d'objet
r передний фокус *m*; фокус в пространстве объекта

* **front focus** → 4036

* **frontier** → 1088

* **frontier** *adj* → 1089

* **frontier point** → 1107

4037 front line; second principal line; second trace parallel
d Frontlinie *f*; zweite Hauptlinie *f*; Hauptlinie zweiter Ordnung
f droite *f* frontale; frontale *f*; deuxième ligne *f* principale
r фронталь *f*; вторая главная линия *f*; прямая *f*, параллельная фронтальной плоскости

4038 front node; forward node
  d vorderer Knotenpunkt *m*
  f nœud *m* antérieur
  r передний узел *m*

4039 front plane; second principal plane
  d Frontplane *f*; zweite Hauptebene *f*;
    Hauptebene zweiter Ordnung
  f plan *m* frontal; deuxième plan principal
  r фронтальная плоскость *f*; вторая главная
    плоскость

4040 front-surface mirror
  d Spiegelabbildung *f* der vorderen Fläche
  f miroir *m* de surface frontale
  r зеркальное отображение *n* фронтальной
    поверхности

4041 front view
  d Frontansicht *f*; Vorderansicht *f*
  f vue *f* frontale
  r фронтальный вид *m*; вид спереди

4042 frozen
  d gefroren
  f figé; congelé; gelé
  r замороженный

  * **frozen frame** → 4018

  * **frozen image** → 4019

4043 frozen layer
  d gefrorene Schicht *f*
  f plan *m* [con]gelé; plan figé
  r замороженный слой *m*

4044 frustum culling
  d Kegelstumpf-Pflücken *n*
  f écartement *m* de tronc; élimination *f* de tronc
  r отстранение *n* усечения

4045 frustum of a cone; truncated cone
  d Kegelstumpf *m*
  f cône *m* tronqué; tronc *m* de cône
  r усеченный конус *m*

4046 frustum of an oblique cone
  d schiefer Kegelstumpf *m*
  f cône *m* oblique tronqué
  r усеченный наклонный конус *m*

4047 frustum of a pyramid; truncated pyramid
  d Pyramidenstumpf *m*
  f pyramide *f* tronquée; tronc *m* de pyramide
  r усеченная пирамида *f*

**4048 frustum of a right cone; truncated right
  cone**
  d gerader Kegelstumpf *m*

  f cône *m* droit tronqué
  r усеченный прямой конус *m*

**4049 frustum of a right pyramid; truncated
  right pyramid**
  d gerader Pyramidenstumpf *m*
  f tronc *m* de pyramide droite; pyramide *f* droite
    tronquée
  r усеченная прямая пирамида *f*

**4050 frustum of circular cone; truncated
  circular cone**
  d Kreiskegelstumpf *m*
  f cône *m* circulaire tronqué; tronc *m* du cône
    circulaire
  r усеченный круговой конус *m*

**4051 frustum of right circular cone; truncated
  right circular cone**
  d gerader Kreiskegelstumpf *m*
  f tronc *m* du cône circulaire droit; cône *m*
    circulaire droit tronqué
  r усеченный прямой круговой конус *m*

  * **frustum of vision** → 1242

4052 full
  d voll; ganz
  f plein; complet
  r полный

4053 full angle
  (= 360°)
  d Vollwinkel *m*
  f angle *m* plein; angle total
  r полный угол *m*

4054 full color; plain color
  d Vollfarbe *f*
  f couleur *f* pleine
  r полный набор *m* цветов

  * **full-color** → 273

4055 full-color bitmap pattern
  d vollfarbes Bitmap-Muster *n*
  f motif *m* bitmap à plein couleur
  r полноцветный растровый мотив *m*

4056 full-color fills
  d Vollfarben-Füllungen *fpl*
  f remplissages *mpl* à plein couleur
  r полноцветные закрашивания *npl*

4057 full-color image
  d Vollfarb[en]bild *n*
  f image *f* à plein couleur
  r полноцветное изображение *n*

4058 full-color printing
  d Vollfarb[en]druck *m*

f impression *f* en pleins couleurs
r полноцветная печать *f*

4059 full-color representation
  d Vollfarb[en]darstellung *f*
  f représentation *f* en plein couleur
  r полноцветное представление *n*

4060 full-face view
  d Gesichtsansicht *f*
  f vue *f* de pleine face
  r лицевой вид *m*

4061 full graphics
  d Vollgrafik *f*
  f graphisme *m* plein
  r полное графическое представление *n*

4062 full image
  d Vollbild *n*
  f image *f* intégrale
  r полное изображение *n*

4063 full-motion digital video; animated digital video
  d animiertes Digitalvideo *n*
  f vidéo *m* numérique animé
  r анимированный цифровой фильм *m*

4064 full-page display
  d Ganzseitendisplay *n*
  f écran *m* à pleine page
  r полностраничный дисплей *m*

4065 full plot preview
  d ganze vorherige Vorschau *f* des Plottens
  f prévisualisation *f* pleine de tracé
  r полный предварительный просмотр *m* черчения

4066 full preview
  d Ganzvorschau *f*
  f prévisualisation *f* pleine
  r полный предварительный просмотр *m*

4067 full scale
  d natürlicher Maßstab *m*
  f grandeur *f* naturelle; échelle *f* réelle
  r натуральный масштаб *m*

4068 full-scale drawing
  d Zeichnung *f* in natürlichem Maßstab
  f dessin *m* en grandeur naturelle; dessin en échelle réelle
  r чертеж *m* в натуральном масштабе

4069 full screen
  d Ganzbildschirm *m*
  f écran *m* plein
  r полный экран *m*

4070 full-screen antialiasing
  d Full-Screen-Antialiasing *n*
  f anticrénelage *m* d'écran plein
  r полноэкранное уменьшение *n* ступенчатости; полноэкранное сглаживание *n*

4071 full-screen mode
  d Ganzbildschirm-Modus *m*
  f mode *m* d'écran plein
  r полноэкранный режим *m*

4072 full-screen preview
  d Ganzbildschirm-Vorschau *f*, Full-Screen-Vorschau *f*
  f prévisualisation *f* d'écran plein
  r полноэкранный предварительный просмотр *m*

4073 full section
  d Ganzschnitt *m*
  f section *f* pleine
  r полное сечение *n*

  * full tone → 2125

4074 full-tone colors; continuous-tone colors
  d Volltonfarben *fpl*
  f couleurs *fpl* de tons continus
  r цвета *mpl* с непрерывными оттенками

4075 full-transparency mapping
  d vollständige Transparenz-Abbildung *f*
  f mappage *m* polyvalent transparent
  r полное отображение *n* с учетом прозрачности

4076 fully desaturated color
  d vollungesättigte Farbe *f*
  f couleur *f* entièrement desaturée
  r вполне ненасыщенный цвет *m*

4077 fully rounded ends
  d vollgerundete Enden *npl*
  f fins *mpl* entièrement arrondis
  r вполне округленные края *mpl*

4078 fully saturated color
  d vollgesättigte Farbe *f*
  f couleur *f* entièrement saturée
  r вполне насыщенный цвет *m*

4079 full zoom; zoom all
  d vollständiges Zoomen *n*
  f zoom *m* total
  r полное динамическое масштабирование *n*

4080 function
  d Funktion *f*

    f fonction *f*
    r функция *f*

4081 functional *adj*
    d funktional
    f fonctionnel
    r функциональный

4082 functional dependence
    d funktionale Abhängigkeit *f*
    f dépendance *f* fonctionnelle
    r функциональная зависимость *f*

4083 functional surface
    d funktionale Fläche *f*
    f surface *f* fonctionnelle
    r функциональная поверхность *f*

4084 function list
    d funktionale Liste *f*
    f liste *f* de fonctions
    r список *m* функций; перечень *f* функций

4085 function name
    d Funktionsname *m*
    f nom *m* de fonction
    r имя *n* функции

    * **fundamental** → **857**

4086 fusing; weld[ing]
    d Verschmelzen *n*; Verschmelzung *f*
    f fusion *f*; soudure *f*
    r плавление *n*; слияние *n*

4087 fuzziness
    d Unbestimmtheit *f*
    f flou *m*
    r нечеткость *f*; нерезкость *f*; размытость *f*;
       расплывчатость *f*

4088 fuzzy; hazy; blurred; non sharp; unsharp
    d unscharf; unbestimmt; Fussy-
    f flou; non distinct
    r размытый; нечеткий; нерезкий; неясный;
       расплывчатый

4089 fuzzy edge
    d unscharfe Kante *f*
    f arête *f* floue
    r размытое ребро *n*; нечеткое ребро

4090 fuzzy graph
    d unbestimmter Graph *m*
    f graphe *m* flou
    r нечеткий граф *m*

4091 fuzzy node
    d unbestimmter Knoten *m*
    f nœud *m* flou

    r нечеткий узел *m*

4092 fuzzy object
    d unbestimmtes Objekt *n*
    f objet *m* flou
    r нерезкий объект *m*; нечеткий объект;
       размытый объект

4093 fuzzy tolerance
    d unbestimmte Toleranz *f*
    f tolérance *f* floue
    r нечеткий допуск *m*

G

4094 gallery
 d Galerie f
 f galerie f
 r галерея f

4095 game-chip
 d Spielchip n
 f puce-jeu f
 r кристалл m игры

4096 game graphics
 d Spielgrafik f
 f graphique m de jeu
 r графика f игр

4097 game in VR
 d virtuelles Spiel n
 f jeu m virtuel
 r игра f в виртуальной реальности

4098 game software
 d Spielsoftware f
 f logiciel m de jeu; ludiciel m
 r программное обеспечение n игры

4099 gamma; gamut
 d Gamma f; Skala f; Gamut n
 f gamme f
 r гамма f; диапазон m; шкала f

4100 gamma adjusting
 d Gamma-Anpassung f
 f ajustage m de gamme; ajustement m de
    gamme
 r настраивание n диапазона

4101 gamma correction
 d Gamma-Korrektur f
 f correction f gamma; gamma-correction f
 r гамма-коррекция f

4102 gamma slider
 d Gamma-Schieber m
 f glisseur m de gamme
 r ползунок m диапазона

 * **gamut → 4099**

 * **gamut mapping → 1469**

4103 ganging
    (the halftone more than one image in only
    one exposure)

 d Vorfach m
 f accouplement m; jumelage m
 r соединение n в комплект; дублирование n;
    сдвоение n

4104 gap
 d Abstand m; Lücke f; Spalte m
 f lacune f; interstice f; fente f
 r промежуток m; зазор m; щель f

4105 gap width
 d Spaltbreite f
 f largeur f d'interstice
 r ширина f зазора; ширина щели

 * **garbage → 6231**

4106 garbage; gibberish; hash
 d Makulatur f; sinnlose Information f;
    Informationsmüll m; bedeutungslose
    Daten npl
 f maculature f; ordure f; données fpl sans
    valeur
 r ненужные данные npl; ненужная
    информация f; мусор m

4107 garbage collection
 d Sammeln n von bedeutungslosen Daten;
    Freispeichersammlung f
 f collection f de maculature; collection
    d'ordures
 r сбор m ненужных данных; очистка f
    памяти

4108 gaseous objects
    (fog, clouds, etc.)
 d gasförmige Objekte npl
 f objets mpl gazeux
 r газообразные объекты mpl

4109 gaseous objects rendering
 d Rendering n der gasförmigen Objekte
 f rendu m d'objets gazeux
 r тонирование n газообразных объектов

 * **gauge v → 1218**

4110 Gaussian blur
 d Gaußsche Unscharfe f; Gauß-Unscharfe f
 f fait m d'embrumer de Gauss
 r гауссовское размывание n; нерезкость f по
    Гауссу

4111 Gaussian blur effect
 d Gauß-Unscharfe-Effekt m
 f effet m flou de Gauss
 r эффект m нерезкости по Гауссу

4112 Gaussian curve
 d Gaußsche Kurve f; Glockenkurve f

f courbe *f* de Gauss; courbe en cloche
r дуга *f* Гаусса

4113 Gaussian distribution
   d Gaußsche Verteilung *f*
   f distribution *f* de Gauss
   r гауссовское распределение *n*

4114 Gaussian filter
   d Gauß-Filter *m*
   f filtre *m* gaussien
   r гауссовский фильтр *m*; фильтр Гаусса

4115 Gaussian noise; random noise; white noise
   d Gaußsches Rauschen *n*
   f bruit *m* gaussien; bruit blanc
   r гауссовский шум *m*

4116 Gaussian optics
   d Gauß-Optik *f*
   f optique *f* gaussienne
   r гауссовская оптика *f*

4117 Gaussian plane
   d Gauß-Ebene *f*
   f plan *m* gaussien
   r гауссовская плоскость *f*

4118 Gaussian sphere
   d Gaußsche Kugel *f*
   f sphère *f* gaussienne
   r гауссова сфера *f*

4119 Gaussian weighted filter
   d bewerteter Gauß-Filter *m*
   f filtre *m* de Gauss pondéré
   r взвешенный гауссовский фильтр *m*

4120 Gauss-Krüger projection
   d Gauß-Krüger-Projektion *f*
   f projection *f* de Gauss-Krüger
   r проекция *f* Гаусса-Крюгера

4121 Gauss lens
   d Gauß-Linse *f*
   f lentille *f* de Gauss
   r гауссовская линза *f*

   * **Gauss point → 1286**

   * **GCR → 4404**

   * **GEM → 4362**

   * **general axonometry → 8759**

4122 general display option
   d allgemeine Darstellungsoption *f*
   f option *f* d'affichage générale
   r общая опция *f* изображений на экране

4123 general format
   d allgemeines Format *n*
   f format *m* général
   r общий формат *m*

4124 general form of the equation of a plane
   d allgemeine Gleichung *f* einer Ebene;
      allgemeine Ebenengleichung *f*; Normalform *f*
      der Ebenengleichung
   f équation *f* générale d'un plan
   r общее уравнение *n* плоскости

**4125 general form of the equation of a second
      order surface**
   d allgemeine Gleichung *f* einer Fläche zweiter
      Ordnung
   f équation *f* générale d'une surface du second
      degré
   r общее уравнение *n* поверхности второго
      порядка

**4126 general form of the equation of a straight
      line**
   d allgemeine Geradengleichung *f*;
      Normalform *f* der Geradengleichung
   f équation *f* générale d'une droite
   r общее уравнение *n* прямой

4127 generalization
   d Generalisierung *f*; Generalisation *f*;
      Verallgemeinerung *f*
   f généralisation *f*
   r генерализация *f*

4128 generalization scale
   d Generalisierungsmaßstab *m*
   f échelle *f* de généralisation
   r масштаб *m* генерализации; масштаб
      обобщения

4129 generalized coordinates
   d generalisierte Koordinaten *fpl*;
      verallgemeinerte Koordinaten *fpl*
   f coordonnées *fpl* généralisées
   r обобщенные координаты *fpl*

4130 generalized cylinder
   d verallgemeinerter Zylinder *m*
   f cylindre *m* généralisé
   r обобщенный цилиндр *m*

4131 generalized Vandermonde matrix
   d generalisierte Vandermonde-Matrix *f*
   f matrice *f* de Vandermonde généralisée
   r обобщенная матрица *f* Вандермонда

4132 general operating preference
   d allgemeine Betriebspräferenz *f*
   f préférence *f* d'opération générale
   r обобщенная операционная поддержка *f*

* **general perspective affinity** → 8766

4133 **general projection algorithm**
  d allgemeiner Projektionsalgorithmus *m*
  f algorithme *m* de projection général
  r общий алгоритм *m* проецирования

4134 **general scaling of gray value**
  d allgemeine Skalierung *f* der Grauwerte
  f mise *f* en échelle générale des valeurs de gris
  r общий пересчет *m* оттенков серого цвета

4135 **general utility function**
  d allgemeine Nutzenfunktion *f*
  f fonction *f* générale d'utilité
  r общая утилитная функция *f*

4136 **generate** *v*
  d generieren; erzeugen
  f générer; engendrer
  r порождать; генерировать; производить

4137 **generating angle**
  (between the axis and the generator of a
  conical surface)
  d erzeugender Winkel *m*
  f angle *m* générateur
  r производящий угол *m*

4138 **generating curve; generating line;
  generatrix; generator**
  d erzeugende Kurve *f*; Erzeugungskurve *f*;
  erzeugende Linie *f*; Erzeugungslinie *f*;
  Mantellinie *f*; Erzeugende *f*
  f courbe *f* génératrice; ligne *f* génératrice;
  génératrice *f*
  r производящая кривая *f*; образующая
  кривая; образующая [линия] *f*;
  генератриса *f*

* **generating line** → 4138

* **generating line of a cone** → 4141

* **generating line of a conical surface** → 4142

* **generating line of a cylinder** → 4143

* **generating line of a cylindrical surface** →
  4144

4139 **generating program; generator**
  d Generierungsprogramm *n*
  f programme *m* de génération; générateur *m*
  r генерирующая программа *f*

* **generating set** → 3702

4140 **generation**
  d Erzeugung *f*; Generierung *f*

  f génération *f*; engendrement *m*
  r порождение *n*; образование *n*

* **generator** → 4138, 4139

4141 **generator of a cone; generating line of a
  cone; generatrix of a cone**
  d Erzeugende *f* eines Kegels
  f génératrice *f* d'un cône
  r образующая *f* конуса

4142 **generator of a conical surface; generating
  line of a conical surface; generatrix of a
  conical surface**
  d Erzeugende *f* einer Kegelfläche
  f génératrice *f* d'une surface conique
  r образующая *f* конической поверхности

4143 **generator of a cylinder; generating line of
  a cylinder; generatrix of a cylinder**
  d Erzeugende *f* eines Zylinders
  f génératrice *f* d'un cylindre
  r образующая *f* цилиндра

4144 **generator of a cylindrical surface;
  generating line of a cylindrical surface;
  generatrix of a cylindrical surface**
  d Erzeugende *f* einer Zylinderfläche
  f génératrice *f* d'une surface cylindrique
  r образующая *f* цилиндрической
  поверхности

* **generatrix** → 4138

* **generatrix of a cone** → 4141

* **generatrix of a conical surface** → 4142

* **generatrix of a cylinder** → 4143

* **generatrix of a cylindrical surface** → 4144

4145 **generic**
  d generisch
  f générique; génératif
  r порождающий

4146 **generic CMYK printer profile**
  d generisches CMYK-Druckerprofil *n*
  f profil *m* d'imprimante CMYK générique
  r порождающий CMYK профиль *m*
  принтера

4147 **generic curve**
  d generische Kurve *f*
  f courbe *f* générique
  r порождающая кривая *f*

* **generic linear complex** → 4148

4148 generic linear complex [of rays]
   d generischer linearer Komplex *m*; generischer
     linearer Strahlenkomplex *m*
   f complexe *m* linéaire générique [de rayons]
   r порождающий линейный комплекс *m*
     [лучей]

4149 generic offset separations profile
   d generisches Profil *n* der Offsetauszüge
   f profil *m* générique de séparations d'offset
   r порождающий профиль *m* офсетных
     отделений

4150 generic profile
   d generisches Profil *n*
   f profil *m* générique
   r порождающий профиль *m*

4151 genus of a surface
   d Geschlecht *n* einer Fläche
   f genre *m* de surface
   r род *m* поверхности

* **geodesic** → **4156**

4152 geodesic; geodetic *adj*
   d geodätisch
   f géodésique
   r геодезический

4153 geodesic circle
   d geodätischer Kreis *m*
   f cercle *m* géodésique
   r геодезическая окружность *f*

4154 geodesic coordinates
   d geodätische Koordinaten *fpl*
   f coordonnées *fpl* géodésiques
   r геодезические координаты *fpl*

4155 geodesic curvature; tangential curvature
   d Tangentialkrümmung *f*
   f courbure *f* géodésique; courbure tangentielle
   r геодезическая кривизна *f*

* **geodesic distance** → **3328**

4156 geodesic [line]
   (of a surface)
   d Geodätische *f*, geodätische Linie *f*; Geodäte *f*
   f géodésique *f*; ligne *f* géodésique
   r геодезическая линия *f*

4157 geodesic mapping; Beltrami['s] mapping
   d geodätische Abbildung *f*; Beltramische
     Abbildung; bahntreue Abbildung
   f application *f* géodésique; application de
     Beltrami
   r геодезическое отображение *n*;
     отображение Бельтрами; отображение,

     сохраняющее траектории

4158 geodesic torsion
   d geodätische Torsion *f*; geodätische Windung *f*
   f torsion *f* géodésique
   r геодезическое кручение *n*

4159 geodesic triangle; geodetic triangle
   d geodätisches Dreieck *n*
   f triangle *m* géodésique
   r геодезический треугольник *m*

4160 geodesy
   d Geodäsie *f*
   f géodésie *f*
   r геодезия *f*

* **geodetic** *adj* → **4152**

* **geodetic triangle** → **4159**

4161 geographic[al] coordinates
   d geografische Koordinaten *fpl*
   f coordonnées *fpl* géographiques
   r географические координаты *fpl*

4162 geographic[al] display
   (mapping geographic location of remote
   server)
   d geografisches Display *n*
   f affichage *m* géographique
   r географический дисплей *m*

4163 geographic[al] information
   d geografische Information *f*
   f information *f* géographique
   r географическая информация *f*

4164 geographic[al] map
   d Landkarte *f*
   f carte *f* géographique
   r географическая карта *f*

4165 geographic[al] view
   d geografische Ansicht *f*
   f vue *f* géographique
   r географическое представление *n*

* **geographic coordinates** → **4161**

* **geographic display** → **4162**

* **geographic information** → **4163**

* **geographic map** → **4164**

* **geographic view** → **4165**

* **geometric** → **4166**

4166 geometric[al]
  d geometrisch
  f géométrique
  r геометрический

4167 geometric[al] axis
  d geometrische Achse *f*
  f axe *m* géométrique
  r геометрическая ось *f*

4168 geometric[al] body
  d geometrischer Körper *m*
  f corps *m* géométrique
  r геометрическое тело *n*

4169 geometric[al] center
  d geometrisches Zentrum *n*
  f centre *m* géométrique
  r геометрический центр *m*

4170 geometric[al] characteristic
  d geometrische Charakteristik *f*
  f caractéristique *f* géométrique
  r геометрическая характеристика *f*

4171 geometric[al] characteristic symbol
  d Symbol *n* der geometrischen Charakteristik
  f symbole *m* de caractéristique géométrique
  r символ *m* геометрической характеристики

4172 geometric[al] concentration
  d geometrische Konzentration *f*
  f concentration *f* géométrique
  r геометрическая концентрация *f*

4173 geometric[al] construction
  d geometrische Konstruktion *f*
  f construction *f* géométrique
  r геометрическое построение *n*

4174 geometric[al] cue
  d geometrisches Zeichen *n*
  f caractère *m* géométrique
  r геометрический знак *m*

4175 geometric[al] data
  d geometrische Daten *npl*
  f données *fpl* géométriques
  r геометрические данные *npl*

4176 geometric[al] database
  d geometrische Datenbasis *f*
  f base *f* de données géométriques
  r база *f* геометрических данных

4177 geometric[al] [data] input
  d geometrischer Eingang *m*; geometrische Dateneingabe *f*
  f entrée *f* de données géométriques; entrée géométrique

  r ввод *m* геометрических данных

4178 geometric[al] [data] output
  d geometrischer Ausgang *m*; geometrischer Datenausgang *m*
  f sortie *f* de données géométriques; sortie géométrique
  r выход *m* геометрических данных

4179 geometric[al] editor
  d geometrischer Editor *m*
  f éditeur *m* géométrique
  r геометрический редактор *m*

4180 geometric[al] element
  d geometrisches Element *n*
  f élément *m* géométrique
  r геометрический элемент *m*

4181 geometric[al] expression
  d geometrischer Ausdruck *m*
  f expression *f* géométrique
  r геометрическое выражение *n*

4182 geometric[al] extent
  d geometrischer Extent *m*
  f étendue *f* géométrique
  r геометрический экстент *m*

4183 geometric[al] figure
  d geometrische Figur *f*
  f figure *f* géométrique
  r геометрическая фигура *f*

4184 geometric[al] graphics
  d Geometrie-Grafik *f*
  f graphique *m* géométrique
  r геометрическая графика *f*

4185 geometric[al] image
  d geometrisches Bild *n*
  f image *f* géométrique
  r геометрическое изображение *n*

4186 geometric[al] locus; locus
  d geometrischer Ort *m*
  f lieu *m* géométrique
  r геометрическое место *m* точек; местоположение *n*

4187 geometric[al] model
  d Geometriemodell *n*
  f modèle *m* géométrique
  r геометрическая модель *f*

4188 geometric[al] modeling
  d geometrische Modellierung *f*
  f modelage *m* géométrique; modélisation *f* géométrique
  r геометрическое моделирование *n*

4189 geometric[al] morphing
   d geometrisches Morphing *n*
   f morphage *m* géométrique
   r геометрический морфинг *m*

4190 geometric[al] object
   d geometrisches Objekt *n*
   f objet *m* géométrique
   r геометрический объект *m*

4191 geometric[al] operations
   d geometrische Operationen *fpl*
   f opérations *fpl* géométriques
   r геометрические операции *fpl*

4192 geometric[al] optics
   d geometrische Optik *f*
   f optique *f* géométrique
   r геометрическая оптика *f*; лучевая оптика

4193 geometric[al] parameters
   d geometrische Parameter *mpl*
   f paramètres *mpl* géométriques
   r геометрические параметры *mpl*

**4194 geometric[al] processor; geometry
       processor**
   d Geometrieprozessor *m*
   f processeur *m* géométrique; processeur de
      géométrie
   r геометрический процессор *m*; процессор
      геометрии

4195 geometric[al] processor chip
   d Chip *m* des Geometrieprozessors
   f puce *f* de processeur géométrique
   r геометрический процессорный чип *m*

4196 geometric[al] relationship
   d geometrischer Zusammenhang *m*
   f relation *f* mutuelle géométrique
   r геометрическая взаимосвязь *f*

4197 geometric[al] server
   d geometrischer Server *m*
   f serveur *m* géométrique
   r геометрический сервер *m*

4198 geometric[al] symbol
   d geometrisches Symbol *n*
   f symbole *m* géométrique
   r геометрический символ *m*

4199 geometric[al] tolerance
   d geometrische Toleranz *f*
   f tolérance *f* géométrique
   r геометрический допуск *m*

4200 geometric[al] transformation
   d Geometrietransformation *f*

   f transformation *f* géométrique
   r геометрическая трансформация *f*

4201 geometric[al] utility function
   d geometrische Nutzenfunkrtion *f*
   f fonction *f* utilitaire géométrique
   r геометрическая утилитная функция *f*

* **geometric axis** → 4167

* **geometric body** → 4168

* **geometric center** → 4169

* **geometric characteristic** → 4170

* **geometric characteristic symbol** → 4171

* **geometric concentration** → 4172

* **geometric construction** → 4173

* **geometric cue** → 4174

* **geometric data** → 4175

* **geometric database** → 4176

* **geometric data input** → 4177

* **geometric data output** → 4178

* **geometric editor** → 4179

* **geometric element** → 4180

* **geometric expression** → 4181

* **geometric extent** → 4182

* **geometric figure** → 4183

* **geometric graphics** → 4184

* **geometric image** → 4185

* **geometric input** → 4177

* **geometric locus** → 4186

* **geometric model** → 4187

* **geometric modeling** → 4188

* **geometric morphing** → 4189

* **geometric object** → 4190

* **geometric operations** → 4191

* **geometric optics** → 4192

* **geometric output** → 4178

* **geometric parameters** → 4193

* **geometric processor** → 4194

* **geometric processor chip** → 4195

* **geometric relationship** → 4196

* **geometric server** → 4197

* **geometric symbol** → 4198

* **geometric tolerance** → 4199

* **geometric transformation** → 4200

* **geometric utility function** → 4201

4202 geometry
  d Geometrie *f*
  f géométrie *f*
  r геометрия *f*

4203 geometry calculator
  d geometrischer Kalkulator *m*
  f calculateur *m* géométrique
  r геометрический калькулятор *m*

4204 geometry cluster
  d geometrischer Cluster *m*
  f grappe *f* de géométrie
  r геометрический блок *m*

4205 geometry compression
  d geometrische Kompression *f*
  f compression *f* géométrique
  r геометрическое уплотнение *n*

4206 geometry of position
  d Geometrie *f* der Lage
  f géométrie *f* de position
  r геометрия *f* положения

4207 geometry of surfaces
  d Flächengeometrie *f*
  f géométrie *f* des surfaces
  r геометрия *f* поверхностей

4208 geometry of the triangle
  d Dreiecksgeometrie *f*; Geometrie *f* des
     Dreiecks
  f géométrie *f* du triangle
  r геометрия *f* треугольника

4209 geometry of webs
  d Webgeometrie *f*

  f géométrie *f* des réseaux
  r геометрия *f* тканей; геометрия сот

* **geometry processor** → 4194

4210 geometry system
  d Geometrie-System *n*
  f système *m* de géométrie
  r геометрическая система *f*

4211 georeference
  d Georeferenz *f*
  f géoréférence *f*
  r географическая ссылка *f*

4212 georeferenced data
  d geografisch codierte Daten *npl*
  f données *fpl* géoréférenciées
  r геореферентные данные *npl*

4213 geospatial database
  d georäumliche Datenbasis *f*
  f base *f* de données géospatiaux
  r геопространственная база *f* данных

4214 germ of mappings; map-germ
  d Keim *m* von Abbildungen
  f germe *m* d'applications
  r класс *m* эквивалентных отображений

4215 gesture
  d Geste *f*
  f geste *m*
  r жест *m*

4216 gesture capturer
  d Gestensammler *m*
  f capteur *m* gestuel
  r уловитель *m* жестов

4217 gesture mode
  d Gestenmodus *m*
  f mode *m* gestuel
  r режим *m* жестов

4218 gesture recognition
  d Gestenerkennung *f*
  f reconnaissance *f* des gestes
  r распознавание *n* жестов

* **ghost** → 7001

* **ghost character** → 4220

* **ghost image** → 7001

4219 ghosting
  d Geistereffekt *m*
  f linéament *m*; dédoublement *m* de l'image

r слабое вторичное изображение *n*;
побочное изображение; появление *n*
ореола

4220 ghost[ing] character
d Geisterzeichen *n*
f caractère *m* fantôme; caractère flou
r фантомный символ *m*

* **gibberish** → 4106

* **GIF** → 4365

4221 GIF file
d GIF-Datei *f*
f fichier *m* GIF
r файл *m* GIF

4222 GIF filter
d GIF-Filter *m*
f filtre *m* GIF
r фильтр *m* GIF

4223 gigapixel
d Gigapixel *n*
f gigapixel *m*
r гигапиксел *m*

* **glancing** *adj* → 8791

4224 glare; reflect; dazzle
d Blendung *f*; Schein *m*
f éblouissement *m*; reflet *m*
r блик *m*; яркий свет *m*; резкий свет;
ослепительный блеск *m*; блескость *f*

* **glare filter** → 449

4225 glare index
d Blend[ungs]index *m*
f indice *m* d'éblouissement
r индекс *m* блика

4226 glass block
d Glasblock *m*
f block *m* en verre
r стеклянный блок *m*

4227 glass block effect
d Glasblock-Effekt *m*
f effet *m* de bloc en verre
r эффект *m* стеклянного блока

4228 glass block filter
d Glasblock-Filter *m*
f filtre *m* de bloc en verre
r фильтр *m* стеклянного блока

* **glass film** → 4229

4229 glass layer; glass film
d Glasschicht *f*
f couche *f* de verre
r стеклянный слой *m*

* **glide** *v* → 8782

4230 glide angle
d Gleitwinkel *m*
f angle *m* de glissement
r угол *m* скольжения

4231 glide path
d Gleitweg *m*
f chemin *m* de glissement
r путь *m* скольжения; глиссада *f*
планирования

4232 glidepoint
d Gleitpunkt *m*
f point *m* de glissement
r точка *f* скольжения

* **glider** → 8788

* **gliding** → 8790

4233 glissete
d Gleitkurve *f*
f glissete *f*
r кривая *f* скольжения; кривая сдвига

4234 global
d global
f global
r глобальный

4235 global attribute
d globales Attribut *n*
f attribut *m* global
r глобальный атрибут *m*

4236 global attribute edit
d Bearbeitung *f* des globalen Attributs
f édition *f* d'attribut global
r редактирование *n* глобального атрибута

* **global coordinate system** → 10471

4237 global illumination
d globale Beleuchtung *f*
f illumination *f* globale
r глобальное освещение *n*

4238 global illumination algorithm
d Algorithmus *m* der globalen Beleuchtung
f algorithme *m* d'illumination globale
r алгоритм *m* глобального освещения

* **global maximum** → 16

* **global minimum** → 17

4239 global scale factor
 d globaler Skalenfaktor m
 f facteur m d'échelle global
 r глобальный коэффициент m
   масштабирования

4240 global section
 d globaler Schnitt m
 f section f globale
 r глобальное сечение n

4241 global variable
 d globale Variable f
 f variable f globale
 r глобальная переменная f

4242 glossary
 d Glossar n; Begriffserklärung f
 f glossaire m
 r глоссарий m; словарь m специальных
   терминов

4243 glossy paper
 d glattes Papier n
 f papier m glacé; papier lustré
 r глянцевая бумага f

4244 glossy print
 (black-and-white print made on glossy paper)
 d Kunstdruckabzug m
 f impression f sur papier glacé
 r печать f на глянцевой бумаге

4245 glove
 d Handschuh m
 f gant m
 r перчатка f

* **glue v together** → 6883

* **gluing** → 6884

* **goal** → 2643

4246 goal hypothesis
 d Zielhypothese f
 f hypothèse f de but; hypothèse d'objectif
 r целевая гипотеза f

4247 goal normalization
 d Zielnormalisierung f
 f normalisation f de but
 r нормирование n цели

4248 goal position
 d Zielposition f
 f position f de cible
 r целевая позиция f

4249 goal seeking
 d Zielsuchen n
 f orientation f au but
 r целенаправленный поиск m

* **going to black** → 3688

4250 golden mean; golden ratio
 d goldenes Mittel n
 f nombre m d'or; proportion f divine
 r золотая середина f; золотая пропорция f

* **golden ratio** → 4250

4251 golden rectangle
 d goldenes Rechteck n
 f rectangle m d'or
 r прямоугольник m с отношением сторон,
   отвечающим золотой пропорции

4252 golden rule
 d goldene Regel f
 f règle f d'or
 r золотое правило n

4253 golden section
 d goldener Schnitt m
 f section f d'or; section dorée
 r золотое сечение n

4254 golden section algorithm
 d Algorithmus m des goldenen Schnitts
 f algorithme m de section d'or
 r алгоритм m золотого сечения

4255 golden section rule
 d Regel f des goldenen Schnitts
 f règle f du nombre d'or; règle de la section
   dorée
 r правило n золотого сечения

4256 golden triangle
 d goldenes Dreieck n
 f triangle m d'or
 r треугольник m с отношением сторон,
   отвечающим золотой пропорции

**4257 goniometry; measurement of angles;
   angular measurement**
 d Winkelmessung f
 f goniométrie f; mesurage m d'angles; mesure f
   des angles
 r измерение n углов; гониометрия f

* **gorge** → 4259

4258 gorge circle of a surface of revolution
 d Kehlkreis m einer Drehfläche; Kehlkreis einer
   Rotationsfläche

f cercle *m* de gorge d'une surface de révolution
r горловая окружность *f* поверхности вращения

4259 gorge [line]; striction line
d Kehllinie *f*; Striktionslinie *f*
f ligne *f* de striction
r горловая линия *f*; стрикционная линия

4260 Gouraud interpolation
d Gouraud-Interpolation *f*
f interpolation *f* Gouraud
r интерполяция *f* Гуро

4261 Gouraud-shaded model
d Gouraud-schattiertes Modell *n*
f modèle *m* ombré Gouraud
r теневая модель *f* Гуро

4262 Gouraud shading
(Lambert or cosine shading plus the representation of specular highlighting)
d Gouraud-Schattierung *f*
f ombrage *m* Gouraud
r оттенение *n* Гуро

* **grabbing** → 1279

* **grad** → 4267

4263 gradation
d Gradation *f*
f gradation *f*
r градация *f*

4264 gradation curve
d Gradationskurve *f*
f courbe *f* de gradation
r кривая *f* градации

4265 gradation filter
d Gradationsfilter *m*
f filtre *m* de gradation
r фильтр *m* градации

4266 grade
d Grad *m*
f degré *m*
r степень *f*

4267 grad[e]
(a unit of an angle)
d Neugrad *m*
f grade *m*
r град *m*

4268 grade; degree
d Grad *m*
f degré *m*; grade *m*
r градус *m*

4269 graded index; gradient index; GRIN
d Gradient[en]index *m*
f gradient *m* d'indice
r градиентный индекс *m*; градиентный показатель *m*

4270 grade measure
d Gradmaß *n*
f mesure *f* en degrés
r градусная мера *f*

4271 grade of darkening; darkening grade
d Schwärzungsgrad *m*
f degré *m* de noircissement
r степень *f* почернения

4272 gradient
d Gradient *m*
f gradient *m*
r градиент *m*

* **gradient angle** → 379

4273 gradient background
d Gradient[en]hintergrund *m*
f fond *m* gradient
r градиентный фон *m*

4274 gradient color
d Gradient[en]farbe *f*
f couleur *f* graduelle
r градиентный цвет *m*

4275 gradient density
d Gradient[en]dichte *f*
f densité *f* graduelle
r градиентная плотность *f*

4276 gradient direction
d Gradient[en]richtung *f*
f direction *f* de gradient
r направление *n* градиента

4277 gradient fill; graduated fill
d Gradient[en]füllung *f*
f remplissage *m* graduel
r градиентное закрашивание *n*; градиентная заливка *f*

* **gradient index** → 4269

* **gradient method** → 4280

4278 gradient of a function
d Gradient *m* einer Funktion
f gradient *m* d'une fonction
r градиент *m* функции

* **gradient scale** → 4283

4279 gradient shading
  d Gradient[en]schattierung *f*
  f ombrage *m* graduel
  r градиентное оттенение *n*

4280 gradient[-step] method
  d Gradient[en]methode *f*;
      Gradient[-Step]-Verfahren *n*
  f méthode *f* des gradients
  r метод *m* градиента; градиентный метод

4281 gradient vector
  d Gradient[en]vektor *m*
  f vecteur *m* gradient
  r градиент-вектор *m*

  * **grading → 1531**

4282 gradually filled
  d allmähliche Füllung *f*
  f rempli graduellement
  r постепенно заполненный

  * **graduate *v* → 1218**

4283 graduated fall line; fall scale; slope scale; gradient scale
  d graduierte Falllinie *f*; Böschungsmaßstab *m*
  f ligne *f* de pente graduée; échelle *f* de pente
  r градуированная линия *f* падения;
      масштаб *m* падения; масштаб наклона

  * **graduated fill → 4277**

4284 graduated filter
  d graduierter Filter *m*
  f filtre *m* gradué
  r градуированный фильтр *m*

4285 graduated line
  d graduierte Linie *f*
  f droite *f* graduée
  r градуированная линия *f*

4286 graduated scale
  d graduierte Skala *f*
  f règle *f* graduée; échelle *f* graduée
  r масштабная линейка *f*

4287 graduation
  d Graduierung *f*
  f graduation *f*
  r градуирование *n*; градуировка *f*

4288 grain
  d Korn *n*
  f grain *m*
  r зерно *n*

4289 grain boundary

4290 graining
  d Korngrenze *f*
  f limite *f* de grains
  r граница *f* зерен

  * **graininess → 4293**

4290 graining
  d Kornbildung *f*; Körnung *f*
  f grenaison *f*; grainage *m*
  r создание *n* зернистости; создание эффекта зернистой поверхности

4291 grain size
  d Korngröße *f*
  f grosseur *f* du grain
  r размер *m* зерен

4292 grammar
  d Grammatik *f*
  f grammaire *f*
  r грамматика *f*

4293 granularity; graininess
  d Körnigkeit *f*
  f granularité *f*
  r зернистость *f*; гранулярность *f*

4294 granular noise
  d Körnrauschen *m*
  f bruit *m* granulaire
  r зернистое искажение *n*

4295 granulated
  d granuliert; körnig
  f à grains
  r зернистый

4296 granulated screen raster
  d granulierter Bildschirmraster *m*
  f trame *f* à grains
  r зернистый растр *m* экрана

4297 granulation
  d Granulation *f*; Körnung *f*
  f granulation *f*; grenu *m*
  r зернение *n*; корнование *n*

  * **graph → 1439**

4298 graph
  d Graph *m*
  f graphe *m*
  r граф *m*

4299 graph drawing
  d Graphzeichnung *f*
  f dessin *m* de graphe
  r чертеж *m* графа

4300 grapheme
  d Grafem *n*

f graphème *m*
r графема *f*

* **graphic** → 1439, 4301

* **graphic accelerator** → 4302

4301 graphic[al] *adj*
d grafisch
f graphique
r графический

4302 graphic[al] accelerator
d grafischer Beschleuniger *m*;
Grafikbeschleuniger *m*
f accélérateur *m* graphique; adaptateur *m* graphique
r графический ускоритель *m*; графический акселератор *m*

4303 graphic animation
d grafische Animation *f*
f animation *f* graphique
r графическая анимация *f*

4304 graphic area; graphics window
d Grafikbereich *m*; Grafikfenster *n*
f domaine *m* graphique; fenêtre *f* graphique
r графическая область *f*; графическое окно *n*

4305 graphic calculation; graphic calculus
d grafisches Rechnen *n*
f calcul *m* graphique
r графическое вычисление *n*

* **graphic calculus** → 4305

* **graphic card** → 10208

4306 graphic card memory
d Grafikkartenspeicher *m*
f mémoire *f* de carte graphique
r память *f* графической карты

4307 graphic character
d grafisches Zeichen *n*; Grafiksymbol *n*
f caractère *m* graphique; symbole *m* graphique
r графический символ *m*

4308 graphic chipset
d grafischer Chipsatz *m*
f jeu *m* de circuit graphique
r набор *m* графических микросхем

4309 graphic cluster
d grafischer Cluster *m*
f grappe *f* graphique
r графический кластер *m*; графический блок *m*

4310 graphic code
d grafischer Code *m*
f code *m* graphique
r графический код *m*

4311 graphic command sequence
d grafische Kommandosequenz *f*
f séquence *f* de commandes graphiques
r последовательность *f* графических команд

4312 graphic communication
d grafische Kommunikation *f*
f communication *f* graphique
r графическая связь *f*

4313 graphic compiler
d Grafikkompilierer *m*
f compilateur *m* graphique
r графический компилятор *m*

4314 graphic computer system
d grafisches Rechnersystem *n*
f système *m* d'ordinateur graphique
r графическая компьютерная система *f*

4315 graphic[s] [co]processor
d Grafik[co]prozessor *m*
f [co]processeur *m* graphique
r графический [co]процессор *m*

4316 graphic data
d grafische Daten *npl*; Grafikdaten *npl*
f données *fpl* graphiques
r графические данные *npl*

4317 graphic [data] input; graphic entry
d grafische Dateneingabe *f*
f entrée *f* de données graphiques
r ввод *m* графических данных

4318 graphic [data] output
d grafische Datenausgabe *f*;
Grafikdatenausgabe *f*
f sortie *f* des données graphiques; émission *f* des données graphiques
r вывод *m* графических данных

4319 graphic [data] transmission
d grafischer Informationsaustausch *m*
f transmission *f* de données graphiques
r передача *f* графической информации

4320 graphic design
d grafisches Design *n*
f dessin *m* graphique
r графическое проектирование *n*

4321 graphic device
d grafisches Gerät *n*

f dispositif *m* graphique
r графическое устройство *n*

4322 graphic display
d grafischer Bildschirm *m*
f afficheur *m* graphique
r графический дисплей *m*

4323 graphic display interface
d Schnittstelle *f* des grafischen Displays
f interface *f* d'afficheur graphique
r интерфейс *m* графического дисплея

4324 graphic editor; graphics editor
d Grafik-Editor *m*
f éditeur *m* graphique
r графический редактор *m*

4325 graphic effect
d grafischer Effekt *m*
f effet *m* [info]graphique
r графический эффект *m*

4326 graphic element
d grafisches Element *n*
f élément *m* graphique
r графический элемент *m*

4327 graphic engine
d grafische Maschine *f*
f moteur *m* graphique
r графическая машина *f*

*   **graphic entry** → **4317**

4328 graphic error
d grafischer Fehler *m*
f erreur *f* graphique
r графическая ошибка *f*

4329 graphic file
d grafische Datei *f*; Grafikdatei *f*
f fichier *m* graphique
r графический файл *m*

4330 graphic font
d grafisches Font *n*
f police *f* graphique
r графический шрифт *m*

4331 graphic font size
d Größe *f* des grafischen Fonts
f taille *f* de la police graphique
r размер *m* графического шрифта; кегль *m*
    графического шрифта

4332 graphic font style
d Stil *m* der grafischen Schrift
f style *m* de police graphique
r стиль *m* графического шрифта

4333 graphic format
d Grafikformat *n*
f format *m* graphique
r графический формат *m*

4334 graphic grammar
d grafische Grammatik *f*
f grammaire *f* graphique
r графическая грамматика *f*

4335 graphic hardware
d grafische Hardware *f*
f matériel *m* graphique
r графическое техническое обеспечение *n*

4336 graphic hyperlink
d Grafik-Hyperlink *n*
f hyperlien *m* graphique
r графическая гиперсвязь *f*

4337 graphic image
d grafisches Bild *n*
f image *f* graphique
r графический образ *m*; графическое
    изображение *n*

4338 graphic information system
d grafisches Informationsystem *n*
f système *m* informatique graphique
r графическая информационная система *f*

*   **graphic input** → **4317**

4339 graphic input/output error
d grafischer Eingabe/Ausgabe-Fehler *m*
f erreur *f* d'entrée/sortie graphique
r ошибка *f* графического ввода/вывода

4340 graphic interactive system
d grafisch-interaktives System *n*
f système *m* interactif graphique
r графическая диалоговая система *f*

4341 graphic interface
d Grafikinterface *n*; Grafikschnittstelle *f*
f interface *f* graphique
r графический интерфейс *m*

4342 graphic interpolation
d grafische Interpolation *f*
f interpolation *f* graphique
r графическая интерполяция *f*

4343 graphic iteration
d grafische Iteration *f*
f itération *f* graphique
r графическая итерация *f*

4344 graphic job processing
d grafische Jobverarbeitung *f*

f traitement *m* de travaux graphiques
r обработка *f* графических заданий

* **graphic language** → 4367

* **graphic library** → 4368

4345 graphic limits
d grafische Grenzen *fpl*
f limites *fpl* graphiques
r границы *fpl* графики

4346 graphic logo
d Grafiklogo *n*
f logo *m* graphique
r графический фирменный знак *m*

4347 graphic method
d grafische Methode *f*
f méthode *f* graphique
r графический метод *m*

4348 graphic mode
d grafischer Modus *m*
f mode *m* graphique
r графический режим *m*

4349 graphic noise
d grafisches Rauschen *n*
f bruit *m* graphique
r искажение *n* графики

4350 graphic object
d Grafikobjekt *n*
f objet *m* graphique
r графический объект *m*

4351 graphic objects embedding
d Grafikobjekte-Einbettung *f*
f emboîtage *m* d'objets graphiques;
encastrement *m* d'objets graphiques
r вложение *n* графических объектов

* **graphic output** → 4318

4352 graphic pipeline
d grafische Pipeline *f*
f pipeline *m* graphique
r графический конвейер *m*

* **graphic primitive** → 7419

* **graphic print** → 4353

4353 graphic print[ing]
d grafischer Druck *m*
f impression *f* graphique
r графическая печать *f*

* **graphic processor** → 4315

4354 graphic projection
d grafische Projektion *f*
f projection *f* graphique
r графическая проекция *f*

4355 graphic representation; diagrammatic representation
d grafische Darstellung *f*
f représentation *f* graphique
r графическое представление *n*

4356 graphics
d Grafik *f*; grafische Mittel *npl*
f graphique *m*
r графика *f*; графические средства *npl*

* **graphics capability** → 4372

* **graphics card** → 10208

4357 graphics coding
d grafische Codierung *f*
f codage *m* graphique
r графическое кодирование *n*

4358 graphics console
d Grafikkonsole *f*
f visu *m* graphique; console *m* graphique
r графическая консоль *f*

4359 graphics controller
d Grafikcontroller *m*
f contrôleur *m* graphique
r графический контроллер *m*

4360 graphics coordinator
d Grafikkoordinator *m*
f coordinateur *m* graphique
r графический координатор *m*

* **graphics coprocessor** → 4315

* **graphics designer** → 3162

* **graphics editor** → 4324

4361 graphic selection
d grafische Auswahl *f*
f sélection *f* graphique
r графический выбор *m*

4362 graphics environment manager; GEM
d Grafik-Umgebung-Manager *m*
f gestionnaire *m* de l'environnement graphique
r менажер *m* графического окружения

* **graphics film recorder** → 7027

4363 graphic sheet
d grafisches Blatt *n*

f feuille *f* graphique
r графический лист *m*

4364 graphics illustration
d grafische Illustration *f*
f illustration *f* graphique
r графическая иллюстрация *f*

4365 graphics interchange format; GIF
d grafisches Austauschformat *n*
f format *m* d'échange graphique
r формат *m* графического обмена

4366 graphics kernel system
d grafisches Kernsystem *n*
f système *m* graphique de noyau
r базовая графическая система *f*

4367 graphic[s] language
d Grafiksprache *f*
f langage *m* [de traitement] graphique
r язык *m* обработки графической
   информации; язык графических символов

4368 graphic[s] library; shape library
d grafische Bibliothek *f*; Bibliothek für
   grafische Grundelemente
f bibliothèque *f* graphique; bibliothèque de
   formes
r библиотека *f* графических фигур

4369 graphic software
d Grafik-Software *f*
f logiciel *m* graphique; grapheur *m*;
   graphiciel *m*
r графическое программное обеспечение *n*

4370 graphic solution
d grafische Lösung *f*
f solution *f* graphique
r графическое решение *n*

4371 graphics page
d grafische Seite *f*
f page *f* graphique
r графическая страница *f*

4372 graphics performance; graphics capability
d Grafikfähigkeit *f*
f productivité *f* graphique
r графическая производительность *f*

* graphics processor → 4315

* graphics primitive → 7419

4373 graphics primitives per second
d grafische Primitivelemente *npl* pro Sekunde
f primitives *fpl* graphiques par seconde
r графические примитивы *mpl* в секунду

4374 graphics printer
d grafischer Drucker *m*
f imprimante *f* graphique
r графический принтер *m*

4375 graphics standards
d grafische Standards *mpl*
f standards *mpl* graphiques
r графические стандарты *mpl*

4376 graphics subsystem
d grafische Untersystem *n*
f sous-système *m* graphique
r графическая подсистема *f*

4377 graphics tablet
d Grafiktablett *n*
f tablette *f* graphique
r графический планшет *m*

4378 graphics text background
d Grafiktext-Hintergrund *m*
f fond *m* de texte graphique
r фон *m* графического текста

4379 graphics text color
d Grafiktextfarbe *f*
f couleur *f* de texte graphique
r цвет *m* графического текста

4380 graphic style
d Grafikstil *m*
f style *m* graphique
r графический стиль *m*

* graphics window → 4304

4381 graphics window background
d Hintergrund *m* des grafischen Fensters
f fond *m* de fenêtre graphique
r фон *m* графического окна

* graphics workstation → 1983

4382 graphic system
d grafisches System *n*
f système *m* graphique
r графическая система *f*

4383 graphic toolbar
d grafischer Werkzeugstreifen *m*
f barre *f* d'outils graphiques
r графическая инструментальная лента *f*;
   панель *f* графических инструментов

4384 graphic toolbox
d grafischer Werkzeugkasten *m*
f boîte *f* à outils graphique
r графический инструментальный ящик *m*

* **graphic transmission** → 4319

4385 graphic units
d Grafikeinheiten *fpl*
f unités *fpl* graphiques
r графические единицы *fpl*

4386 graphic user interface; GUI
d grafische Benutzerschnittstelle *f*
f interface *f* graphique utilisateur
r графический пользовательский
   интерфейс *m*

4387 graphitize *v*
d grafitisieren
f mettre sous forme graphique
r представлять в графическом виде

4388 graph loop
d Graphschleife *f*
f boucle *f* de graphe
r петля *f* графа

4389 graph of a correspondence
d Graph *m* einer Korrespondenz; Graph einer
   Zuordnung
f graphe *m* d'une correspondance
r график *m* соответствия

4390 graph of a function
d Graph *m* einer Funktion; Funktionsgraph *m*
f graphe *m* d'une fonction; courbe *f*
   représentative d'une fonction
r график *m* функции

* **graph of a map** → 4391

4391 graph of a map[ping]
d Graph *m* einer Abbildung;
   Abbildungsgraph *m*
f graphe *m* d'une application
r график *m* отображения

4392 graph of motions
d Bewegungsgraph *m*
f graphe *m* de mouvements
r граф *m* движений

* **graph paper** → 7196

4393 graph parsing
d syntaktische Analyse *f* des Graphs
f analyse *f* syntaxique de graphe
r синтаксический анализ *m* графа

* **graph path** → 6894

4394 graphtals
d Graftale *npl*
f graphtales *fpl*

r графталы *mpl*

4395 graph theory
d Graphentheorie *f*; Theorie *f* der Graphen
f théorie *f* des graphes
r теория *f* графов

4396 graph transformation
d Graph-Transformation *f*
f transformation *f* de graphe
r трансформация *f* графа

4397 graph with loops
d Graph *m* mit Schleifen
f graphe *m* avec boucles
r граф *m* с петлями

* **graph without loops** → 139

* **graticule** → 5789

* **grating** → 5433

4398 grating constant
d Gitterkonstante *f*
f constante *f* de réseau; distance *f* entre lignes
r константа *f* решетки

* **grating generator** → 8107

4399 gravity modeling
d Modellierung *f* der Anziehung
f modelage *m* de gravité
r моделирование *n* притяжения;
   моделирование тяготения

4400 gray; grey
d Grau-; grau
f gris
r серый; теневой

4401 gray balance
d Grauausgleich *m*
f équilibre *m* pour les gris
r баланс *m* по серому

4402 Gray code; reflected binary code
d Gray-Code *m*
f code *m* de Gray; code binaire réfléchi
r код *m* Грея

4403 gray component
d Graukomponente *f*
f composant *m* de gris
r компонента *f* серого

4404 gray component replacement; GCR
d Wechsel *m* der Grauskomponente
f remplacement *m* de composant de gris
r замещение *n* компоненты серого

4405 **grayed icon**
 d abgeblendetes Symbol *n*
 f icône *f* grisée
 r икона *f* в сером

4406 **grayed object**
 d abgeblendetes Objekt *n*
 f objet *m* grisé
 r объект *m* в сером

4407 **gray filter**
 d Graufilter *m*
 f filtre *m* gris
 r серый фильтр *m*; теневой фильтр

 * **gray image** → 4414

4408 **gray image mode**
 d Graubildmodus
 f mode *m* d'image grise
 r режим *m* серого изображения

4409 **gray image morphology**
 d Graubildmorphologie *f*
 f morphologie *f* d'image grise
 r морфология *f* полутонового изображения

4410 **gray level; grey level; shade of gray; gray shade**
 d Graustufe *f*
 f niveau *m* de gris
 r уровень *m* серого; уровень яркости

4411 **gray-level array; gray-level matrix**
 d Graustufenmatrix *f*
 f matrice *f* de niveau de gris
 r матрица *f* [уровней] яркости

 * **gray-level matrix** → 4411

 * **gray picture** → 4414

4412 **gray scale; shading scale**
 d Grau[stufen]skala *f*; Graustufung *f*
 f escalier *m* de demi-teintes gris; échelle *f* des gris
 r шкала *f* яркостей; шкала полутонов; полутоновая шкала; шкала оттенков серого цвета

4413 **gray-scale fitting**
 d Anpassung *f* der Graustufenskala
 f ajustement *m* d'échelle de gris
 r налаживание *n* шкалы полутонов

4414 **gray[-scale] image; gray[-scale] picture; halftone image**
 d Graubild *n*; Halbtonbild *n*
 f image *f* de demi-teinte; image grise; image de niveau gris

 r полутоновое изображение *n*

 * **gray-scale picture** → 4414

4415 **gray-scale shift**
 d Verschiebung *f* der Graustufenskala
 f décalage *m* d'échelle de gris
 r смещение *n* шкалы полутонов

4416 **gray scaling**
 d Grauskalierung *f*
 f mise *f* en échelle grise
 r преобразование *n* цветного изображения в полутоновое; формирование *n* полутонового изображения

 * **gray shade** → 4410

4417 **gray tone**
 d Grauton *m*
 f ton *m* gris
 r серый тон *m*

4418 **gray value**
 d Grauwert *m*
 f valeur *f* de gris
 r код *m* серого; оттенок *m* серого

4419 **gray wedge**
 d Graukeil *m*
 f biseau *m* gris; coin *m* gris
 r серый клин *m* тональности; сенсиметрический клин

4420 **grazing angle**
 d streifender Winkel *m*
 f angle *m* rasant
 r касательный угол *m*

4421 **grazing incidence**
 d streifender Einfall *m*
 f incidence *f* rasante
 r касательное падение *n*

4422 **great circle**
 d Großkreis *m*
 f grand cercle *m*
 r окружность *f* большого круга; большой круг *m*

 * **great circle of the sphere** → 4423

4423 **great circle on a sphere; great circle of the sphere**
 d Großkreis *m* auf der Kugel; Hauptkreis *m* der Kugel
 f grand cercle *m* d'une sphère
 r большой круг *m* сферы

4424 **great display**
 d Großformat-Display *n*

f écran m gros
r широкоформатный дисплей m

* **greek → 4425**

4425 greek[ing]
d Greeking n
f symbolisation f; gris m typographique; faux
texte m
r формирование n строкозаменителей;
имитирование n текста; процесс m
представления текста в виде серых полос
при верстке; грикинг m

4426 green-phosphor display
d grünes Display n; grüner Bildschirm m
f écran m à phosphore; écran à luminophore
vert
r дисплей m зеленого свечения

* **grey → 4400**

* **grey level → 4410**

4427 grid
(of paper)
d Gitter n
f quadrillage m; grille f
r сетка f

* **grid → 7747**

4428 grid bias
d Gitterverschiebung f
f polarisation f de grille
r смещение n сетки; сеточное смещение

* **grid board → 7749**

4429 grid button
d Gitterschaltfläche f
f bouton m de grille
r бутон m растра

* **grid cell → 8106**

4430 grid color
d Gitterfarbe f; Rasterfarbe f
f couleur f de grille
r цвет m сетки; цвет растра

4431 grid coordinates
d Gitterkoordinaten fpl;
Rechtwinkelkoordinaten fpl
f coordonnées fpl rectangulaires
r плоские прямоугольные координаты fpl

4432 grid [element] spacing; grid size
d Raster[element]abstand m
f espacement m de grille

r расстояние n между элементами растра;
шаг m растра

4433 grid field
d Gitterfeld n
f champ m de grille
r растровое поле n

4434 grid-fitting; hinting
d Gitteranpassung f
f ajustage m de précision de grille
r хинтование n

4435 grid graph
d Gittergraph m; Rastergraph m
f graphe m de grille
r граф m сетки; граф решетки

* **gridline → 7768**

4436 grid mask
d Gittermaske f
f masque f de grille
r маска f сетки

4437 grid mode
d Gittermodus m
f mode m de grille
r режим m изображения сетки

4438 grid model
d Gittermodell n
f modèle m de quadrillage; modèle de grille
r модель f решетки; модель сетки

4439 grid origin point
d Gitternullpunkt m; Raster-Ausgangspunkt m
f point m d'origine de grille
r исходная точка f сетки; начальная точка
сетки

4440 grid panel
d Gittertafel f
f panneau m de grille
r панель f сетки

* **grid point → 8366**

4441 grid reference
d Gitterreferenz f
f référence f de grille
r эталон m сетки

4442 grid shape
d Gitterform f
f forme f de grille
r форма f сетки

* **grid size → 4432**

4443 grid snap
 d Gitterfang *m*
 f accrochage *m* à la grille
 r привязка *f* к [координатной] сетке

 * **grid spacing** → **4432**

4444 grid square
 d Gitterquadrat *n*; Netzquadrat *n*
 f carroyage *m*
 r квадрат *m* сетки

4445 grid underlay
 d Gitterunterlage *f*
 f canevas *m* de quadrillage
 r сетевая подкладка *f*; сетевая подстилка *f*

 * **GRIN** → **4269**

 * **grip** *v* → **1280**

4446 grip; handle
 d Griff *m*; Handgriff *m*
 f poignée *f*
 r захват *m*

4447 grip mode
 d Griffmodus *m*; Erfassungsmodus *m*
 f mode *m* de poignée
 r режим *m* захвата

4448 grip size
 d Griffgröße *f*
 f taille *f* de poignée
 r размер *m* захвата

 * **ground line** → **767**

4449 ground-tint
 d Grundton *m*
 f ton *m* de base
 r основной тон *m*

4450 group
 d Gruppe *f*
 f groupe *m*
 r группа *f*

4451 group *v*
 d gruppieren
 f grouper
 r группировать

4452 group box
 d Gruppenkasten *m*; Gruppenfeld *n*
 f zone *f* de groupe; boîte *f* à zone
 r поле *n* группы

4453 group centroid
 d Gruppenzentroid *n*

 f centroïde *m* de groupe
 r центроид *m* группы

4454 group code
 d Gruppencode *m*
 f code *m* de groupe
 r код *m* группы

4455 group collection; collection of groups
 d Gruppensammlung *f*
 f collection *f* de groupes
 r коллекция *f* групп

 * **grouped objects** → **1874**

 * **grouped path** → **1875**

4456 group graph
 d Gruppengraph *m*
 f graphe *m* de groupe
 r граф *m* группы

4457 group heading
 d Gruppenüberschrift *f*
 f en-tête *f* de zone
 r заголовок *m* зоны

4458 group icon
 d Gruppensymbol *n*
 f icône *f* de groupe
 r значок *m* группы

4459 grouping
 d Gruppieren *n*; Gruppierung *f*
 f groupement *m*; groupage *m*
 r группирование *n*; группировка *f*

4460 grouping operator
 d Gruppierungsoperator *m*
 f opérateur *m* de groupement
 r оператор *m* группирования

4461 group object
 d Gruppenobjekt *n*
 f objet *m* groupe
 r объект *m* типа группы

 * **group of curves** → **3701**

4462 group of motions; group of movements
 d Bewegungsgruppe *f*
 f groupe *m* de mouvements
 r группа *f* движений

 * **group of movements** → **4462**

4463 group of paths
 d Weggruppe *f*
 f groupe *m* de chemins
 r группа *f* путей

4464 group of symmetries; symmetry group
  d Symmetriegruppe *f*
  f groupe *m* de symétries
  r группа *f* симметрий

4465 groupoid
  d Gruppoid *n*
  f groupoïde *m*
  r группоид *m*

4466 group selection
  d Auswahl *f* der Gruppe
  f sélection *f* de groupe
  r групповый выбор *m*; выбор группы

4467 group window
  d Gruppenfenster *n*
  f fenêtre *f* de groupe
  r окно *n* группы

  * **guard** → 7604

  * **GUI** → 4386

  * **guide** → 8788

  * **guide bar** → 8788

4468 guideline
  d Leitlinie *f*; Leitgerade *f*; Richtlinie *f*;
    Führungsbahn *f*
  f directive *f*; ligne *f* de conduite; chemin *m* de
    guidage
  r направляющая [линия] *f*

**4469 guide mark; guide score; printed register
mark**
  d Richtpunkt *m*; Führungsstreifen *m*
  f marque *f* de guide
  r приводочная метка *f*

  * **guide score** → 4469

  * **gutter** → 4470

4470 gutter [margin]
  d Bundsteg *m*; Gasse *f* im Satz
  f marge *f* de reliure; gouttière *f*
  r внутреннее корешковое поле *n*; поле
    переплета

4471 gyration
  d Gyration *f*
  f giration *f*; gyration *f*
  r вращение *n*

  * **gyratory motion** → 8193

H

4472 hairline
(thinnest visible space or rule)
d Haarstrich *m*
f trait *m* très fin
r линия *f* толщиной в волос; волосная линия; линия наименьшей толщины

* **half-adjust** *v* → **501**

4473 half-angle
d halber Winkel *m*; Halbwinkel *m*
f demi-angle *m*
r половина *f* угла; полуугол *m*

4474 half-line; ray
d Halbgerade *f*; Strahl *m*
f demi-droite *f*; ligne *f* semi-infinie; rayon *m*
r полупрямая *f*; луч *m*

4475 half-mask
d Halbmaske *f*
f demi-masque *f*
r полумаска *f*

4476 half-plane
d Halbebene *f*
f demi-plan *m*
r полуплоскость *f*

4477 half-section
d Halbsektion *f*
f demi-section *f*
r полусечение *n*

4478 half-section view
d Halbsektionsansicht *f*
f vue *f* de demi-section
r вид *m* полусечения

* **half the perimeter** → **8515**

4479 half-tint; halftone
d Halbton *m*
f demi-teinte *f*; demi-ton *m*
r полутон *m*; полукраска *f*

* **halftone** → **4479**

* **halftone block** → **720**

4480 halftone builder
d Halbtonbilder *m*
f bâtisseur *m* de demi-tons

r программа *f* построения полутонов

4481 halftone cell
d Halbtonzelle *f*
f cellule *f* de demi-teinte
r полутоновая клетка *f*

* **halftone dot** → **8366**

4482 halftone filter
d Halbtonfilter *m*
f filtre *m* de demi-teinte
r фильтр *m* полутонов

* **halftone image** → **4414**

4483 halftone negative
d Halbtonnegativ *n*
f négatif *m* de trame
r растровый негатив *m*

4484 halftone raster; halftone screen
d Halbtonraster *m*
f rastre *m* de demi-teinte; trame *f* simili; trame quartilée
r полутоновый растр *m*

* **halftone screen** → **4484**

4485 halftone screen frequency
d Halbtonrasterfrequenz *f*
f fréquence *f* de trame quartilée
r линиатура *f* растра

4486 halftone screen spot type
d Halbtonrasterpunkttyp *m*
f type *m* de point rastre
r тип *m* растровой точки

4487 halftoning
d Halbtönung *f*; Halftoning *n*
f création *f* de demi-teintes
r образование *n* полутонов

4488 halfwidth
d Halbbreite *f*
f épaisseur *f* à la moitié
r половинная ширина *f*

4489 halo
d Halo *m*; Lichthof *m*
f halo *m*
r гало *n*; ореол *m*; сияние *n*; венчик *m*

4490 halo effect
d Haloeffekt *m*
f effet *m* de halo
r эффект *m* гало

4491 halt; hold; stop
d Halt *m*; Stopp *m*

f arrêt m; halte f; stop m
r останов m

* **hand** adj → 5776

4492 hand
d Hand f
f main f; bras m
r рука f

* **handheld scanner** → 4497

* **handle** → 4446

4493 handle; arm
d Henkel m; Kurbel f; Zeiger m
f anse f; aiguille f
r ручка f; стрелка f [прибора]

4494 handle v; **manipulate** v
d behandeln; handhaben; manipulieren
f traiter; manipuler
r обрабатывать; манипулировать

* **handle of the second kind** → 2300

* **handler** → 4496

4495 handling; manipulation
d Behandlung f; Handhabung f; Manipulieren n
f maniement m; traitement m; manipulation f
r обработка f; манипуляция f

4496 handling program; handler
d Handhabungsprogramm n
f programme m de traitement
r программа f обработки

* **hand-operated** adj → 5776

* **hand-operated scanner** → 4497

* **hand-printed character** → 4502

4497 hand scanner; portable scanner; handheld scanner; hand-operated scanner
d Handabtaster m; Handscanner m
f scanner m à main; scanner manuel
r ручной сканер m

4498 handshake
d Handshake n; Quittierung f
f quittance f
r подтверждение n; квитирование n

4499 hand sketch information
d Handskizzeninformation f
f information f de l'ébauche manuelle
r информация f в виде рисунков; информация в виде эскизов

4500 hand tracking
d Handverfolgung f
f poursuite f à main
r ручное прослеживание n

4501 handwriting recognition
d Handschrifterkennung f
f reconnaissance f d'écriture
r распознавание n рукописного текста

4502 handwritten character; hand-printed character
d handgeschriebenes Zeichen n
f caractère m manuscrit; caractère d'écriture
r рукописный знак m

4503 handwritten digits
d handgeschriebene Ziffern fpl
f chiffres mpl manuscrits
r рукописные цифры fpl

4504 hanging
d hängend; überhängend
f suspendu
r висячий

* **hard** adj → 4509

4505 hard
d hart
f rigide; dur
r жесткий; твердый

4506 hard copy
d Hartkopie f; Druckkopie f
f copie f dure; copie imprimée; copie sur papier; tirage m
r твердая копия f; бумажная копия; печатная копия

* **hard image** → 2155

4507 hard pointer
d Hardwarezeiger m
f pointeur m matériel
r аппаратный указатель m

* **hard space** → 6248

4508 hardware
d Hardware f; Gerätetechnik f
f matériel m; hardware m
r аппаратные средства npl; техническое обеспечение n

4509 hardware; hard adj
d Hardware-; gerätetechnisch
f matériel
r аппаратный

4510 hardware cursor
 d Hardwarecursor *m*
 f curseur *m* matériel
 r аппаратный курсор *m*

4511 hardware geometry processing
 d Hardwareverarbeitung *f* der Geometrie
 f traitement *m* matériel de géométrie
 r аппаратная обработка *f* геометрии

4512 hardware-implemented
 d gerätetechnisch realisiert; Hardware-realisiert
 f réalisé [en] matériel
 r аппаратно-реализованный

4513 hardware lighting
 d Hardwarebeleuchtung *f*
 f éclairage *m* matériel
 r аппаратное освещение *n*

4514 hardware linetype
 d Hardware-Linientyp *m*
 f type *m* de ligne matériel
 r аппаратный тип *m* линии

4515 hardware-supported raytracing
 d Hardware-gestütztes Ray-Tracing *n*
 f raytracing *m* matériel
 r аппаратно-реализованная трассировка *f* лучей

 * **harmonic** → 4517

4516 harmonic *adj*
 d harmonisch
 f harmonique
 r гармонический

4517 harmonic [curve]
 d harmonische Kurve *f*; Harmonische *f*
 f courbe *f* harmonique; harmonique *m*
 r гармоника *f*

4518 harmonicity
 d Harmonizität *f*
 f harmonicité *f*
 r гармоничность *f*

4519 harmonic linearization
 d harmonische Linearisierung *f*
 f linéarisation *f* harmonique
 r гармоническая линеаризация *f*

4520 harmonic oscillation; harmonic vibration
 d harmonische Schwingung *f*
 f oscillation *f* harmonique
 r гармоническое колебание *n*

4521 harmonic proportion
 d harmonische Proportion *f*
 f proportion *f* harmonique
 r гармоническая пропорция *f*

4522 harmonic series
 d harmonische Reihe *f*
 f série *f* harmonique
 r гармонический ряд *m*

 * **harmonic vibration** → 4520

4523 Harvard graphics
 d Harward-Grafik *f*
 f graphique *m* Harvard
 r гарвардская графика *f*

 * **hash** → 4106

 * **hashing** → 7732

 * **hat** → 1289

4524 hatch *v*; **shade** *v*
 d schraffieren
 f hachurer
 r штриховать

4525 hatch; shade
 d Schraffur *f*
 f hachure *f*
 r штриховка *f*

4526 hatch boundary
 d Schraffurgrenze *f*
 f limite *f* de hachure
 r граница *f* штриховки

4527 hatch command
 d Schraffurbefehl *m*
 f commande *f* de hachure
 r команда *f* штриховки

4528 hatch copying
 d Schraffurkopieren *n*
 f copiage *m* de hachure
 r копирование *n* штриховки

4529 hatched; shaded
 d schraffiert
 f hachuré
 r заштрихованный

4530 hatch edit
 d Schraffurbearbeitung *f*
 f édition *f* de hachure
 r редактирование *n* штриховки

4531 hatched rectangle
 d schraffiertes Rechteck *n*

f rectangle *m* hachuré
r заштрихованный прямоугольник *m*

* **hatched rule** → 8571

4532 hatch filling
d Schraffurfüllung *f*
f remplissage *m* par hachure
r заполнение *n* штриховкой

4533 hatch frequency
d Schraffurfrequenz *f*
f fréquence *f* de hachure
r частота *f* штриховки

4534 hatching
d Schraffieren *n*; Schraffen *n*
f hachure *f*
r штриховка *f*; штрихование *n*

4535 hatching method
d Schraffenmethode *f*
f méthode *f* de hachure
r метод *m* штриховки

4536 hatch lines
d Schraffurlinien *fpl*
f lignes *fpl* de hachure
r линии *fpl* штриховки

4537 hatch loop
d Schraffurschleife *f*
f boucle *m* de hachure
r петля *f* штриховки

4538 hatch mode
d Schraffenmodus *m*
f mode *m* de hachure
r режим *m* штриховки

4539 hatch modifying; hatch updating
d Schraffuraktualisierung *f*
f actualisation *f* de hachure
r модифицирование *n* штриховки;
обновление *n* штриховки

4540 hatch object
d Schraffurobjekt *n*
f objet *m* hachure
r объект *m* типа штриховки

4541 hatch option
d Schraffur-Option *f*
f option *f* de la hachure
r опция *f* штриховки

4542 hatch pattern
d Schraffurmuster *n*
f motif *m* de hachure
r модель *f* штриховки; шаблон *m* штриховки

4543 hatch pattern name
d Schraffurmustername *m*
f nom *m* de motif de la hachure
r имя *n* модели штриховки

4544 hatch pattern scale; hatch pattern spacing
d Schraffurmuster-Skala *f*
f échelle *f* de motif de la hachure
r масштаб *m* модели штриховки

* **hatch pattern spacing** → 4544

4545 hatch property
d Schraffureigenschaft *f*
f propriété *f* de hachure
r свойство *n* штриховки; характеристика *f*
штриховки

4546 hatch selecting
d Schraffurauswahl *f*
f sélection *f* de hachure
r выбор *m* штриховки

4547 hatch style
d Schraffurstil *m*
f style *m* de hachure
r стиль *m* штриховки

4548 hatch style code
d Schraffurstil-Code *m*
f code *m* de style de hachure
r код *m* стиля штриховки

* **hatch updating** → 4539

* **hazy** → 4088

4549 head
d Kopf *m*
f tête *f*
r головка *f*; голова *f*

4550 header; heading; title
d Titel *m*; Header *m*; Kopfteil *m*; Überschrift *f*
f header *m*; titre *m*; en-tête *m*
r заголовок *m*; титул *m*

4551 header line; headline; heading line
d Kopfzeile *f*; Anschriftzeile *f*; Titelzeile *f*;
Überschriftzeile *f*
f ligne *f* d'en-tête
r заголовный ряд *m*; строка *f* заголовка

* **heading** → 4550

* **heading line** → 4551

* **headline** → 4551

4552 head-mounted display; HMD; head-up display; HUD; head-mounted screen; videocasque
  d Kopfbildschirm *m*; Videohelm *m*
  f écran *m* monté sur la tête; visiocasque *f*; casque *f* de visualisation; viseur *m* tête-haute; visière *f* stéréoscopique; casque de vision 3D
  r головной экран *m*; видеокаска *f*

  * **head-mounted screen** → 4552

4553 head tracking
  d Kopfverfolgung *f*
  f poursuite *f* de tête
  r прослеживание *n* головой

  * **head-up display** → 4552

4554 heap
  d ungeordnete Datei *f*; Häufung *f*
  f tableau *m* non ordonné
  r неупорядоченный массив *m*

  * **heavy line** → 10420

4555 heavy shadow
  d schwerer Schatten *m*
  f ombre *f* lourde
  r глубокая тень *f*

  * **height** → 303

  * **height line** → 5517

  * **height plane** → 5520

  * **helical** → 4556

  * **helical curve** → 4560

  * **helical displacement** → 4557

  * **helical motion** → 4557

  * **helical surface** → 4558

  * **helical trajectory** → 4559

  * **helicoid** → 4558

4556 helic[oid]al; winding
  d helikoidal; Schrauben-; Wendel-; schraubenförmig
  f hélicoïdal
  r спиральный; винтовой; геликоидальный

  * **helicoidal curve** → 4560

  * **helicoidal displacement** → 4557

4557 helic[oid]al motion; helic[oid]al displacement; screw motion; spiral[l]ing; screwing
  d Schraubenbewegung *f*; Schraubung *f*; spirale Drehung *f*
  f mouvement *m* hélicoïdal; déplacement *m* hélicoïdal; vissage *m*; rotation *f* en spirale
  r винтовое движение *n*; спиральное движение

4558 helic[oid]al surface; helicoid
  d Schraubenfläche *f*; Wendelfläche *f*; Helikoid *n*
  f surface *f* hélicoïdale; hélicoïde *m*
  r винтовая поверхность *f*; геликоид *m*

4559 helic[oid]al trajectory
  d schraubenförmige Bahn *f*; Schraubenbahn *f*
  f trajectoire *f* hélicoïdale
  r винтообразная траектория *f*

4560 helix; cylindrical helix; circular helix; helic[oid]al curve; ordinary helix; screw-line; 3D spiral
  d Schraubenlinie *f*; Schneckenlinie *f*; Böschungslinie *f*; Kurve *f* konstanter Neigung; Loxodrome *f* des Zylinders; Schraub[en]spirale *f*
  f hélice *f* [cylindrique]; hélice circulaire; courbe *f* hélicoïde; spirale *f* cylindrique; ligne *f* de pente constante
  r [цилиндрическая] винтовая линия *f*; винтовая линия на круговом цилиндре; кривая *f* постоянного склона; пространственная спираль *f*; линия ската

  * **helix angle** → 388

  * **help** → 7593

4561 help
  d Hilfe *f*
  f aide *f*
  r помощь *f*; подкрепление *n*; консультация *f*

4562 help file
  d Hilfsdatei *f*
  f fichier *m* d'aide
  r справочный файл *m*

  * **help information** → 7593

4563 help menu
  d Hilfemenü *n*; Bedienungshilfsmenü *n*
  f menu *m* d'aide; menu d'assistance
  r меню *n* подсказки; консультативное меню; справочное меню

4564 help screen
  d Hilfsbildschirm *m*

f écran *m* d'aide
r справочный экран *m*

4565 help text
d Hilfstext *m*
f texte *m* d'aide
r справочный текст *m*

4566 help window
d Hilfefenster *n*
f fenêtre *f* d'aide
r окно *n* подсказки; окно справки

4567 hemisphere
d Halbkugel *f*
f hémisphère *f*
r полусфера *f*; полушар *m*

4568 hemispherical lens
d halbkugelige Linse *f*
f lentille *f* hémisphérique
r полусферическая линза *f*

4569 hendecagon; endecagon
d Elfeck *n*
f hendécagone *m*; endécagone *m*
r одиннадцатиугольник *m*

4570 hendecagonal
d elfeckig; Elfecks-
f hendécagone; endécagonal
r одиннадцатиугольный

4571 hendecahedron; endecahedron
d Elffach *n*
f endécaèdre *m*
r одиннадцатигранник *m*

4572 heptagon
d Heptagon *n*; Siebeneck *n*
f heptagone *m*
r семиугольник *m*

4573 heptagonal
d Heptagonal-; heptagonal
f heptagonal
r семиугольный

4574 heptahedral
d siebenflächig; Siebenflach-
f heptaédrique
r семигранный

4575 heptahedron
d Heptaeder *n*
f heptaèdre *m*
r семигранник *m*; гептаэдр *m*

4576 Hermite form
d Hermite-Form *f*

f forme *f* d'Hermite
r эрмитова форма *f*

4577 Hermite polynomial
d Hermite-Polynom *n*
f polynôme *m* d'Hermite
r эрмитов полином *m*

4578 Hermite spline
d Hermite-Spline *m*
f spline *m* d'Hermite
r эрмитов сплайн *m*

4579 Hermite surface
d Hermite-Fläche *f*
f surface *f* d'Hermite
r эрмитова поверхность *f*

4580 heterogeneous; nonhomogeneous; inhomogeneous
d heterogen; inhomogen; nichthomogen; unhomogen
f hétérogène; non homogène; inhomogène
r гетерогенный; разнородный

4581 heterogeneous simulation
d heterogene Simulation *f*
f simulation *f* hétérogène
r гетерогенная симуляция *f*

4582 heterostructure
d Heterostruktur *f*
f hétérostructure *f*
r гетероструктура *f*

4583 heuristic
d heuristisch
f [h]euristique
r эвристический

4584 heuristic data
d heuristische Daten *npl*
f données *fpl* heuristiques
r эвристические данные *npl*

4585 heuristic routing
d heuristische Routenwahl *f*
f acheminement *m* heuristique
r эвристический выбор *m* маршрута; эвристическая маршрутизация *f*

4586 heuristics
d Heuristik *f*
f heuristique *f*
r эвристика *f*

4587 hexachrome
d Hexachrome-
f hexachrome
r шестицветный

4588 hexachrome color process
(a method of producing virtually any color
using six ink colors: cyan, magenta, yellow,
black, orange and green)
d Hexachrome-Farbprozess *m*
f traitement *m* hexachrome
r шестицветная обработка *f*

4589 hexachrome plate
d Hexachrome-Platte *f*
f plaque *f* hexachrome
r шестицветная плата *f*

4590 hexagon
d Hexagon *n*; Sechseck *n*
f hexagone *m*
r шестиугольник *m*

4591 hexagonal network
d hexagonales Netz *n*
f réseau *m* hexagonal
r шестиугольная сеть *f*

4592 hexagonal prism
d Sechskantprisma *n*
f prisme *m* hexagonal
r шестиугольная призма *f*

4593 hexagram
d Hexagramm *n*
f hexagramme *m*
r гексаграмма *f*

4594 hexahedron
d Hexaeder *n*
f hexaèdre *m*
r гексаэдр *m*; шестигранник *m*

4595 hickey
d Knutschfleck *m*
f plouc *m*; pécquenaud *m*
r марашка *f*; пятнышко *n* краски на оттиске

4596 hidden; covert
d versteckt; verdeckt
f caché; masqué
r скрытый

4597 hidden color
d verdeckte Farbe *f*
f couleur *f* cachée
r скрытый цвет *m*; невидимый цвет

4598 hidden edge
d verdeckte Kante *f*
f arête *f* cachée
r невидимый край *m*; невидимое ребро *n*

4599 hidden image points
d verdeckte Bildpunkte *mpl*

f points *mpl* d'image cachés
r невидимые точки *fpl* изображения

4600 hidden line; invisible line
(of image)
d verdeckte Linie *f*; verdeckte Bildkante *f*
f ligne *f* cachée
r невидимая линия *f*; скрытая линия

* **hidden-line algorithm** → 4604

* **hidden-line elimination** → 4603

4601 hidden-line image
d Bild *n* mit verdeckten Linien
f image *f* à lignes cachées
r изображение *n* скрытыми линиями;
изображение невидимыми линиями

4602 hidden-line playback
d Wiedergabe *f* verdeckter Linien
f reproduction *f* de lignes cachées
r воспроизведение *n* невидимых линий

**4603 hidden-line removal; hidden-line
elimination**
d Entfernung *f* der verdeckten Linien
f élimination *f* de lignes cachées
r устранение *n* скрытых линий; удаление *n*
невидимых линий

4604 hidden-line [removal] algorithm
d Algorithmus *m* zur Entfernung der
verdeckten Linien
f algorithme *m* d'élimination de lignes cachées
r алгоритм *m* удаления невидимых линий

4605 hidden-line wireframe
d Drahtrahmen *m* mit verdeckten Linien
f fil *m* de fer à lignes cachées
r каркас *m* со скрытыми ребрами

4606 hidden surface; invisible surface
d verdeckte Fläche *f*; unsichtbare Fläche
f surface *f* cachée; surface non visible
r скрытая поверхность *f*; невидимая
поверхность

* **hidden-surface algorithm** → 4608

* **hidden-surface elimination** → 4607

**4607 hidden-surface removal; hidden-surface
elimination**
d Entfernung *f* der verdeckten Flächen
f élimination *f* de surfaces cachées
r удаление *n* невидимых поверхностей

4608 hidden-surface [removal] algorithm
d Algorithmus *m* zur Entfernung der
verdeckten Flächen

  f algorithme *m* d'élimination de surfaces
    cachées
  r алгоритм *m* удаления невидимых
    поверхностей

4609 hidden-surface removal processor
  d Prozessor *m* zur Entfernung der verdeckten
    Flächen
  f processeur *m* d'élimination de surfaces
    cachées
  r процессор *m* удаления невидимых
    поверхностей

4610 hide *v*
  d verstecken; verdecken; ausblenden
  f masquer; cacher
  r скрыть

4611 hide button
  d Versteckungsschaltfläche *f*
  f bouton *m* de masquage
  r бутон *m* укрывания

4612 hide command
  d Versteckungsbefehl *m*
  f commande *f* de masquage
  r команда *f* скрытия; команда маскирования

4613 hide *v* **layer**
  d Schicht ausblenden
  f cacher une couche
  r скрыть слой

4614 hiding
  d Versteckung *f*
  f masquage *m*
  r скрытие *n*

4615 hierarchical
  d hierarchisch
  f hiérarchique
  r иерархический

4616 hierarchical classification
  d hierarchische Klassifikation *f*
  f classification *f* hiérarchique
  r иерархическая классификация *f*

4617 hierarchical database
  d hierarchische Datenbasis *f*
  f base *f* de données hiérarchique
  r иерархическая база *f* данных

4618 hierarchical menu
  d hierarchisches Menü *n*
  f menu *m* hiérarchique
  r иерархическое меню *n*

4619 hierarchical objects
  d hierarchische Objekte *npl*

  f objets *mpl* hiérarchiques
  r иерархические объекты *mpl*

4620 hierarchy
  d Hierarchie *f*; Rangordnung *f*; Rangfolge *f*
  f hiérarchie *f*
  r иерархия *f*

4621 high coherence
  d hohe Kohärenz *f*
  f cohérence *f* haute
  r высокая когерентность *f*

4622 high color density
  d hohe Farbdichte *f*
  f densité *f* haute de couleur
  r высокая плотность *f* цвета

4623 high contrast
  d scharfer Kontrast *m*
  f contraste *m* haut
  r высокий контраст *m*

4624 high-contrast bitmap
  d Bitmap *n* mit scharfem Kontrast
  f bitmap *m* à contraste haut
  r высококонтрастное растровое
    изображение *n*

4625 high-contrast image
  d Bild *n* mit scharfem Kontrast
  f image *f* de contraste haut
  r высококонтрастное изображение *n*

4626 high definition
  d hohe Schärfe *f*
  f définition *f* haute
  r высокая четкость *f*

  * **high-definition** *adj* → **4640**

4627 high-end effects; top-of-the-range effects;
    top-of-the-line effects
  d leistungsfähige Effekte *mpl*;
    Spitzeneffekte *mpl*
  f effets *mpl* hauts de gamme
  r эффекты *mpl* высшего класса

4628 high-end scanner
  d leistungsfähiger Scanner *m*
  f scanner *m* haut de gamme
  r сканер *m* высшего класса

4629 high-fidelity geometric models
  d geometrische Modelle *npl* mit hocher
    Genauigkeit
  f modèles *mpl* géométriques de haute précision
  r геометрические модели *fpl* высокой
    точности

4630 highlight *v*; **emphasize** *v*
 d hervorheben
 f mettre en évidence
 r маркировать освещением; подсвечивать; высвечивать

4631 highlighted
 d hervorgehoben
 f en surbrillance; contrasté
 r высвеченный

4632 highlighted area
 d hervorgehobener Bereich *m*; Glanzlichtbereich *m*
 f plage *f* lumineuse
 r подсвеченная область *f*

4633 highlighted background
 d hervorgehobener Hintergrund *m*
 f fond *m* surintensifié; fond contrasté
 r подсвеченный фон *m*

4634 highlighted row
 d hervorgehobene Zeile *f*; Hochlichtzeile *f*; Glanzlichtzeile *f*
 f ligne *f* surintensifiée
 r подсвеченная строка *f*; высвеченная строка

4635 highlighting; emphasis
 d Hervorhebung *f*; Hervorheben *n*; Highlighting *n*
 f mise *f* en évidence; marquage *m* par éclairage
 r маркирование *n* освещением; выделение *n* освещением; подсвечивание *n*; подсветка *f*

4636 highlight *v* **menu**
 d Menü hervorheben
 f mettre en évidence de menu
 r подсвечивать меню; высвечивать меню

4637 high-low graph
 d Hoch-Tief-Graph *m*
 f graphe *m* limité
 r граничный граф *m*; граф в интервале значений

4638 highly transparent
 d hochtransparent
 f de haute transparence; à transparence élevée
 r высокопрозрачный

4639 high-pass filter
 d Hochpassfilter *m*
 f filtre *m* passe-haut
 r фильтр *m* верхних частот

4640 high-resolution; hi-res; high-definition *adj*
 d hochauflösend
 f à résolution élevée; à haute définition
 r с высокой разрешающей способностью; с

высокой резкостью

4641 high-resolution scene
 d hochauflösende Szene *f*
 f scène *f* à haute résolution
 r сцена *f* с высокой разрешающей способностью

4642 high-resolution screen
 d hochauflösender Bildschirm *m*
 f écran *m* à haute résolution
 r экран *m* с высокой разрешающей способностью

4643 highspeed *adj*
 d mit hocher Geschwindigkeit; Hochgeschwindigkeits-
 f à vitesse élevée; à grande vitesse
 r высокоскоростный; быстродействующий

4644 hinge
 d Scharnier *n*; Gelenk *n*
 f charnière *f*
 r шарнир *m*

 * **hinting** → 4434

 * **hi-res** → 4640

 * **histogram** → 827

4645 histogram spikes
 d Spitze *mpl* des Histogramms
 f crêtes *fpl* d'histogramme; sommets *mpl* d'histogramme
 r вершины *fpl* гистограммы

 * **history** → 530

4646 history means
 d Archivierungsmittel *npl*; Vorgeschichtsmittel *npl*
 f moyens *mpl* d'archivage
 r средства *npl* регистрации предыстории; средства архивирования

 * **hit** *v* → 7401

 * **hither plane** → 4029

 * **HLS color model** → 4726

4647 HLS image
 d HLS-Bild *n*
 f image *f* TSL
 r изображение *n* HLS

4648 HLS color wheel
 d HLS-Farb[en]kreis *m*

f roue *f* de couleurs TSL
r цветовое колесо *n* HLS

*HLS model → 4726

4649 HLS/RGB conversion
d HLS/RGB-Konvertierung *f*
f conversion *f* TSL/RGB
r преобразование *n* HLS/RGB

4650 HLS value
d HLS-Wert *m*
f valeur *f* TSL
r значение *n* HLS

* HMD → 4552

* hold → 4491

4651 hole
d Loch *n*; Lochstelle *f*; Stanzstelle *f*
f trou *m*; perforation *f*; bouche *f*
r отверстие *n*; пробивка *f*; дырка *f*

4652 hollow
d hohl
f creux
r полый; пустой; пустотелый; вогнутый

4653 hollow nodes
d hohle Knoten *mpl*
f nœuds *mpl* creux
r пустые узлы *mpl*

4654 hologram
d Hologramm *n*
f hologramme *m*
r голограмма *f*

4655 holographic
d holografisch
f holographique
r голографический

4656 holographic image
d holografisches Bild *n*
f image *f* holographique
r голографический образ *m*

4657 holographic imaging
d holografische Abbildung *f*
f présentation *f* holographique
r голографическое изображение *n*

4658 holographic scanner
d holografischer Scanner *m*
f scanner *m* holographique
r голографический сканер *m*

4659 holography

d Holografie *f*
f holographie *f*
r голография *f*

* holomorphic function → 342

4660 Home key
d Home-Taste *f*; Rückkehrtaste *f*
f touche *f* de renversement; touche de remise en position initiale
r клавиша *f* Home; клавиша возврата в исходное положение

* home location → 4662

4661 home option
d Ausgangsoption *f*
f option *f* initiale
r исходная опция *f*

4662 home position; home location
(on a screen)
d Grundstellung *f*; Ausgangsstellung *f*; Ausgangsposition *f*
f position *f* initiale; position de repos
r исходное положение *n*

4663 homogeneity
d Homogenität *f*
f homogénéité *f*
r однородность *f*

4664 homogeneity condition
d Homogenitätsbedingung *f*
f condition *f* d'homogénéité
r условие *n* однородности

4665 homogeneity relation
d Homogenitätsrelation *f*
f relation *f* d'homogénéité
r [co]отношение *n* однородности

4666 homogeneous
d homogen
f homogène
r однородный; гомогенный

4667 homogeneous coordinates
d homogene Koordinaten *fpl*
f coordonnées *fpl* homogènes
r однородные координаты *fpl*

4668 homogeneous light
d homogenes Licht *n*
f lumière *f* homogène
r гомогенный свет *m*

4669 homogeneous nodes
d homogene Knoten *mpl*

f nœuds *mpl* homogènes
r гомогенные узлы *mpl*

* **homographic division** → 7555

4670 homographic reparametrization
(of a curve)
d homografische Neuparametrisierung *f*
f réparamétrisation *f* homographique
r гомографическая актуализация *f* параметров

4671 homologous
d homolog
f homologue
r гомологичный

* **homology** → 6998

4672 homothetic figures
d homothetische Figuren *fpl*; perspektivähnliche Figuren
f figures *fpl* homothétiques
r гомотетичные фигуры *fpl*; перспективно-подобные фигуры; центрально-подобные фигуры

4673 homothetic ratio; ratio of similitude; similarity coefficient
d Ähnlichkeitsverhältnis *n*; Ähnlichkeitsfaktor *m*; Streckungsfaktor *m*
f coefficient *m* d'homothétie; rapport *m* de similitude; rapport d'homothétie
r коэффициент *m* подобия; коэффициент гомотетии

4674 homothetic transformation
d homothetische Abbildung *f*
f transformation *f* homothétique
r гомотетическое преобразование *n*

4675 homothety
d Homothetie *f*
f homothétie *f*
r гомотетия *f*

4676 homotopy
d Homotopie *f*
f homotopie *f*
r гомотопия *f*

4677 honeycomb pattern
d Honigwabenmuster *n*; hexagonales Netz *n*; Sechsecknetz *n*; Honigwabengitter *n*
f réseau *m* d'hexagones réguliers
r шестиугольная сетка *f*; сотовидный рисунок *m*

4678 honeycomb structure
d Honigwabenstruktur *f*;

Honigwabenkonstruktion *f*
f structure *f* alvéolée
r сотовидная структура *f*

4679 horizon
d Horizont *m*
f horizon *m*
r горизонт *m*

* **horizontal** → 4699

4680 horizontal
d horizontal; waagerecht
f horizontal; de niveau
r горизонтальный

4681 horizontal aberration
d horizontale Aberration *f*
f aberration *f* horizontale
r горизонтальная аберрация *f*

4682 horizontal alignment; horizontal justification
d horizontale Ausrichtung *f*
f alignement *m* horizontal
r горизонтальное выравнивание *n*

4683 horizontal angle
d horizontaler Winkel *m*; Horizontalwinkel *m*
f angle *m* horizontal
r горизонтальный угол *m*

4684 horizontal asymptote
d horizontale Asymptote *f*; waagerechte Asymptote
f asymptote *f* horizontale
r горизонтальная асимптота *f*

4685 horizontal axis
d Horizontalachse *f*
f axe *m* horizontal
r горизонтальная ось *f*

4686 horizontal bar chart
d horizontales Streifendiagramm *n*
f diagramme *m* à bandes horizontaux
r горизонтальная ленточная диаграмма *f*

4687 horizontal coordinates
d horizontale Koordinaten *fpl*; Grundrisskoordinaten *fpl*
f coordonnées *fpl* horizontaux; coordonnées planimétriques
r плоские координаты *fpl*; плановые координаты

4688 horizontal cylinder
d horizontaler Zylinder *m*
f cylindre *m* horizontal
r горизонтальный цилиндр *m*

4689 horizontal deflection
 d horizontale Ablenkung *f*
 f déflexion *f* horizontale
 r горизонтальное отклонение *n*

4690 horizontal dimension
 d horizontale Dimension *f*
 f cotation *f* horizontale; cote *f* horizontale
 r горизонтальное оразмерение *n*

4691 horizontal dimension line
 d horizontale Dimensionslinie *f*
 f trait *m* de cote horizontale
 r горизонтальная размерная линия *f*

4692 horizontal dimension text
 d horizontaler Dimensionstext *m*
 f texte *m* de cote horizontal
 r горизонтальный текст *m* размера

4693 horizontal folding
 d horizontale Faltung *f*
 f plissement *m* horizontal
 r горизонтальная свертка *f*

4694 horizontal frequency
 (of a screen)
 d horizontale Frequenz *f*
 f fréquence *f* horizontale
 r горизонтальная частота *f*

4695 horizontal grid
 d horizontaler Raster *m*
 f grille *f* horizontale
 r горизонтальный растр *m*

4696 horizontal guideline
 d horizontale Richtlinie *f*
 f ligne *f* directrice horizontale; ligne de conduite horizontale
 r горизонтальная направляющая *f*

4697 horizontal interpolation
 d horizontale Interpolation *f*
 f interpolation *f* horizontale
 r горизонтальная интерполяция *f*

4698 horizontal interpolator
 d horizontaler Interpolator *m*
 f interpolateur *m* horizontal
 r горизонтальный интерполятор *m*

 * **horizontal justification → 4682**

4699 horizontal [line]
 d Horizontale *f*
 f horizontale *f*; droite *f* horizontale
 r горизонталь *f*; горизонтальная линия *f*

4700 horizontal list box
 d horizontales Listenfeld *n*
 f zone *f* de liste déroulante horizontale
 r горизонтальное поле *n* списка

4701 horizontal plane
 d horizontale Ebene *f*; waagerechte Ebene
 f plan *m* horizontal
 r горизонтальная плоскость *f*

4702 horizontal plane of projection; horizontal projection plane; first plane of projection
 d Horizontalebene *f*; Grundrissebene *f*; waagerechte Bezugsebene *f*; erste Projektionsebene *f*
 f plan *m* horizontal de projection; premier plan de projection
 r плоскость *f* горизонтальной проекции

4703 horizontal projection; first projection
 (in two-plane projection)
 d Horizontalprojektion *f*; erste Projektion *f*; Grundriss *m*
 f projection *f* horizontale; coupe *f* horizontale
 r горизонтальная проекция *f*; горизонтальный разрез *m*

 * **horizontal projection plane → 4702**

4704 horizontal resolution
 d Horizontalauflösung *f*; Horizontalauflösungsvermögen *n*
 f résolution *f* horizontale
 r разрешающая способность *f* по горизонтали

4705 horizontal retrace
 d Zeilenrücklauf *m*
 f retour *m* [de balayage] horizontal
 r обратный ход *m* по строке; горизонтальный обратный ход

4706 horizontal ruler
 d horizontales Lineal *n*
 f règle *f* horizontale
 r горизонтальная измерительная линейка *f*

4707 horizontal scanning; line scanning; stripe scanning
 d horizontale Abtastung *f*; Zeilenabtastung *f*
 f balayage *m* horizontal; base *f* de temps des lignes; exploration *f* par lignes
 r горизонтальная развертка *f*; строчная развертка

 * **horizontal screen partitioning → 4708**

4708 horizontal screen split; horizontal screen partitioning
 d horizontale Teilung *f* des Bildschirms

    f splittage *m* d'écran horizontal
    r горизонтальное расщепление *n* экрана

4709 horizontal scrollbar
    d horizontale Bildlaufleiste *f*
    f barre *f* de défilement horizontale
    r горизонтальная линейка *f* просмотра

4710 horizontal scrolling; left-right scrolling
    d horizontaler Bildlauf *m*; Bildverschiebung *f*
        von links nach rechts
    f défilement *m* horizontal; déplacement *m*
        horizontal
    r горизонтальная прокрутка *f*

4711 horizontal shading
    d horizontale Schattierung *f*
    f ombrage *m* horizontal
    r горизонтальное затенение *n*

4712 horizontal spacing
    d horizontaler Abstand *m*
    f espacement *m* horizontal
    r горизонтальное расстояние *n*

4713 horizontal split bar
    d horizontaler Fensterteiler *m*
    f barre *f* de fractionnement horizontale
    r горизонтальная линия *f* разбиения

    * **horizontal tab character → 4714**

4714 horizontal tab[ulator] character
    d horizontaler Tabulator *m*
    f caractère *m* de tabulation horizontale
    r знак *m* горизонтальной табуляции

4715 horizontal tangent
    d horizontale Tangente *f*; waagerechte
        Tangente
    f tangente *f* horizontale
    r горизонтальная касательная *f*

    * **horizontal trace line of a plane → 3815**

    * **horizontal trace of a plane → 3815**

4716 horned sphere
    d gehörnte Sphäre *f*
    f sphère *f* à cornes; sphère cornue
    r рогатая сфера *f*

4717 hot colors
    d warme Farben *fpl*
    f couleurs *fpl* chaudes
    r теплые цвета *mpl*

    * **hot image → 1543**

4718 hotspot; clickable area
    d Hotspot *m*; klickbarer Bereich *m*
    f point *m* d'ancrage; point chaud; zone *f*
        sensible; zone cliquable
    r горячее пятно *n*; горячая точка *f*; область *f*
        нажатия кнопки

4719 hotspot angle
    (of spotlights)
    d Hotspot-Winkel *m*
    f angle *m* de zone sensible
    r угол *m* горячего пятна

4720 hotspot area
    d Hotspot-Bereich *m*
    f aire *f* de zone sensible
    r площадь *f* горячего пятна

    * **hotspot cone angle → 870**

4721 hotspot position
    d Hotspot-Position *f*
    f position *f* de point d'ancrage
    r позиция *f* горячего пятна

4722 hourglass pointer
    d Sanduhrzeiger *m*
    f pointeur *m* sablier; sablier *m*
    r указатель *m* типа песочные часы

    * **HSB color model → 4727**

4723 HSB color spread
    d HSB-Farb[en]raum *m*
    f gamme *f* de couleurs TSB
    r цветовая область *f* HSB

    * **HSB model → 4727**

    * **HSV color model → 4728**

4724 HSV color spread
    d HSV-Farb[en]raum *m*
    f gamme *f* de couleurs HSV
    r цветовая область *f* HSV

    * **HSV model → 4728**

    * **HTML → 4769**

    * **HUD → 4552**

    * **hue → 9695**

4725 hueing
    d Farbtönen n; Tönung *f*
    f teinture *f*
    r нюансирование *n*

4726 hue, lightness and saturation model; HLS [color] model
    d Farbton-Helligkeit-Sättigungsmodell *n*;

HLS-Modell *n*
f modèle *m* teinte-luminosité-saturation;
modèle *m* [de couleur] TSL
r цветовая модель *f*
оттенок-яркость-насыщенность; модель
HLS

**4727 hue, saturation and brightness model; HSB
[color] model**
d Farbton-Sättigung-Helligkeitsmodell *n*;
HSB-Modell *n*
f modèle *m* teinte-saturation-brillance; modèle
[de couleur] TSB
r цветовая модель *f*
оттенок-насыщенность-яркость; модель
HSB

**4728 hue-saturation-value model; HSV [color]
model**
d Farbton-Sättigung-Wert-Modell *n*;
HSV-Modell *n*
f modèle *m* [de couleur] HSV
r цветовая модель *f*
оттенок-насыщенность-значение; модель
HSV

4729 hue shift
d Farbtonverschiebung *f*
f décalage *m* de teinte
r смещение *n* оттенка

4730 hue value
d Farbtonwert *m*
f valeur *f* de teinte
r значение *n* оттенка

4731 Hulbert curve
d Hulbert-Kurve *f*
f courbe *f* de Hulbert
r кривая *f* Гилберта

* **hull → 3467**

4732 human behaviour modeling
d Modellierung *f* des Menschenverhaltens
f modelage *m* de comportement humain
r моделирование *n* человеческого поведения

4733 human hand modeling
d Modellierung *f* der Menschenhand
f modelage *m* de la main humaine
r моделирование *n* человеческой руки

4734 human head modeling
d Modellierung *f* des Menschenkopfes
f modelage *m* de la tête humaine
r моделирование *n* человеческой головы

4735 human modeling
d Modellierung *f* des Menschen

f modelage *m* d'homme
r моделирование *n* человека

4736 human skeleton model
d Menschenskelett-Modell *n*
f modèle *m* du squelette humain
r модель *f* человеческого скелета

4737 human visual perception
d visuelle Menschenwahrnehmung *f*
f perception *f* visuelle humaine
r человеческое визуальное восприятие *n*

4738 hybrid
d Hybrid-
f hybride
r гибридный

4739 hybrid color
d Hybridfarbe *f*
f couleur *f* hybride
r гибридный цвет *m*

4740 hybrid lighting calculation
d hybride Lichtberechnung *f*
f calcul *m* d'éclairage hybride
r вычисление *n* гибридного освещения

4741 hyperbola
d Hyperbel *f*
f hyperbole *f*
r гипербола *f*

4742 hyperbolic
d hyperbolisch
f hyperbolique
r гиперболический

4743 hyperbolic catenary
d hyperbolische Kettenlinie *f*
f chaînette *f* hyperbolique; caténaire *f*
hyperbolique
r гиперболическая цепная линия *f*

4744 hyperbolic cone
d hyperbolischer Kegel *m*
f cône *m* hyperbolique
r гиперболический конус *m*

4745 hyperbolic cylinder
d hyperbolischer Zylinder *m*
f cylindre *m* hyperbolique
r гиперболический цилиндр *m*

4746 hyperbolic ellipse
d hyperbolische Ellipse *f*
f ellipse *f* hyperbolique
r гиперболический эллипс *m*

4747 hyperbolic homology; hyperbolic perspectivity
   d hyperbolische Homologie *f*; hyperbolische Perspektivität *f*
   f homologie *f* hyperbolique; perspectivité *f* hyperbolique
   r гиперболическая гомология *f*; гиперболическая перспектива *f*

4748 hyperbolic motion
   d hyperbolische Bewegung *f*; Hyperbelbewegung *f*
   f mouvement *m* hyperbolique
   r гиперболическое движение *n*; движение по гиперболе

4749 hyperbolic paraboloid
   d hyperbolisches Paraboloid *n*
   f paraboloïde *m* hyperbolique
   r гиперболический параболоид *m*

   * **hyperbolic perspectivity** → 4747

4750 hyperbolic point
   d hyperbolischer Punkt *m*
   f point *m* hyperbolique
   r гиперболическая точка *f*

4751 hyperbolic spiral
   d hyperbolische Spirale *f*
   f spirale *f* hyperbolique
   r гиперболическая спираль *f*

4752 hyperboloid
   d Hyperboloid *n*
   f hyperboloïde *m*
   r гиперболоид *m*

4753 hyperboloid of one sheet
   d einschaliges Hyperboloid *n*
   f hyperboloïde *m* à une nappe
   r однополостный гиперболоид *m*

4754 hyperboloid of revolution
   d Rotationshyperboloid *n*; Umdrehungshyperboloid *n*
   f hyperboloïde *m* de révolution
   r гиперболоид *m* вращения

4755 hyperboloid of two sheets
   d zweischaliges Hyperboloid *n*
   f hyperboloïde *m* à deux nappes
   r двуполостный гиперболоид *m*

4756 hypercube
   d Hyperwürfel *m*
   f hypercube *m*
   r гиперкуб *m*

4757 hypergeometric[al] data

   d hypergeometrische Daten *npl*
   f données *fpl* hypergéométriques
   r гипергеометрические данные *npl*

   * **hypergeometric data** → 4757

4758 hypergraph
   d Hypergraph *m*
   f hypergraphe *m*
   r гиперграф *m*

4759 hypergraphics
   d Hypergrafik *f*
   f hypergraphique *m*
   r гиперграфика *f*

4760 hyperimage
   d Hyperbild *n*
   f hyperimage *f*
   r гиперизображение *n*

4761 hyperlink
   d Hyperlink *n*
   f hyperlien *m*
   r гиперсвязь *f*

4762 hypermedia
   d Hypermedien *npl*
   f hypermédia *m*
   r гиперсредства *npl* информации

4763 hyperpatch
   d Hyper-Oberflächenstück *n*
   f hypersurface *f* paramétrique
   r гипер-фрагмент *m*

4764 hyperplane
   d Hyperebene *f*
   f hyperplan *m*
   r гиперплоскость *f*

4765 hyperrelation
   d Hyperrelation *f*
   f hyperrelation *f*
   r гиперреляция *f*

4766 hypersphere
   d Hypersphäre *f*; Hyperkugel *f*
   f hypersphère *f*
   r гиперсфера *f*

4767 hypertext
   d Hypertext *m*
   f hypertexte *m*
   r гипертекст *m*

4768 hypertext link
   d Hypertext-Verknüpfung *f*
   f lien *m* hypertexte
   r гипертекстовая связь *f*

* **hypertext markup language** → 4769

4769 **hypertext metalanguage; hypertext**
markup language; HTML
 d Hypertext-Metasprache *f*;
 Hypertext-Markierungssprache *f*
 f métalangage *m* hypertexte
 r гипертекстовый метаязык *m*

4770 **hypertexture**
 d Hypertextur *f*
 f hypertexture *f*
 r гипертекстура *f*

4771 **hyphen**
 d Bindestrich *m*; Trennstrich *m*; Mittelstrich *m*
 f trait *m* d'union; tiret *m*
 r дефис *m*; тире *n*; знак *m* переноса

4772 **hyphenating; hyphenation**
 d Worttrennung *f*; Silbentrennung *f*
 f coupage *m* de mot; coupure *f* de mot
 r разбивка *f* по слогам; расстановка *f*
 дефисов; перенос *m* слов

* **hyphenation** → 4772

4773 **hypocycloid**
 d Hypozykloide *f*
 f hypocycloïde *f*
 r гипоциклоида *f*

* **hypocycloid of four cusps** → 626

4774 **hypotenuse**
 d Hypotenuse *f*
 f hypoténuse *f*
 r гипотенуза *f*

4775 **hypotrochoid**
 d Hypotrochoide *f*
 f hypotrochoïde *f*
 r гипотрохоида *f*

I

4776 I-beam pointer
 d I-förmiger Mauszeiger *m*
 f pointeur *m* en I
 r указатель *m* луч

4777 icon
 d Ikone *f*
 f icône *f*; graphisme *m*
 r пиктограмма *f*; икона *f*; значок *m*

4778 icon bar
 d Ikonenstreifen *m*; Symbolleiste *n*
 f barre *f* d'icônes
 r полоса *f* икон

4779 icon-driven interface
 d symbolgesteuerte Schnittstelle *f*
 f interface *f* gestionnée par icônes
 r пиктографический интерфейс *m*

4780 iconic
 d ikonisch; Ikonen-
 f iconique
 r иконический; пиктографический

4781 iconic model
 d ikonisches Modell *n*
 f modèle *m* iconique
 r портретная модель *f*

4782 iconic representation; pictogram
 representation
 d ikonische Darstellung *f*
 f représentation *f* iconique
 r иконическое представление *n*;
     пиктографическое представление

4783 iconic technique
 d ikonische Technik *f*
 f technique *f* iconique
 r пиктографическая техника *f*

4784 iconize *v*; stow *v*; shrink *v*
 (of a window)
 d ikonizieren
 f icôniser
 r свертывать в пиктограмму; закрывать

4785 icon menu
 d ikonisches Menü *n*
 f menu *m* iconique
 r пиктографическое меню *n*

 * **iconographic** → 7049

 * **iconology** → 4909

4786 icons arrangement
 d Ikonenanordnung *f*
 f arrangement *m* d'icônes
 r перестановка *f* икон; размещение *n* икон;
     расположение *n* икон

4787 icosahedron
 d Ikosaeder *n*; Zwanzigflächner *m*
 f icosaèdre *m*
 r икосаэдр *m*; двадцатигранник *m*

 * **ID** → 4790

 * **IDB** → 4839

 * **IDE** → 5141

 * **ideal element** → 3347

 * **ideal line** → 5629

 * **ideal plane** → 7142

 * **ideal point** → 7208

4788 identical
 d identisch
 f identique
 r идентичный; тождественный

4789 identification
 d Identifikation *f*; Kennzeichnung *f*
 f identification *f*
 r идентификация *f*; обозначение *n*;
     отождествление *n*

 * **identificator** → 4790

4790 identifier; identificator; ID
 d Identifikator *m*; Bezeichner *m*;
     Identifizierer *m*
 f identificateur *m*
 r идентификатор *m*

4791 identify *v*
 d identifizieren
 f identifier
 r идентифицировать; отождествлять

4792 identity
 d Identität *f*
 f identité *f*
 r тождество *n*; идентитет *m*; идентичность *f*;
     тождественность *f*

 * **identity map** → 4793

4793 identity map[ping]
d identische Abbildung *f*
f application *f* identique
r тождественное отображение *n*

* idle → 990

**4794 idle character; dummy character; blank
    character; ignore character**
d Blindzeichen *n*; Leerzeichen *n*
f caractère *m* inutile; caractère à vide; caractère
    nul; caractère blanc
r фиктивный символ *m*; псевдосимвол *m*;
    пустой символ; отбрасываемый символ

4795 ignore *v*
d ignorieren; fortlassen
f ignorer
r игнорировать; пропускать

* ignore character → 4794

* illegal → 5260

4796 illegal code; false code; forbidden code
d illegaler Code *m*; ungültiger Code;
    unerlaubter Code
f code *m* faux; code interdit
r недействительный код *m*; запрещенный
    код

4797 illegal format
d illegales Format *n*; unerlaubtes Format
f format *m* illégal
r недействительный формат *m*

* illuminance → 5551

* illuminate *v* → 5530

4798 illumination; lighting
d Illumination *f*; Ausleuchtung *f*; Beleuchtung *f*
f illumination *f*; éclairement *m*; éclairage *m*
r иллюминация *f*; освещение *n*

4799 illumination angle
d Illuminationswinkel *m*;
    Ausleuchtungswinkel *m*
f angle *m* d'illumination
r угол *m* освещения

4800 illumination data
d Beleuchtungsdaten *npl*
f données *fpl* d'illumination
r данные *npl* освещения

4801 illumination function
d Ausleuchtungsfunktion *f*
f fonction *f* d'illumination
r функция *f* иллюминации

4802 illumination layer
d Ausleuchtungsschicht *f*
f plan *m* d'illumination
r слой *m* освещения

4803 illumination mirror
d Beleuchtungsspiegel *m*
f réflecteur *m* lumineux
r зеркало *n* освещения

4804 illumination model; lighting model
d Beleuchtungsmodell *n*
f modèle *m* d'illumination
r модель *f* освещения

4805 illumination of lens
d Lichtstärke *f* eines Objektivs
f clarté *f* d'un objectif
r светосила *f* объектива

4806 illumination process
d Beleuchtungsprozess *m*
f processus *m* d'illumination
r процесс *m* освещения

4807 illumination processor
d Beleuchtungsprozessor *m*
f processeur *m* d'illumination
r процессор *m* освещения

4808 illusion
d Illusion *f*
f illusion *f*
r иллюзия *f*

* illusory → 470

4809 illustration
d Illustration *f*
f illustration *f*
r иллюстрация *f*

* illustrational → 7049

4810 illustration gamut mapping
d Illustration-Gamut-Mapping *n*
f chroma-mappage *m* d'illustration
r хроматическое преобразование *n*
    иллюстрации

* illustration program → 1984

* illustrative → 7049

4811 illustrator
    (a software)
d Illustrator *m*
f illustrateur *m*
r иллюстратор *m*

* **illustratory** → 7049

4812 image; pattern; picture
d Bild *n*; Abbild *n*
f image *f*
r образ *m*; изображение *n*

4813 image accumulation
d Bildakkumulation *f*
f accumulation *f* d'images
r накопление *n* изображений

4814 image adjusting
d Bildanpassung *f*
f ajustage *m* d'image
r настройка *f* изображения

4815 image analysis
d Bildanalyse *f*
f analyse *f* d'image
r анализ *m* изображения

4816 image area
d Bildbereich *m*
f aire *f* d'image
r площадь *f* изображения

4817 image attaching
      (to an e-mail message)
d Bildanschluss *m*
f attachement *m* d'image
r присоединение *n* изображения

4818 image attributes
d Bildattribute *npl*
f attributs *mpl* d'image
r атрибуты *mpl* изображения

* **image brightness** → 1142

4819 image browsing
d Bild[er]vorschau *f*
f revue *f* d'images
r просмотр *m* изображений

* **image buffer** → 3982

4820 image button
d Bildschaltfläche *f*
f bouton *m* d'image
r бутон *m* изображения

4821 image capture; frame grabbing
d Bildsammlung *f*
f capture *f* d'image
r захватывание *n* кадра

4822 image capture area
d Bild-Sammelbereich *m*
f domaine *m* de capture d'image

r область *f* улавливания изображения;
   область захватывания кадра

4823 image centroid
d Bildzentroid *n*
f centroïde *m* d'image
r центроид *m* изображения

4824 image clipping; image cropping
d Bildausschnittbestimmung *f*;
   Bildausschnitt *m*; Bild-Beschneiden *n*
f [dé]coupage *m* d'image
r отсекание *n* изображения; кадрировка *f*
   изображения

4825 image coding; picture coding
d Bildcodierung *f*
f codage *m* d'image
r кодирование *n* изображения

4826 image color
d Bildfarbe *f*
f couleur *f* d'image
r цвет *m* изображения

4827 image communication
d Bild[er]kommunikation *f*
f communication *f* par images
r коммуникация *f* с помощью изображений

4828 image comparison
d Bild[er]vergleich *m*
f comparaison *f* d'images
r сравнение *n* изображений

4829 image component
d Bildkomponente *f*
f composant *m* d'image
r компонент *m* изображения; элемент *m*
   изображения

4830 image composition
d Bildsatz *m*
f composition *f* d'image
r состав *m* изображения

4831 image compression; image packing
d Bild-Kompression *f*
f compression *f* d'image
r сжатие *n* изображения; уплотнение *n*
   изображения

4832 image content
d Bildinhalt *m*
f contenu *m* d'image
r содержание *n* изображения

4833 image contrast
d Bildkontrast *m*

  f contraste *m* d'image
  r контраст *m* изображения

4834 image converter
  d Bildumwandler *m*
  f convertisseur *m* d'image
  r преобразователь *m* изображения

4835 image copying
  d Bild-Kopieren *n*
  f copiage *m* d'image
  r копирование *n* изображения

4836 image correlation
  d Bild[er]korrelation *f*
  f corrélation *f* d'images
  r корреляция *f* изображений

4837 image counter
  d Bildzähler *m*
  f compteur *m* d'images
  r счетчик *m* изображений

  * **image cropping** → **4824**

4838 image data
  d Bilddaten *npl*
  f données *fpl* d'image
  r данные *npl* об изображении

4839 image database; IDB
  d Bilder-Datenbasis *f*
  f base *f* de données d'images
  r база *f* данных изображений

4840 image decorrelation
  d Bilddekorrelation *f*
  f décorrélation *f* d'image
  r декорреляция *f* изображения

  * **image definition** → **4915**

4841 image definition area
  d Bildschärfebereich *m*
  f domaine *m* de définition d'image
  r область *f* четкости изображения

4842 image detaching; image unloading
  d Bildtrennung *f*
  f détachement *m* d'image
  r отделение *n* изображения

4843 image detail
  d Bilddetail *n*
  f détail *m* d'image
  r деталь *f* изображения

4844 image dimensions
  d Bilddimensionen *fpl*
  f cotations *fpl* d'image

  r размеры *mpl* изображения

4845 image displacement
  d Bildverschiebung *f*
  f déplacement *m* d'image
  r смещение *n* изображения

  * **image display** → **4846**

4846 image display[ing]
  d Bilddarstellung *f*
  f affichage *m* d'image
  r визуализация *f* изображения

4847 image display process
  d Bilddarstellungsprozess *m*
  f processus *m* d'affichage d'image
  r процесс *m* визуализации изображения

4848 image distance
  d Bildabstand *m*
  f distance *f* d'image
  r расстояние *n* до изображения

4849 image dithering
  (the tradeoff spatial resolution for intensity,
  similar to halftoning)
  d Bildrastern *n*; Bild-Dithering *n*
  f juxtaposition *f* d'image
  r имитация *f* полутонов изображения

  * **image dot** → **7088**

4850 image editing
  d Bildbearbeitung *f*
  f édition *f* d'image
  r редактирование *n* изображения

**4851 image editing program; image editor;
  picture editor**
  d Bildbearbeitungsprogramm *n*; Bildeditor *m*
  f programme *m* d'édition d'images; éditeur *m*
  d'images
  r программа *f* редактирования изображений;
  редактор *m* изображений

  * **image editor** → **4851**

4852 image embedding
  d Bild-Einbetten *n*
  f encastrement *m* d'image
  r вложение *n* изображения

4853 image enhancement
  d Bildverbesserung *f*
  f amélioration *f* d'image
  r улучшение *n* изображения

4854 image feature; feature
  (of a human face)
  d Gesichtszug *m*

f trait *m*
r черта *f*

4855 image feature extraction
  d Bildszüge-Extraktion *f*;
    Gesichtszug-Extraktion *f*
  f extraction *f* de traits faciaux; extraction de
    trats de visage
  r выделение *n* черт образов; выделение черт
    лица

4856 image file
  d Bilddatei *f*
  f fichier *m* d'image
  r файл *m* изображения

4857 image file formats
  d Bilddatei-Formate *npl*
  f formats *mpl* de fichiers d'images
  r форматы *mpl* файлов изображений

4858 image flipping; picture flipping
  d Bildausflippen *n*
  f retournement *m* d'image; rabattement *m*
    d'image
  r переворачивание *n* изображения;
    зеркальное отражение *n* изображения

4859 image focal plane
  d Brennebene *f* des Bilds
  f plan *m* focal d'image
  r фокальная плоскость *f* изображения

4860 image focus
  d Bildbrennpunkt *m*
  f point *m* focal d'image
  r фокус *m* в плоскости изображения

4861 image format; picture format
  d Bildformat *n*
  f format *m* d'image
  r формат *m* изображения; формат образа

4862 image frame
  d Bildrahmen *m*
  f cadre *m* d'image
  r кадр *m* изображения

4863 image framing
  d Bildrahmung *f*
  f cadrage *m* d'image
  r кадрирование *n* изображения

4864 image generation; picture generation
  d Bildgenerierung *f*; Bilderzeugung *f*
  f génération *f* d'images
  r генерирование *n* изображений

4865 image generation frequency
  d Bildgenerierungsfrequenz *f*

f fréquence *f* de génération d'images
r частота *f* генерирования изображений

4866 image generation process
  d Bildgenerierungsprozess *m*
  f processus *m* de génération d'images
  r процесс *m* генерирования изображений

  * **image glow** → 4869

4867 image halftones
  d Bildhalbton *m*
  f demi-teintes *fpl* d'image
  r оттенки *mpl* изображения; нюансы *mpl*
    изображения

4868 image header
  d Bildkopf *m*; Bildtitel *m*
  f en-tête *f* d'image
  r заголовок *m* изображения

4869 image illumination; image glow
  d Bildillumination *f*
  f illumination *f* de l'image
  r освещение *n* изображения

4870 image inserting
  d Bildeinfügung *f*
  f insertion *f* d'image
  r вставка *f* изображения

4871 image inverter
  d Bildinverter *m*
  f inverseur *m* d'image
  r инвертор *m* изображения

4872 image line
  d Bildzeile *f*
  f ligne *f* d'image
  r строка *f* изображения

4873 image listing
  d Bildlistung *f*
  f listage *m* d'image
  r листание *n* изображения

4874 image mailing
  d Bildsendung *f*; Bildeinlieferung *f*
  f publipostage *m* d'image
  r рассылка *f* изображения (электронной
    почтой)

  * **image map** → 1543

4875 image masque
  d Bildmaske *f*
  f masque *f* d'image
  r маска *f* изображения

4876 image model
  d Bildmodell *n*

f modèle *m* d'image
r модель *f* изображения

4877 image modification
  d Bildänderung *f*
  f modification *f* d'image
  r преобразование *n* изображения

4878 image morphing
  d Bild-Morphing *n*
  f morphage *m* d'image
  r морфинг *m* изображения; метаморфоза *f* изображения

  * **image motion** → **4880**

4879 image-motion compensation
  d Kompensation *f* der Bildbewegung
  f compensation *f* de mouvement d'image
  r компенсация *f* сдвига изображения

4880 image moving; image motion
  d Bildbewegung *f*
  f traînée *f* d'image; mouvement *m* d'image
  r сдвиг *m* изображения

4881 image naming
  d Namengebung *f* des Bilds; Bildbenennung *f*
  f désignation *f* d'image
  r наименование *n* изображения

4882 image negative
  d Bildnegativ *n*
  f négatif *m* d'image
  r негатив *m* изображения

4883 image node
  d Knotenpunkt *m* des Bilds
  f nœud *m* d'image
  r узловая точка *f* изображения

4884 image opening
  d Bild[er]öffnung *f*
  f ouverture *f* d'image
  r открытие *n* изображения; отверстие *n* изображения

  * **image packing** → **4831**

4885 image page
  d Bildseite *f*
  f page *f* d'image
  r страница *f* изображения

4886 image parameter
  d Bildparameter *m*
  f paramètre *m* d'image
  r параметр *m* изображения

4887 image plane; picture plane
  d Bildebene *f*; Bildtafel *f*
  f plan *m* [de projection] d'image
  r плоскость *f* [проекции] изображения; картинная плоскость

4888 image positioning
  d Bildpositionierung *f*; Bildpositionieren *n*
  f positionnement *m* d'image
  r позиционирование *n* изображения

4889 image power amplifier; video amplifier
  d Videoverstärker *m*
  f amplificateur *m* vidéo
  r видео-усилитель *m*

  * **image preview** → **4890**

4890 image preview[ing]
  d Bildvorschau *f*
  f prévisualisation *f* d'image
  r предварительный просмотр *m* изображения

4891 image processing; picture processing
  d Bildbearbeitung *f*; Bildverarbeitung *f*
  f traitement *m* d'images
  r обработка *f* изображений

4892 image processing software
  d Bildbearbeitungssoftware *f*
  f logiciel *m* de traitement d'images
  r программное обеспечение *n* обработки изображений

4893 image processor
  d Bildprozessor *m*; Bildrechner *m*
  f processeur *m* d'images
  r процессор *m* изображений

4894 image projection
  d Bildprojektion *f*
  f projection *f* d'image
  r проекция *f* изображения

4895 image quality; picture quality
  d Bildqualität *f*
  f qualité *f* d'image
  r качество *n* изображения

4896 image raster
  d Bildraster *m*
  f rastre *m* d'image
  r растр *m* изображения

  * **image recognition** → **6906**

  * **image refreshing** → **4897**

4897 image regeneration; image refreshing
  d Bildregenerierung *f*; Bildwiederholung *f*; Bildauffrischung *f*

f régénération *f* d'image
r регенерация *f* изображения

4898 image registration
d Bildregistrierung *f*
f enregistrement *m* d'image
r записывание *n* изображения

4899 image rejection
d Bildbeseitigung *f*
f rejet *m* d'image
r отстранение *n* изображения

4900 image rendering
d Bildrendering *n*
f rendu *m* d'image
r тонирование *n* изображения; рендеринг *m* изображения

4901 image resizing
d Bild-Vergrößern/Verkleinern *n*;
   Bild-Größenänderung *f*
f changement *m* de taille d'image
r изменение *n* размера изображения

4902 image resolution
d Bildauflösung *f*
f résolution *f* d'image
r разрешающая способность *f* изображения

4903 image restoration
d Bildwiederherstellung *f*
f restauration *f* d'image
r восстановление *n* изображения

4904 image rotating
d Bilddrehung *f*
f rotation *f* d'image
r вращение *n* изображения

4905 imagery
d Abbildung *f*
f imagerie *f*; visionnique *m*
r изображения *npl*

4906 image saving
d Bildspeicherung *f*
f sauvegarde *f* d'image
r сохранение *n* изображения

4907 image scale
d Abbildungsmaßstab *m*
f échelle *f* d'image
r масштаб *m* изображения

4908 image scaling
d Bildskalierung *f*
f mise *f* en échelle d'image
r масштабирование *n* изображения

* **image scanning** → 7059

* **image scanning method** → 7060

4909 image science; iconology
d Bild[er]erklärung *f*
f iconologie *f*
r иконология *f*

4910 image scrolling
d Bildrollen *n*; Bild[durch]lauf *m*
f défilement *m* d'image
r прокрутка *f* изображения

4911 image security
d Sicherheit *f* des Bilds
f sécurité *f* d'images
r защита *f* изображений; сохранность *f* изображений; секретность *f* изображений

4912 image segmentation
d Bildsegmentierung *f*
f segmentation *f* d'image
r сегментирование *n* изображения

4913 image set
d Bildmenge *f*
f ensemble *m* des images
r множество *n* образов

4914 image shading
d Bildschattierung *f*
f ombrage *m* d'image
r оттенение *n* изображения

4915 image sharpness; image definition
d Bildschärfe *f*
f netteté *f* de l'image; définition *f* de l'image
r четкость *f* изображения; резкость *f* изображения

4916 image sheet
d Bildblatt *n*
f feuille *f* d'image
r лист *m* изображения

4917 image shrinkage; picture shrinkage
d Bildschrumpfung *f*
f contraction *f* d'image
r свертывание *n* изображения; усадка *f* изображения

* **image signature** → 1277

4918 image size
d Bildgröße *f*
f taille *f* d'image
r размер *m* изображения

4919 image slice
d Bildscheibe *f*

f tranche *f* d'image
r вырезка *f* изображения; слой *m* изображения

4920 image sliding
d Bildgleiten *n*; Bildschleifen *n*
f glissement *m* d'image
r скольжение *n* изображения

4921 image smoothing
d Bildglättung *f*
f lissage *m* d'image
r сглаживание *n* изображения

4922 image smudging
d Bildbeschmutzung *f*
f maculage *m* d'image
r [за]пачкание *n* изображения

4923 image space
d Bilderraum *m*
f espace *m* d'images
r пространство *n* образов

4924 image specification
d Bildspezifikation *f*
f spécification *f* d'image
r спецификация *f* изображения

4925 image spreadsheet
d Bilderrechenblatt *n*
f tableur *m* d'images
r электронная таблица *f* изображений

4926 image stability
d Bildstabilität *f*
f stabilité *f* d'image
r устойчивость *f* изображения

4927 image subtraction
d Bild-Subtrahieren *n*
f soustraction *f* d'image
r вычитание *n* изображения

4928 image synthesis
d Bildsynthese *f*
f synthèse *f* d'image
r синтез *m* изображения

4929 image [tele]transmission; picture [remote] transfer
d Bild[fern]übertragung *f*
f [télé]transmission *f* d'images
r [дальняя] передача *f* изображений

4930 image transforms
d Bildtransformationen *fpl*
f transformations *fpl* d'image
r преобразования *npl* изображения

* **image transmission** → 4929

4931 image transparency; pattern transparency
d Bildtransparenz *f*
f transparence *f* d'image
r прозрачность *f* изображения

* **image unloading** → 4842

4932 image vectors
d Bildvektoren *mpl*
f vecteurs *mpl* d'image
r векторы *mpl* изображения

4933 image verification
d Bildüberprüfung *f*
f vérification *f* d'image
r проверка *f* изображения

4934 image visibility
d Bildsichtbarkeit *f*
f visibilité *f* d'image
r видимость *f* изображения

4935 image warping
d Bildverbiegung *f*; Bildverkrümmung *f*
f gauchissement *m* d'image
r неоднородное искажение *n* изображения

4936 image zooming
d Bildzoomen *n*
f zoom *m* d'image
r динамическое масштабирование *n* изображения

4937 imaginary
d imaginär
f imaginaire
r мнимый

4938 imaginary intersection
d imaginäre Schnittmenge *f*
f intersection *f* imaginaire
r мнимое пересечение *n*

4939 imaginary projection
d Imaginärprojektion *f*
f projection *f* imaginaire
r мнимая проекция *f*

4940 imaging
d Abbildung *f*
f imagination *f*; prise *f* d'images; formation *f* d'images; présentation *f* en image
r формирование *n* изображений

4941 imaging artifacts; artifacts
d Artefakte *npl*
f effets *mpl* parasitaires; artéfacts *mpl*
r артефакты *mpl*; ложные изображения *npl*; следы *mpl*

4942 imaging characteristics
  d Abbildungseigenschaften *fpl*
  f caractéristique *f* d'imagination
  r характеристика *f* изображения

4943 imaging cycle
  d Abbildungszyklus *m*
  f cycle *m* d'imagination
  r цикл *m* изображения

4944 immediate; instantaneous
  d unmittelbar; sofortig
  f immédiat; instantané
  r непосредственный; немедленный

4945 immersion
  d Immersion *f*; Eintauchung *f*
  f immersion *f*
  r иммерсия *f*

4946 immersive design
  d eindringender Entwurf *m*
  f dessin *m* immersif
  r иммерсионный проект *m*

4947 immersive design system
  d System *n* des eindringenden Entwurfs
  f système *m* de dessin immersif
  r система *f* иммерсионного проектирования

4948 immiscibility
  d Nichtmischbarkeit *f*
  f immiscibilité *f*
  r несмешаемость *f*

4949 immiscibility analysis
  d Nichtmischbarkeitsanalyse *f*
  f analyse *f* de l'immiscibilité
  r анализ *m* несмешаемости

  * impact → 2274

4950 imperfection
  d Unvollkommenheit *f*
  f imperfection *f*
  r несовершенство *n*; недостаток *m*

4951 impermeable to light; impervious to light; lighttight
  d lichtundurchlässig
  f étanche à la lumière
  r светонепроницаемый

  * impervious to light → 4951

4952 implantation
  d Implantation *f*
  f implantation *f*
  r имплантация *f*

4953 implement *v*
  d ausführen; durchführen
  f implémenter
  r выполнять; осуществлять; претворять

4954 implementation
  d Durchführung *f*
  f implémentation *f*; réalisation *f*; mise *f* en marche
  r реализация *f*; внедрение *n*; ввод *m* в действие

4955 implication
  d Implikation *f*
  f implication *f*
  r импликация *f*

4956 implicator
  d Implikator *m*
  f élément *m* d'implication
  r импликатор *m*

4957 implicit; assumed
  d implizit
  f implicite
  r неявный

4958 implicit form
  d implizite Form *f*
  f forme *f* implicite
  r неявная форма *f*

4959 implicit model
  d implizites Modell *n*
  f modèle *m* implicite
  r неявная модель *f*

4960 implicit representation
  d implizite Darstellung *f*
  f représentation *f* implicite
  r неявное представление *n*

4961 implicit surface
  d implizite Fläche *f*
  f surface *f* implicite
  r неявная поверхность *f*

  * import → 4966

4962 import *v*
  d importieren
  f importer
  r вносить

  * importation → 4966

4963 imported bitmap
  d importiertes Bitmap *n*
  f bitmap *m* importé
  r импортированное растровое отображение *n*

4964 imported image
d importiertes Bild n
f image f importée
r импортированное изображение n

4965 importer
d Importeur m
f importateur m
r вноситель m

4966 import[ing]; importation
d Importieren n
f importation f
r внесение n; импортирование n

4967 import method
d Importmethode f
f méthode f d'importation
r метод m внесения

4968 imprecise; inexact
d ungenau; unexakt; unpräzis[e]
f imprécis; inexact
r неточный; неверный

4969 impression
d Eindruck m
f impression f
r впечатление n; восприятие n

4970 impressionistic effect
d impressionistischer Effekt m
f effet m impressionniste
r импрессионистический эффект m

4971 impressionistic filter
d impressionistischer Filter m
f filtre m impressionniste
r импрессионистический фильтр m

4972 impression of depth
d Tiefeneindruck m
f impression f de profondeur
r впечатление n глубины

4973 impression of space
d Raumeindruck m; Raumvorstellung f
f impression f d'espace; impression
  stéréoscopique
r пространственное восприятие n;
  стереоскопическое восприятие

4974 improper
d uneigentlich; unecht
f impropre
r несобственный

* **improper element** → 3347

* **improper line** → 5629

* **improper plane** → 7142

* **improper point** → 7208

4975 improper subgraph
d unechter Teilgraph m
f sous-graphe m impropre
r несобственный подграф m

4976 improved resolution
d verbesserte Auflösung f
f résolution f améliorée
r улучшенная разрешающая способность f

* **improvement** → 3443

4977 inaccessibility; unavailability;
     unattainability
d Unerreichbarkeit f; Unzugänglichkeit f
f inaccessibilité f; non-disponibilité f
r недостижимость f; недоступность f

4978 inaccessible; unavailable
d unerreichbar
f inaccessible; non accessible
r недостижимый; недоступный

* **inaccessible node** → 9973

4979 inaccuracy; inexactitude
d Ungenauigkeit f; Unexaktheit f
f inexactitude f; imprécision f
r неточность f

4980 inactive
d nichtaktiv; passiv
f inactif; non actif
r неактивный; пассивный

4981 inactive layer
d nichtaktive Schicht f
f couche f inactive
r неактивный слой m

4982 inactive node
d nichtaktiver Knoten m
f nœud m non actif
r неактивный узел m

* **in-betweening** → 6036

* **in-built** → 6186

4983 incentre
d Mittelpunkt m des Inkreises;
  Inkreismittelpunkt m
f centre m du cercle inscrit
r центр m вписанной окружности

4984 inch
d Zoll m

f pouce *m*
r дюйм *m*

* incidence → 4993

4985 incidence
   d Inzidenz *f*
   f incidence *f*
   r инцидентность *f*

* incidence angle → 380

4986 incidence curve
   d Inzidenzkurve *f*
   f courbe *f* d'incidence
   r кривая *f* инцидентности

4987 incidence structure
   d Inzidenzstruktur *f*
   f structure *f* d'incidence
   r структура *f* инцидентности

4988 incidence surface
   d Inzidenzfläche *f*
   f surface *f* d'incidence
   r поверхность *f* инцидентности

* incident direction → 2872

4989 incident light
   d einfallendes Licht *n*
   f lumière *f* incidente
   r падающий свет *m*

4990 incident radiation
   d einfallende Strahlung *f*
   f rayonnement *m* incident; radiation *f* incidente
   r падающее излучение *n*

4991 incident vector
   d Inzidenzvektor *m*
   f vecteur *m* incident
   r инцидентный вектор *m*

4992 incident vertex
   d Inzidenzknoten *m*
   f sommet *m* incident
   r инцидентная вершина *f*

* incircle → 5108

4993 inclination; incidence; slanting
   d Neigung *f*; Steigung *f*
   f inclinaison *f*
   r наклонение *n*; наклон *m*; скос *m*; уклон *m*

* inclination angle → 380

4994 inclination of camera; tilt of camera
   d Neigung *f* der Kamera

f inclinaison *f* de la caméra
r наклон *m* камеры

* inclined → 6411

* inclined line → 6426

4995 inclined plane; oblique plane
   d geneigte Ebene *f*; schiefe Ebene
   f plan *m* incliné; plan oblique
   r наклонная плоскость *f*

* inclined projection → 8768

* include *v* → 3414

4996 included
   d eingeschlossen
   f inclus
   r включенный

4997 inclusion
   d Inklusion *f*; Einfügen *n*; Einfügung *f*
   f inclusion *f*
   r включение *n*

4998 inclusive angles
   d inklusive Winkel *mpl*
   f angles *mpl* inclus
   r включающие углы *mpl*

4999 inclusive segments
   d inklusive Segmente *npl*
   f segments *mpl* inclus; segments incorporés
   r совместимые сегменты *mpl*; включающие сегменты

5000 inclusive tree
   d Einfügungsbaum *m*
   f arbre *m* d'inclusions
   r дерево *n* включений

5001 incoherent
   d inkohärent; nichtkohärent
   f incohérent; non cohérent
   r некогерентный

5002 incoherent light
   d inkohärentes Licht *n*
   f lumière *f* incohérente
   r некогерентный свет *m*

5003 incoherent optics
   d inkohärente Optik *f*
   f optique *f* incohérente
   r некогерентная оптика *f*

5004 incommensurability
   d Inkommensurabilität *f*

f incommensurabilité *f*
r несоизмеримость *f*

5005 incommensurable
d inkommensurabel
f incommensurable
r несоизмеримый

5006 incommensurable quantities
d inkommensurabele Größen *fpl*
f quantités *fpl* incommensurables; grandeurs *fpl* incommensurables
r несоизмеримые величины *fpl*

5007 incomparable
d unvergleichlich
f incomparable
r несравнимый

5008 incomparable quantities
d unvergleichliche Größen *fpl*
f quantités *fpl* incompatibles
r несравнимые величины *fpl*

5009 incompatibility
d Inkompatibilität *f*; Unvereinbarkeit *f*; Unverträglichkeit *f*
f incompatibilité *f*
r несовместимость *f*; несовместность *f*

5010 incomplete
d unvollständig; nichtvollständig
f incomplet; non complet
r неполный

5011 incompleteness
d Unvollständigkeit *f*
f incomplétude *f*
r неполнота *f*; незавершенность *f*

5012 incorporate *v*
d einbauen; aufnehmen; eingliedern
f incorporer
r встраивать; объединять

5013 incorporation
d Einbau *m*; Einlagerung *f*
f incorporation *f*
r встраивание *n*; объединение *n*

5014 incorrect
d unkorrekt; unakkurat; inkorrekt
f incorrect; non correct
r некорректный

5015 incorrect visualization
d unkorrekte Visualisierung *f*
f visualisation *f* non correcte
r некорректная визуализация *f*

5016 increase *v*
d wachsen
f croître; accroître
r расти; возрастать

* **increasing** → 595

5017 increment
d Zuwachs *m*; Inkrement *n*
f incrément *m*; accroissement *m*
r приращение *n*; прирост *m*; инкремент *m*

5018 incremental
d inkrementell; Inkremental-
f incrémental
r инкрементальный; возрастающий

5019 incremental constants
d Inkrementalkonstanten *fpl*
f constantes *fpl* d'incrément
r константы *fpl* инкремента

5020 incremental coordinate
d inkrementelle Koordinate *f*
f coordonnée *f* incrémentale
r инкрементальная координата *f*

5021 incremental direction
d Inkrementalrichtung *f*
f direction *f* d'incrément
r направление *n* нарастания

5022 incremental forming
(layer-by-layer addition of material)
d inkrementelle Formation *f*
f formation *f* incrémentale
r инкрементальное образование *n*

5023 incremental vector
d Inkrementalvektor *m*
f vecteur *m* d'incrément
r вектор *m* приращения

5024 incrustation
d Inkrustation *f*
f incrustation *f*
r врезание *n*

5025 incrustation of image
d Bildinkrustation *f*
f incrustation *f* d'image
r врезание *n* изображения

5026 incrustation of text
d Text-Inkrustation *f*
f incrustation *f* de texte
r врезание *n* текста

* **in-cushion distortion** → 7075

* **indefinite** → 9980

5027 indent
d Einzug *m*
f retrait *m*
r отступ *m*

5028 indentation; indenting
d Einbuchtung *f*; Einkerbung *f*; Einrückung *f*
f décrochement *m*
r отступление *n*; формирование *n* отступа

* **indenting** → 5028

* **independent variable of a function** → 558

5029 indeterminacy; non-determination; undetermination
d Unbestimmtheit *f*; Indeterminiertheit *f*
f indétermination *f*; non-détermination *f*
r неопределенность *f*

5030 index
d Index *m*
f index *m*; indice *m*
r индекс *m*; показатель *m*

5031 indexed color images
d indizierte Farbbilder *npl*
f images *fpl* à couleurs indexées
r индексированные цветные изображения *npl*

5032 indexed colors
d indizierte Farben *fpl*
f couleurs *f* indexées
r индексированные цвета *mpl*

5033 indexing
d Indizieren *n*; Indizierung *f*; Indexierung *f*
f indexage *m*; indexation *f*
r индексация *f*; индексирование *n*

5034 index notation
d Indexbezeichnung *f*; Indexschreibweise *f*
f notation *f* indicielle; écriture *f* indicielle
r индексное обозначение *n*; индексная запись *f*

5035 indication; display
d Indikation *f*; Anzeige *f*; Anzeichen *n*
f indication *f*; affichage *m*
r индикация *f*; показание *n*

5036 indication error
d Anzeigefehler *m*
f erreur *f* d'indication
r ошибка *f* индикации

5037 indicator

d Anzeiger *m*; Indikator *m*
f indicateur *m*
r индикатор *m*; указатель *m*

5038 indirect
d indirekt
f indirect
r косвенный; непрямой

5039 indirect illumination; indirect lighting
d indirekte Beleuchtung *f*
f illumination *f* indirecte; éclairage *m* indirect
r индиректная иллюминация *f*; индиректное освещение *n*

* **indirect lighting** → 5039

5040 indirect scanning
d undirekte Abtastung *f*
f balayage *m* indirect
r индиректное сканирование *n*

5041 individual logo
d individuelles Logo *n*
f logo *m* individuel
r индивидуальное лого *n*

5042 individual selection
d individuelle Selektion *f*
f sélection *f* individuelle
r индивидуальный выбор *m*

5043 indivisibility
d Unteilbarkeit *f*
f indivisibilité *f*
r неделимость *f*

5044 indivisible
d unteilbar
f non divisible; indivisible
r не[раз]делимый

5045 indivisible element
d unteilbares Element *n*
f élément *m* non divisible
r неделимый элемент *m*

* **inductive cone** → 5576

5046 inequality
d Ungleichung *f*
f inéquation *f*; inégalité *f*
r неравенство *n*

5047 inequality sign
d Ungleichheitszeichen *n*
f signe *m* d'inégalité
r знак *m* неравенства

5048 inertia
d Trägheit *f*

  f inertie *f*
  r инерция *f*

5049 inessential; irrelevant
  d unwesentlich
  f insignifiant; non essentiel; sans importance
  r несущественный

  * **inexact → 4968**

5050 inexact dimension
  d inexakte Dimension *f*
  f dimension *f* inexacte
  r неточное измерение *n*

  * **inexactitude → 4979**

5051 infinite; endless
  d unendlich
  f infini; sans fin
  r бесконечный

5052 infinite detail
  (of a fractal)
  d unendliches Detail *n*
  f détail *m* infini
  r бесконечная деталь *f*

  * **infinite element → 3347**

5053 infinite line; constructive line
  d unendliche Linie *f*
  f ligne *f* infinie
  r бесконечная линия *f*

  * **infinite line → 5629**

  * **infinitely distant point → 7208**

  * **infinite plane → 7142**

  * **infinite point → 7208**

5054 infinite structures
  d unendliche Strukturen *fpl*
  f structures *fpl* infinies
  r бесконечные структуры *fpl*

5055 inflate *v* bitmap
  d Bitmap vergrößern
  f hausser un bitmap
  r надувать растровое изображение;
   увеличивать растровое изображение

5056 inflexion; flex
  d Inflexion *f*; Wendung *f*
  f inflexion *f*
  r инфлексия *f*; перегиб *m*

  * **inflexion point → 7218**

  * **influence zone → 10519**

5057 in focus
  d im Fokus; im Brennpunkt
  f au point
  r в фокусе

  * **infography → 1981**

5058 information
  d Information *f*
  f information *f*
  r информация *f*

5059 information density
  d Informationsflussdichte *f*; Datendurchsatz *m*
  f densité *f* du flux d'information
  r интенсивность *f* потока информации

5060 information representation
  d Informationsdarstellung *f*
  f représentation *f* d'information
  r представление *n* информации

5061 information structure; data structure
  d Informationsstruktur *f*; Datenstruktur *f*
  f structure *f* d'information; structure de données
  r структура *f* информации; структура
   данных

5062 information technology
  d Informationstechnologie *f*
  f technologie *f* [de traitement] d'information
  r информационная технология *f*; технология
   обработки информации

5063 information visualization
  d Information-Visualisierung *f*
  f visualisation *f* d'information
  r визуализация *f* информации

5064 infrared; IR
  d Infrarot *n*; IR
  f infrarouge *m*
  r инфракрасный диапазон *m*;
   ИК-диапазон *m*

5065 infrared; IR *adj*
  d Infrarot-; IR-
  f infrarouge
  r инфракрасный; ИК-

5066 infrared image
  d Infrarotbild *n*
  f image *f* infrarouge
  r инфракрасное изображение *n*

5067 infrared response
  d Infrarotempfindlichkeit *f*

f réponse *f* dans l'infrarouge
r чувствительность *f* к инфракрасному
излучению

5068 infrared spectrum
d Infrarotspektrum *n*
f spectre *m* infrarouge
r инфракрасный спектр *m*; ИК-спектр *m*

5069 inherent; inherited
d mitgeschleppt
f inhérent; entraîné; hérité
r исходный; привнесенный

5070 inheritance
d Vererbung *f*; Erbe *n*; Erbschaft *f*
f héritage *m*
r наследование *n*

* **inherited** → 5069

* **inhibit** → 5072

5071 inhibit *v*; **disable** *v*; **disarm** *v*
d sperren; verhindern; unwirksam machen
f inhiber; désactiver
r запрещать; предотвращать

5072 inhibit[ion]; disable
d Inhibition *f*; Verhinderung *f*; Sperrung *f*;
Sperre *f*
f inhibition *f*; interdiction *f*; invalidation *f*
r запрещение *n*; запрет *m*

5073 inhomogeneity
d Inhomogenität *f*
f non-homogénéité *f*
r неоднородность *f*

* **inhomogeneous** → 4580

5074 initial
d Anfangs-
f initial
r начальный

5075 initial coordinates
d Anfangskoordinaten *fpl*
f coordonnées *fpl* initiales
r начальные координаты *fpl*

5076 initialization; initializing
d Initialisierung *f*; Initialisieren *n*; Einleiten *n*
f initialisation *f*
r инициализация *f*; задание *n* начальных
условий

* **initializing** → 5076

* **initial object** → 9161

5077 initial point
d Anfangspunkt *m*
f point *m* initial
r начальная точка *f*

5078 initial segment
d Anfangssegment *n*
f segment *m* initial
r начальный сегмент *m*

5079 initial symbol
d Anfangssymbol *n*
f symbole *m* initial
r начальный символ *m*

* **initiate** *v* → 6631

5080 injection
d Einspritzung *f*
f injection *f*
r впрыск *m*

5081 injection; injective map
d Injektion *f*; injektive Abbildung *f*
f injection *f*; application *f* injective
r инъекция *f*; инъективное отображение *n*

* **injective map** → 5081

5082 ink
d Tinte *f*
f encre *f*
r чернило *n*; печатная краска *f*

5083 ink color
d Tintenfarbe *f*
f couleur *f* d'encre
r цвет *m* чернила

5084 inker
d Farbwerk *n*
f mécanisme *m* d'encrage
r красящий механизм *m*

5085 ink fountain
d Füllreservoir *n*; Farbreservoir *n*
f fontaine *f* d'encre
r источник *m* краски; резервуар *m* краски

5086 inking
d Einfärbung *f*; Inking *n*
f encrage *m*
r намазывание *n* чернилами

**5087 ink-jet printer; bubble-jet printer;
inkwriter**
d Tintenstrahldrucker *m*;
Bubble-Jet-Drucker *m*; Tintenprinter *m*

f imprimante *f* à jet d'encre; imprimante à bulle d'encre
r струйное печатающее устройство *n*; струйный принтер *m*

5088 ink-pot; ink-well
(of ink-jet printer)
d Tintenfass *n*; Farb[en]topf *m*
f encrier *m*
r чернильница *f*

5089 ink ribbon; ribbon
d Farbband *n*
f ruban *m* encreur; ruban d'encrage
r цветная лента *f*; красящая лента; копировальная лента

* **ink-well** → 5088

* **inkwriter** → 5087

5090 inline *adj*
d mitlaufend; schritthaltend
f du même pas; concurrent
r линейный; поточный; сопровождающий

5091 inline; aligned *adj*
d ausgerichtet; Inline-; in einer Linie
f aligné; en série
r выровненный; на одной линии

5092 inline image
d Inline-Bild *n*
f image *f* alignée
r выровненное изображение *n*

* **inner** *adj* → 5186

5093 inner arc
d innerer Bogen *m*
f arc *m* intérieur
r внутренняя дуга *f*

* **inner component** → 5192

5094 inner grid; interior grid
d inneres Gitter *n*
f grille *f* intérieure; première grille
r внутренняя сетка *f*

5095 inner loop
d innere Schleife *f*
f boucle *f* intérieure; boucle mineure
r внутренняя петля *f*

* **inner normal** → 5196

* **inner point** → 5215

5096 inner ring

d innerer Ring *m*; Innerring *m*
f anneau *m* inférieur
r внутреннее кольцо *n*

* **in pairs** → 6754

5097 in-plane
d innerhalb der Ebene
f dans le plan; en plan
r в плоскости

5098 input; entry
d Eingang *m*; Eingabe *f*
f entrée *f*; introduction *f*
r вход *m*; ввод *m*

5099 input data
d Eingabedaten *npl*
f données *fpl* d'entrée
r входные данные *npl*

5100 input light
d Eingangslicht *n*
f lumière *f* d'entrée
r входной свет *m*

5101 input/output; I/O
d Eingabe-Ausgabe *f*; E/A
f entrée-sortie *f*; E/S
r ввод-вывод *m*

5102 input primitive
d Eingabeprimitiv *n*
f primitive *f* d'entrée
r входной примитив *m*

* **inquiry** → 8083

5103 inquiry method
d Abfragemethode *f*
f méthode *f* d'interrogation
r метод *m* запроса

5104 inquiry submenu
d Abfrageuntermenü *n*
f sous-menu *m* d'interrogation
r подменю *n* запроса

5105 inquiry toolbar
d Abfragewerkzeugstreifen *m*
f barre *f* d'outils d'interrogation
r панель *f* инструментов запроса

* **inradius** → 7723, 7724

5106 inscribe *v*
d einschreiben
f inscrire
r вписать

5107 inscribed angle; angle at a circumference
  d einbeschriebener Winkel *m*;
      Umfangswinkel *m*; Peripherienwinkel *m*
  f angle *m* inscrit
  r вписанный угол *m*

5108 inscribed circle; incircle
  d einbeschriebener Kreis *m*; Inkreis *m*
  f cercle *m* inscrit; circonférence *f* inscrite
  r вписанная окружность *f*

5109 inscribed figure
  d einbeschriebene Figur *f*
  f figure *f* inscrite
  r вписанная фигура *f*

5110 inscribed polygon
  d einbeschriebenes Polygon *n*
  f polygone *m* inscrit
  r вписанный многоугольник *m*

5111 inscribed polyhedral
  d einbeschriebenes Polyeder *n*
  f polyèdre *m* inscrit
  r вписанный полиэдр *m*

5112 inscribed quadrangle; inscribed quadrilateral
  d einbeschriebenes Viereck *n*
  f quadrilatère *m* inscrit
  r вписанный четырехугольник *m*

  * **inscribed quadrilateral → 5112**

5113 inscribed sphere; insphere
  d Inkugel *f*
  f sphère *f* inscrite
  r вписанная сфера *f*

5114 inscribed triangle
  d einbeschriebenes Dreieck *n*
  f triangle *m* inscrit
  r вписанный треугольник *m*

5115 insensitiveness
  d Unempfindlichkeit *f*
  f insensibilité *f*
  r нечувствительность *f*

5116 insert *v*; inset *v*; paste *v*
  d einfügen; einschieben
  f insérer; imbriquer
  r вставлять; включать; вкладывать

5117 insert command
  d Einfügungsbefehl *m*; Einfügebefehl *m*
  f commande *f* d'insertion
  r команда *f* вставки; команда включения

  * **inserting → 5118**

5118 insertion; inserting
  d Einsetzen *n*; Einschiebung *f*
  f insertion *f*
  r вставка *f*; вставление *n*

5119 insertion loop
  d Einfügungsschleife *f*
  f boucle *f* d'insertion
  r петля *f* вставки

5120 insertion mode
  d Einfügungsmodus *m*
  f mode *m* d'insertion
  r режим *m* вставки

5121 insertion of text; text insertion
  d Texteinfügung *f*
  f saisie *f* de texte
  r вставка *f* текста

5122 insertion of toolbar
  d Hilfsmittelleiste-Einfügung *f*
  f insertion *f* de barre d'outils
  r вставка *f* панели инструментов

5123 insertion point
  d Einfügungspunkt *m*; Einfügemarke *f*
  f point *m* d'insertion
  r точка *f* вставки; место *n* ввода; позиция *f* ввода

5124 insertion snap
  d Einfügungsfang *m*
  f accrochage *m* d'insertion
  r привязка *f* вставки

5125 Insert key; Ins key
  d Einfügetaste *f*
  f touche *f* d'insertion
  r клавиша *f* Ins

5126 insert *v* new object
  d neues Objekt einfügen
  f insérer un objet neuf
  r вставлять новый объект

5127 insert *v* page
  d Seite einfügen
  f insérer une page
  r вставлять страницу

  * **inset *v* → 5116**

5128 inside boundary
  d innere Grenze *f*; innerhalbe Grenze
  f limite *f* intérieure; limite interne
  r внутренняя граница *f*

5129 inside diameter
  d innerer Durchmesser *m*;
      Innendurchmesser *m*

f diamètre *m* intérieur
r внутренний диаметр *m*

* **Ins key** → 5125

5130 insolubility; undecidability
   d Unlösbarkeit *f*
   f insolubilité *f*
   r неразрешимость *f*

5131 inspection
   d Inspektion *f*
   f inspection *f*
   r инспектирование *n*

* **insphere** → 5113

5132 instable; astable; unstable
   d instabil; unbeständig
   f instable; astable
   r неустойчивый; нестабильный

5133 install *v*
   d einbauen; installieren; aufstellen; montieren
   f installer; monter
   r размещать; располагать; монтировать

5134 installation
   d Anlage *f*; Installierung *f*; Montage *f*
   f installation *f*; montage *m*
   r установка *f*; монтаж *m*

5135 installation component
   d Anlage-Komponente *f*
   f composant *m* d'installation
   r компонента *f* размещения

* **instant** → 6020

* **instantaneous** → 4944

* **in-step** → 9427

* **instruction** → 1877

* **integer** → 5136

5136 integer [value]
   d Ganzwert *m*
   f valeur *f* entière
   r целочисленное значение *n*

5137 integer-valued
   d ganzzahlig; ganzwertig
   f entier; à valeur entière
   r целочисленный; целый

* **integral** *adj* → 3450

5138 integral; integrated
   d integriert; Integral-
   f intégré
   r интегрированный; интегральный

5139 integral curve
   d Integralkurve *f*
   f courbe *f* intégrale
   r интегральная кривая *f*

5140 integral surface
   d Integralfläche *f*
   f surface *f* intégrale
   r интегральная поверхность *f*

* **integrated** → 5138

5141 integrated development environment; IDE
   d integrierte Entwicklungsumgebung *f*
   f environnement *m* de développement intégré
   r интегрированная среда *f* разработки

5142 integrated optics
   d integrierte Optik *f*
   f optique *f* intégrée
   r интегральная оптика *f*

5143 integrated resources
   d integrierte Ressourcen *fpl*
   f ressources *fpl* intégrées
   r интегрированные ресурсы *mpl*

5144 integrating sphere
   d Integrationskugel *f*
   f sphère *f* d'intégration
   r интегрирующая сфера *f*

5145 integrity
   d Ganzheit *f*; Integrität *f*
   f intégrité *f*
   r целостность *f*; сохранность *f*

5146 intelligent; smart
   d intelligent
   f intelligent
   r интеллигентный; интеллектуальный

5147 intelligent vision system
   d intelligentes Sehsystem *n*
   f système *m* de vision intelligent
   r интеллигентная система *f* визуального отображения

5148 intense
   d intensiv; stark; hell
   f intense; intensif
   r сильный; интенсивный

5149 intense color
  d intensive Farbe *f*; helle Farbe
  f couleur *f* intense; couleur intensive
  r сильный цвет *m*; интенсивный цвет

5150 intension
  d Intension *f*
  f intension *f*
  r напряженность *f*; интенсия *f*

5151 intensity
  d Intensität *f*
  f intensité *f*
  r интенсивность *f*

5152 intensity fluctuation
  d Intensitätsschwankung *f*
  f fluctuation *f* d'intensité
  r колебание *n* интенсивности

5153 intensity maximum
  d Intensitätsmaximum *n*
  f maximum *m* d'intensité
  r максимум *m* интенсивности

5154 intensity resolution
  d Intensitätsauflösung *f*
  f résolution *f* d'intensité
  r разрешение *n* интенситета

5155 interact *v*
  d zusammenwirken; wechselwirken
  f interagir; collaborer; dialoguer
  r взаимодействовать

  * interacting → 5156

5156 interaction; interacting
  d interaktiver Betrieb *m*; Wechselwirkung *f*;
     Zusammenarbeit *f*
  f interaction *f*; coopération *f*; dialogue *m*
  r взаимодействие *n*; диалог *m*; взаимосвязь *f*

5157 interactive
  d interaktiv
  f interactif
  r интерактивный; диалоговый

5158 interactive blend tool
  d Hilfsmittel *n* "interaktive Überblendung"
  f outil *m* "dégradé interactif"
  r инструмент *m* интерактивного
     переливания

5159 interactive computer game
  d interaktives Computerspiel *n*
  f jeu *m* d'ordinateur interactif
  r интерактивная компьютерная игра *f*

5160 interactive digitizing

  d interaktive Digitalisierung *f*
  f numérisation *f* interactive
  r диалоговое дигитализирование *n*

5161 interactive display
  d interaktiver Bildschirm *m*
  f afficheur *m* interactif
  r интерактивный дисплей *m*

5162 interactive extrusion
  d interaktive Extrudierung *f*
  f extrusion *f* interactive
  r интерактивная экструзия *f*

5163 interactive extrusion tool
  d Werkzeug *m* der interaktiven Extrudierung
  f outil *m* d'extrusion interactive
  r инструмент *m* диалогового
     экструдирования

5164 interactive fill color
  d interaktive Füll[ungs]farbe *f*
  f couleur *f* de remplissage interactif
  r цвет *m* интерактивного закрашивания

5165 interactive filling
  d interaktive Füllung *f*
  f remplissage *m* interactif
  r интерактивное закрашивание *n*

  * interactive graphics → 1543

5166 interactive image processing
  d interaktive Bildverarbeitung *f*
  f traitement *m* interactif d'images
  r диалоговая обработка *f* изображений

  * interactive mode → 2698

5167 interactive models write-on
  d interaktive Registrierung *f* der Modelle
  f écriture *f* interactive de modèles
  r интерактивная запись *f* модел

5168 interactive presentation
  d interaktive Präsentation *f*
  f présentation *f* interactive
  r диалоговое представление *n*

5169 interactive transparency tool
  d Hilfsmittel *n* "interaktive Transparenz"
  f outil *m* "transparence interactive"
  r инструмент *m* интерактивной
     прозрачности

5170 interactive visual browser
  d interaktiver visueller Browser *m*
  f butineur *m* visuel interactif
  r интерактивный визуальный браузер *m*

5171 interactive visualization
  d interaktive Visualisierung *f*
  f visualisation *f* interactive
  r диалоговая визуализация *f*

  * **intercadre reference** → 5183

5172 intercept
  d Abschnitt *m*; Achsenabschnitt *m*
  f intercepte *m*; segment *m*
  r отрезок *m* [отсекаемый с оси]

  * **interchange** → 3565

  * **interchangeability** → 3566

  * **inter-character space** → 1434

5173 interface
  d Interface *n*; Schnittstelle *f*;
    Anschlussbedingungen *fpl*
  f interface *f*; jonction *f*
  r интерфейс *m*; сопряжение *n*

5174 interface
  (as a surface)
  d Zwischenfläche *f*
  f interface *f*
  r промежуточная поверхность *f*

5175 interfere *v*
  d beeinflussen; beeinträchtigen
  f interférer
  r интерферировать; вмешиваться

5176 interference
  d Interferenz *f*
  f interférence *f*
  r интерференция *f*

  * **interference pattern** → 6019

5177 interference pattern
  d Interferenzmuster *n*; Interferenzbild *n*
  f figure *f* d'interférence
  r интерференционная картина *f*

5178 interferogram
  d Interferogramm *n*
  f interférogramme *m*
  r интерферограмма *f*

5179 interferometer
  d Interferometer *n*
  f interféromètre *m*
  r интерферометр *m*

5180 interferometry
  d Interferometrie *f*
  f interférométrie *f*

  r интерферометрия *f*

5181 interframe compression
  d Zwischenrahmenkompression *f*
  f compression *f* de trames intermédiaires
  r сжатие *n* путем удаления избыточных
    данных с учетом межкадровых переходов

5182 interframe operation
  d Zwischenrahmenoperation *f*
  f opération *f* de trames intermédiaires
  r межкадровая операция *f*

5183 interframe reference; intercadre reference
  d Zwischenrahmenverweis *m*
  f référence *f* entre trames
  r межкадровая ссылка *f*

  * **interframes** → 5208

5184 interframe time fill
  d Füllung *f* der Zeitintervalle der
    Zwischenrahmen
  f temporisation *f* entre trames; remplissage *m*
    de l'intervalle de temps entre les trames
  r заполнение *n* времени межкадровых
    переходах

5185 interior
  d Innere *n*
  f intérieur *m*
  r внутренность *f*

5186 interior; internal; inner *adj*
  d innere; Innen-
  f interne; intérieur
  r внутренний

  * **interior alternate angles** → 297

5187 interior angle
  d innerer Winkel *m*; Innenwinkel *m*
  f angle *m* intérieur
  r внутренний угол *m*

**5188 interior angles of the same side of a
    transversal**
  d innere Winkel *mpl*, die auf derselben Seite
    einer Transversalen liegen
  f angles *mpl* co-internes; angles intérieurs du
    même côté de la sécante
  r внутренние односторонние углы *mpl*

5189 interior area; interior domain
  d innerer Bereich *m*; Innengebiet *n*
  f domaine *m* intérieur; zone *f* intérieure
  r внутренняя область *f*; внутренняя зона *f*

5190 interior bisector; interior bisectrix
  d innere Winkelhalbierende *f*;
    Innenwinkelhalbierende *f*

f bissectrice *f* intérieure
r биссектриса *f* внутреннего угла

* **interior bisectrix** → **5190**

5191 interior clipping
　d inneres Schneiden *n*
　f découpage *m* intérieur
　r внутреннее отсекание *n*

5192 interior component; inner component
　d innere Komponente *f*
　f composante *f* intérieure
　r внутренняя компонента *f*

* **interior domain** → **5189**

5193 interior edge
　d innere Kante *f*
　f arête *f* intérieure
　r внутреннее ребро *n*

* **interior grid** → **5094**

5194 interior map
　d innere Abbildung *f*
　f application *f* intérieure
　r внутреннее отображение *n*

5195 interior node; nonterminal node
　d innerer Knoten *m*
　f nœud *m* intérieur
　r внутренний узел *m*

5196 interior normal; inner normal
　d innere Normale *f*; Innennormale *f*
　f normale *f* intérieure
　r внутренняя нормаль *f*

* **interior point** → **5215**

5197 interior vertex
　d innere Spitze *f*
　f sommet *m* intérieur
　r внутренняя вершина *f*

5198 interlace *v*
　d [sich] verflechten; [sich] verschlingen; [sich] verweben
　f entrelacer; alterner
　r чередовать[ся]; переплетать[ся]; сплетать[ся]

5199 interlaced curves
　d verschlungene Kurven *fpl*
　f courbes *fpl* [mutuellement] entrelacées
　r зацепленные кривые *fpl*

* **interlaced image** → **5201**

5200 interlaced scanning
　d Zeilensprungabtastung *f*
　f balayage *m* entrelacé; balayage intercalé; balayage interligne; interlignage *m*
　r презредовая развертка *f*; презредовое сканирование *n*

5201 interlaced [video]image
　d verschlungenes Videobild *n*
　f image *f* entrelacée
　r зацепленное видеоизображение *n*

5202 interlace line
　d Verschlingungslinie *f*; Zwischenzeile *f*
　f ligne *f* d'entrelacement
　r линия *f* переплетения

5203 interlacing; intertwining; cross interlacing
　d Verschlingung *f*; Verschränkung *f*
　f entrelacement *m*; enlacement *m*; entrelaçage *m*
　r переплетение *n*; сплетение *n*; зацепление *n*; скрещивание *n*

* **interlayer connection** → **9659**

5204 interleaving
　d Abwechseln *n*; Verzahnung *f*
　f alternance *f*; imbrication *f*
　r чередование *n*

* **interline** → **5205**

5205 interline [spacing]; line[-to-line] spacing; vertical line spacing; row pitch
　d Zeilenabstand *m*; Abstand *m* zwischen den Zeilen; Vertikalzeilenschaltung *f*
　f espace[ment] *m* entre lignes; interligne *f*
　r междурядье *n*; интервал *m* между строками; интерлиньяж *m*

5206 intermediate
　d Zwischen-
　f intermédiaire
　r промежуточный

5207 intermediate color
　d Zwischenfarbe *f*
　f couleur *f* intermédiaire
　r промежуточный цвет *m*

5208 intermediate frames; interframes
　d Zwischenrahmen *mpl*
　f cadres *mpl* intermédiaires
　r промежуточные кадры *mpl*; межкадровые переходы *mpl*

5209 intermediate layer
　d Zwischenschicht *f*

f couche *f* intermédiaire
r промежуточный слой *m*

5210 intermediate link
d Zwischenlink *n*
f lien *m* intermédiaire
r промежуточная связь *f*

5211 intermediate node
d Zwischenknoten *m*
f nœud *m* intermédiaire
r промежуточный узел *m*

5212 intermediate objects
d Zwischenobjekte *npl*
f objets *mpl* intermédiaires
r промежуточные объекты *mpl*

5213 intermediate shape
d Zwischenform *f*
f forme *f* intermédiaire
r промежуточная фигура *f*

* **internal** → 5186

5214 internal line
d interne Linie *f*; innere Linie; Innenlinie *f*
f ligne *f* interne
r внутренняя линия *f*

5215 internal point; interior point; inner point
d interner Punkt *m*; innerer Punkt; Innenpunkt *m*
f point *m* intérieur
r внутренняя точка *f*

5216 internal reflection
d interne Reflexion *f*
f réflexion *f* interne
r внутреннее отражение *n*

5217 internal reflector
d interner Reflektor *m*
f réflecteur *m* interne
r внутренний отражатель *m*

5218 internal tangency
d innere Berührung *f*
f tangence *f* intérieure
r внутреннее касание *n*

5219 internal tangent
d innere Tangente *f*; Innentangente *f*
f tangente *f* intérieure
r внутренняя касательная *f*

5220 international settings
d internationale Einrichtungen *fpl*
f paramètres *mpl* internationaux
r международные приложения *npl*

5221 Internet graphics
d Internet-Grafik *f*
f graphique *m* Internet
r Интернет-графика *f*

5222 Internet objects toolbar
d Internet-Objekte-Symbolleiste *f*
f barre *f* d'outils d'objets Internet
r инструментальная панель *f* Интернет-объектов

5223 inter-paragraph spacing
d Absatzabstand *m*
f espace[ment] *m* entre paragraphes
r расстояние *n* между параграфами

5224 interplanar spacing
d Abstand *m* zwischen den Ebenen
f distance *f* entre plans
r расстояние *n* между плоскостями

5225 interpolate *v*
d interpolieren
f interpoler
r интерполировать

5226 interpolated animation
d interpolierte Animation *f*
f animation *f* interpolée
r интерполированная анимация *f*

5227 interpolating function
d Interpolationsfunktion *f*
f fonction *f* d'interpolation
r интерполирующая функция *f*

5228 interpolation
d Interpolation *f*
f interpolation *f*
r интерполяция *f*

5229 interpolation error
d Interpolationsfehler *m*
f erreur *f* d'interpolation
r ошибка *f* интерполяции

* **interpolation fill** → 5230

5230 interpolation fill[ing]
d Interpolationsfüllung *f*
f remplissage *m* interpolé
r интерполяционное заполнение *n*

5231 interpolation formula
d Interpolationsformel *f*
f formule *f* d'interpolation
r формула *f* интерполяции

5232 interpolation method
d Interpolationsverfahren *n*

f méthode *f* d'interpolation
r интерполяционный метод *m*

5233 interpolation node
  d Interpolationsknoten *m*; Stützstelle *f* [der Interpolation]; Stützpunkt *m*
  f nœud *m* d'interpolation
  r узел *m* интерполяции; полюс *m* интерполяции

5234 interpolation of a function
  d Interpolation *f* einer Funktion
  f interpolation *f* d'une fonction
  r интерполяция *f* функции

5235 interpolation polynomial
  d Interpolationspolynom *n*
  f polynôme *m* d'interpolation
  r интерполяционный многочлен *m*

5236 interpolation problem
  d Interpolationsaufgabe *f*; Interpolationsproblem *n*
  f problème *m* d'interpolation
  r интерполяционная задача *f*

5237 interpolation series
  d Interpolationsreihe *f*
  f série *f* d'interpolation
  r интерполяционный ряд *m*

  * **interpolation spline** → 5238

5238 interpolation spline [function]
  d interpolierende Spline-Funktion *f*; Interpolationsspline *m*
  f fonction *f* spline d'interpolation; spline *m* d'interpolation
  r интерполяционный сплайн *m*

5239 interpret *v*
  d interpretieren; deuten
  f interpréter
  r толковать; интерпретировать

5240 interpretation
  d Interpretation *f*; Deutung *f*
  f interprétation *f*
  r интерпретация *f*; истолкование *n*; толкование *n*

5241 interpreter
  d Interpret[ier]er *m*
  f interpré[ta]teur *m*
  r интерпретатор *m*; выполнитель *m*

  * **interrogate *v*** → 7268

  * **interrogation** → 8083

  * **interrupt *v*** → 1129

  * **interruption** → 1130

5242 intersect *v*
  d durchschneiden; kreuzen
  f croiser
  r пересекать

5243 intersect command
  d unterbrechender Befehl *m*
  f commande *f* d'intersection
  r команда *f* пересечения

  * **intersecting circles** → 8416

5244 intersecting faces
  d durchschneidende Flächen *fpl*
  f faces *fpl* sécantes
  r пересекающиеся грани *fpl*

  * **intersecting line** → 9857

  * **intersecting lines** → 2022

5245 intersecting objects
  d sich schneidende Objekte *npl*
  f objets *mpl* sécants; objets en intersection
  r пересекающиеся объекты *mpl*

  * **intersecting plane** → 7146

  * **intersecting planes** → 2416

  * **intersecting surface** → 9369

5246 intersection; crossing
  d Durchschnitt *m*
  f intersection *f*
  r пересечение *n*

  * **intersection angle** → 2311

  * **intersection curve** → 2379

  * **intersection line** → 2379

5247 intersection of a family of sets
  d Durchschnitt *m* einer Mengenfamilie; Durchschnitt eines Mengensystems
  f intersection *f* d'une famille d'ensembles
  r пересечение *n* семейства множеств

5248 intersection of circles
  d Durchschnitt *m* der Kreise
  f intersection *f* de cercles
  r пересечение *n* окружностей

5249 intersection of half-planes
  d Durchschnitt *m* der Halbebenen

ƒ intersection ƒ de demi-plans
r пересечение n полуплоскостей

5250 intersection of line segments
d Durchschnitt m der Liniensegmente
ƒ intersection ƒ de segments d'une ligne
r пересечение n сегментов линии

5251 intersection of two lines
d Durchschnitt m zweier Geraden
ƒ intersection ƒ de deux droites
r пересечение n двух прямых

5252 intersection point; cross-point
d Durchschnittspunkt m
ƒ point m d'intersection; point de concours
r точка ƒ пересечения

5253 intersection snap
d Durchschnittsfang m
ƒ accrochage m vers intersection
r привязка ƒ к пересечениию

5254 intersections of unfinished surfaces
d Durchschnitte mpl unendlicher Flächen
ƒ intersections fpl de surfaces infinies
r пересечения npl бесконечных
поверхностей

* **intertwining** → **5203**

5255 interval; space
(in a text)
d Intervall n
ƒ intervalle m
r интервал m; пропуск m; пробел m

5256 interwindow linking
d Verknüpfung ƒ der Fenster
ƒ liaison ƒ entre fenêtres
r связь ƒ между окнами

5257 intrinsic
d intrinsisch; wesentlich
ƒ intrinsèque
r собственный; внутренний; существенный

5258 intrinsic curvature
d intrinsische Krümmung ƒ
ƒ courbure ƒ intrinsèque
r внутренняя кривизна ƒ

5259 intrinsic geometry
d intrinsische Geometrie ƒ
ƒ géométrie ƒ intrinsèque
r внутренняя геометрия ƒ

* **introduce** v → **3446**

5260 invalid; illegal

d ungültig; unzulässig; illegal; unerlaubt
ƒ invalide; non valable; illégal
r недействительный; неверный;
недопустимый

5261 invalid image
d ungültiges Bild n
ƒ image ƒ non valable
r недействительное изображение n

5262 invariance
d Invarianz ƒ; Unveränderlichkeit ƒ
ƒ invariance ƒ
r инвариантность ƒ

* **inverse** adj → **8123**

* **inversed** adj → **8123**

5263 inverse filtering
d inverse Filtrierung ƒ
ƒ filtrage m inverse
r инверсное фильтрирование n

* **inverse image** → **8124**

5264 inverse linear attenuation
(of light)
d inverse Lineardämpfung ƒ
ƒ atténuation ƒ linéaire inverse
r инверсное линейное затухание n

* **inverse map** → **5265**

5265 inverse map[ping]
d inverse Abbildung ƒ; Umkehrabbildung ƒ
ƒ application ƒ inverse
r обратное отображение n

5266 inverse matrix
d inverse Matrix ƒ
ƒ matrice ƒ inverse
r инверсная матрица ƒ

5267 inverse point
d inverser Punkt m
ƒ point m inverse
r инверсная точка ƒ

5268 inverse square attenuation
(of light)
d inverse Quadratdämpfung ƒ
ƒ atténuation ƒ inverse quadratique
r инверсное квадратичное затухание n

5269 inverse video; reverse video
d inverse Bildschirmdarstellung ƒ; inverses
Video n
ƒ affichage m en négatif; vidéo m inverse
r инверсное видеоизображение n

* inversion → 8129

5270 inversion layer
 d inverse Schicht f
 f couche f d'inversion; couche inverse
 r инверсный слой m

* invert v → 8121

* inverted image → 8124

5271 inverted lens; reversed lens
 d umgekehrte Linse f
 f lentille f renversée
 r перевернутая линза f

* inverted picture → 8124

5272 invisible; nonvisible
 d unsichtbar
 f invisible; non visible
 r невидимый

* invisible line → 4600

5273 invisible object
 d unsichtbares Objekt n
 f objet m invisible
 r невидимый объект m

5274 invisible point
 d unsichtbarer Punkt m
 f point m invisible
 r невидимая точка f

* invisible surface → 4606

* invoke v → 1223

* involute → 3552

* involute of a curve → 3553

* involute of a plane curve → 3553

5275 involution net
 d Involutionsnetz n
 f réseau m d'involution
 r инволюционная сеть f

5276 involutory correspondence
 d involutorische Entsprechung f
 f correspondance f involutive
 r инволютивное соответствие n

5277 involutory homology
 d involutorische Perspektive f
 f perspective f involutive
 r инволютивная гомология f; инволютивная
    перспектива f

* I/O → 5101

5278 I/O port
 d Eingabe-Ausgabe-Port m
 f port m d'entrée-sortie
 r порт m ввода-вывода

* IR adj → 5065

* IR → 5064

5279 irradiance
 d Bestrahlungsstärke f; Beleuchtungsdichte f
 f irradiance f; densité f d'éclairement
 r облученность f; плотность f освещения

5280 irradiance distribution function
 d Verteilungsfunktion f der Beleuchtungsdichte
 f fonction f de distribution d'irradiance
 r функция f распределения облученности

5281 irradiance volume
 d Bestrahlungsstärke-Volumen n
 f volume m d'irradiance
 r объем m облученности

5282 irradiation
 d Bestrahlung f; Einstrahlung f
 f irradiation f
 r облучение n

5283 irrecoverable
 d unverbesserlich; irreparabel
 f irrémédiable; irréparable
 r неисправимый

5284 irrecoverable error
 d unverbesserlicher Fehler m
 f erreur f irrémédiable; erreur irréparable
 r неисправимая ошибка f

5285 irregular
 d unregelmäßig; irregulär
 f irrégulier
 r неправильный; неравномерный;
    нерегулярный

5286 irregular curve
 d unregelmäßige Kurve f
 f courbe f irrégulière
 r нерегулярная кривая f

5287 irregularity
 d Unregelmäßigkeit f; Regellosigkeit f
 f irrégularité f
 r нерегулярность f; неправильность f;
    неравномерность f

5288 irregular polygon
 d unregelmäßiges Polygon n

f polygone *m* irrégulier
r неправильный многоугольник *m*

* **irrelevant** → 5049

5289 irreversible
d irreversibel; nichtumkehrbar
f irréversible
r необратимый

5290 irreversible transformation
d irreversibele Transformation *f*
f transformation *f* irréversible
r необратимая трансформация *f*

5291 irrotational; circular-free
d wirbelfrei
f irrotationnel
r безвихревой

5292 irrotational flow
d wirbelfreie Strömung *f*; Potentialströmung *f*
f écoulement *m* irrotationnel
r безвихревое течение *n*; потенциальное течение

5293 irrotational motion; vortex-free motion
d wirbelfreie Bewegung *f*
f mouvement *m* irrotationnel
r безвихревое движение *n*

5294 island
d Insel *f*
f île *f*
r островок *m*; изолированный участок *m*

5295 island *v*
d isolieren; eine Insel erstellen
f isoler
r изолировать

5296 island detection
d Insel-Detektion *f*; Insel-Erkennung *f*
f détection *f* d'îles
r обнаруживание *n* изолированных участков

5297 island polygon
d Insel-Polygon *n*
f polygone *m* isolé
r изолированный многоугольник *m*

5298 isobaric form
d isobare Form *f*
f forme *f* isobare
r изобарическая форма *f*

* **isobath** → 5517

* **isochrone** → 9503

5299 isochronous
d isochron
f isochrone
r одновременный; изохронный

5300 isocline
d Isokline *f*
f isocline *f*
r изоклина *f*

5301 isogonal
d isogonal
f isogone
r изогональный

5302 isogonal figures
d isogonale Figuren *fpl*
f figures *fpl* isogones
r изогональные фигуры *fpl*

5303 isogonal lines
d isogonale Geraden *fpl*
f droites *fpl* isogones
r изогональные прямые *fpl*

5304 isogonal trajectory
d isogonale Trajektorie *f*; Isogonaltrajektorie *f*; isogonale Bahn *f*
f trajectoire *f* isogone
r изогональная траектория *f*

* **isohypse** → 5517

5305 isolated
d isoliert
f isolé
r изолированный

5306 isolated edge
d isolierte Kante *f*
f arête *f* isolée
r изолированное ребро *n*; изолированная грань *f*

* **isolated point** → 89

5307 isolate *v* **object layer**
d Objektschicht isolieren
f isoler un plan d'objet
r изолировать объектный слой

5308 isolation
d Isolation *f*
f isolation *f*
r изоляция *f*

5309 isolation level
(for query transactions)
d Isolationsniveau *n*

f niveau *m* d'isolation
r уровень *m* изоляции

* **isoline → 5318**

5310 isometric
   d isometrisch
   f isométrique
   r изометрический

5311 isometric arc
   d isometrischer Bogen *m*
   f arc *m* isométrique
   r изометрическая дуга *f*

5312 isometric circle
   d isometrischer Kreis *m*
   f cercle *m* isométrique
   r изометрическая окружность *f*

5313 isometric dimensioning
   d isometrische Dimensionierung *f*
   f dimensionnement *m* isométrique
   r изометрическое оразмерение *n*

5314 isometric drawing
   d isometrische Zeichnung *f*
   f dessin *m* isométrique
   r изометрический чертеж *m*;
      изометрический рисунок *m*

5315 isometric ellipse
   d isometrische Ellipse *f*
   f ellipse *f* isométrique
   r изометрический эллипс *m*

5316 isometric figures
   d isometrische Figuren *fpl*
   f figures *fpl* isométriques
   r изометрические фигуры *fpl*

5317 isometric grid
   d isometrisches Gitter *n*
   f grille *f* isométrique
   r изометрическая сетка *f*

5318 isometric line; isoline
   d Isolinie *f*
   f isoligne *f*
   r изолиния *f*

5319 isometric mapping
   d isometrische Abbildung *f*
   f application *f* isométrique
   r изометрическое отображение *n*

5320 isometric plane
   d isometrische Ebene *f*
   f plan *m* isométrique
   r изометрическая плоскость *f*

5321 isometric projection
   d isometrische Projektion *f*
   f projection *f* isométrique
   r изометрическая проекция *f*

5322 isometric snap grid
   d isometrisches Fanggitter *n*; isometrisches
      Ausrichtgitter *n*
   f grille *f* magnétique isométrique
   r изометрическая сетка *f* привязывания

5323 isometric templates
   d isometrische Schablonen *fpl*
   f maquettes *fpl* isométriques
   r изометрические шаблоны *mpl*

5324 isometric transformation
   d isometrische Transformation *f*
   f transformation *f* isométrique
   r изометрическое преобразование *n*

5325 isometric view
   d isometrische Ansicht *f*
   f vue *f* isométrique
   r изометрический вид *m*

5326 isometry
   d Isometrie *f*
   f isométrie *f*
   r изометрия *f*

5327 isoparametric curve
   d isoparametrische Kurve *f*
   f courbe *f* isoparamétrique
   r изопараметрическая кривая *f*

* **isosceles trapezium → 5328**

5328 isosceles trapezoid; isosceles trapezium
   d gleichschenkliges Trapez *n*
   f trapèze *m* isocèle
   r равнобедренная трапеция *f*

5329 isosceles triangle
   d gleichschenkliges Dreieck *n*
   f triangle *m* isocèle
   r равнобедренный треугольник *m*

* **isothetic quadrilaterals → 6654**

5330 isotropic
   d isotrop
   f isotrope
   r изотропный

5331 isotropic directions
   d isotrope Richtungen *fpl*
   f directions *fpl* isotropes
   r изотропные направления *npl*

5332 isotropy
 d Isotropie *f*
 f isotropie *f*
 r изотропия *f*

5333 item
 d Einzelheit *f*; Einheit *f*; Element *n*
 f article *m*; unité *f*; détail *m*; élément *m*
 r отдельный предмет *m*; элемент *m*;
   единица *f*

5334 iteration
 d Iteration *f*
 f itération *f*
 r итерация *f*

**5335 iteration method; iterative method;
    method of iteration**
 d Iterationsmethode *f*; Iterationsverfahren *n*
 f méthode *f* d'itération; méthode itérative
 r итерационный метод *m*

5336 iteration process
 d Iterationsprozess *m*
 f procédé *m* d'itération
 r процесс *m* итерации

5337 iterative
 d iterativ
 f itératif
 r итеративный; итерационный

 * **iterative method** → **5335**

5338 iterator
 d Iterator *m*
 f itérateur *m*
 r повторитель *m*

J

5339 Jacobian matrix
d Jacobian-Matrix *f*
f matrice *f* jacobienne
r матрица *f* Якоби

5340 jagged edges; jagged lines; jaggies
d gezackte Linien *fpl*; Zacken *mpl*
f marches *fpl* d'escalier; effets *mpl* [de marche]
d'escalier
r неровности *fpl*; ступеньки *fpl*

* **jagged lines** → 5340

* **jaggies** → 5340

* **jam** → 5341

5341 jam[ming]
d Stau *m*
f bourrage *m*
r затор *m*; заклинивание *n*

* **JBIG format** → 5347

5342 jitter
d Zittern *n*; Jitter *n*
f scintillement *m*; ondulation *f* verticale [de
l'image]; tremblement *m*
r дрожание *n*

5343 job
d Arbeitsauftrag *m*; Auftrag *m*; Job *m*
f tâche *f*; travail *m*; job *m*
r задача *f*; задание *n*; работа *f*

* **join** *v* → 612

* **join** → 5345

5344 joining nodes
d vereinigte Knoten *mpl*
f nœuds *mpl* joints
r соединенные узлы *mpl*

* **joint** → 5354

5345 join[t]
d Vereinigung *f*
f raccord *m*; joint *m*
r соединение *n*

5346 joint *adj*
d vereinigt

f joint; uni
r соединенный

**5347 joint bilevel image group format; JBIG
format**
d JBIG-Format *n*
f format *m* JBIG (de compression d'image fixe
en deux tons)
r формат *m* JBIG

**5348 joint photographic expert group format;
JP[E]G format**
d GP[E]G-Format *n*
f format *m* GP[E]G
r формат *m* GP[E]G

5349 joint trajectories
d gemeinsame Trajektorien *fpl*; gemeinsame
Bahnen *fpl*
f trajectoires *fpl* unies
r соединенные траектории *fpl*

5350 joystick
d Joystick *n*; Steuerknüppel *m*; Steuerhebel *m*
f manche *m* à balai; levier *m*; manette *f*;
poignée *f*
r джойстик *m*; рычажный указатель *m*;
координатная ручка *f*

5351 JP[E]G builder
d JP[E]G-Bilder *m*
f bâtisseur *m* JP[E]G
r JP[E]G-построитель *m*

5352 JP[E]G file
d JP[E]G-Datei *f*
f fichier *m* JP[E]G
r файл *m* JP[E]G

* **JPEG format** → 5348

* **JPG builder** → 5351

* **JPG file** → 5352

* **JPG format** → 5348

5353 jump effect
d Springeffekt *m*
f effet *m* de saut; effet de bond
r эффект *m* скока

5354 junction; joint
d Verbindung *f*; Zusammenschaltung *f*;
Kupplung *f*
f jonction *f*; joint *m*
r соединение *n*; связь *f*; стыковка *f*

5355 just
d richtig

f juste
r верный

* * **justification** → 269

* * **justify** *v* → 263

* * **justifying** → 269

* * **juxtaposed** → 178

5356 juxtaposition
d Aneinanderlegung *f*
f juxtaposition *f*
r непосредственное соседство *n*;
  соприкосновение *n*

K

5357 kaleidoscope
d Kaleidoskop *n*
f caléidoscope *m*
r калейдоскоп *m*

5358 kaleidoscope of colors and patterns
d Kaleidoskop *n* der Farben und der Muster
f caléidoscope *m* de couleurs et de motifs
r калейдоскоп *m* красок и очертаний

5359 Kalman filter
d Kalman-Filter *m*
f filtre *m* de Kalman
r фильтр *m* Калмана

5360 kernel; nucleus
d Kern *m*; Nukleus *m*
f noyau *m*; nucléus *m*
r ядро *n*

5361 kernel of polygon
d Polygonkern *m*
f noyau *m* de polygone
r ядро *n* многоугольника

5362 kerning
d Unterschneidung *f*
f crénage *m*; réajustement *m* de l'espace entre caractères
r кернинг *m*; согласование *n* расстояния между буквами

5363 key
d Schlüssel *m*
f clé *f*; clef *f*; chiffre *m*
r ключ *m*; шифр *m*

5364 key; button
d Taste *f*
f touche *f*
r клавиша *f*

5365 keyboard
d Tastatur *f*
f clavier *m*
r клавиатура *f*

* **keyboard shortcuts → 8649**

5366 keyframe animation
d Schlüsselrahmen-Animation *f*
f animation *f* par images clés
r анимация *f* ключевыми кадрами

5367 keyframes
(frames from an animation between which the system calculates the interleaving frames)
d Schlüsselrahmen *mpl*
f images *fpl* clés
r ключевые кадры *mpl*

* **keying → 1468**

5368 keylines
(lines on a negative showing the exact size, shape and location of photographs or other graphic elements)
d Schlüssellinien *fpl*
f lignes *fpl* clés
r ключевые линии *fpl*

5369 keypad
d Kleintastatur *f*; Handtastatur *f*
f pavé *m* du clavier
r специализированная клавиатура *f*; вспомагательная клавиатура

5370 key planes
d Schlüsselebenen *fpl*
f plans *mpl* clés
r ключевые плоскости *fpl*

5371 keystone correction
d Trapezentzerrung *f*
f correction *f* de trapèze
r коррекция *f* трапецеидального искажения

* **keystone distortion → 5372**

5372 keystonning; keystone distortion; trapezium distortion
d Trapezverzerrung *f*; Trapezfehler *f*
f raccourcissement *m* d'image avec déformation partielle; distorsion *f* trapézoïdale; distorsion de trapèze horizontale
r трапецеидальное искажение *n*

5373 key viewport
d Schlüsselansichtsfenster *n*
f clôture-clé *f*
r ключевое окно *n* просмотра; ключевая область *f* просмотра

5374 key viewport layer
d Schicht *f* des Schlüsselansichtsfensters
f plan *m* de clôture-clé
r слой *m* ключевой области просмотра; слой ключевого окна просмотра

* **kind → 8977**

5375 kinematic chain
d kinematische Kette *f*

f chaîne *f* cinématique
r кинематическая цепь *f*

5376 kinematics
   d Kinematik *f*
   f cinématique *f*
   r кинематика *f*

5377 kinematics method
   d kinematische Methode *f*
   f méthode *f* cinématique
   r кинематический метод *m*

5378 kinematics parameters
   d kinematische Parameter *mpl*
   f paramètres *mpl* cinématiques
   r кинематические параметры *mpl*

5379 kinesthesis; sensation of movement
   d Bewegungswahrnehmung *f*;
     Bewegungssehen *n*
   f kinesthésie *f*; sensation *f* de mouvement
   r восприятие *n* движения; ощущение *n*
     движения

   * **kite** → 2598

5380 knife tool
   d Hilfsmittel *n* "Messer"
   f outil *m* "couteau"
   r инструмент *m* "ножик"

   * **knob** → 1201

   * **knock** *v* **out** → 5817

   * **knot** → 6220

5381 knot order; node order
   d Knotenordnung *f*
   f ordre *m* de nœuds
   r порядок *m* узлов

5382 knot sequence
   d Knotensequenz *f*
   f séquence *f* de nœuds
   r последовательность *f* узлов

5383 knot vector
   d Knotenvektor *m*
   f vecteur *m* nodal
   r узловой вектор *m*; вектор узла

5384 Koch curve
   d Koch-Kurve *f*
   f courbe *f* de Koch
   r кривая *f* Коха

5385 k-point perspective
   d k-Point-Perspektive *f*

f perspective *f* à k-points
r k-точечная перспектива *f*

5386 kriging
   d Kriging *n*
   f krigeage *m*
   r кригинг *m*

5387 kurtosis
   d Wölbung *f*
   f kurtosis *m*
   r выпуклость *f*

L

5388 label
d Etikett *n*
f étiquette *f*; label *m*
r метка *f*

* **labeling → 5389**

5389 label[l]ing
d Etikettierung *f*; Beschriftung *f*
f étiquetage *m*; attribution *f* de label
r присваивание *n* меток

5390 label point
d Etikettpunkt *m*
f point *m* d'étiquette
r точка *f* метки

5391 label style
d Etikettstil *m*
f style *m* des étiquettes
r стиль *m* меток

5392 labyrinth
d Labyrinth *n*
f labyrinthe *m*
r лабиринт *m*

* **lag → 2590**

* **lagging → 2590**

5393 Lambert correction
d Lambert-Korrektur *f*
f correction *f* de Lambert
r коррекция *f* Ламберта

5394 Lambertian projection
d Lambert-Projektion *f*
f projection *f* de Lambert
r проекция *f* Ламберта

5395 Lambertian radiosity
d Lambert-Radiosity *n*
f radiosité *f* lambertienne; radiosité de Lambert
r диффузное отражение *n* Ламберта

5396 Lambertian surface
d Lambert-Fläche *f*
f surface *f* de Lambert
r поверхность *f* Ламберта

5397 Lambert shading
d Lambert-Schattierung *f*

f ombrage *m* de Lambert
r оттенение *n* Ламберта

* **landscape → 5401**

5398 landscape
d quer; Quer-
f oblong
r широкий; поперечный

5399 landscape; scenery
d Landschaft *f*
f paysage *m*
r ландшафт *m*; пейзаж *m*

5400 landscape display
d Querformat-Display *n*;
Querformat-Bildschirm *m*
f écran *m* panoramique
r дисплей *m* с изображением, вытянутым по горизонтали

5401 landscape format; landscape [orientation]; landscape layout
d Querformat *n*
f format *m* horizontal; présentation *f* à l'horizontale; présentation à l'italienne
r поперечный формат *m*

* **landscape layout → 5401**

5402 landscape library
d Landschaft-Bibliothek *f*
f bibliothèque *f* de paysages
r ландшафтная библиотека *f*

5403 landscape object
d Landschaftsobjekt *n*
f objet *m* paysager
r объект *m* типа ландшафта

* **landscape orientation → 5401**

5404 landscape paper orientation
d Querseitenausrichtung *f*
f orientation *f* de papier paysage
r ориентация *f* поперек страницы

5405 landscape sketch
d Landschaftsskizze *f*
f dessin *m* perspectif de paysage
r перспективный чертеж *m* местности

5406 language
d Sprache *f*
f langage *m*
r [кодовый] язык *m*

5407 Laplace operator
d Laplace-Operator *m*

f opérateur *m* laplacien
r оператор *m* Лапласа

5408 Laplacian filter
d Laplace-Filter *m*
f filtre *m* laplacien
r фильтр *m* Лапласа

5409 Laplacian pyramid
d Laplace-Pyramide *f*
f pyramide *f* laplacienne
r пирамида *f* Лапласа

5410 large aperture
d große Apertur *f*
f grande ouverture *f*
r большая апертура *f*

5411 large button
d große Taste *f*
f grand bouton *m*
r большой бутон *m*

5412 large-scale graphics
d Großmaßstab-Grafik *f*
f graphique *m* à grande échelle
r крупномасштабная графика *f*

5413 large-scale virtual environment; LSVE
d Großmaßstab-Virtualumgebung *f*
f environnement *m* virtuel à grande échelle
r крупномасштабная виртуальная
реальность *f*

5414 large-screen graphics
d Großbildgrafik *f*; Großschirmgrafik *f*
f graphique *m* à écran large
r широкоэкранная графика *f*

5415 large-screen television
d Großbildfernsehen *n*
f télévision *f* à écran large
r широкоэкранное телевидение *n*

5416 laser[-beam] printer
d Laserdrucker *m*
f imprimante *f* laser
r лазерное печатающее устройство *n*;
лазерный принтер *m*

* **laser disk** → 6545

* **laser display** → 5418

5417 laser pen
d Laserstift *m*
f plume *m* laser
r лазерное перо *n*

* **laser printer** → 5416

5418 laser[-scan] display
d Laserbildschirm *m*
f écran *m* [à rayon] laser
r лазерный экран *m*

5419 laser scanner
d Laserscanner *m*; Laserlesegerät *n*
f scanner *m* laser
r лазерный сканер *m*

5420 laser scanning
d Laserabtasung *f*; Laserscannen *n*
f échantillonnage *m* laser
r лазерное сканирование *n*

5421 last angle
d letzter Winkel *m*
f angle *m* dernier
r концевой угол *m*

5422 last object selection
d Letztobjektselektion *f*
f sélection *f* d'objet dernièr
r выбор *m* последнего объекта

5423 last point
d letzter Punkt *m*
f point *m* dernier
r последняя точка *f*

5424 latency
d Latenz *f*
f latence *f*
r ожидание *n*

5425 latent
d latent
f latent
r скрытый; латентный

5426 latent image
d latentes Bild *n*
f image *f* latente
r латентное изображение

5427 lateral; side
d seitlich; lateral; Seiten-
f latéral
r продольный; боковой

5428 lateral area; lateral surface
d Seitenfläche *f*
f aire *f* latérale; surface *f* latérale
r боковая поверхность *f*

5429 lateral edge; side edge
d Seitenkante *f*
f arête *f* latérale
r боковое ребро *n*

5430 lateral face
d Seitenfläche *f*
f face *f* latérale
r [боковая] сторона *f*; [боковая] грань *f*

* **lateral height** → 8773

5431 lateral structure
d Lateralstruktur *f*
f structure *f* latérale
r продольная структура *f*; продольная конструкция *f*

* **lateral surface** → 5428

5432 lateral tolerance
d Lateraltoleranz *f*
f tolérance *f* latérale
r боковой допуск *m*

* **lateral view** → 8672

* **latitude** → 397

5433 lattice; grating
d Gitter *n*; Gitterrost *m*; Rost *m*
f lattis *m*; treillis *m*; réseau *m*
r решетка *f*; сетка *f*

5434 lattice distribution
d gitterförmige Verteilung *f*
f distribution *f* réticulaire
r решетчатое распределение *n*

5435 latus rectum
d latus *n* rectum; Fokalsehne *f*
f latus *m* rectum; corde *f* focale
r фокальная хорда *f*; хорда, проходящая через фокус и перпендикулярная к фокальной оси

* **layer** → 5514

5436 layer; sheet
(of a drawing)
d Schicht *f*; Ebene *f*
f couche *f*; plan *m*; calque *m*
r слой *m*

5437 layer color
d Schichtfarbe *f*
f couleur *f* du plan
r цвет *m* слоя

* **layer control** → 5448

5438 layer deleting
d Schichtlöschung *f*
f effaçage *m* de plan
r стирание *n* слоя

5439 layered depth image; LDI
d Schichttiefenbild *n*
f image *f* profonde en couches
r расслоенное в глубине изображение *n*

5440 layer effects
d Schichteffekte *mpl*
f effets *mpl* de plan
r эффекты *mpl* слоя

5441 layer filter
d Schichtfilter *m*
f filtre *m* de plan
r фильтр *m* слоев

5442 layer filtering
d Schichtfiltrierung *f*
f filtrage *m* de plan
r фильтрирование *n* слоя; фильтрация *f* слоя

5443 layer index
d Schichtindex *m*
f indice *m* de plan
r индекс *m* слоя

5444 layering
d Schichtenteilung *f*; Schichtung *f*
f division *f* en plans
r разбиение *n* на слои; расслоение *n*

5445 layer linetype
d Linientyp *m* der Schicht
f type *m* de ligne d'un plan
r тип *m* линии слоя

5446 layer list
d Schichtliste *f*
f liste *f* des plans
r список *m* слоев

5447 layer locking
d Schichtsperrung *f*
f verrouillage *m* de plan
r блокирование *n* слоя; запирание *n* слоя

5448 layer management; layer control
d Schichtensteuerung *f*
f gestion *f* des plans; contrôle *m* des plans
r управление *n* слоями

5449 layer manager
d Schichtenmanager *m*
f gestionnaire *m* de plans
r управитель *m* слоев; менажер *m* слоев

5450 layer name
d Schichtname *m*
f nom *m* de plan
r имя *n* слоя

5451 layer object
d Schichtobjekt *n*
f objet *m* plan
r объект *m* типа слоя

5452 layer orientation
d Schichtorientierung *f*
f orientation *f* de plan
r ориентация *f* слоя

5453 layer properties
d Schichteigenschaften *fpl*
f propriétés *fpl* de plan
r свойства *npl* слоя

5454 layer renaming
d Schichtumbenennung *f*
f changement *m* de nom de couche;
changement de nom de plan
r переименование *n* слоя

5455 layers collection object
(all layers in the active drawing)
d Schichtensammlungsobjekt *n*
f objet *m* collection des plans
r объект *m* типа коллекции слоев

5456 layer setting
d Schichteinrichtung *f*
f établissement *m* de plan
r установление *n* параметров слоя

5457 layer thawing
d Schichtauftauen *n*; Schichtaktivierung *f*
f décongélation *f* de plan
r размораживание *n* слоя

5458 layer visibility
d Schichtsichtbarkeit *f*
f visibilité *f* de plan
r видимость *f* слоя

* **layout** → 5460

5459 layout character; format effector
d Anordnungszeichen *n*; Formatsteuerzeichen *n*
f caractère *m* de disposition; caractère de mise
en page
r знак *m* размещения; знак спецификации
формата

5460 layout [chart]; layout plan
(sketch or plan of how a page or sheet will
look when printed)
d topografische Anordnung *f*;
Aufstellungsweise *f*; Layout *n*;
Aufstellungsplan *m*
f disposition *f* [topologique]; layout *m*; carte *f*
de disposition; carte topologique; plan *m* de
montage

r планировка *f*; схема *f* расположения;
топологическая схема; монтажная схема

5461 layout data
d Layoutdaten *npl*
f données *fpl* de disposition
r данные *npl* о размещении

* **layout plan** → 5460

5462 layout style
d Layoutstil *m*
f style *m* de layout
r стиль *m* размещения; стиль расположения

* **LCD** → 5661

* **LDI** → 5439

5463 lead *v*
d führen; leiten
f conduire
r водить

* **leader** → 5466, 5467

5464 leader
d Leiter *m*; Vorlauf *m*
f leader *m*; directeur *m*; apériteur *m*
r водитель *m*

5465 leader length
d Leiterlänge *f*
f longueur *f* de leader
r длина *f* водителя

5466 leader [line]; datum line; reference line
d Führungslinie *f*; Bezugsstrich *m*;
Bezugslinie *f*; Datumszeile *f*
f ligne *f* de rappel de cote; ligne de repère;
ligne de référence
r ведущая линия *f*; начальная линия;
исходная линия; отсчетная линия;
реперная линия

5467 leader [point]
d Führungspunkt *m*
f point *m* de conduite
r ведущая точка *f*

* **leading** → 5756

**5468 leading diagonal; main diagonal; principal
diagonal**
d Hauptdiagonale *f*
f diagonale *f* principale
r главная диагональ *f*

5469 leading dimensions
d Hauptdimensionen *fpl*

f dimensions *fpl* dominantes
r основные размеры *mpl*; габариты *mpl*

5470 leading edge
(of a carrier)
d Vorderkante *f*
f bord *m* avant
r ведущий край *m*

* **lead of the helix** → 7083

5471 leaf
(of a graph)
d Blatt *n*
f feuille *f*
r лист *m*

5472 least-squares fitting
(of curves)
d Ausgleich *m* durch Methode der kleinsten
Quadrate
f ajustage *m* par méthode des moindres carrés
r подбор *m* методом наименьших квадратов

5473 least-squares method
d Methode *f* der kleinsten Quadrate
f méthode *f* des moindres carrés
r метод *m* наименьших квадратов

5474 least upper bound; l.u.b.; supremum; sup
d kleinste obere Schranke *f*; Supremum *n*
f borne *f* supérieure; supremum *m*
r точная верхняя грань *f*; наименьшая
верхняя грань

* **left-aligned** → 5481

* **left alignment** → 5480

5475 left arrow
d Linkspfeil *m*
f flèche *f* à gauche
r левая стрелка *f*

5476 left arrow key
d Linkspfeil-Taste *f*
f touche *f* de flèche à gauche
r клавиша *f* левой стрелки

5477 left edge
d Linkskante *f*
f arête *f* gauche
r левое ребро *n*

5478 left extent
d Links-Extent *m*
f étendue *f* à gauche
r расширение *n* влево

5479 left-handed coordinate system

d linkshändiges Koordinatensystem *n*
f système *m* de coordonnées à gauche
r левая система *f* координат

* **left-handed helix** → 8745

5480 left[-hand] justification; left alignment
d linksbündige Justierung *f*; linksbündige
Ausrichtung *f*
f justification *f* à gauche; alignement *m* à
gauche
r выравнивание *n* влево; левое
выравнивание

* **left helix** → 8745

* **left justification** → 5480

5481 left-justified; left-aligned
d links ausgerichtet
f aligné à gauche
r выравненный влево

5482 left mouse button; primary mouse button
d linke Maustaste *f*
f bouton *m* gauche de souris
r левый бутон *m* мыши

* **left-right scrolling** → 4710

5483 left screw; sinistrorse screw
d Linksschraube *f*
f vis *f* à gauche; vis sinistrorsum
r левый винт *m*

5484 left scroll arrow
d Bildlaufpfeil *m* links
f flèche *f* de défilement à gauche
r стрелка *f* прокрутки влево

5485 left shift
d Linksverschiebung *f*
f décalage *m* vers gauche; déplacement *m* à
gauche
r сдвиг *m* влево

5486 left-side view
d Ansicht *f* der linken Seite
f vue *f* de côté gauche
r левосторонний вид *m*

5487 left stretch
d Linksausdehnung *f*
f étirement *m* à gauche
r вытягивание *m* влево

* **left-twisted helix** → 8745

5488 legend
d Legende *f*

f légende *f*
r легенда *f*

5489 legible
(referring to type having sufficient contrast
with its background)
d leserlich
f lisible
r разборчивый; четкий

* **leg of an angle** → 8665

5490 leg of a right[-angled] triangle
d Kathete *f*
f cathète *f*; côté *f* de l'angle droit
r катет *m*

* **leg of right triangle** → 5490

5491 lemon-shaped solid
d Festkörper *m* mit der Form einer Zitrone
f solide *m* en forme de citron
r плотное тело *n* в форме лимона

**5492 Lempel-Zif-Welch compression; LZW
compression**
d Lempel-Zif-Welch-Kompression *f*
f compression *f* de Lempel-Zif-Welch
r сжатие *n* Лемпеля-Цифа-Вельха

5493 length
d Länge *f*
f longueur *f*
r длина *f*

* **lengthen** *v* → 7591

* **lengthening** → 3382

5494 length of a curve
d Länge *f* der Kurve
f longueur *f* de courbe
r длина *f* кривой

* **length of an arc** → 532

5495 length of a side
d Kantenlänge *f*
f longueur *f* d'un côté
r длина *f* стороны

5496 lens
d Linse *f*
f lentille *f*
r линза *f*

5497 lens
d Objektiv *n*
f objectif *m*
r объектив *m*

5498 lens adjusting
d Linseneinstellung *f*
f ajustage *m* de lentille
r настраивание *n* линзы

5499 lens alignment
d Linsenausgleich *m*
f alignement *m* de lentille
r выравнивание *n* линзы

5500 lens axis
d Linsenachse *f*
f axe *m* de lentille
r ось *f* линзы

5501 lens copying
d Linsenkopierung *f*
f copiage *m* de lentilles
r копирование *n* линз

5502 lens effects
d Linseneffekte *mpl*
f effets *mpl* de lentille
r эффекты *mpl* линзы

5503 lens equation
d Linsengleichung *f*
f équation *f* de la lentille
r уравнение *n* линзы

5504 lenses removing
d Linsenentfernung *f*
f élimination *f* de lentilles
r отстранение *n* линз

5505 lens glare filter
d Linsen-Reflexfilter *m*
f filtre *m* de reflets de lentille
r фильтр *m* бликов линзы

5506 lens glares
d Linsenblendungen *fpl*
f reflets *mpl* de lentille
r блики *mpl* линзы

5507 lens law
d Linsensatz *m*
f loi *f* de lentille
r закон *m* линзы

5508 lens magnification
d Linsenvergrösserung *f*
f grossissement *m* de lentille
r увеличение *n* линзы

5509 lens space
d Linsenraum *m*
f espace *m* lenticulaire
r линзовое пространство *n*

5510 lens' viewpoint
 d Blickpunkt *m* der Linse
 f point *m* de vue de lentille
 r точка *f* зрения линзы

5511 letter; alphabetical character
 d Buchstabe *m*; Schriftzeichen *n*;
    Alphabetzeichen *n*
 f lettre *f*; caractère *m* alphabétique
 r буква *f*; алфавитный символ *m*

 * **letter outline** → 5512

5512 letter shape; letter outline
 d Buchstabenfigur *f*
 f figure *f* de lettre
 r форма *f* буквы; начертание *n* буквы

 * **letter slant** → 5513

5513 letter slant[ing]
 d Buchtaben-Neigung *f*
 f inclinaison *f* de lettres
 r наклонен *m* букв

 * **level** → 5518

5514 level; layer
 d Niveau *n*; Pegel *m*
 f niveau *m*
 r уровень *m*; этаж *m*

 * **level curve** → 5517

5515 level equalization
 d Niveau-Ausgleich *m*
 f égalisation *f* de niveau
 r выравнивание *n* уровня

5516 level equalization filter
 d Filter *m* des Niveauausgleichs
 f filtre *m* d'égalisation de niveau
 r фильтр *m* выравнивания уровня

**5517 level line; level curve; height line;
 isohypse; isobath; contour [elevation];
 stratum**
    (on a map)
 d Höhen[schicht]linie *f*; Schicht[en]linie *f*;
    Isohypse *f*; Isobathe *f*
 f ligne *f* de niveau; courbe *f* de niveau;
    isohypse *f*; isobathe *f*; strate *f*
 r линия *f* уровня; уровневая линия;
    горизонталь *f*; изогипса *f*; изобата *f*; линия
    равных высот; линия равных глубин

5518 level[ling]
 d Nivellierung *f*; Nivellement *n*
 f nivellement *m*; calage *m*
 r нивелирование *n*

5519 level of mapping
 d Abbildungsniveau *n*
 f niveau *m* d'application
 r уровень *m* отображения

5520 level plane; height plane
 d Höhenebene *f*
 f plan *m* de niveau
 r плоскость *f* уровня

5521 level selection
 d Auswahl *f* des Pegels
 f sélection *f* de niveau
 r выбор *m* уровня

 * **level surface** → 3508

5522 Liang-Barsky clipping
 d Liang-Barsky-Schneiden *n*
 f découpage *m* de Liang-Barsky
 r отсекание *n* Лианга-Барского

5523 library
 d Bibliothek *f*
 f bibliothèque *f*
 r библиотека *f*

5524 library directory
 d Bibliotheksverzeichnis *n*;
    Bibliothekskatalog *m*
 f répertoire *m* de bibliothèque; catalogue *m* de
    bibliothèque
 r справочник *m* библиотеки; каталог *m*
    библиотеки; указатель *m* библиотеки

5525 library of materials; materials library
 d Materialienbibliothek *f*
 f bibliothèque *f* de matériaux
 r библиотека *f* материалов

5526 license
 d Lizenz *f*
 f licence *f*; autorisation *f*
 r лицензия *f*

5527 license manager
 d Lizenz-Manager *m*
 f gestionnaire *m* de licence
 r менажер *m* лицензии

 * **lift** *v* → 3352

5528 light
 d Licht *n*
 f lumière *f*
 r свет *m*

5529 light; lightweight *adj*
 d leicht

f léger
r легкий; легковесный

5530 light *v*; lighten *v*; unblank *v*; illuminate *v*
   d beleuchten; erleuchten; erhellen; aufhellen;
      illuminieren
   f éclairer; illuminer
   r освечивать; осветить; освещать

5531 light absorption
   d Lichtabsorption *f*
   f absorption *f* de la lumière; absorption optique
   r поглощение *n* света; светопоглощение *n*

5532 light amplification
   d Lichtverstärkung *f*
   f amplification *f* de lumière
   r усиление *n* света

5533 light area
   d heller Bereich *m*
   f zone *f* claire
   r светлая зона *f*

5534 light beam
   d Lichtstrahl *m*
   f faisceau *m* lumineux
   r световой луч *m*; луч *m* света

5535 light block
   d Lichtblock *m*
   f bloc *m* de sources lumineuses; bloc lumineux
   r блок *m* световых источников; блок
      источников света

5536 light button; virtual pushbutton
   d Lichttaste *f*; Lichtknopf *m*
   f bouton *m* lumineux; touche *f* [de fonction]
      affichable
   r световая кнопка *f*

5537 light calculation
   d Lichtberechnung *f*
   f calcul *m* d'éclairage
   r вычисление *n* освещения

5538 light camera
   d Lichtkamera *f*
   f caméra *f* lumineuse
   r световая камера *f*

5539 light color
   d Lichtfarbe *f*
   f couleur *f* de la lumière
   r цвет *m* света

5540 light compensating filter
   d Lichtausgleich[s]filter *m*
   f filtre *m* de compensation de la lumière
   r световой компенсирующий фильтр *m*

* **light density** → 6543

* **light diffraction** → 6544

5541 light diffusing *adj*
   d lichtstreuend
   f diffusant de lumière
   r светорассеивающий

5542 light emission; light radiation
   d Lichtemission *f*; Lichtstrahlung *f*
   f émission *f* lumineuse; rayonnement *m*
      lumineux
   r световое излучение *n*; излучение света

5543 light emitter
   d Lichtsender *m*; Lichstrahler *m*
   f émetteur *m* de lumière
   r излучатель *m* света

* **lighten *v*** → 5530

* **light filter** → 6549

5544 light focusing
   d Lichtfokussierung *f*
   f focalisation *f* de la lumière
   r фокусировка *f* света; фокусирование *n*
      света

* **lighting** → 4798

5545 lighting effect
   d Beleuchtungseffekt *m*
   f effet *m* d'éclairage
   r эффект *m* освещения

5546 lighting level
   d Beleuchtungsniveau *n*
   f niveau *m* d'éclairage
   r уровень *m* освещения

* **lighting model** → 4804

5547 lighting network
   d Beleuchtungsnetz *n*
   f réseau *m* d'éclairage
   r сеть *f* освещения

5548 lighting node
   d Beleuchtungsknoten *m*
   f nœud *m* d'éclairage
   r узел *m* освещения

5549 lighting simulation
   d Beleuchtungssimulation *f*
   f simulation *f* d'éclairage
   r симуляция *f* освещения

* **light intensity** → 5551

5550 lightness
  d Leichtigkeit *f*
  f légèreté *f*
  r легкость *f*

5551 lightness; luminosity; brightness; illuminance; light intensity
  d Helligkeit *f*; Leuchtstärke *f*; Beleuchtungsstärke *f*; Leuchtkraft *f*; Lichtstärke *f*; Lichtintensität *f*
  f luminosité *f*; intensité *f* de la lumière; intensité lumineuse
  r яркость *f* света [в спектре от черного к белому на мониторе]; освещенность *f*; светимость *f*; сила *f* света; интенсивность *f* света

5552 lightness altering; lightness change
  d Helligkeitsänderung *f*
  f changement *m* de la luminosité
  r изменение *n* яркости света

* **lightness change** → 5552

5553 lightness correction
  d Helligkeitskorrektur *f*
  f correction *f* de la luminosité
  r коррекция *f* яркости света

* **light-obscuration instrument** → 6494

* **light path** → 7796

5554 light pen; light stylus; beam pen; electronic pen; optical wand
  d Lichtgriffel *m*; Lichtstift *m*; elektronischer Stift *m*
  f photostyle *m*; pointeur *m* optique; crayon *m* lumineux; crayon électronique
  r световое перо *n*; световой карандаш *m*

5555 light-pen detection; pen detection; light-pen hit; light-pen strike
  d Lichtgriffeldetektion *f*
  f détection *f* par photostyle; détection par stylet
  r указание *n* световым пером

* **light-pen hit** → 5555

* **light-pen strike** → 5555

5556 light plane
  d Lichtebene *f*
  f plan *m* lumineux
  r световая плоскость *f*

5557 light properties
  d Lichteigenschaften *fpl*
  f propriétés *fpl* de la lumière
  r свойства *npl* света

* **light radiation** → 5542

5558 light-reflected shading
  d Licht-reflektierte Schattierung *f*
  f ombrage *m* réfléchissant la lumière
  r оттенение *n*, отражающее свет

* **light reflection** → 7938

5559 light reflection value
  d Lichtreflektionswert *m*
  f valeur *f* de réflexion lumière
  r значение *f* отражения света

* **light refraction** → 7957

5560 light region
  d Lichtbereich *m*
  f région *f* de la lumière
  r световая зона *f*

* **light scattering** → 8335

5561 light section
  d Lichtschnitt *m*
  f section *f* de la lumière
  r световое сечение *n*

5562 light source; luminous source
  d Lichtquelle *f*
  f source *f* de lumière; source lumineuse; source d'éclairage
  r источник *m* света; световой источник

5563 light source button
  d Lichtquellen-Schaltfläche *f*
  f bouton *m* de source lumineuse
  r бутон *m* светового источника

5564 light source coherence
  d Kohärenz *f* der Lichtquelle
  f cohérence *f* de la source lumineuse
  r когерентность *f* источника света

5565 light source properties
  d Lichtquelleneigenschaften *fpl*
  f propriétés *fpl* de source lumineuse
  r свойства *n* светового источника

5566 light source type
  d Lichtquellentyp *m*
  f type *m* de source lumineuse
  r тип *m* светового источника

5567 light [source] vector
  d Vektor *m* der Lichtquelle; Lichtvektor *m*
  f vecteur *m* de la source lumineuse
  r вектор *m* светового источника

5568 light spot; luminous spot; point of light
  d Leuchtpunkt *m*; Lichtpunkt *m*; Lichtfleck *m*;

Leuchtfleck *m*
f point *m* lumineux; spot *m* lumineux; repère *m* lumineux; tache *f* lumineuse
r световая точка *f*; световое пятно *n*

5569 light stability
d Lichtbeständigkeit *f*
f stabilité *f* de la lumière
r устойчивость *f* света

* **light stylus** → **5554**

5570 light texture
d leichte Textur *f*
f texture *f* légère
r легкая текстура *f*

5571 light threshold
d Lichtschwelle *f*
f seuil *m* lumineux
r порог *m* светового восприятия

* **lighttight** → **4951**

* **light value** → **1147**

* **light vector** → **5567**

* **lightweight** *adj* → **5529**

5572 lightweight polyline
d leichte Polylinie *f*
f polyligne *f* allégée
r легковесная полилиния *f*

* **likelihood** → **7482**

* **likeness** → **8695**

5573 limb
d Limbus *m*
f limbe *m*
r лимб *m*

* **limit** *adj* → **3636**

* **limit** → **1088**

5574 limitation
d Begrenzung *f*
f limitation *f*
r ограничение *n*

* **limit check** → **5575**

5575 limit check[ing]
d Grenzwertprüfung *f*
f vérification *f* aux limites
r граничное испытание *n*; проверка *f* в граничных условиях

* **limited** → **1110**

* **limiter** → **2595**

5576 limiting cone; universal cone; inductive cone
d Limeskegel *m*; universeller Kegel *m*
f cône *m* terminal
r предельный конус *m*; универсальный конус; индуктивный конус

5577 limit object
d Limesobjekt *n*
f objet *m* limitatif
r предельный объект *m*; граничный объект

* **limit superior** → **10074**

5578 limit value
d Grenzwert *m*
f valeur *f* limite
r предельное значение *n*

5579 Lincoln-Wand tablet
d Lincoln-Wand-Tablett *n*
f tablette *f* de [Lincoln-]Wand
r планшет *m* Линкольна-Ванда

* **line** → **9217**

5580 line; row
(in a text)
d Zeile *f*; Reihe *f*
f ligne *f*
r строка *f*; ряд *m*

5581 linear
d linear
f linéaire
r линейный

5582 linear attenuation
(of light)
d Lineardämpfung *f*
f atténuation *f* linéaire
r линейное затухание *n*

5583 linear blend
d lineare Überblendung *f*
f dégradé *m* linéaire
r линейное переливание *n*

5584 linear coefficient
d Linearfaktor *m*
f coefficient *m* linéaire
r линейный коэффициент *m*

5585 linear digital filter
d linearer Digitalfilter *m*

f filtre *m* digital linéaire
r цифровой линейный фильтр *m*

5586 linear dimensions
d lineare Dimensionen *fpl*
f cotations *fpl* linéaires; dimensions *fpl* linéaires
r линейные измерения *npl*

5587 linear eccentricity
d lineare Exzentrizität *f*
f excentricité *f* linéaire
r линейный эксцентрицитет *m*; линейная децентрация *f*

5588 linear extrapolation
d lineare Extrapolation *f*
f extrapolation *f* linéaire
r линейная экстраполяция *f*

5589 linear fill
d lineare Füllung *f*
f remplissage *m* linéaire
r линейное заполнение *n*

5590 linear format
d lineares Format *n*
f format *m* linéaire
r линейный формат *m*

5591 linear hatch
d Linienschraffur *f*
f hachure *f* linéaire
r линейная штриховка *f*

5592 linear hatching
d Linearschraffen *n*
f hachure *f* linéaire
r линейное штрихование *n*

5593 linear interpolation
d lineare Interpolation *f*
f interpolation *f* linéaire
r линейная интерполяция *f*

5594 linearity
d Linearität *f*
f linéarité *f*
r линейность *f*

5595 linearization
d Linearisierung *f*
f linéarisation *f*
r линеаризация *f*

5596 linear magnification
d Linearvergrößerung *f*
f agrandissement *m* linéaire
r линейное увеличение *n*

5597 linear object
d lineares Objekt *n*
f objet *m* linéaire
r линейный объект *m*

5598 linear perspective
d Linienperspektive *f*
f perspective *f* linéaire
r линейная перспектива *f*

5599 linear profile; linear section
d Linienprofil *n*; Linienschnitt *m*
f profil *m* linéaire
r линейный профиль *m*

* **linear projective mapping** → 7577

5600 linear prolongation
d lineare Verlängerung *f*
f allongement *m* linéaire
r линейное удлинение *n*

* **linear raster** → 5632

5601 linear regression
d lineare Regression *f*
f régression *f* linéaire
r линейная регрессия *f*

5602 linear scale
d linearer Maßstab *m*
f échelle *f* linéaire
r линейный масштаб *m*

5603 linear scaling
d lineare Skalierung *f*
f mise *f* à l'échelle linéaire
r линейное масштабирование *n*

* **linear section** → 5599

5604 linear shrinkage
d Linearschrumpfung *f*
f retrait *m* linéaire
r линейное сжатие *n*; линейная усадка *f*

5605 linear space; vector space
d linearer Raum *m*; Vektorraum *m*
f espace *m* linéaire; espace vectoriel
r линейное пространство *n*; векторное пространство

5606 linear spectrum
d Linienspektrum *n*
f spectre *m* linéaire
r линейный спектр *m*

5607 line art
d Strichgrafik *f*

f graphique *m* composé de pixels en deux couleurs
r штриховая графика *f*

5608 linear transformation
d lineare Transformation *f*
f transformation *f* linéaire
r линейная трансформация *f*

5609 linear trend
d linearer Trend *m*; lineare Tendenz *f*
f tendance *f* linéaire
r линейный тренд *m*

5610 line caps
d Linienenden *npl*
f fins *mpl* de lignes
r конечные элементы *mpl* линии

5611 line chart; line graph
d Liniendiagramm *n*
f diagramme *m* linéaire; graphique *m* linéaire
r линейная диаграмма *f*

5612 line deleting
d Linienlöschung *f*
f effacement *m* de ligne
r удаление *n* линии; стирание *n* линии

5613 line drawing
d Linienzeichnen *n*; Linienzug *m*
f tracement *m* de ligne
r черчение *n* линии

5614 line-ending shape
d Form *f* der Linienenden
f forme *f* à l'extrémité de ligne
r форма *f* концов линии

5615 line entity
d Linieneinheit *f*
f entité *f* ligne
r примитив *m* линия

5616 line entity group
d Linieneinheitsgruppe *f*
f groupe *m* d'entités lignes
r группа *f* примитивов линий

5617 line extension
d Linienerweiterung *f*
f extension *f* de ligne
r растяжение *n* линии

5618 line filleting
d Linienabrundung *f*
f filetage *m* de ligne
r округление *n* линии

5619 line folding

d Linienfaltung *m*
f pliage *m* de ligne
r свертка *f* линии

5620 line graph
d Kantengraph *m*
f graphe *m* d'arête
r реберный граф *m*

* **line graph** → 5611

* **line graphics** → 2222

5621 line interlacing
d Linienabwechseln *n*
f entrelaçage *m* de lignes
r чередование *n* линий

5622 line intersection
d Linienüberschneidung *f*
f intersection *f* de lignes
r пересечение *n* линий

5623 line item
d Zeilenposition *f*
f élément *m* de ligne
r элемент *m* строки

* **line length** → 5636

5624 line number; row number
d Zeilennummer *f*
f numéro *m* de lignes
r номер *m* строки

5625 line object
d Linienobjekt *n*
f objet *m* de ligne
r объект *m* типа линии

5626 line of centres; centre line
d Mittelpunktslinie *f*; Zentrale *f*
f ligne *f* des centres
r линия *f* центров

5627 line of curvature on a surface
d Krümmungslinie *f* auf einer Fläche
f ligne *f* de courbure d'une surface
r линия *f* кривизны на поверхности

5628 line of horizon
d Linie *f* des Horizonts
f ligne *f* d'horizon
r линия *f* горизонта

5629 line of infinity; infinite line; ideal line; improper line
d unendlichferne Gerade *f*; Ferngerade *f*; ideale Gerade

f droite *f* de l'infini; droite idéale; droite impropre
r бесконечно удаленная прямая *f*; несобственная прямая

* **line of intersection → 2379**

5630 line of principal curvature
d Hauptkrümmungslinie *f*
f ligne *f* de courbure principale
r линия *f* главной кривизны

5631 line of projection
d Projektionslinie *f*
f ligne *f* de projection
r проектирующая линия *f*

* **line of steepest slope → 3694**

* **line of stream → 3881**

* **line of symmetry → 9416**

* **line scanning → 4707**

5632 line screen; linear raster
d Strichraster *m*; Linienraster *m*
f trame *f* à lignes; trame lignée; rastre *m* linéaire
r линейный растр *m*; линиатура *f*

5633 line segment; straight-line segment
d Geradenabschnitt *m*; Strecke *f*
f segment *m* de droite; segment linéaire
r отрезок *m* [прямой]

5634 line-segment rendering
d Strecken-Rendering *n*
f rendu *m* de segment linéaire
r тонирование *n* отрезка; рендеринг *m* отрезка

5635 line shading
d Linienschattierung *f*
f ombrage *m* linéaire
r линейное оттенение *n*

5636 line size; line length
d Linienlänge *f*
f taille *f* de ligne; longueur *f* de ligne
r размер *m* линии; длина *f* линии

* **line spacing → 5205**

5637 lines per inch; lpi
d Linien *fpl* pro Zoll
f lignes *fpl* par pouce
r линии *fpl* на дюйм

5638 line style

d Linienstil *m*
f style *m* de ligne
r стиль *m* линии

5639 line thinning
d Linienverdünnung *f*
f amincissement *m* de ligne; atténuation *f* de ligne
r утончение *n* линии

* **line-to-line spacing → 5205**

5640 line tracking
d Linienverfolgung *f*
f poursuite *f* de ligne
r прослеживание *n* линии

5641 linetype
d Linientyp *m*
f type *m* de ligne
r тип *m* линии

5642 linetype definition
d Definition *f* des Linientyps
f définition *f* de type de ligne
r определение *n* типа линии

5643 linetype description
d Beschreibung *f* des Linientyps
f description *f* de type de ligne
r описание *n* типа линии

5644 linetype object
d Linientypobjekt *n*
f objet *m* de type de ligne
r объект-тип линии *m*

* **linetype scale → 5645**

5645 linetype scale [factor]
d Linientyp-Maßstab *m*
f facteur *m* d'échelle de type de ligne; échelle *f* de type de ligne
r масштаб *m* типа линии

5646 line width
d Linienbreite *f*
f largeur *f* de ligne
r толщина *f* линии

5647 line with heights; coted line
d kotierte Linie *f*
f ligne *f* cotée
r линия *f* с численными отметками

5648 line wrap
d Zeilenumbruch *m*; Zeilenumhüllung *f*
f enroulement *m* de ligne
r поворот *m* линии

* link $v \rightarrow$ 931

* link $\rightarrow$ 5655

5649 link and node structure
d Struktur *f* der Verbindungen und der Knoten
f structure *f* de liens et de nœuds
r структура *f* узлов и связей

5650 link-based topology
d Verbindung-basierte Topologie *f*
f topologie *f* orientée liaison
r топология *f*, базированная на связей

5651 link color
d Link-Farbe *f*
f couleur *f* de liaison
r цвет *m* связи

5652 linked bitmap
d verknüpftes Bitmap *n*
f bitmap *m* lié
r связанное растровое изображение *n*

5653 linked images
d verknüpfte Bilder *npl*
f images *fpl* liées
r связанные изображения *npl*

5654 linked objects
d verknüpfte Objekte *npl*
f objets *mpl* liés
r связанные объекты *mpl*

5655 link[ing]; bind[ing]
d Verknüpfung *f*; Verbinden *n*; Binden *n*;
Link *n*
f liaison *f*; lien *m*; ligature *f*; embase *f*; reliure *f*
r связь *f*, связывание *n*; звено *n*;
соединение *n*; привязка *f*; связка *f*

5656 link path
d Verbindungsstrecke *f*
f tracé *m* de liaison
r дорожка *f* связи

5657 link path name
d Name *m* der Verbindungsstrecke
f nom *m* de tracé de liaison
r имя *n* дорожки связи

5658 link resistance
d Verbindungsfestigkeit *f*
f résistance *f* de liaison
r устойчивость *f* связи

5659 links available indicator
d Anzeiger *m* der verfügbaren Verbindungen
f indicateur *m* de liaisons accessibles
r индикатор *m* доступных связей

5660 links synchronization
(of a table)
d Link-Synchronisation *f*
f synchronisation *f* de liaisons
r синхронизация *f* связей

5661 liquid-crystal display; LCD; liquid-crystal screen
d Flüssigkristalldisplay *n*;
Flüssigkristallbildschirm *m*
f afficheur *m* à cristaux liquides; indicateur *m* à
cristaux liquides; viseur *m* LCD
r жидкокристаллический дисплей *m*;
индикатор *m* на жидких кристаллах;
жидкокристаллический экран *m*

* liquid-crystal screen $\rightarrow$ 5661

5662 list
d Liste *f*
f liste *f*
r список *m*

5663 list *v*
d listen
f lister
r перелистывать

5664 list box
d Listenfeld *n*
f boîte *f* de liste; zone *f* de liste déroulante
r поле *n* списка; списковое поле

5665 listing
d Listenform *f*; Listing *n*
f listage *m*; listing *m*
r распечатка *f*; листинг *m*

5666 list view
d Listenansicht *f*
f vue *f* de liste
r списковое представление *n*

5667 literal
d Literal *n*; buchstäbliche Konstante *f*
f littéral *m*; libellé *m*; constante *f* littérale
r литерал *m*; литеральная константа *f*

5668 literal *adj*
d buchstäblich; Buchstaben-
f littéral
r буквенный

5669 literal notation
d buchstäbliche Bezeichnung *f*; buchstäbliche
Darstellung *f*
f notation *f* littérale
r буквенное обозначение *n*

* live video $\rightarrow$ 7828

5670 live videotexture samples
  d Muster *npl* der Realzeit-Videotextur
  f modèles *mpl* de vidéotexture vive
  r выборки *fpl* видео-текстуры в реальном
      времени

  * **load → 5673**

5671 load *v*
  d laden; füllen
  f charger
  r нагружать; загружать

5672 loaded shapes
  d geladene Formen *fpl*
  f formes *fpl* chargées
  r загруженные фигуры *fpl*

5673 load[ing]; charge
  d Last *f*, Ladung *f*, Belastung *f*
  f charge *f*
  r груз *m*; нагрузка *f*

5674 load *v* palette
  d Palette laden
  f charger une palette
  r загружать палитры

5675 lobe
  d Keule *f*
  f lobe *m*
  r лепесток *m*

5676 local
  d lokal; örtlich
  f local
  r локальный; местный

5677 local illumination method
  d lokales Beleuchtungsverfahren *n*
  f méthode *f* d'illumination
  r метод *m* локального освещения

  * **localization → 5679**

5678 local shading
  d lokale Schattierung *f*
  f ombrage *m* local
  r локальное оттенение *n*

5679 location; localization; placement
  d Stellung *f*, Lokalisierung *f*, Ortung *f*,
      Plazierung *f*, Aufstellung *f*
  f localisation *f*, location *f*, [em]placement *m*
  r расположение *n*; размещение *n*;
      локализация *f*

5680 locator
  d Lokalisierer *m*
  f relévateur *m* [de coordonnées];

      localisateur *m*; dispositif *m* de location
  r устройство *n* ввода позиции

  * **lock *v* → 1024**

5681 lock
  d Verriegelungsmechanismus *m*; Sperre *f*
  f verrou *m*
  r замок *m*

5682 locked
  d gesperrt; verriegelt
  f verrouillé; bloqué
  r блокированный; запертый

5683 lock[ed] layer
  d blockierte Schicht *f*
  f plan *m* verrouillé; plan bloqué
  r блокированный слой *m*

5684 locked object
  d blockiertes Objekt *n*
  f objet *m* verrouillé
  r блокированный объект *m*

  * **lock-in → 5685, 9424**

5685 locking; lockout; blocking; lock-in
  d Verriegelung *f*; Sperrung *f*; Blockierung *f*
  f verrouillage *m*; blocage *m*
  r запирание *n*; блокирование *n*; блокировка *f*

  * **locking-in → 9424**

  * **lock layer → 5683**

5686 lock *v* object
  d Objekt sperren
  f bloquer un objet
  r блокировать объект

  * **lock-on → 1279**

  * **lockout → 5685**

  * **locus → 4186**

5687 log *v*; register *v*; sign *v* on
  d registrieren; aufzeichnen; aufschreiben
  f enregistrer; inscrire
  r записывать[ся]; регистрировать[ся]

  * **logarithmic → 5688**

5688 logarithmic[al]
  d logarithmisch
  f logarithmique
  r логарифмический

5689 logarithmic curve
  d logarithmische Kurve *f*

f courbe *f* logarithmique
r логарифмика *f*

5690 logarithmic filtering
d logarithmische Filterung *f*
f filtrage *m* logarithmique
r логарифмическое фильтрирование *n*

5691 logarithmic spiral; equiangular spiral; logistic spiral
d logarithmische Spirale *f*; gleichwinklige Spirale
f spirale *f* logarithmique; spirale équiangle
r логарифмическая спираль *f*

5692 log file
d Sicherstellungsdatei *f*
f fichier *m* d'enregistrement
r регистрационный файл *m*

* **logic** → 1070

* **logical** → 1070

5693 logical expression
d logischer Ausdruck *m*
f expression *f* logique
r логическое выражение *n*

5694 logical extent
d logischer Extent *m*
f étendue *f* logique
r логический экстент *m*

5695 logical grouping operator
d Operator *m* der logischen Gruppierung
f opérateur *m* de groupement logique
r оператор *m* логического группирования

5696 logical image
d logisches Bild *n*
f image *f* logique
r логическое изображение *n*

* **logical operation** → 1073

5697 logical query
d logische Abfrage *f*
f interrogation *f* logique
r логический запрос *m*

5698 logical structure
d logische Struktur *f*
f structure *f* logique
r логическая структура *f*

* **logic operation** → 1073

* **logistic spiral** → 5691

* **logo** → 1200

5699 logo screen
d Logo-Schirm *m*
f écran *m* logo
r экран *m* фирменного знака

* **logotype** → 1200

5700 longitude
d Länge *f*
f longitude *f*
r долгота *f*

5701 longitudinal
d longitudinal; Längs-
f longitudinal
r продольный

5702 longitudinal deformation; longitudinal strain
d Längsdeformation *f*
f déformation *f* longitudinale
r продольная деформация *f*

5703 longitudinal direction
d Längsrichtung *f*
f direction *f* longitudinale; sens *m* longitudinal
r продольное направление *n*

5704 longitudinal displacement
d Längsverschiebung *f*
f déplacement *m* longitudinal
r продольное смещение *n*

5705 longitudinal gap
d Längsspalt *m*
f intervalle *m* longitudinal
r продольный зазор *m*

5706 longitudinal profile; longitudinal section
d Längsprofil *n*; Längsschnitt *m*
f profil *m* en long; section *f* longitudinale; coup *m* longitudinal
r продольный профиль *m*; продольное сечение *n*

* **longitudinal section** → 5706

5707 longitudinal shrinkage
d Längsschrumpfung *f*
f retrait *m* longitudinal
r продольное сжатие *n*; продольная усадка *f*

* **longitudinal strain** → 5702

* **long radius** → 7719

5708 long zigzag pattern
d Längenzickzack-Bild *n*

f image *f* zigzag en longueur
r продольное зигзагообразное
изображение *n*

5709 lookup field
d Suchfeld *n*
f champ *m* de recherche
r поле *n* просмотра; просмотровое поле

5710 lookup table
d Lookup-Tabelle *f*; Nachschlagtabelle *f*
f table *f* de référence
r таблица *f* просмотра; просмотровая
таблица; справочная таблица

* **loop** → 434, 1586, 2423

5711 loop button
d Schleifenschaltfläche *f*; Umlauftaste *f*
f bouton *m* de lacet
r бутон *m* вращения; бутон шлейфа

* **loopfree** → 138

5712 Lorenz attractor
d Lorenz-Attraktor *m*
f attracteur *m* de Lorenz
r аттрактор *m* Лоренца

5713 lossless
d verlustfrei; verlustlos
f sans perte
r без потери

5714 lossless compression
d verlustfreie Kompression *f*;
verlustlose Kompaktion *f*
f compression *f* sans perte
r сжатие *n* без потери

5715 lossy compression
d Kompression *f* mit Verlust
f compression *f* avec pertes
r сжатие *n* с потерей

5716 low color density
d niedrige Farbdichte *f*
f densité *f* de couleur basse
r низкая плотность *f* цвета

5717 low contrast
d niedriger Kontrast *m*
f contraste *m* bas
r низкий контраст *m*

5718 low-contrast image
d Bild *n* mit niedrigem Kontrast
f image *f* de contraste bas
r изображение *n* с низким контрастом

5719 lower case
d Kleinschreibung *f*
f registre *m* inférieur
r нижний регистр *m*

5720 lower envelope
d untere Enveloppe *f*
f enveloppe *f* inférieure
r нижняя огибающая *f*

5721 lower half-plane
d untere Halbebene *f*
f demi-plan *m* inférieur
r нижняя полуплоскость *f*

* **lower index** → 9293

5722 lowering; depression
d Erniedrigung *f*; Herunterziehen *n*
f abaissement *m*; dépression *f*
r понижение *n*

5723 low level
d niedriger Pegel *m*; unterer Pegel
f niveau *m* inférieur; niveau bas
r низкий уровень *m*

5724 low-level driver
d Treiber *m* niedrigen Pegels
f driver *m* de niveau bas
r драйвер *m* низкого уровня

5725 low-level image processing
d Bildverarbeitung *f* niedrigen Pegels
f traitement *m* d'images de niveau bas
r обработка *f* изображений низкого уровня

5726 low-pass filter
d Tiefpassfilter *m*
f filtre *m* passe-bas
r фильтр *m* низких частот

5727 low resolution
d niedriges Auflösungsvermögen *n*
f résolution *f* basse
r низкая разрешающая способность *f*

5728 low-resolution image
d Bild *n* mit kleinem Auflösungsvermögen
f image *f* à résolution basse
r изображение *n* с низкой разрешающей
способностью

5729 low-resolution monitor
d Bildschirm *m* mit kleinem
Auflösungsvermögen
f écran *m* à résolution basse
r экран *m* с низкой разрешающей
способностью

* **loxodrome** → 8151

* **loxodromic curve** → 8151

* **loxodromic line** → 8151

* **loxodromic spiral** → 8151

* **lozenge** → 2713

* **lpi** → 5637

* **LSVE** → 5413

* **l.u.b.** → 5474

5730 luminance
(the black-white portion of a video signal)
d Luminanz *f*
f luminance *f*; émittance *f* lumineuse
r световое излучение *n*

5731 luminance coefficient; luminance factor
d Luminanzkoeffizient *m*
f coefficient *m* de luminance; facteur *m* de luminance
r коэффициент *m* светового излучения

5732 luminance component
d Luminanzkomponente *f*
f composante *f* de luminance
r составляющая *f* светового излучения

* **luminance factor** → 5731

5733 luminance meter
d Luminanz-Meter *n*
f mètre *m* de luminance
r измеритель *m* светового излучения

5734 luminance normal
d Luminanznormale *f*
f normale *f* de luminance
r нормаль *f* удельного светового излучения

5735 luminance quantization table
d Luminanzquantisierungstabelle *f*
f table *f* de numérisation de la luminance
r таблица *f* дискретизации светового излучения

* **luminosity** → 5551

5736 luminous area
d beleuchteter Bereich *m*
f zone *f* lumineuse
r освещенная зона *f*

5737 luminous color
d Warnfarbe *f*

f couleur *f* de signalisation
r цвет *m* сигнализации

* **luminous source** → 5562

* **luminous spot** → 5568

5738 lumped
d konzentriert
f localisé; concentré
r сосредоточенный

5739 lune; bit-angle
d Möndchen *n*; Zweieck *n*
f lunule *f*; biangle *m*
r луночка *f*; лунка *f*; двуугольник *m*

* **luster** → 1137

* **lustre** → 1137

* **LZW compression** → 5492

M

5740 machine; engine
   d Maschine *f*
   f machine *f*
   r машина *f*

   * **machine intelligence** → 587

5741 machine vision; artificial vision
   d Maschinensehen *n*; künstliches Sehen *n*
   f vision *f* artificielle
   r машинное зрение *n*; искусственное зрение

5742 macro
   d Makro *n*
   f macro *m*
   r макрос *m*

5743 macrostructure
   d Makrostruktur *f*
   f macrostructure *f*
   r макроструктура *f*

5744 macrostructured texture
   d makrostrukturierte Textur *f*
   f texture *f* macrostructurée
   r макроструктурированная текстура *f*

5745 magic
   d magisch
   f magique
   r магический

5746 magic square
   d magisches Quadrat *n*
   f carré *m* magique
   r магический квадрат *m*

5747 magic wand
   d Zauberstab *m*
   f stylo *m* magique; baguette *f* magique
   r волшебная палочка *f*; магический
   электронный карандаш *m*

5748 magnet
   (an automatic movement of the cursor onto
   the snap point)
   d Magnet *m*
   f aimant *m*
   r магнит *m*

**5749 magnetic capture system; magnetic
     tracking system**
   (for motion capture)

   d magnetisches Sammlungssystem *n*
   f système *m* de capturage magnétique
   r магнитная система *f* улавливания

5750 magnetic photography
   d magnetische Fotografie *f*
   f photographie *f* magnétique
   r магнитная фотосъемка *f*

5751 magnetic resonance imaging; MRI
   d Magnetresonanzbilderzeugung *f*
   f imagination *f* par résonance magnétique;
   imagerie *f* par résonance magnétique
   r изображение *n* магнитным резонансом

   * **magnetic tracking system** → 5749

   * **magnification** → 669

   * **magnification factor** → 1646

5752 magnification level
   d Vergrößerungsniveau *n*
   f niveau *m* de grossissement
   r ниво *n* увеличения

   * **magnifier** → 5753

   * **magnifying** → 669

5753 magnifying glass; magnify lens; magnifier
   d Lupe *f*
   f loupe *f*
   r лупа *f*; увеличительное стекло *n*

   * **magnify lens** → 5753

5754 magnitude
   d Größe *f*
   f grandeur *f*
   r величина *f*

5755 Mahalanobis distance
   d Mahalanobis-Distanz *f*
   f distance *f* Mahalanobis
   r расстояние *n* Махаланобиса

5756 main; principal; master; leading
   d Haupt-; Anfangs-; Leit-; Master-; führend
   f principal; général; maître; dominant; premier
   r главный; ведущий; старший

5757 main application window
   d Hauptanwendungsfenster *n*
   f fenêtre *f* d'application principale
   r главное окно *n* приложения

   * **main diagonal** → 5468

5758 **main direction; principal direction**
  d Hauptrichtung *f*
  f direction *f* principale
  r главное направление *n*

5759 **main menu; root menu**
  d Hauptmenü *n*
  f menu *m* principal; menu de racine
  r главное меню *n*

5760 **main route**
  d Hauptroute *f*
  f route *f* principale
  r главный маршрут *m*

5761 **maintenance; attendance; servicing**
  d Wartung *f*; Instandhaltung *f*; Unterhaltung *f*
  f maintenance *f*; entretien *m*; service *m*
  r поддержка *f*; [техническое] обслуживание *n*; уход *m*

5762 **main window; primary window**
  d Hauptfenster *n*
  f fenêtre *f* principale
  r главное окно *n*

5763 **major axis; principal axis; primary axis**
  d Hauptachse *f*; Primärachse *f*
  f axe *m* majeur; axe principal; axe primaire
  r главная ось *f*

5764 **major axis of an ellipse**
  d große Achse *f* einer Ellipse; Hauptachse *f* einer Ellipse
  f grand axe *m* d'une ellipse; axe focal d'une ellipse; axe principal d'une ellipse
  r большая ось *f* эллипса; главная ось эллипса; фокальная ось эллипса

5765 **major cutting edge**
  d Hauptschnittkante *f*
  f arête *f* de coupe principale
  r главное секущее ребро *n*

5766 **major diameter; outside diameter**
  d Außendurchmesser *m*; Nenndurchmesser *m*
  f diamètre *m* nominal; diamètre extérieur
  r внешний диаметр *m*; наружный диаметр

5767 **major gridlines**
  (in a chart)
  d Hauptrasterlinien *fpl*
  f lignes *fpl* de grille principales
  r главные растровые линии *fpl*

5768 **majority**
  d Majorität *f*; Mehrheit *f*
  f majorité *f*
  r большинство *n*; мажоритарность *f*

5769 **major tick mark**
  d Hauptteilstrich *m*
  f coche *f* maître
  r главная отметка *f*

5770 **management**
  d Leitung *f*; Management *n*
  f direction *f*; gestion *f*; management *m*
  r управление *n*; организация *f*; обслуживание *n*

* **management graphics** → 1199

* **manager** → 5771

5771 **manager [program]**
  d Managerprogramm *n*; Manager *m*
  f programme *m* gestionnaire; gestionnaire *m*
  r управляющая программа *f*; менажер *m*

5772 **Mandelbrot figure**
  d Mandelbrot-Figur *f*
  f figure *f* de Mandelbrot
  r фигура *f* Манделброта

5773 **Mandelbrot set**
  d Mandelbrot-Menge *f*
  f ensemble *m* de Mandelbrot
  r множество *m* Манделброта

* **manifold** → 2245

5774 **manifold; variety**
  d Mannigfaltigkeit *f*
  f variété *f*
  r многообразие *n*

* **manipulate** *v* → 4494

* **manipulation** → 4495

5775 **manual**
  d Handbuch *n*
  f manuel *m*
  r руководство *n*

5776 **manual; hand[-operated]** *adj*
  d Hand-; manuell
  f manuel; à la main
  r ручной

5777 **manual digitizing**
  d manuelle Digitalisierung *f*
  f numérisation *f* manuelle
  r ручное преобразование *n* в цифровую форму

5778 **manual extension line**
  d manuelle Hilfslinie *f*

f ligne *f* d'extension manuelle
r ручная вспомогательная линия *f*

5779 manual scanning
 d manuelle Abtastung *f*
 f échantillonnage *m* manuel
 r ручное сканирование *n*

 * **many-dimensional → 6090**

 * **map → 7528**

5780 map *v*
 d kartografisch darstellen
 f cartographier
 r картографировать

5781 map *v*
 d planen; abbilden
 f faire une projection; établir une correspondance
 r отображать; проецировать

5782 map; chart
 d Karte *f*
 f carte *f*
 r карта *f*

5783 map-coloring problem
 d Färbungsproblem *n* der Karten
 f problème *m* de coloriage des cartes
 r задача *f* о раскрашивании карт

5784 map coordinate system
 d Kartenkoordinatensystem *n*
 f système *m* de coordonnées de la carte
 r координатная система *f* карты

5785 map distortion
 d Abbildungsverzerrung *f*
 f distorsion *f* d'application
 r искажение *n* отображения

 * **map drawing → 1294**

5786 map extent
 d Abbildungsextent *m*
 f étendue *f* d'application
 r экстент *m* отображения

5787 map file
 d Kartendatei *f*
 f fichier *m* de carte
 r картный файл *m*; файл карты

5788 map formatting
 d Kartenformatierung *f*
 f formatage *m* de carte
 r форматирование *n* карты

 * **map-germ → 4214**

5789 map graticule; graticule; cartographical grid
 d Kartennetz *n*; kartografisches Netz *n*; Gitternetz *n*
 f réseau *m* cartographique; réticule *m*
 r картографическая сетка *f*

5790 map library
 d Kartenbibliothek *f*
 f bibliothèque *f* de cartes
 r библиотека *f* карт

5791 map limits
 d Kartengrenzen *fpl*
 f limites *fpl* de carte
 r границы *fpl* карты

 * **mapmaking → 1297**

5792 mapped
 d abgebildet
 f mappé
 r отображенный

5793 mapped buffer
 d Abbildungspuffer *m*; abgebildeter Puffer *m*
 f tampon *m* mappé
 r отображенный буфер *m*

 * **mapping → 1297, 7529**

5794 mapping coordinates
 d Abbildungskoordinaten *fpl*
 f coordonnées *fpl* d'application
 r координаты *fpl* отображения

5795 mapping method
 d Mapping-Verfahren *n*
 f méthode *f* de mappage
 r метод *m* отображения

5796 mapping mode
 d Mapping-Modus *m*
 f mode *m* de mappage
 r режим *m* отображения; режим преобразования

5797 mapping space
 d Abbildungsraum *m*
 f espace *m* des applications
 r пространство *n* отображений

5798 map plane
 d Kartenebene *f*
 f plan *m* de carte
 r плоскость *f* карты

5799 map plotting
 d Kartenplotten *n*

f traçage *m* de carte
r вычерчивание *n* карты

* **map projection** → 1295

5800 map scale
   d Kartenmaßstab *m*
   f échelle *f* de carte
   r масштаб *m* карты

5801 map sheet
   d Kartenblatt *n*
   f feuille *f* de carte
   r лист *m* карты

5802 map sheet boundaries
   d Grenzen *fpl* des Kartenblatts
   f limites *fpl* de feuille de carte
   r границы *fpl* листа карты

5803 map *v* to object
   d dem Objekt zuordnen
   f mapper sur un objet
   r отображать на объект

5804 marble
   d Marmor *m*
   f marbre *m*
   r мрамор *m*

* **marbling** → 6061

* **margin** → 1088

5805 margin
   d Papierrand *m*
   f marge *f*
   r поле *n* [печатной страницы]

* **marginal veil** → 3289

* **mark** → 5809

5806 mark *v*
   d markieren
   f marquer
   r отмечать

* **mark column** → 5807

5807 mark[ed] column
   d markierte Spalte *f*
   f colonne *f* marquée
   r помеченная колонка *f*

5808 marked zones
   d markierte Zonen *fpl*
   f zones *fpl* marquées
   r маркированные зоны *fpl*

5809 mark[er]; buck
   d Marke *f*; Markierungszeichen *n*
   f marque *f*; marqueur *m*
   r пометка *f*; маркер *m*

5810 mark field
   d Markierungsfeld *n*
   f champ *m* de marque
   r поле *n* маркера

5811 marking; flagging
   d Markierung *f*; Kennzeichnung *f*
   f marquage *m*; repérage *m*
   r маркировка *f*; маркирование *n*; разметка *f*

5812 marking sequence
   d Markierungsfolge *f*
   f séquence *f* de marquage
   r последовательность *f* маркировки

5813 marking tolerance
   d Markiertoleranz *f*
   f tolérance *f* de marquage
   r допуск *m* маркировки

5814 Markov chain
   d Markov-Kette *f*; Markovsche Kette *f*
   f chaîne *f* de Markov
   r цепь *f* Маркова; марковская цепь

5815 mark position
   d Markierungsstelle *f*; Markierungsposition *f*
   f position *f* de marque
   r позиция *f* метки

* **mark-space ratio** → 8923

* **mark-to-space ratio** → 8923

5816 mask
   d Maske *f*
   f masque *m*
   r маска *f*

5817 mask *v*; knock *v* out
   (prevent light from reaching part of an image and isolating the remaining part)
   d maskieren; abdecken
   f masquer
   r удалять (дополнительной краской); маскировать

5818 mask aligner
   d Maskenvergleicher *m*
   f aligneur *m* de masques
   r выравнитель *m* масок

* **mask channel** → 289

5819 masking
   d Maskierung *f*; Maskieren *n*; Ausblenden *n*

f masquage *m*
r маскирование *n*; выделение *n* маски; проверка *f* по маске

5820 masking of layer
 d Schichtmaskierung *f*
 f masquage *m* de couche
 r маскирование *n* слоя

5821 mask overlay
 d Maskenüberlagerung *f*
 f recouvrement *m* de masque
 r наложение *n* маски

5822 mask pattern
 d Maskenschablone *f*; Maskenstruktur *f*
 f modèle *m* de masque
 r шаблон *m* маски

5823 mask selection
 d Maskenauswahl *f*
 f sélection *f* de masque
 r выбор *m* маски

5824 mask tool
 d Hilfsmittel *n* "Maske"
 f outil *m* "masque"
 r инструмент *m* "маска"

5825 mask topography
 d Maskentopografie *f*
 f topographie *f* de masque
 r конфигурация *f* маски

5826 mask transformation
 d Maskentransformation *f*
 f transformation *f* de masque
 r трансформация *f* маски

5827 mask transparency
 d Maskentransparenz *f*
 f transparence *f* de masque
 r прозрачность *f* маски

5828 mass
 d Masse *f*
 f masse *f*
 r масса *f*

* **mass center** → 1363

5829 mass properties
 d Masse[n]eigenschaften *fpl*
 f propriétés *fpl* de masse
 r свойства *npl* массы

* **master** → 5756

5830 master desktop plane
 d Hauptdesktop-Ebene *f*

f plan *m* bureautique principal
r главная настольная плоскость *f*

5831 master grid
 d Hauptgitter *n*
 f grille *f* principale
 r главная сетка *f*

5832 master layer
 d Hauptschicht *f*
 f couche *f* principale
 r главный слой *m*; ведущий слой

5833 master node
 d Hauptknoten *m*
 f nœud *m* maître
 r главный узел *m*

5834 master object
 d Hauptobjekt *n*
 f objet *m* principal
 r ведущий объект *m*

5835 master page
 d Hauptseite *f*
 f page *f* principale
 r ведущая страница *f*; главная страница

* **match** *v* → 1657

* **matching** → 1658, 2266

5836 material assignment; material attaching
 d Materialanschluss *m*
 f assignation *m* de matériel; affectation *f* de matériau; attachement *m* de matériel
 r присоединение *n* материала

* **material attaching** → 5836

5837 material attribute
 d Attribut *n* des Materials
 f attribut *m* de matériel
 r атрибут *m* материала

5838 material color
 d Materialfarbe *f*
 f couleur *f* de matériel
 r цвет *m* материала

5839 material coloring
 d Materialfärbung *f*
 f coloriage *m* de matériel
 r раскрашивание *n* материала

5840 material condition
 d Zustand *m* des Materials
 f condition *f* de matériel
 r состояние *n* материала

* **material dispersion** → 5843

5841 material list
d Materialliste f
f liste f des matériaux
r список m материалов

5842 material morphing
d Material-Morphing n
f morphage m de matériaux
r морфинг m материалов

5843 material scattering; material dispersion
d Materialstreuung f
f dispersion f [chromatique] du matériel
r рассеивание n материала

* **materials library** → 5525

5844 mathematical operation
d mathematische Operation f
f opération f mathématique
r математическая операция f

5845 mathematical operator
d mathematischer Operator m
f opérateur m mathématique
r математический оператор m

5846 mathematical symbols
d mathematische Symbole npl
f symboles mpl mathématiques
r математические символы mpl

5847 matrix; array
d Matrix f; Matrize f
f matrice f
r матрица f

5848 matrix calculus
d Matrizenrechnung f; Matrizenkalkül n/m
f calcul m matriciel
r матричное исчисление n

* **matrix display** → 7755

* **matrix dot** → 8366

* **matrix image** → 7762

* **matrix line** → 5849

5849 matrix row; matrix line
d Matrixlinie f; Matrixzeile f
f ligne f de matrice
r строка f матрицы

5850 matrix size
d Matrixgröße f
f dimension f de matrice

r размерность f матрицы

5851 matting
d Mattieren n
f matage m
r матирование n

5852 maximal; maximum
d maximal; Maximal-
f maximal
r максимальный

5853 maximal surface
d Maximalfläche f
f surface f maximale
r максимальная поверхность f

5854 maximize v
d maximieren
f maximaliser
r максимизировать

5855 maximize button
d Schaltfläche f für Maximieren
f bouton m de maximalisation
r кнопка f максимизации (окна)

5856 maximized window
d maximiertes Fenster n
f fenêtre f maximalisée
r максимизированное окно n

* **maximum** → 5852

5857 maximum
d Maximum n
f maximum m
r максимум m; максимальная величина f

5858 maximum active viewpoint
d maximaler aktiver Aug[en]punkt m
f point m de vue actif maximal
r максимальная активная точка f зрения

5859 maximum distance
d Maximaldistanz f; Maximalabstand m
f distance f maximale
r максимальное расстояние n

5860 maximum filter
d Maximumfilter m
f filtre m de maximum
r фильтр m максимума

5861 maximum level of saturation
d maximales Sättigungsniveau n
f niveau m de saturation maximal
r максимальный уровень m насыщения

* **MB** → 5897

* **mean** → 5866

5862 mean; average; medium; middle
d mittler
f moyen; médian; médium
r средний; умеренный

5863 mean coordinates
d mittlere Koordinaten *fpl*
f coordonnées *fpl* moyennes
r средние координаты *fpl*

5864 mean curvature
d mittlere Krümmung *f*
f courbure *f* moyenne
r средняя кривизна *f*

* **mean error** → 733

5865 mean quadratic deviation
d mittlere quadratische Ablenkung *f*
f déviation *f* quadratique moyenne
r среднее квадратическое отклонение *n*

5866 mean [value]; average [value]
d Mittel *n*; Mittelwert *m*
f valeur *f* moyenne; moyenne *f*
r среднее [значение] *n*; средняя величина *f*

5867 measure
d Maß *n*
f mesure *f*
r мера *f*

5868 measured quantity
d Messgröße *f*
f grandeur *f* mesurée
r измеряемая величина *f*

5869 measurement; measuring; metering
d Messung *f*; Abmessung *f*; Messen *n*
f mesurage *m*
r измерение *n*

* **measurement accuracy** → 75

* **measurement of angles** → 4257

* **measurement precision** → 75

5870 measurement system
d Messsystem *n*; System *n* zur Messung
f système *m* de mesurage
r измерительная система *f*

5871 measure of an angle; angle measure; angular measure
d Winkelmaß *n*
f mesure *f* d'angle; mesure angulaire
r угловая мера *f*

5872 measure of an angle in degrees
d Gradmaß *n* des Winkels
f mesure *f* d'un angle en degrés
r градусная мера *f* угла

5873 measure of an angle in radians; radian measure of an angle; circular measure of an angle
d Bogenmaß *n* des Winkels
f mesure *f* d'un angle en radians
r радианная мера *f* угла

5874 measure of dispersion
d Streuungsmaß *n*
f mesure *f* de dispersion
r мера *f* рассеивания

5875 measure of kurtosis
d Wölbungsmaß *n*
f mesure *f* de kurtosis
r мера *f* выпуклости

5876 measure of length
d Längenmaß *n*
f mesure *f* de longueur
r мера *f* длины

5877 measure of location
d Maßzahl *f* der Lage
f mesure *f* de position
r мера *f* расположения

5878 measure of skewness
d Schiefheitsmaß *n*
f mesure *f* d'asymétrie; mesure de dissymétrie
r мера *f* асимметрии

* **measure unit** → 10025

* **measuring** → 5869

5879 measuring data
d Messdaten *npl*
f données *fpl* de mesure
r измерительные данные *npl*

5880 measuring tool
d Messvorrichtung *f*; Messinstrument *n*; Messgerät *n*
f outil *m* de mesure
r инструмент *m* измерения

5881 media
d Medien *npl*
f média *mpl*
r средства *npl* информации; носители *mpl*

5882 medial
d Mitten-; Medial-

    f médial
    r медиальный; серединний

5883 medial triangle; complementary triangle
    d Medialdreieck *n*; Mittendreieck *n*
    f triangle *m* médian; triangle complémentaire
    r серединный треугольник *m*

5884 median
    d Seitenhalbierende *f*; Mediane *f*
    f médiane *f*
    r медиана *f*

5885 median filter
    d Medianfilter *m*
    f filtre *m* médian
    r медианный фильтр *m*

**5886 median of a trapezoid; midline of a
    trapezoid**
    d Mittellinie *f* des Trapezes
    f base *f* moyenne d'un trapèze
    r средняя линия *f* трапеции

5887 median of a triangle
    d Seitenhalbierende *f* des Dreiecks
    f médiane *f* d'un triangle
    r медиана *f* треугольника

    * **mediator** → **5889, 5890**

5888 mediator; bisecting *adj*
    d halbierend
    f médiateur
    r делящий пополам

**5889 mediator [line]; mid-perpendicular; right
    bisector; perpendicular bisector**
    d Mittelsenkrechte *f*; Mittellot *n*
    f médiatrice *f*; perpendiculaire *f* au milieu
    r медиатриса *f*; серединный
    перпендикуляр *m*; симметраль *f*

**5890 mediator [plane]; mid-perpendicular plane
    of a line segment; midplane of a line
    segment**
    d mittelsenkrechte Ebene *f* eines Abschnitts
    f plan *m* médiateur d'un segment
    r медиатрисная плоскость *f* отрезка;
    серединная плоскость отрезка

5891 medical images
    d medizinische Bilder *npl*
    f images *fpl* médicales
    r медицинские изображения *npl*

5892 medical imaging
    d medizinische Abbildung *f*
    f imagerie *f* médicale
    r формирование *n* медицинских

    изображений

5893 medical VR
    d medizinische virtuelle Realität *f*
    f réalité *f* virtuelle médicale
    r виртуальная реальность *f* в медицине

    * **medium** → **5862**

5894 medium
    d Medium *n*
    f médium *m*; milieu *m*
    r среда *f*; средство *n*

5895 medium infrared
    d mittleres Infrarot *n*
    f infrarouge *m* moyen
    r средний инфракрасный диапазон *m*

5896 megabit
    d Megabit *n*
    f mégabit *m*
    r мегабит *m*

5897 megabyte; MB
    d Megabyte *n*; MB
    f méga-octet *m*; Mo
    r мегабайт *m*; Мб

5898 megapixel
    d Megapixel *n*
    f mégapixel *m*
    r мегапиксел *m*

5899 member; term
    d Glied *n*; Teil *m*; Term *m*
    f membre *m*; terme *m*
    r член *m*; терм *m*

5900 member of a group
    d Glied *n* einer Gruppe
    f membre *m* d'un groupe
    r член *m* группы

    * **member of a set** → **3346**

    * **memorization** → **9212**

    * **memorize** *v* → **9213**

5901 memory; storage; store
    d Speicher *m*
    f mémoire *f*
    r память *f*; запоминающее устройство *n*;
    накопитель *m*

5902 mensuration
    d Maßbestimmung *f*
    f détermination *f* métrique
    r определение *n* меры; мероопределение *n*

5903 menu
  d Menü *n*
  f menu *m*
  r меню *n*

5904 menu bar
  d Menüleiste *f*; Menübalken *n*
  f barre *f* des menus
  r меню-лента *f*

5905 menu control
  d Menüsteuerung *f*
  f commande *f* par menu
  r управление *n* с помощью меню

5906 menu customization
  d Menüanpassung *f*
  f personnalisation *f* de menu
  r разработка *f* заказного меню

5907 menu-driven
  d menügeführt; menügesteuert
  f piloté par des menus
  r управляемый через меню

5908 menu group
  d Menügruppe *f*
  f groupe *m* de menus
  r группа *f* меню

5909 menu item; menu point
  d Menüelement *n*; Menüpunkt *m*
  f élément *m* de menu
  r элемент *m* меню

5910 menu option
  d Menüoption *f*
  f option *f* de menu
  r опция *f* меню

  * **menu picking** → 5911

  * **menu point** → 5909

5911 menu selection; menu picking
  d Menüauswahl *f*
  f sélection *f* par menu
  r выбор *m* на основе меню

5912 menu structure
  d Menüstruktur *f*
  f structure *f* du menu
  r структура *f* меню

5913 Mercator projection
  d Merkator-Projektion *f*
  f projection *f* de Mercator
  r проекция *f* Меркатора

5914 merge *v*
  d vermischen; verschmelzen
  f interclasser; fusionner
  r смешивать; сливать

5915 merge group
  d Verschmelzungsgruppe *f*
  f groupe *m* de fusionnement
  r группа *f* слияния

5916 merge mode
  d Verschmelzungsmodus *m*
  f mode *m* de fusionnement
  r режим *m* слияния

5917 merging; meshing
  d Mischen *n*; Zusammenmischen *n*;
     Verschmelzen *n*
  f fusionnement *m*; interclassement *m*
  r слияние *n*; смешивание *n*

5918 merging object
  d Verschmelzungsobjekt *n*
  f objet *m* fusionné
  r сходящийся объект *m*

5919 meridian
  d Meridian *m*
  f méridien *m*
  r меридиан *m*

  * **meridional projection** → 9858

5920 mesh
  d Masche *f*
  f filet *m*; maille *f*; réseau *m* de facettes
  r [простая планарная] сеть *f*; сетка *f*;
     решетка *f*

5921 mesh analysis
  d Maschenanalyse *f*; Netzwerkanalyse *f*
  f analyse *f* de maille
  r анализ *m* сетки

  * **meshbeat** → 6019

5922 mesh[ed] network
  d Maschennetzwerk *n*
  f réseau *m* de mailles
  r сеть *f* с ячеистой топологией; сетчатая
     схема *f*; ячеистая сеть

  * **mesh facet** → 9374

  * **meshing** → 5917

  * **mesh network** → 5922

5923 mesh point
  d Maschenpunkt *m*

 f nœud *m* de maille
 r узел *m* сетки

5924 mesh topology
 d Maschentopologie *f*
 f topologie *f* de maille
 r решетчатая топология *f*; топология типа
  решетки

 * **mesochronous** → 9427

5925 message; notice
 d Nachricht *f*; Meldung *f*; Mitteilung *f*
 f message *m*
 r сообщение *n*; известие *n*

5926 metafile
 d Metadatei *f*
 f métafichier *m*
 r метафайл *m*

5927 metagraph
 d Metagraph *m*
 f métagraphe *m*
 r метаграф *m*

5928 metal rendering
 d Metall-Rendering *n*
 f rendu *m* du métal
 r тонирование *n* металла; металлический
  рендеринг *m*

5929 metamodel
 d Metamodell *n*
 f méta-modèle *m*
 r метамодель *f*

5930 metamorphosis
 d Metamorphose *f*
 f métamorphose *f*
 r метаморфоза *f*

5931 metamorphosis sequence; morph sequence
 d Metamorphosenfolge *f*
 f séquence *f* de métamorphoses
 r последовательность *f* метаморфоз

5932 metaphor
 d Metapher *f*
 f métaphore *f*
 r метафора *f*

 * **metering** → 5869

5933 method
 d Methode *f*; Verfahren *n*
 f méthode *f*; moyen *m*
 r метод *m*; способ *m*

5934 method of approximation; approximation

method; approximate method
 d Approximationsverfahren *n*;
  Approximationsmethode *f*;
  Annäherungsverfahren *n*;
  Näherungsverfahren *n*; Näherungsmethode *f*
 f méthode *f* d'approximation; méthode
  approximative
 r метод *m* аппроксимации; метод
  приближения

 * **method of iteration** → 5335

5935 method of selection; select method
 d Selektionsmethode *f*; Auswahlmethode *f*
 f méthode *f* de sélection
 r селективный метод *m*; метод выборки

5936 metric information
 d metrische Information *f*
 f information *f* métrique
 r метрическая информация *f*; информация в
  метрической системе

5937 metric scales
 d metrische Skalen *fpl*
 f échelles *fpl* métriques
 r метрические масштабы *mpl*

5938 metric space
 d metrischer Raum *m*
 f espace *m* métrique
 r метрическое пространство *n*

5939 metric system
 d metrisches System *n*
 f système *m* métrique
 r метрическая система *f*

5940 metric unit
 d metrische Einheit *f*
 f unité *f* métrique
 r метрическая единица *f*

5941 microfilm
 d Mikrofilm *m*
 f microfilm *m*
 r микрофильм *m*

5942 microframe
 d Mikroframe *n*
 f microtrame *f*
 r микрокадр *m*; кадр *m* микрофильма

5943 micrographics
 d Mikrografik *f*
 f micrographique *m*
 r микрографика *f*

5944 microimage
 d Mikrobild *n*

f micro-image *f*; microvue *f*
r микрообраз *m*; микроизображение *n*

5945 microlens
  d Mikrolinse *f*
  f microlentille *f*
  r микролинза *f*

* **micrometer** → **5946**

5946 micron; micrometer
  d Mikron *n*
  f micron *m*; micromètre *m*
  r микрон *m*

5947 microscanner
  d Mikroscanner *m*
  f microscanner *m*
  r микросканер *m*

* **middle** → **5862**

5948 middle information content of an image
  d mittlerer Informationsgehalt *m* eines Bilds
  f contenu *m* moyen d'information d'une image
  r среднее информационное содержание *n* изображения

5949 middle interior grip
  d mittlerer Innengriff *m*
  f poignée *f* inférieure médiane
  r средний внутренний захват *m*

5950 middle line; midline
  d Mittellinie *f*
  f ligne *f* moyenne
  r средняя линия *f*

5951 middle point; midpoint
  d Mittelpunkt *m*; Mitte *f*
  f point *m* médian; milieu *m*
  r средняя точка *f*; середина *f*

5952 middletones; midtones
  (tones created by dots between 30 percent and 70 percent of coverage, as compared to highlights and shadows)
  d Mitteltöne *mpl*
  f tons *mpl* moyens
  r средние тона *mpl*; значения *npl* градации посередине между ярким светом и тенью

* **midline** → **5950**

* **midline of a trapezoid** → **5886**

* **mid-perpendicular** → **5889**

* **mid-perpendicular plane of a line segment** → **5890**

* **midplane of a line segment** → **5890**

* **midpoint** → **5951**

5953 midpoint slider
  d Mittelpunkt-Schieber *m*
  f glisseur *m* de point médian
  r ползунок *m* средней точки

5954 midrange
  d Mittelbereich *m*
  f champ *m* moyen
  r середина *f* диапазона

5955 midtone adjusting
  d Mitteltonanpassung *f*
  f ajustage *m* de tons moyens
  r наладка *f* средних тонов

5956 midtone area
  d Mitteltonbereich *m*
  f aire *f* de tons moyens
  r область *f* средних тонов

* **midtones** → **5952**

* **military perspective** → **944**

5957 mini-geometry
  d Minigeometrie *f*
  f mini-géométrie *f*
  r мини-геометрия *f*

5958 minimal
  d minimal; Minimal-
  f minimal
  r минимальный

5959 minimal surface
  d Minimalfläche *f*
  f surface *f* minimale
  r минимальная поверхность *f*

5960 minimization; minimizing
  d Minim[is]ierung *f*; Minimalisierung *f*
  f minim[al]isation *f*
  r минимизация *f*

5961 minimize *v*
  d minimieren
  f minimiser
  r минимизировать

5962 minimize button
  d Schaltfläche *f* für Minimieren
  f bouton *m* de minimisation; bouton de réduction
  r бутон *m* минимизирования; бутон свертывания

5963 minimized window
  d minimiertes Fenster n
  f fenêtre f minimisée
  r минимизированное окно n

* **minimizing** → 5960

5964 minimum
  d Minimum n
  f minimum m
  r минимум m

5965 minimum distance
  d Minimaldistanz f; Minimalabstand m
  f distance f minimale
  r минимальное расстояние n

5966 minimum distance classifier
  d Minimum-Distanz-Klassifikator m
  f classeur m de distances minimales
  r классификатор m минимальных
    расстояний

5967 minimum filter
  d Minimumfilter m
  f filtre m de minimum
  r фильтр m минимума

5968 minor
  d minor; geringfügig
  f mineur
  r меньший; подчиненный

5969 minor axis
  d Nebenachse f; kleine Achse f
  f axe m mineur; petit axe
  r побочная ось f; малая ось

5970 minor axis of an ellipse; shorter axis of an ellipse
  d kleine Achse f einer Ellipse; Nebenachse f einer Ellipse; Querachse f einer Ellipse
  f petit axe m d'une ellipse; axe non focal d'une ellipse; axe secondaire d'une ellipse
  r малая ось f эллипса

5971 minority
  d Minorität f
  f minorité f
  r подчиненность f

5972 minor semiaxis of an ellipse; shorter semiaxis of an ellipse
  d kleine Halbachse f einer Ellipse
  f demi-petit axe m d'une ellipse; demi-axe non focal d'une ellipse
  r малая полуось f эллипса

5973 minor structure; substructure
  d Unterstruktur f; Teilstruktur f

  f structure f mineure; structure inférieure; sous-structure f
  r подчиненная структура f; внутренняя структура; подструктура f

* **minus** → 8687

5974 minus color
  d Minusfarbe f
  f couleur f soustractive; moindre couleur
  r комплиментарный цвет m

* **minus sign** → 8687

* **minute** → 5975

5975 minute of a degree; sexagesimal minute; minute
  d Winkelminute f; Minute f
  f minute f [sexagésimale]
  r угловая минута f; дуговая минута

* **mipmap** → 5976

5976 mipmap[ing]
  d Mip-Mapping n
  f mip-mapping m
  r множественное отображение n текстур одного и того же изображения; mip-текстурирование n

5977 mipmap level
  d Mip-Map-Niveau n
  f niveau m de mip-mapping
  r уровень m mip-текстурирования

5978 mirage
  d Luftspiegelung f
  f mirage m
  r мираж m

5979 mirror
  d Spiegel m
  f miroir m
  r зеркало n

5980 mirror button
  d Spiegelschaltfläche f
  f bouton m miroir
  r зеркальная кнопка f

5981 mirror[ed] image
  d Spiegelbild n
  f image f [de] miroir; image spéculaire
  r зеркальное изображение n

* **mirror image** → 5981

* **mirroring** → 9026

5982 mirror line
  d Spiegellinie *f*
  f ligne *f* spéculaire
  r зеркальная линия *f*

* **mirror reflection** → 9026

5983 mirror symmetry
  d Spiegelsymmetrie *f*
  f symétrie *f* spéculaire
  r зеркальная симметрия *f*

* **misalignment** → 747

5984 misframing
  d falsches Framing *n*
  f décadrage *m*
  r ошибочное кадрирование *n*

* **mismatch** → 5985

5985 mismatch[ing]
  d Fehlanpassung *f*; Nichtübereinstimmung *f*
  f déséquilibre *m*; discordance *f*;
    désadaptation *f*; défaut *m* de coordination
  r рассогласование *n*; несовпадение *n*;
    несоответствие *n*

5986 missing data
  d fehlende Daten *npl*; fehlende Angaben *fpl*
  f observation *f* manquante; données *fpl*
    manquantes
  r недостающие данные *npl*

* **miter** → 5988

5987 mit[e]red corner
  d Schrägschnittecke *f*; Schrägschnittwinkel *m*
  f coin *m* coupé d'onglet
  r скошенный угол *m*

5988 miter [join] (US); **mitre [join]** (UK)
  d Gehrung *f*; Gehr[ungs]fuge *f*; Kerbschnitt *m*
  f biseau *m*; jonction *f* de pointe
  r фацетное соединение *n*; соединение в ус;
    скос *m* под углом 45°

* **mitre** → 5988

* **mitre joint** → 5988

* **mitred corner** → 5987

* **mix** → 5995

5989 mix *v*; **blend** *v*
  d mischen; vermischen
  f mixer; confondre; mélanger
  r смешивать; сочетать[ся]

5990 mixed
  d gemischt; Misch-
  f mélangé
  r смешанный

5991 mixed environment
  d gemischte Umgebung *f*
  f environnement *m* mélangé
  r смешанная среда *f*

5992 mixed image
  d Mischbild *n*
  f image *f* mixte
  r смешанное изображение *n*

5993 mixed noise
  d Mischrauschen *n*
  f bruit *m* mixte
  r смешанный шум *m*

5994 mixer
  d Mischer *m*
  f mélangeur *m*; [em]brouilleur *m*
  r смеситель *m*

5995 mix[ing]; blend[ing]
  d Mischung *f*; Vermischen *n*; Mischen *n*
  f mixtion *f*; mixage *m*; mélange *m*
  r смешение *n*; смешивание *n*;
    перемешивание *n*

5996 mixing area
  d Mischbereich *m*
  f domaine *m* de mélange
  r область *f* смешивания; зона *f* смешивания

5997 mixing correlation
  d Mischungsverhältnis *n*
  f corrélation *f* de mélange
  r соотношение *n* смешивания

* **MOB** → 6073

* **mobile** → 7332

* **mobility** → 7331

5998 Möbius band; Möbius surface
  d Möbiusband *n*; Möbiusfläche *f*
  f bande *f* de Möbius; surface *f* de Möbius
  r лента *f* Мебиуса; поверхность *f* Мебиуса

* **Möbius surface** → 5998

5999 modality
  d Modalität *f*
  f modalité *f*
  r модальность *f*

6000 mode
  d Modus *m*; Betriebsart *f*; Betriebsweise *f*

f mode *m*; régime *m*
r режим *m*; способ *m*

6001 model
 d Modell *n*
 f modèle *m*
 r модель *f*

6002 model database
 d Modelldatenbasis *f*
 f base *f* de données de modèle
 r база *f* данных модели

 * **modeler** → 6006

 * **modeling** → 6007

6003 modeling of human visual perception
 d Modellierung *f* der visuellen Menschenwahrnehmung
 f modelage *m* de perception visuelle d'homme
 r моделирование *n* человеческого визуального восприятия

6004 modeling of macrostructured textures
 d Modellierung *f* der makrostrukturierten Texturen
 f modelage *m* de textures à macrostructure
 r моделирование *n* макроструктурных текстур

6005 modeling of plants
 d Pflanzen-Modellierung *f*
 f modelage *m* de plantes
 r моделирование *n* растений

6006 modeling program; modeler
 d Modellierer *m*
 f programme *m* de modelage; modélisateur *m*
 r моделирующая программа *f*

6007 model[l]ing
 d Modellierung *f*; Modellbildung *f*
 f modelage *m*; modélisation *f*; création *f* de modèle
 r моделирование *n*

6008 model reconstruction
 d Rekonstruktion *f* des Modells
 f reconstruction *f* de modèle
 r реконструирование *n* модели

6009 model space
 d Modellraum *m*
 f espace *m* de modèle
 r пространство *n* модели

6010 model's polygon count
 d Zahl *f* der Modellpolygone
 f nombre *m* de polygones de modèle

r число *n* полигонов модели

6011 moderator
 d Moderator *m*
 f animateur *m*
 r замедлитель *m*

 * **modification** → 293

6012 modified conical projection
 d modifizierte konische Projektion *f*; unechte konische Projektion
 f projection *f* mériconique
 r псевдоконическая проекция *f*

6013 modified cylindrical projection
 d modifizierte zylindrische Projektion *f*
 f projection *f* méricylindrique
 r псевдоцилиндрическая проекция *f*

6014 modified polyconical projection
 d modifizierte polykonische Projektion *f*
 f projection *f* polyconique modifiée
 r псевдополиконическая проекция *f*

6015 modifier
 d Modifikator *m*; Modifizierfaktor *m*
 f modificateur *m*
 r модификатор *m*

6016 modular
 d modular; bausteinartig
 f modulaire
 r модульный; блочный

6017 modularity
 d Modularität *f*
 f modularité *f*
 r модульность *f*

6018 module
 d Modul *m*
 f module *m*
 r модуль *m*

 * **moire** → 6019

6019 moire [pattern]; interference pattern; meshbeat
 (undesirable pattern when halftones and screen tints are made with improperly aligned screens)
 d Moiré *m/n*
 f moiré *m*; moirage *m*
 r муар *m*; рябь *f*; оптические искажения *npl*; комбинационные искажения

6020 moment; instant
 d Moment *m*; Zeitpunkt *m*

f moment *m*; instant *m*
r момент *m*

6021 moment of inertia
d Trägheitsmoment
f moment *m* d'inertie
r инерционный момент *m*

* **monitor** → 2927, 6443

6022 monitoring; supervision; surveying
d Monitoring *n*; Überwachung *f*;
Dispatcherverwaltung *f*; Supervision *f*
f monitorage *m*; contrôle *m* [courant];
surveillance *f*; arpentage *m*
r [текущий] контроль *m*; обзор *m*;
обследование *n*

6023 monitor resolution; screen resolution
d Bildschirmauflösung *f*
f résolution *f* d'écran
r разрешающая способность *f* экрана

* **monochromatic** → 6025

6024 monochromaticity
d Einfarbigkeit *f*
f monochromaticité *f*
r монохроматизм *m*; одноцветность *f*

6025 monochrome; monochromatic; one-color
d monochrom[atisch]; einfarbig
f monochrome; monochromatique
r монохромный; монохроматический;
одноцветный

6026 monochrome beam
d monochromatischer Strahl *m*
f faisceau *m* monochromatique
r монохроматический луч *m*

6027 monochrome bitmap
d monochromatisches Bitmap *n*
f bitmap *m* monochrome
r монохроматическое растровое
изображение *n*

6028 monochrome light; one-color light
d monochromatisches Licht *n*; einfarbiges
Licht; einwelliges Licht
f lumière *f* monochromatique
r монохроматический свет *m*; одноцветный
свет

6029 monochrome [light] source
d monochromatische Lichtquelle *f*;
monochromatische Quelle *f*
f source *f* [lumineuse] monochromatique
r монохроматический источник *m* [света]

6030 monochrome monitor
d Monochrom-Monitor *m*;
Schwarzweiß-Monitor *m*
f moniteur *m* monochromatique
r монохромный экран *m*

* **monochrome source** → 6029

6031 monochrome vector
d einfarbiger Vektor *m*
f vecteur *m* monochrome
r монохромный вектор *m*

6032 monoid
(as a hypersurface)
d Monoid *n*; Monoidfläche *f*
f monoïde *m*
r моноид *m*

6033 monoid
(as a curve)
d monoidale Kurve *f*
f courbe *f* monoïdale
r моноид *m*

6034 monospaced font; font with a fixed pitch
d einzelbreite Schrift *f*
f police *f* à espacement fixe
r моноширинный шрифт *m*

6035 monotone polygon
d monotones Polygon *n*
f polygone *m* monotone
r монотонный многоугольник *m*

**6036 morphing; in-betweening; betweening;
tweening**
(generating of additional smoothed frames)
d Morphing *n*
f morphage *m*
r морфинг *m*; заполнение *n* промежуточных
кадров

6037 morphology
d Morphologie *f*
f morphologie *f*
r морфология *f*

* **morph sequence** → 5931

6038 mosaic
d Mosaik-
f mosaïque
r мозаичный

6039 mosaic array
d Mosaikmatrix *f*
f matrice *f* mosaïque
r мозаичная матрица *f*

6040 mosaic graphics; block graphics
(graphical images created in character mode)
  d Mosaikgrafik f
  f graphique m mosaïque
  r блочная графика f

6041 mosaic texture
  d Mosaiktextur f
  f texture f mosaïque
  r мозаичная текстура f

6042 motion; movement
  d Bewegung f
  f mouvement m
  r движение n; ход m; перемещение n

6043 motion analysis system
  d Bewegungsanalysis-System n
  f système m d'analyse de mouvement
  r система f анализа движения

6044 motion blur
  d Bewegungsunschärfe f
  f flou m dû au mouvement
  r размывание n при движении

6045 motion blur effect
  d Bewegung-Unscharfeffekt m
  f effet m de flou dû au mouvement
  r эффект m размывания при движении

6046 motion capture
  d Bewegungssammeln n
  f capture f de mouvement; acquisition f de mouvement; numérisation f de mouvement
  r улавливание n движения; дискретизация f движения

6047 motion-capture system
  d Bewegung-Sammlungssystem n; Bewegungssammelsystem n
  f système m de capture de mouvement
  r система f улавливания движения

6048 motion detection
  d Bewegungsdetektion f
  f détection f de mouvement
  r обнаруживание n движения

6049 motion dynamics
  d Bewegungsdynamik f
  f dynamique f de mouvement
  r динамика f движения

6050 motion geometry
  d Bewegungsgeometrie f
  f géométrie f cinématique
  r геометрия f движения; кинематическая геометрия

6051 motion hierarchy
  d Bewegungshierarchie f
  f hiérarchie f de mouvements
  r иерархия f движений

6052 motion interpolation
  d Bewegungsinterpolation f
  f interpolation f de mouvement
  r интерполяция f движения

6053 motion interpretation of the curvature
  d Bewegungsinterpretation f der Krümmung
  f interprétation f cinématique de la courbure
  r кинематическая интерпретация f кривизны

6054 motion parallax
  d Bewegungsparallaxe f
  f parallaxe m de mouvement
  r параллакс m движения

6055 motion parameters
  d Bewegungsparameter m
  f paramètres mpl de mouvement
  r параметры mpl движения

6056 motion path
  d Bewegungsstrecke f
  f trajectoire f d'un objet animé
  r траектория f движения

6057 motion platform
  d Bewegungsplattform f
  f plate-forme f de mouvement
  r платформа f движения

6058 motion simulation
  d Bewegungssimulierung f
  f simulation f de mouvement
  r симуляция f движения

* motion video → 414

6059 mottle
(spotty, uneven ink absorption)
  d Tupfen m; Sprenkel m
  f marbrure f; bigarrure f
  r пятнышко n; крапинка f; пятнистая окраска f

6060 mottled image
  d geflecktes Bild n; gesprenkeltes Bild
  f image f tachetée; image bigarrée
  r испещренное изображение n

6061 mottling; marbling
  d Sprenkelung f; Besprenkelung f
  f jaspage m; effet m moucheté
  r испещрение n; пятнистость f; крапчатость f

6062 mould v
  d überfluten; formen

f couler
r заливать; формировать

6063 mouse
d Maus *f*; Bedienmaus *f*; Handroller *m*
f souris *f*
r манипулятор *m* типа "мышь"; мышь *f*

6064 mouse button
d Maustaste *f*
f bouton *m* de la souris
r бутон *m* мыши

6065 mouse button release *v*
d Maustaste loslassen
f dégager le bouton de la souris; lâcher le bouton de la souris; répandre le bouton de la souris
r отпускать клавишу мыши

6066 mouse click
d Mausklick *m/n*
f clic *m* de la souris
r нажатие *n* кнопки мыши

6067 mouse configuration
d Mauskonfiguration *f*
f configuration *f* de la souris
r конфигурация *f* мыши

6068 mouse dragging
d Ziehen *n* mittels Maus
f lissage *m* par bouton de souris
r перемещение *n* посредством мыши; буксировка *f* с помощью мыши

6069 mouse dropping
d Mausloslassen *n*
f relâchement *m* par bouton de la souris
r опускание *n* мыши

6070 mouse pointer
d Mauszeiger *m*
f pointeur *m* de la souris; curseur *m* de la souris
r указатель *m* мыши

6071 mouse trail
(on screen)
d Mausspur *f*
f traînée *f* [du curseur] de la souris
r след *m* курсора

6072 movable
d beweglich
f mouvant
r подвижный; передвижной

6073 movable object block; MOB
d beweglicher Objektblock *m*
f unité *f* d'objet mobile

r перемещаемый блок *m* объектов

6074 move *v*
d bewegen; rücken; umsetzen
f déplacer; mouvoir; remuer
r двигать[ся]; передвигать; двинуть

6075 move command
d Bewegungsbefehl *m*; Rückungsbefehl *m*
f commande *f* de mouvement
r команда *f* перемещения; команда движения

* **movement** → 6042

6076 move ruler
d Bewegungslineal *n*
f règle *f* de mouvement
r перемещающаяся измерительная линейка *f*

* **move** *v* **to back** → 1150

* **move** *v* **to front** → 1152

6077 move *v* **to layer**
d zur Schicht rücken
f déplacer vers le plan
r передвигать к слою

6078 movie frame
d Filmaufnahme *f*
f cadre *m* de film
r кадр *m* фильма

6079 movie graphics
d Filmgrafik *f*
f graphique *m* de film
r фильмовая графика *f*

* **moving coordinates** → 8249

6080 moving frame of reference
d bewegtes Bezugssystem *n*; begleitendes Bezugssystem
f repère *m* mobile; système *m* de référence mobile; système d'axes mobiles
r подвижный репер *m*; сопровождающий репер; подвижная система *f* отсчета

6081 moving image; moving picture; animated image
d Animationsbild *n*; Trickbild *n*; Bewegtbild *n*
f image *f* animée; images mobile; image en mouvement
r подвижное изображение *n*; динамическое изображение; оживленное изображение

6082 moving n-hedral
d begleitendes n-Bein *n*

f n-èdre *m* mobile
r сопровождающий n-гранник *m*;
подвижный n-гранник

* **moving picture** → 6081

6083 moving stereo; animated stereo
d Bewegungsstereo *n*; animiertes Stereo *n*
f stéréo *m* en mouvement; stéréo animé
r подвижное стерео *n*; динамическое стерео

**6084 moving trihedral; moving trihedron;
Frenet frame**
d begleitendes Dreibein *n*; Hauptdreikant *n/m*
f trièdre *m* mobile; trièdre principal; trièdre de
[Serret-]Frenet; repère *m* de Frenet; repère
naturel
r подвижный триэдр *m*; сопутствующий
трехгранник *m*; натуральный триэдр
Френе; естественный трехгранник

* **moving trihedron** → 6084

* **MRI** → 5751

6085 multichannel image
d mehrkanaliges Bild *n*
f image *f* multicanale
r многоканальное изображение *n*

6086 multicolor plotter; color plotter
d Mehrfarbenplotter *m*; Farb-Plotter *m*
f traceur *m* en couleurs
r многоцветный графопостроитель *m*

6087 multicolor printer
d Mehrfarbendrucker *m*
f imprimante *f* multicouleur; imprimante à
plusieurs couleurs
r многоцветное печатающее устройство *n*

6088 multicolor printing
d Mehrfarbendruck *m*
f impression *f* multicouleur
r многоцветная печать *f*

6089 multi-column bar chart
d Mehrspalten-Streifendiagramm *n*
f diagramme *m* à barres multiples; graphique *m*
à barres multiples
r многоколонная столбиковая диаграмма *f*

6090 multidimensional; many-dimensional
d mehrdimensional
f multidimensionnel
r многомерный

6091 multidimensional motion interpolation
d mehrdimensionale Bewegungsinterpolation *f*
f interpolation *f* du mouvement

multidimensionnel
r интерполяция *f* многомерного движения

6092 multidimensional views
d mehrdimensionale Ansichten *fpl*
f vues *fpl* multidimensionnelles
r многомерные представления *npl*

* **multidrop** *adj* → 6130

6093 multiframe
d Mehrfachrahmen *m*
f multitrame *f*, supertrame *f*; multicadre *m*
r мультикадр *m*; группа *f* кадров;
многокадровый объект *m*

6094 multiframe alignment
d Mehrrahmenausgleichen *n*
f alignement *m* de multitrame; ajustage *m* de
multitrame
r налаживание *n* группы кадров;
выравнивание *n* многокадрового объекта

6095 multigraph
d Multigraph *m*
f multigraphe *m*
r мультиграф *m*

6096 multi-image
d Multibild *n*; Multi-Image *n*
f multi-image *f*
r множественное изображение *n*

6097 multilayer
d Mehrschicht-; mehrschichtig; Mehrlagen-
f multicouche; multi-plan
r многослойный

6098 multilayer model
d Mehrschichtmodell *n*
f modèle *m* multi-plan
r многослойная модель *f*

6099 multilevel *adj*
d Mehrpegel-
f multi-niveau
r многоуровневой

6100 multiline
d Multilinie *f*; Mehrlinie *f*
f multiligne *f*; lignes *fpl* parallèles multiples
r мультилиния *f*

6101 multiline; multilinear *adj*
d Mehrleitungs-
f multiligne; multilinéaire
r многолинейный; мультилинейный

* **multilinear** *adj* → 6101

6102 multilinearity
d Mehrlinearität f
f multilinéarité f
r мультилинейность f

6103 multilinear mapping
d multilineare Abbildung f
f application f multilinéaire
r мультилинейное отображение n

6104 multiline chart
d Mehrliniendiagramm n
f diagramme m multiligne
r мультилинейная диаграмма f

6105 multiline clipping
d Multilinie-Kappen n
f découpage m de multiligne
r отсекание n мультилинии

6106 multiline cutting
d Mehrlinienschnitt m
f coupe f de multiligne
r срез m мультилинии

6107 multiline intersection
d Mehrliniendurchschnitt m
f intersection f de multilignes
r пересечение n мультилиний

6108 multiline scale
d Mehrlinienmaßstab m
f échelle f de multiligne
r масштаб m мультилинии

6109 multiline style
d Mehrlinienstil m
f style m de multiligne
r стиль m мультилинии

6110 multiline text
d Mehrzeilentext m
f texte m multiligne
r многострочный текст m

* multimedia → 6112

6111 multimedia file
d Multimediendatei f; Multimedia-Datei f
f fichier m multimédia
r мультимедийный файл m

6112 multimedia [system]
d Multimediensystem n
f système m multimédia; multimédia mpl
r мультимедийная система f

6113 multimodality
d Multimodalität f
f multimodalité f
r мультимодальность f

* multinomial adj → 7311

6114 multipage document
d mehrseitiges Dokument n
f document m à plusieurs pages
r многостраничный документ m

6115 multipen plotter
d Plotter m mit mehreren Zeichenstiften
f traceur m multiplume
r многоперьевой графопостроитель m

6116 multiple
d Mehrfach-; mehrfach; vielfach
f multiple
r многократный; множественный

6117 multiple copies
d Mehrfachkopien fpl
f copies fpl multiples
r множество n копий

6118 multiple entity stretch
d Streckung f der Mehrfacheinheiten
f étirement m d'entités multiples
r удлинение n множества примитивов

6119 multiple groups selecting
d Auswahl f der Mehrfachgruppen
f sélection f de groupes multiples
r выбор m множества групп

6120 multiple lights
d mehrfache Lichtquellen fpl
f foyers mpl lumineux multiples
r множественные источники mpl света

6121 multiple material object
d Mehrfachmaterialien-Objekt n
f objet m à matériaux multiples
r многоматериальный объект m

6122 multiple objects
d Mehrfachobjekte npl
f objets mpl multiples
r множественные объекты mpl; множество n объектов

6123 multiple objects selecting
d Auswahl f der Mehrfachobjekte
f sélection f d'objets multiples
r выбор m множества объектов

6124 multiple print
d Mehrfachdruck m
f impression f multiple
r многократная печать f

6125 **multiple reflection**
  d Mehrfachreflexion *f*
  f réflexion *f* multiple
  r многократное отражение *n*

6126 **multiple segmentation primitives**
  d Primitivelemente *npl* der
    Mehrfachsegmentierung
  f primitives *fpl* à segmentation multiple
  r примитивы *mpl* многократным
    сегментированием

6127 **multiple select**
  d Mehrfachauswahl *f*
  f sélection *f* multiple
  r многократный выбор *m*

  * **multiplication sign** → 8686

6128 **multiplier; factor**
  d Multiplikator *m*; Multiplizierer *m*; Faktor *m*;
    Vervielfacher *m*
  f multipli[cat]eur *m*; facteur *m*
  r [у]множитель *m*

6129 **multiply projective space**
  d mehrfach projektiver Raum *m*
  f espace *m* projectif plusieurs fois; espace
    multiprojectif
  r кратно-проективное пространство *n*

6130 **multipoint; multidrop** *adj*
  d Mehrpunkt-
  f multipoint
  r многопозиционный; многоотводный;
    многоточечный

6131 **multiquadratic approximation**
  d multiquadratische Näherung *f*
  f approximation *f* multiquadratique
  r многоквадратичное приближение *n*

6132 **multiresolution**
  d Multiauflösung *f*; Multiresolution *f*
  f résolution *f* multiple
  r многократная разрешающая способность *f*

6133 **multiscanning**
  d Vielfachscannen *n*
  f multi-balayage *m*
  r многократное сканирование *n*

6134 **multispectral image**
  d multispektrales Bild *n*
  f image *f* multispectrale
  r многоспектральное изображение *n*

6135 **multispectral scanner**
  d mehrspektraler Scanner *m*
  f scanner *m* multispectral

  r многоспектральный сканер *m*

6136 **multispectral signature**
  d multispektrale Signatur *f*
  f signature *f* multispectrale
  r многоспектральная подпись *f*

6137 **multitexturing**
  d Multitexturieren *n*
  f multi-texturation *f*
  r мультитекстурирование *n*; создание *n*
    множества текстур

  * **multiwindow** → 6138

6138 **multiwindow[ing]**
  d Bildfenstertechnik *f*; Multiwindowing *n*
  f multifenêtrage *m*; fenêtrage *m* multiple
  r организация *f* полиэкранной работы;
    многооконная работа *f*

6139 **mutation**
  d Mutation *f*
  f mutation *f*
  r мутация *f*

6140 **mutual**
  d wechselseitig; gegenseitig
  f mutuel
  r взаимный

  * **mutually** → 6754

6141 **mutual noises**
  d wechselseitiges Rauschen *n*
  f bruits *mpl* mutuels
  r взаимные помехи *fpl*

N

6142 name
 d Name *m*
 f nom *m*
 r имя *n*

6143 named filter
 d genannter Filter *m*
 f filtre *m* nommé
 r наименованный фильтр *m*

6144 named object
 d genanntes Objekt *n*
 f objet *m* nommé
 r наименованный объект *m*

6145 named object dictionary
 d Wörterbuch *n* der genannten Objekte
 f dictionnaire *m* d'objets nommés
 r словарь *m* наименованных объектов

 * **name domain** → 9701

6146 named reference
 d genannter Verweis *m*
 f référence *f* nommée
 r наименованная ссылка *f*

6147 named UCS
 d genanntes Benutzerkoordinatensystem *n*
 f système *m* de coordonnées utilisateur nommé
 r наименованная координатная система *f* пользователя

6148 named view
 d genannte Ansicht *f*
 f vue *f* nommée
 r наименованное представление *n*; наименованный вид *m*

6149 naming
 d Benennung *f*
 f dénomination *f*; désignation *f*; nommage *m*
 r наименование *n*

6150 nappe; sheet
 d Flächenschale *f*; Schale *f*
 f nappe *f*
 r кора *f*; скорлупа *f*

 * **narrow band** → 6153

6151 narrow domain
 d schmales Gebiet *n*
 f domaine *m* étroite
 r узкая область *f*

6152 narrow spectral width
 d schmale Spektralbreite *f*
 f largeur *f* spectrale étroite
 r узкая ширина *f* спектра

6153 narrow stripe; narrow band
 d schmaler Streifen *m*
 f bande *f* étroite
 r узкая полоса *f*

6154 narrow-stripe geometry
 d Geometrie *f* mit schmalem Streifen; schmale Streifengeometrie *f*
 f géométrie *f* en ruban étroit; géométrie en bande étroite
 r узкополосная геометрия *f*; геометрия с узкой полосой

6155 n-ary domain
 d n-äres Gebiet *n*
 f domaine *m* n-aire
 r n-арная область *f*

6156 natural effects
 d natürliche Effekte *mpl*
 f effets *m* naturels
 r естественные эффекты *mpl*

6157 natural light
 d natürliches Licht *n*
 f lumière *f* naturelle
 r естественный свет *m*

6158 natural pen
 d natürlicher Stift *m*
 f plume *f* naturelle
 r естественное перо *n*

6159 natural pen tool
 d Hilfsmittel *n* "natürlicher Stift"
 f outil *m* "plume naturelle"
 r инструмент *m* "естественное перо"

6160 natural phenomena modeling
 d Modellierung *f* der Naturerscheinungen
 f modelage *m* de phénomènes naturels
 r моделирование *n* естественных явлений

6161 navigate *v*
 d navigieren; befahren
 f naviguer
 r передвигаться; пилотировать

6162 navigation
 d Navigation *f*
 f navigation *f*
 r навигация *f*; передвижение *n*

6163 navigation bar
  d Navigationsstreifen *m*
  f barre *f* de navigation
  r лента *f* навигации

6164 navigation key
  d Navigationstaste *f*
  f touche *f* de navigation
  r клавиша *f* навигации

6165 navigation menu
  d Navigationsmenü *n*
  f menu *m* de navigation
  r меню *n* навигации

6166 navigation tool
  d Navigationshilfsmittel *n*
  f outil *m* de navigation
  r навигационный инструмент *m*

  * **navigator** → 1161

6167 n-chromatic graph
  d n-chromatischer Graph *m*
  f graphe *m* n-chromatique
  r n-хроматический граф *m*

6168 n-coloring
  d n-Färbung *f*
  f n-coloration *f*
  r n-цветная раскраска *f*

6169 n-cube; n-dimensional cube
  d n-dimensionaler Würfel *m*; n-dimensionaler Kubus *m*
  f cube *m* à n dimensions; n-cube *m*
  r n-мерный куб *m*

  * **NDC** → 6300

6170 n-dimensional
  d n-dimensional
  f n-dimensionnel
  r n-мерный

  * **n-dimensional cube** → 6169

6171 n-dimensional Gaussian normal distribution
  d n-dimensionale Gaußsche Normalverteilung *f*
  f distribution *f* normale n-dimensionnelle de Gauss
  r n-мерное нормальное распределение *n* Гаусса

6172 near
  d nah
  f proche
  r близкий

6173 nearest [object] snap
  d nächster Objektfang *m*; nächster Fang *m*
  f accrochage *m* [à l'objet] le plus proche
  r самая близкая [объектная] привязка *f*

  * **nearest snap** → 6173

6174 near-infrared; NIR
  d nahes Infrarot *n*; NIR
  f proche infrarouge *m*
  r ближний инфракрасный диапазон *m*

  * **near plane** → 4029

6175 neat border
  d unvermischte Kante *f*
  f bordure *f* pure
  r чистая кайма *f*; чистое обрамление *n*; чистый бордюр *m*; чистая окантовка *f*

6176 negate *v*
  d negieren
  f nier
  r инвертировать; отрицать

6177 negation
  d Negation *f*
  f négation *f*
  r отрицание *n*

  * **negative** → 6180

6178 negative
  d negativ
  f négatif
  r отрицательный

6179 negative correlation
  d negative Korrelation *f*
  f corrélation *f* négative
  r отрицательная корреляция *f*

6180 negative [photographic image]
  d Negativ *n*
  f négatif *m*
  r негативное фотоизображение *n*; негатив *m*

6181 negative picture signal
  d negatives Bildsignal *n*
  f signal *m* d'image à potentiel négatif
  r отрицательный сигнал *m* изображения

6182 negative printing
  d negativer Druck *m*
  f impression *f* négative
  r негативная печать *f*

6183 negative shape
  d negative Form *f*

f forme *f* négative
r негативная фигура *f*

* **neighborhood** → 7611

6184 neighboring pixel
d Nachbarpixel *n*
f pixel *m* voisin
r соседний пиксел *m*

* **nest** → 6189

6185 nest *v*
d einfügen; einschachteln; verschachteln
f encastrer; emboîter
r вкладывать

6186 nested; in-built; built-in
d eingefügt; eingeschachtelt; verschachtelt; eingebaut
f emboîté; encastré; inséré; imbriqué; incorporé
r гнездовой; вложенный; встроенный

6187 nested blocks
d eingefügte Blöcke *mpl*
f blocs *mpl* encastrés
r вложенные блоки *mpl*

6188 nested images
d eingefügte Bilder *npl*
f images *fpl* encastrées
r вложенные изображения *npl*

6189 nest[ing]; embedding
d Einbettung *f*; Einbetten *n*; Einschachtelung *f*; Verschachtelung *f*; Schachtelung *f*
f encastrement *m*; imbrication *f*; emboîtage *m*; emboîtement *m*; mise *f* en série
r вложение *n*; вложенность *f*; упаковка *f*

* **net** → 6194

6190 net data
d Nettodaten *npl*
f données *fpl* nettes
r чистые данные *npl*

6191 net of curves
d Kurvennetz *n*
f réseau *m* de courbes
r сеть *f* кривых

* **net of lines** → 6192

6192 net of rays; net of lines
d Strahlennetz *n*
f réseau *m* de droites
r сеть *f* лучей; сеть прямых

6193 net of surfaces

d Flächenbündel *n*; Flächennetz *n*
f réseau *m* de surfaces
r связка *f* поверхностей

6194 net[work]
d Netz[werk] *n*
f réseau *m*
r сеть *f*

* **network diagram** → 6196

6195 networked environment
d Netzwerkumgebung *f*
f environnement *m* de réseau
r сетевая среда *f*

6196 network graph; network diagram
d Netzwerkdiagramm *n*
f diagramme *m* de réseau; graphique *m* de réseau
r сетевой график *m*; сетевая модель *f*

6197 network links
d Netzverbindungen *fpl*
f liaisons *fpl* de réseau
r сетевые связи *fpl*

6198 network node; network point
d Netz[werk]knoten *m*
f nœud *m* de réseau
r узел *m* сети

* **network of coordinates** → 2223

* **network point** → 6198

6199 network synthesis
d Netzwerksynthese *f*
f synthèse *f* des réseaux
r синтез *m* сетей

6200 network technique
d Netzwerktechnik *f*; Netzentwicklungstechnik *f*
f technique *f* des réseaux
r техника *f* создания сетей

6201 network theory
d Netzwerktheorie *f*
f théorie *f* des réseaux
r теория *f* сетей

6202 network topology
d Netz[werk]topologie *f*
f topologie *f* de réseau
r топология *f* сети

6203 network visualization
d Netzwerkvisualisierung *f*

f visualisation *f* de réseau
r визуализация *f* сети

6204 neural network; neuronic network
d neuronales Netz *n*
f réseau *m* de neurones
r нейронная сеть *f*

* **neuronic network** → 6204

6205 neutral area
(of an image)
d neutraler Bereich *m*
f zone *f* neutre
r нейтральная зона *f*

6206 neutral colors
d neutrale Farben *fpl*
f couleurs *fpl* neutres
r нейтральные цвета *mpl*

6207 neutral filter
d neutraler Filter *m*
f filtre *m* neutre
r нейтральный фильтр *m*

6208 neutral line; vanishing line
d Verschwindungslinie *f*
f ligne *f* neutre; ligne de fuite
r нейтральная линия *f*

6209 neutral plane; vanishing plane
d Verschwindungsebene *f*
f plan *m* neutre
r нейтральная плоскость *f*

6210 neutral point; vanishing point; VP
d Verschwindungspunkt *m*; Fluchtpunkt *m*
f point *m* neutre; point de fuite; PF
r нейтральная точка *f*

6211 neutral point locked to object
d Fluchtpunkt *m* gesperrt an dem Objekt
f point *m* de fuite verrouillé à l'objet
r нейтральная точка *f*, фиксированная к
  объекту

6212 new color
d neue Farbe *f*
f couleur *f* nouvelle
r новый цвет *m*

6213 new custom color palette
d neue angepaßte Farbpalette *f*
f palette *f* des couleurs nouvelle personnalisée
r новая заказная палитра *f* цветов

* **Newell algorithm** → 6214

6214 Newell[-Sancha] algorithm
d Newell[-Sancha]-Algorithmus *m*

f algorithme *m* de Newell[-Sancha]
r алгоритм *m* Нюел-Санха

6215 n-gon
d n-Eck *n*
f polygone *m* de n côtes
r n-угольник *m*

6216 nib
(of a pen)
d Spitze *f*
f bec *m*; pointe *f* [de stylo]; pointe de plume
r острие *n*; кончик *m* [пера]

6217 nib picker
d Spitzenauswahl-Schaltfläche *f*
f bloc *m* de sélection de pointe de stylo; bloc
  d'initialisation de bec
r бутон *m* выбора кончика

6218 nib shape
d Form *f* der Spitze; Spitzenform *f*
f forme *f* de bec
r форма *f* кончика

* **NIR** → 6174

6219 nodal point
d Knotenpunkt *m*
f point *m* nodal
r узловая точка *f*

6220 node; knot; vertex
d Knoten[punkt] *m*; Ecke *f*
f nœud *m*
r узел *m*

6221 node address
d Knotenadresse *f*
f adresse *f* de nœud
r адрес *m* узла

6222 node addressing
d Knotenadressierung *f*
f adressage *m* de nœud
r адресирование *n* узла

* **node edit** → 6223

6223 node edit[ing]
d Knotenbearbeitung *f*
f édition *f* de nœuds
r редактирование *n* узлов

6224 node of a graph; vertex of a graph
d Knoten[punkt] *m* eines Graphs
f sommet *m* d'un graphe; nœud *m* d'un graphe
r вершина *f* графа

6225 node of a spline
d Spline-Knoten *m*

f nœud *m* de spline
r узел *m* сплайна

* **node order** → 5381

6226 node ordering
d Knotenanordnung *f*
f ordonnancement *m* des nœuds
r упорядочение *n* узлов

6227 node selecting
d Knotenauswahl *f*
f sélection *f* de nœud
r выбор *m* узла

6228 node snap
d Knotenfang *m*
f accrochage *m* au nœud
r привязывание *n* к узлу

6229 node topology
d Knoten-Topologie *f*
f topologie *f* des nœuds
r топология *f* узлов

6230 noise *v*
d rauschen; stören
f bruiter
r шуметь

6231 noise; garbage; perturbation
d Rauschen *n*; Geräusch *n*; Störung *f*
f bruit *m*; brouillage *m*; parasitage *m*; perturbation *f*
r шум *m*; помеха *f*; возмущение *n*; искажение *n*

* **noise density** → 6239

6232 noise effect
d Rauscheffekt *m*; Geräuscheffekt *m*
f effet *m* de bruit
r шумовой эффект *m*; эффект искажения

6233 noise estimation
d Rauschbewertung *f*
f évaluation *f* de bruit
r оценка *f* искажения

6234 noise factor; noise figure
d Rauschfaktor *m*; Rauschzahl *f*; Rauschmaß *n*
f facteur *m* de bruit
r коэффициент *m* возмущения

* **noise figure** → 6234

6235 noise-figure characteristics
d Rauschzahlkennlinie *f*
f caractéristique *f* de facteur de bruit
r характеристика *f* коэффициента искажения

6236 noise filter
d Geräuschfilter *m*; Rauschfilter *m*; Entstörfiter *m*
f filtre *m* de bruit
r фильтр *m* искажения

6237 noise power
d Rauschleistung *f*
f puissance *f* de bruit
r мощность *f* шума; мощность искажения

6238 noise removal and filtering
d Entfernung *f* und Filtrierung *f* des Rauschens
f élimination *f* et filtrage *m* du bruit
r устранение *n* и фильтрирование *n* искажения

6239 noise [spectral] density
d [spektrale] Rauschdichte *f*
f densité *f* [spectrale] de bruit
r [спектральная] плотность *f* искажения

6240 nominal; rated
d nominell; nominal; Nominal-; Soll-; Nenn-
f nominal
r номинальный; расчетный

6241 nominal shapes
d Nominalformen *fpl*
f formes *fpl* nominaux
r номинальные фигуры *fpl*

6242 nominal value; rating
d Nennwert *m*; Sollwert *m*
f valeur *f* nominale
r номинальная величина *f*; номинальное значение *n*

* **nomogram** → 270

6243 non-adjacent edges
(of a graph)
d knotenfremde Kanten *fpl*
f arêtes *fpl* non adjacentes
r несмежные ребра *npl*

6244 nonagon
d Neuneck *n*
f ennéagone *m*
r девятиугольник *m*

6245 non-associative fill
d nichtassoziative Füllung *f*
f remplissage *m* non associatif
r неассоциативное закрашивание *n*; неассоциативное заполнение *n*

6246 non-associative hatch
d nichtassoziative Schraffur *f*

f hachure *f* non associative
r неассоциативная штриховка *f*

6247 non-axial
d nichtaxial
f non axial; désaxé
r неаксиальный

6248 nonbreaking space; hard space
d unzerbrechliche Leerstelle *f*
f espace *m* non interrompu
r неразрывный пробел *m*; твердый пробел

6249 non-connected objects
d nichtverbundene Objekte *npl*
f objets *mpl* non connectés
r несвязные объекты *mpl*

6250 noncoplanar regions
d nichtkomplanare Regionen *fpl*
f régions *fpl* non coplanaires
r некопланарные регионы *mpl*

6251 non-correlative
d unkorreliert
f non corrélatif
r некоррелятивный

6252 non-degeneracy; non-singularity
d Nichtentartung *f*; Nichtausartung *f*
f non-dégénérescence *f*
r невырожденность *f*

6253 non-degenerate; non-singular
d nichtausgeartet; nichtentartet; nichtsingulär
f non dégénéré; non singulier
r невырожденный; несингулярный; необособый

6254 non-degenerate collineation
d nichtausgeartete Kollineation *f*; Kollineation mit regulärer Matrix
f collinéation *f* non dégénérée
r невырожденное проективное отображение *n*

* **non-determination** → 5029

* **non-directed graph** → 6276

6255 non-emissive display
d Display *n* ohne Emission
f afficheur *m* non émissif
r дисплей *m* без эмиссии

6256 non-empty; non-vacuous; nonvoid
d nichtleer
f non vide
r непустой

6257 non-empty set; nonvoid set
d nichtleere Menge *f*
f ensemble *m* non vide
r непустое множество *n*

6258 non-enumerable set
d nichtaufzählbare Menge *f*
f ensemble *m* non énumérable
r неперечислимое множество *n*

6259 non-equilibrium
d Ungleichgewicht *n*; Nichtgleichgewicht *n*
f déséquilibre *m*
r неравновесие *n*

6260 non-equivalence
d Nichtäquivalenz *f*
f non-équivalence *f*
r неэквивалентность *f*; неравнозначность *f*

6261 nonflickering
d flimmerfrei
f sans scintillement
r немерцающий

6262 nonfocal axis
d nichtfokale Achse *f*
f axe *m* non focal
r нефокальная ось *f*

6263 nongraphic attribute
d nichtgrafisches Attribut *n*
f attribut *m* non graphique
r неграфический атрибут *m*

6264 nongraphic object
d nichtgrafisches Objekt *n*
f objet *m* non graphique
r неграфический объект *m*

* **nonhomogeneous** → 4580

6265 nonisometric lines
d nichtisometrische Linien *fpl*
f lignes *fpl* non isométriques
r неизометрические линии *fpl*

* **nonisotropic** → 423

* **nonisotropic line** → 426

* **nonisotropic plane** → 427

6266 nonlinear
d nichtlinear
f non linéaire
r нелинейный

6267 nonlinear animation
d nichtlineare Animation *f*

f animation *f* non linéaire
r нелинейная анимация *f*

6268 nonlinear digital filter
d nichtlinearer digitaler Filter *m*
f filtre *m* numérique non linéaire
r цифровой нелинейный фильтр *m*

6269 non-linearity
d Nichtlinearität *f*
f non-linéarité *f*
r нелинейность *f*

6270 nonlinear optics
d nichtlineare Optik *f*
f optique *f* non linéaire
r нелинейная оптика *f*

6271 nonlinear refraction
d nichtlineare Brechung *f*
f réfraction *f* non linéaire
r нелинейное преломление *n*

6272 nonlinear scattering
d nichtlineare Streuung *f*
f diffusion *f* non linéaire
r нелинейное рассеяние *n*

6273 nonlinear Z buffer
d nichtlinearer Z-Buffer *m*
f Z-buffer *m* non linéaire
r нелинейный Z-буфер *m*

6274 non-orientable surface
d nichtorientierbare Fläche *f*
f surface *f* non orientable
r неориентируемая поверхность *f*

6275 non-oriented angle
d ungerichteter Winkel *m*
f angle *m* non orienté
r неориентированный угол *m*

6276 non-oriented graph; non-directed graph; undirected graph
d ungerichteter Graph *m*
f graphe *m* non orienté
r неориентированный граф *m*

6277 non-orthogonal
d nichtorthogonal
f non orthogonal
r неортогональный

6278 non-orthogonal coordinate system
d nichtorthogonales Koordinatensystem *n*
f système *m* de coordonnées non orthogonaux
r неортогональная система *f* координат

* **non-orthogonal viewports** → 6284

6279 non-overlapping
d nichtüberlappend
f sans recouvrement; sans points intérieurs communs
r неперекрывающийся; не имеющий общих внутренних точек

6280 nonphotorealistic representation
d nichtfotorealistische Darstellung *f*
f représentation *f* non photoréaliste
r нефотореалистическое представление *n*

6281 non-planar graph
d nichtplanarer Graph *m*
f graphe *m* gauche
r неплоский граф *m*

6282 non-printing characters
d nichtdruckbare Zeichen *npl*
f caractères *mpl* non imprimables
r непечатаемые символы *mpl*

6283 non-rectangular bitmap
d nichtrechtwinkliges Bitmap *n*
f bitmap *m* non rectangulaire
r непрямоугольное растровое изображение *n*

6284 non-rectangular viewports; non-orthogonal viewports
d nichtrechtwinklige Ansichtsfenster *npl*
f clôtures *fpl* non rectangulaires
r непрямоугольные области *fpl* просмотра; непрямоугольные окна *npl* просмотра

6285 non-reflecting
d reflexionfrei
f non réfléchissant
r неотражающий

* **non sharp** → 4088

* **non-singular** → 6253

* **non-singularity** → 6252

6286 non-square pixel
d nichtquadratisches Pixel *n*
f pixel *m* non carré
r неквадратный пиксел *m*

6287 non-square pixel geometry
d Geometrie *f* der nichtquadratischen Pixel
f géométrie *f* de pixels non carrés
r геометрия *f* неквадратных пикселов

6288 non-stationary image
d nichtstationäres Bild *n*

f image *f* non fixe
r нестационарное изображение *n*

* **non-symmetric** → 10055

* **non-symmetrical** → 10055

* **nonterminal node** → 5195

6289 non-transparent
  d nichttransparent
  f non transparent
  r непрозрачный

6290 non-transparent texture
  d nichttransparente Textur *f*
  f texture *f* non transparente
  r непрозрачная текстура *f*

6291 nonuniform
  d nichtgleichmäßig; ungleichmäßig
  f non uniforme
  r неравномерный; неоднородный

6292 nonuniform quadratic spline
  d nichtgleichmäßiger quadratischer Spline *m*
  f spline *m* non uniforme quadratique
  r неоднородный квадратичный сплайн *m*

6293 nonuniform rational B-spline surface
  d nichtgleichmäßige rationale
    B-Spline-Fläche *f*
  f surface *f* B-spline rationnelle non uniforme
  r неоднородная рациональная поверхность *f*
    B-сплайна

* **non-vacuous** → 6256

* **nonvisible** → 5272

* **nonvoid** → 6256

* **nonvoid set** → 6257

* **normal** → 6304

6294 normal
  d normal; Normal-
  f normal
  r нормальный

* **normal axonometry** → 6643

* **normal coordinates** → 7858

6295 normal deviation
  d normale Abweichung *f*
  f écart *m* normal
  r нормальное отклонение *n*

6296 normal distribution
  d Normalverteilung *f*
  f distribution *f* normale
  r нормальное распределение *n*

6297 normal hatch style
  d normaler Schraffurstil *m*
  f style *m* de hachure normal
  r нормальный стиль *m* штриховки

* **normalized orthogonal basis** → 6664

6298 normal incidence
  d normaler Einfall *m*; senkrechter Einfall *m*
  f incidence *f* normale
  r нормальное падение *n*; вертикальное
    падение

6299 normalization; normalizing
  d Norm[alis]ierung *f*
  f normalisation *f*; homologation *f*
  r норм[ализ]ирование *n*; нормализация *f*

6300 normalized device coordinate; NDC
  d normierte Gerätekoordinate *f*
  f coordonnée *f* d'appareil normée; coordonnée
    d'appareil normalisée; CAN
  r нормированная координата *f* устройства

6301 normalized direction vector
  d Vektor *m* der normierten Richtung
  f vecteur *m* à direction normalisée
  r вектор *m* нормализованного направления

6302 normalized projection coordinates; NPC
  d normierte Projektionskoordinaten *fpl*
  f coordonnées *fpl* de projection normalisées;
    CPN
  r нормализованные координаты *fpl*
    проекции

6303 normalized transformation
    (of device coordinate)
  d normierte Transformation *f*
  f transformation *f* normée
  r нормализованная трансформация *f*

* **normalizing** → 6299

6304 normal [line]
  d Normale *f*
  f normale *f*
  r нормаль *f*

* **normal orthogonal basis** → 6664

6305 normal plane
  d Normalebene *f*
  f plan *m* normal
  r плоскость *f* нормали

6306 normal to angular point
(of a polygon)
d Eckpunktnormale *f*
f normale *f* au point angulaire
r нормаль *f* к угловой точке

6307 normal to surface; surface normal
d Flächennormale *f*
f normale *f* à la surface
r поверхностная нормаль *f*

6308 normal vector
d Normalenvektor *m*
f vecteur *m* de la normale
r вектор *m* нормали

* **normal-vector interpolation shading →
7008**

6309 normal view
d normale Ansicht *f*; Normalansicht *f*
f vue *f* normale
r нормальный вид *m*

6310 northern light
d Nordlicht *n*
f lumière *f* nord; lumière septentrionale
r северный свет *m*

6311 notation; designation
d Bezeichnung *f*; Schreibweise *f*; Notation *f*
f notation *f*, signification *f*
r обозначение *n*; означение *n*

* **notch** *v* → **2603**

6312 note
d Bemerkung *f*
f note *f*
r примечание *n*

* **notice → 5925**

* **notification → 433**

* **NPC → 6302**

* **nucleus → 5360**

6313 null object
d Nullobjekt *n*
f objet *m* vide; objet nul
r нуль-объект *m*

6314 null plane
d Nullebene *f*
f plan *m* nul
r нулевая плоскость *f*; нуль-плоскость *f*

6315 null point
d Nullpunkt *m*; Ausgangspunkt *m*
f point *m* nul; point zéro
r нулевая точка *f*, нуль-точка *f*;
нуль-пункт *m*; нулевой пункт *m*

6316 null ray
d Nullstrahl *m*; Direktrix *f*
f rayon *m* directeur
r нулевой луч *m*

6317 null value
d Nullwert *m*
f valeur *f* zéro
r нулевое значение *n*

6318 number
d Nummer *f*
f numéro *m*
r номер *m*

6319 number
d Zahl *f*; Anzahl *f*
f nombre *m*
r число *n*

6320 numbering
d Numerierung *f*
f numérotation *f*; numérotage *m*
r нумерирование *n*; нумерация *f*

6321 number of control points
d Steuerpunktzahl *f*; Zahl *f* der Steuerpunkte
f nombre *m* de points de contrôle
r число *n* контрольных точек

6322 number of copies
d Kopienzahl *f*; Zahl *f* der Kopien
f nombre *m* de copies
r число *n* копий

6323 number of fit points
d Zahl *f* der ausgerichteten Punkte
f nombre *m* de points ajustés
r число *n* сглаженных точек

6324 number of loops
d Schleifenzahl *f*; Zahl *f* der Schleifen
f nombre *m* de boucles
r число *n* петель

6325 number of partitions
d Partitionszahl *f*; Zahl *f* der Zerlegungen
f nombre *m* de partitions
r число *n* разбиений

6326 number of regions
d Regionenzahl *f*; Zahl *f* der Regionen
f nombre *m* de régions
r число *n* регионов

6327 **number of repetitions**
  d Wiederholungszahl *f;* Zahl *f* der Wiederholungen
  f nombre *m* de répétitions
  r число *n* повторений

6328 **number of rows; row number**
  (of a rectangular array or of a table)
  d Zeilen[an]zahl *f;* Zahl *f* der Zeilen
  f nombre *m* de lignes; nombre de rangées
  r число *n* строк

  * **numeric** → 6329

6329 **numeric[al]; digital**
  d numerisch; digital
  f numérique; digital
  r численный; цифровой; числовой

  * **numerical data** → 2767

  * **numerical display** → 2770

  * **numerical image** → 2777

6330 **numeric attribute**
  d Zahlenattribut *n*
  f attribut *m* numérique
  r числовой атрибут *m*

6331 **numeric box**
  d numerischer Kasten *m*
  f boîte *f* numérique
  r числовой ящик *m*

6332 **numeric calculation**
  d numerische Berechnung *f*
  f calcul *m* numérique
  r численный расчет *m;* численное вычисление

6333 **numeric chain data**
  d numerische Kettendaten *npl*
  f données *fpl* d'enchaînement numériques
  r данные *npl* типа цифровых строк; числовые строковые данные

6334 **numeric characteristic**
  d Kennziffer *f;* Kennnummer *f*
  f caractéristique *f* numérique
  r числовая характеристика *f*

6335 **numeric database**
  d numerische Datenbasis *f*
  f base *f* de données numérique
  r цифровая база *f* данных

  * **numeric display** → 2770

6336 **numeric expression**

  d numerischer Ausdruck *m*
  f expression *f* numérique
  r цифровое выражение *n*

6337 **numeric format; digital format**
  d numerisches Format *n*
  f format *m* numérique
  r цифровой формат *m*

6338 **numeric function**
  d numerische Funktion *f*
  f fonction *f* numérique
  r цифровая функция *f*

  * **numeric image** → 2777

O

* **OBB** → 6620

6339 obelisk
  d Obelisk *m*
  f obélisque *m*
  r крестик *m*; кинжал *m*; обелиск *m*

6340 object
  d Objekt *n*
  f objet *m*
  r объект *m*

6341 object attributes
  d Objektattribute *npl*; Attribute *npl* des
      Objekts
  f attributs *mpl* d'objet
  r атрибуты *mpl* объекта

6342 object browser
  d Objektbrowser *m*
  f butineur *m* d'objets
  r объектный браузер *m*

6343 object class
  d Objektklasse *f*; Klasse des Objekts
  f classe *f* d'objet
  r класс *m* объекта

6344 object classificator
  d Objektklassifikator *m*
  f classeur *m* d'objets
  r классификатор *m* объектов

6345 object color
  d Objektfarbe *f*
  f couleur *f* d'objet
  r цвет *m* объекта

6346 object conjugating
  d Objektkonjugation *f*
  f conjonction *f* des objets
  r сопряжение *n* объектов

6347 object coordinate system; OCS
  d Objekt-Koordinatensystem *n*
  f système *m* de coordonnées d'objet
  r объектная координатная система *f*;
      объектная система координат

6348 object creating
  d Objekterstellung *f*
  f création *f* d'objet
  r создание *n* объекта

6349 object cutting
  d Objektschnitt *m*
  f coupe *f* d'objet
  r срез *m* объекта

6350 object data
  d Objektdaten *npl*
  f données *fpl* d'objet
  r объектные данные *npl*

6351 object data field
  d Objektdatenfeld *n*; Datenfeld *n* des Objekts
  f champ *m* de données d'objet
  r поле *n* данных объекта

6352 object [data] manager
  d Objekt-Manager *m*
  f gestionnaire *m* [de données] d'objets
  r менажер *m* объектов

6353 object depth
  d Objekttiefe *f*
  f profondeur *f* d'objet
  r глубина *f* объекта

6354 object displacement; object offset[ting]
  d Objektverschiebung *f*
  f déplacement *m* d'objet; décalage *m* d'objet
  r смещение *n* объекта

6355 object dragging
  d Objekt-Ziehen *n*
  f entraînement *m* d'objet
  r таскание *n* объекта

6356 object exporting
  d Objekt-Exportieren *n*
  f exportation *f* d'objets
  r экспортирование *n* объектов

* **object focal plane** → 4035

6357 object format
  d Objektformat *n*
  f format *m* d'objet
  r формат *m* объекта

6358 object grating
  d Objektgitter *n*
  f treillis *m* d'objet
  r решетка *f* объекта

6359 object grip
  d Objektgriff *m*
  f poignée *f* d'objet
  r захват *m* объекта

6360 object group
  d Gruppe *f* der Objekte

 f groupe *m* d'objets
 r группа *f* объектов

6361 object grouping
 d Objektgruppierung *f*; Gruppierung *f* der
  Objekte
 f groupement *m* d'objets
 r группирование *n* объектов

6362 object handling
 d Objekt-Behandlung *f*; Behandlung *f* des
  Objekts
 f traitement *m* d'objet
 r обработка *f* объекта

6363 object height
 d Objekthöhe *f*
 f hauteur *f* d'objet
 r высота *f* объекта

6364 object inserting
 d Objekteinfügung *f*
 f insertion *f* d'objet
 r вставка *f* объекта

 * **objective aperture** → 467

 * **objective lens** → 6367

 * **objective opening** → 467

6365 object labeling
 d Objektmarkierung *f*
 f étiquetage *m* d'objet
 r маркирование *n* объекта

6366 object layer
 d Objektschicht *f*
 f plan *m* d'objet
 r слой *m* объекта

6367 object lens; objective lens
 d Objektivlinse *f*
 f lentille *f* d'objectif
 r линза *f* объектива

6368 object linetype
 d Objekt-Linientyp *m*; Linientyp *m* des Objekts
 f type *m* de ligne d'objet
 r тип *m* линии объекта

6369 object linking
 d Verknüpfen *n* der Objekte
 f liaison *f* d'objets
 r связывание *n* объектов

6370 object linking and embedding; OLE
 d Verknüpfen *n* und Einbetten *n* der Objekte;
  OLE
 f liaison *f* et incorporation *f* d'objets

 r связывание *n* и внедрение *n* объектов

 * **object manager** → 6352

6371 object measuring
 d Objektmessung *f*; Messung *f* des Objekts
 f mesurage *m* d'objets
 r измерение *n* объектов

6372 object merging
 d Objektverschmelzung *f*
 f fusionnement *m* d'objets
 r слияние *n* объектов

6373 object model
 d Objektmodell *n*
 f modèle *m* d'objet
 r модель *f* объекта

6374 object modeler
 d Objekt-Modellierer *m*
 f modélisateur *m* d'objets
 r программа *f* моделирования объектов

6375 object modeling
 d Objektmodellierung *f*
 f modelage *m* d'objet
 r моделирование *n* объекта

6376 object modifying
 d Objektmodifizierung *f*; Modifizierung *f* des
  Objekts
 f modification *f* d'objet
 r модификация *f* объекта

6377 object movement; object moving
 d Objektverschiebung *f*
 f mouvement *m* d'objet
 r движение *n* объекта; перемещение *n*
  объекта

6378 object movement restriction
 d Beschränkung *f* der Objektverschiebung
 f limitation *f* du mouvement d'objet
 r ограничение *n* перемещения объекта

 * **object moving** → 6377

6379 object name
 d Objektname *m*
 f nom *m* d'objet
 r имя *n* объекта

6380 object node
 d Objektknotenpunkt *m*; Knotenpunkt *m* des
  Objekts
 f nœud *m* objet
 r узел *m* объекта

 * **object offset** → 6354

* **object offsetting** → 6354

6381 object orientation
  d Objektorientierung *f*; Orientierung *f* des
      Objekts
  f orientation *f* d'objet
  r ориентация *f* объекта

6382 object-oriented
  d objektorientiert
  f orienté objets
  r объектно-ориентированный

6383 object-oriented graphical language
  d objektorientierte grafische Sprache *f*
  f langage *m* graphique orienté objets; langage
      graphique à objets
  r объектно-ориентированный графический
      язык *m*

6384 object-oriented graphics
  d objektorientierte Grafik *f*
  f graphique *m* orienté objets
  r объектно-ориентированная графика *f*

6385 object-oriented platform
  d objektorientierte Plattform *f*
  f plate-forme *f* orientée objets
  r объектно-ориентированная платформа *f*

6386 object-oriented rendering system
  d objektorientiertes Rendering-System *n*
  f système *m* rendu orienté objets
  r объектно-ориентированная система *f*
      тонирования

6387 object plane
  d Objektebene *f*; Dingebene *f*
  f plan *m* de l'objet; plan-objet *m*
  r предметная плоскость *f*; плоскость объекта

6388 object popping
  d Objekt-Auskellern *n*
  f éclatement *m* d'objet; refoulement *m* d'objet;
      soufflage *m* d'objet
  r выталкивание *n* объекта

6389 object position
  d Objektposition *f*
  f position *f* d'objet
  r позиция *f* объекта

6390 object properties
  d Objekteigenschaften *fpl*
  f propriétés *fpl* d'objet
  r свойства *npl* объекта

6391 object regeneration
  d Objektregenerierung *f*
  f régénération *f* d'objet
  r регенерирование *n* объекта; обновление *n*
      объекта

6392 object renaming
  d Objektumbenennung *f*
  f changement *m* de nom d'objet
  r переименование *n* объекта

6393 object resizing
  d Objekt-Vergrößern/Verkleinern *n*;
      Objekt-Größenänderung *f*
  f changement *m* de taille d'objet
  r переоразмерение *n* объекта

* **object rotating** → 8207

6394 object scaling
  d Objektskalierung *f*
  f mise *f* en échelle d'objet
  r масштабирование *n* объекта

6395 object selection
  d Objektselektion *f*
  f sélection *f* d'objet; choix *m* d'objet
  r выбор *m* объекта

6396 object shape
  d Objektform *f*
  f forme *f* d'objet
  r форма *f* обекта; очертание *n* объекта

* **object snap** → 6398

6397 object snap mode
  d Objektfang-Modus *m*
  f mode *m* d'accrochage aux objets
  r режим *m* привязки к объектам

6398 object snap[ping]; osnap
  d Objektfang *m*
  f accrochage *m* aux objets
  r объектная привязка *f*

6399 object sort
  d Objektsortierung *f*
  f triage *m* d'objets
  r сортировка *f* объектов

6400 object sort order
  d Ordnung *f* der Objektsortierung
  f ordre *m* de triage d'objets
  r порядок *m* сортировки объектов

6401 object space
  d Objektraum *m*; Dingraum *m*
  f espace *m* de l'objet; espace-objet *m*
  r пространство *n* объекта

6402 object splitting
  d Objektaufteilung *f*

f splittage *m* d'objet
r расщепление *n* объекта

6403 object stacking
d Objekt-Kellerung *f*; Objektstapelung *f*
f empilage *m* d'objet
r запись *f* [параметров] объекта в стек

6404 object texture
d Objekt-Textur *f*
f texture *f* d'un objet
r текстура *f* объекта

6405 object transforming
d Objektveränderung *f*
f transformation *f* d'objet
r преобразование *n* объекта

6406 object type
d Objekttyp *m*
f type *m* d'objet
r тип *m* объекта

6407 object width
d Objektbreite *f*
f largeur *f* d'objet
r ширина *f* объекта

6408 oblate; flattened
d abgeplattet; zusammengedrückt
f aplati
r сплюснутый; сплющенный

6409 oblate ellipsoid
d zusammengedrücktes Ellipsoid *n*
f ellipsoïde *m* aplati
r сплющенный эллипсоид *m*

6410 oblate ellipsoid of revolution; oblate spheroid
d zusammengedrücktes Rotationsellipsoid *n*
f ellipsoïde *m* de révolution aplati
r сплющенный эллипсоид *m* вращения

* **oblate spheroid** → 6410

* **oblique** → 6436, 8757

6411 oblique; inclined; slanted; sloping; tilting
d schief; geneigt; schräg; kippbar
f oblique; incliné
r наклонный; косой

6412 oblique affinity
d schiefe Affinität *f*
f affinité *f* oblique
r наклонная аффинность *f*

6413 oblique angle; obliquing angle
d schiefer Winkel *m*

f angle *m* oblique
r косой угол *m*

6414 oblique astroid
d schiefe Astroide *f*
f astroïde *f* oblique
r косая астроида *f*

6415 oblique asymptote; slant asymptote
d schräge Asymptote *f*
f asymptote *f* oblique; asymptote inclinée
r наклонная асимптота *f*

6416 oblique circular cone
d schiefer Kreiskegel *m*
f cône *m* circulaire oblique
r наклонный круглый конус *m*; косой круговой конус

6417 oblique circular cylinder
d schiefer Kreiszylinder *m*
f cylindre *m* circulaire oblique
r наклонный круговой цилиндр *m*

6418 oblique cissoid
d schiefe Zissoide *f*
f cissoïde *f* oblique
r наклонная циссоида *f*

6419 oblique cone; scalene cone
d schiefer Kegel *m*
f cône *m* oblique
r наклонный конус *m*; косой конус

6420 oblique coordinates
d schiefwinklige Koordinaten *fpl*
f coordonnées *fpl* obliques
r косоугольные координаты *fpl*

6421 oblique coordinate system
d schiefwinkliges Koordinatensystem *n*
f système *m* de coordonnées [en axes] obliques
r косоугольная система *f* координат

6422 oblique cylinder
d schiefer Zylinder *m*
f cylindre *m* incliné
r наклонный цилиндр *m*

* **oblique dimension** → 266

6423 oblique font; slanted font
d schräge Schrift *f*
f police *f* oblique
r наклонный шрифт *m*

6424 oblique illumination
d schiefe Beleuchtung *f*
f illumination *f* oblique
r наклонное освещение *n*

6425 oblique incidence
  d schräges Einfallen *n*
  f incidence *f* oblique
  r наклонное падение *n*

6426 oblique [line]; inclined line; slanting line
  d geneigte Gerade *f*
  f droite *f* oblique; oblique *f*; droite inclinée
  r наклонная [прямая] *f*

6427 oblique parallelepiped
  d schiefes Parallelepiped *n*
  f parallélépipède *m* oblique
  r наклонный параллелепипед *m*

  * **oblique plane** → 4995

6428 oblique prism
  d schiefes Prisma *n*
  f prisme *m* oblique
  r наклонная призма *f*; косая призма

  * **oblique projection** → 8768

6429 oblique pyramid
  d schiefe Pyramide *f*
  f pyramide *f* oblique
  r наклонная пирамида *f*; косая пирамида

  * **oblique ray** → 8760

6430 oblique spherical aberration
  d schiefe Kugelaberration *f*
  f aberration *f* sphérique oblique
  r косая сферическая аберрация *f*

6431 oblique stroke
  d Schrägstrich *m*
  f trait *m* oblique
  r косая черта *f*; наклонная черта

6432 oblique stroke arrowhead
  d schiefe Zählpfeilspitze *f*
  f pic *m* de flèche oblique
  r косой конец *m* стрелки

6433 oblique strophoid
  d schräge Strophoide *f*
  f strophoïde *f* oblique
  r косая строфоида *f*

  * **oblique surface** → 8769

6434 oblique symmetry
  d schiefe Symmetrie *f*
  f symétrie *f* oblique
  r косая симметрия *f*

6435 oblique triangle
  d schiefwinkliges Dreieck *n*

  f triangle *m* obliquangle
  r косоугольный треугольник *m*

  * **obliquing angle** → 6413

6436 obscuration
  d Abblendung *f*; Dunkelheit *f*;
     Sichtbehinderung *f*
  f occultation *f*; obscurcissement *m*
  r темнота *f*; потемнение *n*; помрачение *n*;
     смутность *f* очертаний

6437 obscuring; dark *adj*
  d Dunkel-
  f obscur; sombre
  r темный; мрачный; пасмурный

6438 observability
  d Beobachtbarkeit *f*
  f observabilité *f*
  r наблюдаемость *f*

6439 observation
  d Beobachtung *f*
  f observation *f*
  r наблюдение *n*

6440 observational error; error of observation
  d Beobachtungsfehler *m*
  f erreur *f* d'observation
  r ошибка *f* наблюдения; погрешность *f* при
     наблюдении

6441 observe *v*
  d beobachten
  f observer; surveiller
  r наблюдать

6442 observed pattern
  d beobachtetes Muster *n*
  f image *f* observée
  r наблюдаемый образ *m*; наблюдаемая
     картина *f*

6443 observer; monitor; viewer
     (a person)
  d Betrachter *m*; Beobachter *m*
  f observateur *m*; visionneur *m*; visionneuse *f*
  r зритель *m*; наблюдатель *m*

6444 obstacle
  d Hindernis *n*
  f obstacle *m*
  r отражающий объект *m*; препятствие *n*

6445 obtain *v*
  d erreichen
  f obtenir
  r получать; достигать

6446 obtuse
  d stumpf
  f obtus
  r тупой

6447 obtuse angle
  d stumpfer Winkel *m*
  f angle *m* obtus
  r тупой угол *m*

6448 obtuse-angled
  d stumpfwinklig
  f obtusangle
  r тупоугольный

6449 obtuse triangle
  d stumpfwinkliges Dreieck *n*
  f triangle *m* obtusangle
  r тупоугольный треугольник *m*

6450 occlusion
  d Okklusion *f*
  f occultation *f*
  r преграждение *n*; непроходимость *f*

  * **occupancy → 6451**

6451 occupation; occupancy; seizure; seizing
  d Besetzung *f*; Belegung *f*; Ausnutzung *f*;
    Nutzung *f*
  f occupation *f*; encombrement *m*;
    engagement *m*; prise *f*
  r занятие *n*; занятость *f*

  * **OCR → 6540**

6452 OCR font
  d OCR-Schrift *f*
  f fonte *f* à lecture optique; police *f* OCR
  r оптически распознаваемый шрифт *m*

  * **OCS → 6347**

6453 octagon
  d Oktagon *n*; Achteck *n*
  f octogone *m*
  r восьмиугольник *m*

6454 octagonal
  d oktagonal; Oktagonal-
  f octogonal; octogone
  r восьмиугольный

6455 octahedral
  d oktaedral; Oktaeder-
  f octaédrique
  r восьмигранный

6456 octahedron
  d Oktaeder *n*; Achtflach *n*
  f octaèdre *m*
  r восьмигранник *m*

6457 offline; autonomous
  d abgetrennt; getrennt; autonom; Offline-
  f hors ligne; autonome; offline
  r автономный; независимый; офлайн

6458 offset
  d Versatz *m*; Offset *n*
  f offset *m*
  r оффсет *m*

  * **offset → 8643**

6459 offset angle
  d Abweichwinkel *m*; Versatzwinkel *m*
  f angle *m* de décalage
  r угол *m* смещения

6460 offset effect
  d Verschiebungseffekt *m*
  f effet *m* de décalage
  r эффект *m* смещения

6461 offset filter
  d Abstand-Filter *m*
  f filtre *m* de décalage
  r фильтр *m* смещения

6462 offset method
  d Abstand-Methode *f*
  f méthode *f* de décalage
  r метод *m* смещения

6463 offset print
  d Offsetdruck *m*
  f impression *f* offset
  r оффсетная печать *f*

6464 offset snap
  d Abstandsfang *m*
  f accrochage *m* de décalage
  r привязка *f* смещения

  * **OLE → 6370**

6465 OLE automation
  d OLE-Automation *f*
  f automation *f* OLE
  r OLE автоматизация *f*

6466 OLE object
  d OLE-Objekt *n*
  f objet *m* OLE
  r OLE объект *m*

6467 on-demand video
  d mitlaufendes Video *n*

f vidéo *m* à la demande
r заказное видео *n*

6468 one-chip rendering processor
d Einchip-Rendering-Prozessor *m*
f processeur *m* rendu à puce unique
r одночиповый процессор *m* тонирования

* **one-color** → 6025

* **one-color light** → 6028

6469 one-color mode; 1-bit color mode
d Einfarb-Modus *m*
f mode *m* à couleur unique
r одноцветный режим *m*

6470 one-column bar chart
d Einzelspalten-Streifendiagramm *n*
f diagramme *m* à barre unique
r одноколонная столбиковая диаграмма *f*

6471 one-dimensional
d eindimensional
f à une dimension
r одноразмерный

6472 one-dimensional datum
d eindimensionales Datum *n*
f datum *m* à une dimension
r одноразмерное начало *n* отсчета

* **one-directional** → 10004

6473 one-directional linkage
d einseitig gerichtete Verbindung *f*
f liaison *f* à une direction
r однонаправленная связь *f*

6474 one-line text box; text box
d einlineares Textfeld *n*
f zone *f* de texte [simple ligne]; champ *m* de texte monoligne; case *f* de saisie simple; boîte *f* de saisie monoligne
r однолинейное поле *n* текста

6475 one-plane projection
d Eintafelprojektion *f*
f projection *f* sur un [seul] plan
r проекция *f* на одну плоскость; проектирование *n* на одну плоскость

6476 one-point perspective
d Einpunkt-Perspektive *f*
f perspective *f* à un point
r одноточечная перспектива *f*

* **one-sided** → 8742

6477 one-sided surface; unilateral surface;

surface with only one side; surface of one side
d einseitige Fläche *f*
f surface *f* unilatérale
r односторонняя поверхность *f*

6478 one-sided symmetry
d einseitige Symmetrie *f*
f symétrie *f* unilatérale
r односторонняя симметрия *f*

6479 one-to-many correspondence
d ein[-]mehrdeutige Korrespondenz *f*; ein[-]mehrdeutige Zuordnung *f*
f correspondance *f* multivoque
r многозначное соответствие *n*

6480 one-to-one
d eineindeutig; Eins-zu-Eins-
f un à un; biunivoque
r взаимно-однозначный

6481 one-to-one correspondence; univalent correspondence
d eineindeutige Zuordnung *f*; bijektive Zuordnung
f correspondance *f* biunivoque; correspondance bijective
r взаимно-однозначное соответствие *n*; биективное соответствие

6482 one-to-one mapping
d eineindeutige Abbildung *f*; bijektive Abbildung; umkehrbare eindeutige Abbildung
f application *f* biunivoque; application *f* bijective
r взаимно-однозначное отображение *n*

6483 one-to-oneness
d Eineindeutigkeit *f*
f biunivocité *f*
r взаимная однозначность *f*

* **one-way** → 8742, 10004

6484 online
d Online-; mitlaufend; prozessgekoppelt; rechnerverbunden
f en ligne; direct
r неавтономный; управляемый; зависимый; он-лайн

6485 online help
d Online-Hilfe *f*
f aide *f* directe
r неавтономная помощь *f*

6486 online image
d Online-Bild *n*

f image *f* en ligne; graphique *m* en ligne
r неавтономное изображение *n*

6487 online planner
d Online-Planer *m*
f planificateur *m* en ligne
r он-лайн планировщик *m*

6488 on-screen color correction
d Bildschirmfarbkorrektur *f*
f correction *f* de couleur d'écran
r экранная коррекция *f* цвета

6489 on-screen color palette
d Bildschirmfarbpalette *f*
f palette *f* des couleurs de l'écran
r экранная цветовая палитра *f*

6490 on-screen distortion
(of an image)
d Bildschirmverzerrung *f*
f distorsion *f* due à la courbure de l'écran
r экранное искажение *n*

6491 on-screen indicators
d Bildschirmanzeiger *mpl*
f indicateurs *mpl* d'écran
r экранные указатели *mpl*

6492 on-the-fly stretching
d fliegende Ausdehnung *f*
f étirement *m* en marche
r динамическое вытягивание *n*; удлинение *n* "на лету"

6493 on-the-fly texture computation
d fliegende Textur-Rechnung *f*
f calcul *m* en marche
r динамическое вычисление *n* текстуры; вычисление текстуры "на лету"

6494 opacimeter; light-obscuration instrument
d Lichtdurchlässigkeitsmesser *m*; Lichtdurchlässigkeitsprüfer *m*
f opacimètre *m*; instrument *m* de mesure d'opacité
r инструмент *m* измерения непрозрачности

6495 opacity
d Opazität *f*; Deckkraft *f*; Lichtundurchlässigkeit *f*
f opacité *f*
r непрозрачность *f*

6496 opacity determination
d Opazitätsbestimmung *f*
f détermination *f* d'opacité
r определение *n* непрозрачности

6497 opacity map

(a projection of opaque and transparent area onto object)
d Opazitätsabbildung *f*
f projection *f* d'opacité
r проекция *f* непрозрачности

6498 opacity value
d Opazitätswert *m*
f valeur *f* d'opacité
r значение *n* непрозрачности

6499 opaque shadow
d deckender Schatten *m*
f ombre *f* opaque
r непрозрачная тень *f*

6500 open *v*
d öffnen; eröffnen
f ouvrir
r открыть

6501 open
d offen
f ouvert
r открытый; разомкнутый

* open annulus → 6504

6502 open ball
d offene Kugel *f*
f boule *f* ouverte
r открытый шар *m*

6503 open B-spline
d offener B-Spline *m*
f B-spline *m* ouvert
r открытый B-сплайн *m*

* open circle → 6508

6504 open circular ring; open annulus
d offener [ebener] Kreisring *m*
f couronne *f* [circulaire] ouverte
r открытое круговое [плоское] кольцо *n*

6505 open covering
d offene Überdeckung *f*
f recouvrement *m* ouvert
r открытое покрытие *n*

6506 open cross intersection
d offener Querdurchschnitt *m*
f intersection *f* croisée ouverte
r открытое перекрестное пересечение *n*

6507 open curve
d offene Kurve *f*
f courbe *f* ouverte
r разомкнутая кривая *f*; незамкнутая кривая

6508 open disk; open circle
d offene Kreisscheibe f; offener Kreis m
f disque m ouvert
r открытый круг m

6509 open ended extrusion
d Extrusion f mit offenen Enden
f extrusion f ouverte aux extrémités
r экструзия f с открытыми концами

6510 open graphics library
d offene Grafikbibliothek f
f bibliothèque f graphique ouverte
r открытая графическая библиотека f

6511 opening
d Eröffnung f
f ouverture f
r открытие n

6512 open outline
d offene Kontur f
f contour m ouvert
r открытый контур m; разомкнутый контур

6513 open path
d offene Strecke f
f chemin m ouvert
r разомкнутая дорожка f

6514 open polyline
d offene Polylinie f
f polyligne f ouverte
r разомкнутая полилиния f

6515 open sine curve; open sinusoid
d offene Sinuskurve f; offene Sinusoide f
f courbe f sinus[oïdale] ouverte; sinusoïde f ouverte
r разомкнутая синусоида f

* **open sinusoid** → 6515

6516 open space
d offener Raum m
f espace m ouvert
r открытое пространство n

6517 open spherical layer
d offene Kugelschicht f
f couronne f sphérique ouverte
r открытый сферический слой m; открытый шаровой слой

6518 open surface
d offene Fläche f
f surface f ouverte
r открытая поверхность f

6519 open tee intersection

d offener T-förmiger Durchschnitt m
f intersection f en T ouverte
r открытое Т-образное пересечение n

6520 operate v
d betreiben; arbeiten; bedienen
f opérer; travailler; asservir
r оперировать; действовать; работать

6521 operating; operation
d Betrieb m; Betriebsführung f
f exploitation f; fonctionnement m
r эксплуатация f; работа f; оперирование n

6522 operating; operational adj
d Betriebs-; Arbeits-
f opérationnel
r операционный

6523 operating characteristic; operational factor
d Betriebskennlinie f; Arbeitskennlinie f
f caractéristique f d'opération; facteur m opérationnel
r эксплуатационная характеристика f; рабочая характеристика

* **operating data** → 3436

6524 operating system
d Operationssystem n; Betriebssystem n
f système m d'exploitation
r операционная система f

6525 operation
d Operation f
f opération f
r операция f

* **operation** → 6521

* **operational** adj → 6522

* **operational factor** → 6523

6526 operation code
d Operationscode m; Operationsschlüssel m
f code m d'opération
r код m операции

6527 opposite
d entgegengesetzt; gegenüberliegend; Gegen-
f opposé
r противоположный; противолежащий; обратный

6528 opposite angle
d Gegenwinkel m
f angle m opposé
r противолежащий угол m

* opposite angles → 10156

6529 **opposite direction; return direction; back direction**
d entgegengesetzte Richtung f; Rückrichtung f
f sens m opposé; sens contraire; direction f de retour
r противоположное направление n; обратное направление

6530 **opposite face**
d gegenüberliegende Seite f
f face f opposée
r противоположная грань f

6531 **opposite-hand views**
d gegenüberliegende Ansichten fpl
f vues fpl en opposition
r противолежащие представления npl

6532 **opposite leg of a right-angled triangle**
d Gegenkathete f; gegenüberliegende Kathete f
f côté m opposé d'un triangle droit
r противолежащий катет m прямоугольного треугольника

* opposite lighting → 801

* optic → 6533

6533 **optic[al]**
d optisch
f optique
r оптический

6534 **optical access**
d optischer Zugriff m
f accès m optique
r оптический доступ m

6535 **optical axis**
d optische Achse f
f axe m optique
r оптическая ось f

6536 **optical beam scanning**
d optische Strahlabtastung f
f exploration f de faisceau optique
r оптическая развертка f лучом

6537 **optical capture system**
d optisches Sammlungssystem n; optisches Sammelsystem n
f système m de capture optique
r оптическая система f захвата

6538 **optical centre**
d optisches Zentrum n
f centre m optique
r оптический центр m

* optical characteristics → 6563

6539 **optical character reader**
d optischer Klarschriftleser m
f lecteur m de caractères optique
r оптический считыватель m знаков

6540 **optical character recognition; OCR**
d optische Zeichenerkennung f; Mustererkennung f der Zeichen
f reconnaissance f de caractères optique
r оптическое распознавание n символов

6541 **optical code**
d optischer Code m
f code m optique
r оптический код m

* optical coding → 6547

6542 **optical coherence**
d optische Kohärenz f
f cohérence f optique
r оптическая когерентность f; когерентность света

6543 **optical density; light density**
d Lichtdichte f; Schwärzungsdichte f
f densité f optique
r плотность f почернения

6544 **optical diffraction; light diffraction; bending of light**
d optische Beugung f; Lichtablenkung f
f diffraction f optique; diffraction de la lumière
r оптическая дифракция f; дифракция света

6545 **optical disk; videodisk; compact disk; CD; laser disk**
d optischer Disk m; Videodisk m; Kompaktplatte f; Bildplatte f; Videobildplatte f; Laserbildplatte f
f disque m optique; vidéodisque m; disque compact; compact m; disque laser
r оптический диск m; видеодиск m; компактный диск; лазерный диск

6546 **optical document reader; videoscan document reader**
d optischer Dokumentleser m; optischer Belegleser m
f lecteur m de documents optique
r оптический считыватель m документов

6547 **optical [en]coding**
d optische Codierung f; optische Verschlüsselung f
f codage m optique; codification f optique
r оптическое кодирование n

6548 optical equalization
 d optische Entzerrung f
 f égalisation f optique
 r оптическая компенсация f; оптическое
  выравнивание n

6549 optical filter; light filter
 d optischer Filter m; Lichtfilter m
 f filtre m optique
 r оптический фильтр m; светофильтр m

6550 optical font
 d optische Schriftart f; optisch auswertbare
  Schrift f
 f fonte f optique
 r шрифт m для оптического распознавания

6551 optical illusion
 d optische Illusion f
 f illusion f optique
 r оптическая иллюзия f

6552 optical image
 d optisches Bild n
 f image f optique
 r оптическое изображение n

6553 optical image chip
 d Bildwandlerchip n
 f puce f de conversion d'image
 r микросхема f преобразования
  изображения

6554 optical inspection
  (of surface defects)
 d optische Inspektion f
 f inspection f optique
 r оптическая проверка f

6555 optical interference
 d optische Interferenz f
 f interférence f optique
 r оптическая интерференция f

6556 optical lens
 d optische Linse f
 f lentille f optique
 r оптическая линза f

6557 optically-sensed document
 d optisch lesbarer Beleg m
 f document m à lecture optique
 r оптически считываемый документ m

6558 optical mark reader
 d optischer Markierungsleser m
 f lecteur m de marques optique
 r устройство n оптического считывания
  меток

6559 optical measurement
 d optische Messung f
 f mesure f optique
 r оптическое измерение n

6560 optical microphone
 d optisches Mikrofon n
 f microphone m optique
 r оптический микрофон m

6561 optical noise
 d optisches Rauschen n
 f bruit m optique
 r оптический шум m

6562 optical non-linearity
 d optische Nichtlinearität f
 f non-linéarité f optique
 r оптическая нелинейность f

**6563 optical properties; optical characteristics;
 optical specifications**
 d optische Eigenschaften fpl; optische
  Charakteristiken fpl; optische
  Spezifikationen fpl
 f propriétés fpl optiques; caractéristiques fpl
  optiques
 r оптические свойства npl; оптические
  характеристики fpl; оптические
  спецификации fpl

6564 optical radiation
 d optische Strahlung f
 f rayonnement m optique
 r оптическое излучение n

 * **optical reader** → 6570

**6565 optical reading; optical sensing; optical
 scanning**
 d optisches Lesen n
 f lecture f optique
 r оптическое считывание n

6566 optical recording
 d optische Speicherung f
 f enregistrement m optique
 r оптическое записывание n; оптическое
  хранение n

6567 optical reflection
 d optische Reflexion f
 f réflexion f optique
 r оптическое отражение n

6568 optical resolution
 d optische Auflösung f
 f résolution f optique
 r оптическая разрешающая способность f

6569 **optical resonance**
d optische Resonanz f
f résonance f optique
r оптический резонанс m

6570 **optical scanner; visual scanner; optical reader; photoelectric[al] reader**
d optischer Leser m; fotoelektrischer Leser; Klarschriftleser m
f lecteur m optique; balayeur m optique; lecteur photoélectrique
r оптическое считывающее устройство n; оптический сканер m; фотосчитыватель m

* **optical scanning** → 6565

6571 **optical scintillation**
d optische Szintillation f
f scintillation f optique
r оптическая сцинтилляция f

6572 **optical selection**
d optische Selektion f
f sélection f optique
r оптическая выборка f

* **optical sensing** → 6565

6573 **optical signal; visual signal; visible signal**
d optisches Signal n
f signal m optique
r оптический сигнал m

* **optical specifications** → 6563

6574 **optical spectrum analyzer**
d optischer Spektrumanalysator m
f analyseur m de spectre optique
r оптический спектральный анализатор m

6575 **optical tracking**
d optische Verfolgung f
f poursuite f optique
r оптическое прослеживание n

6576 **optical tracking system**
d optisches Verfolgungssystem n
f système m de poursuite optique
r система f оптического прослеживания

* **optical wand** → 5554

6577 **optical window**
d optisches Fenster n
f fenêtre f optique
r оптическое окно n

6578 **optics**
d Optik f
f optique f

r оптика f

6579 **optimal**
d Optimal-
f optimal
r оптимальный

6580 **optimal point**
d Optimalpunkt m
f point m optimal
r оптимальная точка f

6581 **optimal resolution; optimum resolution**
d optimales Auflösungsvermögen n
f résolution f optimale
r оптимальная разрешающая способность f

6582 **optimal trajectory**
d optimale Bahn[kurve] f; optimale Trajektorie f
f trajectoire f optimale
r оптимальная траектория f

6583 **optimal value; optimum [value]**
d Optimalwert m; Optimum n
f valeur f optimum; valeur optimale; optimum m
r оптимальное значение n; оптимальная величина f; оптимум m

* **optimation** → 6584

6584 **optimization; optimation**
d Optimierung f; Optimisierung f; Optimalisierung f
f optimisation f
r оптимизация f

6585 **optimized image; optimized picture**
d optimiertes Bild n
f image f optimisée
r оптимизированное изображение n

* **optimized picture** → 6585

6586 **optimized polyline**
d optimierte Polylinie f
f polyligne f optimisée
r оптимизированная полилиния f

* **optimum** → 6583

* **optimum noise factor** → 6587

6587 **optimum noise figure; optimum noise factor**
d optimale Rauschzahl f
f facteur m de bruit optimum
r оптимальный коэффициент m искажения

* **optimum resolution** → 6581

6588 optimum scanner resolution
   d optimales Scannerauflösungsvermögen *n*
   f résolution *f* de scanner optimale
   r оптимальная разрешающая способность *f* сканера

* **optimum value** → 6583

6589 option
   d Option *f*; Angebot *n*; wahlfreie Möglichkeit *f*
   f option *f*; choix *m*
   r опция *f*; выбор *m*

6590 optional
   d wahlfrei; wahlweise; optional; willkürlich
   f optionnel; aux choix; facultatif
   r необязательный; факультативный; выборочный; выбираемый

6591 optional facility
   d wahlweise Zusatzeinrichtung *f*; wahlweiser Zusatz *m*
   f supplément *m* par option
   r выборочное средство *n*

* **optional sampling** → 6592

6592 optional selection; optional sampling
   d willkürliche Auswahl *f*
   f choix *m* arbitraire; sélection *f* arbitraire
   r произвольный выбор *m*

6593 options dialog box
   d Dialogfeld *n* "Optionen"
   f boîte *f* de dialogue d'options
   r диалоговый ящик *m* выбора

6594 optoacoustic; photoacoustic
   d optoakustisch
   f optoacoustique
   r оптоакустический

6595 optoelectronics
   d Optoelektronik *f*
   f optoélectronique *f*
   r оптоэлектроника *f*

6596 orbit
   d Orbit *m*
   f orbite *f*
   r орбита *f*

6597 orbit plane
   d Orbitalebene *f*
   f plan *m* d'orbite
   r плоскость *f* орбиты

* **orbit space** → 9813

* **order** → 2579, 6602

6598 order
   d Ordnung *f*
   f ordre *m*
   r порядок *m*

6599 order *v*
   d ordnen; anordnen
   f ordonner
   r упорядочивать; располагать в определенном порядке

6600 ordered
   d geordnet
   f ordonné; classé
   r упорядоченный

6601 ordered dithering
   d geordnetes Dithering *n*; geordnetes Rastern *n*
   f juxtaposition *f* ordonnée
   r упорядоченное псевдосмешение *n*

6602 order[ing]
   d Anordnung *f*; Ordnen *n*; Anordnen *n*
   f ordonnance *f*; ordonnancement *m*
   r упорядочение *n*; упорядоченность

* **order of a curve** → 2580

* **order of a surface** → 2582

* **order of precedence** → 6603

6603 order of priority; order of precedence
   d Prioritätsordnung *f*
   f ordre *m* de priorité
   r порядок *m* приоритета; приоритетность *f* [действий]

6604 ordinary
   d gewöhnlich
   f ordinaire
   r обыкновенный; обычный

6605 ordinary branch point
   d gewöhnlicher Verzweigungspunkt *m*
   f point *m* de ramification ordinaire
   r обыкновенная точка *f* разветвления

* **ordinary helix** → 4560

6606 ordinary point; simple point; regular point
   d gewöhnlicher Punkt *m*; einfacher Punkt; regulärer Punkt
   f point *m* ordinaire; point simple; point régulier
   r обыкновенная точка *f*; простая точка; регулярная точка

6607 ordinary ray
   d gewöhnlicher Strahl *m*

f rayon *m* ordinaire
r обыкновенный луч *m*

6608 ordinate
d Ordinate *f*
f ordonnée *f*
r ордината *f*

6609 ordinate dimension
d Ordinaten-Dimension *f*
f cote *f* ordonnée; cotation *f* de points en coordonnées
r ординатное оразмерение *n*; ординатный размер *m*

6610 ordinate of a point; Y coordinate of a point
d Ordinate *f* eines Punktes; Y-Koordinate *f* eines Punktes
f ordonnée *f* d'un point
r ордината *f* точки; Y-координата *f* точки; вторая координата *f* точки

* **ordnance map** → **6611**

6611 ordnance[-survey] map; cadastral survey; cadastral plan
d Kataster[plan]karte *f*; amtliche Landvermessungskarte *f*
f carte *f* de plan cadastral
r карта *f* кадастрального плана

6612 ordnance-survey transfer format
d Katasterkarten-Übertragungsformat *n*
f format *m* de transfert de plan cadastral
r формат *m* переноса кадастральных планов

6613 organization chart
d Organigramm *n*
f organigramme *m*
r органиграмма *f*

* **orgraph** → **2855**

6614 orientable contour
d orientierbare Kontur *f*
f contour *m* orientable
r ориентируемый контур *m*

6615 orientation
d Orientierung *f*
f orientation *f*
r ориентация *f*; ориентировка *f*

6616 orientation margin
d Orientierungsgrenze *f*
f marge *f* d'orientation
r граница *f* ориентации

6617 orientation-preserving *adj*
d orientierungstreu

f préservant l'orientation
r сохраняющий ориентацию

6618 orientation-reversing *adj*
d orientierungsumkehrend
f renversant l'orientation
r обращающий ориентацию

6619 oriented; directed
d orientiert; gerichtet
f orienté; dirigé
r ориентированный; направленный

* **oriented angle** → **2853**

6620 oriented bounded box; OBB
d orientiertes begrenztes Kästchen *n*
f boîte *f* délimitée orientée
r ориентированный ограничивающий ящик *m*

6621 oriented contour
d orientierte Kontur *f*
f contour *m* orienté
r ориентированный контур *m*

6622 oriented curve
d orientierte Kurve *f*
f courbe *f* orientée
r ориентированная кривая *f*

* **oriented graph** → **2855**

* **oriented light** → **2856**

* **oriented line** → **2857**

6623 oriented movement
d orientierte Bewegung *f*
f mouvement *m* orienté
r ориентированное движение *n*

6624 oriented plane
d orientierte Ebene *f*; gerichtete Ebene
f plan *m* orienté
r ориентированная плоскость *f*

6625 oriented space
d orientierter Raum *m*
f espace *m* orienté
r ориентированное пространство *n*

6626 oriented surface
d orientierte Fläche *f*
f surface *f* orientée; nappe *f* orientée
r ориентированная поверхность *f*

* **origin** → **6632, 7219**

6627 original
d Original *n*

f original *m*
r оригинал *m*; подлинник *m*

* **original** → 7410

6628 **original color**
   d Originalfarbe *f*
   f couleur *f* d'origine
   r оригинальный цвет *m*

6629 **original data**
   d Ausgangsdaten *npl*; Ursprungsdaten *npl*
   f données *fpl* originaux; données d'origine
   r исходные данные *npl*; оригинальные
     данные

6630 **original image**
   d Originalbild *n*
   f image *f* originale
   r оригинальное изображение *n*; подлинное
     изображение

6631 **originate** *v*; **initiate** *v*; **begin** *v*
   d beginnen; einleiten
   f commencer; initier
   r начинать; инициировать

6632 **origin[ation]; begin**
   d Ursprung *m*; Beginn *m*; Anfang *m*;
     Entstehung *f*
   f origine *f*; début *m*
   r источник *m*; начало *n* [отсчета]; исход *m*

6633 **origin of coordinates; origin of coordinate**
     system; coordinate origin; coordinate
     source; coordinate fountain
   d Koordinatenursprung *f*; Nullpunkt *m* des
     Koordinatensystems;
     Koordinatenanfangspunkt *m*
   f origine *f* de coordonnées; origine du système
     de coordonnées
   r начало *n* координат; начало координатной
     системы

* **origin of coordinate system** → 6633

6634 **origin offset**
   d Ausgangspunkt-Abstand *m*
   f décalage *m* d'origine
   r смещение *n* нулевой точки

* **origin point** → 7219

6635 **ornament**
   d Ornament *n*
   f ornement *m*
   r орнамент *m*

6636 **ornamentation**
   d Ornamentik *f*

f ornementation *f*
r орнаментация *f*

* **ortho** → 6652

6637 **orthocenter; orthocentre**
   (of a triangle)
   d Höhenpunkt *m*; Orthozentrum *n*
   f orthocentre *m*
   r ортоцентр *m*

* **orthocentre** → 6637

6638 **orthochromatic**
   d orthochromatisch
   f orthochromatique
   r ортохроматический

6639 **orthodiagonal quadrangle**
   d orthodiagonales Viereck *n*
   f quadrilatère *m* orthodiagonal
   r ортодиагональный четырехвершинник *m*

6640 **orthogonal; perpendicular** *adj*
   d orthogonal; perpendikulär
   f orthogonal; perpendiculaire
   r ортогональный; перпендикулярный

6641 **orthogonal affinity**
   d orthogonale Affinität *f*
   f affinité *f* orthogonale
   r ортогональная аффинность *f*

6642 **orthogonal axes**
   d orthogonale Achsen *fpl*; Orthogonalachsen *fpl*
   f axes *mpl* orthogonaux
   r ортогональные оси *fpl*

6643 **orthogonal axonometry; normal**
     axonometry
   d orthogonale Axonometrie *f*; senkrechte
     Axonometrie
   f axonométrie *f* orthogonale; axonométrie
     normale
   r ортогональная аксонометрия *f*

6644 **orthogonal circles**
   d orthogonale Kreise *mpl*
   f cercles *mpl* orthogonaux
   r ортогональные окружности *fpl*

6645 **orthogonal coordinate system**
   d orthogonales Koordinatensystem *n*
   f système *m* de coordonnées orthogonaux
   r ортогональная система *f* координат

6646 **orthogonal curves**
   d orthogonale Kurven *fpl*
   f courbes *fpl* orthogonaux
   r ортогональные кривые *fpl*

6647 orthogonal 2D model
 d orthogonales 2D-Modell *n*
 f modèle *m* 2D orthogonal
 r двумерная ортогональная модель *f*

6648 orthogonal function
 d Orthogonalfunktion *f*
 f fonction *f* orthogonale
 r ортогональная функция *f*

6649 orthogonality; perpendicularity
 d Orthogonalität *f*
 f orthogonalité *f*; perpendicularité *f*
 r ортогональность *f*; перпендикулярность *f*

6650 orthogonalization
 d Orthogonalisierung *f*
 f orthogonalisation *f*
 r ортогонализация *f*

 * **orthogonal lines** → 6976

6651 orthogonal matrix
 d orthogonale Matrix *f*
 f matrice *f* orthogonale
 r прямоугольная матрица *f*

6652 orthogonal mode; ortho
 d orthogonaler Modus *m*
 f mode *m* orthogonal
 r ортогональный режим *m*; режим
   вычерчивания перпендикулярных линий

 * **orthogonal planes** → 6977

**6653 orthogonal projection; perpendicular
   projection; orthographic projection**
 d orthogonale Projektion *f*;
   Orthogonalprojektion *f*; senkrechte
   Parallelprojektion *f*
 f projection *f* orthogonale
 r ортогональная проекция *f*; прямоугольная
   проекция; ортогональное
   проектирование *n*

**6654 orthogonal quadrilateral; isothetic
   quadrilateral**
 d orthogonales Vierseit *n*
 f quadrilatère *m* orthogonal
 r ортогональный четырехсторонник *m*

6655 orthogonal surfaces
 d Orthogonalflächen *fpl*
 f surfaces *fpl* orthogonaux
 r ортогональные поверхности *fpl*

6656 orthogonal symmetry
 d orthogonale Symmetrie *f*
 f symétrie *f* orthogonale
 r ортогональная симметрия *f*

6657 ortho[gonal] tool
 d orthogonales Hilfsmittel *n*
 f outil *m* orthogonal
 r ортогональный инструмент *m*

6658 orthogonal transformation
 d orthogonale Transformation *f*
 f transformation *f* orthogonale
 r ортогональная трансформация *f*

6659 orthogonal vector
 d orthogonaler Vektor *m*
 f vecteur *m* orthogonal
 r ортогональный вектор *m*

6660 orthogonal view
 d orthogonale Ansicht *f*
 f vue *f* orthogonale
 r ортогональный вид *m*

 * **orthogonal window** → 7872

6661 orthographic corrector; spell[ing] checker
 d orthografischer Korrektor *m*;
   Rechschreibkorrektor *m*
 f correcteur *m* orthographique
 r корректор *m* правописания;
   грамматический корректор; правописный
   словарь *m*

 * **orthographic projection** → 6653

6662 orthographic view
 d orthografische Ansicht *f*
 f vue *f* orthographique
 r прямоугольный вид *m*

 * **orthomorphic projection** → 2039

6663 orthonormal
 d orthonormiert; orthonormal
 f orthonormal; orthonormé
 r ортонормированный

**6664 orthonormal basis; normal[ized]
   orthogonal basis**
 d orthonormale Basis *f*; orthonormierte Basis
 f base *f* orthonormale; base orthonormée
 r ортонормированный базис *m*

6665 orthonormalization
 d Orthonormierung *f*
 f orthonormalisation *f*
 r ортонормирование *n*; ортонормализация *f*

6666 orthophotograph
 d Orthofotografie *f*; Orthofoto *n*
 f orthophoto[graphie] *f*
 r ортоснимок *m*

* **ortho tool** → 6657

6667 **oscillate** *v*
  d oszillieren; schwanken
  f osciller
  r осциллировать; колебаться

6668 **oscillation**
  d Schwankung *f*; Oszillation *f*
  f oscillation *f*
  r осцилляция *f*, колебание *n*

* **osculating circle** → 1484

6669 **osculating conic**
  d Schmieg[ungs]kegelschnitt *m*; oskulierender Kegelschnitt *m*
  f conique *f* osculatrice
  r соприкасающееся коническое сечение *n*

6670 **osculating curve**
  d oskulierende Kurve *f*
  f courbe *f* osculatrice
  r соприкасающаяся кривая *f*; оскулирующая кривая

6671 **osculating helix**
  d Schmiegschraubenlinie *f*
  f hélice *f* osculatrice
  r соприкасающаяся винтовая линия *f*

6672 **osculating plane**
  d Schmieg[ungs]ebene *f*; Oskulationsebene *f*
  f plan *m* osculateur
  r соприкасающаяся плоскость *f*

6673 **osculating sphere**
  d Schmiegkugel *f*
  f sphère *f* osculatrice
  r соприкасающаяся сфера *f*

6674 **osculating tangent**
  d Schmiegtangente *f*
  f tangente *f* osculatrice
  r соприкасающаяся касательная *f*

* **osnap** → 6398

6675 **osnap settings**
  d Objektfang-Einrichtung *f*
  f paramètres *mpl* d'accrochage aux objets
  r параметры *mpl* привязки к объектам

* **outer** → 3602

6676 **outer arc**
  d äußerer Bogen *m*
  f arc *m* externe
  r внешняя дуга *f*

6677 **outer edge; outside edge**
  (of a graph)
  d äußere Kante *f*
  f arête *f* externe; arête extérieure
  r внешнее ребро *n*

6678 **outer hatch style**
  d äußerer Schraffurstil *m*
  f style *m* externe de hachure
  r внешний стиль *m* штриховки

6679 **outer loop**
  d äußere Schleife *f*
  f boucle *f* externe
  r внешняя петля *f*

6680 **outgoing radiosity**
  d Ausgangsradiosity *n*
  f radiosité *f* sortante
  r исходящее диффузное отражение *n*

* **outline** → 2129

6681 **outline attributes; contour attributes**
  d Umrissattribute *npl*; Konturattribute *npl*
  f attributs *mpl* de contour
  r атрибуты *mpl* контура

* **outline color** → 2132

6682 **outline font**
  d Konturschrift *f*
  f police *f* de contour
  r контурный шрифт *m*

6683 **outline pen**
  d Konturstift *m*
  f plume *f* de contour
  r перо *n* контура

6684 **outline properties; contour characteristics**
  d Umrisseigenschaften *fpl*
  f propriétés *fpl* de contour; caractéristiques *fpl* de contour
  r свойства *npl* контура

6685 **outline symbol**
  d konturiertes Symbol *n*
  f symbole *m* de contour
  r контурный символ *m*

* **outline thickness** → 6687

6686 **outline tool; contour tool**
  d Hilfsmittel *n* "Umriss"
  f outil *m* "contour"
  r инструмент *m* "контур"

6687 **outline width; outline thickness**
  d Umrissbreite *f*

f largeur *f* de contour; largeur de bordure;
épaisseur *f* de contour
r ширина *f* контура; толщина *f* контура

* **outlining** → 2140

6688 out-of-focus
d ohne Fokus
f défocalisé; décentré
r дефокусированный

6689 out-of-frame
d außerhalb des Rahmens
f décadré
r вне кадра

6690 out-of-gamut color
d außerhalb des Gamuts liegende Farbe *f*
f couleur *f* hors de la gamme
r цвет *m* вне диапазона

* **output** → 3570

6691 output
(of data)
d Ausgabe *f*
f extraction *f*; émission *f*; sortie *f*
r вывод *m*

* **output angle** → 3571

* **output primitive** → 7419

6692 output shape
d Ausgangsfigur *f*
f figure *f* de sortie; forme *f* sortante
r выходная фигура *f*

6693 output spectrum
d Strahlungsspektrum *n*
f spectre *m* d'émission
r спектр *m* излучения

* **outside** → 3602, 3603

6694 outside boundary
d Außengrenze *f*
f limite *f* extérieure
r наружная граница *f*

* **outside diameter** → 5766

* **outside edge** → 6677

* **outward** *adj* → 3602

6695 oval; bowl
d Eilinie *f*; Oval *n*
f ovale *m*
r овал *m*

6696 overall scale
d gemeinsamer Maßstab *m*
f échelle *f* générale
r обобщенный масштаб *m*

6697 overbar; overline
d Strich *m* über eine Größe
f ligne *f* sur une grandeur
r черта *f* сверху; штрих *m* над величиной

6698 overflow
d Überlauf *m*; Bereichsüberschreitung *f*
f dépassement *m*; débordement *m*
r переполнение *n*

* **overlap** → 6700

6699 overlap *v*
d überlappen
f recouvrir; chevaucher
r налагать; перекрывать; совмещать; иметь
общую внутреннюю часть; покрывать

6700 overlap[ping]
d Überlappung *f*
f chevauchement *m*; recouvrement *m*
r перекрытие *n*; совмещение *n*

6701 overlapping faces
d sich überlappende Flächen *fpl*
f faces *fpl* de chevauchement
r перекрывающиеся грани *fpl*

6702 overlapping line
d überlappende Linie *f*
f ligne *f* de chevauchement
r перекрывающая линия *f*

6703 overlay
d Overlay *n*
f calque *m*; décalque *m*; segment *m* de
recouvrement; overlay *m*
r оверлей *m*

6704 overlaying
d Überlagerung *f*
f recouvrement *m*; superposition *f*;
revêtement *m*
r наложение *n*; перекрытие *n*

* **overline** → 6697

6705 overload *v*
d über[be]lasten; überbeanspruchen
f surcharger
r перегружать

* **overprint** → 6709

6706 overprint *v*
d überdrucken

f surimprimer
r надпечатывать; печатать поверх [текста]

6707 overprint color
  d überdruckte Farbe f
  f couleur f surimprimée
  r надпечатанный цвет m

6708 overprinted objects
  d überdruckte Objekte npl
  f objets mpl surimprimés
  r надпечатанные объекты mpl

6709 overprint[ing]
  d Überdruckung f
  f surimpression f
  r надпечатание n

6710 override v
  d aufheben
  f casser; abolir; abroger
  r подменять; игнорировать

6711 overriding
  d Aufhebung f
  f asservissement m
  r подмена f; отмена f

6712 oversampling
  d Überabtastung f
  f suréchantillonnage m
  r сверхразвертка f; сверхсканирование n

6713 overstrike v
  d überdrucken
  f superposer
  r набирать лишние символы; налагать знаки

6714 overview
  d Überblick m; Übersicht f
  f vue f synoptique; survol m; aperçu m
  r обзор m

P

6715 pack *v*
d verdichten; konzentrieren; packen
f empaqueter; emballer; condenser; compresser
r уплотнять; упаковывать; упаковать

* **pack** → 6716

* **package** → 3413

6716 pack[age]; packet
d Paket *n*; Stapel *m*
f paquet *m*
r пакет *m*

6717 packed data
d gepackte Daten *npl*
f données *fpl* paquetées
r данные *npl* в упакованном формате

* **packet** → 6716

6718 packing
d Packung *f*; Verpackung *f*
f empilement *m*
r упаковка *f*

6719 packing of spheres; sphere packing; system of spheres
d Kugelpackung *f*
f empilement *m* de sphères; paquet *m* de sphères; système *m* de sphères
r упаковка *f* сфер; шаровая упаковка

* **pad** → 6720

6720 pad[ding]
d Auffüllung *f*
f remplissage *m*
r заполнение *n*; набивка *f*

6721 page
d Seite *f*
f page *f*
r страница *f*

6722 page border
d Seitenrahmen *m*
f bordure *f* de page
r кайма *f* страницы

6723 page break
d Seitenumbruch *m*
f interruption *f* de page
r прерывание *n* страницы

6724 page curl
d Seitenaufrollen *n*
f roulage *m* de page; tuilage *m* de page; ondulation *f* de page
r завиток *m* страницы

6725 page cut
d Seitenschnitt *m*
f coupe *f* de page
r срез *m* страницы

6726 page cut effect
d Effekt *m* des Seitenschnitts
f effet *m* de coupe de page
r эффект *m* среза страницы

6727 Page Down key; PgDn key
d Bild-nach-unten-Taste *f*
f touche *f* de pageage en arrière
r клавиша *f* листания назад

6728 page exporting
d Seiten-Exportieren *n*
f exportation *f* de page
r экспортирование *n* страницы

6729 page format
d Seitenformat *n*
f format *m* de la page
r формат *m* страницы

6730 page frame
d Seitenrahmen *m*; Seitenfach *n*
f cadre *m* de page; trame *f* de page
r блок *m* страницы; страничный блок

6731 page header
d Seitentitel *m*
f en-tête *f* de page
r заголовок *m* страницы

6732 page image format; PIF
d Seitendarstellungsformat *n*
f format *m* d'image de page
r формат *m* изображения страницы

6733 page-layout
d Seitenanordnung *f*; Seitentopologie *f*
f disposition *f* de pages; topologie *f* de pages
r макет *m* страницы; топология *f* страницы

6734 page number
d Seitennummer *f*
f numéro *m* de page
r номер *m* страницы

6735 page setting
d Seiteneinrichtung *f*

f établissement *m* de page; mise *f* en page
r установление *n* параметров страницы

6736 page setup *v*
  d Seite einrichten
  f mettre en page
  r установлять параметры страницы

6737 page size
  d Seitengröße *f*
  f taille *f* de page
  r размер *m* страницы

6738 page table
  d Seitentabelle *f*
  f table *f* de pages
  r таблица *f* страниц

6739 page template
  d Seitenschablone *f*
  f maquette *f* de page
  r шаблон *m* страницы

6740 Page Up key; PgUp key
  d Bild-nach-oben-Taste *f*
  f touche *f* de pageage en avant; touche de page
     précédente
  r клавиша *f* листания вперед; клавиша PgUp

6741 paint *v*; **fill** *v*
  d färben
  f peindre; dépeindre
  r закрашивать

6742 paint *v*; **design** *v*
  d malen; zeichnen
  f dessiner; brosser
  r рисовать

6743 paintbrush; brush
  d Paint-Brush *n*; Pinsel *m*
  f pinceau *m*; brosse *f*
  r кисть *f* (для рисования); кисточка *f*

6744 paintbrush properties
  d Eigenschaften des Pinsels
  f propriétés *fpl* de pinceau
  r свойства *npl* кисти

6745 paintbrush tool; brush tool
  d Hilfsmittel *n* "Pinsel"
  f outil *m* "brosse"
  r инструмент *m* "кисть"

6746 paint color
  d Malfarbe *f*
  f couleur *m* de peinture
  r цвет *m* рисования

6747 paint color swatch

d Malfarbe-Musterstreifen *m*
f échantillon *m* de couleur de peinture
r образчик *m* цвета рисования

6748 painter palette
  d Malerpalette *f*
  f palette *f* de peinture
  r палитра *f* для рисования

6749 painting
  d Malen *n*
  f peinture *f*
  r рисование *n*

6750 painting technique
  d Maltechnik *f*
  f technique *f* de peinture
  r техника *f* рисования

6751 paint mode
  d Malmodus *m*
  f mode *m* de peinture
  r режим *m* рисования

  * **paint program** → 1984

6752 paint system
  d Malsystem *n*
  f système *m* de peinture
  r система *f* рисования

6753 pair; couple
  d Paar *n*
  f paire *f*; couple *m*
  r пара *f*

6754 pairwise; in pairs; mutually
  d paarweise
  f deux à deux; deux par deux; mutuellement
  r попарно; парами

6755 palette
  d Palette *f*
  f palette *f*
  r палитра *f*

6756 palette animation
  d Palettenanimation *f*
  f animation *f* de palette
  r анимация *f* палитрой

6757 palette color mode
  d Palettenfarbmodus *m*
  f mode *m* couleur de palette
  r цветовой режим *m* палитры

  * **paletted color** → 6759

  * **paletted texture** → 6760

6758 **palette editor**
  d Paletteneditor *m*
  f éditeur *m* de palette
  r редактор *m* палитры

6759 **palett[iz]ed color**
  d palettisierte Farbe *f*
  f couleur *f* palettisée
  r палетизированный цвет *m*

6760 **palett[iz]ed texture**
  d palettisierte Textur *f*
  f texture *f* palettisée
  r палетизированная текстура *f*

6761 **palindrome**
  d Palindrom *n*
  f palindrome *m*
  r палиндром *m*

  * **pan** → 6765

6762 **pan** *v*
  d bildverschieben
  f faire un pan[oramique]; effectuer un
    panoramique; panoramiquer
  r панорамировать

  * **pane** → 9322

6763 **panel**
  d Frontplatte *f*; Bedienungsfeld *n*; Pult *n*
  f panneau *m*; pupitre *m*
  r панель *f*; пульт *m*; стенд *m*

6764 **pan function**
  d Bildverschiebungsfunktion *f*
  f fonction *f* panoramique
  r функция *f* панорамирования

6765 **pan[ning]**
  d Verschieben *n*; Schwenken *n*
  f panoramique *m*; mouvement *m* panoramique;
    pan *m*
  r панорамирование *n*

6766 **panning effect**
  d Schwenkeffekt *m*
  f effet *m* de panoramique
  r эффект *m* панорамирования

  * **panorama** → 6771

  * **panorama camera** → 6767

6767 **panoramic camera; panorama camera**
  d Panoramakamera *f*; Rundblickkamera *f*
  f caméra *f* panoramique
  r панорамная камера *f*

6768 **panoramic distortion**
  d Panoramaverzerrung *f*
  f distorsion *f* panoramique
  r панорамное искажение *n*

6769 **panoramic lens**
  d Panoramalinse *f*
  f lentille *f* panoramique
  r панорамная линза *f*

  * **panoramic picture** → 6771

6770 **pan[oramic] tool**
  d Panoramahilfsmittel *n*
  f outil *m* panoramique
  r инструмент *m* панорамирования

6771 **pan[oramic] view; panoramic picture;**
    panorama
  d Panoramaansicht *f*; Rundbildaufnahme *f*;
    Panoramabild *n*; Panorama *n*
  f vue *f* panoramique; panorama *m*
  r панорамное изображение *n*; панорамный
    вид *m*; панорама *f*

6772 **pan[oramic] zoom**
  d Panorama-Zoomen *n*
  f zoom *m* panoramique
  r панорамное динамическое
    масштабирование *n*

6773 **pantograph**
  d Pantograph *m*
  f pantographe *m*
  r пантограф *m*

6774 **pantone color marker**
  d Pantone-Farbmarker *m*
  f marqueur *m* de couleur pantone
  r маркер *m* цвета pantone

6775 **pantone colors**
    (a set of printing colors, signed by numbers)
  d Pantone-Farben *fpl*
  f couleurs *fpl* pantones
  r цвет *m* pantone

  * **pan tool** → 6770

  * **pan view** → 6771

  * **pan zoom** → 6772

6776 **paper**
  d Papier *n*
  f papier *m*
  r бумага *f*

  * **paper advance** → 6779

6777 **paper color**
    d Papierfarbe *f*
    f couleur *f* du papier
    r цвет *m* бумаги

6778 **paper color swatch**
    d Papierfarben-Musterstreifen *m*;
       Papierfarben-Probestreifen *m*
    f échantillon *m* de couleur de papier
    r образчик *m* цвета бумаги

6779 **paper feed; paper advance**
    d Papierzuführung *f*
    f avancement *m* de papier; acheminement *m* de
       papier
    r подача *f* бумаги; протяжка *f* бумаги

6780 **paperless**
    d papierlos
    f sans papier
    r безбумажный

6781 **paper orientation**
    d Papierorientierung *f*
    f orientation *f* de papier
    r ориентация *f* бумаги

6782 **paper selection**
    (for printer)
    d Papierauswahl *f*
    f sélection *f* de papier
    r выбор *m* бумаги

6783 **paper size**
    d Papierformat *n*
    f taille *f* de papier
    r размер *m* бумаги

6784 **paper space**
    d Papierraum *m*
    f espace *m* papier
    r бумажное пространство *n*

6785 **paper space properties**
    d Papierraumeigenschaften *fpl*
    f propriétés *fpl* d'espace papier
    r характеристики *fpl* бумажного
       пространства

6786 **parabola**
    d Parabel *f*
    f parabole *f*
    r парабола *f*

6787 **parabolic**
    d parabolisch
    f parabolique
    r параболический

6788 **parabolic arc**
    d Parabelbogen *m*
    f arc *m* parabolique
    r дуга *f* параболы

6789 **parabolic bundle of circles; parabolic sheaf
      of circles; parabolic star of circles**
    d parabolisches Kreisbündel *n*
    f étoile *f* de cercles paraboliques
    r параболическая связка *f* окружностей

6790 **parabolic cone**
    d parabolischer Kegel *m*
    f cône *m* parabolique
    r параболический конус *m*

6791 **parabolic curve**
    d parabolische Kurve *f*
    f courbe *f* parabolique
    r параболическая кривая *f*

6792 **parabolic cylinder**
    d parabolischer Zylinder *m*
    f cylindre *m* parabolique
    r параболический цилиндр *m*

6793 **parabolic homology; parabolic
      perspectivity**
    d parabolische Homologie *f*; parabolische
       Perspektivität *f*
    f homologie *f* parabolique
    r параболическая гомология *f*

6794 **parabolic hyperbola**
    d parabolische Hyperbel *f*
    f hyperbole *f* parabolique
    r параболическая гипербола *f*

6795 **parabolic movement**
    d parabolische Bewegung *f*
    f mouvement *m* parabolique
    r параболическое движение *n*

6796 **parabolic operator**
    d parabolischer Operator *m*
    f opérateur *m* parabolique
    r параболический оператор *m*

   * **parabolic perspectivity** → 6793

6797 **parabolic profile**
    d parabolisches Profil *n*
    f profil *m* parabolique
    r параболический профиль *m*

   * **parabolic sheaf of circles** → 6789

6798 **parabolic spiral**
    d parabolische Spirale *f*
    f spirale *f* parabolique
    r параболическая спираль *f*

* **parabolic star of circles** → 6789

6799 **paraboloid**
  d Paraboloid *n*
  f paraboloïde *m*
  r параболоид *m*

6800 **paraboloidal surface**
  d parabolische Fläche *f*
  f surface *f* paraboloïdale
  r параболоидная поверхность *f*

6801 **paraboloid of revolution**
  d Rotationsparaboloid *n*; Drehparaboloid *n*
  f paraboloïde *m* de révolution
  r параболоид *m* вращения

6802 **paragraph**
  d Absatz *m*; Paragraph *m*
  f paragraphe *m*
  r параграф *m*; абзац *m*

6803 **paragraph aligning**
  d Absatzausrichtung *f*
  f alignement *m* de paragraphe
  r выравнивание *n* параграфа

6804 **paragraph beginning**
  d Absatzbeginn *m*
  f début *m* de paragraphe
  r начало *n* параграфа

6805 **paragraph editing**
  d Absatzbearbeitung *f*
  f édition *f* de paragraphe
  r редактирование *n* параграфа

6806 **paragraph [end] mark**
  d Absatzendmarke *f*
  f marque *f* de fin de paragraphe
  r маркер *m* конца параграфа

6807 **paragraph formatting**
  d Absatzformatierung *f*
  f formatage *m* de paragraphe
  r форматирование *n* параграфа

6808 **paragraph justifying**
  d zweiseitige Absatz-Ausrichtung *f*
  f justification *f* de paragraphe
  r выравнивание *n* параграфа по обеим
    границам

* **paragraph mark** → 6806

6809 **paragraph properties**
  d Absatzeigenschaften *fpl*
  f propriétés *fpl* de paragraphe
  r свойства *npl* параграфа

6810 **paragraph sign**
  d Paragraphenzeichen *n*
  f marque *f* de paragraphe
  r символ *m* параграфа

6811 **paragraph text**
  d Absatztext *m*
  f texte *m* courant
  r текст *m* параграфа

6812 **paragraph text frame**
  d Absatztextrahmen *m*
  f cadre *m* de texte courant
  r рамка *f* текста параграфа

* **parallactic angle** → 374

6813 **parallax**
  d Parallaxe *f*
  f parallaxe *m*
  r параллакс *m*

6814 **parallax correction**
  d Parallaxen-Korrektion *f*
  f correction *f* de parallaxe
  r коррекция *f* параллакса

6815 **parallel**
  d parallel
  f parallèle
  r параллельный

6816 **parallel axes**
  d parallele Achsen *fpl*
  f axes *mpl* parallèles
  r параллельные оси *fpl*

6817 **parallel curves**
  d parallele Kurven *fpl*
  f courbes *fpl* parallèles
  r параллельные кривые *fpl*

6818 **parallel dimensioning**
  d parallele Dimensionierung *f*
  f cotation *f* parallèle; dimension *f* parallèle
  r параллельное оразмерение *n*

* **parallel displacement of the system of
  coordinates** → 9831

6819 **parallel edge extraction**
  d parallele Kantenextraktion *f*
  f extraction *f* d'arêtes parallèle
  r параллельное извлечение *n* ребер

6820 **parallelepiped; box**
  d Parallelepiped[on] *n*; Parallelflach *n*; Spat *m*
  f parallélépipède *m*
  r параллелепипед *m*

6821 parallel graphic processor
d Parallelgrafikprozessor *m*
f processeur *m* graphique parallèle
r параллельный графический процессор *m*

6822 paralleling
d Parallellauf *m*
f parallélisation *f*
r распараллеливание *n*

6823 parallel interface
d parallele Schnittstelle *f*; Parallelschnittstelle *f*
f interface *f* parallèle
r параллельный интерфейс *m*

6824 parallelism
d Parallelität *f*
f parallélisme *m*
r параллелизм *m*

6825 parallel lines
d parallele Linien *fpl*
f lignes *fpl* parallèles
r параллельные линии *fpl*

6826 parallelogram
d Parallelogramm *n*
f parallélogramme *m*
r параллелограмм *m*

6827 parallelogram method
d Methode des Parallelogramms
f méthode *f* de parallélogramme
r метод *m* параллелограмма

6828 parallelohedron
d Paralleloeder *n*
f paralléloèdre *m*
r параллелоэдр *m*

6829 parallelotope
d Parallelotop *n*
f parallélotope *m*
r параллелотоп *m*; гиперпараллелепипед *m*

6830 parallel perspective
d Parallelperspektive *f*
f perspective *f* parallèle
r параллельная перспектива *f*

6831 parallel planes
d parallele Ebenen *fpl*
f plans *mpl* parallèles
r параллельные плоскости *fpl*

6832 parallel port
d Parallelport *m*; parallele Anschlussstelle *f*
f port *m* parallèle
r параллельный порт *m*

6833 parallel projection
d Parallelprojektion *f*
f projection *f* parallèle
r параллельная проекция *f*

6834 parallel scanning
d Parallelabtastung *f*
f échantillonnage *m* parallèle
r параллельное сканирование *n*

6835 parallel slit
d Parallelschlitz *m*
f fente *f* parallèle
r параллельный разрез *m*; параллельный надрез *m*

6836 parallel slit domain
d Parallelschlitzgebiet *n*
f plan *m* muni de fentes parallèles
r область *f* с параллельными разрезами

6837 parallel straight lines
d parallele Geraden *fpl*
f droites *fpl* parallèles
r параллельные прямые *fpl*

6838 parallel stripe
d Parallelstreifen *m*
f bande *f* parallèle
r полоса *f*, ограниченная параллелями

* parallel vectors → 1687

6839 parameter
d Parameter *m*
f paramètre *m*
r параметр *m*

6840 parametric coordinates
d parametrische Koordinaten *fpl*
f coordonnées *fpl* paramétriques
r параметрические координаты *fpl*

6841 parametric curve
d parametrische Kurve *f*
f courbe *f* paramétrique
r параметрическая кривая *f*

6842 parametric drawing
d parametrische Zeichnung *f*
f dessin *m* paramétrique
r параметрическое черчение *n*

6843 parametric form
d Parameterform *f*
f forme *f* paramétrique
r параметрическая форма *f*

6844 parametric keyframe animation
d parametrische Schlüsselbilder-Animation *f*

f animation *f* paramétrique par images clées
r параметрическая анимация *f* ключевых
кадров

6845 parametric model
d parametrisches Modell *n*
f modèle *m* paramétrique
r параметрическая модель *f*

6846 parametric rasterization
d parametrische Rasterung *f*
f rastérisation *f* paramétrique
r параметрическая растеризация *f*;
параметрическое растрирование *n*

6847 parametric space
d parametrischer Raum *m*
f espace *m* de paramètres
r параметрическое пространство *n*

6848 parametrization
d Parametrisierung *f*
f paramétrisation *f*; paramétrage *m*
r параметризация *f*

6849 parametrized curve
d parametrisierte Kurve *f*
f courbe *f* paramétrisée
r параметризированная кривая *f*

6850 parametrized geometric objects
d parametrisierte geometrische Objekte *npl*
f objets *mpl* géométriques paramétrisés
r параметризированные геометрические
объекты *mpl*

6851 parent
d Eltern-; übergeordnet; Stamm-
f parent
r родительский

6852 parent color
d Elternfarbe *f*; übergeordnete Farbe *f*;
Stammfarbe *f*
f couleur *f* parente
r родительский цвет *m*

6853 parent dimension
d übergeordnete Dimension *f*
f dimension *f* parente
r родительский размер *m*

6854 parent group
d Stammgruppe *f*
f groupe *m* parent
r родительская группа *f*

6855 parentheses; round brackets
d runde Klammern *fpl*
f parenthèses *fpl* [rondes]

r круглые скобки *fpl*

6856 parent node
d Stammknoten *m*
f nœud *m* parent
r родительский узел *m*

6857 parsing
d Parsing *n*; syntaktische Analyse *f*
f analyse *f* lexicale
r параметрический анализ *m*;
синтаксический анализ; синтаксический
разбор *m*

6858 parsing algorithm
d Algorithmus *m* der syntaktischen Analyse
f algorithme *m* d'analyse lexicale
r алгоритм *m* синтаксического анализа

6859 parsing of random graph
(for scene analysis)
d syntaktische Analyse *f* des zufälligen Graphs
f analyse *f* de graphe aléatoire
r синтаксический разбор *m* стохастического
графа

* **part** → 6861

6860 part
d Teil *m*; Bauteil *m*
f partie *f*
r часть *f*

6861 part[ial]
d partiell; teilweise
f partiel; en partie
r частичный; парциальный

6862 partial coherence
d partielle Kohärenz *f*
f cohérence *f* partielle
r частичная когерентность *f*

6863 partially oriented surface
d teilweise orientierte Fläche *f*
f surface *f* localement orientée
r частично ориентированная поверхность *f*

6864 partially rounded ends
d teilweise abgerundete Enden *npl*
f fins *mpl* arrondis partiellement
r частично округленные края *mpl*

* **partial map** → 6865

6865 partial map[ping]
d partielle Abbildung *f*
f application *f* partielle
r частичное отображение *n*

6866 partial open
(of a drawing)
d partielle Öffnung *f*; partieller Schnitt *m*
f ouverture *f* partielle
r частичное открытие *n*

6867 partial plot preview
d partielle vorherige Vorschau *f* des Plottens
f prévisualisation *f* de tracement partielle
r частичный предварительный просмотр *m*
черчения

6868 partial tone reversal
d teilweise Tonumkehrung *f*
f inversion *f* de nuances partielle
r частичное инвертирование *n* оттенков

6869 partial views
d partielle Ansichten *fpl*; Teilansichten *fpl*
f vues *fpl* partielles
r частичные виды *mpl*

6870 particle
d Bruchteil *m*
f particule *f*; grain *m*
r частица *f*

6871 particular; special
d partikulär; speziell
f particulier
r частный; отдельный; конкретный

* **partition** → 6874

6872 partition *v*
d aufteilen; unterteilen; untergliedern
f partager; segmenter
r разделять; расчленять; разбивать

6873 partitioned
d aufgeteilt; untergliedert
f partagé; divisé
r разделенный; расчлененный

6874 partition[ing]
d Partition *f*; Zerlegung *f*
f partition *f*; partage *m*
r разбиение *n*; расчленение *n*

* **part list** → 6876

6875 part number
d Teilnummer *f*
f numéro *m* de pièce; numéro d'identification
r номер *m* части; номер детали

6876 part[s] list
d Stückliste *f*; Teilliste *f*
f liste *f* des pièces détachées
r спецификация *f*; список *m* деталей

6877 pass; passage
d Durchgang *m*; Übergang *m*
f passage *m*; pas *m*; trajet *m*
r проход *m*; переход *m*; прогон *m*

* **passage** → 6877

6878 passive [computer] graphics
d passive Rechnergrafik *f*
f infographie *f* passive
r пассивная компьютерная графика *f*

* **passive graphics** → 6878

6879 passive matrix
d Passivmatrix *f*
f matrice *f* passive
r пассивная матрица *f*

6880 passive-matrix color display
d Passivmatrix-Farbdisplay *n*
f écran *m* couleur à matrice passive
r [жидкокристаллический] цветной
дисплей *m* с пассивной матрицей

6881 pass *v* **through a point**
d durch einen Punkt gehen
f passer par un point
r проходить через точку

* **paste** *v* → 5116

6882 paste *v* **special**
d speziell einfügen
f insérer spécialement
r вкладывать специально

6883 paste *v* **together; patch** *v* **together; piece** *v*
together; glue *v* **together; sew** *v*
d zusammenkleben
f coller
r склеи[ва]ть; приклеивать; клеить

6884 pasting together; gluing
d Zusammenkleben *n*; Kleben *n*
f collage *m*; recollement *m*
r склеивание *n*

6885 patch *v*
d flicken; ausflicken; einsetzen
f corriger; compléter; rapiécer
r ставить заплаты (в программе)

* **patch** → 1178, 9374

6886 patch-based modeling
d Stück-basierte Modellierung *f*
f modélisation *f* orientée aux surfaces
paramétriques
r фрагментное моделирование *n*

6887 patch fitting
   d Oberflächenstück-Anpassung *f*
   f déformation *f* sur une surface paramétrique
   r налаживание *n* фрагментов; налаживание
      кусков

   * **patch** *v* **together** → **6883**

6888 patch visibility
   d Sichtbarkeit *f* der Oberflächenstücke
   f visibilité *f* de surfaces paramétriques
   r видимость *f* фрагментов; видимость
      кусков

6889 path adjustment
   d Wegeinstellung *f*
   f ajustement *m* de tracé
   r настройка f дорожки

   * **path** → **8228**

6890 path button
   d Schaltfläche *f* der Strecke
   f bouton *m* [de] tracé
   r кнопка *f* дорожки

6891 path curve
   d Bahnkurve *f*
   f courbe *f* de tracé
   r кривая *f* трассы

6892 path data; path information
   d Weginformation *f*
   f information *f* de chemin
   r маршрутные данные *npl*; информация *f* о
      маршруте

6893 path image
   d Weg[ab]bild *n*
   f image *f* de chemin
   r изображение *n* дорожки

6894 path in a graph; graph path
   d Graphenweg *m*
   f chemin *m* dans un graphe
   r путь *m* в графе

   * **path information** → **6892**

6895 path segment
   d Wegsegment *n*
   f segment *m* de chemin
   r сегмент *m* дорожки

6896 path tracing
   d Weg-Trassieren *n*
   f traçage *m* de chemin
   r трассировка *f* дорожки

6897 path transformations
   d Wegtransformationen *fpl*
   f transformations *fpl* de chemin
   r трансформации *fpl* дорожки

6898 pattern
   d Motiv *n*
   f motif *m*; forme *f* [géométrique régulière]
   r мотив *m*; узор *m*; рисунок *m*

   * **pattern** → **4812, 9512**

6899 pattern block
   d Motivblock *m*
   f bloc *m* mosaïque; bloc de formes
   r блок *m* рисунок

6900 pattern density
   d Motivdichte *f*
   f densité *f* de motif
   r плотность *f* рисунка

6901 pattern[ed] fill[ing]
   d Musterfüllung *f*
   f remplissage *m* par motif
   r заполнение *n* шаблона; закрашивание *n*
      шаблона

6902 pattern feature
   d Schablonengestaltung *f*; Schablonenraster *m*
   f aspect *m* de modèle; rastre *m* de modèle
   r вид *m* шаблона; растр *m* шаблона

6903 pattern file
     (.pat)
   d Musterdatei *n*
   f fichier *m* de modèles
   r файл *m* шаблонов

   * **pattern fill** → **6901**

6904 pattern generator
   d Mustergenerator *m*
   f générateur *m* d'images; générateur de
      configurations
   r генератор *m* изображений; генератор
      образов

   * **pattern match** → **6905**

6905 pattern match[ing]
   d Musteranpassung *f*
   f appariement *m* de formes
   r соответствие *n* изображений

6906 pattern recognition; image recognition; PR
   d Bilderkennung *f*; Mustererkennung *f*;
      Gestalterkennung *f*
   f reconnaissance *f* d'images; reconnaissance de
      modèles; reconnaissance de formes
   r распознавание *n* образов; распознавание
      изображений; распознавание формы

6907 pattern regularity
(of a texture)
  d Motivregelmäßigkeit *f*
  f régularité *f* de motif
  r регулярность *f* мотива

6908 pattern selection
  d Musterauswahl *f*
  f sélection *f* de modèle
  r выбор *m* шаблона; выбор модели

6909 pattern surface
  d Musterfläche *f*
  f surface *f* de modèle
  r поверхность *f* модели

6910 pattern table
  d Motivtabelle *f*
  f table *f* des motifs
  r таблица *f* узоров

  *   **pattern transparency → 4931**

6911 pattern type
  d Mustertyp *m*; Schablonentyp *m*
  f type *m* de motif; type de modèle
  r тип *m* рисунка; тип модели

6912 pause
  d Pause *f*
  f pause *f*
  r пауза *f*

6913 pausing
  d Pausieren *n*
  f mise *f* en pause
  r установление *n* паузы

  *   **paving → 9681**

  *   **PCD → 7010**

6914 PCD file
  d PCD-Datei *f*
  f fichier *m* PCD
  r файл *m* PCD

6915 PCD image
  d PCD-Bild *n*
  f image *f* PCD
  r изображение *n* PCD

6916 peak; spike
  d Spitze *f*; Scheitel *m*
  f crête *f*; pic *m*; top *m*; aiguille *f*; pointe *f*
  r пик *m*; верх *m*; выброс *m*; острие *n*

6917 peak intensity
  d höchste Intensität *f*
  f intensité *f* de crête

  r максимальная интенсивность *f*

  *   **peak point → 2388**

6918 Peano's curve
  d Peanosche Kurve *f*
  f courbe *f* de Peano
  r кривая *f* Пеано

6919 pedal
  d Fußpunkt-
  f podaire; pédal
  r подерный; подэрный

6920 pedal curve
  d Fußpunktkurve *f*
  f courbe *f* podaire; podaire *f*
  r подерная кривая *f*; подэра; подера *f*;
     подошвенная кривая

  *   **pel → 7088**

6921 pen; stylus
  d Schreibfeder *f*; Griffel *m*
  f stylo *m*; plume *f*
  r перо *n*

6922 pen-based data entry
  d Stift-basierte Dateneingabe *f*
  f entrée *f* de données par plume
  r ввод *m* данных световым пером

6923 pen capping
  d Stiftdeckung *f*
  f rebouchage *m* de plume
  r перекрытие *n* пера

6924 pen carriage; pen holder
  d Stiftträger *m*
  f porte-plume *f*, support *m* de plume
  r перьевой держатель *m*; перьевая каретка *f*

6925 pencil
  d Stift *m*
  f crayon *m*
  r карандаш *m*

6926 pencil; sheaf; bundle; bunch
  d Büschel *n*; Bündel *n*; Garbe *f*
  f faisceau *m*; pinceau *m*; gerbe *f*
  r пучок *m*; связка *f*

**6927 pencil of circles; bundle of circles; sheaf of
     circles; star of circles**
  d Kreisbüschel *n*; Kreisbündel *n*
  f faisceau *m* de cercles; gerbe *f* de cercles;
     réseau *m* de cercles
  r пучок *m* окружностей; связка *f*
     окружностей

6928 pencil of complexes
  d Komplexbüschel *n*
  f faisceau *m* de complexes
  r пучок *m* комплексов

6929 pencil of conics
  d Kegelschnittbüschel *n*
  f faisceau *m* de coniques
  r пучок *m* конических сечений; связка *f* коник

6930 pencil of light; cone of light
  d Lichtbüschel *n*; Lichtbündel *n*; Lichtkegel *m*
  f cône *m* lumineux; cône de lumière; faisceau *m* de rayons
  r пучок *m* лучей; конус *m* лучей

  * **pencil of lines** → 1196

6931 pencil of parallel lines
  d Parallelstrahlenbüschel *n*
  f faisceau *m* de droites parallèles
  r пучок *m* параллельных прямых

6932 pencil of planes; bundle of planes; sheaf of planes; star of planes
  d Ebenenbüschel *n*; Ebenenbündel *n*
  f faisceau *m* de plans; gerbe *f* de plans; étoile *f* de plans
  r пучок *m* плоскостей; связка *f* плоскостей

  * **pencil of points** → 7742

  * **pencil of rays** → 1196

  * **pencil of spheres** → 1197

6933 pencils of conjugate circles
  d Bündel *npl* der konjugierten Kreise
  f faisceaux *mpl* de cercles conjugués
  r связки *fpl* сопряженных окружностей

6934 pencil tool
  d Hilfsmittel *n* "Stift "
  f outil *m* "crayon"
  r инструмент *m* "карандаш"

6935 pen configuration
  d Stiftkonfiguration *f*
  f configuration *f* de plume
  r конфигурация *f* пера

  * **pen detection** → 5555

6936 pen down *v*
  d Stift absetzen
  f baisser de plume
  r снимать перо

6937 penetration

  d Eindringen *n*; Eindringtiefe *f*; Durchdringung *f*
  f pénétration *f*
  r проникновение *n*; проницаемость *f*

  * **pen holder** → 6924

6938 pen icon
  d Stiftikone *f*
  f icône *f* de stylo
  r икона *f* пера

6939 penless plotter
  d Plotter *m* ohne Stifte; stiftfreier Plotter
  f traceur *m* sans plumes
  r безперьевой графопостроитель *m*

6940 pen motion; pen movement
  d Stiftbewegung *f*
  f déplacement *m* de plume; mouvement *m* de plume
  r движение *n* пера; перемещение *n* пера

  * **pen movement** → 6940

6941 pen number
  d Stiftnummer *f*
  f numéro *m* de style
  r номер *m* пера

6942 pen parameter
  d Stiftparameter *m*
  f paramètre *m* de plume
  r параметр *m* пера

6943 pen plotter
  d Zeichenstift-Plotter *m*; Stiftplotter *m*
  f traceur *m* à plumes
  r перьевой графопостроитель *m*

  * **pen rate** → 6946

6944 pen settings
  d Stifteinrichtungen *fpl*
  f paramètres *mpl* de plume
  r перьевые назначения *npl*

6945 pen size
  d Stiftgröße *f*
  f taille *f* de plume
  r размер *m* пера

6946 pen speed; pen rate
  d Stiftgeschwindigkeit *f*
  f vitesse *f* de plume
  r скорость *f* [движения] пера

6947 pentagon
  d Fünfeck *n*; Pentagon *n*

f pentagone *m*
r пятиугольник *m*; пентагон *m*

6948 pentagonal
d fünfeckig; pentagonal
f pentagonal
r пятиугольный; пентагональный

6949 pentagonal prism
d pentagonales Prisma *n*
f prisme *m* pentagonale
r пятиугольная призма *f*

6950 pen up *v*
d Stift [an]heben
f lever de plume
r поднимать перо

6951 pen width
d Stiftbreite *f*
f largeur *f* de plume
r толщина *f* пера

* **per cent** → 6952

* **percent** → 6955

6952 percent; per cent
d Prozent *n*
f pourcentage *m*; pour-cent *m*
r процент *m*

6953 percentage bar chart
d prozentuales Streifendiagramm *n*
f diagramme *m* de pourcentage à barres
r процентная столбиковая диаграмма *f*

6954 percentage slider
d prozentualer Schieber *m*
f glisseur *m* de pourcentage
r ползунок *m* процентов

6955 percent [sign]; percent symbol
(%)
d Prozentzeichen *n*
f signe *m* de pourcentage; symbole *m* de pourcentage
r знак *m* процента

* **percent symbol** → 6955

6956 percept
d Wahrnehmungsobjekt *n*
f objet *m* de perception
r объект *m* восприятия

6957 perception
d Perzeption *f*; Wahrnehmung *f*
f perception *f*
r перцепция *f*; восприятие *n*; ощущение *n*

6958 perfect
d perfekt; vollkommen
f parfait; idéal
r совершенный; точный

* **perfect match** → 6959

6959 perfect match[ing]
d vollkommene Übereinstimmung *f*
f coïncidence *f* parfaite
r точное совпадение *n*

6960 perfect restitution
d vollkommene Wiedergabe *f*
f reproduction *f* parfaite
r точное воспроизведение *n*

6961 performance
d Leistung *f*; Leistungsvermögen *n*
f performance *f*; productivité *f*
r производительность *f*

6962 performance chart; performance curve
d Arbeitsdiagramm *n*
f diagramme *m* de marche; courbe *f* de réponse
r рабочая диаграмма *f*

* **performance curve** → 6962

6963 perimeter
d Umfang *f*; Perimeter *m*
f périmètre *m*
r периметр *m*

6964 period
d Periode *f*; Zeitraum *m*
f période *f*
r период *m*

6965 periodic
d periodisch
f périodique
r периодический

6966 periodic prolongation
d periodische Fortsetzung *f*
f prolongation *f* périodique
r периодическое продолжение *n*

6967 periodic spectral filter
d periodischer Spektralfilter *m*
f filtre *m* spectral périodique
r периодический спектральный фильтр *m*

* **peripheral** → 6969

6968 peripheral
d peripher
f périphérique
r периферийный; внешний

6969 peripheral device; peripheral [unit]
 d periphere Einheit *f*; Peripheriegerät *n*;
 Anschlussgerät *n*
 f dispositif *m* périphérique; unité *f*
 périphérique; périphérique *m*
 r периферийное устройство *n*; внешнее
 устройство

* **peripheral unit** → 6969

6970 periphery
 d Peripherie *f*
 f périphérie *f*
 r периферия *f*

6971 Perlin noise function
 d Perlin-Rauschfunktion *f*
 f fonction *f* de bruit de Perlin
 r функция *f* искажения Перлина

6972 permanent topology
 d permanente Topologie *f*
 f topologie *f* permanente
 r устойчивая топология *f*

* **permissibility** → 200

* **permissible** → 201

* **permissible value** → 205

6973 permission; allowance
 d Erlaubnis *n*
 f permission *f*
 r разрешение *n*; позволение *n*

6974 permutation
 d Permutation *f*; Vertauschung *f*
 f permutation *f*
 r перестановка *f*; размен *m*

6975 permute *v*
 d permutieren; vertauschen; versetzen
 f permuter
 r переставлять; менять местами

* **perpendicular** → 6979

* **perpendicular** *adj* → 6640

* **perpendicular bisector** → 5889

* **perpendicularity** → 6649

6976 perpendicular lines; orthogonal lines
 d perpendikuläre Geraden *fpl*
 f droites *fpl* perpendiculaires; droites
 orthogonaux
 r перпендикулярные прямые *fpl*

6977 perpendicular planes; orthogonal planes
 d perpendikuläre Ebenen *fpl*; orthogonale
 Ebenen
 f plans *mpl* perpendiculaires; plans
 orthogonaux
 r перпендикулярные плоскости *fpl*;
 ортогональные плоскости

* **perpendicular projection** → 6653

6978 perpendicular snap
 d perpendikulärer Fang *m*
 f accrochage *m* au perpendiculaire
 r привязывание *n* к перпендикуляру

6979 perpendicular [straight line]
 d perpendikuläre Linie *f*
 f perpendiculaire *f*; droite *f* perpendiculaire
 r перпендикуляр *m*; перпендикулярная
 прямая *f*

6981 persistence; retention
 (of a screen)
 d Nachleuchtdauer *f*
 f persistance *f*; traînage *m*; rémanence *f*
 r послесвечение *n*

6980 persistence; persistency
 d Stetigkeit *f*
 f persistance *f*
 r устойчивость *f*

* **persistency** → 6980

6982 personalizing
 d Personifizierung *f*
 f personnification *f*
 r олицетворение *n*

* **perspective** → 1383

6983 perspective adjustment
 d Anpassung *f* der Perspektive
 f ajustage *m* de perspective
 r настраивание *n* перспективы

* **perspective affine correspondence** → 6984

**6984 perspective affine relation; perspective
 affine correspondence; affine relation**
 d [perspektiv-]affine Beziehung *f*;
 [perspektiv-]affine Relation *f*
 f relation *f* [perspective] affine;
 correspondance *f* [perspective] affine
 r [перспективно-]аффинное соотношение *n*;
 [перспективно-]аффинное соответствие *n*;
 родственное соотношение

6985 perspective affinity
 d perspektive Affinität *f*; Affinität bei
 perspektiver Lage

f affinité *f* perspective
r аффинно-перспективное преобразование *n*

6986 perspective collineation
d perspektive Kollineation *f*
f collinéation *f* perspective
r перспективная коллинеация *f*

6987 perspective cone of rays
d perspektives Strahlenbündel *n*
f faisceau *m* lumineux perspectif
r перспективный световой пучок *m*

6988 perspective correction
d Perspektivkorrektur *f*
f correction *f* de perspective
r коррекция *f* перспективы

6989 perspective effect
d Perspektiveffekt *m*
f effet *m* de perspective
r эффект *m* перспективы

**6990 perspective figures; figures in central
projection; figures in central perspective**
d perspektive Figuren *fpl*;
zentral-perspektivische Figuren;
zentral-kollineare Figuren
f figures *fpl* perspectives; figures en projection
centrale; figures dans la perspective centrale;
figures homologues
r перспективные фигуры *fpl*; фигуры в
центральной проекции; фигуры в
центральной перспективе

6991 perspective filter
d Perspektive-Filter *m*
f filtre *m* de perspective
r фильтр *m* перспективы

6992 perspective having no vanishing point
d Perspektive *f* ohne Fluchtpunkte
f perspective *f* sans point de fuite
r перспектива *f*, не имеющая точки схода

* **perspective image** → 6994

6993 perspective involution
d perspektive Involution *f*
f involution *f* perspective
r перспективная инволюция *f*;
перспективное инволюционное
преобразование *n*

* **perspective mapping** → 1383

6994 perspective picture; perspective image
d perspektiv[isch]es Bild *n*
f image *f* perspective

r перспективный образ *m*; перспективное
изображение *n*

* **perspective plane** → 7143

* **perspective point** → 7225

* **perspective projection** → 1383

6995 perspective tetrahedra
d perspektive Tetraeder *npl*
f tétraèdres *mpl* perspectifs
r перспективные тетраэдры *mpl*;
перспективные четырехгранники *mpl*

6996 perspective triangles
d perspektive Dreiecke *npl*
f triangles *mpl* perspectifs; triangles
homologiques réciproques
r перспективные треугольники *mpl*

6997 perspective window
d Perspektive-Fenster *n*
f fenêtre *f* de vue en perspective
r окно *n* перспективы

**6998 perspectivity; central collineation;
homology**
d Perspektivität *f*; zentrale Kollineation *f*;
Zentralkollineation *f*; perspektive
Abbildung *f*; Homologie *f*
f perspectivité *f*; collinéation *f* centrale;
homologie *f*
r перспективное соответствие *n*;
центральная коллинеация *f*; гомология *f*

* **perturbation** → 6231

6999 perturbation coefficient
d Störungskoeffizient *m*
f coefficient *m* de perturbation
r коэффициент *m* возмущений

* **PgDn key** → 6727

* **p-graph** → 7608

* **PgUp key** → 6740

7000 phantom
d Phantom *n*
f fantôme *m*
r фантом *m*

7001 phantom image; ghost [image]
d Phantombild *n*; Geisterbild *n*; Nebenbild *n*
f image *f* fantôme
r фантомное изображение *n*

7002 phantom line
d Phantomlinie *f*

f ligne *f* fantôme
r фантомная линия *f*

7003 phantom view
d Phantomdarstellung *f*
f vue *f* fantôme
r фантомный вид *m*

7004 phase
d Phase *f*
f phase *f*
r фаза *f*

7005 phenomenon
d Erscheinung *f*
f phénomène *m*
r явление *n*; феномен *m*

7006 Phong light model equation
d Phongsche Lichtmodellgleichung *f*
f équation *f* de modèle d'éclairage de Phong
r уравнение *n* модели освещения Фонга

7007 Phong method
d Verfahren *n* von Phong; Phongsche
   Methode *f*
f méthode *f* de Phong
r метод *m* Фонга

* **Phong rendering** → 7008

**7008 Phong shading; Phong rendering; normal-
   vector interpolation shading**
   (Lambert or cosine shading plus smoothing
   and specularity of faceted surfaces)
d Phong-Schattierung *f*; Phong-Rendering *n*
f ombrage *m* de Phong; ombrage par
   interpolation de vecteurs de la normale
r затенение *n* методом Фонга; рендеринг *m*
   Фонга

7009 Phong-shading processor
d Phong-Schading-Prozessor *m*
f processeur *m* d'ombrage de Phong
r процессор *m* затенения методом Фонга

* **phonic** → 90

* **photo** → 7018

* **photoacoustic** → 6594

7010 photo-CD; PCD
d Foto-Kompaktdisk *m*
f disque *m* optique photo
r фото-компактдиск *m*

7011 photocomposition; phototypesetting
d Fotosatz *m*
f photocomposition *f*

r фотонабор *m*

7012 photocomposition system
d Fotosatzsystem *n*
f système *m* de photocomposition
r фотонаборная система *f*

7013 photocopier
d Fotokopierer *m*
f photocopieur *m*; photocopieuse *f*
r фотокопирующее устройство *n*

* **photoelectrical reader** → 6570

* **photoelectric reader** → 6570

7014 photographic
d fotografisch
f photographique
r фотографический

* **photographic chroma mapping** → 7015

**7015 photographic color mapping;
   photographic chroma mapping**
d fotografische Farbabbildung *f*
f chroma-mappage *m* photographique;
   mappage *m* photographique en couleurs
r фотографическое цветное отображение *n*

7016 photographic realism; photorealism
d fotografischer Realismus *m*; Fotorealismus *m*
f réalisme *m* photographique; photoréalisme *m*
r фотографический реализм *m*;
   фотореализм *m*; фотореалистичность *f*

7017 photographic source page
d fotografisches Quellblatt *n*
f page *f* de source photographique
r фотографическая исходная страница *f*

7018 photo[graphy]
d Fotografie *f*; Foto *n*; Aufnahme *f*
f photo[graphie] *f*
r фотография *f*; фотосъемка *f*; снимок *m*

7019 photography importing
d Foto-Importieren *n*
f importation *f* de photo[graphie]
r импортирование *n* фотографии

* **photolithographic mask** → 7026

* **photomask** → 7026

7020 photo-mechanical transfer; PMT
d fotomechanische Übertragung *f*
f transfert *m* photo-mécanique
r фото-механический перенос *m*

7021 photometric
d fotometrisch
f photométrique
r фотометрический

7022 photometric texture data
d fotometrische Texturdaten *npl*
f données *fpl* de texture photométriques
r фотометрические данные *npl* текстуры

7023 photometry
d Fotometrie *f*
f photométrie *f*
r фотометрия *f*

7024 photon tracing
d Foton-Tracing *n*
f tracement *m* de photon
r фотонная трассировка *f*

7025 photonumeric
d fotonumerisch
f photonumérique
r фотоцифровой

7026 photo pattern; photolithographic mask; photomask
d Fotoschablone *f*; fotolithografische Maske *f*
f modèle *m* photographique; masque *f* photolithographique; photomasque *f*
r фотошаблон *m*; фотолитографическая маска *f*; фотомаска *f*

7027 photoplotter; graphics film recorder; film recorder; video hard copy unit
d Fotoplotter *m*
f phototraceur *m*; système *m* de phototraçage
r фотоплоттер *m*; фотопостроитель *m*

* **photorealism** → 7016

7028 photorealistic
d fotorealistisch
f photoréaliste
r фотореалистический

7029 photorealistic image
d fotorealistisches Bild *n*
f image *f* photoréaliste
r фотореалистическое изображение *n*

7030 photorealistic model
d fotorealistisches Modell *n*
f modèle *m* photoréaliste
r фотореалистическая модель *f*

* **photorealistic render** → 7031

7031 photorealistic render[ing]
d fotorealistisches Rendering *n*

f rendu *m* photoréaliste
r фотореалистическое тонирование *n*; фотореалистический рендеринг *m*

7032 photorealistic representation
d fotorealistische Darstellung *f*
f représentation *f* photoréaliste
r фотореалистическое представление *n*

7033 photorealistic texture
d fotorealistische Textur *f*
f texture *f* photoréaliste
r фотореалистическая текстура *f*

7034 photo reproduction
d Fotoreproduktion *f*
f photoreproduction *f*
r фоторепродукция *f*

7035 photoscanner
d Fotoscanner *m*
f scanner *m* d'images photo; photoscanner *m*
r фото-сканер *m*

7036 photos scrapbook
d Fotoskizzenbuch *n*
f classeur *m* de photos
r буферный файл *m* фотографий

* **phototypesetting** → 7011

7037 physical optics
d physische Optik *f*
f optique *f* physique
r физическая оптика *f*

7038 pica
(1/6 inch or 1/72 foot)
d Pica
f pica
r пика

7039 pick *v*
d auswählen
f désigner
r отбирать; выбирать

7040 pickbox; selection box
d Auswahlkasten *m*; Auswahlfeld *n*
f boîte *f* de sélection; boîte de désignation
r ящик *m* отбора

7041 pick button
d Auswahl-Schaltfläche *f*
f bouton *m* de désignation; bouton sélecteur
r кнопка *f* выбора; бутон *m* выбора

7042 pick device; picker
d Picker *m*

f dispositif *m* de désignation
r устройство *n* указания; подборщик *m*

* **picker** → 7042

7043 **picking**
(the elements on the screen)
d Identifizierung *f*
f désignation *f*
r указание *n*; отбор *m*; подбор *m*

7044 **pick point**
d Auswahlpunkt *m*
f point *m* de sélection
r точка *f* отбора; точка выбора

7045 **pick set; selection set**
d Auswahlsatz *m*
f ensemble *m* sélectionné; ensemble de
sélection
r совокупность *f* отбора

7046 **pick tool; selection tool**
d Auswahl-Hilfsmittel *n*; Auswahlwerkzeug *n*
f outil *m* sélecteur
r инструмент *m* отбора; инструмент выбора

* **pickup** → 8528

7047 **pictogram**
d Piktogramm *n*
f pictogramme *m*
r пиктограмма *f*

* **pictogram representation** → 4782

7048 **pictography**
d Piktografie *f*; Bilderschrift *f*
f pictographie *f*
r пиктография *f*

7049 **pictorial; pictoric; iconographic;**
illustrational; illustrative; illustratory
d piktografisch; bildlich; bildhaft; malerisch
f pictural
r наглядный; изобразительный;
иллюстрированный; графический

7050 **pictorial diagram**
d bildliches Diagramm *n*
f schéma *m* synoptique
r иллюстрированная диаграмма *f*

7051 **pictorial representation**
d bildliche Darstellung *f*
f représentation *f* picturale
r картинное представление *n*

* **pictoric** → 7049

* **picture** → 4812

7052 **picture black**
(in a fax)
d Bildschwarz *n*; Schwarzpegel *m*
f niveau *m* de noir le plus profond
r уровень *m* черного изображения

7053 **picture block**
d Bildblock *m*
f bloc *m* d'images
r блок *m* изображений

7054 **picture box**
d Bildkasten *m*
f zone *f* d'image
r ящик *m* изображения

* **picture catalog** → 1310

* **picture cell** → 7088

* **picture coding** → 4825

* **picture dot** → 7088

* **picture editor** → 4851

* **picture element** → 7088

* **picture flipping** → 4858

* **picture format** → 4861

7055 **picture frequency**
d Bildfrequenz *f*
f fréquence *f* d'image
r частота *f* смены изображения

* **picture generation** → 4864

7056 **picture lock**
d Bildsperre *f*
f calage *m* de l'image
r блокирование *n* изображения; замок *m*
изображения

7057 **picture number**
d Bildzahl *f*
f numéro *m* de trame
r номер *m* кадра

* **picture plane** → 4887

* **picture processing** → 4891

* **picture quality** → 4895

7058 **picture quality scale**
d Bildqualität-Skala *f*

f échelle *f* de qualité d'image
r шкала *f* качества изображения

* **picture remote transfer** → 4929

7059 picture scanning; image scanning
d Bildabtastung *f*; Bildscannen *n*
f exploration *f* d'image; balayage *m* d'image;
échantillonnage *m* d'image
r сканирование *n* изображения

7060 picture scanning method; image scanning
method
d Bildabtastungsmethode *f*
f méthode *f* d'exploration d'images
r метод *m* сканирования изображений

* **picture setting** → 7061

7061 picture setup; picture setting
d Bildaufbau *m*
f établissement *m* d'image
r установка *f* изображения

* **picture shrinkage** → 4917

7062 picture symbol
d Abbildungssymbol *n*
f symbole *m* d'image
r символ *m* изображения

* **picture transfer** → 4929

7063 picture white
(in a fax)
d Bildweiß *n*; Weißpegel *m*
f niveau *m* du blanc le plus clair
r уровень *m* белого изображения

7064 piece
d Stück *n*; Glied *n*
f pièce *f*; morceau *m*
r кусок *m*

* **piece** *v* **together** → 6883

7065 piecewise
d stückweise; abteilungsweise; abschnittsweise
f en morceaux; par morceaux; par tranches
r кусочно

7066 piecewise Bézier polygon
d stückweise zusammengestelltes
Bézier-Polygon *n*
f polygone *m* de Bézier en morceaux; polygone
de Bézier par tranches
r кусочный многоугольник *m* Безье

7067 piecewise linear interpolation
d stückweise basierte lineare Interpolation *f*

f interpolation *f* linéaire par tranches
r кусочно-линейная интерполяция *f*

7068 piecewise linear object
d stückweise zusammengestelltes lineares
Objekt *n*
f objet *m* linéaire par tranches
r кусочно-линейный объект *m*

7069 piecewise polynomial model
d stückweise zusammengestelltes
polynomisches Modell *n*
f modèle *m* polynomial en morceaux
r кусочно-полиномная модель *f*

7070 piecewise polynomials
d stückweise zusammengestellte Polynome *npl*
f polynômes *mpl* par tranches
r кусочные полиномы *mpl*

7071 pie chart; pie graph; circular chart; circle
graph; sector diagram
d Kreisdiagramm *n*; Sektordiagramm *n*;
Tortengrafik *f*
f diagramme *m* circulaire; diagramme à
secteurs; graphique *m* circulaire; graphique
sectoriel; camembert *m*
r круговая диаграмма *f*; секторная
диаграмма

* **pie graph** → 7071

7072 piercing point; trace [point]
(a point at which a line intersects one of the
coordinate planes)
d Spurpunkt *m*; Durchstoßpunkt *m*
f point *m* [de] trace
r точечный след *m*; след точки; точка-след *f*
(в картинной плоскости)

7073 pie slice; pie wedge
d Tortengrafik-Sektor *m*
f secteur *m* de camembert; secteur de
graphique circulaire
r сектор *m* круговой диаграммы

* **pie wedge** → 7073

* **PIF** → 6732

7074 pigment color
d Pigmentfarbe *f*
f couleur *m* de pigment
r цвет *m* пигментирования

7075 pillow distortion; in-cushion distortion
d Kissenverzerrung *f*; kissenförmige
Verzerrung *f*
f distorsion *f* en coussinet
r подушкообразная дисторсия *f*

7076 **pilot** *v*
  d vorsteuern
  f piloter
  r управлять

7077 **pinch effect**
  d Klemmeffekt *m*; Pinch-Effekt *m*
  f effet *m* de pince[ment]; effet de striction
  r эффект *m* пинцирования; эффект чеканки

7078 **pinhole**
  d Pinloch *n*
  f trou *m* de pointe
  r точечное отверстие *n*

7079 **pipe**
  (of tore)
  d Rohr *n*
  f tuyau *m*
  r труба *f*

7080 **pipeline**
  d Pipeline *f*; Fließband *n*
  f pipeline *m*; chaîne *f*; conveyor *m*
  r конвейер *m*

7081 **pipeline processing; pipelining**
  d Pipelineverarbeitung *f*;
    Fließbandarbeitsweise *f*
  f traitement *m* pipeline; pipelinage *m*
  r конвейерная обработка *f*; конвейеризация *f*

  * **pipelining** → 7081

  * **pipe-shaped** → 8872

7082 **pitch**
  d Ganghöhe *f*; Gang *m*; Stufe *f*
  f pas *m*; entraxe *m*
  r шаг *m*; ход *m*

  * **pitch** → 8376, 8795

7083 **pitch of the helix; screw pitch; lead of the helix**
  d Schraubengang *m*; Schraubensteigung *f*;
    Gang *m* der Schraube
  f pas *m* d'hélice; pas de la vis; hauteur *f* de pas
    de la vis
  r шаг *m* винтовой линии; ход *m* винта;
    оборот *m* винта; поступь *m* винта

  * **pivot** → 7085

7084 **pivot**
  d Pivot *m/n*
  f pivot *m*
  r поворот *m*

7085 **pivot[al]**

  d Pivot-
  f pivotant
  r ведущий; направляющий

  * **pivot axis** → 769

  * **pivot center** → 1367

7086 **pivoting; tourning; swivelling**
  d Pivotisierung *f*; Schwenkung *f*
  f pivotement *m*
  r вращение *n* вокруг оси; крепление *n* на оси

7087 **pivoting window; single-action window**
  d Pivotfenster *n*; Fenster *n* mit einfacher
    Bewegung
  f fenêtre *f* pivotante
  r направляющее окно *n*

7088 **pixel; picture element; pel; picture cell; image dot; picture dot**
  d Pixel *n*; Bildpunkt *m*; Bildelement *n*
  f pixel *m*; élément *m* pictural; élément d'image
  r пиксел *m*; элемент *m* растра; точка *f*
    изображения

7089 **pixel address; pixel position**
  d Pixel-Adresse *f*; Pixelposition *f*
  f adresse *f* de pixel; position *f* de pixel
  r адрес *m* пиксела

  * **pixel arithmetic** → 7090

7090 **pixel arithmetic[s]**
  d Pixel-Arithmetik *f*
  f arithmétique *f* de pixel
  r пиксельная арифметика *f*

7091 **pixelate effect**
  d Mosaikeffekt *m*
  f effet *m* pixélisé
  r мозаичный эффект *m*

7092 **pixelate filter**
  d Mosaikfilter *m*
  f filtre *m* pixélisé
  r фильтр *m* мозаики

7093 **pixel block**
  d Pixel-Block *m*
  f trame *f* de pixels
  r блок *m* пикселов

7094 **pixel-by-pixel panning**
  d bildpunktweises Schwenken *n*
  f panoramique *m* par pixels
  r поэлементная прокрутка *f*; прокрутка
    пиксел за пикселом

7095 **pixel cache**
  d Pixel-Cache *m*

f cache *f* de pixels
r кэш-память *f* пикселов

7096 pixel caching
d Pixel-Schreiben *n* im Cache
f mise *f* en cache de pixels
r кэширование *n* пикселов

* **pixel clock** → 7100

7097 pixel color
d Pixel-Farbe *f*
f couleur *f* de pixel
r цвет *m* пиксела

7098 pixel color values
d Farbwerte *mpl* eines Pixels
f valeurs *fpl* des couleurs d'un pixel
r коды *mpl* цветов пиксела

* **pixel depth** → 1734

7099 pixel engine
d Pixel-Maschine *f*
f moteur *m* pixel
r пиксельная машина *f*

7100 pixel frequency; pixel clock
(number of pixels drawn per second in MHz)
d Pixelfrequenz *f*; Pixeluhr *f*
f fréquence *f* de pixels
r частота *f* пикселов

* **pixel graphics** → 7759

7101 pixel intensity
d Pixel-Intensität *f*
f intensité *f* de pixel
r интенситет *m* пиксела

7102 pixel interpolator
d Pixel-Interpolator *m*
f interpolateur *m* de pixels
r интерполятор *m* пикселов

7103 pixelization; space quantization
d Bildpunktverarbeitung *f*
f pixélisation *f*
r разбиение *n* на пикселы; пространственное
квантование *n* [изображения]

7104 pixel matrix
d Pixelmatrix *f*
f matrice *f* de pixels
r пиксельная матрица *f*

7105 pixel node
d Pixel-Knoten *m*
f nœud *m* de pixel
r узел *m* пиксела

7106 pixel normal
d Pixel-Normale *f*
f normale *f* au pixel
r нормаль *f* пиксела; пиксельная нормаль

7107 pixel normal interpolation
d Pixel-Normalen-Interpolation *f*
f interpolation *f* de normale au pixel
r интерполяция *f* пиксельной нормали

7108 pixel pattern
d Pixelmuster *n*
f modèle *m* de pixel
r шаблон *m* пиксела; образец *m* пиксела;
модель *f* пиксела

7109 pixel-phasing
d Pixel-Phasing *n*
f phasage *m* de pixels
r фазировка *f* пикселов; фазирование *n*
пикселов

7110 pixel plane
d Pixel-Ebene *f*
f plan *m* de pixel
r плоскость *f* пиксела

* **pixel position** → 7089

7111 pixel processor
d Pixel-Prozessor *m*
f processeur *m* de pixels
r процессор *m* элементов изображения

7112 pixel processor pipeline
d Pixel-Prozessor-Pipeline *f*
f pipeline *m* de processeur de pixels
r конвейер *m* процессора обработки
пикселов

7113 pixel rendering
d Pixel-Rendering *n*
f rendu *m* pixel
r пиксельное тонирование *n*; пиксельный
рендеринг *m*

7114 pixel resolution
d Pixel-Auflösungsvermögen *n*
f résolution *f* pixel; nombre *m* de pixels
r пиксельная разрешающая способность *f*

7115 pixel set
d Pixelmenge *f*
f ensemble *m* de pixels
r множество *n* пикселов

7116 pixel shading
d Pixel-Schattierung *f*
f ombrage *m* pixel
r пиксельное оттенение *n*

7117 pixels per inch; PPI
d Pixel *npl* pro Zoll
f pixels *mpl* par pouce
r пикселы *mpl* на дюйм

7118 pixel-to-pixel coherence
d Pixel-zu-Pixel-Kohärenz *f*
f cohérence *f* pixel à pixel
r двухпиксельная когерентность *f*

7119 pixel value
d Pixelwert *m*
f valeur *f* de pixel
r значение *n* пиксела

7120 place; position; point
d Platz *m*; Stelle *f*; Position *f*; Ort *m*
f place *f*; position *f*; endroit *m*
r пункт *m*; место *n*; позиция *f*

7121 placeholder
d Stellenhalter *m*
f zéro *m* structurel; zéro teneur de place
r структурный нуль *m*

* placement → 5679

7122 placement algorithm
d Plazierungsalgorithmus *m*
f algorithme *m* de placement
r алгоритм *m* размещения

7123 placement of views
d Ansichten-Plazierung *f*
f placement *m* de vues
r размещение *n* представлений

7124 placement speed
d Plazierungsgeschwindigkeit *f*
f vitesse *f* de placement
r скорость *f* размещения

7125 place *v* camera
d Kamera aufstellen
f placer une caméra
r размещать камеру

* plain color → 4054

7126 plain text
d Klarschrift *f*; Klartext *m*
f texte *m* clair; texte en format ASCII
r незашифрованный текст *m*

* plan → 2628

7127 planar; plane; flat
d planar; eben; flach; platt
f plat; plan; flat
r плоский; планарный; плоскостный

* planar angle → 7134

7128 planar area
d flacher Bereich *m*
f aire *f* plane
r плоская область *f*

* planar convex hull → 2505

7129 planar graph; plane graph
d Planargraph *m*
f graphe *m* plan; graphe plat
r планарный граф *m*; плоский граф

7130 planar model
d Planarmodell *n*
f modèle *m* plat
r планарная модель *f*

* planar patch → 3100

7131 planar polygon
d Planarpolygon *n*
f polygone *m* plan
r планарный многоугольник *m*; плоский
многоугольник

7132 planar projection
d Planarprojektion *f*
f projection *f* plane
r планарная проекция *f*; плоская проекция

* planar surface → 7149

7133 plane
d Ebene *f*
f plan *m*; plaine *f*
r плоскость *f*

* plane → 7127

7134 plane angle; planar angle
d ebener Winkel *m*
f angle *m* plan
r плоский угол *m*

7135 plane coordinates; coordinates in the plane
d ebene Koordinaten *fpl*;
Ebenenkoordinaten *fpl*; Koordinaten in der
Ebene
f coordonnées *fpl* planes; coordonnées dans le
plan
r координаты *fpl* на плоскости; плоскостные
координаты

7136 plane curve; flat curve
d ebene Kurve *f*; flache Kurve
f courbe *f* plane
r плоская кривая *f*

7137 plane dihedral angle
  d Schnittwinkel *m* zweiter Ebenen
  f angle *m* dièdre plan; rectiligne *m* d'un dièdre;
    angle rectiligne d'un dièdre
  r линейный угол *m* двугранного угла

7138 plane field of lines
  d ebenes Geradenfeld *n*
  f champ *m* de droites plan
  r плоское поле *n* прямых

  * **plane figure** → 2672

7139 plane geometry; planimetry
  d Planimetrie *f*
  f géométrie *f* plane; planimétrie *f*
  r планиметрия *f*

  * **plane graph** → 7129

7140 plane mirroring
  d Ebenenspiegelung *f*
  f réflexion *f* spéculaire de plan
  r зеркальное отражение *n* плоскости

  * **plane of homology** → 7143

7141 plane of incidence
  d Einfallsebene *f*
  f plan *m* d'incidence
  r плоскость *f* падения

**7142 plane of infinity; infinite plane; ideal
    plane; improper plane**
  d unendlichferne Ebene *f*; uneigentliche Ebene;
    ideale Ebene; Fernebene *f*
  f plan *m* à l'infini; plan de l'infini; plan idéal;
    plan impropre
  r бесконечно удаленная плоскость *f*;
    несобственная плоскость

**7143 plane of perspectivity; perspective plane;
    plane of homology**
  d Ebene *f* der Perspektivität; perspektivische
    Ebene; Perspektivitätsebene *f*;
    Perspektivebene *f*
  f plan *m* de perspectivité; plan perspectif; plan
    d'homologie
  r плоскость *f* перспективы; плоскость
    гомологии

**7144 plane of reference; reference plane; datum
    plane**
  d Bezugsebene *f*; Bezugsfläche *f*;
    Referenzebene *f*; Vergleichsebene *f*
  f plan *m* de référence; plan de comparaison
  r плоскость *f* относимости; начальная
    плоскость; плоскость отсчета; относимая
    плоскость

  * **plane of support** → 9343

7145 plane of symmetry
  d Symmetrieebene *f*; Spiegelebene *f*
  f plan *m* de symétrie
  r плоскость *f* симметрии

  * **plane of the cut** → 7146

**7146 plane of the section; section[al] plane;
    plane of the cut; cut plane; cutting plane;
    intersecting plane**
  d Schnittebene *f*; schneidende Ebene *f*
  f plan *m* de la section; plan de la coupe; plan
    sécant
  r плоскость *f* сечения; секущая плоскость;
    плоскость разреза

**7147 plane projective geometry; projective
    geometry in the plane; projective plane
    geometry**
  d ebene projektive Geometrie *f*; projektive
    Geometrie in der Ebene
  f géométrie *f* plane projective; géométrie
    projective dans le plan
  r проективная геометрия *f* на плоскости;
    плоская проективная геометрия

7148 plane section
  d Ebenenschnitt *m*
  f section *f* plane
  r плоское сечение *n*

7149 plane surface; planar surface
  d planare Fläche *f*
  f surface *f* plane
  r плоская поверхность *f*

  * **plane symmetry** → 9420

7150 plane trigonometry
  d ebene Trigonometrie *f*
  f trigonométrie *f* plane
  r плоская тригонометрия *f*

7151 plane view
  d ebene Ansicht *f*
  f vue *f* plane
  r плоский вид *m*; плоское представление *n*

  * **planimetric accuracy** → 76

7152 planimetric scale
  d Grundrissmaßstab *m*
  f échelle *f* planimétrique
  r плановый масштаб *m*

  * **planimetry** → 7139

7153 planisphere
  d Planisphäre *f*

f planisphère f
r планисфера m

7154 planner
d Planer m
f planificateur m
r планировщик m; чертежник m

7155 planning
d Planung f
f planage m; planification f; planning m
r планирование n; проектирование n

7156 plant design
d Pflanzendesign n
f dessin m de plantes
r проектирование n растений

7157 plant visualization
d Pflanzenvisualisierung f
f visualisation f de plantes
r визуализация f растений

7158 plasma display
d Plasmadisplay n; Plasmabildschirm m
f afficheur m à plasma; écran m à plasma
r плазменный экран m

7159 platform
d Plattform f
f plate[-]forme f
r платформа f

7160 plausible
d plausibel; glaubwürdig
f plausible
r правдоподобный

7161 plausible dimension
d plausibele Dimension f
f dimension f plausible
r правдоподобное измерение n

7162 playback
d Playback n; nochmalige Wiedergabe f
f reproduction f; play-back m
r воспроизведение n; проигрывание n

7163 playback control
d Wiedergabe-Steuerung f
f commande f de reproduction
r управление n воспроизведением

* **plot** → **1439, 7188**

7164 plot v
d plotten; grafisch darstellen; maschinell
zeichnen; mit einem Kurvenschreiber
aufzeichnen
f tracer

r представлять графически; чертить;
вычерчивать; строить

* **plot area** → **7189**

* **plot area adjusting** → **7190**

* **plot area deleting** → **7191**

7165 plot boundary polyline
d Polylinie f der Plott-Grenze
f polyligne f frontière de traçage
r полилиния f границы вычерчивания

7166 plot configuration file
d Konfigurationdatei f des Plottens
f fichier m de configuration de traçage
r конфигурационный файл m вычерчивания

7167 plot configuration parameter
d Konfigurationsparameter m des Plottens
f paramètre m de configuration de traçage
r параметр m конфигурации вычерчивания

7168 plot file; drawing file
d Zeichnungsdatei f
f fichier m de tracé; fichier de dessin
r файл m чертежа; чертежный файл

* **plot head** → **7192**

7169 plot layout
d Plott-Layout n
f maquette f de traçage
r макет m вычерчивания

7170 plot orientation
d Plott-Orientierung f
f orientation f de traçage
r ориентация f вычерчивания

7171 plot origin
d Ausgangspunkt m des Plottens
f origine f de traçage
r начало n вычерчивания

7172 plot preview
d Vorschau f des Plottens
f prévisualisation f de tracé
r предварительный просмотр m чертежа

* **plot program** → **7197**

7173 plot rotation
d Drehung f des Plottens
f rotation f de tracé
r ротация f чертежа

* **plot scale** → **7198**

7174 plot set
  d Plott-Parametersatz *m*
  f ensemble *m* des paramètres de traçage
  r установка *f* параметров вычерчивания

7175 plot set definition
  d Definition *f* der Plott-Parameter
  f définition *f* de paramètres de traçage
  r определение *n* параметров вычерчивания

7176 plot size; drawing size
  d Zeichnungsgröße *f*
  f taille *f* de dessin
  r размер *m* чертежа; размер рисунка

7177 plot spooling
  d Plott-Spulung *f*; Plott-Spulen *n*
  f spoulage *m* de traçage
  r спулинг *m* черчения; буферизированный
      выход *m* на графопостроитель

7178 plotted output; plotting output
  d Plottausgabe *f*
  f sortie *f* de traçage
  r вывод *m* на графопостроитель

7179 plotter
  d Plotter *m*; Kurvenschreiber *m*
  f traceur *m* [de courbes]; traceur graphique
  r графопостроитель *m*

7180 plotter configuration
  d Plotterkonfiguration *f*
  f configuration *f* de traceur
  r конфигурация *f* графопостроителя

7181 plotter drawing
  d Plotterzeichnung *f*
  f dessin *m* par traceur
  r черчение *n* графопостроителем

7182 plotter linetype
  d Plotterlinientyp *m*
  f type *m* de ligne de traceur
  r тип *m* линии графопостроителя

7183 plotter manager
  d Plotter-Manager *m*
  f gestionnaire *m* de traçage
  r менажер *m* графопостроителя

7184 plotter name
  d Plottername *m*
  f nom *m* de traceur
  r имя *n* графопостроителя

7185 plotter screen
  d Plotterbildschirm *m*
  f écran *m* de traceur
  r экран *m* графопостроителя

7186 plotter speed
  d Plotter-Geschwindigkeit *f*
  f vitesse *f* de traceur
  r скорость *f* графопостроителя

7187 plotter step size
  d Plotterschrittweite *f*
  f pas *m* de traceur
  r шаг *m* графопостроителя

7188 plot[ting]
  d Plotten *n*; maschinelles Zeichnen *n*;
      Ausdruck *m* des Kurvenschreibers
  f traçage *m*; tracement *m*; pointage *m*
  r машинное нанесение *n*; [машинное]
      вычерчивание *n*

7189 plot[ting] area
  d Plottbereich *m*
  f aire *f* de traçage; zone *f* de traçage
  r область *f* вычерчивания

7190 plot[ting] area adjusting
  d Einstellung *f* des Plottbereichs
  f ajustage *m* de zone de traçage
  r наладка *f* области вычерчивания

7191 plot[ting] area deleting
  d Löschung *f* des Plottbereichs
  f effaçage *m* de zone de traçage
  r стирание *n* области вычерчивания

7192 plot[ting] head
  d Schreibkopf *m*; Plotterkopf *m*
  f tête *f* traçante; tête de traçage; tête de tracé
  r пишущий узел *m* графопостроителя;
      пишущая головка *f*

7193 plotting of a curve
  d Kurvenplotten *n*
  f traçage *m* d'une courbe
  r вычерчивание *n* кривой

7194 plotting of points
  d Punktauftragung *f*
  f tracement *m* de points
  r вычерчивание *n* точек

7195 plotting order
  d Plottenfolge *f*
  f ordre *m* de traçage
  r порядок *m* вычерчивания

  * **plotting output** → 7178

7196 plotting paper; graph paper
  d Millimeterpapier *n*
  f papier *m* millimétré
  r миллиметровая бумага *f*

7197 **plot[ting] program**
 d Plottprogramm *n*
 f programme *m* de traçage; programme de tracement
 r программа *f* машинного вычерчивания

7198 **plot[ting] scale**
 d Plott-Maßstab *m*
 f échelle *f* de traçage
 r масштаб *m* вычерчивания

7199 **plotting tolerance**
 d Plotttoleranz *f*
 f tolérance *f* de traçage
 r допуск *m* вычерчивания

 * **plot units** → 3167

 * **pluggable** → 7200

7200 **plug-in; pluggable**
 d austauschbar; steckbar
 f enfichable; changeable; remplaçable
 r сменный; съемный

7201 **plug-in filter**
 d austauschbarer Filter *m*
 f filtre *m* changeable
 r сменный фильтр *m*

 * **plus** → 7203

7202 **plus/minus tolerance symbol; plus or minus symbol**
 (+/-)
 d Plus-Minus-Zeichen *n*
 f symbole *m* plus/moins
 r символ *m* плюс-минус

 * **plus or minus symbol** → 7202

7203 **plus [sign]**
 (+)
 d Plus[zeichen] *n*
 f signe *m* plus; plus *m*
 r знак *m* плюс; плюс *m*

 * **PMT** → 7020

7204 **pocket size**
 d Taschenformat *n*
 f taille *f* de poche
 r карманный размер *m*

 * **poid** → 1388

 * **Poinsot polyhedron** → 9156

 * **Poinsot's polyhedron** → 9156

 * **point** *v* → 3052

7205 **point**
 (a sign)
 d Punkt *m*
 f point *m*
 r точка *f*

 * **point** → 7120

7206 **point** *v*
 d indizieren
 f montrer; indiquer
 r указать; направлять

7207 **point accessibility**
 d Erreichbarkeit *f* des Punkts
 f accessibilité *f* de point
 r достижимость *f* точки

7208 **point at infinity; infinite point; ideal point; improper point; infinitely distant point**
 d unendlichferner Punkt *m*; uneigentlicher Punkt; idealer Punkt; Fernpunkt *m*
 f point *m* à l'infini; point de l'infini; point idéal; point impropre
 r бесконечно удаленная точка *f*; идеальная точка; несобственная точка

7209 **point backspacing**
 d Rücksetzen *n* um einen Punkt
 f rappel *m* d'un point
 r возврат *m* на одну точку

7210 **pointed cone**
 d spitzer Kegel *m*
 f cône *m* pointé
 r заостренный конус *m*

7211 **pointed corner**
 d spitze Ecke *f*, Spitzecke *f*
 f coin *m* pointé
 r заостренный угол *m*

7212 **pointer**
 d Zeiger *m*; Hinweis *m*; Pointer *m*
 f pointeur *m*; aiguille *f*
 r указатель *m*

7213 **pointer shape**
 d Zeigerform *f*
 f forme *f* de pointeur
 r форма *f* указателя

 * **point filter** → 2217

 * **point light** → 7228

 * **pointlike** → 7232

7214 point list
  d Liste *f* der Punkte
  f liste *f* de points
  r список *m* точек

* **point map** → 7215

7215 point map[ping]
  d Punktabbildung *f*
  f application *f* ponctuelle
  r точечное отображение *n*

7216 point marker
  d Punkt-Marker *m*
  f marqueur *m* de point
  r маркер *m* точки

7217 point object
  d Punktobjekt *n*
  f objet *m* point
  r объект *m* типа точки

* **point of adherence** → 174

* **point of contact** → 7223

7218 point of inflexion; inflexion point; flex point
  d Wendepunkt *m*; Inflexionspunkt *m*
  f point *m* d'inflexion
  r точка *f* перегиба

* **point of light** → 5568

* **point of origin** → 7219

7219 point of origin[ation]; origin [point]
  d Entstehungsort *m*
  f point *m* d'origine; point-origine *m*
  r точка *f* источника; начальная точка

7220 point of reference; reference point; datum point; datum mark
  d Bezugspunkt *m*; Referenzpunkt *m*; Stützpunkt *m*
  f point *m* de référence; point de départ; point de repère
  r опорная точка *f*; исходная точка; относимая точка; исходный пункт *m*

7221 point of self-intersection; self-intersection point
  d Selbstschnittpunkt *m*; Selbstdurchdringungspunkt *m*
  f point *m* d'auto-intersection; point de self-intersection
  r точка *f* самопересечения

7222 point of self-tangency; self-tangency point
  d Selbstberührungspunkt *m*

  f point *m* autotangentiel
  r точка *f* самоприкосновения; точка самокасания

* **point of sight** → 7225

7223 point of tangency; point of contact
  d Berührungspunkt *m*
  f point *m* de tangence; point de contact
  r точка *f* касания; точка [со]прикосновения

7224 point of vantage; vantage point
  (a position that affords a broad overall view or perspective)
  d günstige Stellung *f*
  f position *f* avantageuse
  r позиция *f* наблюдения; точка расположения камеры

7225 point of view; viewpoint; perspective point; sighting point; point of sight; eye position
  d Aug[en]punkt *m*; Blickzentrum *n*
  f point *m* de vue; position *f* de l'œil
  r точка *f* зрения; положение *n* глаза; центр *m* глаз

7226 point pair
  d Punktepaar *n*
  f couple *m* de points
  r пара *f* точек

7227 point-plane distance
  d Punkt-Ebene-Distanz *f*
  f distance *f* point-plan
  r расстояние *n* точка-плоскость

* **point range** → 7742

* **point sequence** → 8541

* **point source** → 7228

7228 point source [of light]; point light
  d Punktquelle *f*; Punktlicht *n*; punktförmiges Licht *n*
  f source *f* [lumineuse] ponctuelle; lumière *f* point
  r точечный источник *m* [света]; точкообразный источник [света]

7229 point style
  d Stil *m* des Punkts
  f style *m* de point
  r стиль *m* точки

* **point symmetry** → 9421

7230 point system
  d Punkt[e]system *n*

f système *m* de points
r типометрическая система *f*; типографская система мер

7231 point transformation
   d Punkttransformation *f*
   f transformation *f* de point; transformation ponctuelle
   r трансформация *f* точки; точечное преобразование *n*

7232 pointwise; pointlike; punctiform *adj*
   d punktweise
   f ponctuel; point par point
   r [по]точечный

7233 pointwise curve
   d punktweise Kurve *f*
   f courbe *f* ponctuelle
   r точечная кривая *f*

7234 pointwise curve drawing
   d Zeichnen *n* der punktweisen Kurve
   f tracement *m* de courbe ponctuelle
   r черчение *n* точечной кривой

   * **pointwise reproduction** → **3058**

7235 point with height; coted height
   d kotierter Punkt *m*
   f point *m* coté
   r точка *f* с численной отметкой

   * **polar** → **7253**

7236 polar
   d polar
   f polaire
   r полярный

7237 polar angle
   d Polarecke *f*
   f angle *m* polaire; coin *m* polaire
   r полярный угол *m*

7238 polar array
   d Polarfeld *n*
   f réseau *m* polaire; tableau *m* polaire
   r круговой массив *m*

7239 polar axis
   d Polarachse *f*
   f axe *m* polaire
   r полярная ось *f*

7240 polar coordinates
   d Polarkoordinaten *fpl*
   f coordonnées *fpl* polaires
   r полярные координаты *fpl*

   * **polar coordinates in the space** → **9049**

7241 polar coordinate system
   d Polarkoordinatensystem *n*
   f système *m* de coordonnées polaires
   r полярная координатная система *f*

7242 polar equation; equation in a polar coordinate system
   d Polargleichung *f*
   f équation *f* polaire
   r полярное уравнение *n*

7243 polar form
   d polare Form *f*; Polarform *f*
   f forme *f* polaire
   r полярная форма *f*

   * **polar grid** → **7254**

7244 polarity
   d Polarität *f*
   f polarité *f*
   r полярность *f*

7245 polarization
   d Polarisation *f*
   f polarisation *f*
   r поляризация *f*

7246 polarization dispersion
   d Polarisationsdispersion *f*
   f dispersion *f* de la polarisation
   r дисперсия *f* поляризации

7247 polarization effects
   d Polarisationseffekte *mpl*
   f effets *mpl* de la polarisation
   r поляризационные эффекты *mpl*

7248 polarization ellipse
   d Polarisationsellipse *f*
   f ellipse *f* de la polarisation
   r поляризационный эллипс *m*

7249 polarization filter
   d Polarisationsfilter *m*
   f filtre *m* de polarisation
   r фильтр *m* поляризации

7250 polarization parameter
   d Polarisationsparameter *m*
   f paramètre *m* de la polarisation
   r параметр *m* поляризации

7251 polarized light
   d polarisiertes Licht *n*
   f lumière *f* polarisée
   r поляризованный свет *m*

7252 polarized light projection
d Projektion *f* mit polarisiertem Licht
f projection *f* par lumière polarisée
r проекция *f* поляризованным светом

7253 polar [line]
d polare Gerade *f*; Polargerade *f*; Polare *f*
f droite *f* polaire; polaire *f*
r полярная прямая *f*; поляра *f*

7254 polar net; polar grid
d Polarnetz *n*; Polarraster *m*
f grille *f* polaire
r полярная [растровая] сеть *f*

7255 polar normal
d Polarnormale *f*
f normale *f* polaire
r полярная нормаль *f*

7256 polar plane
d Polarebene *f*
f plan *m* polaire
r полярная плоскость *f*

7257 polar radius
d Polarradius *m*
f rayon *m* polaire
r полярный радиус *m*

7258 polar reciprocation
d Polar[en]reziprozität *f*; Polar[en]korrelation *f*
f réciprocité *f* polaire; corrélation *f* involutive
r полярное соответствие *n*; полярная корреляция *f*

* **polar simplex → 8493**

7259 polar solid angle
d supplementäre dreiseitige Ecke *f*; supplementäres Trieder *n*
f angle *m* solide polaire; trièdre *m* supplémentaire
r полярный телесный угол *m*

7260 polar surface
d Polarfläche *f*
f surface *f* polaire
r полярная поверхность *f*

7261 polar tangent
d Polartangente *f*
f tangente *f* polaire
r полярная касательная *f*

7262 polar tetrahedron
d Polartetraeder *n*
f tétraèdre *m* polaire
r полярный тетраэдр *m*

7263 polar triangle
d Polardreieck *n*
f triangle *m* polaire
r полярный треугольник *m*

7264 polar trihedral
d Poldreikant *n/m*; Poldreiflach *n*
f trièdre *m* polaire
r полярный трехгранник *m*

7265 polar vector
d polarer Vektor *m*
f vecteur *m* polaire
r полярный вектор *m*

7266 pole
d Pol *m*
f pôle *m*
r полюс *m*

7267 pole of rotation
d Drehpol *m*
f pôle *m* de rotation
r полюс *m* вращения

* **polhode → 1388**

7268 poll *v*; interrogate *v*
d zyklisch abfragen; zyklisch abrufen; ausgewählt abfragen
f interroger; sonder
r опрашивать; запрашивать

7269 polyarc
d Polybogen *m*
f polyarc *m*
r полидуга *f*

7270 polychromatic
d polychromatisch
f polychromatique
r полихроматический

7271 polyconic projection
d polykonische Projektion *f*
f projection *f* polyconique
r поликоническая проекция *f*

7272 polyeder; polyhedron
d Polyeder *n*; Vielflach *n*; Vielflächner *m*
f polyèdre *m*
r многогранник *m*; полиэдр *m*

7273 polyface mesh
d Polyflächenmasche *f*
f maille *f* polyface
r многогранная сеть *f*

7274 polygon
d Vieleck *n*; Polygon *n*

f polygone *m*
r многоугольник *m*; полигон *m*

7275 polygon[al] clipping
    d Polygonkappen *n*; Polygonschnitt *m*
    f découpage *m* d'un polygone
    r отсекание *n* многоугольника; отсекание
    полигона

7276 polygon[al] clipping boundary; clip
    polygon
    d Polygongrenze *f* des Kappens; Polygongrenze
    des Schnitts
    f limite *f* de découpage polygonale;
    polygone *m* de découpage
    r многоугольная грань *f* отсекания;
    полигональная отсекающая грань

7277 polygonal line
    d Polygonlinie *f*
    f ligne *f* polygonale
    r многоугольная линия *f*; линия полигона

7278 polygon[al] mesh
    d Polygonmasche *f*
    f maille *f* polygonale; maillage *m* par
    polygones
    r многоугольная сеть *f*;
    полигональная сетка *f*

7279 polygonal model
    d Polygonmodell *n*
    f modèle *m* polygonal
    r многогоугольная модель *f*; полигональная
    модель

7280 polygonal net
    d Polygonnetz *n*
    f réseau *m* de polygones
    r сетка *f* полигонов

7281 polygon[al] selection window
    d Polygonfenster *n* der Auswahl
    f fenêtre *f* de sélection polygonale
    r многоугольное окно *n* отбора

7282 polygonal traverses; traverses
    d Polygonzüge *mpl*
    f cheminements *mpl* polygonaux
    r полигональные ходы *mpl*

7283 polygon-arc topology
    d Polygon-Bogen-Topologie *f*
    f topologie *f* polygone-arc
    r топология *f* многоугольников и дуг

* **polygon as star** → 9155

7284 polygon-based modeling
    d Polygon-basierte Modellierung *f*

f modélisation *f* orientée aux polygones;
    modélisation polygonale
r моделирование *n* [поверхности объекта] с
    помощью многоугольников;
    полигональное моделирование

* **polygon clipping** → 7275

* **polygon clipping boundary** → 7276

7285 polygon edge
    d Polygonkante *f*
    f arête *f* de polygone
    r ребро *n* многоугольника; ребро полигона

7286 polygon editor
    d Polygoneditor *m*
    f éditeur *m* de polygones
    r редактор *m* многоугольников; редактор
    полигонов

7287 polygon filling
    d Polygonfüllung *f*
    f remplissage *m* de polygones
    r закрашивание *n* многоугольников;
    заполнение *n* полигонов

7288 polygon-filling unit
    d Polygonfüll[ungs]block *m*;
    Polygonfüll[ungs]einheit *f*
    f bloc *m* de remplissage de polygones
    r блок *m* [сплошного] закрашивания
    многоугольников; блок заполнения
    полигонов

7289 polygon generation
    d Polygongenerierung *f*
    f génération *f* de polygones
    r генерирование *n* многоугольников;
    генерирование полигонов

7290 polygonization
    d Polygonzerlegung *f*
    f polygonisation *f*
    r разделение *n* на многоугольники;
    разделение на полигоны

7291 polygon manager
    d Polygon-Manager *m*
    f gestionnaire *m* de polygones
    r менажер *m* многоугольников; менажер
    полигонов

* **polygon mesh** → 7278

7292 polygon mesh deformation
    d Polygonmaschendeformation *f*
    f déformation *f* de maille polygonale
    r деформация *f* многоугольной сети

7293 polygon overlay
  d Polygonüberlagerung *f*
  f recouvrement *m* de polygone
  r полигональное перекрытие *n*

7294 polygon reduction
  d Polygonverkleinerung *f*
  f réduction *f* de polygone
  r уменьшение *n* многоугольника;
       уменьшение полигона

7295 polygon rendering
  d Polygon-Rendering *n*
  f rendu *m* de polygones
  r рендеринг *m* полигонов

**7296 polygon rendering chip; polygon rendering
        processor**
  d Polygon-Rendering-Chip *m*;
       Polygon-Rendering-Prozessor *m*
  f processeur *m* de rendu de polygones
  r процессор *m* тонирования полигонов;
       процессор рендеринга полигонов

  * **polygon rendering processor** → 7296

  * **polygon selection window** → 7281

7297 polygon tool
  d Hilfsmittel *n* "Polygon"
  f outil *m* "polygone"
  r инструмент *m* "полигон"

7298 polygon topology
  d Polygontopologie *f*
  f topologie *f* de polygone
  r топология *f* полигона

7299 polyhedral angle
  d polyedrale Ecke *f*
  f angle *m* polyèdre; angle polyédrique
  r многогранный угол *m*

7300 polyhedral surface
  d Polyederfläche *f*
  f surface *f* polyédrique
  r многогранная поверхность *f*

7301 polyhedral topology
  d Polyedertopologie *f*
  f topologie *f* polyédrique
  r топология *f* полиэдров

7302 polyhedric projection
  d Polyederabbildung *f*; polyedrische
       Abbildung *f*
  f projection *f* polyédrique
  r полиэдрическая проекция *f*

  * **polyhedron** → 7272

7303 polyline
  d Polylinie *f*
  f polyligne *f*
  r полилиния *f*; ломаная линия *f*

7304 polyline curve segment
  d Polylinienkurvensegment *n*
  f segment *m* courbe de polyligne
  r криволинейный сегмент *m* полилинии

7305 polyline entity group code
  d Code *m* der Polylinieneinheitsgruppe
  f code *m* de groupe d'entité polyligne
  r код *m* группы примитивов полилинии

7306 polyline object
  d Polylinienobjekt *n*
  f objet *m* polyligne
  r объект *m* типа полилинии

7307 polyline segment
  d Polyliniensegment *n*
  f segment *m* de polyligne
  r сегмент *m* полилинии

7308 polymesh
  d Polymasche *f*
  f polymaille *f*
  r полисетка *f*; полисеть *f*

7309 polymorphic system
  d polymorphes System *n*
  f système *m* polymorphe
  r полиморфная система *f*

7310 polymorphism
  d Polymorphismus *m*
  f polymorphisme *m*
  r полиморфизм *m*

  * **polynomial** → 7312

7311 polynomial; multinomial *adj*
  d polynomisch; multinomial
  f polynomial; multinomial
  r полиномиальный; мультиномиальный

7312 polynomial [expression]
  d Polynom *n*
  f polynôme *m*
  r полином *m*; многочлен *m*

7313 polynomial interpolation
  d polynom[isch]e Interpolation *f*
  f interpolation *f* polynomiale
  r полиномиальная интерполяция *f*

7314 polynomial model
  d polynom[isch]es Modell *n*

f modèle *m* polynomial
r полиномиальная модель *f*

7315 polynomial trendline
  d polynom[isch]e Trendlinie *f*
  f ligne *f* de tendance polynôme
  r полиномиальная тренд-линия *f*

7316 polyspiral
  d Polyspirale *f*
  f polyspirale *f*
  r полиспираль *f*

7317 polytope
  d Polytop *n*
  f polytope *m*
  r политоп *m*

7318 pool
  d Pool *m*
  f pool *m*
  r пул *m*; накопитель *m*; буфер *m*

7319 pooling of data; data pooling
  d Zusammenfassen *n* von Daten
  f réunion *f* de données
  r объединение *n* данных

7320 poor color
  d schwache Farbe *f*
  f couleur *f* pauvre
  r плохой цвет *m*

  * **poor painting** → 8393

7321 pop
  d Auskellern *n*; Entkellern *n*
  f dépilage *m*; dépilement *m*
  r извлечение *n*; выталкивание *n*

7322 population
  d Population *f*; Gesamtheit *f*
  f population *f*
  r популяция *f*; совокупность *f*

7323 popup
  d Popup-
  f relevant
  r всплывающий

7324 popup button
  d Popup-Taste *f*
  f bouton *m* flash; bouton relevant
  r всплывающая кнопка *f*

7325 popup help
  d Popup-Hilfe *f*
  f aide *f* relevante
  r всплывающая помощная информация *f*

7326 popup menu
  d Popup-Menü *n*; Auftauch-Menü *n*
  f menu *m* relevant; menu à liste directe; menu superposable; menu en incrustation
  r всплывающее меню *n*

7327 popup palette
  d Popup-Palette *f*
  f palette *f* relevante
  r всплывающая палитра *f*

7328 popup slider
  d Popup-Schieber *m*
  f règle *f* en incrustation
  r всплывающий ползунок *m*

7329 popup window
  d Aufspringfenster *n*
  f fenêtre *f* à liste directe; fenêtre flash; fenêtre en incrustation
  r всплывающее окно *n*

7330 port
  d Port *m*; Anschlussstelle *f*
  f port *m*
  r порт *m*; место *n* подключения

7331 portability; transportability; relocatability; mobility
  d Portabilität *f*; Transportierbarkeit *f*; Übertragbarkeit *f*; Verschieblichkeit *f*
  f portabilité *f*; transportabilité *f*; relogeabilité *f*; mobilité *f*
  r переносимость *f*; перемещаемость *f*; мобильность *f*

7332 portable; transportable; relocatable; mobile
  d tragbar; übertragbar; verschiebbar; versetzbar; mobil
  f portable; relogeable; translatable; déplaçable; transportable; mobile
  r портативный; переносной; переносимый; перемещаемый; мобильный

  * **portable scanner** → 4497

7333 portion of a curve
  d Kurvenausschnitt *m*
  f portion *f* de courbe
  r кусок *m* кривой

7334 portrait display
  d Hochformat-Display *n*; Hochformatbildschirm *m*
  f écran *m* portrait
  r дисплей *m* с изображением, вытянутым по вертикали

  * **portrait format** → 7335

* portrait layout → 7335

7335 portrait [paper] orientation; portrait
format; portrait layout; vertical format;
upright format
  d Hochformat-Orientierung *f*
  f orientation *f* [de papier] portrait; orientation
  verticale; format *m* vertical; présentation *f* à
  verticale; présentation à la française
  r ориентация *f* вдоль страницы

* portrait orientation → 7335

* position → 7120

7336 positional accuracy
  d Positionsgenauigkeit *f*;
  Positioniergenauigkeit *f*
  f exactitude *f* de position
  r позиционная точность *f*

7337 positional tolerance
  d Positionstoleranz *f*; Positioniertoleranz *f*
  f tolérance *f* de position
  r позиционный допуск *m*

7338 positioned text
  d positionierter Text *m*
  f texte *m* positionné
  r позиционированный текст *m*

7339 position indicator
  d Positionsindikator *m*
  f indicateur *m* de position
  r индикатор *m* местоположения

7340 positioning
  d Positionierung *f*; Positionieren *n*
  f positionnement *m*
  r позиционирование *n*

7341 position plane
  (in central projection)
  d Positionsebene *f*; Standebene *f*
  f plan *m* de position
  r плоскость *f* позиционирования

7342 position point; standpoint
  (in central projection)
  d Standpunkt *m*
  f point *m* de position
  r основание *n* центра проекции; основание
  глаза

7343 position rollup
  d Positionsrollup *n*
  f déroulement *m* séquentiel ascendant de la
  position
  r свертывание *n* позиции

7344 position sensor
  d Positionssensor *m*; Lagesensor *m*
  f transmetteur *m* de position
  r датчик *m* положения

7345 position trigger
  d Positionstrigger *m*
  f basculeur *m* de position
  r триггер *m* положения

7346 positive
  d positiv
  f positif
  r положительный

7347 positive affine isometry
  d positive affine Isometrie *f*
  f isométrie *f* affine positive
  r положительная аффинная изометрия *f*

7348 positive angle
  d positiver Winkel *m*
  f angle *m* positif
  r положительный угол *m*

7349 positive correlation
  d positive Korrelation *f*
  f corrélation *f* positive
  r положительная корреляция *f*

7350 positive direction; positive sense
  d positive Richtung *f*
  f direction *f* positive; sens *m* positif
  r положительное направление *n*

7351 positive image
  d Positivbild *n*
  f image *f* positive
  r позитивное изображение *n*

7352 positive position
  d positive Position *f*
  f position *f* positive
  r положительная позиция *f*

7353 positive position of X axis
  d positive Position *f* der Achse X
  f position *f* positive d'axe X
  r положительная позиция *f* оси X

7354 positive right angle
  d positiver rechter Winkel *m*
  f angle *m* droit positif
  r положительный прямой угол *m*

* positive sense → 7350

* pstedit → 7355

7355 postedit[ing]
  d Nacheditieren *n*

f édition *f* postérieure
r постредактирование *n*; заключительное редактирование *n*

7356 poster; affiche
d Plakat *n*; Anschlag *m*
f affiche *f*; placard *m*
r афиша *f*, плакат *m*

7357 posterization
d Farb[en]zahl-Reduzierung *f*
f postérisation *f*
r уменьшение *n* числа цветов; огрубение *n* [изображения]

7358 posterize *v* colors
d Farb[en]zahl reduzieren
f posteriser des couleurs
r уменьшать число цветов

7359 postfiltering
d Nachfiltrierung *f*
f filtrage *m* postérieur
r последующее фильтрирование *n*

* **postfocalization** → 7360

7360 postfocusing; postfocalization
d Nachfokussierung *f*
f postfocalisation *f*
r фокусировка *f* после отклонения луча

7361 postluminescence
d Nachleuchten *n*
f postluminescence *f*
r послесвечение *n*; остаточное свечение *n*

* **Postscript** → 7368

7362 PostScript file
d PostScript-Datei *f*
f fichier *m* PostScript
r Postscript файл *m*

* **Postscript fill** → 7363

7363 PostScript fill[ing]
d PostScript-Füllung *f*
f remplissage *m* de texture PostScript
r заполнение *n* с PostScript текстурой

7364 PostScript fill pattern
d PostScript-Füllmuster *n*
f motif *m* de remplissage PostScript
r PostScript шаблон *m* закраски

7365 PostScript font
d PostScript-Schrift *f*
f police *f* PostScript
r PostScript шрифт *m*

7366 PostScript halftone screen
d PostScript-Halbtonbildschirm *m*
f écran *m* demi-teinte PostScript
r полутоновый PostScript экран *m*

7367 PostScript image
d PostScript-Bild *n*
f image *f* PostScript
r PostScript изображение *n*

7368 PostScript [language]
d PostScript-Sprache *f*
f langage *m* PostScript
r язык *m* Postscript; язык описания страниц

7369 PostScript pattern
d PostScript-Motiv *n*
f motif *m* PostScript
r PostScript мотив *m*

7370 PostScript printer
d PostScript-Drucker *m*
f imprimante *f* [dotée de] PostScript
r PostScript принтер *m*

7371 PostScript texture
d PostScript-Textur *f*
f texture *f* PostScript
r PostScript текстура *f*

* **potential line** → 3507

* **potential surface** → 3508

7372 power
d Potenz *f*; Leistung *f*
f puissance *f*
r мощность *f*

* **power** → 9339

* **PPI** → 7117

* **PR** → 6906

7373 precede *v*
d vorangehen; vorausgehen
f précéder
r предшествовать

7374 precedence
d Vorhergehen *n*; Präzedenz *f*
f précédence *f*
r предшествование *n*

7375 precession; precessional motion
d Präzession *f*; Präzessionsbewegung *f*
f précession *f*, mouvement *m* de précession
r прецессия *f*; прецессионное движение *n*

* **precessional motion** → 7375

* **precision** → 71

* **precision of measurement** → 75

7376 **predefined variable**
   d im voraus definierte Variable *f*
   f variable *f* prédéfinie
   r предварительно дефинированная
      переменная *f*

7377 **predictable color**
   d vorhersagbare Farbe *f*
   f couleur *f* prévisible
   r прогнозируемый цвет *m*

* **prediction** → 3930

7378 **pre-editing**
   d Voreditieren *n*
   f préédition *f*
   r предварительное редактирование *n*;
      предредактирование *n*

7379 **preference**
   d Präferenz *f*, Vorzug *m*; Bevorzugung *f*
   f préférence *f*
   r преференция *f*; предпочтение *n*

7380 **prefiltering**
   d Vorfiltrierung *f*
   f filtrage *m* préalable
   r предварительное фильтрирование *n*

7381 **prefix**
   d Präfix *n*
   f préfixe *m*
   r приставка *f*; префикс *m*

* **preformat** → 7382

7382 **preformat[ting]**
   d Vorformatieren *n*
   f préformatage *m*
   r предварительное форматирование *n*

7383 **pre-image; before-image**
   d Urbild *n*; vorheriges Bild *n*
   f image *f* anticipée; pré-image *f*
   r праобраз *m*; первообраз *m*;
      предварительное изображение *n*

7384 **preloaded**
   d im voraus eingerichtet
   f préchargé
   r предварительно загруженный

7385 **preloaded font**
   d im voraus eingerichtetes Font *n*

   f fonte *f* préchargée
   r предварительно загруженный шрифт *m*

7386 **preparation; preparing**
   d Vorbereitung *f*
   f préparation *f*
   r подготовка *f*

* **preparing** → 7386

7387 **preprinted form**
   d Vorabdruck *m*
   f prétirage *m*; formulaire *m* préimprimé
   r предпечатный формуляр *m*

7388 **presence**
   d Präsenz *f*, Anwesenheit *f*
   f présence *f*
   r присутствие *n*; наличие *n*

7389 **presentation**
   d Präsentation *f*
   f présentation *f*
   r представление *n*

7390 **presentation drawing**
   d Präsentationszeichnung *f*
   f dessin *m* présentatif
   r представительный чертеж *m*

* **presentation graphics** → 1199

7391 **presentation graphics software**
   d Präsentationsgrafik-Software *f*
   f logiciel *m* de graphique de présentation
   r программное обеспечение *n* деловой
      графики

7392 **presentation image**
   d Präsentationsbild *n*; Darstellungsbild *n*
   f image *f* de présentation
   r представительное изображение *n*

7393 **preservation of area**
   d Flächentreue *f*
   f conservation *f* de l'aire
   r сохранение *n* площади

7394 **preservation of length**
   d Längentreue *f*
   f conservation *f* de la longueur
   r сохранение *n* длины

* **preset** → 7398

7395 **preset** *v*
   d voreinstellen
   f ajuster d'avance; présélectionner; prérégler;
      prépositionner
   r предварительно установлять

7396 preset fountain fill
 d voreingestellte Verlaufsfüllung *f*
 f remplissage *m* par dégradé prédéfini
 r предварительно установленный
    источник *m* закраски

7397 preset parameter
 d voreingestellter Parameter *m*; vorgegebener
    Parameter
 f paramètre *m* prédéfini; paramètre établi
 r заданный параметр *m*; предварительно
    установленный параметр

7398 preset[ting]
 d Voreinstellung *f*; Voreinstellen *n*; Festlegen *n*
    von Anfangsbedingungen
 f forçage *m*; établissement *m* d'avance;
    présélection *f*; prédéfinition *f*; fixation *f* d'une
    condition initiale
 r предварительная установка *f*

7399 preshaded image
 d vorschattiertes Bild *n*
 f image *f* pré-ombrée
 r предварительно затушеванное
    изображение *n*

7400 preshaded surface texture
 d vorschattierte Flächentextur *f*
 f texture *f* de surface pré-ombrée
 r предварительно затушеванная текстура *f*
    поверхности

7401 press *v*; hit *v*
 d pressen; drücken
 f presser; appuyer; serrer
 r нажимать

7402 pressed button
 d gedrückte Schaltfläche *f*
 f bouton *m* enfoncé
 r нажатый бутон *m*

7403 pressure-sensitive pen settings
 d druckempfindliche Stifteinrichtungen *fpl*
 f paramètres *mpl* de plume, dépendants de la
    pression
 r параметры *mpl* пера, зависимые давлением

* **preview → 7406**

7404 preview *v*
 d im voraus besichtigen
 f prévisualiser
 r предварительно просматривать

7405 preview area; preview zone
 d Vorschauzone *f*
 f zone *f* d'aperçu; zone de prévisualisation

 r зона *f* предварительного просмотра

7406 preview[ing]
 d Vorschau *f*
 f prévisualisation *f*; vision *f* avant impression
 r предварительный просмотр *m*

7407 preview of selected objects
 d Vorschau *f* der ausgewählten Objekte
 f prévisualisation *f* d'objets sélectionnés
 r предварительный просмотр *m* выбранных
    объектов

* **preview zone → 7405**

7408 previous object
 d voriges Objekt *n*; vorhergehendes Objekt
 f objet *m* antérieur; objet précédent
 r предыдущий объект *m*

7409 prewarping
 d vorherige Verbiegung *f*
 f gauchissement *m* d'avance; gauchissement
    préalable
 r предварительное искажение *n*

7410 primary; prime; original
 d primär; ursprünglich
 f primaire; de départ; original
 r первичный; первоначальный; исходный;
    примарный

* **primary axis → 5763**

7411 primary colors
 d Primärfarben *fpl*; Normfarben *fpl*
 f couleurs *fpl* primaires
 r первичные цвета *mpl*

7412 primary color space
 d Primärfarbraum *m*; Normfarbraum *m*
 f espace *m* de couleurs primaires
 r пространство *n* первичных цветов

7413 primary data
 d Primärdaten *npl*
 f données *fpl* primaires
 r первоначальные данные *npl*; первичные
    данные

7414 primary display
 d Erstmonitor *m*; Primärmonitor *m*
 f écran *m* primaire
 r первичный дисплей *m*

* **primary mouse button → 5482**

7415 primary point
 d Primärpunkt *m*

f point *m* primaire
r первичная точка *f*

7416 primary units
d primäre Einheiten *fpl*
f unités *fpl* primaires
r первичные [мерные] единицы *fpl*

* **primary window** → 5762

* **prime** → 7410, 7417

7417 prime [sign]; prime symbol
(')
d Strich *m*; Strichsymbol *n*
f prime *f*
r прим *m*; штрих *m*

* **prime symbol** → 7417

* **primitive** → 7419

7418 primitive *adj*
d primitiv
f primitif
r примитивный

7419 primitive [element]; graphic[s] primitive; output primitive
d primitives Element *n*; Primitiv *n*; Grafikgrundelement *n*
f élément *m* primitif; primitive *f* [graphique]
r примитивный элемент *m*; базисный элемент; [графический] примитив *m*

* **principal** → 5756

7420 principal arc
d Hauptbogen *m*
f arc *m* principal
r главная дуга *f*

* **principal axis** → 5763

7421 principal branch
d Hauptzweig *m*; Hauptast *m*
f branche *f* principale
r главная ветвь *f*

7422 principal curvature
d Hauptkrümmung *f*
f courbure *f* principale
r главная кривизна *f*

* **principal diagonal** → 5468

* **principal direction** → 5758

7423 principal direction of curvature
d Hauptkrümmungsrichtung *f*

f direction *f* de courbure principale
r главное направление *n* кривизны

7424 principal image plane
d Bildhauptebene *f*
f plan *m* d'image principal
r главная плоскость *f* изображения

7425 principal image point
d Bildhauptpunkt *m*
f point *m* d'image principal
r главная точка *f* изображения

7426 principal moment
d Hauptmoment *m*
f moment *m* principal
r главный момент *m*; основной момент

7427 principal neutral point
d Hauptverschwindungspunkt *m*; Hauptneutralpunkt *m*
f point *m* principal neutre
r главная нейтральная точка *f*

7428 principal normal
d Hauptnormale *f*
f normale *f* principale
r главная нормаль *f*

7429 principal normal plane
d Hauptnormalebene *f*
f plan *m* de normale principale
r плоскость *f* главной нормали

7430 principal normal section
d Hauptkrümmungsschnitt *m*
f section *f* normale principale
r сечение *n* главной кривизны

7431 principal object plane
d Objekthauptebene *f*
f plan *m* d'objet principal
r главная плоскость *f* объекта

7432 principal object point
d Objekthauptpunkt *m*
f point *m* d'objet principal
r главная точка *f* объекта

7433 principal plane
d Haupt[symmetrie]ebene *f*
f plan *m* principal
r плоскость *f* главной симметрии

7434 principal point
d Hauptpunkt *m*
f point *m* principal
r главная точка *f*

* **principal radius of curvature** → 7718

* principal ray → 738

7435 **principal surface**
  d Hauptfläche *f*
  f surface *f* principale
  r главная поверхность *f*

7436 **principal tangent**
  d Haupttangente *f*
  f tangente *f* principale
  r главная касательная *f*

7437 **principal trace**
  d Hauptspur *f*
  f trace *f* principale
  r главный след *m*

7438 **principal vanishing point**
  d Hauptfluchtpunkt *m*
  f point *m* de fuite principal
  r главная точка *f* схода

7439 **principle of abstraction**
  d Abstraktionsprinzip *n*
  f principe *m* d'abstraction
  r принцип *m* абстракции

7440 **principle of construction**
  d Konstruktionsprinzip *n*
  f principe *m* de construction
  r принцип *m* конструирования

7441 **principle of duality; duality principle**
  (of projective geometry)
  d Prinzip *n* der Dualität; Dualitätsprinzip *n*
  f principe *m* de dualité
  r принцип *m* двойственности; дуальный
    принцип

* print → 7465

7442 **print** *v*
  d drucken
  f imprimer
  r печатать

7443 **printable area**
  d druckbarer Bereich *m*
  f zone *f* imprimable
  r печатаемая зона *f*; печатаемая область *f*;
    область печати

7444 **printable background**
  d druckbarer Hintergrund *m*
  f fond *m* imprimable
  r печатаемый фон *m*

7445 **printable page**
  d druckbare Seite *f*
  f page *m* imprimable

r печатаемая страница *f*

7446 **print [column] spacing; character pitch**
  d Druckspaltenteilung *f*,
    Druckspaltenabstand *m*
  f partage *m* de colonne d'impression
  r расстояние *n* между столбцами печати

7447 **printed form**
  d gedruckte Form *f*
  f forme *f* imprimée
  r отпечатанная форма *f*

* **printed register mark** → 4469

7448 **printer**
  d Drucker *m*; Printer *m*
  f imprimante *f*; imprimeur *m*
  r печатающее устройство *n*; принтер *m*

7449 **printer adjustment**
  d Druckereinstellung *f*
  f ajustement *m* d'imprimante
  r настраивание *n* принтера

7450 **printer calibration**
  d Druckerkalibrierung *f*
  f calibrage *m* d'imprimante
  r калибровка *f* принтера

7451 **printer color profile**
  d Druckerfarbprofil *n*
  f profil *m* de couleurs d'imprimante
  r цветовой профиль *m* принтера

7452 **printer colors**
  d Druckerfarben *fpl*
  f couleurs *fpl* d'imprimante
  r цвета *mpl* принтера

7453 **printer configuration**
  d Druckerkonfiguration *f*
  f configuration *f* d'imprimante
  r конфигурация *f* принтера

7454 **printer driver**
  d Druck[er]treiber *m*
  f excitateur *m* d'impression; pilote *m*
    d'imprimante; driver *m* d'imprimante
  r драйвер *m* принтера; драйвер печати

7455 **printer font**
  d Druckerschrift *f*
  f police *f* d'imprimante
  r шрифт *m* принтера; принтерный шрифт

7456 **printer gamut**
  d Drucker-Gamut *n*
  f gamme *f* d'imprimante
  r цветовой диапазон *m* принтера

7457 printer icon
d Druckersymbol *n*
f icône *f* d'imprimante
r икона *f* принтера

7458 printer interface
d Druckerschnittstelle *f*
f interface *f* d'imprimante
r интерфейс *m* принтера

7459 printer layout; print format
d Druckformat *n*; Druckform *f*
f format *m* d'impression
r формат *m* печати; формат распечатки;
макет *m* печати

7460 printer model
d Druckermodell *n*
f modèle *m* d'imprimante
r модель *f* принтера

7461 printer resolution
d Druckerauflösung *f*
f résolution *f* d'imprimante
r разрешающая способность *f* принтера

7462 printer settings
d Druckereinrichtungen *fpl*
f paramètres *mpl* d'imprimante
r параметры *mpl* принтера

7463 printer's mark
d Druckermarke *f*; Druckerzeichen *n*
f marque *f* d'imprimante
r маркер *m* принтера

7464 print file
d Druckdatei *f*
f fichier *m* d'impression
r файл *m* печати

* **print format → 7459**

7465 print[ing]
d Druck *m*; Drucken *n*
f impression *f*
r печатание *n*

7466 printing colors
d Druckfarben *fpl*
f couleurs *fpl* d'impression
r цвета *mpl* печати

7467 print[ing] quality
d Druckqualität *f*
f qualité *f* d'impression
r качество *m* печати

7468 printing speed
d Druckgeschwindigkeit *f*

f vitesse *f* d'impression
r скорость *f* печати

7469 print job
d Druckauftrag *m*
f tâche *f* d'impression
r задание *n* печати

7470 print merge
d Druckvereinigung *f*
f fusionnement *m* d'impression
r слияние *n* печата; объединение *n* печата

7471 printout
d Ausdruck *m*; Druckbild *n*; Druck[er]ausgabe *f*
f impression *f*; aspect *m* d'impression; sortie *f*
par impression
r распечатка *f*; отпечаток *m*; вывод *m* на
печать

7472 print preview
d Druckvorschau *f*
f aperçu *m* avant impression
r предпечатное представление *n*

* **print quality → 7467**

7473 print script
d Druckskript *n*
f script *m* d'impression
r принтерный скрипт *m*

7474 print setting; print setup
d Druckeinrichtung *f*
f établissement *m* d'impression
r установка *f* печати

* **print setup → 7474**

* **print spacing → 7446**

7475 print spool file
d Druckspoolerdatei *f*
f fichier *m* de spoulage d'impression
r файл *m* спулера печатания

7476 print style
d Druckstil *m*
f style *m* d'impression
r стиль *m* печатания

7477 print *v* to a file
d in einer Datei drucken
f imprimer dans un fichier
r печатать в файле

7478 prism
d Prisma *n*
f prisme *m*
r призма *f*

7479 prismatic surface
 d prismatische Fläche *f*; Prismenfläche *f*
 f surface *f* prismatique
 r призматическая поверхность *f*

7480 prism grating
 d Prismenraster *m*
 f réseau *m* à prismes
 r призматический растр *m*

7481 probabilistic
 d probabilistisch
 f probabilistique
 r вероятностный

7482 probability; likelihood
 d Wahrscheinlichkeit *f*
 f probabilité *f*
 r вероятность *f*

7483 probe
 d Taster *m*; Sonde *f*
 f sonde *f*; palpeur *m*
 r пробник *m*; зонд *m*

7484 problem; task
 d Problem *n*; Task *f*; Aufgabe *f*
 f problème *m*; tâche *f*; devoir *m*
 r задача *f*

7485 problem data; task data
 d Problemdaten *npl*; Aufgabedaten *npl*
 f données *fpl* de problème
 r данные *npl* задачи

 * **problem of coloration** → 1771

 * **problem of coloring maps in four colors** →
   3959

7486 problem of projectivity
   (in the plane or in the space)
 d Problem *n* der Projektivität
 f problème *m* de projectivité
 r задача проективности

7487 procedural animation
 d prozedurale Animation *f*
 f animation *f* procédurale
 r процедурная анимация *f*

7488 procedural material
 d prozedurales Material *n*
 f matériau *m* procédural
 r процедурный материал *m*

7489 procedural textures
 d prozedurale Texturen *fpl*
 f textures *fpl* procéduraux
 r процедурные текстуры *fpl*

7490 procedure
 d Prozedur *f*
 f procédure *f*; procédé *m*
 r процедура *f*

7491 process
 d Prozess *m*
 f processus *m*
 r процесс *m*

7492 processed image
 d verarbeitetes Bild *n*
 f image *f* traitée; image dépouillée
 r обработанное изображение *n*

7493 processing; treatment
 d Verarbeitung *f*; Bearbeitung *f*
 f traitement *m*
 r обработка *f*

7494 processor
 d Prozessor *m*
 f processeur *m*
 r процессор *m*

7495 product
 d Produkt *n*
 f produit *m*
 r произведение *n*

7496 product modeling
 d Produktmodellierung *f*
 f modélisation *f* de produit
 r моделирование *n* продукта

7497 professional-quality bitmap
 d Bitmap *n* in professioneller Qualität
 f image *f* bitmap à qualité professionnelle
 r растровое изображение *n*
   профессионального качества

7498 profile
 d Profil *n*
 f profil *m*
 r профиль *m*

 * **profile** *v* → **8601**

7499 profile deleting
 d Profillöschung *f*
 f effacement *m* de profil
 r стирание *n* профиля

7500 profile image
 d Profil-Bild *n*
 f image *f* de profil
 r изображение *n* профиля

7501 profile importing
 d Profilimportieren *n*

f importation *f* de profil
r внесение *n* профиля

7502 profile line
   d Linie *f* des Profils
   f droite *f* de profil
   r линия *f* профиля

7503 profile optimization
   d Profiloptimierung *f*
   f optimisation *f* du profil
   r оптимизация *f* профиля

7504 profile parameter
   d Profilparameter *m*
   f paramètre *m* du profil
   r параметр *m* профиля

7505 profile plane
   d Profilebene *f*
   f plan *m* de profil
   r профильная плоскость *f*

7506 profile setup
   d Profileinrichtung *f*
   f établissement *m* de profil
   r установление *n* профиля

7507 profile view
   d Profilansicht *f*
   f vue *f* de profil
   r профильное представление *n*

 * **prognosis → 3930**

7508 program
   d Programm *n*
   f programme *m*
   r программа *f*

7509 program credit
       (on the screen)
   d Programmkredit *m*
   f titre *m* de programme
   r программный кредит *m*; программный
       титр *m*

7510 program folder
   d Programm-Mappe *f*
   f dossier *m* de programme
   r программная папка *f*

7511 programming
   d Programmierung *f*; Programmieren *n*
   f programmation *f*
   r программирование *n*

7512 program parameter
   d Programmparameter *m*
   f paramètre *m* de programme

r программный параметр *m*

7513 program window
   d Programmfenster *n*
   f fenêtre *f* de programme
   r окно *n* программы

7514 progress bar
   d Fortschrittsbalken *m*
   f barre *f* de progression
   r полоса *f* продвижения; полоса движения
       вперед

7515 progressive refinement
   d Progressiv-Refinement *n*
   f raffinement *m* progressif
   r прогрессивное усовершенствование *n*

 * **project → 2628**

 * **project *v* → 2629**

7516 project database
   d Datenbasis *f* des Projekts
   f base *f* de données de projet
   r база *f* данных проекта

 * **projected light → 7523**

7517 projected tolerance
   d projektierte Toleranz *f*
   f tolérance *f* projective
   r проективный допуск *m*

7518 projected tolerance symbol
   d Zeichen *n* der projektierten Toleranz
   f symbole *m* de tolérance projective
   r символ *m* проективного допуска

7519 projected tolerance zone
   d Zone *f* der projektierten Toleranz
   f zone *f* de tolérance projective
   r зона *f* проективного допуска

7520 projected video wall
   d projektierte Videowand *f*
   f mur *m* vidéo projectif
   r проективная видеостена *f*

7521 project file
   d Projektdatei *f*
   f fichier *m* de projet
   r проектный файл *m*

 * **projecting → 7529**

 * **projecting beam → 7527**

7522 projecting cone; projective cone
   d projizierender Kegel *m*; Strahlenkegel *m*

f cône *m* projetant; cône projectif
r проектирующий конус *m*; проективный
конус

7523 projecting light; projection light; projected light
    d Projektionslicht *n*; projektiertes Licht *n*
    f lumière *f* de projection; lumière projetée
    r проективный свет *m*

7524 projecting line
    d projizierende Gerade *f*; Projektionsgerade *f*
    f droite *f* projetante; droite de projection
    r проектирующая прямая *f*; прямая
    проекции

7525 projecting plane; projection plane
    d projizierende Ebene *f*; Sehebene *f*;
    Projektionsebene *f*
    f plan *m* projetant; plan de projection
    r проектирующая плоскость *f*; плоскость
    проекции

7526 projecting process; projection process
    d Projektionsprozess *m*
    f processus *m* de projet
    r процесс *m* проектирования

7527 projecting ray; projecting beam; projector
    d Projektionsstrahl *m*; Sehstrahl *m*;
    Perspektivitätsstrahl *m*; Projektor *m*
    f rayon *m* projetant; rayon de projection;
    projecteur *m*
    r проектирующий луч *m*; луч зрения;
    проектор *m*

7528 projection; map
    (as an image)
    d Projektion *f*; projektives Bild *n*; Abbild *n*;
    Einteilungsübersicht *f*
    f projection *f*; mappe *f*
    r проекция *f*; отображение *n*

7529 projection; projecting; mapping
    (as an operation)
    d Projizieren *n*; Abbildung *f*; Mapping *n*
    f projection *f*; application *f*; mappage *m*;
    mapping *m*
    r проектирование *n*; проецирование *n*;
    операция *f* проецирования; отображение *n*;
    наложение *n*

* **projection axis** → 767

7530 projection coordinates
    d Projektionskoordinaten *fpl*
    f coordonnées *fpl* de projection
    r координаты *fpl* проекции

7531 projection cylinder

    d Projektionszylinder *m*
    f cylindre *m* de projection
    r цилиндр *m* проекции

* **projection light** → 7523

7532 projection mask
    d Projektionsmaske *f*
    f masque *m* de projection
    r проекционная маска *f*; проекционный
    шаблон *m*

7533 projection mode
    d Projektionsmodus *m*
    f mode *m* de projection
    r режим *m* проекции

7534 projection on an axis
    d Achsenprojektion *f*; Projektion *f* auf einer
    Achse
    f projection *f* sur un axe
    r проекция *f* на ось

7535 projection on a plane
    d Projektion *f* auf einer Ebene
    f projection *f* sur un plan
    r проекция *f* на плоскость

* **projection operator** → 7581

* **projection plane** → 7525

7536 projection point
    d Projektionspunkt *m*
    f point *m* de projection
    r проекционная точка *f*

* **projection process** → 7526

7537 projection raster
    d Projektionsraster *m*
    f rastre *m* de projection
    r растр *m* проекции

* **projection scale** → 8301

7538 projection sphere
    d Projektionssphäre *f*
    f sphère *f* de projection
    r сфера *f* проекции

7539 projection square
    d Projektionsquadrat *n*
    f carré *m* de projection
    r квадрат *m* проекции

7540 projection system
    d Projektionssystem *n*
    f système *m* de projection
    r система *f* проекции

* **projection with heights** → 9739

7541 projective assembly; projective group
  d projektive Gruppe *f*
  f ensemble *m* projectif; groupe *m* projectif
  r проективная группа *f*

7542 projective axioms of incidence; axioms of incidence in projective geometry
  d projektive Verknüpfungsaxiome *npl*; Verknüpfungsaxiome in der projektiven Geometrie
  f axiomes *mpl* d'incidence projectifs; axiomes d'incidence dans la géométrie projective
  r проективные аксиомы *fpl* инцидентности; аксиомы инцидентности проективной геометрии; проективные   аксиомы сочетания

7543 projective base
  d projektive Basis *f*
  f base *f* projective; repère *m* projectif
  r проективная база *f*

7544 projective collineation
  d projektive Kollineation *f*
  f collinéation *f* projective
  r проективная коллинеация *f*

* **projective cone** → 7522

7545 projective conic; conic section in projective geometry
  d projektiver Kegelschnitt *m*
  f conique *f* projective; section *f* conique projective
  r проективная коника *f*; проективное коническое сечение *n*

7546 projective connection
  d projektiver Zusammenhang *m*
  f connexion *f* projective
  r проективная связность *f*

7547 projective coordinates
  d projektive Koordinaten *fpl*
  f coordonnées *fpl* projectives
  r проективные координаты *fpl*

7548 projective [coordinate] system; set of projective coordinates
  d projektives Koordinatensystem *n*; projektives System *n*
  f système *m* de coordonnées projectives; système [de coordonnées] projectif
  r проективная система *f* [координат]; система проективных координат

7549 projective correspondence
  d projektive Zuordnung *f*

  f correspondance *f* projective
  r проективное соответствие *n*

7550 projective curvature
  d projektive Krümmung *f*
  f courbure *f* projective
  r проективная кривизна *f*

7551 projective curve
  d projektive Kurve *f*
  f courbe *f* projective
  r проективная кривая *f*

7552 projective deformation; projective development
  d projektive Deformation *f*; projektive Abwicklung *f*
  f déformation *f* projective; développement *m* projectif
  r проективное деформирование *n*; проективное развертывание *n*; проективная развертка *f*

* **projective development** → 7552

7553 projective dimension
  d projektive Dimension *f*
  f dimension *f* projective
  r проективная размерность *f*

7554 projective displacement; projective transfer
  d projektive Verschiebung *f*; projektive Übertragung *f*
  f transport *m* projectif; transfert *m* projectif
  r проективное перенесение *n*

7555 projective division; related division; homographic division
  d homografische Teilung *f*
  f division *f* homographique
  r гомографическое деление *n*

7556 projective generation
  d projektive Erzeugung *f*
  f génération *f* projective
  r проективное порождение *n*

7557 projective generator
  d projektiver Generator *m*
  f générateur *m* projectif
  r проективный образующий *m*

7558 projective geometry
  d projektive Geometrie *f*
  f géométrie *f* projective
  r проективная геометрия *f*

* **projective geometry in the plane** → 7147

* **projective group** → 7541

7559 projective line
d projektive Gerade *f*
f droite *f* projective
r проективная прямая *f*

7560 projectively flat space
d projektiv-ebener Raum *m*
f espace *m* projectivement plat
r проективно плоское пространство *n*

7561 projectively independent points
d projektiv-unabhängige Punkte *mpl*
f points *mpl* projectivement indépendants
r проективно независимые точки *fpl*

7562 projective manifold; projective variety
d projektive Mannigfaltigkeit *f*
f variété *f* projective
r проективное многообразие *n*

* **projective map** → 7563

7563 projective map[ping]
d projektive Abbildung *f*
f application *f* projective
r проективное отображение *n*

* **projective mensuration** → 7564

7564 projective metric; projective mensuration
d projektive Metrik *f*, projektive Maßbestimmung *f*
f métrique *f* projective
r проективная метрика *f*; проективное мероопределение *n*

7565 projective minimal surface
d Projektivminimalfläche *f*
f surface *f* projective minimale
r проективная минимальная поверхность *f*

7566 projective module
d projektiver Modul *m*
f module *m* projectif
r проективный модуль *m*

7567 projective object
d projektives Objekt *n*
f objet *m* projectif
r проективный объект *m*

7568 projective parameter
d projektiver Parameter *m*
f paramètre *m* projectif
r проективный параметр *m*

7569 projective pencil of lines
d projektives Geradenbüschel *n*

f faisceau *m* de rayons homographique
r проективный пучок *m* прямых

7570 projective plane
d projektive Ebene *f*
f plan *m* projectif
r проективная плоскость *f*

* **projective plane geometry** → 7147

7571 projective point ranges
d projektive Punktreihen *fpl*
f ponctuelles *fpl* projectives
r проективные ряды *mpl* точек

7572 projective property
d projektive Eigenschaft *f*
f propriété *f* projective
r проективное свойство *n*

7573 projective quadric
d projektive Quadrik *f*
f quadrique *f* projective
r проективная квадрика *f*

7574 projective space
d projektiver Raum *m*
f espace *m* projectif
r проективное пространство *n*

* **projective system** → 7548

7575 projective tensor
d projektiver Tensor *m*
f tenseur *m* projectif
r проективный тензор *m*

7576 projective theorem
d projektiver Satz *m*
f théorème *m* projectif
r проективная теорема *f*

* **projective transfer** → 7554

7577 projective transformation; linear projective mapping; collineatory transformation
d projektive Transformation *f*; lineare projektive Abbildung *f*; kollineare Abbildung
f transformation *f* projective; application *f* projective linéaire; transformation colinéaire
r проективное преобразование *n*; линейное проективное отображение *n*; коллинеарное преобразование

* **projective variety** → 7562

7578 projective vector
d projektiver Vektor *m*
f vecteur *m* projectif

r проективный вектор *m*; вектор
проецирования

7579 projectivity
d Projektivität *f*
f projectivité *f*
r проективность *f*

7580 project name
d Projektname *m*
f nom *m* de projet
r имя *n* проекта

* **projector** → 7527

7581 projector; projection operator
d Projektor *m*; Projektionsoperator *m*
f projecteur *m*; opérateur *m* de projection
r проектор *m*; проекционный оператор *m*;
оператор проектирования

7582 projector light
d Projektorlicht *n*
f lumière *f* de projecteur
r свет *m* проектора

7583 project planning
d Planung *f* des Projekts
f planification *f* de projet
r планирование *n* проекта

7584 prolate; extended; stretched; elongated; prolonged
d verlängert; gestreckt
f allongé
r удлиненный

7585 prolate cycloid; extended cycloid
d verlängerte Zykloide *f*
f cycloïde *f* allongée
r удлиненная циклоида *f*

7586 prolate ellipsoid of revolution; prolate spheroid
d langgestrecktes Rotationsellipsoid *n*
f ellipsoïde *m* de révolution allongé
r вытянутый эллипсоид *m* вращения

7587 prolate epicycloid; extended epicycloid
d verlängerte Epizykloide *f*
f épicycloïde *f* allongée
r удлиненная эпициклоида *f*

7588 prolate hypocycloid; extended hypocycloid
d verlängerte Hypozykloide *f*
f hypocycloïde *f* allongée
r удлиненная гипоциклоида *f*

* **prolate spheroid** → 7586

* **prolog** → 7590

7589 prolog section
d Prologsektion *f*
f section *f* de prologue
r вводная секция *f*

7590 prolog[ue]
d Prolog *m*; Einleitungsteil *m*
f prologue *m*
r вводная часть *f*

7591 prolong *v*; elongate *v*; lengthen *v*; enlarge *v*
d verlängern
f allonger; prolonger; élargir
r удлинять; продолжать

* **prolongation** → 2113, 3382

* **prolonged** → 7584

7592 prolonged object
d verlängertes Objekt *n*
f objet *m* allongé
r удлиненный объект *m*

* **prompt** → 7594

7593 prompt; help [information]
d Prompt *n*; Hinweis *m*; Hilfsinformation *f*
f consigne *f*; prompt *m*; invite *f*; information *f* d'aide
r подсказка *f*; указание *n*; помощная
информация *f*; консультативная
информация

7594 prompt [character]
d Aufforderungszeichen *n*;
Bereitschaftszeichen *n*; Hinweiszeichen *n*
f caractère *m* de consigne
r знак *m* подсказки; приглашение *n*

7595 prompting
d Bedienerführung *f* [mittels Hinweiszeichen]
f incitation *f*; guidage *m*
r выдача *f* подсказки

7596 propagation
d Ausbreitung *f*; Verbreitung *f*; Fortpflanzung *f*
f propagation *f*
r распространение *n*

* **property** → 3719

7597 property bar
d Eigenschaftsleiste *f*
f barre *f* des propriétés
r лента *f* признаков

7598 property setting
d Eigenschaft-Einrichtung *f*

f établissement *m* de propriété
r установление *n* признака

7599 proportion
d Proportion *f*
f proportion *f*
r пропорция *f*

7600 proportional
d proportional; proportionell
f proportionnel
r пропорциональный

7601 proportionality
d Proportionalität *f*
f proportionnalité *f*
r пропорциональность *f*

* **proportionality factor** → 1647

7602 proportionally object resizing
d proportionale Objekt-Größenänderung *f*
f redimensionnement *m* proportionnellement d'objet
r пропорциональное переоразмерение *n* объекта

7603 proportionally spaced font
d Proportionalschriftsatz *m*
f police *f* à espacement proportionnel
r шрифт *m* с пропорциональной разрядкой

7604 protection; guard
d Schutz *m*
f protection *f*; garde *f*
r защита *f*

7605 protection key
d Schutzschlüssel *m*
f clé *f* de protection
r ключ *m* защиты

7606 prototype
d Prototyp *m*
f prototype *m*
r прототип *m*; [опытный] образец *m*

* **prototype drawing** → 3159

7607 prototype drawing file; seat file
d Prototypzeichnung-Datei *f*
f fichier *m* du dessin de base; fichier du dessin prototype
r файл *m* с чертежом-прототипом

7608 prototype graph; p-graph
d Graph *m* des Prototyps
f graphe *m* prototype
r граф *m* прототипа

7609 prototyping

d Prototypherstellung *f*
f maquettage *m*
r макетирование *n*

7610 provisional coordinates
d vorläufige Koordinaten *fpl*
f coordonnées *fpl* provisoires
r неуточненные координаты *fpl*; приближенные координаты

7611 proximity; vicinity; neighborhood
d Nachbarschaft *f*; Nähe *f*; Näherung *f*
f proximité *f*; ambiance *f*
r близость *f*; соседство *n*

7612 proximity zone
d Näherungszone *f*
f zone *f* de proximité
r зона *f* близости

7613 proxy graphics
d Proxy-Grafik *f*
f graphique *m* proximal; graphique de serveur mandaté
r графика *f* прокси-сервера

7614 proxy object
d Proxy-Objekt *n*
f objet *m* proximal
r объект *m* типа прокси-сервера

* **pseudo-** → 3226

7615 pseudocolor
d Pseudofarbe *f*; Falschfarbe *f*
f pseudocouleur *f*
r псевдоцвет *m*

7616 pseudocolor enhancement
d Pseudofarb[en]-Anreicherung *f*; Pseudofarb[en]-Erhöhung *f*
f amélioration *f* de pseudocouleur
r улучшение *n* псевдоцвета; расширение *n* псевдоцвета; псевдоцветное добавление *n*

7617 pseudocolor image
d Pseudofarb[en]bild *n*
f image *f* pseudocouleur
r псевдоцветное изображение *n*

7618 pseudocolor representation
d Falschfarb[en]darstellung *f*; Pseudofarb[en]darstellung *f*
f représentation *f* pseudocouleur
r псевдоцветное представление *n*

7619 pseudocolor transform
d Pseudofarb[en]-Änderung *f*
f transformation *f* pseudocouleur
r трансформация *f* псевдоцвета

7620 pseudo-3D graphics
  d Pseudo-3D Grafik *f*
  f graphique *m* pseudo-tridimensionnel
  r псевдо-3D графика *f*

7621 pseudo-3D image
  d Pseudo-3D-Bild *n*
  f image *f* pseudo 3D
  r псевдо-3D изображение *n*

7622 pseudographics; quasi graphics; character graphics
  d Pseudografik *f*; Quasi-Grafik *f*;
      Zeichengrafik *f*; Symbolgrafik *f*
  f pseudographique *m*; graphique *m* par
      caractères
  r псевдографика *f*

7623 pseudo-image
  d Pseudobild *n*
  f pseudo-image *f*
  r псевдо-изображение *n*; псевдообраз *m*

7624 pseudonode
  d Pseudoknoten *m*
  f pseudo-nœud *m*
  r псевдо-узел *m*

  * **pseudo-perspective** → 3700

7625 pseudo-skeleton
  d Pseudoskelett *n*
  f pseudo-squelette *f*
  r псевдо-скелет *m*

7626 pseudo-sphere
  d Pseudokugel *f*
  f pseudo-sphère *f*
  r псевдо-сфера *f*

7627 pseudo-square
  d Pseudoquadrat *n*
  f pseudo-carré *m*
  r псевдо-квадрат *m*

7628 psychedelic
  d psychedelisch
  f psychédélique
  r флюоресцирующий; яркий; броский;
      галлюциногенный

7629 psychedelic color
  d psychedelische Farbe *f*
  f couleur *f* psychédélique
  r флюоресцирующий цвет *m*

7630 psychedelic effect
  d psychedelischer Effekt *m*
  f effet *m* psychédélique
  r галлюциногенный эффект *m*

7631 publishing
  d Publizieren *n*; Publishing *n*; Verlagsgewerbe *f*
  f publication *f*
  r публикование *n*; издание *n*

  * **puck** → 2306

7632 pulldown list
  d Pulldown-Liste *f*
  f liste *f* déroulante
  r падающий список *m*

7633 pulldown menu; dropdown menu; tear-off menu
  d Pulldown-Menü *n*; Dropdown-Menü *n*;
      Rollmenü *n*
  f menu *m* déroulant
  r развернутое меню *n*; падающее меню;
      спускающееся меню

7634 pulldown window
  d Pulldown-Fenster *n*
  f fenêtre *f* déroulante
  r раскрывающееся [вниз] окно *n*; падающее
      окно

7635 punch effect
  d Punch-Effekt *m*
  f effet *m* de poinçonnage
  r эффект *m* штампа; штамповальный эффект

  * **punctiform** *adj* → 7232

  * **punctuate** *v* → 3052

7636 punctuation marks
  d Satzzeichen *npl*
  f signes *mpl* de ponctuation
  r знаки *mpl* препинания

7637 pure color
  d klare Farbe *f*; reine Farbe
  f couleur *f* pure
  r чистый цвет *m*

7638 purge command
  d Reinigungsbefehl *m*
  f commande *f* de purification
  r команда *f* очистки

  * **purging** → 1535

  * **purification** → 1535

7639 push *v*
  d hinzufügen
  f pousser; ajouter
  r толкать; прибавлять

7640 puzzle
  d Rätsel *n*; Puzzle *n*

f casse-tête *m*; énigme *f*; puzzle *m*
r картинка-загадка *f*

7641 puzzle filter
  d Puzzle-Filter *m*
  f filtre *m* d'énigme
  r фильтр *m* загадки

7642 pyramid
  d Pyramide *f*
  f pyramide *f*
  r пирамида *f*

7643 pyramidal chart
  d pyramidales Diagramm *n*
  f diagramme *m* pyramidal
  r пирамидальная диаграмма *f*

7644 pyramidal filtering
  d pyramidale Filtrierung *f*
  f filtrage *m* pyramidal
  r пирамидальное фильтрирование *n*

7645 pyramidal surface
  d Pyramidenfläche *f*; Pyramidenoberfläche *f*
  f surface *f* pyramidale
  r пирамидальная поверхность *f*

Q

7646 quad density
d Vierfachdichte *f*
f densité *f* quadruple
r четырехкратная плотность *f*

7647 quadrangle; quad; tetragon
d Viereck *n*; Quadrangel *n*
f quadrangle *m*; quad *m*
r четырехвершинник *m*; четырехугольник *m*

7648 quadrangular
d viereckig
f quadrangulaire
r четырехугольный

7649 quadrangular prism
d Vierkantprisma *n*; viereckiges Prisma *n*; vierseitiges Prisma
f prisme *m* quadrangulaire
r четырехугольная призма *f*

7650 quadrangular pyramid
d vierseitige Pyramide *f*
f pyramide *f* quadrangulaire; pyramide tétraédrique
r четырехугольная пирамида *f*; четырехгранная пирамида

7651 quadrant
d Quadrant *m*
f quadrant *m*
r квадрант *m*

7652 quadrant snap
d Quadrantfang *m*
f accrochage *m* au quadrant
r привязка *f* к квадранту

7653 quadr[at]ic; square-low
d quadratisch
f quadratique
r квадрат[ич]ный; квадратурный

7654 quadratic smoothing
d quadratische Glättung *f*
f lissage *m* quadratique
r квадратичное сглаживание *n*

7655 quadratic spline
d quadratischer Spline *m*
f spline *m* quadratique
r квадратический сплайн *m*

7656 quadrichromy
d Quadrichromie *f*
f quadrichromie *f*
r четырехцветность *f*

7657 quadric shape
d Quadriform *f*
f forme *f* quadratique
r четырехсторонняя фигура *f*

7658 quadrifolium
d Quadrifolium *n*; Vierblatt *n*
f quadrifolium *m*
r четырехлистник *m*

7659 quadrilateral *adj*
d vierseitig
f quadrilatéral
r четырехсторонний

7660 quadrilateral
d Vierseit *n*
f quadrilatère *m*
r четырехсторонник *m*

7661 quadrilateral solid fill
d Füllung *f* des vierseitigen Körpers
f remplissage *m* de solide quadrilatéral
r закрашивание *n* четырехстороннего монолитного тела

7662 quadtone
(four inks)
d Vierfachton *m*
f quad-ton *m*
r черно-белое полутоновое изображение *n*, отпечатанное четырьмя красками

7663 quadtree
d Quad-Tree *n*; Viererbaum *m*
f arbre *m* quaternaire; quad-tree *m*
r квадритомическое дерево *n*

7664 quality
d Güte f; Qualität f
f qualité f
r качество n; добротность f

7665 quality inspection
d Prüfung f der Qualität
f inspection f de qualité
r проверка f качества

* **quantifier → 2800**

7666 quantitative character
d quantitatives Merkmal n
f caractère m quantitatif
r количественный признак m

7667 quantitative estimation
d quantitative Schätzung f
f estimation f quantitative
r количественная оценка f

7668 quantity
d Quantität f
f quantité f
r количество n

* **quantization → 2901**

* **quantization distortion → 7670**

* **quantization noise → 7670**

7669 quantization step; quantizing step; quantizing value
d Quantisierungsschritt m;
  Quantisierungswert m
f pas m de quantification
r шаг m квантования

* **quantizing → 2901**

7670 quantizing distortion; quantizing noise; quantization distortion; quantization noise
d Quantisierungsverzerrung f;
  Quantisierungsgeräusch n;
  Quantisierungsrauschen n
f distorsion f de quantification; bruit m de quantification
r искажение n квантования

7671 quantizing interval
d Quantisierungsintervall n
f intervalle m de quantification
r интервал m квантования

* **quantizing noise → 7670**

* **quantizing step → 7669**

* **quantizing value → 7669**

7672 quantum
d Quantum n; Quant n
f quantum m
r квант m

7673 quantum noise
d Quantenrauschen n
f bruit m quantique
r квантовый шум m

* **quasi graphics → 7622**

7674 quasi-harmonic
d quasiharmonisch
f quasi-harmonique
r квазигармонический

7675 quasilinear
d quasilinear
f quasi-linéaire
r квазилинейный

7676 quasi-monochromatic
d quasimonochromatisch
f quasi-monochromatique
r квазимонохроматический

7677 quasi-optical
d quasioptisch
f quasi-optique
r квазиоптический

7678 quaternary
d quaternär
f quaternaire
r четверичный; квартерный

7679 quaternary domain
d quaternäres Gebiet n
f domaine m quaternaire
r кватернарная область f

* **query → 8083**

7680 query by image content; QBIC
d bildinhaltliche Abfrage f
f interrogation f par le continu d'image
r запрос m содержанием изображения

7681 query criteria
d Abfrage-Kriterium n
f critère m d'interrogation
r критерий m запроса

7682 query server
d Abfrage-Server m

  f serveur *m* d'interrogation

  r сервер *m* опросов

7683 query transaction

  d Abfrage-Transaktion *f*

  f transaction *f* d'interrogation

  r транзакция *f* запроса

7684 question mark

  (?)

  d Fragezeichen *n*

  f point *m* d'interrogation

  r вопросительный знак *m*

7685 queue; waiting line

  d Warteschlange *f*

  f queue *f*; file *f* d'attente

  r очередь *f*

7686 quick digitalization

  d Schnelldigitalisierung *f*

  f digitalisation *f* rapide

  r быстрое оцифрование *n*

7687 quick reference

  d schneller Verweis *m*

  f référence *f* rapide

  r быстрая ссылка *f*

7688 quick snap

  d schneller Fang *m*

  f accrochage *m* rapide

  r быстрое привязывание *n*

7689 quick view

  d Schnellansicht *f*

  f vue *f* rapide

  r быстрый просмотр *m*

  * **quit → 3570**

7690 quota

  d Quote *f*

  f quota *m*

  r процентная часть *f*, доля *f*, квота *f*

  * **quotation mark → 469**

  * **quotation marks → 3090**

  * **quote marks → 3090**

  * **quotes → 3090**

R

* **rad** → 7698

7691 radial
 d radial; Radial-
 f radial
 r радиальный

7692 radial basic function
 d radiale Basisfunktion *f*
 f fonction *f* de base radiale
 r радиальная базисная функция *f*

7693 radial B-spline
 d radialer B-Spline *m*
 f B-spline *m* radial
 r радиальный В-сплайн *m*

7694 radial component
 d Radialkomponente *f*
 f component *m* radial
 r радиальный элемент *m*

7695 radial dimensions
 d Radialdimensionen *fpl*
 f cotations *fpl* de rayon; dimensions *fpl* radiaux
 r радиальное оразмерение *n*; размеры *mpl* радиуса

7696 radial fill
 d Radialfüllung *f*
 f remplissage *m* radial
 r радиальное заполнение *n*

* **radial network** → 9168

7697 radial slit domain
 d Radialschlitzgebiet *n*; Radialschlitzbereich *m*
 f plan *m* muni de fentes radiaux
 r область *f* с радиальными разрезами

7698 radian; rad
 d Radiant *m*
 f radian *m*
 r радиан *m*

7699 radiance; radiant emittance; radiant intensity
 d Strahl[en]dichte *f*; Strahlungsdichte *f*; Strahlstärke *f*; Strahlungsintensität *f*
 f radiance *f*; intensité *f* de rayonnement; intensité radiante
 r яркость *f* излучения; плотность *f* луча; интенситет *m* излучения; лучистость *f*

7700 radiance equation
 d Gleichung *f* der Strahl[en]dichte
 f équation *f* de radiance
 r уравнение *n* интенситета излучения

7701 radian measure; circular measure
 d Bogenmaß *n*
 f mesure *f* en radians
 r радианная мера *f*

* **radian measure of an angle** → 5873

* **radiant** → 3398

7702 radiant efficiency; radiative efficiency
 d Strahlungseffektivität *f*
 f rendement *m* en radiation
 r эффективность *f* излучения; коэффициент *m* полезного действия источника излучения

* **radiant emittance** → 7699

* **radiant intensity** → 7699

7703 radiate *v*
 d ausstrahlen; strahlen
 f radier; rayonner; émettre
 r излучать

* **radiated** → 7705

7704 radiation
 d Strahlung *f*
 f radiation *f*; rayonnement *m*
 r радиация *f*

* **radiation angle** → 3394

7705 radiative; radiated; emissive
 d Strahlung-
 f radiatif; émissif
 r излучаемый; излучательный

* **radiative efficiency** → 7702

7706 radical axis
 d Potenzgerade *f*; Potenzlinie *f*; Chordale *f*
 f axe *m* radical; cordale *f*
 r радикальная ось *f*

7707 radical axis of two circles
 d Potenzlinie *f* zweier Kreise
 f axe *m* radical de deux cercles
 r радикальная ось *f* двух окружностей

7708 radical centre
 d Potenzzentrum *n*; Potenzpunkt *m*
 f centre *m* radical
 r радикальный центр *m*

7709 radical plane
d Potenzebene *f*
f plan *m* radical
r радикальная плоскость *f*

7710 radio button
d Radioschaltfläche *f*; rundes Optionsfeld *n*
f bouton *m* radio; bouton d'option; cercle *m* d'option
r радиокнопка *f*; зависимая кнопка *f*

7711 radiosity; adaptive meshing
(of global illumination model)
d Radiosity *n*
f radiosité *f*
r диффузное отражение *n*; излучательность *f*

7712 radiosity algorithm
d Radiosity-Algorithmus *m*
f algorithme *m* de radiosité
r алгоритм *m* диффузного отражения

7713 radiosity model
d Radiosity-Modell *n*
f modèle *m* de radiosité
r модель *f* излучательности; модель диффузного отражения

7714 radius
d Radius *m*; Halbmesser *m*
f rayon *m*
r радиус *m*

* **radius at bend** → 7715

7715 radius of curvature; curvature radius; bend[ing] radius; radius at bend
d Krümmungsradius *m*; Biegeradius *m*; Krümmungshalbmesser *m*
f rayon *m* de courbure
r радиус *m* изгиба; радиус кривизны

7716 radius of curvature of the parabola
d Krümmungsradius *m* der Parabel
f rayon *m* de courbure de la parabole
r радиус *m* кривизны параболы

7717 radius of gyration
d Gyrationsradius *m*; Gyroradius *m*
f rayon *m* de giration
r радиус *m* кругового движения; радиус круговращательного движения; радиус циркуляции

7718 radius of principal curvature; principal radius of curvature
d Hauptkrümmungsradius *m*
f rayon *m* de courbure principal
r радиус *m* главной кривизны

7719 radius of the circumscribed circle; circumradius; long radius
d Radius *m* des Umkreises; Umkreisradius *m*
f rayon *m* du cercle circonscrit
r радиус *m* описанной окружности

7720 radius of the circumsphere; circumradius
d Radius *m* der Umkugel; Umkugelradius *m*
f rayon *m* de la sphère circonscrite
r радиус *m* описанной сферы

7721 radius of the escribed circle; exradius
d Ankreisradius *m*
f rayon *m* du cercle exinscrit
r радиус *m* вневписанной окружности

7722 radius of the escribed sphere; exradius
d Ankugelradius *m*
f rayon *m* de la sphère exinscrite
r радиус *m* вневписанной сферы

7723 radius of the inscribed circle; inradius
d Inkreisradius *m*; Radius *m* des Inkreises
f rayon *m* du cercle inscrit
r радиус *m* вписанной окружности

7724 radius of the inscribed sphere; inradius
d Inkugelradius *m*; Radius *m* der Inkugel
f rayon *m* de la sphère inscrite
r радиус *m* вписанной сферы

7725 radius of torsion; torsion radius
d Torsionsradius *m*; Windungsradius *m*
f rayon *m* de torsion
r радиус *m* кручения

7726 rainbow color map
d Regenbogen-Farbkarte *f*
f carte *f* de couleurs d'arc-en-ciel
r таблица *f* цветов радуги

7727 rainbow colors
d Regenbogenfarbe *fpl*
f couleurs *fpl* d'arc-en-ciel
r цвета *mpl* радуги

* **ramification** → 1124

7728 random; aleatory; stochastic; accidental; arbitrary
d zufällig; Zufalls-; willkürlich; stochastisch
f aléatoire; arbitraire; accidentel; fortuit; stochastique
r случайный; стохастический; произвольный

7729 random access
d wahlfreier Zugriff *m*
f accès *m* aléatoire
r произвольный доступ *m*

7730 **random color**
   d zufällige Farbe *f*
   f couleur *f* arbitraire; couleur aléatoire
   r случайный цвет *m*

7731 **random graph**
   d zufälliger Graph *m*
   f graphe *m* arbitraire
   r стохастический граф *m*

   * **randomization** → 7732

7732 **randomizing; randomization; hashing**
   d willkürliche Verteilung *f*; Randomisierung *f*;
      Hashing *n*
   f randomisation *f*; arrangement *m* au hasard;
      hashing *m*; transformation *f* aléatoire
   r рандомизация *f*; хэширование *n*;
      расположение *n* в случайном порядке

7733 **randomness**
   d Wahllosigkeit *f*
   f aspect *m* aléatoire; caractère *m* aléatoire
   r стохастичность *f*; случайность *f*

   * **random noise** → 4115

7734 **random point**
   d zufälliger Punkt *m*
   f point *m* aléatoire
   r случайная точка *f*

7735 **random point selection**
   d Auswahl *f* des zufälligen Punkts
   f sélection *f* de point aléatoire
   r выбор *m* случайной точки

7736 **random scan**
   d zufälliges Scannen *n*
   f balayage *m* cavalier
   r свободное сканирование *n*; произвольное
      сканирование

7737 **random texture**
   d zufällige Textur *f*
   f texture *f* arbitraire
   r произвольная текстура *f*

7738 **range**
   d Umfang *m*; Reichweite *f*; Wertebereich *m*;
      Diapason *m*
   f plage *f*; rangée *f*
   r охват *m*; область *f* значений; диапазон *m*

   * **range** → 8936, 10518

7739 **range kerning**
   d Umfang-Unterschneidung *f*
   f interlettrage *m* de diapason; crénelage *m* de
      plage

   r кернинг *m* диапазона; кернинг интервала;
      уменьшение *n* межзнакового интервала

7740 **range of colors; color gamma; color
      gamut; color range**
   d Farb[en]umfang *f*; Farben-Gamut *n*;
      Farbgamut *n*
   f gamme *f* de couleurs
   r диапазон *m* цветов; хроматический
      диапазон

7741 **range of magnification**
   d Vergrößerungsbereich *m*
   f latitude *f* d'agrandissement; limite *f*
      d'augmentation
   r граница *f* увеличения; степень *f*
      увеличения

7742 **range of points; point range; series of
      points; row of points; pencil of points**
   d Punktreihe *f*; Punkt[e]büschel *n*
   f ponctuelle *f*; division *f* rectiligne
   r ряд *m* точек

7743 **range of sight; range of visibility; range of
      vision**
   d Sehweite *f*
   f portée *f* de la vue; portée de visibilité
   r дальность *f* видимости; предел *m*
      видимости; расстояние *n* видимости

   * **range of visibility** → 7743

   * **range of vision** → 7743

7744 **range selection**
   d Bereichsauswahl *f*
   f sélection *f* de rangée
   r выбор *m* охвата

7745 **rank**
   d Rang *m*
   f rang *m*
   r ранг *m*

7746 **ranking**
   d Rangierung *f*
   f rangement *m*
   r ранжирование *n*; упорядочение *n*

7747 **raster; scan pattern; grid**
      (of a screen)
   d Raster *m*; Grid *n*
   f trame *f*; rastre *m*; grille *f*
   r растр *m*; решетка *f*; сетка *f*

7748 **raster angle; screen angle**
   d Rasterwinkel *m*
   f angle *m* de rastre; angle de trame
   r угол *m* [поворота] растра; угол установки
      растра

7749 raster board; grid board
d Raster[leiter]platte *f*
f plaque *f* à trame; plaque à grille
r плата *f* с координатной сеткой

7750 raster conversion
d Rasterkonvertierung *f*
f conversion *f* rastre
r растровое преобразование *n*

7751 raster count
d Rasterzahl[ung] *f*
f nombre *m* de pixels de trame; comptage *m* de grilles; définition *f* de trame
r число *n* элементов растра; отсчет *m* адресуемых координат

7752 raster data model
d Modell *n* der Rasterdaten
f modèle *m* de données de trame
r модель *f* данных растра

7753 raster density
d Rasterdichte *f*
f densité *f* de rastre; densité de trame
r плотность *f* растра

7754 raster direction
d Rasterrichtung *f*
f direction *f* de rastre
r направление *n* растра

7755 raster display; matrix display; raster monitor
d Rasterbildschirm *m*; Rasterdisplay *n*; Rastermonitor *m*; Matrixanzeige *f*
f écran *m* dot-matrice; écran à balayage tramé; écran à balayage récurrent; visu *m* matriciel; visu à quadrillage
r растровый дисплей *m*; матричный дисплей; мозаичный индикатор *m*

7756 raster file
d Rasterdatei *f*
f fichier *m* rastre; fichier trame
r растровый файл *m*

7757 raster file format
d Format *n* der Rasterdatei
f format *m* de fichier rastre
r формат *m* растрового файла

7758 raster font
d Rasterschrift *f*
f police *f* de caractères tramés; police de caractères en mode points
r растровый фонт *m*

7759 raster graphics; bitmap[ped] graphics; pixel graphics; scan graphics
d Rastergrafik *f*; Bitmap-Grafik *f*; Pixel-Grafik *f*; Punktgrafik *f*
f graphique *m* rastre; graphique trame; infographie *f* par quadrillage; infographie par balayage tramé; graphique bitmap; graphique de visualisation par bits; graphique à pixels
r растровая графика *f*; графика с растровым отображением; точечная графика

7760 raster graphics system
d rastergrafisches System *n*
f système *m* graphique trame
r растровая графическая система *f*

7761 raster grid
d Rastergitter *n*
f grille *f* rastre
r растровая сетка *f*

7762 raster image; matrix image; bitmap [image]
d Rasterbild *n*; Bitmap *n*; Bitmap-Bild *n*
f image *f* matricielle; image rastre; image pixélisée; image à points; bitmap *m*
r растровое изображение *n*; побитовое отображение *n*; поразрядное отображение; точечное изображение

7763 raster image file format; RIFF
d RIFF-Format *n*
f format *m* RIFF
r формат *m* RIFF

7764 raster image memory
d Rasterbildspeicher *m*
f mémoire *f* d'images rastres
r память *f* растровых изображений

7765 raster-image processor
d Raster-Image-Prozessor *m*
f processeur *m* d'images matricielles
r процессор *m* растровых изображений

7766 rasterization
d Rasterung *f*
f rastérisation *f*
r растеризация *f*; растрирование *n*

7767 rasterize *v*
d rastern
f rastériser
r растеризовать; преобразовывать в растровый формат

7768 raster line; gridline
d Rasterlinie *f*
f ligne *f* de rastre; ligne de trame; ligne de grille
r линия *f* растра; растровая линия; линия сетки

* **raster monitor** → 7755

7769 raster object; bitmap object
d Rasterobjekt n; Bitmap-Objekt n
f objet m rastre; objet bitmap
r растровый объект m; точечный объект

* **raster overlay** → 7771

7770 raster pattern
d Rastermuster n
f modèle m trame
r растровая модель f

7771 raster[-pattern] overlay
d Rastermuster-Overlay n
f recouvrement m de [modèle] trame
r перекрытие n растровой модели

7772 raster plotter
d Rasterplotter m
f traceur m par ligne; traceur à trame
r растровый графопостроитель m

7773 raster plotting
d Rasterplotten n
f traçage m par ligne; traçage à trame
r растровое вычерчивание n

* **raster point** → 8366

7774 raster printer
d Rasterdrucker m
f imprimante f rastre
r растровый принтер m

* **raster scan** → 7776

7775 raster-scan device
d Rasterscan-Gerät n
f dispositif m à balayage de trame
r растровое сканирующее устройство n

7776 raster scan[ning]
d Rasterscannen n; Rasterabtastung f
f balayage m ligne par ligne; balayage
récurrent; balayage de trame
r растровое сканирование n

7777 raster-scan writing
d Rasterscan-Schreiben n
f enregistrement m trame
r растровая запись f

7778 raster to vector conversion; raster-vector conversion
d Raster-Vertor-Konvertierung f
f conversion f de rastre en vecteur
r растрово-векторное преобразование n

7779 raster unit
d Rastereinheit f
f unité f de trame
r растровая единица f

* **raster-vector conversion** → 7778

* **rate** → 1641, 9029

* **rated** → 6240

* **rating** → 6242

7780 ratio
d Verhältnis n; Wechselbeziehung f
f rapport m
r отношение n; соотношение n

7781 rational Bézier curves
d rationale Bézier-Kurven fpl
f courbes fpl de Bézier rationnelles
r рациональные кривые fpl Безье

* **ratio of foreshortening** → 7782

7782 ratio of reduction; ratio of foreshortening
(in axonometry)
d Verkürzungsverhältnis n;
Reduktionsverhältnis n
f rapport m de réduction
r [co]отношение n редуцирования;
отношение уменьшения

* **ratio of similitude** → 4673

7783 ratio of slope
d Neigungsverhältnis n
f rapport m de pente
r [co]отношение n уклона

* **ray** → 869, 4474

7784 ray casting
d Ray-Casting n
f transtypage m de rayons; lancer m de rayons
r отслеживание n лучей

7785 ray-casting technique
d Ray-Casting-Technik f
f technique f de transtypage
r техника f отслеживания лучей

7786 ray-convex polygon intersection
d Strahl-Konvexpolygon-Durchschnitt m
f intersection f rayon-polygone convexe
r пересечение n луча и выпуклого
многоугольника

7787 ray direction
d Strahlrichtung f

f direction *f* de rayon
r направление *n* луча

7788 ray equation
d Strahlengleichung *f*
f équation *f* des rayons
r лучевое уравнение *n*

7789 ray object; beam object
d Strahlobjekt *n*
f objet *m* rayon
r объект *m* типа луча

7790 ray-object intersection
d Strahl-Objekt-Durchschnitt *m*
f intersection *f* rayon-objet
r пересечение *n* луч-объект

* **ray of similarity** → 8696

* **ray path** → 7796

7791 ray-plane intersection
d Strahl-Ebene-Durchschnitt *m*
f intersection *f* rayon-plan
r пересечение *n* луч-плоскость

7792 raytrace rendering
d Ray-Trace-Rendering *n*
f rendu *m* lancé de rayons
r тонирование *n* трассировкой лучей;
рендеринг *m* трассировкой лучей

7793 raytracing
d Ray-Tracing *n*; Strahlverfolgungstechnik *f*
f raytracing *m*; lancé *m* de rayons
r трассировка *f* лучей

7794 raytracing application
d Ray-Tracing-Anwendung *f*
f application *f* de raytracing
r приложение *n* трассировки лучей

7795 raytracing method
d Ray-Tracing-Methode *f*
f méthode *f* de raytracing
r метод *m* трассировки лучей

7796 ray trajectory; ray path; light path
d Strahlengang *m*; Strahlenbahn *f*;
Strahlenverlauf *m*; Strahlweg *m*
f trajectoire *f* des rayons [optiques]; trajet *m* de
lumière; trajet de rayons; marche *f* de rayons
r ход *m* лучей

7797 ray-triangle intersection
d Strahl-Dreieck-Durchschnitt *m*
f intersection *f* rayon-triangle
r пересечение *n* луч-треугольник

* **reachability** → 55

* **read** → 7800

7798 read *v*; **sense** *v*
d lesen; ablesen
f lire
r читать; считывать

7799 readability
d Lesbarkeit *f*
f lisibilité *f*
r удобочитаемость *f*

7800 read[ing]; sensing
d Lesen *n*; Ablesen *n*; Ablesung *f*
f lecture *f*
r чтение *n*; считывание *n*

7801 reading line
d Ablesestrich *m*
f division *f* de lecture; trait *m* de repère
r отсчетный штрих *m*

7802 read[ing] rate; read[ing] speed
d Lesegeschwindigkeit *f*; Leserate *f*
f vitesse *f* de lecture
r скорость *f* чтения; скорость считывания

* **reading speed** → 7802

* **read rate** → 7802

* **read speed** → 7802

7803 real
d real; Real-; reell; Echt-
f réel
r реальный; вещественный

7804 real image
d reales Bild *n*
f image *f* réelle
r действительное изображение *n*; реальное
изображение

7805 realism
d Realismus *m*
f réalisme *m*
r реализм *m*

7806 realistic
d realistisch
f réaliste
r реалистический; реалистичный

7807 realistic computer graphics
d realistische Computergrafik *f*
f graphique *m* d'ordinateur réaliste
r реалистическая компьютерная графика *f*

7808 realistic image
   d realistisches Bild *n*
   f image *f* réaliste
   r реалистическое изображение *n*

7809 realistic image synthesis
   d Synthese *f* des realistischen Bilds
   f synthèse *f* d'image réaliste
   r синтез *m* реалистического изображения

7810 realistic representation
   d realistische Darstellung *f*; realitätsnahe Darstellung
   f représentation *f* réaliste
   r реалистическое представление *n*

7811 realistic view
   d realistische Ansicht *f*; realistischer Ausblick *m*
   f aspect *m* réaliste
   r реалистический вид *m*

7812 realistic virtual human; avatar
   (virtual human representing the user)
   d Avatar *m*
   f avatar *m*
   r аватар *m*; олицетворение *n* пользователя; воплощение *n* пользователя (в виртуальной реальности)

7813 reality
   d Realität *f*; Wirklichkeit *f*
   f réalité *f*
   r действительность *f*; реальность *f*; вещественность *f*

7814 real reverse[d] image
   d reales umgekehrtes Bild *n*
   f image *f* réelle renversée
   r действительное перевернутое изображение *n*

   * **real reverse image**→ 7814

7815 realtime animation
   d Realzeitanimation *f*
   f animation *f* en temps réel
   r анимация *f* в реальном времени

7816 realtime blending
   d Realzeitmischung *f*
   f mélange *m* en temps réel
   r смешение *n* в реальном времени

7817 realtime [computer] graphics
   d Realzeitgrafik *f*; Echtzeit-Computer-Grafik *f*
   f graphique *m* en temps réel
   r графика *f* в реальном времени

7818 realtime 3D shared virtual world
   d gemeinschaftliche 3D-Realzeit-Virtualwelt *f*
   f monde *m* virtuel 3D partagé en temps réel
   r общедоступный трехмерный виртуальный мир *m* в реальном времени

7819 realtime 3D virtual world
   d Realzeit-3D-Virtualwelt *f*
   f monde *m* virtuel 3D en temps réel
   r трехмерный виртуальный мир *m* в реальном времени

7820 realtime 3D visualization
   d Realzeit-3D-Visualisierung *f*
   f visualisation *f* tridimensionnelle en temps réel
   r трехмерная визуализация *f* в реальном времени

7821 realtime gesture recognition system
   d Realzeit-Gestenerkennungsystem *n*
   f système *m* de reconnaissance des gestes en temps réel
   r система *f* распознавания жестов в реальном времени

   * **realtime graphics** → 7817

7822 realtime imaging
   d Echtzeit-Abbildung *f*
   f imagerie *f* en temps réel
   r изображение *n* в реальном времени

7823 realtime-oriented 3D graphics toolkit
   d Realzeit-orientierter 3D-Grafikwerkzeugsatz *m*
   f kit *m* d'instruments de graphique 3D en temps réel
   r инструментальный набор *m* трехмерной графики в реальном времени

7824 realtime processing
   d Echtzeitverarbeitung *f*; Realzeitverarbeitung *f*
   f traitement *m* en temps réel
   r обработка *f* в реальном времени

7825 realtime rendering
   d Realzeitrendering *n*
   f rendu *m* en temps réel
   r тонирование *n* в реальном времени; рендеринг *m* в реальном времени

7826 realtime sampling
   d Realzeit-Stichprobenauswahl *f*
   f échantillonnage *m* en temps réel
   r выборка *f* в реальном времени

7827 realtime surface shading
   d Realzeit-Flächenschattierung *f*
   f ombrage *m* de surface en temps réel
   r оттенение *n* поверхности в реальном времени

7828 **realtime video; live video**
  d Realzeit-Video *n*
  f vidéo *m* en temps réel
  r реальное видео *n*; видео в реальном
     [масштабе] времени; "живое" видео

7829 **realtime video image mapping**
  d Realzeitmapping *n* der Videobilder
  f mappage *m* de vidéo-image en temps réel
  r отображение *n* видеоизображения в
     реальном времени

7830 **realtime virtual-human body**
  d virtueller menschlicher Körper *m* in Realzeit
  f corps *m* d'homme virtuel en temps réel
  r тело *n* виртуального человека в реальном
     времени

7831 **realtime virtual humans**
  d virtuelle Menschen *mpl* in Realzeit
  f hommes *mpl* virtuels en temps réel; monde *m*
     virtuel en temps réel
  r виртуальные люди *pl*в реальном времени

7832 **realtime visual simulation**
  d visuelle Simulation *f* in Realzeit
  f simulation *f* visuelle en temps réel
  r визуальная симуляция *f* в реальном
     времени

7833 **realtime zooming**
  d Realzeitzoomen *n*
  f zoom *m* en temps réel
  r масштабирование *n* в реальном времени

7834 **real world**
  d reale Welt *f*
  f monde *m* réel
  r реальный мир *m*

7835 **real-world object**
  d Objekt *n* der realen Welt
  f objet *m* de monde réel
  r объект *m* реального мира

7836 **real-world studio**
  d Studio *n* der realen Welt
  f studio *m* de monde réel
  r студия *f* реального мира

7837 **rear focus**
  d hinterer Brennpunkt *m*
  f foyer *m* postérieur
  r задний фокус *m*

7838 **rear node**
  d hinterer Knotenpunkt *m*
  f nœud *m* postérieur; nœud arrière
  r задняя узловая точка *f*

* **rear projection** → 7839

7839 **rear [screen] projection; background
     projection**
  d Rückprojektion *f*;
     Hinterleinwand-Projektion *f*;
     Durchprojektion *f*
  f projection *f* postérieure; projection par
     transparence
  r задняя проекция *f*; рирпроекция *f*

7840 **rear view; back view**
  d hintere Ansicht *f*; Rückansicht *f*
  f vue *f* arrière
  r задний вид *m*; вид сзади

* **recept** → 7841

7841 **recept[ion]**
  d Empfang *m*; Aufnahme *f*
  f réception *f*
  r прием *m*; получение *n*

7842 **receptor**
  d Rezeptor *m*
  f récepteur *m*
  r рецептор *m*

* **reciprocation** → 3220

* **reciprocity** → 3220

* **reckon** *v* → 1214

7843 **recognition**
  d Erkennung *f*
  f reconnaissance *f*
  r распознавание *n*; различение *n*

7844 **recognition logic**
  d Erkennungslogik *f*
  f logique *f* de reconnaissance
  r логика *f* распознавания

7845 **recognize** *v*
  d erkennen
  f reconnaître
  r распознавать

7846 **recognizer**
  d Erkennungseinrichtung *f*
  f reconnaisseur *m*
  r устройство *n* распознавания

7847 **recoloring**
  d wiederholte Färbung *f*
  f récoloriage *m*
  r повторное раскрашивание *n*; повторная
     раскраска *f*

7848 reconfiguration; reconfiguring
   d Rekonfigurierung *f*
   f reconfiguration *f*
   r реконфигурация *f*

   * **reconfiguring** → **7848**

   * **record** *v* → **10480**

   * **recording** → **10481**

7849 recover *v*; **restore** *v*
   d wiederherstellen; wiedereinsetzen
   f récupérer; regagner; restaurer; restituer; remettre
   r восстанавливать

7850 rectangle
   d Rechteck *n*
   f rectangle *m*
   r прямоугольник *m*

7851 rectangle corner
   d Rechteckecke *f*
   f coin *m* rectangulaire
   r прямоугольная вершина *f*

7852 rectangle of selection
   d Auswahlrechteck *n*
   f rectangle *m* de sélection
   r прямоугольник *m* выбора

7853 rectangle tool
   d Rechteck-Hilfsmittel *n*
   f outil *m* "rectangle"
   r инструмент *m* черчения прямоугольника

7854 rectangle with rounded corners
   d Rechteck *m* mit abgerundeten Ecken
   f rectangle *m* à coins arrondis
   r прямоугольник *m* с округленными углами

7855 rectangular; right-angled
   d rechtwinklig; rechteckig; Rechteck-
   f rectangulaire
   r прямоугольный

7856 rectangular area
   d rechteckiger Bereich *m*
   f zone *f* rectangulaire
   r прямоугольная область *f*

7857 rectangular array
   d rechteckiges Feld *n*
   f réseau *m* rectangulaire; tableau *m* rectangulaire
   r прямоугольный массив *m*

7858 rectangular [Cartesian] coordinates; normal coordinates

   d rechtwinklige [kartesische] Koordinaten *fpl*
   f coordonnées *fpl* [cartésiennes] rectangulaires
   r прямоугольные [декартовы] координаты *fpl*

7859 rectangular [Cartesian] coordinate system
   d rechtwinkliges [kartesisches] Koordinatensystem *n*
   f système *m* de coordonnées [cartésiennes] rectangulaires
   r [декартова] прямоугольная система *f* координат

7860 rectangular cell
   d rechtwinklige Zelle *f*
   f cellule *f* rectangulaire
   r прямоугольная клетка *f*

7861 rectangular clipping boundary
   d Grenze *f* des rechtwinkligen Schneidens
   f limite *f* de découpage rectangulaire
   r прямоугольная граница *f* отсекания

   * **rectangular coordinates** → **7858**

   * **rectangular coordinate system** → **7859**

7862 rectangular cross-section
   d rechteckiger Querschnitt *m*
   f section *f* rectangulaire
   r прямоугольное поперечное сечение *n*

   * **rectangular hyperbola** → **3501**

7863 rectangularity
   d Rechtwinkligkeit *f*
   f rectangularité *f*
   r свойство *n* быть прямоугольным

7864 rectangular mesh
   d rechteckige Masche *f*
   f maille *f* rectangulaire
   r прямоугольная сеть *f*

7865 rectangular parallelepiped; cuboid
   d Quader *m*; Rechtkant *m*
   f parallélépipède *m* rectangle; quadrone *m*
   r прямоугольный параллелепипед *m*; кубоид *m*

7866 rectangular parametrization
   d rechtwinklige Parametrisierung *f*
   f paramétrisation *f* rectangulaire
   r прямоугольная параметризация *f*

7867 rectangular polyline
   d rechtwinklige Polylinie *f*
   f polyligne *f* rectangulaire
   r прямоугольная полилиния *f*

7868 rectangular prism; right[-angled] prism
  d rechtwinkliges Prisma *n*
  f prisme *m* rectangulaire; prisme rectangle
  r прямоугольная призма *f*

7869 rectangular space coordinates
  d rechtwinklige Raumkoordinates *fpl*
  f coordonnées *fpl* spatiaux rectangulaires
  r прямоугольные пространственные
       координаты *fpl*

7870 rectangular trapezium
  d rechtwinkliges Trapez *n*
  f trapèze *m* rectangle
  r прямоугольная трапеция *f*

7871 rectangular viewport
  d rechtwinkliges Ansichtsfenster *n*
  f clôture *f* rectangulaire
  r прямоугольная область *f* просмотра;
       ортогональное окно *n* просмотра

7872 rectangular window; orthogonal window
  d rechtwinkliges Fenster *n*
  f fenêtre *f* rectangulaire; fenêtre orthogonale
  r прямоугольное окно *n*

7873 rectifiable curve
  d rektifizierbare Kurve *f*; streckbare Kurve
  f courbe *f* rectifiable
  r спрямляемая кривая *f*

7874 rectification
       (of a curve)
  d Rektifikation *f*; Bogenberechnung *f*
  f rectification *f*
  r спрямление *n*; ректификация *f*

7875 rectify *v*
  d rektifizieren
  f rectifier; redresser
  r спрямлять; ректифицировать

7876 rectifying plane
  d rektifizierende Ebene *f*
  f plan *m* rectifiant
  r спрямляющая плоскость *f*

7877 rectifying straight-line
  d rektifizierende Gerade *f*
  f droite *f* rectifiante
  r спрямляющая прямая *f*

7878 rectilinear coordinates
  d geradlinige Koordinaten *fpl*
  f coordonnées *fpl* rectilignes
  r прямолинейные координаты *fpl*

7879 rectilinear motion; straight-line motion
  d geradlinige Bewegung *f*

  f mouvement *m* rectiligne
  r прямолинейное движение *n*

7880 recurrence point
  d Rekurrenzpunkt *m*; Wiederkehrpunkt *m*
  f point *m* de récurrence; point de retour
  r точка *f* возврата; точка возвращения

7881 recursion
  d Rekursion *f*
  f récursion *f*
  r рекурсия *f*

7882 recursive raytracing
  d rekursives Ray-Tracing *n*
  f raytracing *m* récursif
  r рекурсивная трассировка *f* лучей

**7883 recursive stochastic sampling of
       illumination**
  d rekursive stochastische Stichprobenauswahl *f*
       der Illumination
  f échantillonnage *m* récursif stochastique
       d'illumination
  r рекурсивная стохастическая
       дискретизация *f* освещения

7884 recursivity
  d Rekursivität *f*
  f récursivité *f*
  r рекурсивность *f*

7885 redefinition
  d Umdefinieren *n*; Neufestlegung *f*
  f rédéfinition *f*
  r переопределение *n*

7886 redesign
  d Neuentwurf *m*; Reentwurf *m*
  f projet *m* nouveau
  r реконструкция *f*; переделка *f*

7887 red filter
  d Rotfilter *m*
  f filtre *m* rouge
  r красный фильтр *m*

7888 red, green and blue; RGB
  d Rot, Grün und Blau; RGB
  f rouge, vert et bleu; RVB
  r красный, зеленый и синий

7889 redimension *v*
  d wiederaufmessen
  f redimensionner
  r переоразмерять

7890 redirection
  d Richtungsänderung *f*; Veränderung *f* der
       Richtung

f rédirection *f*; changement *m* de direction
r изменение *n* направления

7891 redisplay *v*
d wiederdarstellen
f réafficher
r повторно изображать

7892 redo *v*
d wiederherstellen
f rétablir (la dernière opération annulée)
r переделывать

7893 redo command
d Wiederherstellungsbefehl *m*
f commande *f* de rétablissement
r команда *f* переделывания

7894 redraw *v*
d zeichnen im Weiterschlag; ziehen im Nachzug
f redessiner; refaire; retracer
r перечерчивать; перерисовывать

7895 reduce *v*
d reduzieren; verringern
f réduire
r приводить; сокращать; редуцировать

* reduced → 1

7896 reduced
d reduziert
f réduit
r приведенный; уменьшенный

7897 reduced data
d reduzierte Daten *npl*; verdichtete Daten
f données *fpl* réduites
r сжатые данные *npl*

7898 reduced scale
d reduzierter Maßstab *m*
f échelle *f* réduite
r уменьшенный масштаб *m*

7899 reduced view
d reduzierte Ansicht *f*
f vue *f* réduite
r уменьшенный вид *m*

* reducing → 7900

7900 reduction; reducing; foreshortening
d Reduktion *f*; Reduzierung *f*; Verkleinerung *f*; Verringerung *f*
f réduction *f*
r редукция *f*; уменьшение *n*; понижение *n*; приведение *n*; сокращение *n*

* reduction factor → 1648

7901 reduction of angles
d Winkelreduktion *f*
f réduction *f* des angles
r редукция *f* углов

7902 reduction of contrast
d Kontrastminderung *f*; Schwärzungsabfall *m*
f réduction *f* du contraste
r понижение *n* контраста

7903 reduction of data
d Reduktion *f* der Daten
f réduction *f* des données
r сокращение *n* данных

7904 reduction of gray value
d Reduktion *f* des Grauwerts
f réduction *f* de valeur de gris
r уменьшение *n* оттенка серого

* redundant → 39

* redundant replica → 3231

7905 reference
d Referenz *f*; Verweis *m*
f référence *f*
r ссылка *f*; обращение *n*

7906 reference
d Bezug *m*
f référence *f*
r эталон *m*; опора *f*

7907 reference angle
d Bezugswinkel *m*
f angle *m* de référence
r эталонный угол *m*

7908 reference area
d Bezugsgebiet *n*
f domaine *m* de référence
r эталонная область *f*

* reference axis → 756

7909 reference beam
d Referenzstrahl *m*
f faisceau *m* de référence
r опорный луч *m*; эталонный луч

7910 reference color
d Referenzfarbe *f*
f couleur *f* de référence
r эталонный цвет *m*

7911 reference data
d Bezugsdaten *npl*

f données *fpl* de référence
r справочные данные *npl*; эталонные данные

7912 reference datum
d Bezugswert *m*
f repère *m* de référence
r эталонное начало *n* отсчета

7913 reference direction
d Bezugsrichtung *f*
f direction *f* de repérage; direction de référence
r начальное направление *n*

7914 reference edge
d Bezugskante *f*; Bezugsrand *m*
f marge *f* de référence
r опорный край *m*

* **reference frame → 3988**

7915 reference length
d Bezugslänge *f*
f longueur *f* de référence
r эталонная длина *f*

* **reference line → 5466**

* **reference mark → 2338**

7916 reference object
(in array command)
d Bezugsobjekt *n*
f objet *m* de référence
r эталонный объект *m*

7917 reference pattern; reference picture
d Bezugsmuster *n*; Referenzmuster *n*
f échantillon *m* de référence; image *f* de référence
r эталонный образ *m*; образец *m*

* **reference picture → 7917**

* **reference plane → 7144**

* **reference point → 7220**

7918 reference surface
d Bezugsoberfläche *f*
f surface *f* de référence
r опорная поверхность *f*; эталонная поверхность

* **reference system → 9440**

7919 reference tool
d Referenz-Hilfsmittel *n*
f outil *m* de référence
r эталонный инструмент *m*

7920 reference toolbar
d Referenz-Hilfsmittelstreifen *m*
f barre *f* d'outils de référence
r инструментальная панель *f* ссылок

7921 reference voxel
d Referenz-Voxel *n*
f pixel *m* 3D de référence
r эталонный трехмерный пиксел *m*

7922 refined data
d verfeinerte Daten *npl*
f données *fpl* raffinées
r уточненные данные *npl*

7923 refinement; refining
d Verfeinigung *f*; Verfeinerung *f*
f raffinement *m*; raffinage *m*
r измельчение *n*; усовершенствование *n*; детализация *f*

* **refining → 7923**

* **reflect → 4224**

7924 reflectance; reflectivity
d Reflexionsvermögen *n*; Reflexibilität *f*; Reflektanz *f*
f réflectance *f*; réflexivité *f*
r отражательная способность *f*

7925 reflectance matrix
d Reflektanzmatrix *f*
f matrice *f* de réflectance
r матрица *f* отражательной способности

7926 reflected beam; reflected ray
d reflektierter Strahl *m*
f rayon *m* réfléchi; faisceau *m* réfléchi; raie *f* réfléchie
r отраженный луч *m*

* **reflected binary code → 4402**

7927 reflected image
d reflektiertes Bild *n*
f image *f* réfléchie
r отраженное изображение *n*

7928 reflected light
d reflektiertes Licht *n*
f lumière *f* réfléchie
r отраженный свет *m*

* **reflected ray → 7926**

7929 reflected ray direction vector
d Richtungsvektor *m* des reflektierten Strahls
f vecteur *m* de direction de rayon réfléchi
r направляющий вектор *m* отраженного луча

7930 reflected view vector
 d Vektor *m* der reflektierten Ansicht
 f vecteur *m* de vue réfléchie
 r вектор *m* отраженного представления

* **reflecting angle** → 383

7931 reflecting colors
 d reflektive Farben *fpl*
 f couleurs *fpl* réfléchissantes
 r отражающие цвета *mpl*

7932 reflecting surface; reflective surface
 d Reflexionsfläche *f*; reflektive Fläche *f*
 f surface *f* réfléchissante
 r отражающая поверхность *f*

7933 reflection
 d Reflexion *f*; Rückstrahlung *f*
 f réflexion *f*
 r отражение *n*

7934 reflection coefficient; reflection factor
 d Reflexionskoeffizient *m*; Reflexionsfaktor *m*
 f coefficient *m* de réflexion; facteur *m* de réflexion
 r коэффициент *m* отражения

7935 reflection color
 d Reflexionsfarbe *f*
 f couleur *f* de réflexion
 r цвет *m* отражения

* **reflection factor** → 7934

7936 reflection mapping
 d Reflexionsabbildung *f*
 f mappage *m* de réflexions
 r построение *n* отражений

7937 reflection model
 d Reflexionsmodell *n*
 f modèle *m* de réflexion
 r модель *f* отражения

7938 reflection of light; light reflection
 d Lichtreflexion *f*
 f réflexion *f* de la lumière
 r отражение *n* света

7939 reflections map
 d Reflexionskarte *f*
 f carte *f* des réflexions
 r карта *f* отражений

7940 reflection spectrometry
 d Reflexionsspektrometrie *f*
 f spectrométrie *f* par réflexion
 r спектрометрия *f* отражением

7941 reflection spectrum
 d Reflexionsspektrum *n*
 f spectre *m* de réflexion
 r спектр *m* отражения

* **reflection with respect to a plane** → 9420

* **reflective** → 7948

7942 reflective marker; reflective spot
 d reflektiver Marker *m*
 f marqueur *m* réfléchissant
 r отражающий маркер *m*

7943 reflective planar surface
 d reflektive planare Fläche *f*
 f surface *f* planaire réfléchissante
 r плоская отражающая поверхность *f*

7944 reflective sphere
 d reflektive Sphäre *f*
 f sphère *f* réfléchissante
 r отражающая сфера *f*

* **reflective spot** → 7942

* **reflective surface** → 7932

7945 reflective surface geometry
 d Geometrie *f* der reflexiven Fläche
 f géométrie *f* de surface réfléchissante
 r геометрия *f* отражающей поверхности

* **reflectivity** → 7924

7946 reflectometry
 d Reflektometrie *f*; Reflexionsmesstechnik *f*
 f réflectométrie *f*
 r рефлектометрия *f*; техника *f* измерения отражения

7947 reflector
 d Reflektor *m*
 f réflecteur *m*
 r отражатель *m*; рефлектор *m*

7948 reflexive; reflective
 d reflexiv; reflektiv
 f réfléchissant; réflexible
 r рефлексивный; отражающий; отражательный

7949 refocusing
 d Refokussierung *f*
 f refocalisation *f*
 r повторная фокусировка *f*

* **reformat** → 7950

7950 reformat[ting]
 d Umformatieren *n*; Formatänderung *f*

f reformatage *m*; modification *f* du format
r переформатирование *n*; изменение *n* формата

7951 refract *v*
 d brechen
 f réfracter
 r преломлять

7952 refracted light
 d refraktiertes Licht *n*
 f lumière *f* réfractée
 r преломленный свет *m*

7953 refracted ray
 d gebrochener Strahl *m*
 f rayon *m* réfracté
 r преломленный луч *m*

 * **refracting angle** → 384

7954 refracting surface
 d Refraktionsfläche *f*
 f surface *f* de réfraction
 r поверхность *f* преломления

7955 refraction
 d Brechung *f*; Refraktion *f*
 f réfraction *f*
 r преломление *n*; рефракция *f*

 * **refraction angle** → 384

7956 refraction error
 d Brechungsfehler *m*
 f erreur *f* de réfraction
 r ошибка *f* преломления

7957 refraction of light; light refraction
 d Lichtbrechung *f*
 f réfraction *f* de la lumière
 r рефракция *f* света

7958 refraction of material
 d Materialbrechung *f*
 f réfraction *f* de matériel
 r рефракция *f* материала

7959 refractive index
 d Brechungsindex *m*
 f indice *m* de réfraction
 r индекс *m* рефракции

7960 refractivity
 d Brechungsvermögen *n*
 f réfrangibilité *f*
 r преломляющая способность *f*

7961 refractometer
 d Refraktometer *n*

f réfractomètre *m*
r рефрактометр *m*

7962 reframe *v*
 d Aufnahmen wiederherstellen
 f recadrer
 r повторно кадрировать

7963 reframing
 d Aufnahmen-Wiederherstellung *f*; Rahmenänderung *f*
 f retramage *m*; recadrage *m*
 r повторное формирование *n* кадра; повтор *m* кадрирования

 * **refresh** → 7966

7964 refresh *v*; **freshen** *v* **up**
 d auffrischen; erneuern
 f rafraîchir
 r обновлять; освежать

7965 refresh display
 d Bildschirm *m* mit Bildwiederholung; Refresh-Display *n*
 f écran *m* à rafraîchissement d'image
 r дисплей *m* с регенерацией изображения

7966 refresh[ing]; refreshment
 d Auffrischung *f*; Refresh *n*
 f rafraîchissement *m*
 r обновление *n*; регенерация *f*

 * **refreshment** → 7966

7967 refresh rate
 (of an image)
 d Auffrischrate *f*; Refresh-Rate *f*; Wiederholfrequenz *f*; Wiederholrate *f*
 f fréquence *f* de rafraîchissement
 r частота *f* регенерации

7968 regenerate *v*
 d regenerieren
 f régénérer
 r регенерировать

7969 regenerated drawing
 d regenerierte Zeichnung *f*
 f dessin *m* régénéré
 r регенерированный рисунок *m*; регенерированный чертеж *m*

7970 regenerate *v* **texture**
 d Füllmuster regenerieren
 f régénérer une texture
 r регенерировать текстуру

7971 regeneration
 d Regenerierung *f*; Regeneration *f*

f régénération f
r регенерация f; повторная генерация f; восстановление n

7972 region; area
(as a georeferenced object)
d Region f
f région f
r регион m; район m

7973 regionalization
d Bereichsunterteilung f
f régionalisation f
r разбиение n на регионы; разбиение на области

7974 region fill; area fill
d Bereichsfüllen n; Regionfüllung f
f remplissage m de zones; remplissage de régions
r заполнение n областей; закрашивание n регионов

7975 region object
d Region-Objekt n
f objet m région
r объект m типа региона

7976 region specification
d Regionsspezifikation f
f spécification f de région
r спецификация f региона

* **register** v → **5687**

7977 register
d Register n
f registre m
r регистр m

7978 registered application
d registrierte Anwendung f
f application f enregistrée
r регистрированное приложение n

7979 registered status
d registrierter Status m
f état m enregistré
r регистрированное состояние n

* **registration** → **10481**

7980 registration marks
(for aligning color separation)
d Registriermarken fpl
f marques fpl de repérage
r пасеры mpl; метки fpl обреза листа

7981 registration problem
d Registrierproblem n

f problème m d'enregistrement
r проблема f регистрации

7982 regression
d Regression f
f régression f
r регрессия f

7983 regular
d regulär; regelmäßig
f régulier
r регулярный; правильный

7984 regular cell structure
d reguläre Zell[en]struktur f; regelmäßige Zell[en]struktur
f structure f de cellule régulière
r регулярная клеточная структура f

7985 regular color mapping
d regelmäßige Farbabbildung f
f mappage m de couleurs régulier
r равномерное отображение n цветов; обычное отображение цветов

7986 regular curve
d reguläre Kurve f
f courbe f régulière
r регулярная кривая f

7987 regular font
d regelmäßige Schrift f
f police f régulière
r нормальный шрифт m

* **regular function** → **342**

7988 regularity
d Regularität f
f régularité f
r регулярность f; правильность f

7989 regularization; regulation
d Regularisierung f; Regulierung f; Regelung f
f régularisation f; régulation f; réglage m
r регулирование n

* **regular point** → **6606**

* **regular polygon** → **3502**

7990 regular polyhedron
d regelmäßiges Polyeder n
f polyèdre m régulier
r правильный многогранник m

7991 regular prism
d regelmäßiges Prisma n
f prisme m régulier
r правильная призма f

7992 regular pyramid
d reguläre Pyramide *f*
f pyramide *f* régulière
r правильная пирамида *f*

7993 regular representation
d reguläre Darstellung *f*
f représentation *f* régulière
r регулярное представление *n*

7994 regular routing
d reguläre Leitweglenkung *f*
f routage *m* régulier
r регулярная маршрутизация *f*

7995 regular surface
d reguläre Fläche *f*
f surface *f* régulière
r регулярная поверхность *f*

  * **regular triangle** → 3503

  * **regulate** *v* → 195

  * **regulation** → 7989

  * **reject** → 7997

7996 reject *v*; **discard** *v*; **throw** *v* **off**
d beseitigen; verwerfen; ablehnen
f rejeter; repousser; refuser; décliner
r отбрасывать; выбрасывать; отклонять

7997 reject[ion]
d Verwerfen *n*; Rückweisung *f*; Ablehnung *f*
f rejet *m*
r отбрасывание *n*; отказ *m*; непринятие *n*

7998 rejection filter
d Sperrfilter *m*
f filtre *m* de rejet [de bande]; circuit *m* éliminateur; circuit rejeteur
r режекционный фильтр *m*

  * **related division** → 7555

7999 relation
d Relation *f*; Beziehung *f*
f relation *f*; rapport *m*
r реляция *f*; отношение *n*

8000 relation character; relation symbol
d Relationszeichen *n*
f caractère *m* de relation; symbole *m* relationnel
r знак *m* отношения; символ *m* [операции] отношения

8001 relationship
d Zusammenhang *m*

f relation *f* [mutuelle]
r взаимоотношение *n*; взаимосвязь *f*

  * **relation symbol** → 8000

8002 relative
d relativ
f relatif
r относительный

8003 relative accuracy
d relative Genauigkeit *f*
f précision *f* relative
r относительная точность *f*

8004 relative angles
d relative Winkel *mpl*
f angles *mpl* relatifs
r относительные углы *mpl*

8005 relative Cartesian coordinates
d relative kartesische Koordinaten *fpl*
f coordonnées *fpl* cartésiennes relatives
r относительные декартовы координаты *fpl*

8006 relative command
d relativer Befehl *m*
f commande *f* relative
r относительная команда *f*

8007 relative coordinates
d relative Koordinaten *fpl*
f coordonnées *fpl* relatives
r относительные координаты *fpl*

8008 relative curvature
d relative Krümmung *f*; Relativkrümmung *f*
f courbure *f* relative
r относительная кривизна *f*

8009 relative polar coordinates
d relative Polarkoordinaten *fpl*
f coordonnées *fpl* relatives polaires
r относительные полярные координаты *fpl*

8010 relative spectral sensitivity
d relative spektrale Empfindlichkeit *f*
f sensibilité *f* spectrale relative
r относительная спектральная чувствительность *f*

8011 relative vector
d relativer Vektor *m*
f vecteur *m* relatif
r относительный вектор *m*

8012 relaxation
d Relaxation *f*
f relaxation *f*
r релаксация *f*

* release → 10142

8013 reliability
d Betriebssicherheit *f*; Zuverlässigkeit *f*
f fiabilité *f*
r надежность *f*; безотказность *f*

8014 relief
d Relief *n*
f relief *m*
r рельеф *m*

8015 relief carte; relief map; feature map
d Reliefkarte *f*
f carte *f* en relief
r рельефная карта *f*

8016 relief color
d Relieffarbe *f*
f couleur *f* de relief
r цвет *m* рельефа

8017 relief drawing
d Reliefzeichnung *f*
f dessin *m* altimétrique
r рисовка *f* рельефа

* relief effect → 3389

* relief lining → 8078

* relief map → 8015

8018 relief model
d Reliefmodell *n*
f modèle *m* du relief
r модель *f* рельефа

8019 relief printing
d Hochdruck *m*
f impression *f* en relief
r рельефная печать *f*; высокая печать

8020 relief text
d Relieftext *m*
f texte *m* en relief
r рельефный текст *m*

* reload → 8021

8021 reload[ing]
d Neuladen *n*
f rechargement *m*
r повторная загрузка *f*; перезагрузка *f*

* relocatability → 7331

* relocatable → 7332

8022 relocation

d Umsied[e]lung *f*; Versetzung *f*
f relocation *f*; relogement *m*
r перемещение *n*; настройка *f* по месту

* remap → 8023

8023 remap[ping]
d Neukartierung *f*
f nouvelle cartographie *f*; remappage *m*
r пересоставление *n* карты

8024 remark
d Bemerkung *f*
f remarque *f*
r примечание *n*; комментарий *m*

8025 remarkable line
d ausgezeichnete Gerade *f*
f droite *f* remarquable
r прямая *f*, занимающая особое положение

8026 remarkable plane
d ausgezeichnete Ebene *f*
f plan *m* remarquable
r плоскость *f*, занимающая особое положение

8027 remote sensing
d Fernerkundung *f*; Fernablesung *f*; Fernabtastung *f*
f télédétection *f*; détection *f* à distance
r дистанционное зондирование *n*

8028 removal; removing
d Entfernung *f*; Aussonderung *f*; Beseitigung *f*
f suppression *f*; enlèvement *m*; dégagement *m*
r удаление *n*; устранение *n*

* remove *v* → 1536

8029 remove *v* face
d Fläche entfernen
f supprimer une face
r удалить грани

8030 remove *v* hidden lines
d verdeckte Linien entfernen
f éliminer les lignes cachées; supprimer les lignes cachées
r удалить скрытые линии; удалить невидимые линии

8031 remove *v* noise
d Rauschen entfernen
f supprimer le bruit
r удалить шумовой эффект

* removing → 8028

8032 rename *v*
d neubenennen; umbenennen

f changer de nom; renommer
r переименовать

8033 rename *v* **page**
  d Seite umbenennen
  f renommer une page
  r переименовать страницу

8034 render *v*
  d rendern
  f rendre
  r тонировать

8035 render background color
  d Hintergrundfarbe *f* des Renderings
  f couleur *f* de fond de rendu
  r фоновый цвет *m* тонирования

8036 render block
  d Rendering-Block *m*
  f bloc *m* de rendu
  r блок *m* тонирования; блок рендеринга

8037 render [display] window
  d Rendering-Fenster *n*
  f fenêtre *f* [d'affichage] de rendu
  r окно *n* тонирования; окно рендеринга

8038 rendered image
  d gerendertes Bild *n*
  f image *f* rendue
  r тонированное изображение *n*

8039 rendered object
  d gerendertes Objekt *n*
  f objet *m* rendu
  r тонированный объект *m*

8040 rendered sphere
  d gerenderte Kugel *f*
  f sphère *f* rendue
  r тонированная сфера *f*

8041 rendered texture
  d gerenderte Textur *f*
  f texture *f* rendue
  r тонированная текстура *f*

8042 render effects
  d Rendering-Effekte *mpl*
  f effets *mpl* de rendu
  r эффекты *mpl* тонирования; эффекты рендеринга

8043 renderer
  d Rendering-Programm *n*
  f fournisseur *m*; moteur *m* de rendu
  r программа *f* рендеринга

8044 render file
  d Rendering-Datei *n*
  f fichier *m* de rendu
  r рендеринг-файл *m*

8045 render imitation
  d Rendering-Imitation *f*
  f imitation *f* de rendu
  r симулирование *n* тонирования; симулирование рендеринга

8046 rendering
  d Rendern *n*; Rendering *n*
  f rendu *m*
  r тонирование *n*; рендеринг *m*

8047 rendering algorithm
  d Rendering-Algorithmus *m*
  f algorithme *m* de rendu
  r алгоритм *m* тонирования; алгоритм рендеринга

8048 rendering attribute
  d Renderingsattribut *n*
  f attribut *m* de rendu
  r атрибут *m* тонирования; атрибут рендеринга

8049 rendering equation
  d Rendering-Gleichung *f*
  f équation *f* de rendu
  r уравнение *n* тонирования; уравнение рендеринга

8050 rendering filter
  d Rendering-Filter *m*
  f filtre *m* de rendu
  r фильтр *m* рендеринга

8051 rendering pipeline
  (a series of 2D views, separated from 3D model)
  d Rendering-Fließband *n*
  f conveyor *m* de rendu
  r конвейер *m* тонирования; конвейер рендеринга

8052 rendering process
  d Rendering-Prozess *m*
  f processus *m* de rendu
  r процесс *m* тонирования; процесс рендеринга

8053 rendering processor
  d Rendering-Prozessor *m*
  f processeur *m* rendu
  r тонирующий процессор *m*; рендеринг-процессор *m*

8054 rendering speed
  d Renderingsgeschwindigkeit *f*

f vitesse *f* de rendu
r скорость *f* тонирования; скорость
рендеринга

8055 rendering system
d Renderingssytem *n*
f système *m* de rendu
r система *f* тонирования; система
рендеринга

8056 rendering technology
d Rendering-Technologie *f*
f technologie *f* de rendu
r техника *f* тонирования; технология
рендеринга

8057 render quality
d Render-Qualität *f*
f qualité *f* de rendu
r качество *n* тонирования; качество
рендеринга

8058 render toolbar
d Rendering-Hilfsmittelstreifen *m*
f barre *f* d'outils de rendu
r инструментальная панель *f* тонирования

* **render window** → 8037

* **reorder** → 8060

8059 reorder *v*
d neuordnen; umordnen
f réarranger
r переупорядочивать

8060 reorder[ing]
d Umordnung *f*
f reclassement *m*; réarrangement *m*
r переупорядочение *n*

8061 reorient *v*
d wiederorientieren
f réorienter
r переориентировать

8062 repair *v*
d reparieren
f réformer; remédier
r исправлять; восстанавливать

8063 repeat *v*
d wiederholen
f répéter
r повторять[ся]

8064 repeat reading; repeat scanning
d wiederholte Abtastung *f*; wiederholtes
Ablesen *n*
f exploration *f* répétée

r повторное сканирование *n*; повторный
отсчет *m*

* **repeat scanning** → 8064

* **repertoire** → 8065

8065 repertory; repertoire
d Vorrat *m*; Repertoire *n*
f répertoire *m*; stock *m*
r перечень *m*; список *m*; реестр *m*; опись *f*

8066 repetition
d Repetition *f*; Wiederholung *f*
f répétition *f*
r повторение *n*

8067 repetition centre
(a center of object's array)
d Wiederholungszentrum *n*
f centre *f* de répétition
r центр *m* повторения

8068 replace *v*
d ersetzen
f remplacer; substituer
r подставлять; заменять

8069 replace *v* **color**
d Farbe ersetzen
f remplacer de couleur
r замещать цвет

8070 replace *v* **color filter**
d Farbfilter ersetzen
f remplacer un filtre de couleur
r замещать фильтр цвета

8071 replacement
d Ersetzung *f*; Ersatz *m*
f remplacement *m*
r замена *f*

8072 replacer
d Umsetzgerät *n*; Austauscher *m*
f substitueur *m*
r устройство *n* замещения; заменитель *m*

8073 replace *v* **text**
d Text ersetzen
f remplacer de text
r замещать текст

* **replication** → 3095

8074 report
d Report *m*; Liste *f*; Bericht *m*
f rapport *m*; liste *f*
r отчет *m*

8075 **repositioning**
   d Wiederpositionierung *f*; Verstellung *f*
   f repositionnement *m*
   r повторное позиционирование *n*

8076 **representation; view**
   d Darstellung *f*; Repräsentation *f*
   f représentation *f*
   r представление *n*

8077 **representation of relief by contours**
   d Reliefdarstellung *f* durch Höhenlinien
   f relief *m* en courbes de niveau
   r изображение *n* рельефа горизонталями

8078 **representation of relief by hachures; relief lining**
   d Reliefdarstellung *f* durch Schraffen
   f relief *m* en hachures
   r изображение *n* рельефа штрихами

8079 **representation of terrain; representation of topographical surfaces**
   d Geländedarstellung *f*
   f représentation *f* du terrain; représentation de surfaces topographiques
   r представление *n* местности; представление топографических поверхностей

   * **representation of topographical surfaces** → 8079

8080 **representative point**
   d Darstellungspunkt *m*; Abbildungspunkt *m*
   f point *m* représentatif
   r изображающая точка *f*

8081 **representative sample**
   d repräsentative Stichprobe *f*
   f échantillon *m* représentatif
   r представительная выборка *f*

8082 **reproduction**
   d Reproduktion *f*
   f reproduction *f*
   r воспроизведение *n*; репродукция *f*

8083 **request; interrogation; demand; inquiry; enquiry; query**
   d Abfrage *f*; Anfrage *f*; Auftrag *m*
   f requête *f*; interrogation *f*; question *f*; demande *f*
   r запрос *m*; опрос *m*; заказ *m*; справка *f*

8084 **requirement; demand**
   d Forderung *f*; Anforderung *f*; Bedarf *m*; Erfordernis *n*
   f nécessité *f*; exigence *f*
   r требование *n*; потребность *f*

8085 **requirement description**
   d Bedarfsdeskription *f*
   f description *f* des nécessités
   r описание *n* требований; техническое задание *n*

8086 **reroute** *v*
   d umsteuern; umleiten
   f rerouter
   r перенаправлять; обходить

8087 **rerouting; alternative routing**
   d Umsteuerung *f*
   f déroutement *m*; détournement *m*
   r перенаправление *n*; обход *m*

8088 **resample** *v*
   d wieder abfragen; wieder abtasten; wieder probieren
   f rééchantillonner
   r делать повторную выборку [изображения]; сделать перевыборку

8089 **resampling**
   d wiederholte Stichprobenauswahl *f*
   f rééchantillonnage *m*
   r повторная выборка *f*

8090 **rescale** *v*
   d Skale ändern
   f changer d'échelle
   r перемасштабировать

8091 **rescanning**
   d Wiederabtastung *f*; Wiederabfrage *f*
   f balayage *m* répétitif; exploration *f* répétitive
   r повторный просмотр *m*

8092 **research**
   d Forschung *f*; Suche *f*
   f recherche *f*
   r исследование *n*; поиск *m*

8093 **reselection**
   d wiederholte Selektion *f*
   f resélection *f*
   r повторный выбор *m*

8094 **reservation**
   d Reservation *f*; Reservierung *f*
   f réservation *f*
   r резервирование *n*

8095 **reset** *v*
   d zurücksetzen
   f réinitialiser
   r переустановлять

   * **reset** *v* → 1261, 3356

* reset → 8110

* resetting → 8110

8096 reshape *v*
  d wieder formieren
  f remettre en forme; reconstruire
  r повторно формировать

8097 resident
  d resident
  f résident
  r резидентный

8098 resident fonts
  d Residentschriften *fpl*
  f polices *fpl* résidentes
  r резидентные шрифты *mpl*

8099 residual
  d Rest-
  f résiduel
  r остаточный

8100 residual distortion
  d Restverzerrung *f*
  f distorsion *f* résiduelle
  r остаточное искажение *n*

* resistance → 9230

8101 resize *v*
  d Größe verändern
  f changer la taille
  r изменять размер

8102 resizing
  d Größenänderung *f*; Vergrößern/Verkleinern *n*
  f changement *m* de taille
  r изменение *n* размера

8103 resizing handle
  d Größenänderungsgriff *m*; Ziehpunkt *m* der Größenänderung
  f poignée *f* de changement de taille
  r захват *m* изменения размера

8104 resizing the printed image
  d Größenänderung *f* des gedruckten Bilds
  f changement *m* de taille d'image imprimée
  r изменение *n* размера печатаемого изображения

* resolution → 2534, 8105

8105 resolution [capability]; resolution power; resolving power
  d Auflösungsvermögen *n*
  f pouvoir *m* de résolution; puissance *f* de résolution; résolution *f*

r разрешающая способность *f*

8106 resolution cell; grid cell
  d Rasterzelle *f*; Gitterzelle *f*; Auflösungsraumelement *n*
  f point *m* de trame; point de résolution; cellule *f* de grille
  r клетка *f* растра

* resolution power → 8105

8107 resolution target; definition chart; grating generator
  d Auflösungstestfigur *f*
  f mire *f* de résolution
  r мира *f* для определения разрешающей способности

* resolving power → 8105

8108 resource
  d Ressource *f*; Systemmittel *n*
  f ressource *f*
  r ресурс *m*

8109 response
  d Reaktion *f*; Wirkung *f*
  f réponse *f*; réaction *f*
  r реакция *f*; ответ *m*; отклик *m*

* response → 1422

* response curve → 1422

* responsivity → 8526

8110 restoration; reset[ting]
  d Wiederherstellung *f*; Wiederaufbau *m*; Zurücksetzen *n*
  f restauration *f*; restitution *f*; remise *f* [en état]; retour *m*; rétablissement *m*
  r восстановление *n*; возврат *m*

* restore *v* → 7849

* restrain *v* → 2092

* restrict *v* → 2092

* restricted → 1110

8111 restriction; constraint
  d Restriktion *f*; Einschränkung *f*; Beschränkung *f*
  f restriction *f*; contrainte *f*
  r ограничение *n*; рестрикция *f*

* retention → 6981

8112 reticular
  d netzförmig

f réticulaire
r сетчатый

8113 reticular distance; reticular spacing
d Netzabstand *n*
f intervalle *f* réticulaire
r промежуток *m* в сетке

* **reticular spacing** → 8113

* **retouch** → 8115

8114 retouch *v*
d retuschieren
f retoucher
r ретушировать

8115 retouch[ing]
d Retusche *f*
f retouche *f*
r ретушь *f*; ретуширование *n*

8116 retouching program
d Retuschier-Programm *n*
f programme *m* de retouche
r программа *f* ретуширования

* **retrace** → 3885

* **retrenchment** → 8651

8117 return button; return key
d Rückrichtung-Taste *f*
f bouton *m* de retour; touche *f* de retour
r кнопка *f* возврата

* **return direction** → 6529

* **return key** → 8117

8118 reuse window
d Wiederverwendung-Fenster *n*
f fenêtre *f* réutilisable
r многократно используемое окно *n*

8119 reversal
d Umkehrung *f*; Wendung *f*
f retournement *m*; redressement *m*
r реверсирование *n*; изменение *n*
направления на обратное

8120 reversal finder
d Umkehr[ungs]finder *m*;
Umschwung-Finder *m*
f viseur-redresseur *m*
r реверсивный визир *m*

* **reverse** → 8123

8121 reverse *v*; **invert** *v*

d umkehren; umdrehen; invertieren
f reverser; invertir
r обращать; реверсировать; инвертировать

8122 reverse clipping
d inverses Schneiden *n*
f découpage *m* inverse
r реверсивное отсекание *n*; перевернутое
отсекание

8123 reverse[d]; inverse[d] *adj*
d umgekehrt; invers
f reverse; inverse; renversé; rétroactif
r обратный; инверсный; перевернутый;
реверсивный

**8124 reverse[d] image; inverse image; flip
image; inverted image; inverted picture;
upside[-down] image**
d umgekehrtes Bild *n*; inverses Bild
f image *f* renversée; image inverse
r перевернутое изображение *n*; инверсное
изображение; инвертированное
изображение; реверсивное изображение;
реверс *m*

* **reversed lens** → 5271

* **reverse image** → 8124

8125 reverse projection
d inverse Projektion *f*
f projection *f* reverse
r обратная проекция *f*; реверсная проекция

8126 reverse-projection processor
d Prozessor *m* der inversen Projektionen
f processeur *m* de projections reverses
r процессор *m* реверсных проекций

8127 reverse quote
(`)
d Gegenquote *f*; Rückwärtsquote *f*
f guillemet *m* renversé
r обратная кавычка *f*

* **reverse scan** → 8128

8128 reverse scan[ning]
d umgekehrte Abtastung *f*
f balayage *m* inverse
r обратное сканирование *n*; сканирование с
возвратом; обратное считывание *n*

* **reverse video** → 5269

8129 reversion; inversion
d Invertierung *f*; Inversion *f*
f réversion *f*; renversement *m*; inversion *f*
r перевращение *n*; обращение *n*; инверсия *f*;
инвертирование *n*

8130 **revert** *v*
d zurückgeben; zurückkehren
f retourner; revenir
r возвращаться

8131 **review**
d Rundschau *f*
f revue *f*
r просмотр *m*

* **revision** → 666

8132 **revision number**
d Revisionsnummer *f*
f numéro *m* de révision
r номер *m* ревизии

8133 **revision tracking**
d Revisionsverfolgung *f*
f poursuite *f* de révision
r прослеживание *n* ревизии

* **revolution** → 8200

8134 **revolution speed**
d Drehgeschwindigkeit *f*
f vitesse *f* de révolution
r скорость *f* вращения

8135 **revolution tolerance**
d Drehungstoleranz *f*
f tolérance *f* de révolution
r допуск *m* вращения

* **revolve** *v* → 1511

* **revolved solid** → 8893

* **revolved surface** → 9371

* **revolving** → 8198

* **RGB** → 7888

8136 **RGB bitmap**
d RGB-Bitmap *n*
f bitmap *m* RVB
r растровое изображение *n* RGB

8137 **RGB color**
d RGB-Farbe *f*
f couleur *f* RVB
r цвет *m* RGB

8138 **RGB color coordinates**
d RGB-Farbkoordinaten *fpl*
f coordonnées *fpl* de couleur RVB
r координаты *fpl* цветов RGB

8139 **RGB color format**

d RGB-Farbformat *n*
f format *m* de couleurs RVB
r цветной формат *m* RGB

8140 **RGB color mode**
d RGB-Farbmodus *m*
f régime *m* de couleurs RVB
r цветной режим *m* RGB

8141 **RGB [color] model**
d RGB-Farbmodell *n*; RGB-Modell *n*
f modèle *m* [de couleur] RVB
r цветовая модель *f* RGB

8142 **RGB color restitution**
d RGB-Farbwiedergabe *f*
f restitution *f* de couleur RVB
r восстановление *n* цвета RGB

8143 **RGB color space**
d RGB-Farbraum *m*
f espace *m* de couleur RVB
r цветовое пространство *n* RGB

8144 **RGB color system**
d RGB-Farbsystem *n*
f système *m* de couleurs RVB
r цветовая система *f* RGB

8145 **RGB color value**
d RGB-Farbwert *m*
f valeur *f* RVB
r код *m* цвета RGB

8146 **RGB image**
d RGB-Bild *n*
f image *f* RVB
r изображение *n* RGB

* **RGB model** → 8141

8147 **RGB slider**
d RGB-Schieber *m*
f curseur *m* RVB
r ползунок *m* RGB

8148 **RGB/XYZ matrix**
d RGB/XYZ-Matrix *f*
f matrice *f* RGB/XYZ
r матрица *f* RGB/XYZ

* **rhomb** → 2713

8149 **rhombohedron**
d Rhomboeder *n*; Rautenflächner *m*
f rhomboèdre *m*
r ромбоэдр *m*

8150 **rhomboid**
d Rhomboid *n*

f rhomboïde *m*
r ромбоид *m*

* **rhombus** → 2713

**8151 rhumb line; spherical helix; loxodrome;
loxodromic spiral; loxodromic line;
loxodromic curve**
(on a sphere or on the earth's surface)
d Rhumblinie *f*; Loxodrome *f* auf der Erdkugel;
Schieflaufende *f*
f loxodromie *f*; ligne *f* loxodromique; hélice *f*
sphérique; loxodrome *m*
r локсодрома *f*; локсодромная спираль *f*

* **ribbon** → 5089

* **RIFF** → 7763

8152 right
d recht; gerade
f droit
r правый; прямой

* **right-aligned** → 8166

8153 right alignment
d rechtsbündige Ausrichtung *f*
f alignement *m* à droite
r выравнение *n* по правому краю

8154 right angle
d rechter Winkel *m*
f angle *m* droit
r прямой угол *m*

* **right-angled** → 7855

* **right-angled prism** → 7868

8155 right[-angled] triangle
d rechtwinkliges Dreieck *n*
f triangle *m* rectangle
r прямоугольный треугольник *m*

8156 right arrow key
d Rechtspfeil-Taste *f*
f touche *f* à flèche droite
r клавиша *f* правой стрелки

* **right bisector** → 5889

8157 right circular cone
d gerader Kreiskegel *m*
f cône *m* droit à base circulaire
r прямой круговой конус *m*

8158 right-click
(of the mouse)
d Klick *m* auf der rechten Maustaste

f clic *m* sur le bouton droit
r щелчок *m* правой кнопки

8159 right cone; direct cone
d gerader Kegel *m*
f cône *m* droit
r прямой конус *m*

8160 right cylinder
d gerader Zylinder *m*
f cylindre *m* droit
r прямой цилиндр *m*

8161 right extent
d Rechtsextent *m*
f étendue *f* droite
r расширение *n* вправо

8162 right-handed coordinate system
d Rechtskoordinatensystem *n*; Rechtskreuz *n*
f système *m* de coordonnées dextrorsum
r правая система *f* координат

* **right-handed curve** → 2667

* **right-handed helix** → 2668

8163 right-handed rotation
d Rechtsdrehung *f*
f rotation *f* droite
r правое вращение *n*; правый поворот *m*

* **right-handed screw** → 2669

8164 right-hand[ed screw] rule
d Rechte-Hand-Regel *f*; Schraubregel *f*;
Dreifingerregel *f*
f règle *f* du tire-bouchon; règle de la main
droite
r правило *n* трех пальцев; правило [правого]
вращения

* **right-hand helix** → 2668

* **right-hand rule** → 8164

8165 right isotropic line
d Rechtsisotrope *f*
f droite *f* isotrope à droite
r правая изотропная прямая *f*

8166 right-justified; right-aligned
d rechts ausgerichtet; rechtsbündig
f serré à droit; aligné à droit
r выравненный вправо

8167 right mouse button
d rechte Maustaste *f*
f bouton *m* droit de souris
r правый бутон *m* мыши

8168 **right prism**
  d gerades Prisma *n*
  f prisme *m* droit
  r прямая призма *f*

8169 **right pyramid**
  d gerade Pyramide *f*
  f pyramide *f* droite
  r прямая пирамида *f*

  * **right screw** → 2669

8170 **right scroll arrow**
  d Bildlaufpfeil *m* rechts
  f flèche *f* de défilement à droit
  r стрелка *f* прокрутки вправо

8171 **right shift; shift right**
  d Rechtsverschiebung *f*
  f décalage *m* à droit
  r сдвиг *m* вправо

8172 **right-side view**
  d Ansicht *f* der rechten Seite; rechte Ansicht
  f vue *f* de côté droit
  r вид *m* справа

  * **right prism** → 7868

  * **right triangle** → 8155

  * **rigid body** → 8873

8173 **rigid body motion**
  d Bewegung des festen Körpers
  f mouvement *m* de solide
  r перемещение *n* жесткого тела

  * **ring** → 434

8174 **ring**
  d Ring *m*
  f anneau *m*; bague *f*
  r кольцо *m*

  * **ring domain** → 435

  * **ring-shaped** → 434

  * **ring shift** → 1508

8175 **ring topology**
  d Ringtopologie *f*
  f topologie *f* en anneau
  r кольцевая топология *f*

8176 **ripple; wavelet**
  d kleine Welle *f*; Rippel *n*
  f petite ride *f*; petit plissé *m*; ondelette *f*
  r рябь *f*; зыбь *f*; пульсация *f*; волна *f*

8177 **rippled surface**
  d wellige Oberfläche *f*; gewellte Oberfläche
  f surface *f* ondulée
  r волнистая поверхность *f*

8178 **ripple effect**
  d Welleneffekt *m*; Rippel-Effekt *m*
  f effet *m* de petites rides; effet de petits plissés; effet d'ondulation
  r волнообразный эффект *m*; волновой эффект

8179 **ripple filter**
  d Wellenfilter *m*; Pulsierfilter *m*
  f filtre *m* d'ondulation; uniformisateur *m*
  r фильтр *m* волнистости

  * **rising branch** → 596

  * **RMS** → 8190

  * **robot** → 235

8180 **roll**
  d Rolle *f*
  f rouleau *m*
  r ролик *m*; валик *m*; рулон *m*

8181 **roll** *v*
  d rollen
  f dérouler; rouler
  r крутить

8182 **rollback**
  d Rückkehr *f*
  f recul *m*; roulement *m* en arrière
  r откат *m*; отмена *f*

8183 **rolling**
  d Rundbiegen *n*; Wälzen *n*
  f roulage *m*; roulement *m*; cintrage *m*; cylindrage *m*; laminage *m*
  r прокрутка *f*; качание *n*; ролинг *m*

  * **rolling** *adj* → 8198

8184 **rolling ball; trackball [mouse]; tracker ball; control ball**
  d Trackball *m*; Rollkugel *f*
  f trackball *m*; souris *f* trackball; boule *f* roulante; boule de commande
  r [координатный] шар *m*; шаровой указатель *m*; трекбол *m*

8185 **rolling mouse**
  d Rollmaus *f*
  f souris *f* roulante
  r вращающаяся мышь *f*

8186 **rollup**
  d Roll[-]up *n*

f déroulement *m* séquentiel ascendant; cumul *m*
r свертывание *n* строк (на экране дисплея)

8187 rollup group
 d Rollup-Gruppe *f*
 f groupe *m* déroulant
 r закатывающаяся группа *f*; поднимающаяся группа

8188 Roman numeral
 d römisches Numerale *n*; römisches Zahlsymbol *n*
 f chiffre *m* romain; symbole *m* numérique romain; numéral *m* romain
 r римская цифра *f*

8189 root
 d Wurzel *f*
 f racine *f*; radical *m*
 r корень *m*

8190 root-mean-square; RMS
 d quadratischer Mittelwert *m*
 f moyenne *f* quadratique
 r среднеквадратичное значение *n*; среднее квадратичное *n*

 * **root menu** → 5759

8191 root of a tree
 d Wurzel *f* eines Baums
 f racine *f* d'un arbre
 r корень *m* дерева

8192 rosette
 d Rosette *f*
 f rosette *f*
 r [растровая] розетка *f*

8193 rotary motion; rotating motion; gyratory motion
 d Drehbewegung *f*; Rotationsbewegung *f*
 f mouvement *m* giratoire; mouvement gyroscopique
 r вращательное движение *n*

 * **rotate** *v* → 1511

8194 rotated dimension
 d gedrehte Dimension *f*; rotierte Dimension; Rotationsdimension *f*
 f dimension *f* par rotation; dimension circulaire
 r перевернутый размер *m*

8195 rotated object
 d gedrehtes Objekt *n*
 f objet *m* en rotation
 r перевернутый объект *m*

8196 rotated snap angle
 d gedrehter Fangwinkel *m*
 f angle *m* d'accrochage en rotation
 r перевернутый угол *m* привязки

8197 rotate method
 d Drehmethode *f*
 f méthode *f* de rotation
 r метод *m* вращения

8198 rotating; revolving; rolling *adj*
 d umlaufend; sich drehend
 f roulant
 r вращающий[ся]

 * **rotating motion** → 8193

8199 rotating vector; vector rotating in a circular motion
 d drehender Vektor *m*; Drehvektor *m*
 f vecteur *m* tournant; vecteur qui décrit un cercle
 r ротационный вектор *m*

8200 rotation; revolution
 d Rotation *f*; Umdrehung *f*; Drehung *f*; Drehen *n*
 f rotation *f*; tour *m*; révolution *f*
 r вращение *n*; поворот *m*

8201 rotation about a point
 d Rotation *f* um einen Punkt; Drehung *f* um einen Punkt
 f rotation *f* autour d'un point
 r вращение *n* вокруг точки

 * **rotational** → 10361

 * **rotational axis** → 769

 * **rotationally symmetric surface** → 9371

 * **rotation angle** → 385

8202 rotation direction
 d Dreh[ungs]richtung *f*
 f direction *f* de rotation
 r направление *n* вращения; направление поворота

8203 rotation grip
 (twisted two-directional arrow)
 d Umdrehungsgriff *m*
 f poignée *f* de rotation
 r захват *m* вращения

8204 rotation matrix
 d Drehungsmatrix *f*; Rotationsmatrix *f*
 f matrice *f* de rotation
 r матрица *f* вращения; матрица поворота

8205 **rotation of axes; rotation of coordinate system; coordinate system rotating**
  d Drehung *f* des Koordinatensystems; Drehung der Koordinatenachsen
  f rotation *f* des axes de coordonnées; rotation d'un système de coordonnées
  r поворот *m* координатных осей; поворот осей координат; вращение *n* координатной системы

8206 **rotation of block; block rotation**
  d Blockrotation *f*
  f rotation *f* de bloc
  r вращение *n* блока; поворот *m* блока

  * **rotation of coordinate system** → 8205

8207 **rotation of object; object rotating**
  d Objektrotation *f*
  f rotation *f* d'objet
  r вращение *n* объекта; поворот *m* объекта

8208 **rotation point**
  d Drehpunkt *m*
  f point *m* de rotation
  r точка *f* поворота; точка вращения

8209 **rotation point marking**
  d Drehpunkt-Markierung *f*
  f marquage *m* de point de rotation
  r маркирование *n* точки поворота

8210 **rotation slider**
  d Drehungsschieber *m*
  f glisseur *m* de rotation
  r ползунок *m* вращения

8211 **rotation through an angle**
  d Drehung *f* um einen Winkel
  f rotation *f* à un angle
  r вращение *n* на угол; поворот *m* на угол

  * **rotor** → 2341

8212 **rough; draft**
  d roh; grob; rauh
  f rugueux; brut
  r шероховатый

8213 **rough approximation; crude approximation**
  d rohe Approximation *f*
  f approximation *f* grossière
  r грубое приближение *n*

  * **rough draft** → 8214

8214 **rough drawing; rough draft; draft; sketch; draught**
  d Rohentwurf *m*; Rohlayout *n*; [flüchtige]

Skizze *f*; Kroki *n*; Riss *m*
  f esquisse *f*; ébauche *f*; croquis *m*
  r грубый чертеж *m*; скица *f*; эскиз *m*; кроки *n*

8215 **roughness; unevenness** (of materials or surfaces)
  d Rauhigkeit *f*; Unebenheit *f*
  f rugosité *f*
  r шероховатость *f*

8216 **rough shape**
  d rauhe Form *f*
  f forme *f* rugueuse
  r шероховатая фигура *f*

  * **rough sketch** → 9662

8217 **round** *v*
  d abrunden; runden
  f arrondir
  r округлять

8218 **round; curly**
  d rund
  f rond
  r круглый

8219 **round beam**
  d Punktstrahl *m*
  f faisceau *m* rond
  r круглый луч *m*

  * **round brackets** → 6855

  * **round dots** → 1506

8220 **rounded**
  d abgerundet; gerundet
  f arrondi
  r округленный

8221 **rounded corner**
  d abgerundete Ecke *f*
  f coin *m* arrondi; angle *m* arrondi
  r округленная вершина *f* угла

8222 **rounded edge**
  d abgerundete Kante *f*
  f joint *m* arrondi; arête *f* arrondie
  r округленное ребро *n*

8223 **rounded line caps**
  d gerundete Linienenden *npl*
  f fins *mpl* de lignes arrondis
  r округленные конечные элементы *mpl* линии

8224 **round function**
  d Rundungsfunktion *f*

f fonction *f* d'arrondissement
r функция *f* округления

8225 rounding; roundness; round-off
    d Rundung *f*; Runden *n*; Abrundung *f*
    f arrondissement *m*
    r округление *n*

    * **roundness** → **8225**

    * **round-off** → **8225**

    * **round screen** → **1506**

8226 round shapes
    d gerundete Formen *fpl*
    f formes *fpl* arrondies
    r округленные формы *fpl*

8227 route *v*
    d leiten
    f router
    r маршрутизировать; направлять

8228 route; path; way
    d Leitweg *m*; Weg *m*; Bahn *f*; Strecke *f*
    f route *f*; chemin *m*; voie *f*; cours *m*; tracé *m*
    r маршрут *m*; путь *m*; дорога *f*; курс *m*; направление *n* [связи]; дорожка *f*; трасса *f*

8229 router
    d Router *m*
    f traceur *m*
    r трассировщик *m*

8230 routing
    d Leitweglenkung *f*; Leitwegsuchen *n*; Wegewahl *f*; Lenkung *f*; Routing *n*
    f acheminement *m*; choix *m* d'itinéraire; routage *m*
    r маршрутизация *f*; выбор *m* пути

8231 routing grid
    d Rastergitter *n* für Routing; Routing-Grid *n*
    f grille *f* de routage
    r сетка *f* для трассировки

8232 row
    (in a table)
    d Zeile *f*
    f ligne *f*; enregistrement *m*
    r строка *f*; запись *f*

    * **row** → **5580**

    * **row edit** → **8233**

8233 row edit[ing]
    d Zeilenbearbeitung *f*
    f édition *f* de rangée

r редактирование *n* строки

    * **row length** → **8235**

    * **row number** → **5624, 6328**

8234 row offset
    d Zeilenverschiebung *f*
    f décalage *m* de lignes
    r смещение *n* строк

    * **row of points** → **7742**

    * **row pitch** → **5205**

8235 row size; row length
    d Zeilenlänge *f*
    f longueur *f* de ligne
    r длина *f* строки

8236 row vector
    d Zeilenvektor *m*
    f vecteur *m* de ligne
    r вектор *m* строки

8237 rubber band
    d Gummiband *n*
    f fil *m* élastique; élastique *m*
    r резиновая нить *f*

8238 rubber-band graphics
    d Gummibandgrafik *f*
    f graphique *m* à fil élastique
    r эластичная графика *f*; графика с резиновой нитью

8239 rubber-banding
    d Einpassen *n* mit Gummibandfunktion
    f étirement *m* par fil élastique
    r эластичное соединение *n*; соединение резиновой нитью

8240 rubber-band line
    d Gummibandlinie *f*
    f ligne *f* du fil élastique
    r линия *f* резиновой нити

8241 rubber-band selection
    d Gummiband-Auswahl *f*
    f sélection *f* par fil élastique
    r выбор *m* методом резиновой нити

8242 rubric
    (a subarea of dialog box)
    d Rubrik *f*
    f rubrique *f*
    r рубрика *f*

8243 rule
    d Regel *f*

f règle *f*

r правило *n*

8244 ruled surface

d geregelte Oberfläche *f*; beherrschte Oberfläche

f surface *f* réglée [entre deux courbes]

r линованная поверхность *f*

8245 ruler

d Zeilenlineal *n*; Lineal *n*

f ruleur *m*; règle *f*

r [измерительная] линейка *f*

8246 ruler crosshair

d Lineal-Fadenkreuz *n*

f viseur *m* de réticule en croix

r крест *m* нитей измерительной линейки

8247 ruler showing

d Anzeigen *n* des Lineals

f apparence *f* de ruleur

r показ *m* измерительной линейки

* **run → 8248**

* **runner → 8788**

8248 run[ning]

d Durchlauf *m*; Lauf *m*; Ausführung *f*

f marche *f*; passage *m*; cours *m*

r прогон *m*; выполнение *n*

8249 running coordinates; current coordinates; moving coordinates

d laufende Koordinaten *fpl*

f coordonnées *fpl* courantes

r текущие координаты *fpl*

8250 running point

d laufender Punkt *m*

f point *m* courant

r бегущая точка *f*

8251 run *v* script

d Skript ausführen

f exécuter de script

r выполнять скрипт

8252 runway

d Weglaufen *n*

f passage *m* hors contrôle

r выход *m* из-под контроля

S

8253 saddle
d   Sattel *m*
f   col *m*; selle *f*
r   седло *n*; седловина *f*

8254 saddle point
d   Sattelpunkt *m*; Jochpunkt *m*
f   point *m* [de] col; point de selle
r   точка *f* перевала

8255 saddle point method
d   Sattelpunktmethode *f*; Pass[punkt]methode *f*
f   méthode *f* du col
r   метод *m* перевала

*   **safety** → 8443

*   **sagittal** → 581

*   **salient point** → 399

8256 sample
d   Stichprobe *f*; Probe *f*; Abtastwert *m*
f   échantillon *m* [d'essai]; modèle *m* d'essai; étalon *m*
r   образец *m*; выборка *f*; проба *f*; отсчет *m*

8257 sample code
d   Stichprobencode *m*
f   code *m* d'échantillon
r   код *m* выборки

8258 sample color
d   Probenfarbe *f*
f   couleur *f* d'échantillon
r   выборочный цвет *m*; примерный цвет

8259 sampled data
d   Stichprobendaten *npl*
f   données *fpl* échantillonnées; données d'exploration
r   выборочные данные *npl*

8260 sample distribution; sampling distribution
d   Stichprobenverteilung *f*
f   distribution *f* d'échantillonnage
r   распределение *n* выборки

8261 sample point
d   Abtastpunkt *m*
f   point *m* d'échantillonnage
r   точка *m* выборки

*   **sampler** → 8264

*   **sample rate** → 8268

8262 samples per second
d   Stichproben *fpl* pro Sekunde
f   échantillons *fpl* par seconde
r   выборки *fpl* в секунду

8263 sampling
d   Stichprobenauswahl *f*; Stichprobenerhebung *f*; Abtastung *f*
f   échantillonnage *m*; prélèvement *m* d'échantillons
r   процесс *m* выборки; опробирование *n*; отбор *m* выборок

*   **sampling distribution** → 8260

8264 sampling facility; sampler
d   Abtasteinrichtung *f*; Abtaster *m*; Quantisierer *m*
f   dispositif *m* d'exploration; explorateur *m*; échantillonneur *m*; balayeur *m*
r   опробирующее устройство *n*; квантизатор *m*

8265 sampling instant
d   Abtastzeitpunkt *m*
f   instant *m* d'échantillonnage
r   момент *m* выборки

8266 sampling latitude
d   Abtastumfang *m*
f   latitude *f* d'échantillonnage
r   охват *m* выборки; диапазон *m* выборки

8267 sampling method
d   Stichprobenverfahren *n*
f   méthode *f* d'échantillonnage
r   выборочный метод *m*

8268 sampling rate; sample rate; scan[ning] frequency; scanning rate; sensing rate
d   Abtastrate *f*; Scanrate *f*; Abtastfrequenz *f*
f   taux *m* d'échantillonnage; fréquence *f* d'échantillonnage; fréquence de balayage; fréquence d'exploration; cote *f* de scrutation
r   частота *f* взятия отсчетов; частота развертки; скорость *f* выборки

8269 sampling time; scanning time
d   Abtastzeit *f*
f   temps *m* d'échantillonnage
r   время *n* выборки

8270 sampling window
d   Abtastfenster *n*
f   fenêtre *f* d'échantillonnage
r   окно *n* выборки

8271 saturated; saturating
 d saturiert; gesättigt
 f saturé
 r насыщенный

8272 saturated colors
 d gesättigte Farben *fpl*
 f couleurs *fpl* saturées
 r насыщенные цвета *mpl*

 * **saturating** → 8271

8273 saturation
 d Sättigung *f*; Saturation *f*
 f saturation *f*
 r насыщение *n*; насыщенность *f*

8274 save *v*
 d aufbewahren; sicherstellen
 f conserver; sauvegarder
 r сохранять

8275 save area
 d Sicherstell[ungs]bereich *m*
 f zone *f* de sauvegarde; champ *m* de sauvegarde
 r область *f* сохранения

8276 save command
 d Speichern-Befehl *m*
 f commande *f* de sauvegarde
 r команда *f* сохранения

8277 saw-tooth waveform
 d Sägezahnkurve *f*
 f courbe *f* en dents de scie
 r пилообразная кривая *f*

8278 scalable font; vector font
 d vektorielle Schrift *f*; Vektorschrift *f*
 f police *f* vectorisée; police de taille variable; police vectorielle
 r векторный шрифт *m*; масштабируемый фонт *m*

 * **scalable graphics** → 10121

8279 scalable rendering processor
 d Vektorrendering-Prozessor *m*
 f processeur *m* de rendu vectorisé
 r процессор *m* масштабируемого оттенения

 * **scalar** → 8285

8280 scalar *adj*
 d skalar
 f scalaire
 r скалярный

8281 scalar approximation
 d skalare Näherung *f*
 f approximation *f* scalaire
 r скалярная аппроксимация *f*

8282 scalar field
 d skalares Feld *n*
 f champ *m* scalaire
 r скалярное поле *n*

8283 scalar model
 d skalares Modell *n*
 f modèle *m* scalaire
 r скалярная модель *f*

8284 scalar optics
 d skalare Optik *f*
 f optique *f* scalaire
 r скалярная оптика *f*

8285 scalar [quantity]
 d Skalar *m*; skalare Größe *f*
 f scalaire *m*; grandeur *f* scalaire
 r скаляр *m*; скалярная величина *f*

8286 scale
 d Maßstab *m*
 f échelle *f*
 r масштаб *m*

8287 scale
 d Skala *f*; Skale *f*
 f échelle *f*; graduation *f*
 r шкала *f*

8288 scale *v*; **size** *v*
 d skalieren; Maßstab ändern
 f modifier à l'échelle
 r масштабировать

8289 scale *v* **down**
 d Maßstab verkleinern
 f réduire à l'échelle
 r уменьшать масштаб

8290 scaled value
 d skalierter Wert *m*
 f valeur *f* réduite
 r приведенное к масштабу значение *n*

8291 scale error
 d Maßstabsfehler *m*; Skalenfehler *m*
 f erreur *f* d'échelle
 r погрешность *f*, вносимая шкалой

8292 scale factor; scaling factor; scaling multiplier
 d Skalenfaktor *m*; Maßstabsfaktor *m*
 f facteur *m* d'échelle
 r масштабный коэффициент *m*; масштабный множитель *m*

8293 scale graduation
  d Skalen[ein]teilung *f*
  f graduation *f* d'échelle
  r [раз]деление *n* шкалы; градуировка *f* шкалы

8294 scalene; scalenous
  d ungleichseitig
  f scalène
  r разносторонний; неравносторонний

  * **scalene cone → 6419**

8295 scalene triangle
  d ungleichseitiges Dreieck *n*
  f triangle *m* scalène
  r неравносторонний треугольник *m*

  * **scalenous → 8294**

8296 scale of drawing; drawing scale
  d Zeichenmaßstab *m*; Zeichnungsmaßstab *m*
  f échelle *f* de dessin
  r масштаб *m* чертежа

8297 scale of heights; vertical scale
  d Höhenskala *f*; Höhenmaßstab *m*
  f échelle *f* des hauteurs; échelle des altitudes
  r масштаб *m* высот; вертикальный масштаб

8298 scale of lengths
  d Längenskala *f*; Längenmaßstab *m*
  f échelle *f* des longueurs
  r масштаб *m* долгот

8299 scale of magnification
  d Vergrößerungsmaßstab *m*
  f échelle *f* d'agrandissement
  r масштаб *m* увеличения

8300 scale of model
  d Modellmaßstab *m*
  f échelle *f* de modèle
  r масштаб *m* модели

8301 scale of projection; projection scale
  d Projektionsmaßstab *m*
  f échelle *f* de projection
  r масштаб *m* проекции

8302 scale of reduction
  d Verkleinerungsmaßstab *m*
  f échelle *f* de réduction
  r масштаб *m* уменьшения

8303 scale parameter
  d Skalenparameter *m*
  f paramètre *m* d'échelle; paramètre d'étalement
  r масштабный параметр *m*

8304 scale-preserving mapping
  d maßstab[s]treue Abbildung *f*
  f transformation *f* conservante l'échelle
  r отображение *n*, сохраняющее масштаб

8305 scale proportion; scale ratio
  d Maßstabsverhältnis *n*
  f rapport *m* d'échelle
  r масштабное отношение *n*

  * **scale ratio → 8305**

8306 scaling
  d Skalierung *f*; Maßstabsänderung *f*
  f mise *f* à l'échelle; choix *m* d'échelle
  r масштабирование *n*; выбор *m* масштаба; пересчет *m*

  * **scaling factor → 8292**

  * **scaling multiplier → 8292**

  * **scan → 8320**

8307 scan *v*
  d abtasten; scannen
  f balayer; explorer; lire
  r сканировать; развертывать

8308 scan converter
  d Scankonverter *m*
  f convertisseur *m* de balayage
  r сканирующий преобразователь *m*

  * **scan cycle → 8322**

  * **scan frequency → 8268**

  * **scan graphics → 7759**

  * **scan line → 8324**

8309 scan-line spacing; scanning pitch
  d Abtastzeilenabstand *m*
  f espacement *m* entre lignes de balayage
  r расстояние *n* между строками сканирования

8310 scanned image
  d Scanbild *n*
  f image *f* balayée
  r сканированное изображение *n*

8311 scanned surface
  d Scanfläche *f*
  f surface *f* balayée
  r сканированная поверхность *f*

8312 scanner
  d Scanner *m*

f scanner *m*
r сканер *m*; сканирующее устройство *n*

8313 scanner calibration
  d Scanner-Kalibrierung *f*
  f calibrage *m* de scanner
  r калибровка *f* сканера

8314 scanner characteristics
  d Scanner-Merkmale *npl*
  f caractéristiques *fpl* de scanner
  r характеристики *fpl* сканера

8315 scanner configuration
  d Scanner-Konfiguration *f*
  f configuration *f* de scanner
  r конфигурация *f* сканера

8316 scanner file
  d Scanner-Datei *f*
  f fichier *m* de scanner
  r файл *m* сканера

8317 scanner resolution
  d Scannerauflösungsvermögen *n*
  f résolution *f* de scanner
  r разрешающая способность *f* сканера

8318 scanner software
  d Scannersoftware *f*; Programmierhilfen *fpl* des Scanners
  f logiciel *m* de scanner
  r программное обеспечение *n* сканера

8319 scanner transfer mode
  d Transferbetriebsweise *f* des Scanners
  f mode *m* de transfert de scanner
  r режим *m* передачи сканера

8320 scan[ning]; exploration; exploring
  d Abtastung *f*; Abtasten *n*; Scanning *n*; Scannen *n*; Scan *n*
  f balayage *m*; scrutation *f*; exploration *f*
  r сканирование *n*

8321 scanning beam
  d Abtaststrahl *m*
  f faisceau *m* de balayage
  r сканирующий луч *m*

8322 scan[ning] cycle
  d Abtastzyklus *m*
  f cycle *m* de balayage
  r цикл *m* сканирования; цикл развертки

  * **scanning frequency → 8268**

8323 scanning input
  d Abtasteingang *m*
  f entrée *f* de balayage
  r сканирующий вход *m*

8324 scan[ning] line
  d Abtastlinie *f*; Abtastzeile *f*
  f ligne *f* de balayage; ligne d'exploration; ligne de lecture
  r строка *f* развертки; полоса *f* сканирования

8325 scanning mechanism
  d Abtastungsmechanismus *m*
  f mécanisme *m* de balayage
  r механизм *m* сканирования

  * **scanning method → 8328**

8326 scanning parameter
  d Abtastungsparameter *m*
  f paramètre *m* d'exploration
  r параметр *m* сканирования

  * **scanning pitch → 8309**

  * **scanning rate → 8268**

8327 scanning speed; sensing speed
  d Abtastgeschwindigkeit *f*
  f vitesse *f* d'exploration
  r скорость *f* сканирования

8328 scanning technique; scanning method
  d Abtastverfahren *n*
  f méthode *f* de balayage
  r метод *m* сканирования

  * **scanning time → 8269**

  * **scan pattern → 7747**

  * **scatter** *v* **→ 2738**

8329 scatter chart; scatter plot; scatter diagram; dispersion diagram
  d Streu[ungs]diagramm *n*
  f graphique *m* de dispersion; diagramme *m* de dispersion; nuage *m* de points
  r диаграмма *f* разброса; диаграмма рассеивания

  * **scatter diagram → 8329**

8330 scattered
  d diffus; verstreut; zerstreut
  f diffus; dispersé
  r рассеянный

8331 scattered beam
  d gestreuter Strahl *m*
  f faisceau *m* diffusé
  r рассеянный луч *m*

* scattered light → 2741

8332 scattered radiation
    d Streustrahlung *f*
    f rayonnement *m* diffusé
    r рассеяное излучение *n*

8333 scattered sheaf; flabby sheaf; weak sheaf
    d gestreute Garbe *f*
    f faisceau *m* flasque
    r вялый пучок *m*

* scattering → 2908

* scattering coefficient → 2752

8334 scattering loss
    d Streu[ungs]verlust *m*
    f pertes *fpl* par diffusion
    r потери *fpl* на рассеивание

8335 scattering of light; light scattering
    d Lichtstreuung *f*
    f diffusion *f* de la lumière; dispersion *f* de la lumière
    r рассеивание *n* света

8336 scattering particles
    d streuende Teilchen *npl*
    f particules *fpl* diffusantes
    r рассеивающиеся частицы *fpl*

* scatter plot → 8329

8337 scenario; script
    d Szenarium *n*
    f scénario *m*
    r сценарий *m*

8338 scene
    d Szene *f*
    f scène *f*
    r сцена *f*

8339 scene analysis
    d Szenenanalyse *f*
    f analyse *f* de scène
    r анализ *m* сцены

8340 scene builder
    d Szenenbildner *m*
    f bâtisseur *m* de scène
    r компоновщик *m* сцен; разработчик *m* сцен; построитель *m* сцен

8341 scene description
    d Szenenbeschreibung *f*
    f description *f* de scène
    r описание *n* сцены

8342 scene digitalization
    d Szenendigitalisierung *f*
    f numérisation *f* de scène
    r оцифрование *n* сцены

8343 scene geometry
    d Szenegeometrie *f*
    f géométrie *f* de scène
    r геометрия *f* сцены

8344 scene graph
    (directed acyclic graph whose nodes contain geometry and texture information for components)
    d Szenengraph *m*
    f graphe *m* de scène
    r граф *m* сцены

8345 scene management
    d Szenenmanagement *n*
    f gestion *f* de scène
    r обработка *f* сцены

8346 scene modeling
    d Szenenmodellierung *f*
    f modelage *m* de scène
    r моделирование *n* сцены

* scenery → 5399

8347 scenes view
    d Szenenansicht *f*
    f vue *f* de scènes
    r вид *m* сцен

8348 scene synthesis
    d Szenensynthese *f*
    f synthèse *f* de scène
    r синтез *m* сцены

8349 schedule; timetable
    d Ablaufplan *m*; Zeitplan *m*
    f table *f* de temps; plan *m* [de déroulement]; horaire *m*
    r расписание *n*; график *m*

8350 scheduling
    d Ablauf[folge]planung *f*
    f planification *f* de séquence
    r составление *n* графика

8351 schema; scheme
    d Schema *n*
    f schéma *m*; schème *m*
    r схема *f*; план *m*

8352 schematic design
    d Schaltungsentwurf *m*
    f conception *f* de circuiterie
    r схемотехническое проектирование *n*

8353 schematic map
d schematische Karte *f*
f carte *f* schématique
r схематическая карта *f*

8354 schematic visualization
d schematische Visualisierung *f*
f visualisation *f* schématique
r схематическая визуализация *f*

* **scheme** → 8351

* **scissoring** → 1558

8355 scope
d Spielraum *m*; Gültigkeitsbereich *m*;
Wirkungsbereich *m*; Sichbarkeitsbereich *m*
f domaine *m* d'action; domaine d'application;
champ *m* de validité
r область *f* действия; диапазон *m* действия

8356 score
d Häkchen *n*; Note *f*
f score *m*; note *f*, enregistrement *m*
r оценка *f*; отметка *f*

* **scrambler** → 8357

8357 scrambler [circuit]
d Verwürfler *m*; Scrambler *m*
f embrouilleur *m*; circuit *m* brouilleur;
brasseur *m*
r скрэмблер *m*

8358 scrambling
d Verwürfelung *f*
f embrouillage *m*; mélange *m*
r запутывание *n*; размешивание *n*;
перемешивание *n*; зашумление *n*

8359 scrapbook
d Skizzenbuch *n*
f classeur *m*
r текстографический буферный файл *m*

8360 scratch
d Zug *m*; Furche *f*; Spur *f*
f sillon *m*
r борозда *f*; царапина *f*

* **scratch area** → 10460

8361 screen
d Bildschirm *m*
f écran *m*
r экран *m*

* **screen angle** → 7748

* **screen buffer** → 2920

8362 screen capture; screen dump; screenshot
d Bildschirm-Sammeln *n*
f capture *f* d'écran; copie *f* d'écran
r зэкранный дамп *m*; скриншот *m*

8363 screen capturer
d Bildschirmsammler *m*
f capteur *m* d'écran
r экранный уловитель *m*

8364 screen coordinates
d Bildschirmkoordinaten *fpl*
f coordonnées *fpl* d'écran
r экранные координаты *fpl*

8365 screen diagonal
d Bildschirmdiagonale *f*
f diagonale *f* d'écran
r диагональ *m* экрана

8366 screen dot; matrix dot; halftone dot; dot; grid point; raster point
d Rasterpunkt *m*; Halbtonpunkt *m*;
Gitterpunkt *m*
f point *m* rastre; point d'écran; point de grille
r точка *f* растра; растровая точка

8367 screen dot pitch; dot pitch; pitch
d Bildschirmpunktabstand *m*; Pixelabstand *m*;
Punktabstand *m*; Rastermaß *n*; Pitch *m*
f pas *m* de masque; espacement *m* entre pixels;
distance *f* entre points; pitch *m*
r расстояние *n* между точками изображения
на экране; шаг *m* расположения
[растровых] точек; шаг растра

* **screen driver** → 2928

* **screen dump** → 8362

8368 screen editor
d Bildschirmeditor *m*
f éditeur *m* d'écran
r экранный редактор *m*

8369 screen factor
d Schirmfaktor *m*
f facteur *m* d'écran
r коэффициент *m* экранирования

* **screen flicker** → 8370

8370 screen flicker[ing]
d Bildschirmblinken *n*
f scintillement *m* d'écran
r мигание *n* экрана

8371 screen font
d Bildschirmschrift *f*

f police *f* d'écran
r экранный шрифт *m*

8372 screen formatting
d Bildschirmformatierung *f*
f formatage *m* d'écran
r форматирование *n* изображения на экране

8373 screen frequency
d Bildschirmfrequenz *f*
f fréquence *f* d'écran
r частота *f* экрана

8374 screen function
d Bildschirmfunktion *f*
f fonction *f* d'écran
r экранная функция *f*

8375 screen grid
d Bildschirm-Gitter *n*
f grille-écran *f*
r экранная решетка *f*

* **screening → 8641**

8376 screen menu
d Bildschirm-Menü *n*
f menu *m* d'écran
r экранное меню *n*

8377 screen mode
d Bildschirmmodus *m*
f mode *m* d'écran
r экранный режим *m*

8378 screen overlay
d Bildschirm-Overlay *n*
f recouvrement *m* d'écran
r перекрытие *n* экрана

8379 screen painter
d Bildschirmmaler *m*
f unité *f* de coloriage de l'écran
r экранный оформитель *m*; блок *m*
   раскраски изображения на экране

8380 screen palette
d Bildschirmpalette *f*
f palette *f* d'écran
r экранная палитра *f*

8381 screen photography
d Bildschirmfoto *n*
f photographie *f* d'écran
r снимок *m* экрана

8382 screen preview
d Bildschirmvorschau *f*
f aperçu *m* d'écran
r экранный предварительный просмотр *m*

* **screen redraw → 8383**

8383 screen redraw[ing]
d Bildschirmauffrischung *f*
f retraçage *m* d'écran; reconstruction *f* d'écran
r обновление *n* изображения на экране

* **screen resolution → 6023**

8384 screen ruling
d Rasterwinkelung *f*; Rasterdehnung *f*;
   Rasterlage *f*
f orientation *f* de trame
r ориентация *f* экранного растра

8385 screen saver
d Bildschirmsparer *m*
f économiseur *m* d'écran
r экранный сберегатель *m*

* **screenshot → 8362**

8386 screen size
d Bildschirmgröße *f*
f taille *f* d'écran
r размер *m* экрана

8387 screen snapshot
d Bildschirm-Schnappschuss *m*
f image *f* instantanée sur l'écran
r моментальный снимок *m* экрана

* **screen split → 8388**

8388 screen split[ting]
d Teilung *f* des Bildschirms
f splittage *m* d'écran
r расщепление *n* экрана

8389 screen view; display view
d Bildschirmansicht *f*
f vue *f* d'écran
r экранный вид *m*

8390 screen window
d Bildfenster *n*
f fenêtre *f* d'écran
r экранное окно *n*

8391 screw
d Schraube *f*
f vis *f*
r винт *m*

* **screwing → 4557**

* **screw-line → 4560**

* **screw motion → 4557**

* **screw pitch** → 7083

8392 scribble *v*
d kritzeln
f griffonner
r писать неразборчиво

8393 scribble; poor painting
d grafische Layoutskizze *f*
f gribouillage *m*; griffonnage *m*
r небрежное рисование *n*; неразборчивое
рисование

* **script** → 8337

8394 script editor
d Schrift *f*
f éditeur *m* de scripts
r редактор *m* скриптов

8395 script file
d Skriptdatei *f*
f fichier *m* de script
r скрипт-файл *m*; файл сценария

8396 script manager
d Skript-Manager *m*
f gestionnaire *m* de scripts
r программа *f* управления скриптов

* **scroll** → 8401

8397 scrollable window
d rollbares Bildfenster *n*
f fenêtre *f* défilable
r прокручиваемое окно *n*

8398 scroll arrow
d Bildlaufpfeil *m*
f flèche *f* de défilement
r стрелка *f* прокрутки

8399 scrollbar; elevator
d Rollbalken *n*; Bildlaufleiste *f*
f barre *f* de défilement; ascenseur *m*
r лента *f* прокручивания; линейка *f*
просмотра

8400 scroll box
d Bildlauffeld *n*
f boite *f* de défilement; curseur *m* de défilement
r бегунок *m*

8401 scroll[ing]
d Rollen *n*; Blättern *n*
f défilement *m*
r прокрутка *f*; прокручивание *n*;
скроллинг *m*

8402 scrolling text box

d Durchlauftextfeld *n*
f champ *m* de texte déroulant; zone *f* de texte
multiligne; case *f* de saisie multiple
r ящик *m* прокручивания [многострочного]
текста

8403 sculptor program
d Bildhauerprogramm *n*
f programme *m* sculpteur
r программа *f* скульптор

* **SDF** → 8921

8404 seam
d Naht *f*; Fuge *f*; Saum *m*
f joint *m*
r шов *m*; рубец *m*; прослойка *f*

8405 seam *v*
d nähen
f joindre
r набороздить; сшить; сшивать

8406 seamless
d spaltfrei; nahtlos
f sans soudure
r без шва; из одного куска; цельнотянутый;
цельнокроенный

8407 seamless background
d spaltfreier Hintergrund *m*
f fond *m* sans soudure
r непрерывный фон *m*; цельнокроенный фон

* **search** → 8409

8408 search algorithm
d Suchalgorithmus *m*
f algorithme *m* de recherche
r алгоритм *m* поиска

8409 search[ing]; seek[ing]
d Suche *f*; Suchen *n*; Untersuchung *f*
f recherche *f*
r поиск *m*; искание *n*

8410 searching strategy
d Suchstrategie *f*
f stratégie *f* de recherche
r стратегия *f* поиска

8411 search key
d Suchschlüssel *m*
f clé *f* de recherche
r ключ *m* поиска

8412 search path
d Suchweg *m*
f chemin *m* de recherche
r маршрут *m* поиска

8413 search procedure
d Suchverfahren *n*
f procédure *f* de recherche
r процедура *f* отыскания; процедура поиска

8414 search process
d Suchprozess *m*
f processus *m* de recherche
r процесс *m* отыскания; процесс поиска

8415 search string
d Such[zeichen]kette *f*
f chaîne *f* de recherche
r строка *f* поиска

* **seat file** → 7607

* **secant** → 9857

8416 secant circles; intersecting circles
d sich schneidende Kreise *mpl*
f cercles *mpl* sécants
r пересекающиеся окружности *fpl*

8417 secant curve
d Sekanskurve *f*; Sekansoide *f*
f courbe *f* sécante; sécantoïde *f*
r секансоида *f*

* **secant line** → 9857

* **second** → 401

8418 secondary
d sekundär; Zweit-
f secondaire; deuxième
r вторичный; второстепенный; второй

8419 secondary axis
d Sekundärachse *f*
f axe *m* secondaire
r вторичная ось *f*; вспомагательная ось

8420 secondary chart axes
d Sekundärachsen *fpl* des Diagramms
f axes *m* de diagramme secondaires
r вторичные оси *fpl* диаграммы

* **secondary color** → 1916

8421 secondary diagonal
d Nebendiagonale *f*
f diagonale *f* secondaire
r побочная диагональ *f*; вторичная
   диагональ

8422 secondary polygonal traverse
d Nebenpolygonzug *m*
f cheminement *m* polygonal secondaire
r вторичный полигональный ход *m*

8423 secondary ray
d Sekundärstrahl *m*
f rayon *m* secondaire
r вторичный луч *m*

8424 secondary triangulation
d Kleintriangulation *f*
f triangulation *f* secondaire
r малая триангуляция *f*; триангуляция
   нисшего класса

* **second curvature** → 9778

8425 second normal form
d zweite Normalform *f*
f deuxième forme *f* normale
r вторая нормальная форма *f*

8426 second order effect
d Effekt *m* zweiter Ordnung
f effet *m* d'ordre secondaire
r вторичный эффект *m*

* **second plane of projection** → 10181

* **second principal line** → 4037

* **second principal plane** → 4039

* **second projection** → 10180

* **second trace parallel** → 4037

* **second trace point** → 8427

8427 second trace point [of a line]
d zweiter Spurpunkt *m* [der Linie]
f second point *m* de trace [de ligne]
r второй след *m* [прямой]; вертикальный
   след [прямой]

8428 second window
d zweites Fenster *n*
f deuxième fenêtre *f*
r второе окно *n*

8429 section
d Abschnitt *m*; Abteilung *f*
f partie *f*
r раздел *m* [документа]; секция *f*

8430 section; cut
d Sektion *f*; Schnitt *m*
f section *f*; coupe *f*
r сечение *n*; разрез *m*

8431 sectional drawing
d Querschnittzeichnung *f*
f dessin *m* en coupe
r чертеж *m* в разрезе

8432 sectional object; cutting object
 d Schnittobjekt *n*
 f objet *m* de la coupe
 r секущий объект *m*

8433 sectional view
 d Schnittansicht *f*
 f vue *f* en coupe; vue transversale
 r вид *m* в разрезе

8434 section header; section title
 d Abschnittskopf *m*; Abteilungstitel *m*
 f tête *f* de section
 r заголовок *m* секции; заголовок раздела

8435 sectioning
 d Sektionierung *f*
 f sectionnement *m*
 r секционирование *n*

8436 section length
 d Schnittlänge *f*
 f longueur *f* de section
 r длина *f* сечения

8437 section of a sheaf
 d Schnitt *m* einer Garbe
 f section *f* d'un faisceau
 r сечение *n* пучка

* section plane → 7146

* section title → 8434

8438 sector
 d Sektor *m*
 f secteur *m*
 r сектор *m*

8439 sector angle
 d Sektorwinkel *m*
 f angle *m* du secteur
 r угол *m* сектора

* sector diagram → 7071

8440 sector exploding
 d Sektor-Explodieren *n*
 f décomposition *f* de secteur
 r развязка *f* сектора

8441 sector of a circle; circular sector
 d Kreisabschnitt *m*; Kreisausschnitt *m*;
   Kreissektor *m*
 f secteur *m* de cercle; secteur circulaire
 r круговой сегмент *m*

8442 sector of a sphere; spherical sector
 d Kugelsektor *m*; Kugelausschnitt *m*
 f secteur *m* de la sphère; secteur sphérique

 r сектор *m* сферы; сферический сектор;
   шаровой сектор

8443 security; safety
 d Sicherheit *f*; Schutz *m*
 f sécurité *f*; sûreté *f*
 r безопасность *f*; защита *f*

* seek → 8409

* seeking → 8409

* seeming → 470

8444 segment
 d Segment *n*; Abschnitt *m*
 f segment *m*
 r сегмент *m*; отрезок *m*

8445 segmentation
 d Segmentierung *f*
 f segmentation *f*
 r сегментирование *n*; сегментация *f*

8446 segmentation and block formation
 d Segmentierung *f* und Blockbildung *f*
 f segmentation *f* et formation *f* des blocs
 r сегментирование *n* и формирование *n*
   блоков

8447 segment attribute
 d Segment-Attribut *n*
 f attribut *m* de segment
 r атрибут *m* сегмента

8448 segment of a circle; circle segment
 d Kreissegment *n*
 f segment *m* de cercle
 r сегмент *m* круга

8449 segment of a sphere; spherical segment
 d Kugelabschnitt *m*; Kugelsegment *n*
 f segment *m* sphérique
 r шаровой сегмент *m*; сферический сегмент

8450 seize *v*
 d belegen; einnehmen
 f occuper; gripper
 r занять; занимать; захватывать

* seizing → 6451

* seizure → 6451

* select → 8460

8451 select *v*; choose *v*
 d auswählen; wählen; selektieren
 f sélectionner; choisir
 r выбирать; отбирать; избирать

8452 selectable
  d wählbar
  f sélectable
  r выбираемый

8453 select *v* all
  d alles auswählen
  f sélectionner tout
  r выбирать все

8454 selected
  d ausgewählt; markiert
  f sélectionné
  r выбранный

8455 selected area
  d ausgewählter Bereich *m*
  f aire *f* sélectionnée
  r выбранная область *f*

8456 selected grips
  d markierte Griffe *mpl*
  f poignées *fpl* sélectionnées
  r выбранные захваты *mpl*

8457 selected object
  d ausgewähltes Objekt *n*
  f objet *m* sélectionné
  r выбранный объект *m*

8458 selected text characters
  d Zeichen *npl* des markierten Texts
  f caractères *mpl* de texte sélectionné
  r символы *mpl* выбранного текста

  * **selecting → 8460**

8459 selecting bar
  d Auswahl-Balken *n*
  f barre *f* de sélection
  r полоса *f* выбора

8460 selection; select[ing]; choice
  d Auswahl *f*; Wahl *f*; Selektion *f*
  f sélection *f*; choix *m*
  r выбор *m*; выборка *f*; отбор *m*; селекция *f*

  * **selection box → 7040**

8461 selection check
  d Wahlprüfung *f*
  f essai *m* de sélection
  r проверка *f* выбора

8462 selection cursor; element cursor
  d Auswahlkursor *m*
  f curseur *m* de sélection
  r курсор *m* выбора

8463 selection cycling

  d zyklische Wiederholung *f* der Auswahl
  f bouclage *m* de sélection
  r зацикливание *n* выбора

8464 selection ellipse
  d Ellipse *f* der Auswahl
  f ellipse *f* de sélection
  r эллипс *m* выборки

8465 selection feature
  d Wahlmerkmal *n*; Auswahlwerkzeug *m*
  f moyen *m* de sélection
  r средство *n* выбора

8466 selection form
  d Auswahlformular *n*
  f formulaire *m* de sélection
  r формуляр *m* выборки

8467 selection format
  d Wahlformat *n*
  f format *m* de sélection
  r формат *m* выбора

  * **selection frame → 8474**

8468 selection mode
  d Selektionsbetriebsart *f*
  f mode *m* de sélection
  r режим *m* выборки

8469 selection procedure
  d Wahlverfahren *n*
  f procédure *f* de sélection
  r процедура *f* выбора

8470 selection process
  d Auswahlprozess *m*; Auswahlvorgang *m*
  f processus *m* de sélection
  r процесс *m* выбора

8471 selection radius
  d Auswahlradius *m*
  f rayon *m* de sélection
  r радиус *m* выбора

  * **selection set → 7045**

8472 selection target
  d Auswahlziel *n*
  f cible *f* de sélection; destination *f* de sélection
  r цель *f* выбора

  * **selection tool → 7046**

8473 selection tree
  d Selektorbaum *m*
  f arbre *m* de sélection
  r дерево *n* выбора; дерево-селектор *n*

8474 **selection window; selection frame**
d Auswahlfenster *n*
f fenêtre *f* de sélection; cadre *f* de sélection
r окно *n* выбора

8475 **selective absorption**
d selektive Absorption *f*
f absorption *f* sélective
r селективное поглощение *n*

8476 **selective filter**
d Selektivfilter *m*
f filtre *m* sélectif
r селективный фильтр *m*

8477 **selectivity**
d Selektivität *f*
f sélectivité *f*
r селективность *f*; избирательность *f*

* **select method** → 5935

8478 **selector; choice device**
d Selektor *m*; Auswähler *m*; Wähler *m*
f sélecteur *m*
r селектор *m*; искатель *m*

8479 **self-absorption**
d Selbstabsorption *f*; Eigenabsorption *f*
f auto-absorption *f*
r самопоглощение *n*

* **self-acting** → 688

8480 **self-adapting; auto-adapting**
d selbsteinstellend
f auto-adaptatif
r самоадаптирующийся;
самоприспосабливающийся

8481 **self-adjusting** *adj*
d selbstanpassend
f auto-ajustable; autoréglable
r самонастраивающийся

8482 **self-aligning; auto-aligning** *adj*
d selbstausrichtend
f auto-alignant
r самовыравнивающийся

8483 **self-alignment**
d Selbstausrichtung *f*
f auto-alignement *m*
r самовыравнивание *n*

8484 **self-calibrating**
d Selbstkalibrierung *f*
f calibrage *m* automatique
r автоматическое калибрирование *n*

8485 **self-checking; self-testing; auto-checking; auto-testing**
d selbstprüfend
f autocontrôlé
r самопроверяющийся;
самоконтролирующийся

8486 **self-checking code**
d selbstprüfender Code *m*
f code *m* de autovérification; code autocontrôlé
r самоконтролирующийся код *m*; код с самопроверкой

8487 **self-correcting code**
d selbstkorrigierender Code *m*
f code *m* autocorrecteur
r самокорректирующийся код *m*

* **self-corresponding point** → 3840

* **self-focus** → 677

* **self-focusing** → 678

* **self-focusing** *adj* → 679

8488 **self-focusing effect**
d Selbstfokussierungseffekt *m*
f effet *m* d'autofocalisation
r эффект *m* самофокусирования

8489 **self-intersection**
d Selbstschnitt *m*
f auto-intersection *f*
r самопересечение *n*

* **self-intersection point** → 7221

8490 **self-overlapping**
d Selbstüberlappung *f*; Selbstüberschneidung *f*
f auto-recouvrement *m*; auto-chevauchement *m*
r авто-перекрытие *n*; авто-перекрывание *n*;
авто-накладывание *n*; авто-наложение *n*

8491 **self-polarity**
d Selbstpolarität *f*; Autopolarität *f*
f autopolarité *f*
r автополярность *f*

8492 **self-polar polygon**
(of a quadric)
d selbstpolares Vieleck *n*; Polarvieleck *n*;
Polvieleck *n*
f polygone *m* autopolaire
r автополярный полигон *m*

8493 **self-polar simplex; polar simplex**
d selbstpolares Simplex *n*; Polarsimplex *n*
f simplexe *m* [auto]polaire
r автополярный симплекс *m*

8494 self-polar tetrahedron
  d selbstpolares Tetraeder *n*; Polvierflach *n*
  f tétraèdre *m* autopolaire
  r автополярный тетраэдр *m*

  * **self-polar triad of lines → 8495**

8495 self-polar trilateral; self-polar triad of lines
  d Polardreiseit *n*
  f trilatère *m* polaire
  r автополярный трехсторонник *m*;
     автополярный трехугольник *m*

  * **self-replication → 8496**

8496 self-reproduction; self-replication
  d Selbstreproduktion *f*
  f autoreproduction *f*
  r самовоспроизведение *n*

  * **self-tangency point → 7222**

  * **self-testing → 8485**

8497 semantic
  d semantisch
  f sémantique
  r семантический

8498 semantic node
  d semantischer Knoten *m*
  f nœud *m* sémantique
  r узел *m* семантической сети

8499 semantics
  d Semantik *f*
  f sémantique *f*
  r семантика *f*

  * **semaphore → 8500**

8500 semaphore [variable]
  d Semaphor *m*; Semaphorvariable *f*
  f sémaphore *m*; variable *f* sémaphore
  r семафор *m*; семафорная переменная *f*

8501 semi-automated digitizing
  d halbautomatische Digitalisierung *f*
  f numérisation *f* demi-auto
  r полуавтоматизированное оцифрование *n*

8502 semiaxis
  d Halbachse *f*
  f demi-axe *m*
  r полуось *f*

8503 semicircle
  d Halbkreis *m*
  f demi-cercle *m*
  r полукруг *m*

8504 semicolon
  (;)
  d Semikolon *n*
  f point-virgule *m*
  r точка *f* с запятой

8505 semiconjugate axis
  (of a hyperbola)
  d imaginäre Halbachse *f*
  f demi-axe *m* non transverse
  r мнимая полуось *f* гиперболы

8506 semicubic parabola
  d halbkubische Parabel *f*
  f parabole *f* semi-cubique
  r полукубическая парабола *f*

  * **semi-focal chord → 3900**

8507 semi-gloss surfaces
  d Halbglanzflächen *fpl*
  f surfaces *fpl* semi-brillantes
  r полуглянцевые поверхности *fpl*;
     полугладкие поверхности

8508 semijoin
  d Halbverbindung *f*
  f semi-jonction *f*
  r полуобъединение *n*

8509 semimajor axis
  (of a conic section)
  d große Halbachse *f*
  f demi-grand axe *m*; demi-axe *m* focal
  r большая полуось *f*

8510 semimean axis
  (of an ellipsoid)
  d mittlere Halbachse *f*
  f demi-axe *m* moyen
  r средняя полуось *f*

8511 semiminor axis
  (of an ellipse or ellipsoid)
  d kleine Halbachse *f*
  f demi-petit axe *m*; demi-axe *m* non focal
  r малая полуось *f*

8512 semiocclusion
  d Halbokklusion *f*
  f demi-occultation *f*
  r полупреграждение *n*;
     полунепроходимость *f*

8513 semiordered
  d halbgeordnet
  f demi-ordonné
  r полуупорядоченный

8514 semiordered vector space
  d halbgeordneter Vektorraum *m*

f espace *m* vectoriel demi-ordonné
r полуупорядоченное векторное пространство *n*

8515 semiperimeter; half the perimeter
   d halber Umfang *m*
   f demi-périmètre *m*
   r полупериметр *m*

8516 semi-polar coordinates
   d Halbpolarkoordinaten *fpl*
   f coordonnées *fpl* semi-polaires
   r полуполярные координаты *fpl*

8517 semi-reflecting; semi-reflective
   d halbreflektierend
   f semi-réfléchissant
   r полуотражающий; частично отражающий

8518 semi-reflecting mirror
   d halbreflektierender Spiegel *m*
   f miroir *m* semi-réfléchissant
   r полуотражающее зеркало *n*

   * **semi-reflective** → 8517

8519 semi-space
   d Halbraum *m*
   f demi-espace *m*
   r полупространство *n*

8520 semi-transparent
   d halbtransparent
   f semi-transparent
   r полупрозрачный

8521 semi-transparent mirror
   d halbtransparenter Spiegel *m*
   f miroir *m* semi-transparent
   r полупрозрачное зеркало *n*

8522 semitransverse axis
   (of a hyperbola)
   d reale Halbachse *f*
   f demi-axe *m* focal; demi-axe transverse
   r действительная полуось *f*

8523 send *v*
   d senden; aussenden; abgeben
   f envoyer; émettre; transférer
   r отправлять; посылать

8524 send *v* to bottom
   d nach unten senden
   f envoyer en bas
   r посылать вниз

   * **sensation of movement** → 5379

   * **sense** → 2862

   * **sense *v*** → 7798

8525 sense *v*
   d abtasten; ablesen
   f palper; explorer
   r воспринимать; опознавать; считывать

8526 sensibility; sensitivity; responsivity
   d Empfindlichkeit *f*
   f sensibilité *f*
   r чувствительность *f*

8527 sensing
   d Abfühlen *n*; Wahrnehmen *n*
   f palpage *m*; exploration *f*; saisie *f*
   r ощущение *n*; опознавание *n*

   * **sensing** → 7800

   * **sensing device** → 8528

8528 sensing element; sensing device; sensor; pickup
   d Fühlelement *n*; Messfühler *m*; Geber *m*; Sensor *m*; Aufnehmer *m*; Messwertaufnehmer *m*
   f élément *m* sensible; capteur *m* [de mesure]; senseur *m*
   r чувствительный элемент *m*; считывающий элемент; сенсор *m*; датчик *m*

   * **sensing rate** → 8268

   * **sensing speed** → 8327

8529 sensitive image
   d empfindliches Bild *n*
   f image *f* sensitive
   r чувствительное изображение *n*

   * **sensitive screen** → 9790

   * **sensitivity** → 8526

8530 sensitivity loss
   d Empfindlichkeitsverlust *m*
   f perte *f* de sensibilité
   r потеря *f* чувствительности

8531 sensitivity range
   d Empfindlichkeitsbereich *m*
   f gamme *f* de sensibilité
   r диапазон *m* чувствительности

   * **sensor** → 8528

   * **sensor glove** → 2481

   * **sentinel** → 3843

8532 separate *v*
   d trennen
   f séparer
   r отделять

8533 separated point
   d getrennter Punkt *m*; separierter Punkt
   f point *m* séparé
   r отделимая точка *f*

   * **separating** → 8535

8534 separating filter
   d Trennungsfilter *m*
   f filtre *m* de séparation
   r разделительный фильтр *m*

8535 separation; separating
   d Auszug *m*; Trennung *f*; Separation *f*
   f séparation *f*
   r разделение *n*; отделение *n*; сепарация *f*

8536 separation function
   d Trenn[ungs]funktion *f*
   f fonction *f* de séparation
   r функция *f* разделения

8537 separations printer
   d Auszugsdrucker *m*
   f imprimante *f* de séparations
   r цветоотделительный принтер *m*

   * **separation symbol** → 8538

8538 separator symbol; separation symbol; delimiter sign
   d Trennzeichen *n*; Trennsymbol *n*;
      End[e]zeichen *n*; Begrenzungssymbol *n*
   f signe *m* séparateur; symbole *m* délimiteur
   r знак *m* ограничения; разделительный
      символ *m*

8539 sequence
   d Folge *f*; Reihenfolge *f*; Sequenz *f*
   f séquence *f*; suite *f*
   r последовательность *f*; порядок *m*
      [следования]

8540 sequence of edges; walk
   d Kantenfolge *f*; Kantenzug *m*
   f chaîne *f* de côtes
   r последовательность *f* ребер; обход *m* ребер

8541 sequence of points; point sequence
   d Punktfolge *f*
   f suite *f* de points
   r последовательность *f* точек

8542 sequencing
   d Reihenfolgebestimmung *f*;

Sequentialisieren *n*
   f détermination *f* de séquence
   r установление *n* последовательности

8543 sequent
   (in a lattice)
   d oberer Nachbar *m*
   f voisin *m* supérieur
   r верхний сосед *m*

   * **sequential** → 8545

8544 sequential sampling
   d sequentielle Stichprobenauswahl *f*
   f échantillonnage *m* séquentiel
   r последовательный выбор *m*

8545 serial; sequential
   d seriell; sequentiell
   f sériel; séquentiel
   r последовательный; серийный

8546 serial edge extraction
   d sequentielle Kantenextraktion *f*
   f extraction *f* d'arêtes séquentielle
   r последовательное извлечение *n* ребер

8547 serial images
   d serielle Bilder *npl*
   f images *fpl* sérielles
   r последовательные изображения *npl*

8548 serial number
   d Seriennummer *f*
   f nombre *m* sériel
   r серийный номер *m*

8549 serial port
   d serieller Port *m*
   f port *m* sériel
   r серийный порт *m*

8550 series; train
   d Reihe *f*
   f série *f*; train *m*
   r ряд *m*; серия *f*

8551 series of coordinates
   d Reihe *f* der Koordinaten
   f série *f* de coordonnées
   r ряд *m* координат

8552 series of frames
   d Reihe *f* der Bilder
   f série *f* de cadres
   r ряд *m* кадров

   * **series of points** → 7742

   * **serpentine** → 8837

8553 **server**
  d Server *m*; Zubringer *m*
  f serveur *m*
  r сервер *m*

8554 **service program; service routine; utility [program]**
  d Dienstprogramm *n*
  f programme *m* de service; utilitaire *m*
  r обслуживающая программа *f*; сервисная программа; утилит *m*

  * **service routine** → 8554

  * **servicing** → 5761

8555 **session**
  d Session *f*; Sitzung *f*
  f session *f*; séance *f*
  r сессия *f*; сеанс *m*

  * **set** *v* → 1940

  * **set** → 8561

8556 **set** *v*
  d setzen; einstellen
  f établir
  r устанавливать

8557 **set; ensemble**
  d Menge *f*; Satz *m*
  f ensemble *m*
  r множество *n*; комплект *m*

8558 **set** *v* **fill color**
  d Füllungsfarbe einstellen
  f établir une couleur de remplissage
  r устанавлять цвета заливки; устанавливать цвет закрашивания

  * **set of projective coordinates** → 7548

8559 **set** *v* **outline color**
  d Konturfarbe einstellen
  f établir une couleur de bordure
  r устанавливать цвет контура

8560 **set point**
  d Einstellpunkt *m*
  f point *m* établi
  r заданная точка *f*

  * **set time** → 8563

8561 **set[ting]; setup; establishment**
  d Einstellung *f*; Einstellen *n*; Einrichtung *f*
  f établissement *m*
  r установление *n*; установка *f*

8562 **setting the constrain angle**
  d Beschränkungswinkel-Einstellung *f*
  f ajustage *m* d'angle constraint
  r установление *n* ограничивающего угла

8563 **set[ting] time**
  d Einstell[ungs]zeit *f*
  f temps *m* d'établissement
  r время *n* установления

  * **setup** → 8561

8564 **setup** *v* **guidelines**
  d Leitlinien einstellen
  f configurer les lignes de conduite; configurer les lignes directrices
  r установление *n* направляющих линий

8565 **set value**
  d Einstellwert *m*
  f valeur *f* établie; valeur de consigne; grandeur *f* de consigne
  r заданное значение *n*

  * **sew** *v* → 6883

  * **sexagesimal minute** → 5975

  * **sexagesimal second** → 401

8566 **shade** *v*
  d schattieren; beschatten; überschatten
  f ombrer
  r затенять; оттенять

  * **shade** *v* → 4524

  * **shade** → 4525, 8583, 9695

8567 **shaded**
  d schattiert; beschattet
  f ombré
  r теневой; затененный; затушеванный; с тенями

  * **shaded** → 4529

8568 **shaded blend**
  d schattierte Überblendung *f*
  f dégradé *m* ombre
  r затененное переливание *n*

  * **shaded font** → 8572

8569 **shaded image**
  d schattiertes Bild *n*
  f image *f* ombrée
  r теневое изображение *n*; изображение с тенями

8570 **shaded region**
   d schraffiertes Gebiet *n*
   f région *f* hachurée
   r заштрихованная область *f*

8571 **shaded rule; hatched rule**
   d schraffierte Strichlinie *f*
   f ligne *f* hachurée
   r затененная линия *f*

8572 **shaded type; shaded font**
   d Schattenschrift *f*; lichte Schrift *f* mit Fallschatten
   f police *f* ombrée
   r затушеванный фонт *m*

8573 **shaded viewing**
   d schattierte Visualisierung *f*
   f visionnement *m* ombré
   r затушеванная визуализация *f*

8574 **shaded watermark**
   d Schattenwasserzeichen *n*
   f filigrane *m* ombré
   r водяной знак *m* с тенями

   * **shade of gray** → 4410

8575 **shader**
   d Schattierungsprogramm *n*
   f programme *m* d'ombrage
   r программа *f* построения теней

8576 **shading**
   d Schattierung *f*; Schattieren *n*; Abschattung *f*
   f ombrage *m*
   r оттенение *n*; затенение *n*

8577 **shading calculation**
   d Schattierungsberechnung *f*
   f calcul *m* d'ombrage
   r вычисление *n* затенения

8578 **shading extrusions**
   d schattierende Extrusionen *fpl*
   f extrusions *fpl* ombrées
   r оттененные экструзии *fpl*

8579 **shading layer**
   d schattierende Schicht *f*
   f plan *m* d'ombrage
   r слой *m* оттенения

8580 **shading mask; shadow mask**
   d Schattenmaske *f*
   f masque *f* d'ombrage; masque d'ombre
   r маска *f* затенения

8581 **shading processor**
   d Schattierungsprozessor *m*

   f processeur *m* d'ombrage
   r процессор *m* оттенения; процессор затенения

   * **shading scale** → 4412

8582 **shading table**
   d Schattierungstabelle *f*
   f tableau *m* d'ombrage
   r таблица *f* оттенения

8583 **shadow; shade**
   d Schatten *m*
   f ombre *f*
   r тень *f*

8584 **shadow anchor**
   d Schattenanker *m*; Verankerung *f* des Schattens
   f ancrage *m* d'ombre
   r закрепление *n* тени

8585 **shadow area**
   d Schattenfläche *f*
   f aire *f* d'ombre
   r площадь *f* тени

8586 **shadow attenuation**
   d Dämpfung *f* des Schattens
   f atténuation *f* d'ombre
   r затухание *n* тени

8587 **shadow boundaries**
   d Grenzen *fpl* des Schattens
   f limites *fpl* d'ombre
   r границы *fpl* тени

8588 **shadow casting**
   d Schatteneinbau *m*; Schattenguss *m*
   f moulage *m* d'ombres
   r построение *n* теней

   * **shadow character** → 8591

8589 **shadow color**
   d Schattenfarbe *f*
   f couleur *f* d'ombre
   r цвет *m* тени

8590 **shadow contours**
   d Umrisse *mpl* des Schattens
   f contours *mpl* d'ombre
   r контуры *mpl* тени

8591 **shadow[ed] character**
   d schattiertes Zeichen *n*
   f caractère *m* ombré
   r оттененный символ *m*; символ с тенью

8592 **shadow effect**
   d Schatteneffekt *m*

f effet *m* d'ombre
r эффект *m* тени; теневой эффект

8593 shadow form
d Schattenform *f*
f forme *f* d'ombre
r форма *f* тени

8594 shadow generation
d Schattengenerierung *f*
f génération *f* d'ombre
r генерирование *n* тени

8595 shadow intersections
d Durchschnitte *mpl* der Schatten
f intersections *fpl* d'ombres
r [взаимные] пересечения *npl* теней

* **shadow map** → 8596

8596 shadow map[ping]
d Schattenabbildung *f*
f mappage *m* d'ombre
r отображение *n* тени

* **shadow mask** → 8580

8597 shadow node
d Schattenknoten *m*
f nœud *m* d'ombre
r узел *m* тени

8598 shadow offset
d Schattenabstand *m*
f décalage *m* d'ombre
r смещение *n* тени

8599 shadow region
d Schattenbereich *m*
f zone *f* d'ombre
r зона *f* затемнения; зона тени

8600 shadow software
d Schattierungssoftware *f*
f logiciel *m* d'ombrage
r программное обеспечение *n* затенения

* **shape** → 3939

8601 shape *v*; **profile** *v*
d formen
f profiler
r профилировать

* **shape** → 3939

8602 shape abstraction
d Formabstraktion *f*
f abstraction *f* de forme
r абстракция *f* формы

8603 shape analysis
d Form[en]analyse *f*
f analyse *f* de formes
r анализ *m* форм

8604 shape construction
d Konstruktion *f* der Form
f construction *f* de forme
r конструкция *f* формы

8605 shape correction
d Korrektur *f* der Form
f correction *f* de forme; conformation *f*
r коррекция *f* формы

8606 shape data
d Formdaten *npl*
f données *fpl* de forme
r данные *npl* формы

8607 shaped beam
d geformter Strahl *m*
f faisceau *m* formé; faisceau profilé
r сформированный луч *m*;
профилированный луч

8608 shape editing
d Formbearbeitung *f*
f édition *f* de forme
r редактирование *n* формы

8609 shape file
d Formendatei *f*
f fichier *m* de formes
r файл *m* графичных форм

8610 shape interpolation
d Forminterpolation *f*
f interpolation *f* des formes
r интерполяция *f* форм

* **shape library** → 4368

8611 shape mapping
d Formabbildung *f*
f mappage *m* de forme
r отображение *n* формы

8612 shape modeling
d Formmodellierung *f*
f modelage *m* de formes
r моделирование *n* форм

8613 shape number
d Formnummer *f*
f numéro *m* de forme
r номер *m* формы

8614 shape object
d Formobjekt *n*

f objet *m* forme
r объект *m* типа формы

8615 shaper; former
   d Form[ier]er *m*; Formierungseinrichtung *f*
   f formateur *m*; dispositif *m* de formation
   r формирователь *m*

8616 shape recognition
   d Formerkennung *f*
   f reconnaissance *f* des formes
   r распознавание *n* форм

8617 shape reconstruction
   d Formrekonstruktion *f*
   f reconstruction *f* de forme
   r реконструкция *f* формы

8618 shape reconstruction algorithm
   d Algorithmus *m* der Formrekonstruktion
   f algorithme *m* de reconstruction de formes
   r алгоритм *m* реконструкции форм

8619 shape tool
   d Hilfsmittel *n* "Form"
   f outil *m* "forme"
   r инструмент *m* [вычерчивания] форм

8620 shaping
   d Formgebung *f*; Verformung *f*; Formen *n*
   f mise *f* à la forme; formage *m*
   r формирование *n*

8621 shaping filter
   d Formgebungsfilter *m*
   f filtre *m* de formage
   r формирующий фильтр *m*

8622 share *v*
   d teilen; gemeinsam benutzen
   f partager; utiliser en commun
   r разделять; совместно использовать

   *   shareable file → 8623

8623 shared file; shareable file
   d gemeinsam benutzte Datei *f*;
     gemeinschaftliche Datei
   f fichier *m* [utilisé en] commun; fichier partagé
   r коллективный файл *m*; файл совместного
     пользования

8624 shared virtual environment
   d gemeinschaftliche Virtualumgebung *f*
   f environnement *m* virtuel partagé
   r распределенная виртуальная среда *f*

8625 shared worlds
   d gemeinschaftliche Welten *fpl*
   f mondes *mpl* partagés

   r распределенные миров *mpl*

8626 sharp area
   d scharfe Zone *f*
   f zone *f* brusque
   r крутая зона *f*

8627 sharp bend
   d scharfes Knick *m*
   f coude *m* brusque
   r крутой изгиб *m*

8628 sharp[ed] mask
   d scharfe Maske *f*
   f masque *f* distincte
   r резкая маска *f*

8629 sharpen *v*
   d schärfen
   f affûter; aiguiser; appointer
   r острить

8630 sharpen brush
   d scharfer Pinsel *m*
   f brosse *f* distincte
   r резкая кисть *f*

   *   sharpen effect → 8636

8631 sharpen filter
   d Schärfefilter *m*
   f filtre *m* distinct
   r фильтр *m* резкости

8632 sharpening
   (of an image)
   d Scharfschleifen *n*; Schärfeeinstellung *f*
   f affûtage *m*; retaillage *m*; émouture *f*
   r увеличение *n* резкости

8633 sharpening
   d Anspitzung *f*
   f piquage *m*; amincissement *m*
   r заострение *n*; утончение *n*

   *   sharpening effect → 8636

8634 sharpen tool
   d Schärfewerkzeug *n*
   f outil *m* d'affûtage
   r инструмент *m* резкости

   *   sharp mask → 8628

8635 sharpness; definition
   d Schärfe *f*
   f netteté *f*; définition *f*
   r четкость *f*; резкость *f*; ясность *f*

8636 sharpness effect; sharpen[ing] effect
   d Schärfeeffekt *m*

f effet *m* de netteté
r эффект *m* четкости; эффект резкости

* **sheaf** → 6926

* **sheaf of circles** → 6927

* **sheaf of complexes** → 1194

* **sheaf of curves** → 1195

* **sheaf of lines** → 1196

* **sheaf of planes** → 6932

* **sheaf of spheres** → 1197

8637 shear
d Scherung *f*
f cisaillement *m*
r срез *m*

* **sheet** → 3467, 5436, 6150

8638 sheet
d Blatt *n*; Vordruck *m*
f feuille *f*; formulaire *m*
r лист *m*; бланк *m*; перечень *m* [документов]

8639 sheet-feed plotter
d Plotter *m* mit Blattzuführung
f traceur *m* en feuilles
r графопостроитель *m* с полистовой подачей

8640 sheet size
d Blattgröße *f*
f taille *f* de feuille
r размер *m* листа

* **shell** → 1276, 3467, 8754

8641 shielding; screening
d Schirmung *f*; Abschirmung *f*
f blindage *m*
r экранирование *n*

* **shift** → 8643

8642 shifted text
d verschobener Text *m*
f texte *m* décalé
r перемещенный текст *m*; сдвинутый текст

8643 shift[ing]; displacement; offset
d Verschiebung *f*; Schieben *n*; Schiftung *f*; Verlagerung *f*
f décalage *m*; déplacement
r сдвиг *m*; смещение *n*

8644 shifting character

d Verschiebungszeichen *n*
f caractère *m* de décalage
r символ *m* сдвига; знак *m* смещения

8645 Shift key
d Schift-Taste *f*
f touche *f* Maj; touche de commutation
r клавиша *f* Shift

* **shift operator** → 9833

* **shift right** → 8171

8646 shooting
d Filmaufnahme *f*
f prise *f* de vue
r киносъемка *f*

8647 short
d kurz
f court; bref
r короткий

8648 shortcut
d Shortcut *n*; schneller Zugang *m*
f accès *m* rapide
r быстрый доступ *m*

* **short-cut** → 2364

8649 shortcut keys; keyboard shortcuts
d Shortcut-Tasten *fpl*
f touches *fpl* d'accès rapide
r клавиши *fpl* быстрого доступа

8650 shorten *v*
d verkürzen
f raccourcir
r укорачивать

* **shortened** → 2364

8651 shortening; retrenchment
d Verkürzung *f*
f raccourcissement *m*
r сокращение *n*

* **shorter axis of an ellipse** → 5970

* **shorter semiaxis of an ellipse** → 5972

8652 shortest path
d kürzeste Strecke *f*
f chemin *m* le plus court
r кратчайшая дорожка *f*

8653 short precision
d niedrige Genauigkeit *f*
f précision *f* écourtée; précision limitée
r ограниченная точность *f*

8654 **shot block**
d Aufnahme[n]block *m*
f bloc *m* de cadres
r блок *m* кадров

8655 **show *v* layer**
d Ebene anzeigen
f montrer une couche; désigner une couche
r показывать слой

8656 **show *v* raster image**
d Rasterbild anzeigen
f montrer une image rastre
r показывать растровое изображение

8657 **shrink *v***
d schrumpfen; kleiner werden
f contracter; déformer
r сжимать

* **shrink *v* → 4784**

* **shrinkage → 8658**

8658 **shrinking; shrinkage; contraction**
d Schrumpfung *f*, Schwinden *n*; Schwund *m*;
Kontraktion *f*
f retrait *m*; rétrécissement *m*; contraction *f*
r сокращение *n*; свертывание *n*;
контракция *f*

8659 **shrink lens; anamorphic lens**
d anamorphische Linse *f*
f lentille *f* anamorphique
r анаморфная линза *f*

8660 **shrink *v* to a point; collapse *v* to a point;
deform *v* continuously to a point**
d auf einen Punkt schrumpfen; auf einen Punkt
zusammenziehen; kontinuierlich zu einem
Punkt deformieren
f déformer en un point
r стягивать в [одну] точку

8661 **shutter**
d Verschluss *m*; Schließklappe *f*
f obturateur *m*
r затвор *m* объектива; обтюратор *m*

* **side → 5427**

8662 **side**
d Seite *f*; Schenkel *m*
f côté *m*
r сторона *f*; бок *m*

8663 **side band**
d Seitenband *n*
f bande *f* latérale
r боковая полоса *f*

* **side edge → 5429**

8664 **side handle**
d seitlicher Griff *m*; Seitengriff *m*
f poignée *f* latérale
r боковой захват *m*

8665 **side of an angle; arm of an angle; leg of an
angle**
d Winkelschenkel *m*; Schenkel *m*
f côté *m* d'un angle
r сторона *f* угла

8666 **side of a polygon**
d Polygonseite *f*
f côté *m* d'un polygone
r сторона *f* многоугольника

* **side plane → 8668**

8667 **side profile**
d seitliches Profil *n*
f profil *m* latéral
r боковой профиль *m*

8668 **side [projection] plane; third plane**
(of a projection)
d Seitenrissebene *f*; dritte Projektionsebene *f*
f plan *m* latéral; troisième plan de projection
r плоскость *f* боковой проекции

8669 **side sectional view**
d Seitenschnittansicht *f*
f coupe *f* longitudinale
r боковой вид *m* в разрезе

8670 **side trace line**
(of a plane)
d Seitenspurlinie *f*; dritte Spurlinie *f*
f trace *f* de profil; troisième trace
r профильный след *m* плоскости

8671 **side vector**
d Seitenvektor *m*
f vecteur *m* latéral
r боковой вектор *m*

8672 **side view; lateral view**
d laterale Ansicht *f*; Seitenansicht *f*
f vue *f* latérale
r боковой вид *m*

8673 **side viewing angle**
d Seitenbetrachtungswinkel *m*
f angle *m* de visionnement latéral
r боковой угол *m* зрения

* **sift → 8674**

8674 **sift[ing]**
d Siebung *f*; Durchsiebung *f*

f tamisage *m*; criblage *m*
r отсеивание *n*; просеивание *n*

8675 sight
d Blick *m*; Einblick *m*
f regard *m*; vue *f*; coup *m* d'œil
r взгляд *m*; прицел *m*

* **sighting direction** → 245

* **sighting line** → 243

* **sighting mark** → 247

* **sighting point** → 7225

8676 sighting ray
d Zielstrahl *m*
f rayon *m* de visée
r радиус *m* визирования

8677 sigmoid curve; S-shaped curve
d Sigmoidkurve *f*; S-förmige Kurve *f*
f courbe *f* sigmoïde; courbe en S
r сигмоидная кривая *f*; S-образная кривая

8678 sign
d Zeichen *n*; Vorzeichen *n*
f signe *m*
r знак *m*

8679 signature
d Signatur *f*; Unterschrift *f*
f signature *f*; empreinte *f*
r сигнатура *f*; подпись *f*

8680 signature capture tablet; signature tablet
d Signatur-Sammlungstablett *n*
f tablette *f* de signature
r сигнатурный планшет *m*

8681 signature layout
d Signaturaufstellung *f*
f disposition *f* de la signature
r размещение *n* сигнатуры

* **signature tablet** → 8680

8682 signed curvature
d vorzeichenbehaftete Krümmung *f*
f courbure *f* signé
r кривизна *f* со знаком

8683 significance
d Signifikanz *f*; Bedeutsamkeit *f*
f signification *f*; importance *f*
r значимость *f*

8684 significant; essential
d wesentlich; bedeutsam

f significatif; essentiel; important
r значащий; значимый; существенный

* **significant singularity** → 3534

8685 sign of intersection; cap
d Zeichen *n* der Durchschnittsbildung
f signe *m* d'intersection
r знак *m* пересечения

8686 sign of multiplication; multiplication sign
d Multiplikationszeichen *n*; Malzeichen *n*
f signe *m* de multiplication
r знак *m* умножения

8687 sign of subtraction; subtraction sign; minus [sign]
d Subtraktionszeichen *n*; Minuszeichen *n*; Differenzzeichen *n*; Minus *n*
f signe *m* moins; signe de soustraction; moins *m*
r знак *m* вычитания; [знак] минус *m*

8688 sign of union; cup
d Zeichen *n* der Vereinigungsbildung
f signe *m* d'union
r знак *m* объединения

* **sign *v* on** → 5687

8689 silhouette
d Silhouette *f*; Schattenriss *m*
f silhouette *f*
r силуэт *m*

8690 silhouette curve
d Schattenrisskurve *f*
f courbe *f* de silhouette
r кривая *f* силуэта

8691 silhouette halftone
d Schattenrisshalbton *m*
f demi-teinte *f* de silhouette
r полутон *m* силуэта

8692 silhouette technique
d Schattenbildtechnik *f*
f technique *f* de silhouette
r силуэтная техника *f*

8693 similar
d ähnlich
f semblable
r подобный

8694 similar figures
d ähnliche Figuren *fpl*
f figures *fpl* semblables
r подобные фигуры *fpl*

8695 similarity; similitude; likeness
   d Ähnlichkeit *f*
   f similarité *f*; similitude *f*; ressemblance *f*
   r подобие *n*; сходство *n*

   * **similarity coefficient** → 4673

8696 similarity ray; ray of similarity
   d Ähnlichkeitsstrahl *m*
   f rayon *m* de similitude
   r луч *m* подобия

8697 similarity transformation; transformation of similitude
   d Ähnlichkeitstransformation *f*
   f transformation *f* par similitude
   r подобное преобразование *n*

8698 similar polygons
   d ähnliche Polygone *npl*
   f polygones *mpl* semblables
   r подобные многоугольники *mpl*

8699 similar triangles
   d ähnliche Dreiecke *npl*
   f triangles *mpl* semblables
   r подобные треугольники *mpl*

   * **similitude** → 8695

8700 simple
   d einfach
   f simple
   r простой

8701 simple closed curve
   d einfache geschlossene Kurve *f*
   f courbe *f* simple fermée
   r простая замкнутая кривая *f*

8702 simple curve
   d einfache Kurve *f*
   f courbe *f* simple
   r простая кривая *f*

8703 simple edge
   d einfache Kante *f*
   f arête *f* simple
   r простое ребро *n*

8704 simple image
   d einfaches Bild *n*
   f image *f* simple
   r простое изображение *n*

8705 simple image registration
   d Registrierung *f* des einfachen Bilds
   f enregistrement *m* d'image simple
   r запись *f* простого изображения

8706 simple lens
   d einfache Linse *f*
   f lentille *f* simple
   r простая линза *f*

8707 simple line
   d einfache Linie *f*
   f ligne *f* simple
   r простая линия *f*

8708 simple linetype
   d einfacher Linientyp *m*
   f type *m* de ligne simple
   r простой тип *m* линии

   * **simple point** → 6606

8709 simple quadrangle
   d einfaches Viereck *n*
   f quadrangle *m* simple
   r простой четырехугольник *m*

8710 simple quadrilateral
   d einfaches Vierseit *n*
   f quadrilatère *m* simple
   r простой четырехсторонник *m*

8711 simple surface
   d schlichte Fläche *f*
   f surface *f* de genre nul
   r простая поверхность *f*

8712 simple wireframe
   d einfacher Drahtrahmen *m*
   f fil *m* de fer simple
   r простой каркас *m*

8713 simplification
   d Vereinfachung *f*
   f simplification *f*
   r упрощение *n*

8714 simplification strategies
   d Vereinfachungsstrategien *fpl*
   f stratégies *fpl* de simplification
   r стратегии *fpl* упрощения

8715 simulated printer colors
   d simulierte Druck[er]farben *fpl*
   f couleurs *fpl* de l'imprimante simulées
   r симулированные цвета *mpl* принтера

8716 simulated society
   d simulierte Gesellschaft *f*
   f société *f* simulée
   r симулированное общество *n*

8717 simulated white light source
   d simulierte weiße Lichtquelle *f*

 f source *f* d'éclairage blanche simulée
 r симулированный источник *m* белого света

8718 simulate *v* walking
 d Gang simulieren
 f simuler de pas
 r симулировать походку; симулировать
  ходьбу

8719 simulation
 d Simulation *f*; Simulierung *f*
 f simulation *f*; imitation *f*
 r [имитационное] моделирование *n*;
  имитация *f*

8720 simulation methodology
 d Simulierungsmethodologie *f*
 f méthodologie *f* de simulation
 r методология *f* симуляции

8721 simulator
 d Simulator *m*; Simulationseinrichtung *f*
 f simulateur *m*; imitateur *m*
 r симулятор *m*; имитатор *m*

8722 simultaneity
 d Gleichzeitigkeit *f*
 f simultanéité *f*
 r одновременность *f*; совместность *f*

 * **simultaneous → 2021**

8723 simultaneous mode
 d Simultanbetrieb *m*
 f mode *m* parallèle
 r режим *m* параллельной обработки

 * **sine curve → 8746**

 * **sine line → 8746**

8724 sine spiral
 d Sinusspirale *f*
 f spirale *f* sinusoïdale
 r синусоидальная спираль *f*

8725 single
 d einzeln; Einzel-; allein
 f seul; unique; singulier
 r один; отдельный; единственный;
  самостоятельный

 * **single-action window → 7087**

8726 single click
 d Einzelklick *m*
 f clic *m* unique
 r одиночное нажатие *n* кнопки

8727 single cut

 d Einzelschnitt *m*
 f coupe *f* unique
 r одиночное прерывание *n*

8728 single frame
 d Einzelrahmen *m*
 f trame *f* unique
 r одиночный кадр *m*

8729 single-frame mode; single-frame operation
 d Einzelblockverfahren *n*;
  Einfachrahmen-Modus *m*
 f mode *m* à trame unique
 r однокадровый режим *m*

 * **single-frame operation → 8729**

8730 single line
 d Einzellinie *f*
 f ligne *f* unique
 r отдельная линия *f*

8731 single number
 d Einzelzahl *f*
 f nombre *m* individuel; nombre unique
 r отдельное число *m*

8732 single object
 d Einzelobjekt *n*
 f objet *m* unique
 r отдельный объект *m*; самостоятельный
  объект

8733 single-pass
 d Einweg-; Einschritt-
 f à pas unique
 r однопассовый; одношаговый

8734 single-pass algorithm
 d Einwegalgorithmus *m*
 f algorithme *m* à pas unique
 r однопассовый алгоритм *m*

8735 single-pass multitexturing
 d Einweg-Multitexturieren *n*
 f multi-texturation *f* simple-passe;
  multi-texturation à pas unique
 r создание *n* множества текстур за один шаг

8736 single-pass segmentation
 d Einwegsegmentierung *f*
 f segmentation *f* à pas unique
 r однопассовое сегментирование *n*

**8737 single-pass segmentation of 3D
  pseudo-manifolds**
 d Einwegsegmentierung *f* der
  3D-Pseudo-Kopien

f segmentation *f* à pas unique de pseudo-copies 3D
r однопассовое сегментирование *n* трехмерных псевдо-копий

8738 single-pass trilinear filtering
d Einweg-Trilinear-Filtering *n*
f filtrage *m* trilinéaire simple-passe
r одношаговое трилинейное фильтрирование *n*

8739 single-pen plotter
d Plotter *m* mit einfachem Zeichenstift
f traceur *m* à plume unique
r одноперьевой графопостроитель *m*

8740 single point
d Einzelpunkt *m*
f point *m* unique
r отдельная точка *f*

8741 single screen
d Einzelbildschirm *m*
f écran *m* unique
r одиночный экран *m*

8742 single-sided; one-sided; one-way; unilateral
d einseitig; unilateral
f unilatéral; à un seul côté
r односторонний

8743 singular; degenerate
d singulär; ausgeartet; entartet
f singulier; dégénéré
r сингулярный; особый; вырожденный

* **singular complex of rays** → 8973

* **singular conic** → 2576

* **singular conic section** → 2576

8744 singular form
d ausgeartete Form *f*; singuläre Form
f forme *f* singulière; forme dégénérée
r вырожденная форма *f*; сингулярная форма

* **sinistrorse** → 447

8745 sinistrorse helix; left[-handed] helix; left-twisted helix
d linksgängige Schraubenlinie *f*; linkswendige Schraubenlinie
f hélice *f* sinistrorsum; hélice à gauche
r завитая влево винтовая линия *f*; левая винтовая линия

* **sinistrorse screw** → 5483

* **sinistrorsum** *adj* → 447

* **sinusoid** → 8746

8746 sinusoidal curve; sinusoidal line; sine curve; sine line; sinusoid
d sinusförmige Kurve *f*; Sinusoide *f*; Sinuskurve *f*; Sinuslinie *f*
f courbe *f* sinusoïdale; courbe sinus; ligne *f* sinusoïdale; ligne sinus; sinusoïde *f*
r синусоидальная кривая *f*; синусоидальная линия *f*; синусоида *f*

* **sinusoidal line** → 8746

8747 sinusoidal motion
d sinusförmige Bewegung *f*
f mouvement *m* sinusoïdal
r синусоидальное движение *n*

8748 site
d Lage *f*; Ortslage *f*; Standort *m*
f site *m*
r местоположение *n*

8749 site map
d Karte *f* der Lage
f carte *f* de site; plan *m* de site
r карта *f* местоположения

8750 size
d Größe *f*
f taille *f*
r размер *m*; величина *f*

* **size** *v* → 8288

8751 skeletal
d Skelett-
f squelettique; de squelette
r остовный; скелетный; каркасный

8752 skeletal animation; wireframe animation
d Skelettanimation *f*; Drahtrahmenanimation *f*
f animation *f* de squelette; animation filaire; animation en fil de fer
r скелетная анимация *f*; каркасная анимация

8753 skeletal code
d Skelettcode *m*; Drahtrahmencode *m*
f code *m* squelettique
r скелетный код *m*

8754 skeleton; shell
d Skelett *n*; Gerüst *n*
f squelette *m*
r скелет *m*; остов *m*

8755 skeleton model
d Skelettmodell *n*

f modèle *m* squelettique
r скелетная модель *f*

* **sketch → 8214**

8756 sketch line
d Linie *f* der Skizze
f ligne *f* d'esquisse
r эскизная линия *f*

* **skew** *adj* → 627

* **skew** *v* → 9682

8757 skew; oblique
d Schrägverzerrung *f*; Schrägversatz *m*; Schräglauf *m*
f distorsion *f* oblique; gâchissement *m*; déjettement *m*
r перекос *m*; наклон *m*

8758 skew anchor point
d schräger Ankerpunkt *m*
f point *m* d'ancrage oblique
r косая точка *f* закрепления

8759 skew axonometry; general axonometry
d schräge Axonometrie *f*; allgemeine Axonometrie
f axonométrie *f* oblique; axonométrie générale
r косоугольная аксонометрия *f*; общая аксонометрия

* **skew curve → 8919**

8760 skew[ed] ray; oblique ray
d schiefer Strahl *m*; Nichtmeridianstrahl *m*
f rayon *m* oblique; rayon non méridien
r наклонный луч *m*; немередианный луч; немеридиональный луч

8761 skewing
d Schrägverstellung *f*
f désalignement *m*; mise *f* en travers
r скрещивание *n*; скашивание *n*; плохое выравнивание *n*; деформация *f* сдвигом

8762 skewing bitmaps
d windschiefe Bitmaps *npl*
f bitmaps *mpl* désalignés
r скрещивающиеся растровые изображения *npl*

8763 skewing nodes
d windschiefe Knoten *mpl*
f nœuds *mpl* désalignés
r скрещивающиеся узлы *mpl*

8764 skewing objects
d windschiefe Objekte *npl*

f objets *mpl* désalignés
r скрещивающиеся объекты *mpl*

8765 skew lines
d windschiefe Geraden *fpl*; sich kreuzende Geraden
f droites *fpl* gauches; droites non coplanaires
r скрещивающиеся прямые *fpl*

* **skewness → 629**

8766 skew perspective affinity; general perspective affinity
d schiefe perspektive Affinität *f*; allgemeine perspektive Affinität
f affinité *f* perspective générale
r косое перспективно-аффинное преобразование *n*; общее перспективно-аффинное преобразование

8767 skew polygon
d windschiefes Vieleck *n*; Vieleck im Raum
f polygone *m* spatial
r пространственный многоугольник *m*

8768 skew projection; oblique projection; inclined projection
d schiefwinklige Projektion *f*; schiefe Projektion; Schrägprojektion *f*
f projection *f* oblique
r косая проекция *f*; косоугольная проекция; скошенная проекция; наклонная проекция

**skew ray → 8760

8769 skew surface; oblique surface
d schiefe Fläche *f*
f surface *f* oblique
r асимметричная поверхность *f*; косая поверхность

* **skew-symmetric → 457**

8770 skip
d Übersprung *m*; Auslassung *f*
f saut *m*; manque *m*; omission *f*
r проскок *m*; пропуск *m*; перескок *m*

* **slant angle → 380**

* **slant asymptote → 6415**

* **slanted → 6411**

* **slanted dimension → 266**

8771 slanted dimension line
d geneigte Dimensionslinie *f*
f ligne *f* de cotation inclinée
r наклонная размерная линия *f*

* **slanted font** → 6423

8772 slanted guideline
d geneigte Richtlinie *f*
f ligne *f* directrice oblique; ligne de conduite oblique
r наклонная направляющая *f*

8773 slant height; lateral height; altitude of a face
d Höhe *f* der Seitenfläche
f hauteur *f* de pente; hauteur latérale
r боковая высота *f*

* **slanting** → 4993

* **slanting line** → 6426

8774 slanting object
d geneigtes Objekt *n*
f objet *m* oblique
r наклонный объект *m*

8775 slash; forward slash
d Schrägstrich *m*; Slash *n*
f barre *f* oblique; barre penchée
r [прямая] косая черта *f*

8776 slave
d untergeordnet; Slave-
f esclave; asservi
r подчиненный; ведомый

8777 slave node
d Slave-Knoten *m*
f nœud *m* esclave
r подчиненный узел *m*

8778 slice
d Scheibe *f*; Scheibenteil *m*
f tranche *f*
r слой *m*; вырезка *f*; секция *f*; разрез *m*

8779 slice architecture
d Scheibenarchitektur *f*
f architecture *f* en tranches
r секционированная архитектура *f*; слоистая архитектура

8780 slicing
d Aufschneiden *n*; Schneiden *n*
f mise *f* en tranches
r расслоение *n*; секционирование *n*

* **slide** → 8788

8781 slide; diapositive
d Schlitten *n*; Diapositiv *n*
f diapositive *f*
r диапозитив *m*; слайд *m*;

прозрачная пленка *f*

8782 slide *v*; **glide** *v*; **slip** *v*
d gleiten; abgleiten; rutschen
f glisser
r скользить; глиссировать

* **slide bar** → 8788

8783 slide file
d Diapositivdatei *f*
f fichier *m* de diapositive
r файл *m* слайда; диапозитивный файл

8784 slide file format
d Diapositivdateiformat *n*
f format *m* de fichiers de diapositives
r формат *m* диапозитивных файлов

8785 slide finder
d Diapositivsucher *m*
f viseur *m* de diapositive
r указатель *m* слайда

8786 slide library
d Diapositivbibliothek *f*
f bibliothèque *f* de diapositives
r библиотека *f* слайдов

8787 slide master
d Diapositiv-Meister *m*
f maître *m* de diapositives
r мастер *m* диапозитивов

8788 slide[r]; slide bar; runner; guide [bar]; glider
d Schieber *m*; Läufer *m*; Gleiter *m*
f glissière *f*; glisseur *m*; curseur *m* [de réglage]; coulisseau *m*; réglette *f*, coulisse *f*
r ползунок *m*; движок *m*; слайдер *m*

8789 slide sorter
d Diapositiv-Sortierer *m*
f trieur *m* de diapositives
r сортировщик *m* слайдов

8790 sliding; gliding; slipping[-down]
d Gleiten *n*; Gleitung *f*; Rutschen *n*; Rutschung *f*; Schleifen *n*
f glissement *m*; glissage *m*; dérapage *m*
r скольжение *n*; соскальзывание *n*; плавное движение *n*

8791 sliding; slipping; glancing *adj*
d gleitend; verschieblich
f glissant
r скользящий

8792 sliding vector
d gleitender Vektor *m*; linienflüchtiger Vektor

f vecteur *m* glissant
r скользящий вектор *m*

* **slip** *v* → **8782**

* **slipping** → **8790, 8791**

* **slipping-down** → **8790**

* **slit** → **8799**

8793 slit domain; slit region
d Schlitzgebiet *n*
f domaine *m* avec coupures; domaine muni de fentes
r область *f* с разрезами; область с надрезами

8794 slit mask
d Schlitzmaske *f*
f masque *f* de fente
r маска *f* отверстия; маска разреза

* **slit region** → **8793**

* **slope** *v* → **9682**

8795 slope; tilt; pitch
d Böschung *f*; Schräge *f*
f talus *m*; pente *f*
r наклон *m*; уклон *m*; откос *m*

8796 slope arrow
d Schrägpfeil *m*
f flèche *f* inclinée
r наклонная стрелка *f*

8797 slope calculation
d Neigungsberechnung *f*
f calcul *m* d'inclinaison
r вычисление *n* наклона

8798 slope of line
d Neigung *f* der Linie
f inclinaison *f* de ligne
r наклон *m* линии

* **slope scale** → **4283**

* **sloping** → **6411**

8799 slot; throat; slit
d Schlitz *m*; Ritze *f*; Steckplatz *m*
f prise *f* femelle; place *f* à enficher; fente *f*; créneau *m*; logement *m*; gorge *f*
r [щелевое] отверстие *n*; щель *f*; канал *m*; надрез *m*; гнездо *n*; горло *n*

8800 slow-motion images
d langsambewegliche Bilder *npl*
f images *fpl* retardées

r медленно передвигающиеся изображения *npl*

* **slow-time scale** → **3598**

8801 small capitals; small caps
d Kapitälchen *npl*
f petits capitaux *mpl*; majuscules *fpl* petites
r уменьшенные заглавные буквы *fpl*; малые прописные буквы

* **small caps** → **8801**

8802 small circle
d Kleinkreis *m*
f petit cercle *m*
r малый круг *m*

8803 small icon
(representing a folder or a file)
d kleine Ikone *f*; kleines Symbol *n*
f miniature *f*
r малая пиктограмма *f*

* **smart** → **5146**

8804 smear *v*
d beschmieren; schmieren
f étaler; enduire
r [на]мазать; измаз[ыв]ать

8805 smear
d Fleck *m*
f traînée *f* [lumineuse verticale]
r пятно *n*; мазок *m*

8806 smiley; emoticon
d Emoticon *n*
f émoticône *m*; binette *f*; sourire *m*; mimique *f*; rictus *m*; faciès *m*
r смайлик *m*; ухмылочка *f*; эмограмма *f*; пиктограмма *f* для передачи эмоций

8807 Smith chart
d Smith-Diagramm *n*
f diagramme *m* de Smith
r график *m* Смита

8808 smoke *v*
d rauchen
f fumer
r курить; дымить

8809 smoked glass filter
d Filter *m* des dunklen Glases
f filtre *m* de verre fumé
r фильтр *m* темного стекла

8810 smoking effect
d Raucheffekt *m*

f effet *m* de fumée
r эффект *m* дыма

8811 smooth *adj*
d glatt
f lisse
r гладкий

8812 smooth *v*
d glätten
f lisser
r сглаживать

8813 smooth area
d glatte Fläche *f*
f zone *f* lisse
r гладкая область *f*

8814 smooth blur effect
d Glätten-Unschärfe-Effekt *m*
f effet *m* de brouillage lissé
r эффект *m* плавной размытости; эффект гладкой расплывчатости

8815 smooth contour
d glatte Kontur *f*
f contour *m* régulier
r гладкий контур *m*; регулярный контур

8816 smooth curve
d glatte Kurve *f*
f courbe *f* lisse
r гладкая кривая *f*

8817 smooth effect
d Glättungseffekt *m*
f effet *m* de lissage
r эффект *m* сглаживания

8818 smooth face
d glatte Seite *f*
f face *f* lisse
r гладкая сторона *f*; гладкая грань *f*

8819 smoothing
d Glättung *f*
f lissage *m*
r сглаживание *n*

8820 smoothing angle
d Glättungswinkel *m*
f angle *m* de lissage
r угол *m* сглаживания

8821 smoothing coefficient; smoothing factor
d Glättungskoeffizient *m*
f coefficient *m* de lissage
r коэффициент *m* сглаживания

* **smoothing factor → 8821**

8822 smoothing filter
d Glättungsfilter *m*
f filtre *m* de lissage
r сглаживающий фильтр *m*

8823 smooth Lambertian surface
d glatte Lambert-Fläche *f*
f surface *f* lambertienne lisse
r гладкая поверхность *f* Ламберта

8824 smooth model
d glattes Modell *n*
f modèle *m* lisse
r гладкая модель *f*

8825 smooth model transitions
d glatte Transitionen *fpl* des Modells
f transitions *fpl* de modèle lisses
r плавные [цветовые] переходы *mpl* модели

8826 smooth motion
d glatte Bewegung *f*
f mouvement *m* lisse
r гладкое движение *n*

8827 smoothness
d Glätte *f*
f apparence *f* lisse; égalité *f*
r гладкость *f*

8828 smoothness criterion
d Glättekriterium *n*
f critère *m* de lissage
r критерий *m* гладкости

* **smooth node → 8829**

8829 smooth node [point]
d glatter Knoten[punkt] *m*
f point *m* nodal lisse; nœud *m* lisse
r гладкая узловая точка *f*; гладкий узел *m*

8830 smooth scrolling
d stetiger Schriftbildlauf *m*; stetige Bildverschiebung *f*; ununterbrochenes Rollen *n*
f évolution *f* continue d'écriture; défilement *m* lent
r непрерывное изображение *n* в рулонном режиме

8831 smooth shading
d glatte Schattierung *f*
f ombrage *m* lisse
r гладкое оттенение *n*

8832 smooth transition
d glatte Transition *f*

f transition *f* lisse
r плавное перемещение *n*;
плавный переход *m*

8833 smudge
d Schmutzfleck *m*
f maculage *m*
r грязное пятно *n*

8834 smudge *v*
d [be]schmutzen; beschmieren
f maculer
r загрязнять; [ис]пачкать; мазать

8835 smudge tool
d Beschmutzungsmittel *n*
f outil *m* de maculage
r инструмент *m* загрязнения

8836 smudging
d Beschmutzung *f*
f détérioration *f* [d'image]; salissure *f*
r загрязнение *n*; запачкивание *n*

8837 snakelike; serpentine; wound; coiled
d schlangenförmig; schlangenartig
f serpentin
r змеевидный

8838 snakelike curve
d Schlangenlinie *f*; schlangenförmige Kurve *f*
f courbe *f* du dragon
r змеевидная кривая *f*

* **snap → 8846**

8839 snap *v*
(on the screen grid)
d fangen; [zu]schnappen; [zer]springen
f attirer; accrocher
r фиксировать; привязывать; запирать;
ухватываться; защелкивать; прыгать;
перепрыгивать

8840 snap angle
d Fangwinkel *m*
f angle *m* de magnétisme; angle d'accrochage
r угол *m* привязки

8841 snap base point
d Fang-Basispunkt *m*
f point *m* de base magnétique; point de base
d'accrochage
r базовая точка *f* привязки

* **snap distance → 8854**

8842 snap function
d Fangfunktion *f*
f fonction *f* magnétique; fonction d'accrochage

r функция *f* привязки

* **snap interval → 8854**

8843 snap mode
d Fangmodus *m*
f mode *m* magnétique; mode d'accrochage
r режим *m* привязки

8844 snap object
d Fangobjekt *n*
f objet *m* magnétique
r объект *m* типа привязки

8845 snap origin point
d Fangnullpunkt *m*
f point *m* magnétique d'origine; point d'origine
d'accrochage
r начальная точка *f* привязки

8846 snap[ping]
d Fangen *n*; Griff *m*
f magnétisme *m*; accrochage *m*; croquage *m*
r привязка *f*; привязывание *n*; защелка *f*;
прыжок *m*

* **snapping distance → 8854**

8847 snapping object to other objects
d an [anderen] Objekten Objektfang *m*
f accrochage *m* d'objet vers [d'autres] objets
r привязывание *n* объекта к другим
объектам

8848 snapping object to the grid
d an dem Gitter Objektfang *m*;
Objektrasterfang *m*
f accrochage *m* d'objet vers la grille
r привязывание *f* объекта к сетке

8849 snapping object to the guideline
d an der Richtlinie Objektfang *m*
f accrochage *m* d'objet vers ligne directrice
r привязывание *n* объекта к направляющей
линии

8850 snap point
d Fangpunkt *m*
f point *m* magnétique; point d'accrochage
r точка *f* привязки

8851 snap rotation angle
d Fang-Dreh[ungs]winkel *m*
f angle *m* de rotation de magnétisme; angle de
rotation d'accrochage
r угол *m* поворота сети привязки

8852 snapshot
d Schnappschuss *m*

f image *f* instantanée; photo[graphie] *f*
  instantanée
r моментальный снимок *m*

8853 snapshot key
  d Schnappschuss-Taste *f*
  f touche *f* d'images instantanées
  r клавиша *f* моментального снимка

**8854 snap spacing; snap interval; snap[ping]
    distance**
  d Fangabstand *m*
  f intervalle *m* de magnétisme; espacement *m*
    magnétique
  r интервал *m* привязки

8855 snaptip
  d Fangende *f*
  f info-bulle *f* magnétique
  r кончик *m* привязки

8856 snap *v* to the grid
  d an dem Gitter fangen
  f accrocher à la grille
  r привязывать к [координатной] сетке;
    ухватываться за сетку

8857 snap *v* to the guideline
  d an der Hilfslinie fangen; an der Richtlinie
    fangen
  f accrocher à la ligne directrice; accrocher à la
    ligne conduite
  r привязывать к направляющей линии

8858 snap *v* to objects
  d an Objekten fangen
  f accrocher aux objets
  r привязывать к объектам

  * **Snell's law → 8859**

8859 Snell's law [of refraction]
  d Snelliussches Brechungsgesetz *n*
  f loi *f* de réfraction de Descartes[-Snell]
  r закон *m* преломления Снеллиуса[-Декарта]

8860 soft copy; transient copy
  d nichtdauerhafte Kopie *f*; Bildschirmkopie *f*;
    Softcopy *n*
  f copie *f* non dure; copie sur écran
  r недокументальная копия *f*; экранная
    копия; мягкая копия

8861 soft image
  d Nichtkontrast-Bild *n*
  f image *f* sans contraste; image grisâtre
  r неконтрастное изображение *n*

8862 softness
    (of materials or surfaces)

  d Weichheit *f*
  f douceur *f*; souplesse *f*; mollesse *f*
  r мягкость *f*

  * **soft patch → 1178**

8863 soft pointer
  d programmierbarer Zeiger *m*
  f pointeur *m* programmable
  r программируемый указатель *m*

8864 soft reflections
  d programmierbare Reflexionen *fpl*
  f réflexions *fpl* programmables
  r программируемые отражения *npl*

8865 soft scrolling
  d gleichmäßige Bildverschiebung *f*
  f défilement *m* mesuré
  r плавная прокрутка *f*

8866 soft shadows
  d Nichtkontrast-Schatten *mpl*
  f ombres *fpl* non contrastes
  r мягкие тени *fpl*; неконтрастные тени

8867 software
  d Software *f*; Programmierhilfen *fpl*
  f logiciel *m*; software *m*
  r программное обеспечение *n*

8868 solarization
  d Solarisation *f*; Überbelichtung *f*
  f solarisation *f*
  r соляризация *f*

8869 solarization color transform
  d Solarisationfarben-Änderung *f*
  f transformation *f* de couleur de solarisation
  r преобразование *n* цвета соляризации

8870 solarize effect
  d Überbelichtungseffekt *m*
  f effet *m* de solarisation
  r эффект *m* соляризации

8871 solenoid
  d Solenoid *n*
  f solénoïde *m*
  r соленоид *m*

8872 solenoidal; pipe-shaped
  d solenoidal
  f solénoïdal
  r соленоидальный

8873 solid; rigid body; body
  d [fester] Körper *m*; Festkörper *m*

f solide *m*; corps *m* [solide]
r [твердое] тело *n*; монолитное тело; жесткое тело

8874 solid angle
    d räumlicher Winkel *m*; Raumwinkel *m*
    f angle *m* solide
    r телесный угол *m*

8875 solid background
    d Vollhintergrund *m*
    f fond *m* solide
    r плотный фон *m*

    * **solid black** → 8876

8876 solid black [color]
    d vollschwarze Farbe *f*
    f couleur *f* noire solide
    r плотный черный цвет *m*

8877 solid box
    d Vollparallelflach *n*
    f boîte *f* solide
    r монолитный параллелепипед *m*

8878 solid brush
    d dichter Pinsel *m*
    f brosse *f* solide
    r сплошная кисть *f*

8879 solid color
    d Vollfarbe *f*
    f couleur *f* solide
    r плотный цвет *m*

8880 solid cone
    d Vollkegel *m*
    f cône *m* solide
    r монолитный конус *m*

8881 solid coordinates
    d Koordinaten *fpl* des Körpers
    f coordonnées *fpl* de solide
    r координаты *fpl* тела

8882 solid cylinder
    d Vollzylinder *m*
    f cylindre *m* solide
    r монолитный цилиндр *m*

    * **solid entity** → 1056

8883 solid fill
    d Vollfüllung *f*
    f remplissage *m* solide
    r плотное заполнение *n*

8884 solid fill boundary
    d Vollfüllungsgrenze *f*

f limite *f* de remplissage solide
r граница *f* плотного заполнения

8885 solid-filled circle
    d vollgefüllter Kreis *m*
    f cercle *m* rempli
    r плотно закрашенная окружность *f*

8886 solid-filled polygon
    d vollgefülltes Polygon *n*
    f polygone *m* rempli
    r плотно закрашенный многоугольник *m*

8887 solid font
    d Festschrift *f*
    f police *f* solide
    r монолитный шрифт *m*

8888 solid graphics
    d Körpergrafik *f*
    f graphique *m* solide
    r графика *f* монолитных тел

8889 solid line
    d Vollinie *f*
    f ligne *f* solide
    r плотная линия *f*; монолитная линия

    * **solid model** → 3204

8890 solid modeler
    d Körper-Modellierer *m*
    f modélisateur *m* de solides
    r программа *f* моделирования плотных тел

8891 solid modeling technology
    d Technologie *f* der Körper-Modellierung
    f technologie *f* de modelage de solides
    r технология *f* моделирования плотных тел

8892 solid of projection
    d Projektionskörper *m*
    f solide *m* de projection
    r тело *n* проекции

8893 solid of revolution; body of revolution; revolved solid
    d Rotationskörper *m*; Drehungskörper *m*; Umdrehungskörper *m*
    f solide *m* de révolution; corps *m* de révolution
    r тело *n* вращения

8894 solid projection
    d Projektion *f* des Körpers
    f projection *f* de solide
    r проекция *f* плотного тела

8895 solid sectioning
    d Körper-Sektionierung *f*

f sectionnement *m* de solide
r сечение *n* плотного тела

8896 solid-state
  d Festkörper-
  f [à l'état] solide
  r твердотельный

8897 solid texture
  d kompakte Textur *f*
  f texture *f* solide
  r текстура *f* твердого тела; текстура объемного объекта

  * **solution** → 2534

8898 solution error
  d Lösungsfehler *m*
  f erreur *f* de solution
  r погрешность *f* решения

8899 solvability
  d Lösbarkeit *f*; Auflösbarkeit *f*
  f résolubilité *f*
  r разрешимость *f*

  * **sort** → 8904

8900 sort *v*
  d sortieren
  f trier
  r сортировать

8901 sort *v* **colors**
  d Farben sortieren
  f trier des couleurs
  r сортировать цвета

8902 sort *v* **facets**
  d Facetten sortieren
  f trier des facettes
  r сортировать фацеты

8903 sort function
  d Sortierfunktion *f*
  f fonction *f* de triage
  r функция *f* сортировки

8904 sort[ing]
  d Sortierung *f*; Sortieren *n*
  f tri[age] *m*
  r сортировка *f*; сортирование *n*

8905 sort order
  d Sortierungsordnung *f*; Ordnung *f* der Sortierung
  f ordre *m* de triage
  r порядок *m* сортировки

8906 sound

d Schall *m*
f son *m*
r звук *m*

  * **sound** → 90

8907 sound and video options
  d Schall- und Videooptionen *fpl*
  f options *fpl* vidéo et son
  r звуковые и видео опции *fpl*

8908 source
  d Quelle *f*
  f source *f*
  r источник *m*; исток *m*

8909 source configuration
  d Quellenkonfiguration *f*
  f configuration *f* de la source
  r конфигурация *f* источника

8910 source coordinate system
  d Quellenkoordinatensystem *n*
  f système *m* de coordonnées source
  r исходная координатная система *f*

8911 source document
  d Ursprungsbeleg *m*; Primärbeleg *m*
  f document *m* d'origine; document de base
  r исходный документ *m*; первичный документ

8912 source drawing
  d Quellenzeichnung *f*
  f dessin *m* d'origine
  r исходный чертеж *m*

8913 source image
  d Quellenbild *n*
  f image *f* d'origine
  r исходное изображение *n*

8914 space
  d Raum *m*
  f espace *m*
  r пространство *n*

8915 space *v*
  d auseinanderlegen
  f espacer
  r располагать с интервалами; располагать вразрядку; оставлять пробел

  * **space** → 5255, 8917, 8940

8916 space adjustment
  d Abstand-Justierung *f*
  f ajustage *m* d'espacement
  r настройка *f* расстояния

* space bar → 8924

8917 space [character]; blank [character]
d Leerzeichen *n*; Zwischenraumzeichen *n*;
  Lückenzeichen *n*
f caractère *m* d'espace[ment]
r знак *m* пробела; знак пропуска

8918 space code
d Abstandscode *m*; Pausencode *m*
f code *m* d'espace
r код *m* интервала

* space configuration → 8944

**8919 space curve; spatial curve; curve in space;
twisted curve; skew curve**
d räumliche Kurve *f*; Raumkurve *f*; Kurve
  doppelter Krümmung; Kurve im Raum
f courbe *f* spatiale; courbe à double courbure;
  courbe gauche
r пространственная кривая *f*; кривая
  двоякой кривизны; кривая в пространстве;
  изогнутая кривая

8920 space deformation
d räumliche Deformation *f*
f déformation *f* spatiale
r пространственная деформация *f*

8921 space-delimited format; SDF
d räumlich begrenztes Format *n*;
  Platz-abgegrenztes Format
f format *m* délimité en espace
r пространственно-ограниченный формат *m*

8922 space division
d Raumteilung *f*
f répartition *f* dans l'espace
r пространственное [раз]деление *n*;
  пространственное уплотнение *n*

**8923 space factor; filling factor; duty factor;
mark[-to]-space ratio**
d Füllfaktor *m*;
  Zeichen-Zwischenraum-Verhaltnis *n*
f taux *m* de remplissage
r коэффициент *m* заполнения

* space image → 8951

8924 space key; space bar
d Leertaste *f*; Space-Taste *f*;
  Zwischenraumtaste *f*
f touche *f* de vide; touche d'espacement
r клавиша *f* пробела; кнопка *f* пропуска

8925 space lattice
d Raumgitter *n*
f réseau *m* spatial

r пространственная решетка *f*

8926 space layer
d Raumschicht *f*
f couche *f* spatial
r разделительный слой *m*

8927 space model
d räumliches Modell *n*
f modèle *m* spatial
r пространственная модель *f*

* space modeling → 10346

8928 space mouse; spatial mouse
d räumliche Maus *f*
f souris *f* spatiale
r пространственная мышь *f*

8929 space object
d räumliches Objekt *n*
f objet *m* spatial
r пространственный объект *m*

8930 space orientation
d räumliche Orientierung *f*
f orientation *f* spatiale
r пространственная ориентация *f*

* space quantization → 7103

8931 space sharing
d Raumaufteilung *f*
f partage *m* d'espace
r разделение *n* пространства

8932 spacing
d Abstandsbestimmung *f*; Anordnung *f* mit
  Zwischenraumzeichen
f espacement *m*; allocation *f* espacée
r расположение *n* с интервалами

8933 spacing after paragraphs
d Abstand *m* nach Absätzen
f espacement *m* devant les paragraphes
r расстояние *n* после параграфов

8934 spacing before paragraphs
d Abstand *m* vor Absätzen
f espacement *m* après les paragraphes
r расстояние *n* перед параграфами

* spacing between words → 10458

8935 span *v*
d aufspannen
f étendre
r охватывать; распространять

8936 span; range
d Spannweite *f*; Variationsbreite *f*

f portée *f*; étendue *f*
r размах *m*; протяжение *n*; полоса *f* захвата

8937 spangle
d Flitter *m*; Schimmer *m*
f paillette *f*
r блестка *f*; блеск *m*; сверкание *n*

8938 spangle *v*
d mit Flitter besetzen; schmücken
f pailleter; briller
r украшать блестками; [фигурально]
усеивать; сверкать

8939 span parameter
d Diapason-Parameter *m*
f paramètre *m* de plage
r параметр *m* диапазона

8940 spatial; space
d räumlich; Raum-; spatial
f spatial; de l'espace; dans l'espace
r пространственный

8941 spatial autocorrelation
d räumliche Autokorrelation *f*
f autocorrélation *f* spatiale
r пространственная автокорреляция *f*

8942 spatial coherence
d räumliche Kohärenz *f*
f cohérence *f* spatiale
r пространственная когерентность *f*

8943 spatial cohesion
d räumliche Kohäsion *f*
f cohésion *f* spatiale
r пространственное сцепление *n*

8944 spatial configuration; space configuration
d räumliche Konfiguration *f*
f configuration *f* spatiale
r пространственная конфигурация *f*

* **spatial coordinates** → 2230

8945 spatial correlation
d räumliche Korrelation *f*
f corrélation *f* spatiale
r пространственная корреляция *f*

* **spatial curve** → 8919

8946 spatial dimension
d räumliche Dimension *f*
f dimension *f* spatiale
r пространственный размер *m*

8947 spatial display
d räumlicher Bildschirm *m*

f affichage *m* spatial
r пространственный дисплей *m*

8948 spatial domain
d Raumgebiet *n*; Gebiet *n* des Raums;
räumliches Gebiet
f domaine *m* dans l'espace [tridimensionnel];
domaine à trois dimensions
r пространственная область *f*

8949 spatial filtering
d räumliche Filtrierung *f*
f filtrage *m* spatial
r пространственная фильтрация *f*

8950 spatial frequency
d spatiale Frequenz *f*; Raumfrequenz *f*
f fréquence *f* spatiale
r пространственная частота *f*

8951 spatial image; space image; stereo[scopic] image
d Raumbild *n*; stereoskopisches Bild *n*
f image *f* en relief; image stéréo[scopique]
r пространственное изображение *n*;
стерео[скопическое] изображение

8952 spatial index
d Raumindex *m*
f indice *m* spatial
r пространственный индекс *m*

8953 spatial information
d Rauminformation *f*
f information *f* spatiale
r пространственная информация *f*

8954 spatial information system
d räumliches Informationsystem *n*
f système *m* d'information spatial
r пространственная информационная
система *f*

8955 spatial interaction model
d räumliches Wechselwirkungsmodell *n*
f modèle *m* d'interaction spatiale
r модель *f* пространственного
взаимодействия

8956 spatial intersection
d räumlicher Durchschnitt *m*
f intersection *f* spatiale
r пространственное пересечение *n*

8957 spatial location
d räumliche Position *f*
f position *f* spatiale
r пространственное расположение *n*

8958 spatially uniform light emission
d räumlich homogene Lichtemission *f*

    f émission *f* lumineuse spatialement uniforme
    r пространственно-гомогенное световое
        излучение *n*

8959 spatial mark
    d räumliche Messmarke *f*; Raummarke *f*;
        wandernde Messmarke
    f index *m* de pointe spatiale; index de pointe
        stéréoscopique
    r пространственная [измерительная] марка *f*;
        мнимая марка

    * **spatial modeling** → 10346

    * **spatial mouse** → 8928

8960 spatial navigation
    d räumliche Navigation *f*
    f navigation *f* spatiale
    r передвижение *n* в пространстве

8961 spatial perception
    d räumliche Wahrnehmung *f*
    f perception *f* spatiale
    r пространственное ощущение *n*

8962 spatial point
    d räumlicher Punkt *m*
    f point *m* spatial
    r пространственная точка *f*

8963 spatial resolution
    d räumliche Auflösung *f*
    f résolution *f* spatiale
    r пространственное разрешение *n*

8964 spatial scale
    d räumlicher Maßstab *m*
    f échelle *f* spatiale
    r пространственный масштаб *m*

8965 spatial set operations
    (union, intersection and subtraction)
    d Operationen *fpl* der räumlichen Mengen
    f ensemble *m* d'opérations sur objets spatiaux
    r операции *fpl* с пространственными
        объектами

8966 spatial smoothing
    d räumliche Glättung *f*
    f lissage *m* spatial
    r пространственное сглаживание *n*

8967 spatial unit
    d räumliche Einheit *f*
    f unité *f* spatiale
    r пространственная единица *f*

8968 spatial vision
    d räumliches Sehen *n*

    f vision *f* spatiale
    r пространственное зрение *n*

8969 spatio-temporal data
    d spatio-zeitliche Daten *npl*
    f données *fpl* spatio-temporelles
    r пространственно-временные данные *npl*

8970 spatio-temporal database
    d spatio-zeitliche Datenbasis *f*
    f base *f* de données spatio-temporelles
    r база *f* пространственно-временных данных

8971 speaker
    d Sprecher *m*
    f parleur *m*
    r динамик *m*; громкоговоритель *m*;
        акустическая колонка *f*

    * **special** → 6871

8972 special character
    d Sonderzeichen *n*
    f caractère *m* spécial
    r специальный символ *m*

**8973 special complex of lines; singular complex
of rays**
    d spezieller Geradenkomplex *m*; singulärer
        Strahlenkomplex *m*
    f complexe *m* de droites spécial; complexe des
        rayons singulier
    r специальный комплекс *m* прямых;
        сингулярный комплекс лучей

8974 special effect
    d Spezialeffekt *m*
    f effet *m* spécial
    r специальный эффект *m*

8975 special effects filter
    d Spezialeffekte-Filter *m*
    f filtre *m* d'effets spéciaux
    r фильтр *m* специальных эффектов

    * **special map** → 9631

8976 special views
    d spezielle Ansichten *fpl*; Sonderansichten *fpl*
    f vues *fpl* spéciaux
    r специальные представления *npl*

8977 species; kind
    d Sorte *f*; Art *f*
    f espèce *f*
    r вид *m*; род *m*

8978 specification
    d Spezifikation *f*

f spécification *f*
r спецификация *f*

8979 specificator; specifier
d Spezifikator *m*
f spécificateur *m*
r спецификатор *m*

8980 specific curvature
d spezifische Krümmung *f*
f courbure *f* spécifique
r удельная кривизна *f*

8981 specified behaviour
d vorgegebenes Verhalten *n*; vorgeschriebenes Verhalten
f comportement *m* spécifié
r предписанное поведение *n*

*   **specifier → 8979**

8982 speckle pattern
d Granulationsmuster *n*
f spectre *m* de tacheture
r пятнистая картина *f*

8983 speckles
d Sprenkel *mpl*; Tüpfelchen *npl*
f tacheture *f*
r спеклы *npl*; пятна *npl*

8984 spectral
d Spektral-; spektral
f spectral
r спектральный

8985 spectral absorptance
d spektraler Absorptionsgrad *m*
f facteur *m* d'absorption spectral
r спектральный коэффициент *m* поглощения

*   **spectral absorption analysis → 29**

8986 spectral analysis
d Spektralanalysis *f*; Spektralanalyse *f*
f analyse *f* spectrale
r спектральный анализ *m*

8987 spectral attenuation
d Spektraldämpfung *f*
f atténuation *f* spectrale; affaiblissement *m* spectral
r спектральное затухание *n*

8988 spectral [band]width
d spektrale Bandbreite *f*; Spektralbreite *f*
f largeur *f* [de la bande] spectrale
r спектральная ширина *f* полосы; ширина спектра

8989 spectral brightness sensitivity
d spektrale Helligkeitsempfindlichkeit *f*
f sensitivité *f* de brillance spectrale
r спектральная чувствительность *f* яркости

8990 spectral characteristics; spectral response
d Spektralcharakteristik *f*
f caractéristique *f* spectrale; réponse *f* spectrale
r спектральная характеристика *f*

8991 spectral color
d Spektralfarbe *f*
f couleur *f* du spectre
r спектральный цвет *m*

8992 spectral curve
d Spektralkurve *f*
f courbe *f* spectrale
r спектральная кривая *f*

8993 spectral decomposition; chromatic decomposition
d spektrale Zerlegung *f*; Spektralzerlegung *f*; Spektralentwicklung *f*
f décomposition *f* spectrale; développement *m* spectral
r спектральное разложение *n*

8994 spectral density
d Spektraldichte *f*
f densité *f* spectrale
r спектральная плотность *f*

*   **spectral displacement → 9012**

8995 spectral distribution
d spektrale Verteilung *f*
f distribution *f* spectrale; répartition *f* spectrale
r спектральное распределение *n*

8996 spectral emissivity
d spektraler Emissionsgrad *m*; spektrale Emissionsfähigkeit *f*
f émissivité *f* spectrale; pouvoir *m* émissif spectral
r спектральный коэффициент *m* излучения; спектральная излучательная способность *f*

8997 spectral family
d Spektralschar *f*
f famille *f* spectrale
r спектральное семейство *n*

8998 spectral feature
d spektrales Merkmal *n*
f signe *m* spectral
r спектральный признак *m*

8999 spectral filter
d Spektralfilter *m*

f filtre *m* spectral
r спектральный фильтр *m*

9000 spectral function
d Spektralfunktion *f*
f fonction *f* spectrale
r спектральная функция *f*

9001 spectral invariant
d Spektralinvariante *f*
f invariant *m* spectral
r спектральный инвариант *m*

9002 spectral irradiance
d spektrale Bestrahlungsstärke *f*
f irradiance *f* spectrale
r спектральная облученность *f*

9003 spectral line; emission line
d Spektrallinie *f*; Emissionlinie *f*
f raie *f* spectrale
r спектральная линия *f*

9004 spectral measure
d Spektralmaß *n*
f mesure *f* spectrale
r спектральная мера *f*

9005 spectral measurement
d spektrale Messung *f*
f mesurage *m* spectrale
r измерение *n* спектра

9006 spectral radiance
d spektrale Strahl[en]dichte *f*; spezifische spektrale Ausstrahlung *f*
f densité *f* spectrale de luminance [énergétique]; radiance *f* spectrale; luminance *f* spectrale énergétique
r спектральная яркость *f* [излучения]; спектральная плотность *f* излучения; удельное спектральное излучение *n*

9007 spectral range; spectral region
d Spektralbereich *m*; Spektralgebiet *n*
f domaine *m* spectral; région *f* de spectre
r спектральная область *f*

* **spectral region** → 9007

9008 spectral representation
d Spektraldarstellung *f*
f représentation *f* spectrale
r спектральное представление *n*

9009 spectral resolution
d Spektralauflösung *f*
f résolution *f* spectrale
r спектральная разрешающая способность *f*

* **spectral response** → 8990

9010 spectral response curve; spectral sensitivity curve
d spektrale Empfindlichkeitskurve *f*
f courbe *f* de réponse spectrale; courbe de sensibilité spectrale
r кривая *f* спектральной чувствительности

9011 spectral responsivity; spectral sensitivity
d Spektralempfindlichkeit *f*; spektrale Empfindlichkeit *f*
f sensibilité *f* spectrale
r спектральная чувствительность *f*

* **spectral sensitivity** → 9011

* **spectral sensitivity curve** → 9010

9012 spectral shift; spectral displacement
d Spektralverschiebung *f*
f déplacement *m* spectral; décalage *m* spectral
r спектральное смещение *n*; спектральный сдвиг *m*

9013 spectral signature
d spektrale Unterschrift *f*
f signature *f* spectrale
r спектральная подпись *f*

9014 spectral spread
d spektraler Umfang *m*
f étalement *m* spectral
r спектральный охват *m*

* **spectral width** → 8988

9015 spectral window
d Spektralfenster *n*
f fenêtre *f* spectrale
r спектральное окно *n*

* **spectre** → 9018

9016 spectrometry
d Spektrometrie *f*
f spectrométrie *f*
r спектрометрия *f*

9017 spectroscopy
d Spektroskopie *f*
f spectroscopie *f*
r спектроскопия *f*

9018 spectrum; spectre
d Spektrum *n*
f spectre *m*
r спектр *m*

9019 spectrum light source
d Quelle *f* des Spektrallichts

f source *f* lumineuse spectrale
r источник *m* спектрального цвета

9020 spectrum locus
d Spektralort *m*
f lieu *m* géométrique du spectre
r местоположение *n* спектра

9021 specular
d spiegelnd
f spéculaire
r зеркальный

9022 specular body
d spiegelnder Körper *m*
f corps *m* spéculaire
r зеркальное тело *n*

* **specular highlight** → 9023

9023 specular highlight[ing]; specular lighting
d spiegelnde Beleuchtung *f*; spiegelnde
Leuchtung *f*
f mise *f* en évidence spéculaire
r зеркальное высвечивание *n*

* **specular lighting** → 9023

9024 specular lighting function
d Funktion *f* der spiegelnden Beleuchtung
f fonction *f* d'éclairage spéculaire
r функция *f* зеркального освещения

9025 specular power coefficient
d spiegelnder Leistungskoeffizient *m*
f coefficient *m* de puissance spéculaire
r коэффициент *m* зеркальной мощности

**9026 specular reflection; mirror reflection;
mirroring**
d Spiegelreflexion *f*; Normalreflexion *f*;
gerichtete Reflexion *f*; Spiegeln *n*;
Spiegelung *f*
f réflexion *f* spéculaire; réflexion dirigée
r зеркальное отражение *n*; нормальное
отражение

9027 specular reflector
d Spiegelreflektor *m*
f réflecteur *m* spéculaire
r зеркальный отражатель *m*

9028 specular surface
d Spiegelfläche *f*
f surface *f* spéculaire
r зеркальная поверхность *f*

9029 speed; rate; velocity
d Geschwindigkeit *f*
f vitesse *f*; rapidité *f*

r скорость *f*; быстрота *f*

* **spell checker** → 6661

9030 spelling
d Rechtschreibung *f*
f orthographie *f*; écriture *f*
r правописание *n*; орфография *f*

* **spelling checker** → 6661

9031 sphere
d Kugel *f*
f sphère *f*
r сфера *f*

* **sphere packing** → 6719

9032 spherical angle
d sphärischer Winkel *m*; Kugelwinkel *m*
f angle *m* sphérique
r сферический угол *m*

9033 spherical annulus; spherical ring
d Kugelring *m*
f anneau *m* sphérique
r шаровое кольцо *n*; сферическое кольцо

9034 spherical calotte; spherical cap
d Kugelkappe *f*; Kalotte *f*
f calotte *f* sphérique
r сферическая шапка *f*

* **spherical cap** → 9034

* **spherical coordinates** → 9049

9035 spherical coordinate system
d sphärisches Koordinatensystem *n*
f système *m* de coordonnées sphériques
r сферическая координатная система *f*

9036 spherical curvature
d sphärische Krümmung *f*
f courbure *f* sphérique
r сферическая кривизна *f*

9037 spherical diffuse lighting
d sphärische diffuse Beleuchtung *f*
f éclairage *m* diffus sphérique
r сферическое диффузное освещение *n*

9038 spherical diffuse lighting table
d Tafel *f* der sphärischen diffusen Beleuchtung
f table *f* d'éclairage diffus sphérique
r таблица *f* сферического диффузного
освещения

* **spherical distance** → 1464

9039 spherical domain
 d Kugelgebiet *n*
 f domaine *m* sphérique
 r шаровая область *f*

9040 spherical geometry
 d sphärische Geometrie *f*
 f géométrie *f* sphérique
 r сферическая геометрия *f*

9041 spherical gradient
 d sphärischer Gradient *m*
 f gradient *m* sphérique
 r сферический градиент *m*

9042 spherical grid
 d sphärisches Gitter *n*
 f grille *f* sphérique
 r сферическая сеть *f*

 * **spherical helix** → 8151

9043 spherical layer; spherical shell
 d Kugelschicht *f*; Hohlkugel *f*; Kugelschale *f*
 f couronne *f* sphérique; couche *f* sphérique
 r шаровой слой *m*; сферический слой; полый шар *m*

9044 spherical lens; ball lens
 d Kugellinse *f*
 f lentille *f* sphérique; lentille boule
 r шаровая линза *f*

 * **spherical map** → 9045

9045 spherical map[ping]
 d sphärische Abbildung *f*
 f application *f* sphérique
 r сферическое отображение *n*

9046 spherical mirror
 d sphärischer Spiegel *m*
 f miroir *m* sphérique
 r сферическое зеркало *n*

9047 spherical neighborhood
 d sphärische Umgebung *f*
 f voisinage *m* sphérique
 r сферическая окрестность *f*

 * **spherical neighborhood of radius** → 3484

9048 spherical polar angle
 d sphärischer Polarwinkel *m*
 f angle *m* polaire sphérique
 r полярный сферический угол *m*

9049 spherical [polar] coordinates; polar coordinates in the space
 d sphärische Polarkoordinaten *fpl*; sphärische Koordinaten *fpl*; Kugelkoordinaten *fpl*; räumliche Polarkoordinaten *fpl*
 f coordonnées *fpl* sphériques [polaires]
 r сферические координаты *fpl*; полярные координаты в пространстве

9050 spherical polar mapping
 d sphärische Polarabbildung *f*
 f mappage *m* polaire sphérique
 r сферическое полярное отображение *n*

9051 spherical polar parametrization
 d sphärische Polarparametrisierung *f*
 f paramétrisation *f* polaire sphérique
 r сферическая полярная параметризация *f*

9052 spherical polygon
 d sphärisches Polygon *n*
 f polygone *m* sphérique
 r сферический многоугольник *m*

9053 spherical projection
 d sphärische Projektion *f*
 f projection *f* sphérique
 r сферическая проекция *f*

9054 spherical pyramid
 d sphärische Pyramide *f*
 f pyramide *f* sphérique
 r сферическая пирамида *f*

9055 spherical reflection
 d sphärische Reflexion *f*
 f réflexion *f* sphérique
 r сферическое отражение *n*

9056 spherical reflection image
 d sphärisches Reflexionsbild *n*
 f image *f* de réflexion sphérique
 r изображение *n* сферического отражения

9057 spherical reflection mapping
 d Abbildung *f* der sphärischen Reflexion
 f mappage *m* de réflexion sphérique
 r отображение *n* сферического отражения

 * **spherical ring** → 9033

 * **spherical sector** → 8442

 * **spherical segment** → 8449

 * **spherical shell** → 9043

9058 spherical triangle
 d sphärisches Dreieck *n*; Kugeldreieck *n*
 f triangle *m* sphérique
 r сферический треугольник *m*

9059 spherical trigonometry
 d sphärische Trigonometrie *f*

f trigonométrie *f* sphérique
r сферическая тригонометрия *f*

9060 spherical wavelets
   d sphärische Elementarwellen *fpl*
   f ondelettes *fpl* sphériques
   r сферические пульсации *fpl*

9061 spherical wedge
   d Kugelkeil *m*
   f biseau *m* sphérique; coin *m* sphérique
   r шаровой клин *m*

9062 spherical zone
   d Kugelzone *f*
   f zone *f* sphérique
   r шаровой пояс *m*; [шаровая] зона *f*

9063 spherocylinder
   d Sphärozylinder *m*
   f sphérocylindre *m*
   r сфероцилиндр *m*

9064 spheroid
   d Drehellipsoid *n*
   f sphéroïde *m*
   r сфероид *m*

9065 spider web effect
   d Spinnweben-Effekt *m*
   f effet *m* de toile d'araignée
   r паучковый эффект *m*

   * **spike** → 6916

9066 spiral
   d Spirale *f*
   f spirale *f*
   r спираль *f*

9067 spiral *adj*
   d spiral
   f spiral
   r спиральный

   * **spiral angle** → 388

   * **spiraling** → 4557

   * **spiralling** → 4557

9068 spiral scanning
   d Spiralabtastung *f*
   f échantillonnage *m* spiral
   r спиральное сканирование *n*

9069 spiral tool
   d Spiralwerkzeug *m*
   f outil *m* spirale
   r инструмент *m* [вычерчивания] спиралей

   * **spline** → 9071

9070 spline approximation
   d Spline-Approximation *f*
   f approximation *f* par une fonction spline
   r сплайн-аппроксимация *f*

9071 spline [curve]
   d Spline *m*
   f spline *m*
   r сплайн *m*

9072 splined polyline; spline-fit polyline
   d Polylinie *f* mit Form des Splines
   f polyligne *f* [lissée] en spline
   r сглаженная полилиния *f*; полилиния, сглаженная сплайном

   * **spline-fit polyline** → 9072

9073 spline fitting
   d Spline-Anpassung *f*; Spline-Fitten *n*
   f déformation *f* sur un spline; ajustement *m* de points par fonction spline
   r аппроксимация *f* сплайна; сглаживание *n* сплайна

9074 spline function
   d Spline-Funktion *f*
   f fonction *f* spline
   r сплайн-функция *f*

9075 spline interpolation
   d Spline-Interpolation *f*
   f interpolation *f* [par une fonction] spline
   r сплайн-интерполяция *f*

9076 spline leader
   d Spline-Vorlauf *m*
   f apériteur *m* de spline; directeur *m* de spline
   r начало *n* сплайна; заголовок *m* сплайна

   * **spline map** → 9077

9077 spline map[ping]
   d Spline-Abbildung *f*
   f application *f* de spline
   r отображение *n* сплайна

9078 spline modeler
   d Spline-Modellierer *m*
   f modélisateur *m* de splines
   r программа *f*, моделирующая сплайны

9079 spline object
   d Spline-Objekt *n*
   f objet *m* spline
   r объект *m* типа сплайна

9080 spline processor
   d Spline-Prozessor *m*

f spline-processeur *m*
r сплайн-процессор *m*

* split → 9093

9081 split *v*
d zerspalten; zersplittern; zerteilen
f scinder; fractionner
r расщеплять; дроблять; разделять

9082 split *adj*
d spaltend; zerlegbar; zerfallend
f scindé
r расщепляемый

9083 split bar
(of the window)
d Fensterteiler *m*
f barre *f* de fractionnement
r разделительная линейка *f*

9084 split box
d Teilungsfeld *n*
f curseur *m* de fractionnement
r маркер *m* разбиения

9085 split field
d geteiltes Feld *n*
f champ *m* divisé
r разделенное поле *n*

9086 split lens
d geteiltes Objektiv *n*
f lentille *f* divisée
r разделенная линза *f*; расщепленная линза

9087 split line
d Aufteilungslinie *f*
f ligne *f* de séparation
r линия *f* разбиения

9088 split method
d Aufteilungsmethode *f*
f méthode *f* de splittage
r метод *m* разбиения; метод дробления

9089 split mode
d Aufteilungsbetriebsweise *f*
f mode *m* de splittage
r режим *m* разбиения; режим расщепления

9090 split screen; divided screen
d geteilter Bildschirm *m*
f écran *m* partagé; écran divisé; écran
dédoublé; écran fractionné
r разделенный экран *m*; полиэкран *m*

9091 split-screen format
d geteiltes Bildschirmformat *n*
f format *m* multifenêtre

r полиэкранный формат *m*; многооконный
формат

9092 splitter bar
d Aufteilungsleiste *f*
f barre *f* de splittage
r лента *f* разбиения

9093 split[ting]
d Aufteilung *f*; Aufteilen *n*; Spaltung *f*;
Splitting *n*; Splitten *n*
f splittage *m*; scindement *m*; fractionnement *m*;
scission *f*
r расщепление *n*; дробление *n*; разбиение *n*

9094 spontaneous optical radiation
d spontane optische Strahlung *f*
f rayonnement *m* optique spontané
r спонтанное оптическое излучение *n*

9095 spontaneous request
d spontane Anforderung *f*
f interrogation *f* spontanée
r случайный запрос *m*

9096 spooled plotting
d spulendes Plotten *n*
f traçage *m* tamponné
r буферизированное вычерчивание *n*

9097 spooling
d Spooling *n*; Spulen *n*; Spulung *f*
f spoulage *m*
r спулинг *m*; буферирование *n*

9098 sporting graphics
d Sportgrafik *f*
f graphique *m* sportif
r спортивная графика *f*

9099 spot
d Fleck *m*
f tache *f*; spot *m*
r пятно *n*

9100 spot color
d Punktfarbe *f*
f couleur *f* du spot
r цвет *m* пятна

9101 spot-color reproduction
d Punktfarb[en]-Reproduktion *f*
f reproduction *f* de couleur du spot
r воспроизведение *n* цвета пятна

9102 spot diameter
d Fleck[en]durchmesser *m*
f diamètre *m* de tache
r диаметр *m* пятна

9103 **spotlight**
   d Spotlight *n*; Spot-Licht *n*; Streiflicht *n*
   f projecteur *m* à faisceau concentré; projecteur
      spot; projecteur convergent; projecteur
      intensif
   r прожектор *m*

9104 **spotlight cone**
   d Spotlight-Kegel *m*
   f cône *m* d'éclairage
   r конус *m* прожектора

9105 **spot size**
   d Fleck[en]größe *f*
   f taille *f* du spot
   r размер *m* пятна

9106 **spot texture**
   d Fleck[en]textur *f*
   f texture *f* de tache
   r текстура *f* пятна

   * **spray** → **9109**

9107 **spray** *v*
   d sprühen
   f pulvériser; atomiser
   r распылять

9108 **spray**
   d Spray *n*; Spritz *m*; Aerosol *m*
   f spray *m*; aérosol *m*
   r распыленная краска *f*; аэрозоль *m*

   * **spraycan** → **250**

9109 **spray[ing]**
   d Pulverisierung *f*
   f pulvérisation *f*; atomisation *f*
   r распыление *n*

   * **spread** → **9110**

9110 **spread[ing]**
   d Ausdehnung *f*; Spreizung *f*
   f étalement *m*; propagation *f*
   r протягивание *n*; распространение *n*;
      разброс *m*

   * **spreadsheet** → **3340**

   * **spreadsheet program** → **3340**

9111 **sprite**
      (small pictogram, used in games; graphical
      image that can move within a larger graphic)
   d Geist *m*
   f sprite *m*; lutin *m*; démon *m*
   r динамический графический элемент *m*;
      спрайт *m*

9112 **spurious**
   d parasitär; Parasiten-
   f parasite; erroné; faux
   r паразитный; ложный

9113 **spurious polygon**
   d Parasitenpolygon *n*
   f polygone *m* parasite
   r паразитный полигон *m*

   * **SQL** → **9258**

9114 **SQL driver**
   d SQL-Treiber *m*
   f driver *m* SQL
   r драйвер *m* SQL

9115 **SQL editor**
   d SQL-Editor *m*
   f éditeur *m* SQL
   r редактор *m* SQL

9116 **SQL file**
   d SQL-Datei *f*
   f fichier *m* SQL
   r файл *m* SQL

9117 **SQL query**
   d SQL-Abfrage *f*
   f interrogation *f* SQL; requête *f* SQL
   r запрос *m* SQL

9118 **square; quadrate**
   d Quadrat *n*
   f carré *m*
   r квадрат *m*

9119 **square attenuation**
      (of light)
   d Quadratdämpfung *f*
   f atténuation *f* quadratique
   r квадратичное затухание *n*

9120 **square brackets**
      ([ ])
   d eckige Klammern *fpl*
   f crochets *mpl*
   r квадратные скобки *fpl*

9121 **square cap**
   d eckiges Kappen *n*
   f rebouchage *m* carré
   r квадратное перекрытие *n*

9122 **square cell**
   d eckige Zelle *f*
   f cellule *f* carrée
   r квадратная клетка *f*

9123 **square fill**
   d Quadratfüllung *f*

f remplissage *m* de carré
r закрашивание *n* квадрата

* **square grid** → 9124

* **square-low** → 7653

9124 square[-mesh] grid
d quadratisches Netz *n*; Quadratnetz *n*
f réseau *m* quadratique; quadrillage *m*
r квадратная сетка *f*; квадратная сеть *f*

9125 square pixel
d eckiges Pixel *n*
f pixel *m* carré
r квадратный пиксел *m*

9126 square pyramid
d eckige Pyramide *f*
f pyramide *f* carrée
r квадратная пирамида *f*

9127 squaring; quadrature
d Quadratur *f*
f quadrature *f*
r квадратура *f*

* **S-shaped curve** → 8677

9128 stability
d Stabilität *f*
f stabilité *f*
r устойчивость *f*

9129 stable
d stabil
f stable
r устойчивый

9130 stack frame
d Stack-Rahmen *m*
f échelon *m* de pile
r граница *f* стека

9131 stacking order
d Aufstapeln-Ordnung *f*
f ordre *m* d'empilage
r порядок *m* записи в стек

* **stage** → 1300

9132 stage
d Stadium *m*
f stade *m*; étape *f*
r стадия *f*; этап *m*

9133 staggering
d Verstimmung *f*
f désordre *m*
r расстройство *n*

9134 stainless steel effect
d Effekt *m* des rostfreien Stahls
f effet *m* d'acier inoxydable
r эффект *m* нержавеющей стали

* **stairstepping** → 259

9135 stand-alone
d unabhängig; selbständig
f indépendant
r самостоятельный; независимый

9136 standard
d Standard *m*; Norm *f*
f standard *m*
r стандарт *m*

9137 standard deviation
d Standardabweichung *f*
f écart *m* type
r стандартное отклонение *n*

9138 standard deviation report
d Bericht *m* der Standardabweichung
f rapport *m* d'écart type
r отчет *m* стандартного отклонения

9139 standard for drawing; drawing standard
d Zeichenstandard *m*
f standard *m* de dessin
r чертежный стандарт *m*

9140 standard form
d Standardform *f*; Grundform *f*
f forme *f* standard
r стандартная форма *f*; общий вид *m*

9141 standard graphics; default graphics
d Standardgrafik *f*
f graphique *m* standard
r стандартная графика *f*

9142 standard[ized] mode
d Standardmodus *m*; normierter Modus *m*
f mode *m* standard
r стандартный режим *m*; нормальный режим

9143 standardized raster graphics
d Standardrastergrafik *f*
f graphique *m* rastre standardisé
r стандартная растровая графика *f*

9144 standard keyboard
d Standardtastatur *f*
f clavier *m* standard
r стандартная клавиатура *f*

9145 standard library
d Standardbibliothek *f*

f bibliothèque *f* standard
r библиотека *f* стандартных модулей

9146 standard library file
d standardmäßige Bibliotheksdatei *f*
f fichier *m* de bibliothèque standard
r стандартный библиотечный файл *m*

*   **standard mode** → 9142

9147 standard model
d Standardmodell *n*
f modèle *m* standard
r стандартная модель *f*

9148 standard paper size
d Papier-Normalformat *n*
f format *m* de papier standard
r стандартный формат *m* бумаги

9149 standard profile
d Standardprofil *n*
f profil *m* standard
r стандартный профиль *m*

9150 standard representation
d Standarddarstellung *f*
f représentation *f* type
r стандартное представление *n*

9151 standard toolbar
d Standardhilfsmittelstreifen *m*
f barre *f* d'outils standard
r стандартная инструментальная лента *f*;
    стандартная панель *f* инструментов

*   **standpoint** → 7342

9152 star
d Stern *m*
f étoile *f*
r звезда *f*

*   **star domain** → 9153

9153 star[-like] domain; star region
d Sternbereich *m*; Sterngebiet *n*
f domaine *m* étoilé
r звездообразная область *f*; звездная
    область; звездчатая область

*   **star network** → 9168

*   **star of circles** → 6927

*   **star of planes** → 6932

*   **star of rays** → 1196

*   **star of spheres** → 1197

9154 star pentagon
d Sternfünfeck *n*
f pentagone *m* étoilé
r звездчатый пятиугольник *m*

**9155 star polygon; asterisk-shaped polygon;
        polygon as star**
d Sternvieleck *n*; Sternpolygon *n*
f polygone *m* étoilé; polygone en forme d'étoile
r звездчатый многоугольник *m*

**9156 star polyhedron; stellated polyhedron;
        Poinsot['s] polyhedron**
d Sternvielflach *n*; Sternpolyeder *n*
f polyèdre *m* étoilé
r звездчатый многогранник *m*;
    многогранник Пуансо

*   **star region** → 9153

9157 start
d Start *m*; Starten *n*; Anfang *m*
f départ *m*; début *m*
r запуск *m*; старт *m*; пуск *m*; начало *n*

*   **start head character** → 9163

9158 starting color
d Anfangsfarbe *f*
f couleur *f* de départ
r начальный цвет *m*

9159 starting width
d Anfangsbreite *f*
f largueur *f* initiale
r начальная ширина *f*

9160 start node
d Anfangsknoten *m*
f nœud *m* initial
r начальный узел *m*

9161 start object; initial object
    (of blending)
d Anfangsobjekt *n*
f objet *m* initial
r начальный объект *m*; стартовый объект

9162 start of frame; frame start
d Rahmenbeginn *m*
f démarrage *m* de trame; début *m* de cadre
r старт *m* фрейма; старт кадра

**9163 start-of-heading character; start head
        character**
d Kopfanfangszeichen *n*; Startkopfzeichen *n*
f caractère *m* de début d'en-tête
r символ *m* начала заголовка

9164 **start of text**
  d Textanfang *m*; Textbeginn *m*
  f début *m* de texte
  r начало *n* текста; старт *m* текста

9165 **startup**
  d Anlauf *m*; Einleitung *f*
  f démarrage *m*
  r пуск *m*

9166 **startup angle**
  d Anlauf[s]winkel *m*
  f angle *m* de démarrage
  r пусковой угол *m*

9167 **startup point**
  d Anlauf[s]punkt *m*
  f point *m* de démarrage
  r точка *f* запуска

9168 **star[-wired] network; radial network**
  d Sternnetz *f*; Netz *f* mit Sternstruktur
  f réseau *m* en étoile; réseau radial
  r звездообразная сеть *f*; радиальная сеть

9169 **state; status**
  d Zustand *m*; Status *m*
  f état *m*; statut *m*
  r состояние *n*

9170 **state diagram**
  d Zustandsdiagramm *n*
  f diagramme *m* d'état
  r диаграмма *f* состояния

9171 **static; stationary; steady-state**
  d statisch; stationär; stehend; ortsfest
  f statique; stationnaire; établi; permanent
  r статический; постоянный; стационарный; стоячий; установленный

9172 **static image; static picture; static pattern; still[-frame] image; background [display image]; fixed image**
  d Standbild *n*; Stehbild *n*; statisches Bild *n*
  f image *f* statique; image fixe
  r статичное изображение *n*

9173 **static information**
  d statische Information *f*
  f information *f* fixe; information statique
  r постоянная информация *f*; установленная информация

9174 **static model**
  d statisches Modell *n*
  f modèle *m* statique
  r статичная модель *f*

  * **static pattern** → 9172

9175 **static-pattern compression; still-image compression**
  d Kompression *f* der statischen Bilder
  f compression *f* d'images statiques
  r сжатие *n* статичных изображений

  * **static picture** → 9172

9176 **static-picture transmission; still-image transmission**
  d Standbildübertragung *f*; Stehbildübertragung *f*
  f transmission *f* d'images statiques; transmission d'images fixes
  r передача *f* статичных изображений

9177 **static threshold; fixed threshold**
  d statischer Schwellwert *m*; fixer Schwellwert
  f seuil *m* statique; seuil fixe
  r статический порог *m*

  * **stationary** → 9171

9178 **stationary point**
  d stationärer Punkt *m*
  f point *m* stationnaire
  r стационарная точка *f*

  * **statistic** → 9179

9179 **statistic[al]**
  d statistisch
  f statistique
  r статистический

9180 **statistical analysis**
  d statistische Analyse *f*
  f analyse *f* statistique
  r статистический анализ *m*

9181 **statistical pattern**
  d statistische Bilder *npl*
  f images *fpl* statistiques
  r статистические изображения *npl*

9182 **statistical surface**
  d statistische Fläche *f*
  f surface *f* statistique
  r статистическая поверхность *f*

9183 **statistics**
  d Statistik *f*
  f statistique *f*
  r статистика *f*

  * **status** → 9169

9184 **status bar**
  d Statusleiste *f*
  f barre *f* d'état
  r лента *f* состояния; строка *f* статуса; строка состояния

9185 status character
   d Zustandszeichen *n*
   f caractère *m* d'état
   r знак *m* состояния

9186 status information
   d Zustandsinformation *f*; Statusinformation *f*
   f information *f* d'état
   r информация *f* о состоянии

9187 status line
   d Statuslinie *f*
   f ligne *f* d'état
   r линия *f* состояния

9188 status table
   d Zustandstabelle *f*
   f table *f* d'état
   r таблица *f* состояния

   * **steady-state** → 9171

   * **steepest line** → 3694

   * **stellated polyhedron** → 9156

9189 stencil
   (special information for each pixel, whether
   and how it is drawn and redrawn)
   d Matritze *f*; Stencil *n*
   f stencil *m*
   r узор *m*

   * **stencil** → 9512

9190 stencil buffer
   d Stencil-Puffer *m*
   f tampon *m* de stencil
   r буфер *m* шаблонов

9191 step
   d Schritt *m*
   f pas *m*
   r шаг *m*

9192 step-by-step; stepped; stepwise
   d schrittweise; stufenweise
   f pas à pas
   r пошагово

9193 step length
   d Schrittlänge *f*; Schrittweite *f*
   f longueur *f* de pas; longueur d'étape
   r длина *f* шага

   * **stepped** → 9192

   * **stepwise** → 9192

9194 steradian

9195 stereocamera
   d Stereokamera *f*
   f stéréocaméra *f*
   r стереокамера *f*

9196 stereogram
   d Stereogramm *n*
   f stéréogramme *m*
   r стереограмма *f*

9197 stereographic
   d stereografisch
   f stéréographique
   r стереографический

9198 stereographic image
   d stereografisches Bild *n*
   f image *f* stéréographique
   r стереографическое изображение *n*

9199 stereographic projection; azimuthal
   orthomorphic projection; zenithal
   orthomorphic projection
   d stereografische Projektion *f*; winkeltreue
   Azimutalprojektion *f*; Kugelprojektion *f*;
   stereografische Abbildung *f*
   f projection *f* stéréographique; représentation *f*
   stéréographique
   r стереографическая проекция *f*

   * **stereo image** → 8951

9200 stereometric camera
   d stereometrische Kamera *f*;
   Stereomesskamera *f*
   f caméra *f* stéréométrique
   r стереометрическая камера *f*

9201 stereophotography
   d Stereoaufnahme *f*
   f stéréophoto[graphie] *f*
   r стереоскопический снимок *m*

9202 stereoscopic
   d stereoskopisch
   f stéréoscopique
   r стереоскопический

9203 stereoscopic casque
   d stereoskopischer Helm *m*
   f casque *f* stéréoscopique
   r стереоскопическая каска *f*

   * **stereoscopic image** → 8951

9204 stereoscopic plotter
   d stereoskopischer Plotter *m*

d Steradian *m*
f stéradian *m*
r стерадиан *m*

f traceur *m* stéréoscopique
r стереоскопический графопостроитель *m*

9205 stereoscopic vision
    d stereoskopische Vision *f*; stereoskopisches
    Sehen *n*
    f vision *f* stéréoscopique
    r стереоскопическое зрение *n*

9206 stereoscopy
    d Stereoskopie *f*
    f stéréoscopie *f*
    r стереоскопия *f*

9207 stereo TV
    d Stereofernsehen *n*
    f télévision *f* stéréoscopique; télévision en
    relief; télévision en trois dimensions
    r объемное телевидение *n*;
    стереотелевидение *n*

9208 stereoview
    d Stereosicht *f*
    f stéréovue *f*
    r стереопредставление *n*; стереовид *m*

9209 stick diagram
    d Stabdiagramm *n*
    f diagramme *m* à barres; diagramme en bâtons
    r палочковая диаграмма *f*

  * **sticking** → 176

  * **still-frame image** → 9172

  * **still image** → 9172

  * **still-image compression** → 9175

  * **still-image transmission** → 9176

  * **stochastic** → 7728

9210 stochastic modeling
    d stochastische Modellierung *f*
    f modelage *m* stochastique
    r стохастическое моделирование *n*

9211 stochastic relaxation
    d stochastische Relaxation *f*
    f relaxation *f* stochastique
    r стохастическая релаксация *f*

  * **stop** → 4491

  * **storage** → 5901

9212 storage; storing; store; memorization
    d Speichern *n*; Speicherung *f*
    f stockage *m*; mémorisation *f*; emmagasinage *m*

    r хранение *n*; запоминание *n*

  * **store** → 5901, 9212

9213 store *v*; **memorize** *v*
    d [ein]speichern; merken
    f mémoriser; stocker; emmagasiner
    r запоминать; хранить

  * **stored error** → 69

  * **storing** → 9212

  * **stow** *v* → 4784

9214 straight angle; flat angle
    d gestreckter Winkel *m*
    f angle *m* plat
    r развернутый угол *m*; выпрямленный угол

9215 straightening
    d Geraderichten *n*; Ausrichten *n*
    f redressage *m*
    r выпрямление *n*; выстраивание *n* [в линию]

9216 straight-forward design
    d geradliniger Entwurf *m*
    f conception *f* linéaire
    r прямой метод *m* проектирования

9217 straight line; line
    d Gerade *f*; Linie *f*
    f ligne *f* droite; droite *f*
    r прямая [линия] *f*

  * **straight-line knurling** → 9218

9218 straight-line moire; straight-line knurling
    d geradliniger Moiré *m*
    f moletage *m* droit
    r линейный муар *m*

  * **straight-line motion** → 7879

9219 straight-line section
    d direkte Sektion *f*; geradlinige Sektion
    f coupe *f* rectiligne; section *f* rectiligne
    r прямолинейный срез *m*; прямолинейное
    отсекание *n*

  * **straight-line segment** → 5633

9220 straight-line threshold
    d geradlinige Schwelle *f*
    f seuil *m* rectiligne
    r прямолинейный порог *m*

9221 stranding
    d Zusammendrehung *f*

f toronnage *m*
r скручивание *n*

9222 strap
  d Riemen *m*; Gurt *m*
  f corde *f*; cordon *m*
  r канат *m*; провод *m*; ремень *m*

9223 strategy
  d Strategie *f*
  f stratégie *f*
  r стратегия *f*

9224 strategy of viewpoints selection
  d Strategie *f* der Augenpunkte-Auswahl
  f stratégie *f* de sélection des points de vue
  r стратегия *f* выбора точек зрения

9225 stratification
  d Stratifikation *f*
  f stratification *f*
  r стратификация *f*; наслоение *n*

9226 stratified sample
  d stratifizierte Stichprobe *f*
  f échantillon *m* stratifié
  r наслоенная выборка *f*

  * **stratum** → 5517

9227 stray
  d Irrfahrt *f*; Störung *f*
  f errance *f*; brouillage *m*; parasite *m*
  r блуждание *n*; возмущение *n*

9228 stray rays
  d Streustrahlen *mpl*
  f rayons *mpl* dispersés; rayons diffusés
  r паразитные лучи *mpl*; рассеянное
    излучение *n*

  * **stream** → 3877

  * **stream line** → 3881

9229 streamlined form
  d Stromlinienform *f*
  f forme *f* aérodynamique
  r упрощенная форма *f*; аэродинамическая
    форма; обтекаемая форма

9230 strength; resistance; endurance
  d Festigkeit *f*
  f résistance *f*
  r прочность *f*; крепкость *f*

9231 stretch *v*
  d strecken; [aus]dehnen; spannen
  f étirer; tendre
  r растягивать; вытягивать

9232 stretch *v* arrowhead
  d Pfeilspitze strecken; größere Pfeilspitze
    erstellen
  f étirer un pic de flèche
  r вытаскивать конец стрелки

  * **stretched** → 7584

9233 stretching
  d Strecken *n*; Streckung *f*; Ausdehnung *f*;
    Dehnung *f*
  f étirage *m*; écrouissage *m*; étirement *m*
  r вытягивание *n*; растягивание *n*;
    удлинение *n*

9234 stretch *v* object
  d Objekt strecken
  f étirer un objet
  r вытаскивать объект

9235 strict
  d streng; strikt
  f strict
  r строгий

  * **striction line** → 4259

  * **strike *v* out** → 9236

9236 strike *v* through; strike *v* out; expunge *v*
  d durchstreichen
  f barrer; rayer
  r зачеркивать; удалять

9237 strikethrough text
  d durchgestrichener Text *m*
  f texte *m* barré
  r зачеркнутый текст *m*

9238 string
  d String *m*; Kette *f*; Zeichenkette *f*
  f chaîne *f*; ordre *m* symbolique
  r строка *f*; цепочка *f* символов

9239 string conversion
  d Stringkonvertierung *f*; Kettenkonvertierung *f*
  f conversion *f* de chaîne
  r преобразование *n* строки

9240 string data
  d Stringdaten *npl*
  f données *fpl* de [type de] chaîne
  r строковые данные *npl*

9241 string quotes
  d Kettenanführungszeichen *npl*
  f guillemets *mpl* de chaîne
  r ведущие кавычки *fpl* строки

9242 string value
  d Wert *m* der Kette

f valeur *f* de chaîne
r значение *n* строки; строковое значение

* **strip → 821**

9243 strip *v*
d abstreifen
f retirer; dénuder; détacher
r зачищать; снимать

* **stripe → 821**

9244 stripe geometry
d Streifengeometrie *f*
f géométrie *f* en ruban; géométrie en bande
r полосковая геометрия *f*

* **stripe scanning → 4707**

* **stroke → 2274**

9245 stroke; bar; dash
d Strich *m*; Stab *m*
f trait *m*; barre *f*; raie *f*
r черта *f*; штрих *m*; тире *n*

9246 stroke device
d Liniengeber *m*
f lecteur *m* de courbes
r устройство *n* ввода последовательности позиций

9247 stroked writing
d Strichschreiben *n*
f écriture *f* hachurée
r штриховая запись *f*

9248 stroke generator
d Strich[zeichen]generator *m*
f générateur *m* de traits
r генератор *m* штрихов

* **stroke marking → 2466**

9249 stroke thickness
d Strichstärke *f*
f épaisseur *f* de trait
r толщина *f* штриха

9250 stroke width
d Strichbreite *f*
f largeur *f* trait; largeur de raie
r ширина *f* штриха; ширина черты

9251 strophoid
d Strophoide *f*
f strophoïde *f*
r строфоида *f*

9252 structural

d Struktur-; strukturell
f structural
r структурный; строительный

9253 structural features
d Strukturierungsmöglichkeiten *fpl*
f facilités *fpl* structuraux
r возможности *fpl* структурирования

9254 structural parameter
d Strukturparameter *m*
f paramètre *m* de structure
r параметр *m* структуры

9255 structure
d Struktur *f*
f structure *f*
r структура *f*; конструкция *f*

9256 structured data
d strukturierte Daten *npl*
f données *fpl* structurées
r структурированные данные *npl*

9257 structured query
d strukturierte Abfrage *f*
f interrogation *f* structurée
r структурированный запрос *m*

9258 structured query language; SQL
d Sprache *f* der strukturierten Abfragen
f langage *m* de requête structurée
r язык *m* структурированных запросов

9259 structured walkthrough; walkthrough
d strukturierte Durchgangsprüfung *f*
f parcours *m* structural de part en part
r сквозной структурный контроль *m*

9260 Stucky filter
d Stucky-Filter *m*
f filtre *m* de Stucky
r фильтр *m* Стаки

9261 studio
d Studio *n*
f studio *m*
r студия *f*

* **stuff → 9262**

9262 stuff[ing]
d Auffüllen *n*; Stopfen *n*
f intercalation *f*; bourrage *m*
r заполнение *n*; вставка *f*; вставление *n*; стаффинг *m*

9263 stunning images
d Betäubungsbilder *npl*

f images *fpl* étourdissantes
r ошеломляющие изображения *npl*

9264 style
  d Stil *m*
  f style *m*
  r стиль *m*

9265 style deleting
  d Stillöschung *f*
  f effacement *m* de style
  r устранение *n* стиля

9266 style gallery
  d Stilgalerie *f*
  f galerie *f* de styles
  r галерея *f* стилей

9267 style library
  d Stilbibliothek *f*
  f bibliothèque *f* de styles
  r библиотека *f* стилей

9268 style list
  d Stilliste *f*
  f liste *f* de styles
  r список *m* стилей

9269 style manager
  d Stil-Manager *m*
  f gestionnaire *m* de styles
  r стилевой менажер *m*

9270 style name
  d Stilname *m*
  f nom *m* de style
  r имя *n* стиля

9271 style properties
  d Stileigenschaften *fpl*
  f propriétés *fpl* de style
  r характеристики *fpl* стиля; свойства стиля

  * **style selection** → 1462

9272 styles page
  d Stilseite *f*
  f page *f* de styles
  r страница *f* стилей

9273 style template
  d Stilschablone *f*
  f modèle *m* de style
  r шаблон *m* стиля; стилевой макет *m*

  * **stylus** → 6921

  * **subarea** → 9279

  * **subassembly** → 1606

9274 subbody; subsolid
  d Unterkörper *m*
  f sous-corps *m*
  r подтело *n*

  * **subchain** → 9307

9275 subclass
  d Unterklasse *f*; Teilklasse *f*
  f sous-classe *f*
  r подкласс *m*

9276 subclass data marker
  d Marker *m* der Unterklassen-Daten
  f marqueur *m* de données de sous-classe
  r маркер *m* данных подкласса

9277 subdirectory
  d Unterkatalog *m*; Teilverzeichnis *n*
  f sous-catalogue *m*; sous-répertoire *m*; sous-dossier *m*
  r подкаталог *m*; подсправочник *m*

9278 subdivision
  d Unterteilung *f*
  f subdivision *f*
  r подразделение *n*; подразбиение *n*

9279 subdomain; subregion; subarea
  d Unterbereich *m*; Teilbereich *m*; Teilgebiet *n*
  f sous-domaine *m*
  r подобласть *f*

9280 sub-entity
  (block attributs, segments of line etc.)
  d Untereinheit *f*
  f sous-entité *f*
  r подпримитив *m*

9281 subframe
  d Unteraufnahme *f*; Subframe *n*
  f sous-trame *f*; sous-cadre *m*
  r подкадр *m*

9282 subgroup
  d Untergruppe *f*
  f sous-groupe *m*
  r подгруппа *f*

9283 subharmonic
  d Subharmonische *f*
  f sous-harmonique *m*
  r субгармоника *f*

  * **subheading** → 9309

9284 subimage; subpicture
  d Teilbild *n*
  f sous-image *f*
  r [составная] часть *f* изображения

9285 sublattice
  d Untergitter *n*; Teilgitter *n*
  f sous-lattis *m*; sous-treillis *m*
  r подрешетка *f*

9286 sublayer
  d Unterschicht *f*
  f sous-niveau *m*; sous-couche *f*
  r подуровень *m*

9287 submenu
  d Untermenü *n*
  f sous-menu *m*
  r подменю *n*

9288 subobject
  d Unterobjekt *n*; Teilobjekt *n*
  f sous-objet *m*
  r подобъект *m*

9289 subpath
  d Unterstrecke *f*
  f sous-tracé *m*
  r поддорожка *f*; подмаршрут *m*

  * **subpicture** → 9284

9290 subplane
  (of a projective plane)
  d Unterebene *f*
  f sous-plan *m*
  r подплоскость *f*

9291 subrange
  d Unterdiapason *m*; Teildiapason *m*
  f sous-rangée *f*
  r поддиапазон *m*

  * **subregion** → 9279

9292 subscript *v*
  d tiefstellen
  f indicer
  r индицировать

9293 subscript; lower index
  d unterer Index *m*; tiefgestellter Index
  f indice *m* inférieur; indice en bas
  r нижний индекс *m*; подстрочный индекс

9294 subscript brackets
  d Indexklammern *fpl*
  f accolades *fpl* indiquées; crochets *mpl*
    indiqués
  r индексные скобки *fpl*

9295 subscript expression
  d Indexausdruck *m*
  f expression *f* indiquée; expression indexée

  r выражение *n* с индексами; индексное
    выражение

9296 subscripting
  d Tiefstellen *n*
  f indexation *f*
  r индицирование *n*

9297 subsection
  d Teilabschnitt *m*
  f sous-section *f*
  r подраздел *m*

9298 subsequence
  d Teilfolge *f*
  f sous-suite *f*
  r подпоследовательность *f*

9299 subsequent; consequent
  d folgend; nachfolgend; konsequent
  f subséquent; conséquent; postérieur; ultérieur
  r следующий; последующий

9300 subsequent equalization
  d folgender Ausgleich *m*
  f égalisation *f* postérieure
  r последующее выравнивание *n*

9301 subsequent modification
  d folgende Modifizierung *f*
  f modification *f* ultérieure
  r последующая модификация *f*

9302 subset
  d Untermenge *f*; Teilmenge *f*
  f sous-ensemble *m*; sous-multitude *f*
  r подмножество *n*

9303 subshape
  d Teilform *f*
  f sous-forme *f*
  r часть *f* формы

  * **subsolid** → 9274

9304 subspace
  d Unterraum *m*
  f sous-espace *m*
  r подпространство *n*

9305 substitution
  d Substitution *f*; Ersetzung *f*; Ersetzen *n*
  f substitution *f*
  r подстановка *f*; субституция *f*

9306 substrate
  d Substrat *n*; Trägerschicht *f*; Unterlage *f*
  f substrat *m*; galette *f*
  r подставка *f*; основание *n*

9307 substring; subchain
  d Teil[zeichen]kette *f*; Teilstring *m*
  f sous-chaîne *f*, sous-ligne *f*
  r подцепочка *f*; подстрока *f*

  * **substructure** → **5973**

9308 subsystem
  d Teilsystem *n*; Untersystem *n*; Subsystem *n*
  f sous-système *m*
  r подсистема *f*

9309 subtitle; subheading
  d Zwischenüberschrift *f*; Untertitel *m*
  f sous-titre *m*
  r подзаголовок *m*

9310 subtracting; subtraction
  d Subtraktion *f*; Subtrahieren *n*
  f soustraction *f*
  r вычитание *n*

  * **subtraction** → **9310**

  * **subtraction sign** → **8687**

9311 subtractive
  d subtraktiv
  f soustractif
  r вычитаемый

9312 subtractive blend
  d subtraktive Überblendung *f*
  f dégradé *m* soustractif
  r вычитаемое переливание *n*

9313 subtractive chromatic system
  d subtraktives Farbsystem *n*
  f système *m* chromatique soustractif
  r вычитаемая хроматическая система *f*

9314 subtractive colorimetric system
  d subtraktives kolorimetrische System *n*
  f système *m* colorimétrique soustractif
  r вычитаемая колориметрическая система *f*

9315 subtractive color mixing
  d subtraktive Farbmischung *f*
  f mélange *m* de couleurs soustractif
  r вычитаемое смешивание *n* цветов

9316 subtractive color model
  d subtraktives Farbmodell *n*
  f modèle *m* de couleur soustractif
  r вычитаемая цветовая модель *f*

9317 subtractive color process
  d subtraktiver Farbprozess *m*
  f processus *m* couleur soustractif
  r вычитаемая цветовая обработка *f*

9318 subtractive mask mode
  d Modus *m* der subtraktiven Maske
  f mode *m* de masque soustractif
  r режим *m* вычитаемой маски

9319 subtractive primary colors
  d subtraktive Primärfarben *fpl*
  f couleurs *fpl* primaires soustractives
  r вычитаемые основные цвета *mpl*

9320 subtriangles
  d Unterdreiecke *npl*
  f sous-triangles *mpl*
  r под-треугольники *mpl*

9321 subtype
  d Untertyp *m*
  f sous-type *m*
  r подтип *m*

9322 subwindow; pane
  d Unterfenster *n*; Fensterausschnitt *m*
  f sous-fenêtre *f*
  r подокно *n*

9323 succession
  d Nachfolge *f*
  f succession *f*
  r последовательность *f*; приемственность *f*; наследование *n*

9324 successive
  d aufeinanderfolgend; sukzessiv
  f successif
  r последовательный

9325 successive layers
  d aufeinanderfolgende Schichten *fpl*
  f plans *mpl* successifs
  r последовательные слои *mpl*

9326 suffix
  d Suffix *n*
  f suffixe *m*
  r суффикс *m*

9327 suffixing
  d Suffigierung *f*
  f suffixation *f*
  r суффиксация *f*

9328 sum
  d Summe *f*
  f somme *f*
  r сумма *f*

  * **summation** → **149**

  * **summing** → **149**

9329 sunlight
  d Sonnenlicht *n*
  f lumière *f* solaire; éclairage *m* naturel
  r солнечный свет *m*

* **sup** → 5474

* **super index** → 9335

* **superior limit** → 10074

9330 superposable
  d deckungsgleich; formengleich; überdeckbar
  f superposable
  r накладывающийся; наложимый

9331 superpose *v*
  d überlagern; superponieren
  f superposer
  r накладывать; совмещать; суперпозировать

9332 superposed figures
  d zusammengesetzte Figuren *fpl*
  f figures *fpl* superposables
  r наложимые фигуры *fpl*

9333 superposition
  d Superposition *f*
  f superposition *f*
  r суперпозиция *f*

9334 super-sampling
  d Super-Stichprobenauswahl *f*
  f super-échantillonnage *m*
  r супер-опробирование *n*; супер-
    квантование *n*; супер-выборка *f*

9335 superscript; super index
  d Index *m* rechts oben; oberer Index;
    hochgestellter Index
  f index *m* supérieur
  r верхний индекс *m*

9336 superstructure
  d Superstruktur *f*
  f superstructure *f*
  r сверхструктура *f*

* **supervision** → 6022

9337 supplement
  d Supplement *n*; Zusatz *m*
  f supplément *m*
  r добавление *n*

9338 supplementary angles
  d Supplementwinkel *mpl*
  f angles *mpl* supplémentaires
  r дополнительные до 180° углы *mpl*

9339 supply; power
  d Versorgung *f*
  f alimentation *f*
  r питание *n*

* **support** → 1290

9340 support *v*
  d unterstützen
  f supporter; soutenir; appuyer
  r поддерживать; обеспечивать

9341 support
  d Stütze *f*
  f appui *m*
  r опора *f*

9342 supporting line
  d Stützlinie *f*
  f droite *f* d'appui
  r опорная линия *f*

9343 supporting plane; plane of support
  d Stützebene *f*
  f plan *m* d'appui
  r опорная плоскость *f*

9344 supporting position
  d Stützstelle *f*
  f position *f* d'appui
  r опорная позиция *f*

9345 supporting triangle; triangle of support
  d Stützdreieck *n*
  f triangle *m* d'appui
  r опорный треугольник *m*

9346 suppose *v*; **assume** *v*
  d annehmen; voraussetzen; vermuten
  f supposer; admettre
  r допускать; предполагать

9347 suppression
  d Unterdrückung *f*
  f suppression *f*
  r подавление *n*

* **supremum** → 5474

9348 surface
  d Fläche *f*; Oberfläche *f*
  f surface *f*
  r поверхность *f*

* **surface area** → 552

* **surface chart** → 546

9349 surface color
  d Flächenfarbe *f*

ƒ couleur *f* de surface
r цвет *m* поверхности

9350 surface color variation
  d Flächenfarb[en]-Variation *f*
  f variation *f* de couleur de surface
  r вариация *f* цвета поверхности

9351 surface construction
  d Flächenstrukturierung *f*
  f construction *f* de surfaces
  r конструирование *n* поверхностей;
    построение *n* поверхностей

9352 surface construction algorithm
  d Flächenstrukturierungsalgorithmus *m*
  f algorithme *m* de construction de surfaces
  r алгоритм *m* конструирования
    поверхностей

9353 surface correlation
  d Flächenkorrelation *f*
  f corrélation *f* de surface
  r корреляция *f* поверхности

  * **surface curl** → 2342

9354 surface design
  d Flächendesign *n*
  f conception *f* de surface
  r дизайн *m* поверхности

9355 surface detection
  d Flächendetektion *f*
  f détection *f* de surfaces
  r обнаруживание *n* поверхностей

  * **surface element** → 3345

9356 surface fitting
  d Flächenanpassung *f*; Flächenausgleich *m*;
    Flächenausgleichung *f*
  f ajustage *m* de surface
  r аппроксимация *f* поверхности;
    сглаживание *n* поверхности

9357 surface geodesy
  d Flächengeodäsie *f*
  f géodésie *f* d'une surface
  r геодезия *f* поверхности

  * **surface graph** → 546

9358 surface grid
  d Flächengitter *n*
  f grille *f* surfacique
  r поверхностная сетка *f*

  * **surface in relief** → 3390

9359 surface interpolation
  d Flächeninterpolation *f*
  f interpolation *f* de surface
  r интерполяция *f* поверхности

9360 surface irregularity
  d Flächenunregelmäßigkeit *f*
  f irrégularité *f* de surface
  r нерегулярность *f* поверхности

9361 surface layer
  d Oberflächenschicht *f*
  f couche *f* de surface; couche superficielle
  r поверхностный слой *m*; покрытие *n*

9362 surface mesh
  d Flächenmasche *f*
  f maille *f* surfacique; maille superficielle;
    surface *f* maillée
  r сеточная поверхность *f*

9363 surface mesh modeling
  d Modellierung *f* der Flächenmasche
  f modelage *m* de maille surfacique
  r моделирование *n* сеточной поверхности

9364 surface model
  d Flächenmodell *n*
  f modèle *m* surfacique
  r модель *f* поверхности

  * **surface normal** → 6307

9365 surface normal vector
  d Vektor *m* der Flächennormale;
    Flächennormalenvektor *m*
  f vecteur *m* de normale à surface
  r вектор *m* поверхностной нормали

9366 surface of an object
  d Fläche *f* eines Objekts
  f surface *f* d'un objet
  r поверхность *f* объекта

9367 surface of constant curvature
  d Fläche *f* konstanter Krümmung
  f surface *f* à courbure constante
  r поверхность *f* постоянной кривизны

9368 surface of contact
  d Berührungsfläche *f*
  f surface *f* de contact
  r поверхность *f* соприкосновения;
    площадка *f* касания

9369 surface of intersection; intersecting surface
  d Schnittfläche *f*
  f surface *f* d'intersection
  r поверхность *f* пересечения

* surface of one side → 6477

9370 surface of projection
 d Projektionsfläche *f*
 f surface *f* projetée; surface de projection; surface par projection
 r поверхность *f* проекции

* surface of revolution → 9371

9371 surface of rotation; surface of revolution; rotationally symmetric surface; revolved surface
 d Rotationsfläche *f*; Dreh[ungs]fläche *f*, rotationssymmetrische Fläche *f*
 f surface *f* [à symétrie] de révolution
 r поверхность *f* вращения; вращательно-симметричная поверхность

9372 surface of slope
 d Böschungsfläche *f*
 f surface *f* de pente
 r поверхность *f* откоса

9373 surface orientation
 d Flächenorientierung *f*
 f orientation *f* d'une surface
 r ориентация *f* поверхности

9374 surface patch; area patch; patch; mesh facet
 (piece of a surface bounded by a closed curve)
 d Oberflächenstück *n*; Flächenstück *n*
 f surface *f* paramétrique; portion *f*; morceau *m* de surface limité par une courbe fermée
 r фрагмент *m*; кусок *m* поверхности

9375 surface patch normal
 (a normal to mesh facet)
 d Oberflächenstück-Normale *f*
 f normale *f* à une surface paramétrique
 r нормаль *f* к фрагменту

9376 surface profile
 d Flächenprofil *n*
 f profil *m* de surface
 r профиль *m* поверхности

9377 surface quality
 d Flächenqualität *f*
 f qualité *f* de surface
 r качество *n* изображения поверхности

9378 surface reflection
 d Flächenreflexion *f*
 f réflexion *f* de surface
 r поверхностное отражение *n*

9379 surface roughness
 d Oberflächenrauheit *f*
 f rugosité *f* de la surface
 r шероховатость *f* поверхности

9380 surface smoothness
 d Flächenglätte *f*
 f égalité *f* de la surface
 r гладкость *f* поверхности

9381 surface structure
 d Oberflächenstruktur *f*
 f structure *f* de la surface
 r структура *f* поверхности

9382 surface tangent
 d Flächentangente *f*
 f tangente *f* à une surface
 r касательная *f* к поверхности

9383 surface tension
 d Oberflächenspannung *f*
 f tension *f* superficielle; tension de la surface
 r поверхностное напряжение *n*

9384 surface texture
 d Flächentextur *f*; Oberflächentextur *f*
 f texture *f* de surface
 r текстура *f* поверхности

9385 surface treatment
 d Oberflächenbehandlung *f*
 f traitement *m* de surface
 r обработка *f* поверхности; поверхностная обработка

9386 surface type
 d Flächentyp *m*
 f type *m* de surface
 r тип *m* поверхности

* surface with only one side → 6477

* surface with two sides → 9959

* surround → 9388

9387 surround *v*
 d umgeben
 f entourer
 r окружать

9388 surround[ing]
 d Umgebung *f*
 f entourage *m*
 r окружение *n*

9389 survey
 (in geodesy)
 d Aufnahme *f*

f levé *m* [du terrain]
r съемка *f*

* **surveying → 6022**

9390 Sutherland-Hodgman clipping
   d Sutherland-Hodgman-Schneiden *n*
   f découpage *m* de Sutherland-Hodgman
   r отсекание *n* Садерланда-Ходжмана

* **swap → 9391**

9391 swap[ping]
   d Austausch *m*; Wechsel *m*; Swapping *n*
   f échange *m*; swapping *m*; alternance *f*
   r перекачка *f*; [взаимный] обмен *m*;
      свопинг *m*

9392 swatch
   (a square containing color in color palette)
   d Musterstreifen *m*; Probenstreifen *m*
   f coupon *m*; échantillon *m*; swatch *m*
   r образчик *m*

* **sweep → 882**

9393 sweep generator
   d Kippgenerator *m*; Ablenkgenerator *m*
   f générateur *m* de balayage
   r генератор *m* развертки

* **sweep rate → 9394**

9394 sweep speed; sweep rate
   d Ablenkgeschwindigkeit *f*
   f vitesse *f* de balayage
   r скорость *f* развертки

9395 sweep surface
   d Krümmungsfläche *f*
   f surface *f* de courbure
   r поверхность *f* кривизны

9396 swinging
   d Schwingung *f*; Einpendeln *n*
   f balancement *m*
   r качание *n*; колебание *n*

9397 swirl
   d Wirbel *m*
   f tourbillon *m*
   r вихрь *m*

9398 swirl bitmap
   d Wirbel-Bitmap *n*
   f bitmap *m* tourbillonné
   r вихревое растровое изображение *n*

9399 swirl effect
   d Wirbeleffekt *m*

f effet *m* de tourbillonnement
r вихревой эффект *m*

9400 switching
   d Schalten *n*; Durchschalten *n*;
      Durchschaltung *f*
   f commutation *f*
   r переключение *n*; коммутация *f*

* **swivelling → 7086**

* **symbol → 1409**

* **symbol bar → 1411**

* **symbol font → 1417**

9401 symbolic
   d symbolisch
   f symbolique
   r символический

9402 symbolic description
   d symbolische Beschreibung *f*
   f description *f* symbolique
   r символьное описание *n*

9403 symbolic description of volumetric data
   d symbolische Beschreibung *f* der räumlichen
      Daten
   f description *f* symbolique de données
      volumétriques
   r символьное описание *n* пространственных
      данных

9404 symbolic processing
   d Symbolverarbeitung *f*
   f traitement *m* symbolique
   r обработка *f* символьной информации

9405 symbol library
   d Symbolbibliothek *f*
   f bibliothèque *f* de symboles
   r библиотека *f* символов

9406 symbol name
   d Symbolname *m*
   f nom *m* symbolique
   r имя *n* символа; наименование *n* символа

9407 symbology
   d Symbolik *f*
   f symbolique *f*
   r символика *f*

* **symbol table → 1428**

* **symmetric → 9408**

9408 symmetric[al]
   d symmetrisch

f symétrique
r симметрический; симметричный

9409 symmetrical deviation
d symmetrische Ablenkung *f*
f déviation *f* symétrique
r симметричное отклонение *n*

9410 symmetrical figures
d symmetrische Figuren *fpl*
f figures *fpl* symétriques
r симметричные фигуры *fpl*

9411 symmetrical form
d symmetrische Form *f*
f forme *f* symétrique
r симметрическая форма *f*

* **symmetrical node → 9412**

9412 symmetrical node [point]
d symmetrischer Knoten[punkt] *m*
f nœud *m* symétrique; point *m* nodal
symétrique
r симметричный узел *m*

9413 symmetrical polygon
d symmetrisches Polygon *n*
f polygone *m* symétrique
r симметрический полигон *m*

9414 symmetrical spirals
d symmetrische Spiralen *fpl*
f spirales *fpl* symétriques
r симметрические спирали *fpl*

9415 symmetry
d Symmetrie *f*; Spiegelgleichheit *f*
f symétrie *f*
r симметрия *f*

* **symmetry group → 4464**

9416 symmetry line; line of symmetry
d Linie *f* der Symmetrie; Symmetrielinie *f*
f ligne *f* de symétrie
r линия *f* симметрии

9417 symmetry of rotation
d Rotationssymmetrie *f*
f symétrie *f* de rotation
r симметрия *f* вращения

9418 symmetry symbol
d Zeichen *n* der Symmetrie
f symbole *m* de symétrie
r символ *m* симметрии

9419 symmetry with respect to a line
d Symmetrie *f* bezüglich einer Geraden;

Spiegelung *f* an einer Geraden
f symétrie *f* par rapport à une droite
r симметрия *f* относительно прямой

**9420 symmetry with respect to a plane;
reflection with respect to a plane; plane
symmetry**
d Symmetrie *f* bezüglich einer Ebene;
Spiegelung *f* an einer Ebene;
Ebenensymmetrie *f*
f symétrie *f* par rapport à un plan; réflexion *f*
par rapport à un plan
r симметрия *f* относительно плоскости;
отображение *n* относительно плоскости

**9421 symmetry with respect to a point; point
symmetry**
d Symmetrie *f* bezüglich eines Punkts;
Punktsymmetrie *f*
f symétrie *f* par rapport à un point
r симметрия *f* относительно точки

9422 symmetry with respect to the origin
d Symmetrie *f* bezüglich des
Koordinatenursprungs
f symétrie *f* par rapport à l'origine des
coordonnées
r симметрия *f* относительно начала
координат

9423 symptom
d Symptom *m*
f symptôme *m*
r симптом *m*

9424 synchronism; lock[ing]-in
d Synchronismus *m*; Synchronität *f*;
Gleichlauf[zwang] *m*
f synchronisme *m*; mise *f* au pas
r синхронизм *m*; синхронность *f*

9425 synchronization; synchronizing
d Synchronisation *f*; Gleichlaufsteuerung *f*
f synchronisation *f*
r синхронизация *f*

9426 synchronize *v*
d synchronisieren
f synchroniser
r синхронизировать

* **synchronizing → 9425**

9427 synchronous; in-step; mesochronous
d synchron; gleichlaufend
f synchrone; au pas
r синхронный

* **synclinal line → 9629**

* **syncline** → 9629

* **synectic plane** → 1424

9428 synonym
 d Synonym *n*
 f synonyme *m*
 r синоним *m*

9429 syntax
 d Syntax *f*
 f syntaxe *f*
 r синтаксис *m*

9430 syntax error
 d Syntaxfehler *m*
 f erreur *f* syntaxique
 r синтаксическая ошибка *f*

9431 synthesis
 d Synthesis *f*; Synthese *f*
 f synthèse *f*
 r синтез *m*

9432 synthetic actor; actor
 d Akteur *m*
 f actor *m*; acteur *m*
 r синтетический действующий субъект *m*;
 актор *m*

* **synthetic image** → 1979

9433 system
 d System *n*
 f système *m*
 r система *f*

9434 system color
 d Systemfarbe *f*
 f couleur *f* de système
 r системный цвет *m*

9435 system data
 d Systemdaten *npl*
 f données *fpl* de système
 r системные данные *npl*

9436 system directory
 d Systemkatalog *m*
 f catalogue *m* de système
 r системная директория *f*

9437 system environment
 d Systemumgebung *f*
 f environnement *m* de système
 r системная среда *f*

9438 system failure
 d Systemstörung *f*
 f erreur *f* système

 r системная ошибка *f*

9439 system menu
 d Systemmenü *n*
 f menu *m* système
 r системное меню *n*

* **system of curves** → 3701

9440 system of reference; reference system
 d Bezugssystem *n*; Referenzsystem *n*
 f système *m* de référence
 r система *f* отсчета

* **system of spheres** → 6719

9441 system printer
 d Systemdrucker *m*
 f imprimante *f* système
 r системный принтер *m*

9442 system tables
 d Systemtabellen *fpl*
 f tables *fpl* de système
 r системные таблицы *fpl*

9443 system variable
 d Systemvariable *f*
 f variable *f* système
 r системная переменная *f*

T

* tab → 9462

9444 Tab key
d Tabulatortaste f
f touche f Tab
r клавиша f Tab

9445 table
d Tabelle f; Tafel f
f table f; tableau m
r таблица f

9446 table cell
d Tabellenfeld n
f case f d'un tableau
r клетка f таблицы; ячейка f таблицы

9447 tablecloth
d Tischdecke f; Tischtuch f
f nappe f [de table]
r скатерть f

9448 table column
d Tabellenspalte f
f colonne f de table
r колонка f таблицы

9449 table data
d Tabellendaten npl
f données fpl de tableau
r табличные данные npl

9450 table row
d Tabellenzeile f
f ligne f de table
r строка f таблицы

9451 table synchronization
d Tabellensynchronisation f
f synchronisation f de table
r синхронизация f таблицы

* tablet → 2804

9452 tablet menu
d Tablettmenü n
f menu m de tablette
r меню n планшета

9453 tablet menu area
d Gebiet n des Tablettmenüs
f zone f de menu de tablette
r область f меню планшета

9454 tablet mode
d Tablettmodus m
f mode m de tablette
r режим m планшета

9455 tablet transformation
d Tabletttransformation f
f transformation f de tablette
r трансформация f планшета

9456 tabular
d tabellarisch; tafelmäßig
f tabulaire
r табличный

9457 tabular dimensioning
d tabellarische Dimensionierung f
f cotation f tabulaire
r табличное оразмерение n

9458 tabulate v
d tabulieren
f tabuler
r табулировать

9459 tabulated surface
d tabulierte Fläche f
f surface f tabulée; surface extrudée à partir d'un chemin courbe et d'un vecteur de direction
r табулированная поверхность f

9460 tabulated surface mesh
d tabulierte Flächenmasche f
f maille f surfacique tabulée
r табулированная сеточная поверхность f

* tabulating → 9461

9461 tabulation; tabulating
d Tabulierung f; Darstellung f in Tabellenform; tabellarische Darstellung
f tabulation f; mise f en table
r табулирование n; табуляция f; составление n таблицы

9462 tabulator; tab
d Tabulator m
f tabulateur m
r табулятор m

* tactile display → 9790

* tactile-type sensor → 9791

9463 tag
d Tag n
f tag m; balise f
r тег m; метка f

9464 tag bit
   d Etikettbit *n*; Anhängerbit *n*
   f bit *m* de tag
   r теговый бит *m*

9465 tagged image
   d gekennzeichnetes Bild *n*
   f image *f* libellée
   r отмеченное изображение *n*; помеченное изображение

9466 tagged image file format; TIF[F]
   d TIF[F]-Format *n*
   f format *m* TIF[F]
   r формат *m* TIF[F]

9467 tally; count
   d Zahleinheit *f*; Gesamtbetrag *m*; Gesamtergebnis *n*
   f unité *f* de comptage; total *m*
   r единица *f* счета; итог *m*

   * **talweg** → 9629

9468 tangency; contact
   d Berührung *f*
   f tangence *f*; contact *m*
   r касание *n*

   * **tangent** → 9473, 9480

9469 tangent circles
   d Tangentenkreise *mpl*
   f cercles *mpl* tangents
   r касательные окружности *fpl*

9470 tangent cone
   (of a surface)
   d Tangentenkegel *m*; Tangentialkegel *m*; Berührungskegel *m*
   f cône *m* tangentiel
   r касательный конус *m*

9471 tangent conical projection
   d Berührungskegelprojektion *f*
   f projection *f* conique tangente
   r тангенциальная коническая проекция *f*

9472 tangent curve; tangentoid
   d Tangentialkurve *f*; Tangensoide *f*
   f courbe *f* tangente; tangentoïde *f*
   r тангенсоида *f*

   * **tangent edge** → 9476

9473 tangent[ial]
   d tangential
   f tangentiel

   r тангенциальный; касательный

9474 tangential approximation
   d Approximation *f* durch Tangenten
   f approximation *f* tangentielle
   r тангенциальная аппроксимация *f*

9475 tangential coordinates
   d Tangentenkoordinaten *fpl*
   f coordonnées *fpl* tangentielles
   r тангенциальные координаты *fpl*

   * **tangential curvature** → 4155

9476 tangent[ial] edge
   d Tangentialkante *f*
   f arête *f* tangente
   r касательное ребро *n*

9477 tangent[ial] plane
   d Berührungsebene *f*; Tangentialebene *f*; Tangentenebene *f*
   f plan *m* tangent
   r касательная плоскость *f*

9478 tangent[ial] point
   d Tangentialpunkt *m*
   f point *m* tangentiel
   r тангенциальная точка *f*

9479 tangent[ial] surface
   d Tangentialfläche *f*
   f surface *f* tangentielle
   r касательная поверхность *f*

9480 tangent [line]
   d Tangente *f*; Berührende *f*
   f tangente *f*; droite *f* tangente
   r касательная *f*

9481 tangent [line] to a curve
   d Tangente *f* einer Kurve; Tangente an einer Kurve; Kurventangente *f*
   f tangente *f* à une courbe; tangente d'une courbe; droite *f* tangente à une courbe
   r касательная *f* к кривой

   * **tangentoid** → 9472

   * **tangent plane** → 9477

   * **tangent plane projection** → 9739

   * **tangent point** → 9478

9482 tangent snap
   d Tangentialfang *m*
   f accrochage *m* à une tangente
   r привязка *f* к касательной

* **tangent surface** → 9479

9483 tangent to a circle
d Tangente *f* an einem Kreis
f tangente *f* à un cercle
r касательная *f* к окружности

* **tangent to a curve** → 9481

9484 tangent to the vertex
d Scheiteltangente *f*
f tangente *f* au sommet
r касательная *f* к вершине

9485 tangent vector
d Tangentenvektor *m*; Tangentialvektor *m*
f vecteur *m* tangent
r касательный вектор *m*

* **tap** → 9491

9486 taper *v*
d zuspitzen; spitzzulaufen
f effiler
r сходиться на конус; сводить на конус;
сужаться; заострять

9487 tapered
d zugespitzt
f aigu[isé]; affûté; pointu; conique
r заостренный; конический;
конусообразный; сужающийся к концу

9488 tapered extrusion
d zugespitzte Extrusion *f*
f extrusion *f* conique
r конусообразная экструзия *f*

9489 tapered polyline segment
d zugespitztes Poliliniensegment *n*
f segment *m* de polyligne conique
r заостренный сегмент *m* полилинии;
конусообразный сегмент полилинии

9490 tapering
d zuspitzend
f effilement *m*
r конусность *f*; конусообразность *f*;
заострение *n*

9491 tap[ping]
d Abgreif *m*
f prise *f*; branchement *m*; dérivation *f*
r ответвление *n*; отвод *m*; разветвление *n*

9492 tapping point
d Abgreifpunkt *m*
f prise *f* de dérivation
r точка *f* разветвления; точка отпайки; точка
отвода

9493 target
d Ziel *n*
f cible *f*; destination *f*
r мишень *f*; цель *f*

9494 target angle
d Zielwinkel *m*
f angle *m* de cible
r целевой угол *m*

9495 target attribute
d Zielattribut *n*
f attribut *m* de la cible
r целевой атрибут *m*

9496 target box
d Zielkasten *m*
f boîte *f* de la cible
r целевой ящик *m*

9497 target color
d Zielfarbe *f*
f couleur *f* de la cible
r цвет *m* цели

9498 target distance
d Zielabstand *m*; Zielentfernung *f*
f distance *f* de la destination
r расстояние *n* до цели

9499 target object
d Zielobjekt *n*
f objet *m* cible
r целевой объект *m*

* **target point** → 248

9500 target radial speed vector visualization
d Visualisierung *f* des
Radialgeschwindigkeitsvektors des Ziels
f visualisation *f* du vecteur de vitesse radiale de
la cible
r визуализация *f* вектора радиального
ускорения цели

* **task** → 7484

9501 taskbar
d Taskstreifen *m*; Taskleiste *f*
f barre *f* de tâches
r лента *f* задач

9502 taskbar button
d Taskstreifentaste *f*
f bouton *m* d'outil de tâches
r кнопка *f* ленты задач

* **task data** → 7485

9503 tautochrone; isochrone
d Tautochrone *f*; Isochrone *f*

f courbe *f* tautochrone; courbe isochrone;
isochrone *f*
r изохронная кривая *f*

9504 taxonomy of projections
d Taxonomie *f* der Projektionen
f taxonomie *f* des projections
r таксономия *f* проекций

* **teardrop** → 819

* **tear-off menu** → 7633

9505 technical drawing
d technische Zeichnung *f*
f dessin *m* technique
r техническое черчение *n*

9506 technical illustrations
d technische Illustrationen *fpl*
f illustrations *fpl* techniques
r технические иллюстрации *fpl*

9507 technology
d Technologie *f*
f technologie *f*
r технология *f*

9508 tee intersection
d T-Durchschnitt *m*
f intersection *f* en T
r пересечение *n* типа T; T-образное
пересечение

9509 telemanipulation
d Telemanipulation *f*
f télémanipulation *f*
r телеобработка *f*

9510 telepresence
d Telepräsenz *f*
f téléprésence *f*
r дистанционное присутствие *n*

9511 televirtuality
d Televirtualität *f*
f télévirtualité *f*
r дистанционная виртуальность *f*

9512 template; stencil; pattern
d Schablone *f*; Schrittschablone *f*; Vorlage *f*;
Formatbild *n*
f maquette *f*; modèle *m*
r шаблон *m*; траффарет *m*; макет *m*;
образец *m*; модель *f*

9513 template file
d Datei *f* der Schablone
f fichier *m* de maquettes
r макетный файл *m*

9514 template wizard
d Schablonen-Assistent *m*
f assistant *m* de maquettes
r советник *m* создания шаблона

9515 temporal; temporary
d zeitlich; zeitweilig
f temporel; temporaire
r временный

9516 temporal accuracy
d zeitliche Genauigkeit *f*
f exactitude *f* temporaire
r временная точность *f*

9517 temporal coherence
d zeitliche Kohärenz *f*
f cohérence *f* temporelle
r временная когерентность *f*

9518 temporal compression
d zeitliche Kompression *f*
f compression *f* temporelle
r временное сжатие *n*

9519 temporal database
d zeitliche Datenbasis *f*
f base *f* de données temporelle
r временная база *f* данных

9520 temporal extent
d zeitlicher Extent *m*
f étendue *f* temporelle
r временное расширение *n*

* **temporary** → 9515

9521 temporary file
d zeitliche Datei *f*
f fichier *m* temporaire
r временный файл *m*

9522 temporary reference point
d zeitlicher Referenzpunkt *m*
f point *m* de référence temporaire
r временная эталонная точка *f*

9523 temporary topology
d zeitliche Topologie *f*
f topologie *f* temporaire
r временная топология *f*

9524 tension
d Spannung *f*; Zug *m*
f tension *f*
r растяжение *n*; натяжение *n*; напряжение *n*

* **term** → 5899

9525 terminal *adj*
d terminal; End-

f terminal
r конечный; терминальный; последний

9526 terminal edge
d Endkante *f*
f arête *f* terminale
r концевое ребро *n*

* **terminal node** → 9527.

* **terminal object** → 3426

* **terminal point** → 3428

9527 terminal vertex; terminal node; end vertex
d Endknoten *m*
f sommet *m* terminal
r концевая вершина *f*

9528 terminate *v*
d beenden
f terminer
r завершить

9529 termination; finishing
d Beendigung *f*; Termination *f*; Vollendung *f*; Fertigbearbeitung *f*
f terminaison *f*; achèvement *m*; suspension *f*; finissage *m*
r окончание *n*; завершение *n*

9530 terminator
(a sign)
d Beendigungszeichen *n*; Beendigungssymbol *n*
f symbole *m* de terminaison; signe *m* de fin
r символ *m* окончания; знак *m* завершения

9531 ternary
d ternär
f ternaire
r троичный

9532 terrain
d Gelände *n*; Bodenform *f*; Terrain *n*
f terrain *m*
r конфигурация *f* местности; формы *fpl* местности

9533 terrain creation
d Terrainerstellung *f*
f création *f* de terrain
r создание *n* конфигурации местности

9534 terrain display system
d Terraindarstellungssystem *n*
f système *m* d'affichage de terrain
r система *f* визуализации местности

9535 terrain geometry
d Terraingeometrie *f*

f géométrie *f* de terrain
r геометрия *f* местности

9536 terrain model
d Geländemodell *n*; Terrainmodell *n*
f modèle *m* du terrain
r макет *m* местности

9537 terrain visualization
d Terrainvisualisierung *f*
f visualisation *f* de terrain
r визуализация *f* местности

9538 terrestrial coordinates
d terrestrische Koordinaten *fpl*
f coordonnées *fpl* terrestres
r наземные координаты *fpl*

* **tessellation** → 9681

9539 test
d Test *m*; Prüfung *f*
f essai *m*; test *m*
r тест *m*; испытание *n*

* **test** *v* → 1450

9540 tether *v*
d anbinden; festbinden
f attacher
r привязывать; ограничивать; ставить предел

9541 tethered
d angebunden; verankert
f captif; amarré; attaché; lié
r привязанный

9542 tethering
d Anbindung *f*
f attachement *m*; arrimage *m*
r привязывание *n*

* **tetracuspid** → 626

9543 tetrad
d Tetrade *f*
f tétrade *f*
r тетрада *f*; четверка *f*

* **tetragon** → 7647

9544 tetrahedral
d tetraedral
f tétraédrique
r четырехгранный

9545 tetrahedral complex
d tetraedraler Komplex *m*

f complexe *m* tétraédrique
r четырехгранный комплекс *m*

* **tetrahedron** → 9891

* **texel** → 9605

9546 text
d Text *m*
f texte *m*
r текст *m*

9547 text alignment; text justification
d Textanpassung *f*; Textausrichtung *f*
f alignement *m* de texte
r выравнивание *n* текста

9548 text along arc; arc aligned text
d Text *m* auf der Länge des Bogens
f texte *m* à l'arc
r текст *m* возле дуги

* **text area** → 9549

9549 text block; text area
d Textblock *m*
f bloc *m* de texte
r текстовой блок *m*; текстовое поле *n*

9550 text boundaries
d Textgrenzen *fpl*
f limites *fpl* de texte
r границы *fpl* текста

* **text box** → 6474

9551 text carrier
d Textträger *m*
f porteur *m* de texte
r носитель *m* текста

9552 text color
d Textfarbe *f*
f couleur *f* de texte
r цвет *m* текста

9553 text data
d Textdaten *npl*
f données *fpl* de texte
r текстовые данные *npl*

9554 text editing
d Textbearbeitung *f*
f édition *f* de texte
r редактирование *n* текста

9555 text editor
d Texteditor *m*; Textbearbeitungsprogramm *n*
f éditeur *m* de texte
r текстовой редактор *m*

9556 text envelope
d Texthülle *f*
f enveloppe *f* de texte
r оболочка *f* текста

9557 text exploding
d Textexplodieren *n*
f décomposition *f* de texte
r развязывание *n* текста

9558 text field
d Textfeld *n*
f champ *m* de texte
r поле *n* текста

9559 text file
d Textdatei *f*
f fichier *m* de texte
r текстовой файл *m*

9560 text fitting
d Textanpassung *f*
f ajustage *m* de texte
r налаживание *n* текста

* **text flow** → 9628

9561 text font
d Textschrift *f*
f police *f* de texte
r текстовой шрифт *m*

9562 text font compressing
d Kompression *f* der Textschrift
f compression *f* de la police de texte
r сжатие *n* текстового шрифта

9563 text formatting
d Textformatierung *f*; Textformatieren *n*
f formatage *m* de texte
r форматирование *n* текста

9564 text frame
d Textrahmen *m*
f encadré *f* de texte
r текстовой кадр *m*; рамка *f* текста

9565 text gap
d Textabstand *m*
f intervalle *m* de texte
r интервал *m* в тексте

9566 text generation flag
d Textgenerierungskennzeichen *n*
f repérage *m* de génération de texte
r флаг *m* генерирования текста

9567 text height
d Texthöhe *f*
f hauteur *f* de texte
r высота *f* текста

* **text insertion** → 5121

9568 text insertion point
 d Texteinfügungspunkt *m*
 f point *m* d'insertion de texte
 r точка *f* вставки текста

* **text justification** → 9547

9569 text label
 d Textkennzeichen *n*
 f étiquette *f* texte
 r текстовая метка *f*

9570 text mask
 d Textmaske *f*
 f masque *f* de texte
 r текстовая маска *f*

9571 text object
 d Textobjekt *n*
 f objet *m* texte
 r объект *m* типа текста

9572 text obliquing angle
 d Schrägwinkel *m* des Textes
 f angle *m* d'inclinaison de texte
 r угол *m* наклона текста

9573 text orientation
 d Textorientierung *f*
 f orientation *f* de texte
 r ориентация *f* текста

9574 text page
 d Textseite *f*
 f page *f* de texte
 r текстовая страница *f*; страница текста

9575 text path
 (on an image)
 d Textweg *m*
 f chemin *m* de texte
 r текстовая дорожка *f*

9576 text position
 d Textposition *f*
 f position *f* de texte
 r позиция *f* текста; расположение *n* текста

9577 text processing; word processing
 d Textverarbeitung *f*; Wortverarbeitung *f*
 f traitement *m* de texte; traitement de mots
 r обработка *f* текста; обработка слов

9578 text resizing
 d Textgrößenänderung *f*
 f changement *m* de taille de texte
 r изменение *n* размера текста

9579 text rotation
 d Textdrehung *f*
 f rotation *f* de texte
 r ротация *f* текста; поворот *m* текста

9580 text selecting
 d Textauswahl *f*
 f sélection *f* de texte
 r выбор *m* текста

9581 text size
 d Textgröße *f*
 f taille *f* de texte
 r размер *m* текста

9582 text slanting
 d Textneigung *f*
 f inclinaison *f* de texte
 r наклонение *n* текста

9583 text statistics
 d Textstatistik *f*
 f statistique *f* de texte
 r статистика *f* текста

9584 text style
 d Textstil *m*
 f style *m* de texte
 r текстовой стиль *m*

9585 text template
 d Textschablone *f*
 f maquette *f* de texte
 r текстовой шаблон *m*

9586 textual fidelity
 d textuelle Genauigkeit *f*; Textrichtigkeit *f*
 f fidélité *f* textuelle
 r текстовая точность *f*; текстовая верность *f*

9587 textual selection
 d textuelle Auswahl *f*
 f sélection *f* textuelle
 r текстовой выбор *m*

9588 text underscoring
 d Text-Unterstreichung *f*
 f soulignement *m* de texte
 r подчеркивание *n* текста

9589 texture
 d Textur *f*; Füllmuster *n*
 f texture *f*
 r текстура *f*; побитовая ткань *f*

9590 texture analysis
 d Textur-Analyse *f*
 f analyse *f* de texture
 r анализ *f* текстуры

9591 texture blend
  d Textur-Überblendung *f*
  f dégradé *m* de texture
  r переливание *n* текстуры

9592 texture characteristics
  d Texturmerkmale *npl*
  f caractéristiques *fpl* de la texture
  r характеристики *fpl* текстуры

9593 texture compression
  d Textur-Kompression *f*;
     Texturenkomprimierung *f*
  f compression *f* de texture
  r сжатие *n* текстуры

9594 texture coordinates
  d Texturkoordinaten *fpl*
  f coordonnées *fpl* de la texture
  r координаты *fpl* текстуры

9595 texture depth
  d Texturen-Tiefe *f*
  f profondeur *f* de texture
  r глубина *f* текстуры

9596 texture design
  d Textur-Design *n*
  f conception *f* de texture
  r проектирование *n* текстуры; дизайн *m*
     текстуры

9597 texture[d] fill[ing]
  d Texturauffüllen *n*
  f remplissage *m* texturiel
  r заполнение *n* текстурой

9598 textured image
  d Bild *n* mit einer Textur
  f image *f* à texture; image texturée
  r изображение *n* с текстурой

9599 textured image segmentation
  d Segmentierung *f* des Bilds mit einer Textur
  f segmentation *f* d'image texturée
  r сегментация *f* текстурированного
     изображения

9600 textured material
  d Material *n* mit einer Textur
  f matériel *m* à texture; matériel texturé
  r материал *m* с текстурой

9601 textured model
  d Modell *n* mit einer Textur
  f modèle *m* texturé
  r модель *f* с текстурой

9602 textured object
  d Objekt *n* mit einer Textur

  f objet *m* texturé
  r объект *m* с текстурой

9603 textured polygon
  d Polygon *n* mit einer Textur
  f polygone *m* à texture; polygone texturé
  r полигон *m* с текстурой

9604 texture edge
  d Texturkante *f*
  f arête *f* de texture
  r грань *f* текстуры

9605 texture element; texel
  d Textur-Element *n*; Texel *n*
  f élément *m* de texture
  r элемент *m* текстуры; тексел *m*

  * **texture fill** → 9597

9606 texture filtering
  d Texturen-Filtrierung *f*
  f filtrage *m* de textures
  r фильтрирование *n* текстур

9607 texture format
  d Format *n* der Textur
  f format *m* de texture
  r формат *m* текстуры

9608 texture level
  d Texturen-Niveau *n*
  f niveau *m* de texture
  r уровень *m* текстуры

9609 texture library
  d Füllmusterbibliothek *f*; Texturbibliothek *f*
  f bibliothèque *f* de textures
  r библиотека *f* текстур

9610 texture list
  d Texturliste *f*
  f liste *f* de textures
  r список *m* текстур

  * **texture map** → 9611

9611 texture map[ping]
  d Texturenabbildung *f*
  f mappage *m* de texture
  r отображение *n* текстуры; наложение *n*
     текстуры

9612 texture mapping hardware
  d Texturenabbildungshardware *f*
  f matériel *m* de mappage de texture
  r аппаратное обеспечение *n* отображения
     текстуры

9613 texture maps
  d Textur-Karten *fpl*

ƒ cartes *fpl* de textures
r текстурные карты *fpl*

9614 texture marker
d Texturmarker *m*
ƒ marqueur *m* de texture
r маркер *m* текстуры

9615 texture memory
d Texturspeicher *m*
ƒ mémoire *f* de textures
r память *f* текстур

9616 texture mipmapping
d Textur-Mip-Mapping *n*
ƒ mip-mapping *m* de texture
r множественное отображение *n* текстуры

9617 texture modulation
d Textur-Modulation *f*
ƒ modulation *f* de textures
r модуляция *f* текстур

9618 texture morphing
d Textur-Morphing *n*
ƒ morphage *m* de texture
r морфинг *m* текстуры

9619 texture options
d Füllmusteroptionen *fpl*
ƒ options *fpl* de la texture
r опции *fpl* текстуры

9620 texture pattern
d Textur-Motiv *n*
ƒ motif *m* de texture
r шаблон *m* текстуры

9621 texture pattern coordinates
d Textur-Motiv-Koordinaten *fpl*
ƒ coordonnées *fpl* de motif de texture
r координаты *fpl* текстурного шаблона

9622 texture reverse projection processor
(performs nonlinear positioning from device to texture or video pattern coordinates)
d Prozessor *m* der inversen Textur-Projektionen
ƒ processeur *m* de projections reverses des textures
r процессор *m* инверсных проекций текстур

* **texture speckiness** → 9625

9623 texture swapping
d Texturen-Swapping *n*
ƒ swapping *m* de texture
r своппинг *m* текстуры

9624 texture transparency
d Textur-Transparenz *f*

ƒ transparence *f* de texture
r прозрачность *f* текстуры

9625 texture variegation; texture speckiness
d Fleckigkeit *f* einer Textur
ƒ bigarrure *f* d'une texture; bariolage *m* d'une texture
r испещрение *n* текстуры

9626 texturing
d Texturieren *n*; Texturierung *f*
ƒ texturation *f*
r текстурирование *n*

9627 text window
d Textfenster *n*
ƒ fenêtre *f* de texte
r текстовое окно *n*

* **text wrap** → 9628

9628 text wrap[ping]; text flow
d Textumhüllung *f*
ƒ habillage *m* de texte
r размещение *n* текста вокруг [изображения]; заверстывание *n* текста; оборка *f* текстом

9629 t[h]alweg; synclinal line; syncline
(of a surface)
d Talweg *m*; Muldenlinie *f*
ƒ ligne *f* de t[h]alweg; ligne de synclinal; ligne d'écoulement des eaux d'une surface
r тальвег *m*; синклинальная линия *f*; ось *f* долины

* **thaw** → 9630

9630 thaw[ing]
d Auftauen *n*
ƒ décongélation *f*; dégel *m*
r размораживание *n*

9631 thematic map; special map
d thematische Karte *f*; Themakarte *f*
ƒ mappe *f* thématique
r тематическая карта *f*

9632 thematic mapper; TM
d thematischer Kartograph *m*
ƒ cartographe *m* thématique; mappeur *m* thématique; scanner *m* multibande pour thèmes multiples
r устройство *n* изготовления тематических карт

9633 thematic range
d thematischer Diapason *m*
ƒ rangée *f* thématique
r тематический диапазон *m*

9634 **theory**
  d Theorie f
  f théorie f
  r теория f

9635 **thermal paper**
  d thermisches Papier n
  f papier m thermique
  r термографическая бумага f

9636 **thermal printer; thermoprinter; electrothermic printer**
  d Thermodrucker m; elektrothermischer Drucker m
  f imprimante f thermique; imprimante thermographique
  r термографический принтер m; устройство n термопечати

  * **thermoprinter → 9636**

9637 **thesaurus**
  d Thesaurus m; Sprachthesaurus m
  f thésaurus m
  r тезаурус m

9638 **thick black arrow**
  d dicker Schwarzpfeil m
  f flèche f noire épaisse
  r толстая черная стрелка f

9639 **thickening**
  d Verdickung f
  f épaississement m
  r утолщение n

9640 **thickness**
  d Stärke f; Dicke f
  f épaisseur f
  r толщина f

9641 **Thiessen polygon**
  d Thiessen-Polygon n
  f polygone m de Thiessen
  r многоугольник m Тиссена; полигон m Тиссена

9642 **thin band**
  d dünner Streifen m
  f barre f mince
  r тонкая лента f

9643 **thin-window display**
  d Kleinformat-Display n
  f écran m à fenêtre mince
  r узкоформатный дисплей m

9644 **third-party effect**
  d Drittwirkung f
  f effet m de tiers

  r посторонний эффект m

  * **third plane → 8668**

9645 **third principal line; third trace parallel**
  d dritte Hauptlinie f
  f troisième ligne f principale
  r третья главная линия f

9646 **third principal plane**
  (in two-plane projection)
  d dritte Hauptebene f
  f troisième plan m principal
  r третья главная плоскость f

  * **third trace parallel → 9645**

  * **third trace point → 9647**

9647 **third trace point [of a line]**
  d dritter Spurpunkt m [der Linie]
  f troisième point m de trace [de ligne]
  r третий след m [прямой]; профильный след [прямой]

9648 **thorn**
  d Dorn m
  f épine f
  r шип m; колючка f

9649 **three-dimensional; tri-dimensional; 3D**
  d dreidimensional; 3D
  f tridimensionnel; à trois dimensions; [en] 3D
  r трехмерный; 3D

9650 **three-plane projection**
  d Dreitafelprojektion f
  f projection f sur trois plans
  r проектирование n на три плоскости

9651 **three-point perspective**
  d Dreipunkte-Perspektive f
  f perspective f à trois points
  r трехточечная перспектива f

9652 **three-tuple; triplet**
  d Tripel n; Drilling m
  f triplet m
  r тройка f; триплет m

  * **threshold → 9658**

9653 **threshold angle**
  d Schwellenwinkel m
  f angle m de seuil
  r пороговый угол m

9654 **threshold conversion**
  d Schwellkonvertierung f

f conversion *f* de seuil
r пороговая конверсия *f*

9655 threshold dithering
   d Schwell-Dithering *n*; Schwellrastern *n*
   f juxtaposition *f* de seuil
   r пороговое псевдосмешение *n*

9656 threshold filter
   d Schwellenfilter *m*
   f filtre *m* de seuil
   r пороговый фильтр *m*

9657 threshold of color vision
   d Schwelle *f* der Farb[en]wahrnehmung
   f seuil *m* de vision de couleurs
   r порог *m* восприятия цветов

9658 threshold [value]
   d Schwell[en]wert *m*; Schwelle *f*
   f valeur *f* de seuil; seuil *m*
   r пороговая величина *f*; порог *m*

   * **throat → 8799**

9659 through-connection; interlayer connection
   d Durchkontaktierung *f*
   f connexion *f* entière
   r сквозное отверстие *n*; сквозное
      соединение *n*

9660 throughput
   d Durchlässigkeit *f*; Durchlassfähigkeit *f*
   f rendement *m*; débit *m*
   r пропускная способность *f*; прохождение *n*

   * **throw *v* off → 7996**

9661 thumb
   d Thumb *n*; Daumen *m*
   f pouce *m*
   r перст *m* (курсор с вытянутым
      указательным пальцем)

   * **thumbnail → 9662**

**9662 thumbnail [image]; thumbnail
         representation; rough sketch**
   d Thumbnail *n*; Umrissskizze *f*; Kennsatz *m*
   f onglet *m*; croquis *m* [minuscule]; image *f*
      timbre poste; image miniature; image vignette
   r набросок *m*; свернутое [в пиктограмму]
      изображение *n*

   * **thumbnail representation → 9662**

9663 thumbnail review
   d Thumbnail-Übersicht *f*
   f revue *f* de croquis minuscules; revue d'images

miniatures; revue d'images vignettes
   r просмотр *m* свернутых изображений

9664 thumbscanner
   d Thumbscanner *m*
   f scanner *m* dactyloscopique
   r дактилоскопический сканер *m*

9665 thumb wheel
   d Daumenrad *n*
   f molette *f*
   r устройство *n* типа "колесо"; координатный
      манипулятор *m* (для управления курсором)

   * **tick → 9666**

9666 tick [mark]
   (on the graph axis)
   d Teilstrich *m*; Skalenstrich *m*
   f coche *f*
   r отметка *f* (на оси графика); птичка *f*;
      галочка *f*; деление *n*

9667 tick-mark label
   d Teilstrichetikett *n*
   f étiquette *f* de coche
   r этикет *m* отметки

9668 tie point; attachment point
   d Anschlusspunkt *m*; Verbindungspunkt *m*
   f point *m* d'attachement; point de raccordement
   r связующая точка *f*; точка скрепления

   * **TIF → 9466**

   * **TIFF → 9466**

   * **tight coupling → 1575**

9669 tilde; wave
   (~)
   d Tilde *f*
   f tilde *m*
   r тильда[-эллипсис] *f*

9670 tile; tiled pattern
   d nebeneinander angeordnetes Muster *n*;
      Musterkachel *f*
   f mosaïque *f*
   r неперекрывающийся образец *m*;
      мозаичный шаблон *m*; мозаика *f*

9671 tiled horizontally
   d nebeneinander angeordnet
   f disposé en mosaïque horizontalement
   r горизонтально неперекрывающийся

9672 tiled maps
   d nebeneinander angeordnete Karten *fpl*

f cartes *fpl* disposées en mosaïque
r неперекрывающиеся карты *fpl*

9673 tiled pages
d nebeneinander angeordnete Seiten *fpl*
f pages *fpl* en mosaïque
r неперекрывающиеся страницы *fpl*

* **tiled pattern → 9670**

9674 tiled terrain model
d nebeneinander angeordnetes Geländemodell *n*
f modèle *m* de terrain disposé en mosaïque
r модель *f* неперекрывающихся форм местности

9675 tiled vertically
d untereinander angeordnet
f disposé en mosaïque verticalement
r вертикально непекрывающийся

9676 tiled viewports
d nebeneinander angeordnete Ansichtsfenster *npl*
f clôtures *fpl* en mosaïque
r неперекрывающиеся области *fpl* просмотра; неперекрывающиеся окна *npl* просмотра

9677 tiled wallpaper
d nebeneinander angeordnete Tapeten *fpl*
f image *f* en mosaïque de fond
r неперекрывающийся экранный фон *m*; неперекрывающиеся обои *pl*

9678 tiled windows
d nebeneinander angeordnete Fenster *npl*
f fenêtres *fpl* [disposées] en mosaïque
r неперекрывающиеся окна *npl*; окна мозаикой

9679 tile size
d Kachelgröße *f*
f taille *f* de mosaïque
r размер *m* мозаичного шаблона

9680 tile width
d Kachelbreite *f*
f largeur *f* de mosaïque
r ширина *f* мозаичного шаблона

9681 tiling; tessellation; paving; covering of the plane with tiles
d Nebeneinander-Anordnung *f*; Musterkachelung *f*; Parkettierung *f*
f pavage *m*; dallage *m*; tessellation *f*; disposition *f* en mosaïque
r разбиение *n* плоскости на многоугольники; покрытие *n* плоскости многоугольниками; мозаичное

размещение *n*; неперекрывающееся размещение; тасселяция *f*

* **tilt → 8795**

9682 tilt *v*; slope *v*; skew *v*; tip *v*
d neigen
f incliner
r наклонять

* **tilt angle → 380**

* **tilting → 6411**

* **tilt of camera → 4994**

9683 time
d Zeit *f*
f temps *m*
r время *n*; период *m* времени; момент *m* времени

9684 time base; time scale
d Zeitbasis *f*; Zeitskala *f*
f base *f* de temps
r линия *f* развертки во времени; шкала *f* времени; масштаб *m* [по оси] времени

9685 time chart; timing chart; timing sheet; timing diagram
d Zeitdiagramm *n*
f diagramme *m* de temps; chronogramme *m*
r времедиаграмма *f*; временная диаграмма *f*

9686 time code; timing code
d Zeitcode *m*; Timecode *m*
f code *m* temporel; code horaire; temps-code *m*
r временный код *m*

9687 time filter
d Zeitfilter *m*
f filtre *m* de temps
r фильтр *m* хронирования

9688 time-line
d Zeitlinie *f*
f ligne *f* de temps
r линия *f* времени

9689 timeout
d Zeitsperre *f*; Auszeit *f*; Timeout *n*
f temps *m* inexploitable; temps de suspension
r превышение *n* лимита времени; блокировка *f* по времени; тайм-аут *m*

9690 time-path diagram
d Zeit-Weg-Diagramm *n*
f diagramme *m* temps-chemin
r время-маршрутная диаграмма *f*

* **time scale** → 9684

9691 time scale axes
   d Achsen *fpl* der Zeitskala
   f axes *mpl* de l'échelle du temps
   r оси *fpl* шкалы времени

* **timetable** → 8349

9692 time warping
   d Zeitverbiegung *f*
   f gauchissement *m* de temps
   r искажение *n* времени

* **timing chart** → 9685

* **timing code** → 9686

9693 timing curve
   d Timing-Kurve *f*
   f courbe *f* de synchronisation; courbe de chronométrage
   r синхронизирующая кривая *f*; кривая хронирования

* **timing diagram** → 9685

9694 timing offset
   d Synchronisationsverschiebung *f*
   f désynchronisation *f*
   r смещение *n* синхронизации

* **timing sheet** → 9685

9695 tint; shade; hue; dye; color cast
   d Nuance *f*
   f teinte *f* [légère]; nuance *f*
   r оттенок *m*; нюанс *m*; подцветка *f*

9696 tint block
   d Tonplatte *f*
   f bloc *m* de teintes
   r блок *m* красок; блок оттенков

9697 tint slider
   d Tonwert-Schieber *m*
   f glisseur *m* de teintes
   r ползунок *m* оттенков

* **tip** *v* → 9682

* **tip** → 9730

* **title** → 4550

9698 title bar
   d Titelleiste *f*; Titel-Balken *n*
   f barre *f* de têtes; barre d'en-têtes; barre de titre
   r полоса *f* заголовка; строка *f* заголовка

9699 title bar text
   d Titelleistetext *m*
   f texte *m* de barre de têtes
   r текст *m* полосы заголовка

9700 title block
   d Titelblock *m*
   f bloc *m* de têtes
   r блок *m* заголовка

9701 title domain; name domain
   d Titelbereich *m*; Gültigkeitsbereich *m* der Namens
   f domaine *m* de noms
   r область *f* заголовок; область названий

* **TM** → 9632

9702 toggle button
   d Kippschalter *m*
   f bouton *m* bascule
   r тумблер *m*

9703 tolerance
   d Toleranz *f*
   f tolérance *f* [dimensionnelle]
   r допуск *m*; допустимый предел *m*; погрешность *f*

9704 tolerance limit
   d Toleranzgrenze *f*
   f limite *f* de tolérance
   r граница *f* допуска; толерантный предел *m*

9705 tolerance scheme
   d Toleranzschema *n*
   f schéma *m* de tolérance
   r схема *f* допуска

9706 tolerance symbol
   d Toleranzzeichen *n*
   f symbole *m* de tolérance
   r символ *m* допуска

9707 tolerance zone
   d Toleranzzone *f*
   f zone *f* de tolérance
   r зона *f* допуска

9708 tolerancing
   d Toleranzfestlegung *f*
   f mise *f* à la tolérance
   r определение *n* допуска

9709 tomogram
   d Tomogramm *n*
   f tomogramme *m*
   r томограмма *f*

9710 tonal correction
  d Tonkorrektion *f*
  f correction *f* de tonalité
  r тональная коррекция *f*

9711 tonal range
  d Farbtonbreite *f*
  f rangée *f* tonale
  r диапазон *m* цветового оттенка

9712 tonal rendering
  d Ton-Rendering *n*
  f rendu *m* de tonalité
  r тональный рендеринг *m*

  * tonal scale → 9720

9713 tonal value
  d Tonwert *m*
  f valeur *f* tonale
  r оттеночное значение *n*

  * tone → 90

9714 tone
  (of a color)
  d Ton *m*
  f ton *m*
  r тон *m*

9715 tone adjustment
  d Tonausgleichung *f*; Tonausgleich *m*
  f ajustage *m* de ton
  r выравнивание *n* тона

9716 tone compensation
  d Farbtonkompensation *f*
  f compensation *f* de ton
  r компенсация *f* тона

9717 tone curve
  d Tonkurve *f*
  f courbe *f* de tonalité
  r градационная кривая *f*; тональная кривая

9718 tone curve filter
  d Tonkurvenfilter *m*
  f filtre *m* de courbe de tonalité
  r фильтр *m* тональной кривой

9719 toner
  d Toner *m*
  f toner *m*
  r тонер *m*

9720 tone scale; tonal scale
  d Tonskala *f*
  f échelle *f* des tons
  r тональная шкала *f*; шкала тонов

9721 tone-scale adjustment
  d Tonskala-Ausgleichung *f*
  f ajustage *m* d'échelle de tonalité
  r выравнивание *n* шкалы тонов

9722 tool
  d Werkzeug *n*; Hilfsmittel *n*; Instrument *n*
  f outil *m*; instrument *m*
  r средство *n*; инструмент *m*

9723 toolbar
  d Werkzeugstreifen *m*; Hilfsmittelsleiste *f*;
     Symbolleiste *f*
  f barre *f* d'outils
  r инструментальная лента *f*; панель *f*
     инструментов

9724 toolbar button; toolbar item
  d Hilfsmittel-Schaltfläche *f*;
     Hilfsmittelsstreifenelement *n*
  f bouton *m* de barre d'outils
  r кнопка *f* панели инструментов

  * toolbar item → 9724

9725 toolbox
  d Werkzeugkasten *m*
  f boîte *f* à outils
  r инструментальный ящик *m*; меню *n*
     операций

9726 tool icon
  d Hilfsmittelssymbol *n*
  f icône *f* d'outil
  r икона *f* инструмента

9727 toolkit
  d Werkzeugsatz *m*
  f kit *m* d'instruments
  r инструментальный пакет *m*;
     инструментальный набор *m*

9728 tool palette
  d Hilfsmittelspalette *f*
  f palette *f* d'outils
  r палитра *f* инструментов

9729 tool property
  d Hilfsmitteleigenschaft *f*
  f propriété *f* d'outil
  r свойство *n* инструмента; характеристика *f*
     инструмента

9730 tooltip; tip
  d Tip *m*
  f info-bulle *f*
  r сведение *n* инструментальной кнопки

  * top → 1289

9731 top extent
   d Extent *m* nach oben
   f étendue *f* du haut
   r расширение *n* вверх

   * **top margin** → 10074

9732 top node
   d oberer Knoten *m*
   f nœud *m* du haut
   r верхний узел *m*

   * **top-of-the-line effects** → 4627

   * **top-of-the-range effects** → 4627

9733 topographical database
   d topografische Datenbasis *f*
   f base *f* de données topographiques
   r топографическая база *f* данных

9734 topographical drawing
   d topografische Zeichnung *f*
   f dessin *m* topographique
   r топографический чертеж *m*;
      топографический рисунок *m*

9735 topographical element; feature
   d topografisches Element *n*
   f élément *m* topographique
   r топографический элемент *m*

9736 topographical map
   d topografische Karte *f*
   f carte *f* topographique
   r топографическая карта *f*

9737 topographical plane
   d topografische Ebene *f*
   f plan *m* topographique
   r топографическая плоскость *f*

9738 topographical point
   d topografischer Punkt *m*
   f point *m* topographique
   r топографическая точка *f*

9739 topographic[al] projection; tangent plane projection; ; projection with heights; coted projection
   d topografische Projektion *f*, kongruente Projektion; kotierte Projektion
   f projection *f* topographique; projection sur un plan tangent; projection cotée
   r топографическая проекция *f*; проекция с числовыми отметками

9740 topographical relief model
   d topografisches Reliefmodell *n*
   f modèle *m* de relief topographique
   r топографическая модель *f* рельефа

9741 topographical surface
   d topografische Fläche *f*; Geländefläche *f*
   f surface *f* topographique
   r топографическая поверхность *f*

9742 topographical view
   d topografische Ansicht *f*
   f vue *f* topographique
   r топографический вид *m*

   * **topographic projection** → 9739

9743 topography
   d Topografie *f*
   f topographie *f*; схема *f* размещения
   r топография *f*; схема *f* размещения

   * **topography texture map** → 9744

9744 topography texture map[ping]
   d topografische Texturenabbildung *f*
   f application *f* de texture topographique
   r топографическое отображение *n* текстуры

9745 topological analysis
   d topologische Analyse *f*
   f analyse *f* topologique
   r топологический анализ *m*

9746 topological cell
   d topologische Zelle *f*; krumme Zelle
   f cellule *f* topologique
   r топологическая клетка *f*; кривая клетка

9747 topological circle
   d topologische Kreisscheibe *f*
   f cercle *m* topologique
   r топологический круг *m*

9748 topological circumference
   d topologischer Kreis *m*
   f circonférence *f* topologique
   r топологическая окружность *f*

9749 topological closure
   (as a operation)
   d topologische Hüllenoperation *f*
   f opération *f* de fermeture topologique
   r топологическая операция *f* замыкания

9750 topological display
   d topologischer Bildschirm *m*
   f afficheur *m* topologique
   r топологический дисплей *m*

9751 topological error
   d topologischer Fehler *m*

f erreur *f* topologique
r топологическая ошибка *f*

9752 topological graph
  d topologischer Graph *m*
  f graphe *m* topologique
  r топологический граф *m*

9753 topological group
  d topologische Gruppe *f*
  f groupe *m* topologique
  r топологическая группа *f*

9754 topological information
  d topologische Information *f*
  f information *f* topologique
  r топологическая информация *f*

9755 topologically complex objects
  d topologische Komplexobjekte *npl*
  f objets *mpl* topologiquement complexes
  r топологически комплексные объекты *mpl*

9756 topologically structured data
  d topologisch strukturierte Daten *npl*
  f données *fpl* structurées topologiquement
  r топологически структурированные данные *npl*

9757 topological modeling
  d topologische Modellierung *f*
  f modelage *m* topologique
  r топологическое моделирование *n*

9758 topological sort
  d topologisches Sortieren *n*
  f tri[age] *m* topologique
  r топологическая сортировка *f*

9759 topological space
  d topologischer Raum *m*
  f espace *m* topologique
  r топологическое пространство *n*

9760 topological structure
  d topologische Struktur *f*
  f structure *f* topologique
  r топологическая структура *f*

9761 topology
  d Topologie *f*
  f topologie *f*
  r топология *f*

9762 topology auditing
  d topologische Revision *f*
  f inspection *f* de topologie
  r топологическая ревизия *f*; контроль *m* топологии

9763 topology description
  d topologische Beschreibung *f*
  f description *f* de topologie
  r топологическое описание *n*

9764 topology element
  d topologisches Element *n*
  f élément *m* de topologie
  r элемент *m* топологии

9765 topology function
  d topologische Funktion *f*
  f fonction *f* topologique
  r топологическая функция *f*

9766 topology name
  d topologischer Name *m*
  f nom *m* de topologie
  r топологическое имя *n*

9767 topology object data
  d topologische Objektdaten *npl*
  f données *fpl* d'objets topologiques
  r данные *npl* топологических объектов

9768 topology property
  d topologische Eigenschaft *f*
  f propriété *f* topologique
  r свойство *n* топологии

9769 topology query
  d topologische Abfrage *f*
  f interrogation *f* topologique
  r топологический запрос *m*

9770 topology statistics
  d topologische Statistik *f*
  f statistique *f* topologique
  r топологическая статистика *f*

9771 topology type code
  d topologischer Typcode *m*
  f code *m* de type de topologie
  r код *m* типа топологии

9772 topology variable
  d topologische Variable *f*
  f variable *f* topologique
  r топологическая переменная *f*

9773 top surface
  d obere Fläche *f*
  f surface *f* supérieure
  r верхняя поверхность *f*

* **tore → 9781**

9774 toroid
  (as a surface)
  d Toroid *n*

f toroïde *f*
r тороид *m*

9775 toroid
(as a curve)
d Toroide *f*
f toroïde *f*
r тороида *f*

9776 toroidal
d toroidisch
f torique
r тороидальный

9777 toroidal polygon mesh
d toroidische Polygonmasche *f*
f maille *f* polygonale torique
r тороидальная многоугольная сеть *f*

9778 torsion; second curvature
d Windung *f*; Torsion *f*; Schmiegung *f*; zweite Krümmung *f*
f torsion *f*; deuxième courbure *f*; seconde courbure; courbure de seconde espèce
r кручение *n*; вторая кривизна *f*

* **torsion coefficient** → 1651

* **torsion radius** → 7725

9779 torsion ring
d Torsionsring *m*
f anneau *m* en torsion
r крутильное кольцо *n*

9780 torsion strength; twist strength
d Torsionsfestigkeit *f*; Verdrehungsfestigkeit *f*
f résistance *f* à la torsion; tenue *f* en torsion
r крутильная плотность *f*

9781 torus; anchor ring; tore
(as a solid)
d Torus *m*; Ringkörper *m*; Kreistorus *m*; Kreisring *m*
f tore *m* [circulaire]; tore de révolution
r тор *m* [вращения]; баранка *f*; бублик *m*; круговой тор

9782 torus diameter
d Torusdurchmesser *m*
f diamètre *m* de tore
r диаметр *m* тора

9783 torus radius
d Torusradius *m*
f rayon *m* de tore
r радиус *m* тора

9784 total internal reflection
d innere Totalreflexion *f*

f réflexion *f* interne totale
r полное внутреннее отражение *n*

9785 total radiation
d Gesamtstrahlung *f*
f rayonnement *m* total; radiation *f* totale
r полное излучение *n*

9786 total reflection
d totale Reflexion *f*; Totalreflexion *f*
f réflexion *f* totale
r полное отражение *n*

* **total surface area** → 1923

* **touch device** → 9789

* **touch display** → 9790

9787 touchpad; touch-sensitive tablet; trackpad
d Touchpad *n*
f trackpad *m*
r сенсорная панель *f*

9788 touch scanner
d Berührungsscanner *m*
f scanner *m* tactile
r сенсорный сканер *m*

* **touch screen** → 9790

9789 touch[-sensitive] device
d Gerät *n* mit Berührungseingabe; Sensor-Gerät *n*
f unité *f* sensorielle; unité tactile; élément *m* sensitif
r сенсорное устройство *n*; сенсорный элемент *m*

9790 touch[-sensitive] screen; sensitive screen; touch[-sensitive] display; tactile display
d Berührungsbildschirm *m*; Sensor-Bildschirm *m*; Touchscreen *n*
f écran *m* sensoriel; écran tactile
r сенсорный экран *m*; тактильный экран

* **touch-sensitive display** → 9790

* **touch-sensitive tablet** → 9787

9791 touch sensor; tactile-type sensor
d Berührungssensor *m*; taktiler Sensor *m*
f capteur *m* [du type] tactile; senseur *m* tactile
r тактильный датчик *m*

* **tourning** → 7086

9792 tourning handle
d Drehgriff *m*

f poignée *f* tournante
r вращающийся захват *m*

* **tps** → **9882**

* **trace** → **3129, 7072**

* **trace** *v* → **9810**

9793 trace; trail
   d Spur *f*; Ablauffolge *f*
   f trace *f*; poursuite *f* de déroulement; droite *f* de
      suite
   r след *m*; трасса *f*

9794 trace; tracing
   d Trassieren *n*; Tracing *n*; Aufzeichnung *f*;
      Durchzeichnung *f*
   f traçage *m*; tracement *m*
   r трассирование *n*; трассировка *f*

9795 trace command
   d Tracing-Befehl *m*
   f commande *f* de traçage
   r команда *f* трассировки

9796 trace curve
   d Spurkurve *f*
   f courbe *f* trace
   r след *m* поверхности; кривая *f* типа следа

9797 trace device; tracer
   d Folgeeinrichtung *f*; Nachlaufeinrichtung *f*
   f unité *f* de traçage; dispositif *m*
      d'asservissement; localisateur *m* de la trace
   r следящее устройство *n*

9798 trace fill
   d Spurfüllung *f*
   f remplissage *m* de trace
   r заполнение *n* трассы

9799 trace line
   d Spurlinie *f*; Spurgerade *f*
   f ligne *f* trace; droite *f* trace; ligne pleine
   r след *m* плоскости; линия *f* типа следа;
      основание *n* картинной плоскости;
      основание картины

9800 trace object
   d Spurobjekt *n*
   f objet *m* trace
   r объект *m* типа следа

9801 trace of a line
   d Spur *f* einer Linie
   f trace *f* d'une droite
   r след *m* линии

9802 trace parameter

d Spurparameter *m*
f paramètre *m* de trace
r параметр *m* трассы

* **trace point** → **7072**

9803 trace program; tracing program; tracer
   d Folgeprüfprogramm *n*;
      Ablaufverfolgungsprogramm *n*;
      Trace-Programm *n*
   f programme *m* de traçage; programme de
      poursuite; programme de dépistage
   r программа *f* трассировки; программа
      прослеживания

* **tracer** → **9797, 9803**

* **tracing** → **9794**

9804 tracing; tracking
   d Folgen *n*; Nachführen *n*; Verfolgung *f*;
      Ablaufverfolgung *f*; Spurverfolgung *f*
   f poursuite *f*; suivi *m*
   r слежение *n*; прослеживание *n*

9805 tracing accuracy
   d Verfolg[ungs]genauigkeit *f*
   f exactitude *f* de poursuite
   r точность *f* слежения

9806 tracing geometry
   d Tracing-Geometrie *f*
   f géométrie *f* de traçage
   r геометрия *f* трассировки

9807 tracing model
   d Verfolgungsmodell *n*
   f modèle *m* de traçage
   r модель *f* трассировки; модель
      прослеживания

9808 tracing model element
   d Element *n* des Verfolgungsmodells
   f élément *m* de modèle de traçage
   r элемент *m* модели прослеживания

* **tracing program** → **9803**

9809 tracing symbol
   d Verfolgungssymbol *n*
   f symbole *m* de poursuite
   r символ *m* прослеживания

9810 track *v*; **trace** *v*
   d folgen; verfolgen
   f suivre; tracer
   r следить

* **trackball** → **8184**

* **trackball mouse** → 8184

* **tracker ball** → 8184

* **tracking** → 9804

* **trackpad** → 9787

* **trail** → 9793

* **train** → 8550

9811 training pattern
   d Ausbildungsmuster *n*
   f image *f* enseignante
   r обучающий образ *m*

9812 trajectory
   d Trajektorie *f*
   f trajectoire *f*
   r траектория *f*

9813 trajectory space; orbit space
   d Raum *m* der Trajektorien; Bahnenraum *m*
   f espace *m* des trajectoires
   r пространство *n* траекторий

9814 transaction
   d Vorgang *m*; Transaktion *f*
   f transaction *f*
   r входное сообщение *n*; информационный обмен *m*; транзакция *f*

9815 transcribe *v*
   d umschreiben; eintragen
   f transcrire
   r перезаписывать; описывать

* **transcribing** → 9816

9816 transcription; transcribing
   d Umschreibung *f*
   f transcription *f*
   r перезапись *f*; транскрипция *f*

* **transfer** → 9817

9817 transfer[ing]
   d Transfer *m*; Übertragung *f*; Übergabe *f*
   f transfert *m*; lancement *m*
   r перенос *m*

* **transform** → 9820

9818 transform *v*
   d transformieren; umwandeln; umformen
   f transformer
   r преобразовывать; трансформировать

9819 transformability

   d Transformiertbarkeit *f*
   f transformabilité *f*
   r преобразуемость *f*

9820 transform[ation]
   d Umwandlung *f*; Umsetzung *f*; Transformation *f*
   f transformation *f*
   r преобразование *n*; трансформация *f*

9821 transformation matrix; transition matrix
   d Transformationsmatrix *f*
   f matrice *f* des transformations
   r матрица *f* преобразований

9822 transformation of coordinate system; coordinate system transformation
   d Transformation *f* des Koordinatensystem
   f transformation *f* de système de coordonnées
   r преобразование *n* координатной системы

* **transformation of similitude** → 8697

9823 transformation origin
   d Transformationsursprung *m*
   f origine *f* de transformation
   r начало *n* трансформации

9824 transformation to principal axes
   d Hauptachsentransformation *f*
   f transformation *f* aux axes principaux; réduction *f* aux axes principaux
   r приведение *n* к главным осям

9825 transformed
   d transformiert
   f transformé
   r преобразованный; трансформированный

* **transient copy** → 8860

9826 transition
   d Transition *f*; Übergang *m*
   f transition *f*
   r переход *m*

9827 transition blending
   d Transitionsüberblendung *f*
   f dégradé *m* transitoire
   r переходное переливание *n*

* **transition matrix** → 9821

* **translating** → 9828

9828 translation; translating
   d Translation *f*; Übersetzung *f*
   f translation *f*
   r трансляция *f*; сдвиг *m*

9829 translation of axes
d Translation *f* der Achsen
f translation *f* des axes
r трансляция *f* осей

9830 translation of coordinates; coordinate translation
d Koordinatentranslation *f*
f translation *f* de coordonnées
r трансляция *f* координат

9831 translation of the coordinate system; translation of the system of coordinates; parallel displacement of the system of coordinates
d Parallelverschiebung *f* des Koordinatensystems; Translation *f* des Koordinatensystems
f translation *f* du système des coordonnées; déplacement *m* parallèle du système des coordonnées
r трансляция *f* системы координат; параллельный перенос *m* системы координат

9832 translation of the origin
d Nullpunktverschiebung *f*; Nullpunkttransformation *f*; Verschiebung *f* des Nullpunkts
f changement *m* d'origine
r перенос *m* начала [координат]

** * translation of the system of coordinates → 9831**

9833 translation operator; shift operator; displacement operator
d Translationsoperator *m*; Verschiebungsoperator *m*
f opérateur *m* de translation; opérateur de déplacement
r оператор *m* сдвига

9834 translation parameter
d Verschiebungsparameter *m*
f paramètre *m* de translation
r параметр *m* сдвига

9835 translucency
d Transluzenz *f*; Durchscheinfähigkeit *f*
f translucidité *f*
r полупрозрачность *f*

9836 translucency effect
d Transluzenz-Effekt *m*
f effet *m* de translucidité
r эффект *m* полупрозрачности

9837 translucent
d lichtdurchlässig; durchscheinend;

durchsichtig
f translucide
r полупрозрачный; просвечивающий

9838 translucent body
d durchscheinender Körper *m*
f corps *m* translucide
r полупрозрачное тело *n*

9839 translucent objects
d durchscheinende Objekte *npl*
f objets *mpl* translucides
r полупрозрачные объекты *mpl*

9840 transparency
d Transparenz *f*; Durchsichtigkeit *f*
f transparence *f*
r прозрачность *f*

9841 transparency coefficient
d Transparenzfaktor *m*
f coefficient *m* de transparence
r коэффициент *m* прозрачности

9842 transparency mapping
d Transparenz-Abbildung *f*
f mappage *m* transparent
r отображение *n* с учетом прозрачности

9843 transparency of material
d Materialtransparenz *f*
f transparence *f* du matériel
r прозрачность *f* материала

9844 transparency unit
d Transparenzeinheit *f*
f unité *f* de transparence
r единица *f* прозрачности

9845 transparency window
d Transparenzfenster *n*
f fenêtre *f* de transparence
r окно *n* прозрачности

9846 transparent
d transparent
f transparent
r прозрачный

9847 transparent background
d transparenter Hintergrund *m*
f fond *m* transparent
r прозрачный фон *m*

9848 transparent color
d transparente Farbe *f*
f couleur *f* transparente
r прозрачный цвет *m*

9849 transparent command
d transparenter Befehl *m*

f commande *f* transparente
r прозрачная команда *f*

9850 transparent data
d transparente Daten *npl*
f données *fpl* transparentes
r прозрачные данные *npl*

9851 transparent plane
d transparente Ebene *f*
f plan *m* transparent
r прозрачная плоскость *f*

9852 transparent section
(of picture)
d transparente Sektion *f*
f section *f* transparente
r прозрачная секция *f*

9853 transparent texture
d transparente Textur *f*
f texture *f* transparente
r прозрачная текстура *f*

* **transportability** → 7331

* **transportable** → 7332

9854 transposed map
d transponierte Abbildung *f*
f application *f* transposée
r транспонированное отображение *n*

9855 transposition
d Transposition *f*
f transposition *f*
r транспозиция *f*; перемещение *n*

9856 transposition code
d Transpositionscode *m*
f code *m* de transposition
r код *m* транспозиции

* **transversal** → 9860

9857 transversal; secant [line]; intersecting line
d Transversale *f*; Treffgerade *f*; Sekante *f*
f transversale *f*; droite *f* sécante; sécante *f*
r трансверсаль *f*; пересекающая линия *f*; секант[а] *m/f*

9858 transversal projection; meridional projection
d querachsige Projektion *f*
f projection *f* transversale; projection méridienne
r поперечная проекция *f*; меридиональная проекция

9859 transversal through a vertex

d Ecktransversale *f*
f transversale *f* à travers un sommet
r трансверсаль *f*, проведенная через вершину [треугольника]

9860 transverse; transversal; cross
d transversal; Quer-
f transversal; croisé
r поперечный; перекрестный

9861 transverse axis of a hyperbola
d Hauptachse *f* der Hyperbel; reelle Achse *f* der Hyperbel
f axe *m* transverse d'une hyperbole; axe focal d'une hyperbole
r главная ось *f* гиперболы; фокальная ось гиперболы

9862 transverse chromatic aberration
d transversale chromatische Aberration *f*
f aberration *f* chromatique transversale
r поперечная хроматическая аберрация *f*

9863 transverse diameter
d Hauptdurchmesser *m*
f diamètre *m* principal; diamètre transverse; diamètre focal
r главный диаметр *m*

* **transverse profile** → 2317

* **trap** → 9865

9864 trapezium (UK); trapezoid (US)
d Trapez *n*
f trapèze *m*
r трапеция *f*

* **trapezium distortion** → 5372

9865 trap[ping]
d Trapp *m*; Falle *f*
f trappe *f*; piège *m*
r ловушка *f*; улавливание *n*

9866 traverse *v*
d durchlaufen
f traverser; pointer en direction
r пересекать; проходить

* **traverse** → 2310

* **traverses** → 7282

9867 traversing
d Polygonierung *f*; Polygonzugmessung *f*
f cheminement *m*; polygonation *f*
r измерение *n* полигонального хода

* **treatment** → 7493

9868 tree
  d Baum *m*
  f arbre *m*
  r дерево *n*

9869 tree chart
  d Baumdiagramm *n*
  f diagramme *m* arborescent
  r древовидная диаграмма *f*

9870 tree[-coded] menu
  d baumförmiges Menü *n*
  f menu *m* arborescent
  r древовидное меню *n*

  * tree menu → 9870

9871 tree structure
  d Baumstruktur *f*
  f structure *f* d'arbre; structure arborescente
  r древовидная структура *f*

9872 tree view
  d Baumansicht *f*
  f vue *f* d'arbre; vue arborescente
  r древовидное представление *n*

  * trefoil → 9873

9873 trefoil [knot]; cloverleaf
  d Kleeblattschlinge *f*
  f nœud *m* de trèfle
  r трилистная петля *f*; узел-трилистник *m*

9874 trefoil symmetry
  d Kleeblattsymmetrie *f*
  f symétrie *f* à trois feuilles
  r трилистная симметрия *f*

9875 trend
  d Trend *m*; Tendenz *f*; Richtung *f*
  f tendance *f*; direction *f*
  r тренд *m*

9876 trendline
  d Trendlinie *f*
  f ligne *f* de tendance
  r тренд-линия *f*; линия *f* тренда

  * trial → 640

9877 triangle
  d Dreieck *n*
  f triangle *m*
  r треугольник *m*

9878 triangle decomposition
  d Dreieckszerlegung *f*
  f décomposition *f* de triangles
  r разбиение *n* треугольников

9879 triangle edge
  d Dreieckkante *f*
  f arête *f* de triangle
  r ребро *n* треугольника

9880 triangle filter
  d Dreieckfilter *m*
  f filtre *m* triangle
  r фильтр *m* треугольников

  * triangle of support → 9345

9881 triangle rendering
  d Dreieckrendering *n*
  f rendu *m* triangulaire
  r треугольное тонирование *n*; рендеринг *m* треугольников

9882 triangles per second; tps
  d Dreiecke *npl* pro Sekunde
  f triangles *mpl* par seconde
  r треугольники *mpl* в секунду

9883 triangle surface
  d Dreieckfläche *f*
  f surface *f* de triangle
  r площадь *f* треугольника

9884 triangle vertices
  d Dreieckknotenpunkte *mpl*
  f sommets *mpl* de triangle
  r вершины *fpl* треугольника

9885 triangular
  d dreieckig
  f triangulaire
  r треугольный

9886 triangular area
  d Dreiecksfläche *f*
  f aire *f* triangulaire
  r треугольная площадь *f*

9887 triangular B-spline patches
  d dreieckige B-Spline-Oberflächenstücke *npl*
  f surfaces *fpl* de B-spline paramétriques triangulaires
  r B-сплайновые треуголные фрагменты *mpl*

9888 triangular 3D face
  d dreieckige 3D-Fläche *f*
  f face *f* triangulaire 3D
  r треугольная 3D грань *f*

9889 triangular mesh
  d dreieckige Masche *f*
  f maille *f* triangulaire
  r сеть *f* треугольников; треугольная сетка *f*

9890 triangular prism
  d dreieckiges Prisma *n*

f prisme *m* triangulaire
r треугольная призма *f*

9891 triangular pyramid; tetrahedron
   d dreiseitige Pyramide *f*; Tetraeder *n*;
      Vierflach *n*
   f pyramide *f* triangulaire; tétraèdre *m*
   r треугольная пирамида *f*; тетраэдр *m*;
      четырехгранник *m*

9892 triangulation
   d Triangulation *f*
   f triangulation *f*
   r триангуляция *f*

9893 triangulation-based digitizer
   d Triangulation-basierter Digitalgeber *m*
   f numériseur *m* orienté à triangulation
   r дигитайзер *m*, базированный на
      триангуляции

9894 triangulation factor
   d Triangulationsfaktor *m*
   f coefficient *m* de triangulation
   r коэффициент *m* триангуляции

9895 triangulation scanner
   d Triangulationscanner *m*
   f scanner *m* de triangulation
   r триангуляционный сканер *m*

9896 triaxial
   d dreiachsig
   f à trois axes
   r трехосный

9897 trichromatic color
   d dreichromatische Farbe *f*
   f couleur *f* trichrome
   r трихроматический цвет *m*

   * **tri-dimensional** → 9649

9898 trifolium
   d Dreiblatt *n*; Trifolium *n*
   f trifolium *m*
   r трилистник *m*

   * **trigonometric** → 9899

9899 trigonometric[al]
   d trigonometrisch
   f trigonométrique
   r тригонометрический

9900 trigonometric[al] function; circular function
   d trigonometrische Funktion *f*; Kreisfunktion *f*
   f fonction *f* trigonométrique; fonction circulaire

r тригонометрическая функция *f*; круговая
   функция

   * **trigonometric function** → 9900

9901 trigonometry
   d Trigonometrie *f*
   f trigonométrie *f*
   r тригонометрия *f*

   * **trihedral** → 9903

9902 trihedral angle
   d dreiseitige Körperecke *f*; Triederwinkel *m*;
      Dreikant *n/m*
   f angle *m* trièdre
   r трехгранный угол *m*

9903 trihedron; trihedral
   d Dreibein *n*
   f trièdre *m*
   r триэдр *m*

9904 trilateral
   d Dreiseit *n*
   f trilatère *m*
   r трехсторонник *m*

9905 trilinear filtering
   d Trilinear-Filtering *n*
   f filtrage *m* trilinéaire
   r трилинейное фильтрирование *n*;
      трилинейная фильтрация *f*

9906 trilinear interpolator
   d Trilinear-Interpolator *m*
   f interpolateur *m* trilinéaire
   r трилинейный интерполятор *m*

9907 trilinear mipmapping
   d Trilinear-Mip-Mapping *n*
   f mip-mapping *m* trilinéaire
   r трилинейное mip-текстурирование *n*

9908 trilinear texture
   d Trilinear-Textur *f*
   f texture *f* trilinéaire
   r трилинейная текстура *f*

9909 trilinear texture filtering
   d Trilinear-Textur-Filtering *n*
   f filtrage *m* de texture trilinéaire
   r фильтрирование *n* трилинейной текстуры

   * **trim** → 9912

9910 trim *v*; **crop** *v*
   d beschneiden; zuschneiden
   f tronquer
   r обрезать; подрезать; удалять; отсекать;
      вырезать; стричь

9911 trimmed surface
  d beschnittene Fläche *f*
  f surface *f* tronquée
  r обрезанная поверхность *f*

9912 trim[ming]; crop[ping]
  d Beschneidung *f*; Zuschneidung *f*;
      Beschneiden *n*; Zuschneiden *n*
  f tronque *f*; coupure *f*
  r обрезание *n*; обрезка *f*; укорачивание *n*

9913 triple buffering
  d dreifache Pufferung *f*
  f tamponnage *m* triple
  r тройное буферирование *n*; тройная
      буферизация *f*

  *   **triplet** → 9652

9914 trisection
  d Dreiteilung *f*; Trisektion *f*
  f trisection *f*
  r трисекция *f*

9915 trisection of the angle
  d Winkeldreiteilung *f*; Trisektion *f* des Winkels
  f trisection *f* de l'angle
  r трисекция *f* угла

9916 trisectrix
  d Trisektrix *f*
  f trisectrice *f*
  r трисектриса *f*

9917 tritone
      (three inks)
  d Triton *m*
  f trois tons *mpl*
  r триплекс *m*

9918 trochoid
  d Trochoide *f*
  f trochoïde *f*
  r трохоида *f*

9919 tropism
  d Tropismus *m*
  f tropisme *m*
  r тропизм *m*

9920 troubleshooting
  d Fehlersuche *f*; Störungssuche *f*
  f recherche *f* de pannes
  r поиск *m* неисправностей

  *   **trucking shot** → 3046

9921 true
      (as a logical value)
  d Wahrheit *f*

  f vrai *m*
  r истина *f*; логическая единица *f*

9922 true color
  d Echtfarbe *f*
  f couleur *f* vraie
  r реалистичный цвет *m*

9923 true color representation
  d True-Color-Darstellung *f*;
      Echtfarb[en]darstellung *f*
  f représentation *f* en couleurs vraies
  r реалистичное цветовоспроизведение *n*

9924 true edge
  d wahrer Rand *m*
  f côte *f* vraie
  r истинный край *m*

9925 true intersection
  d wahrer Durchschnitt *m*
  f intersection *f* vraie
  r истинное пересечение *n*

  *   **true representation** → 3692

9926 true shape
  d wahre Gestalt *f*
  f vraie forme *f*
  r истинная форма *f*

9927 TrueType font
  d TrueType-Schrift *f*
  f police *f* TrueType
  r TrueType шрифт *m*

9928 truncated
  d abgeschnitten; abgestumpft; trunkiert
  f tronqué
  r усеченный

  *   **truncated circular cone** → 4050

  *   **truncated cone** → 4045

9929 truncated corner
  d abgeschnittene Ecke *f*
  f coin *m* tronqué
  r усеченный угол *m*

9930 truncated cylinder
  d abgeschnittener Zylinder *m*
  f cylindre *m* tronqué
  r усеченный цилиндр *m*

9931 truncated line caps
  d abgeschnittene Linienenden *npl*
  f fins *mpl* de lignes tronqués
  r усеченные конечные элементы *mpl* линии

* **truncated pyramid** → 4047

* **truncated right circular cone** → 4051

* **truncated right cone** → 4048

* **truncated right pyramid** → 4049

9932 truncation
  d Abschneiden *n*
  f tronquage *m*; troncature *f*
  r усечение *n*

9933 tube
  d Rohr *n*
  f tube *m*
  r труба *f*

9934 tube diameter
  d Rohrdurchmesser *m*
  f diamètre *m* de tube
  r диаметр *m* трубы

9935 tube radius
  d Rohrradius *m*
  f rayon *m* de tube
  r радиус *m* трубы

9936 tubular light source
  d röhrenförmige Lichtquelle *f*
  f source *f* lumineuse tubulaire
  r трубообразный источник *m* света

9937 tumbing
  d Taumeln *n*
  f culbute *f*
  r кувыркание *n*

* **tune** *v* → 195

9938 turbulence
  d Turbulenz *f*
  f turbulence *f*
  r турбуленция *f*

9939 turbulence of the marble
  d Marmorturbulenz *f*
  f turbulence *f* du marbre
  r турбуленция *f* мрамора

* **turbulent** → 10361

9940 turbulent model
  d Turbulenzmodell *n*
  f modèle *m* turbulent
  r турбулентная модель *f*

9941 turtle geometry
  d Turtle-Geometrie *f*
  f géométrie *f* de la tortue

  r "черепашья" геометрия *f*

9942 turtle graphics
  d Turtle-Grafik *f*
  f graphique *m* de la tortue
  r "черепашья" графика *f*

* **tweening** → 6036

9943 twirl *v*
  d [herum]drehen
  f tournoyer
  r вертеть[ся]; крутить[ся]; кружить

9944 twirling baton
  d drehender Stab *m*; Drehstab *m*; wirbelnder Stab
  f bâton *m* tournoyant
  r вращающаяся палочка *f*; крутящийся жезл *m*

9945 twist *v*
  d verdrehen
  f tordre; torsader
  r закручивать; сплетаться; виться

9946 twist
  d Verdrehung *f*
  f carotte *f*; torsion *f*; vrillage *m*
  r [за]крутка *f*; кручение *n*; сучение *n*

* **twist angle** → 388

9947 twisted black arrow
  d verdrehter Schwarzpfeil *m*; verdrillter Schwarzpfeil
  f flèche *f* noire tordue
  r изогнутая черная стрелка *f*

* **twisted curve** → 8919

9948 twisted surface
  d verdrehte Fläche *f*
  f surface *f* tordue; surface torsadée; surface vrillée
  r извилистая поверхность *f*; сплетенная поверхность

9949 twisted torus
  d verdrehter Torus *m*
  f tore *m* tordu
  r закрученный тор *m*

* **twist strength** → 9780

9950 two-color bitmap pattern fill
  d Zweifarben-Bitmap-Musterfüllung *f*
  f remplissage *m* par motif bitmap à deux couleurs
  r заполнение *n* двухцветным точечным мотивом

9951 two-color combination
  d Zweifarbenkombination *f*
  f combinaison *f* en deux couleurs
  r комбинация *f* двух цветов

9952 two-color effect
  d Zweifarbeneffekt *m*
  f effet *m* bicouleur
  r двухцветный эффект *m*

9953 two-color fountain
  d zweifarbiger Verlauf *m*;
      Zweifarben-Verlauf *m*
  f source *f* bicouleur
  r двухцветный источник *m*

9954 two-color pattern; bicolor pattern
  d Zweifarbenmuster *n*; Zweifarben-Motiv *n*
  f motif *m* en deux couleurs; motif bicolore
  r двухцветный мотив *m*; двухцветный
      рисунок *m*

9955 two-color pattern editor
  d Zweifarbenmuster-Editor *m*
  f éditeur *m* de motifs en deux couleurs
  r редактор *m* двухцветных мотивов

9956 two-dimensional; bidimensional; 2D
  d zweidimensional
  f à deux dimensions; bidimensionnel; [en] 2D
  r двумерный; двудимензионный

  *   **two-directional → 910**

9957 two-point perspective
  d Zweipunkt-Perspektive *f*
  f perspective *f* à deux points
  r двухточечная перспектива *f*

9958 two-segment callout
  d Zweisegmentlegende *f*
  f légende *f* à deux segments
  r двусегментная легенда *f*

  *   **two-sided → 917**

**9959 two-sided surface; bilateral surface;
        surface with two sides**
  d bilaterale Fläche *f*
  f surface *f* bilatérale
  r двусторонняя поверхность *f*

9960 two-view drawings
  d Zwei-Ansicht-Zeichnung *f*
  f dessins *mpl* à deux vues
  r чертеж *m* в двух представлениях

  *   **two-way → 910**

  *   **type → 1417**

9961 type
  d Typ *m*
  f type *m*
  r тип *m*; вид *m*

9962 typed objects
  d typisierte Objekte *npl*
  f objets *mpl* typiques
  r типизированные объекты *mpl*

  *   **typeface → 9963**

  *   **type font → 1417**

9963 type of [font] style; typeface; font style
  d Schrifttyp *m*; Schriftform *f*; Typenart *f*
  f type *m* de caractères; œil *m* du caractère;
      espèce *f* de caractère; style *m* de jeu de
      caractères; genre *m* de caractères; relief *m* de
      caractères
  r вид *m* шрифта; начертание *n* шрифта;
      рисунок *m* шрифта

9964 type of projection
  d Projektionstyp *m*
  f type *m* de projection
  r тип *m* проекции

  *   **type of style → 9963**

9965 type set; typesetting
  d Typensatz *m*; Schriftsatz *m*
  f jeu *m* de types
  r набор *m* шрифтов

  *   **typesetting → 9965**

  *   **type style → 1417**

9966 typography
  d Typografie *f*
  f typographie *f*
  r типография *f*; построение *n* шрифтов

U

* **UCR → 9982**

* **UCS → 10084**

9967 UCS icon
   d Symbol *n* des Benutzerkoordinatensystems
   f icône *f* de système de coordonnées utilisateur
   r икона *f* координатной системы
      пользователя

9968 UCS orientation
   d Benutzerkoordinatensystem-Orientierung *f*
   f orientation *f* de système de coordonnées
      utilisateur
   r ориентация *f* пользовательской
      координатной системы

9969 UCS toolbar
   d Hilfsmittelstreifen *m* des
      Benutzerkoordinatensystems
   f barre *f* d'outils de système de coordonnées
      utilisateur
   r панель *f* инструментов пользовательской
      координатной системы

9970 ultraviolet; UV
   d ultraviolett; UV
   f ultraviolet; UV
   r ультрафиолетовый; УВ

9971 unary
   d unitär; einstellig
   f unitaire; monoplace
   r унарный; одноместный

9972 unassigned
   d nichtzugeordnet
   f non assigné
   r незакрепленный; неназначенный

* **unattainability → 4977**

* **unavailability → 4977**

* **unavailable → 4978**

9973 unavailable node; inaccessible node
   d unerreichbarer Knoten *m*
   f nœud *m* inaccessible; nœud non accessible
   r недоступный узел *m*; недостижимый узел

9974 unbalance
   d Ungleichgewicht *n*

   f déséquilibrage *m*
   r разбаланс *m*; дисбаланс *m*;
      рассоглосование *n*

9975 unbiased
   d nichtvorgespannt; biasfrei
   f sans biais
   r несмещенный

* **unblank *v* → 5530**

* **unblock *v* → 10035**

* **unblock → 10037**

* **unblocking → 10037**

* **unbounded → 1117**

9976 unclosed
   d ungeschlossen
   f non fermé
   r незамкнутый

9977 unclosed contour
   d offene Höhenlinie *f*
   f courbe *f* de niveau non fermé
   r незамкнутая горизонталь *f*

9978 unclosed [polygonal] traverse
   d offener Polygonzug *m*
   f cheminement *m* polygonal non fermé
   r висячий полигонный ход *m*

* **unclosed traverse → 9978**

9979 unconditional
   d unbedingt
   f inconditionnel
   r безусловный

* **undecidability → 5130**

9980 undefined; undetermined; unidentifiable; indefinite
   d undefiniert; undeterminiert; unbestimmt
   f non défini; indéfini; non déterminé;
      indéterminé
   r недефинированный; неопределенный

9981 undefined object
   d undefiniertes Objekt *n*
   f objet *m* non défini
   r недефинированный объект *m*

9982 undercolor removal; UCR; undercolor separation
   d Unterfarbenbeseitigung *f*; UCR
   f séparation *f* de couleurs parasites

r удаление *n* паразитных цветов;
вычитание *n* цветов из-под черного

* **undercolor separation** → 9982

9983 underline *v*; **underscore** *v*; **emphasize** *v*
d unterstreichen
f souligner
r подчеркивать

9984 underlined text
d unterstrichener Text *m*
f texte *m* souligné
r подчеркнутый текст *m*

* **underscore** *v* → 9983

* **underscore** → 9985

9985 underscore [sign]
d Unterstreichungszeichen *n*
f signe *m* de soulignement
r знак *m* подчеркивания; символ *m* подчеркивания

9986 underscoring
d Unterstreichung *f*
f soulignement *m*
r подчеркивание *n*

* **undetermination** → 5029

* **undetermined** → 9980

9987 undirected
d ungerichtet
f non orienté
r ненаправленный; неориентированный

9988 undirected edge
d ungerichtete Kante *f*
f arête *f* non orientée
r ненаправленное ребро *n*

* **undirected graph** → 6276

9989 undirected light
d ungerichtetes Licht *n*
f lumière *f* non orientée
r неориентированный свет *m*

* **undo** → 9991

9990 undo *v*
d rückgängig machen; rückgängig erstellen; den vorherigen Zustand wiederherstellen
f annuler; défaire
r отменять последнее действие

9991 undo[ing]
d Rückgang *m*

f annulation *f*
r возврат *m*; откат *m*; отмена *f* последнего действия

9992 undoing actions
d rückgängige Wirkungen *fpl*
f actions *fpl* d'annulation
r отменяющие действия *npl*; возвратные действия

* **unevenness** → 8215

9993 unfreeze *v*
d auftauen; Fixierung aufheben
f dégeler; décongeler; débloquer
r размораживать; расфиксировать; отменить фиксацию

9994 unfreeze *v* **layers**
d Schichten auftauen
f dégeler des plans; débloquer des calques
r размораживать слои

9995 unfreeze *v* **panes**
d Unterfenster auftauen
f libérer des sous-fenêtres
r размораживать подокна; расфиксировать подокна

9996 ungroup *v*
d Gruppierung aufheben
f dégrouper
r разгруппировать

9997 ungrouped objects
d nichtgruppierte Objekte *npl*
f objets *mpl* dégroupés
r разгруппированные объекты *mpl*

9998 ungula
d Huf *m*
f onglet *m*
r часть *f* тела вращения, заключенная между двумя полуплоскостями, исходящими из оси вращения

9999 uniaxial
d einachsig
f uniaxial; uniaxe
r одноосный

* **unicode** → 10031

10000 Unicode character
d Unicode-Zeichen *n*; Universalcode-Zeichen *n*
f caractère *m* Unicode
r уникодовый символ *m*

10001 Unicode character map
d Unicode-Zeichentabelle *f*

f table *f* de caractères Unicode
r таблица *f* уникодовых символов; таблица символов шрифта Unicode

10002 Unicode character string
 d Unicode-Zeichenkette *f*
 f chaîne *f* de caractères Unicode
 r цепочка *f* уникодовых символов

10003 Unicode font
 d Universalcode-Schrift *f*
 f police *f* Unicode
 r уникодовый фонт *m*

 * **unidentifiable → 9980**

10004 unidirectional; one-directional; one-way
 d unidirektional; einseitig gerichtet; Einweg-; einfach gerichtet
 f à une direction; unidirectionnel
 r однонаправленный; однопроходный

10005 unidirectional dimensioning
 d einseitig gerichtete Dimensionierung *f*
 f cotation *f* à une direction
 r однонаправленное оразмерение *n*

10006 unification
 d Unifikation *f*
 f unification *f*
 r унификация *f*

10007 uniform
 d gleichmäßig; gleichförmig; uniform
 f uniforme
 r равномерный; однородный; однообразный

10008 uniform chromaticity
 d gleichmäßige Farbart *f*; gleichförmige Chromazität *f*
 f chromaticité *f* uniforme
 r однородная цветность *f*; однородный хроматизм *m*

10009 uniform color
 d Standardfarbe *f*
 f couleur *f* uniforme; couleur unie
 r равномерный цвет *m*; стандартный цвет

10010 uniform color space
 d gleichförmiger Farb[en]raum *m*
 f espace *m* chromatique uniforme
 r однородное цветовое пространство *n*

10011 uniform continuity of mapping
 d gleichmäßige Stetigkeit *f* einer Abbildung
 f continuité *f* uniforme d'une application
 r однородная непрерывность *f* отображения

 * **uniform fill → 10012**

10012 uniform fill[ing]
 d gleichmäßige Füllung *f*
 f remplissage *m* uniforme; remplissage uni
 r равномерное заполнение *n*

10013 uniform outline
 d gleichmäßiger Umriss *m*
 f contour *m* uniforme
 r однородный контур *m*; однородное представление *n*; однородный макет *m*

10014 uniform scale
 d gleichmäßige Skala *f*
 f échelle *f* uniforme
 r равномерная шкала *f*

10015 uniform scaling
 d gleichmäßige Skalierung *f*
 f mise *f* à l'échelle uniforme
 r однородное масштабирование *n*

10016 uniform spectrum
 d gleichmäßiges Spektrum *n*
 f spectre *m* uniforme
 r равномерный спектр *m*

10017 uniform surface
 d gleichförmige Fläche *f*
 f surface *f* uniforme
 r однородная поверхность *f*

10018 uniform transparency
 d gleichmäßige Transparenz *f*
 f transparence *f* uniforme
 r равномерная прозрачность *f*

 * **unilateral → 8742**

 * **unilateral surface → 6477**

10019 union
 d Vereinigung *f*
 f [ré]union *f*
 r объединение *n*

10020 union command
 d Vereinigungsbefehl *m*
 f commande *f* d'union
 r команда *f* объединения

10021 unit
 (as a part of construction)
 d Geräteinheit *f*; Block *m*; Baustein *m*
 f unité *f*; bloc *m*; module *m*
 r устройство *n*; блок *m*; модуль *m*

10022 unit
 (as a measure)
 d Einheit *f*; Einer *m*

f unité *f*
r единица *f*

10023 unit circle
d Einheitskreis *m*
f cercle *m* unité
r единичная окружность *f*

10024 unit of length
d Längeneinheit *f*
f unité *f* de longueur
r единица *f* длины

* **unit of measure → 10025**

10025 unit of measure[ment]; measure unit
d Messeinheit *f*
f unité *f* de mesure
r единица *f* измерения; мерная единица

10026 unit point
d Einheitspunkt *m*
f point *m* unitaire
r единичная точка *f*

10027 unit sphere
d Einheitskugel *f*
f sphère *f* unitaire
r единичная сфера *f*

10028 unit tangent vector
d Tangenteneinheitsvektor *m*
f vecteur *m* unitaire tangent
r касательный единичный вектор *m*

10029 unit vector
d Einheitsvektor *m*; Grundvektor *m*;
Koordinateneinheitsvektor *m*
f vecteur *m* unité; vecteur unitaire
r единичный вектор *m*; основной вектор;
орт *m*

* **univalent correspondence → 6481**

10030 universal
d universell; Universal-
f universel
r универсальный; всеобщий

10031 universal code; unicode
d Universalcode *m*
f code *m* universel
r универсальный код *m*

* **universal cone → 5576**

* **universal filter → 283**

10032 universe
d Universum *n*

f univers *m*
r универсальное множество *n*; генеральная
совокупность *f*

* **unlabeled → 10033**

10033 unlabel[l]ed
d nichtetikettiert
f sans label; non étiqueté
r непомеченный

* **unlimited → 1117**

10034 unload; discharge
d Entladung *f*; Entlastung *f*
f déchargement *m*
r разгрузка *f*; разряд *m*

* **unlock → 10037**

10035 unlock *v*; **unblock** *v*
d freigeben; befreien; entsperren
f déverrouiller; débloquer; libérer; ouvrir
r разблокировать

10036 unlocked
d freigegeben; entsperrt
f unverrouillé; débloqué
r разблокированный

10037 unlock[ing]; unblock[ing]
d Entsperrung *f*; Entsperren *n*; Entblockung *f*
f déverrouillage *m*; déblocage *m*
r снятие *n* блокировки; разблокирование *n*;
деблокирование *n*

10038 unmarked
d nichtmarkiert; unbezeichnet;
nichtgekennzeichnet
f sans marque; non marqué
r немаркированный

10039 unmask *v*
d demaskieren
f démasquer
r снимать маску; размаскировать

10040 unmoved
d unbeweglich; unbewegt; ungerührt
f non mouvant
r неперемещаемый

* **unnamed block → 438**

* **unpack → 10043**

10041 unpack *v*
d auspacken; entpacken

f déballer; dépaqueter
r распаковывать

10042 unpacked
  d entpackt
  f dépaqueté
  r распакованный

10043 unpack[ing] .
  d Entpacken *n*
  f dépaquetage *m*
  r распаковка *f*

10044 unrealistic
  d unrealistisch
  f non réaliste
  r нереалистический

10045 unrendered texture
  (texture that has not yet been converted into a bitmap)
  d nichtgerenderte Textur *f*
  f texture *f* non rendu
  r нетонированная текстура *f*

10046 unrendered texture design
  d Design *n* der nichtgerenderten Textur
  f dessin *m* de texture non rendu
  r дизайн *m* нетонированной текстуры

10047 unrounded
  d nichtgerundet; nichtabgerundet
  f non arrondi
  r неокругленный

10048 unsaved change
  d nichterlöste Änderung *f*
  f change *m* non archivé
  r неархивированная перемена *f*

10049 unscaled
  d nichtskaliert
  f sans échelle
  r немасштабированный

10050 unselected
  d nichtausgewählt; ungewählt
  f non sélectionné
  r невыбранный

10051 unselected grips
  d nichtausgewählte Griffe *mpl*
  f poignées *fpl* non sélectionnées
  r невыбранные захваты *mpl*

  * **unsharp** → 4088

10052 unsharp contour
  d unscharfe Kontur *f*
  f contour *m* flou
  r нечеткий контур *m*

  * **unsharped mask** → 446

10053 unsharp filter
  d unscharfer Filter *m*
  f filtre *m* non distinct
  r нерезкий фильтр *m*

10054 unsharp image
  d unscharfes Bild *n*
  f image *f* non distincte
  r нечеткое изображение *n*; нерезкое изображение

  * **unsharp mask** → 446

  * **unstable** → 5132

  * **unsymmetric** → 10055

10055 unsymmetric[al]; non-symmetric[al]
  d unsymmetrisch
  f non symétrique
  r несимметрический; несимметричный

10056 unsymmetry
  d Unsymmetrie *f*
  f non-symétrie *f*
  r отсутствие *n* симметрии

10057 untrace *v*
  d Ablaufverfolgung abschalten
  f invalider le suivi
  r сбрасывать режим прослеживания; отбрасывать прослеживание

10058 untraceable
  d unauffindbar
  f introuvable
  r непрослеживаемый

10059 unwanted feature
  d unerwünschtes Merkmal *n*
  f particularité *f* non désirée; signe *m* non désiré
  r нежелательный признак *m*

10060 unwanted noise
  d Parasitenrauschen *n*
  f bruit *m* parasite; bruit non désiré
  r нежелательный шум *m*; нежелательная помеха *f*

  * **unzoom** *v* → 10533

  * **unzoom** → 10532

  * **up** → 10079

10061 updatable
  d aktualisierbar; veränderlich; änderbar

f actualisable
r обновляемый; скорректированный; регенерируемый

10062 updatable drawing
d aktualisierbare Zeichnung *f*
f dessin *m* actualisable
r обновляемый чертеж *m*

10063 update *v*
d aktualisieren; ändern
f actualiser
r обновлять; актуализировать; модернизировать

* update → 10067

10064 update cursor
d Aktualisierungscursor *m*
f curseur *m* d'actualisation
r курсор *m* обновления

10065 update method
d Aktualisierungsmethode *f*
f méthode *f* d'actualisation
r метод *m* обновления

10066 update region
d aktualisierte Region *f*; aktualisiertes Gebiet *n*
f région *f* de mise à jour
r актуализированный регион *m*

10067 updating; update
d Aktualisierung *f*; Änderung *f*
f mise *f* à jour; mise au niveau; actualisation *f*
r корректировка *f*; обновление *n*; актуализация *f*; модернизация *f*

10068 up-down bars
d Vorwärts-Rückwärts-Streifen *mpl*
f barres *fpl* réversibles
r реверсивные полосы *fpl*

10069 uppercase alphabet
d Großbuchstabenalphabet *n*
f alphabet *m* du registre supérieur
r алфавит *m* верхнего регистра

10070 uppercase letter; capital letter
d Großbuchstabe *m*
f lettre *f* du registre supérieur; lettre majuscule; majuscule *f*
r буква *f* верхнего регистра; прописная буква; большая буква; заглавная буква

10071 upper envelope
d obere Hülle *f*
f enveloppe *f* supérieure
r верхняя огибающая *f*

10072 upper half-plane
d obere Halbebene *f*
f demi-plan *m* supérieur
r верхняя полуплоскость *f*

10073 upper left corner
d Ecke *f* oben links
f coin *m* à gauche supérieur
r верхний левый угол *m*

10074 upper limit; limit superior; superior limit; top margin
d obere Grenze *f*
f limite *f* supérieure; marge *f* du haut
r верхний предел *m*; верхняя грань *f*

10075 upper right corner
d Ecke *f* oben rechts
f coin *m* à l'endroit supérieur
r верхний правый угол *m*

10076 upper surface
d Deckfläche *f*
f surface *f* à haut
r верхнее основание *n*

* upright format → 7335

* upright image → 3521

10077 up scroll arrow
d Bildlaufpfeil *m* aufwärts
f flèche *f* de défilement vertical
r стрелка *f* прокрутки вверх

* upside-down image → 8124

* upside image → 8124

10078 upside view
d umgekehrte Ansicht *f*
f vue *f* de hausse; vue renversée
r инвертированный вид *m*

* uptime → 3330

* upward → 10079

10079 upward[s]; up
d nach oben
f vers le haut
r вверх

* usage → 10080

10080 use; utilization; usage; using
d Benutzung *f*; Nutzung *f*; Auslastung *f*
f usage *m*; utilisation *f*
r пользование *n*; употребление *n*

10081 user; consumer
- *d* Benutzer *m*; Anwender *m*; Nutzer *m*
- *f* utilisateur *m*; usager *m*
- *r* пользователь *m*; потребитель *m*

10082 user arrow
- *d* Benutzerpfeil *m*; benutzerbestimmter Pfeil *m*
- *f* flèche *f* personnalisée
- *r* заказная стрелка *f*

10083 user coordinate
- *d* Anwenderkoordinate *f*
- *f* coordonnée *f* d'utilisateur
- *r* координата *f* пользователя

10084 user coordinate system; UCS
- *d* Benutzerkoordinatensystem *n*
- *f* système *m* de coordonnées utilisateur; SCU
- *r* координатная система *f* пользователя; пользовательская система координат

10085 user-defined
- *d* benutzerdefiniert
- *f* défini par l'utilisateur
- *r* определяемый пользователем

10086 user[-defined] library
- *d* Anwenderbibliothek *f*
- *f* bibliothèque *f* de l'utilisateur
- *r* библиотека *f* пользователя

10087 user-dependent
- *d* benutzerabhängig
- *f* dépendant par utilisateur
- *r* зависимый от пользователя

10088 user-dependent parameter
- *d* benutzerabhängiger Parameter *m*
- *f* paramètre *m* dépendant de l'utilisateur
- *r* параметр *m*, зависимый от пользователя

10089 user dimension text
- *d* Benutzerdimensionstext *m*
- *f* texte *m* de cotation personnalisé
- *r* заказной оразмерительный текст *m*

10090 user-input function
- *d* Benutzereingangsfunktion *f*
- *f* fonction *f* d'entrée de l'utilisateur
- *r* функция *f* пользовательского ввода

* **user library** → 10086

10091 user options
- *d* Anwenderoptionen *fpl*
- *f* options *fpl* d'utilisateur
- *r* возможности *fpl*, доступные для пользователя

10092 user-positioned text
- *d* vom Benutzer positionierter Text *m*
- *f* texte *m* positionné par utilisateur
- *r* текст *m*, позиционированный пользователем

* **using** → 10080

* **utility** → 8554

10093 utility function
- *d* Nutzenfunktion *f*; Dienstfunktion *f*
- *f* fonction *f* d'utilité
- *r* утилитная функция *f*; служебная функция

* **utility program** → 8554

* **utilization** → 10080

* **UV** → 9970

V

* **vacant** → 990

* **vague** → 313

* **vagueness** → 312

10094 valid
  d gültig
  f valable; valide
  r правильный; справедливый; верный;
     истинный

* **validate** *v* → 2036

10095 valid data; clean data
  d gültige Daten *npl*; fehlerlose Daten
  f données *fpl* valables; données valides;
     données pures
  r правильные данные *npl*; достоверные
     данные

* **valuation** → 3537

10096 valuator
  d Wertgeber *m*
  f comparateur *m*
  r устройство *n* ввода числа

10097 value
  d Wert *m*
  f valeur *f*
  r значение *n*

10098 value axes
  d Wertachsen *fpl*
  f axes *mpl* des valeurs
  r оси *fpl* значений

* **vanishing line** → 6208

* **vanishing plane** → 6209

* **vanishing point** → 6210

* **vantage point** → 7224

10099 variability
  d Variabilität *f*
  f variabilité *f*
  r изменчивость *f*; разнообразие *n*

10100 variable
  d Variable *f*; Veränderliche *f*

  f variable *f*
  r переменная *f*

10101 variable attribute
  d veränderliches Attribut *n*
  f attribut *m* variable
  r переменный атрибут *m*

10102 variable coefficient
  d veränderlicher Faktor *m*
  f coefficient *m* variable
  r переменный коэффициент *m*

10103 variable frequency display; VFD
  d Variable-Frequenz-Monitor *m*; VFD
  f afficheur *m* de fréquence variable
  r дисплей *m* переменной частоты

10104 variable units
  d veränderliche Einheiten *fpl*
  f unités *fpl* variables
  r переменные единицы *fpl*

10105 variance
  d Varianz *f*
  f variance *f*
  r [среднее] отклонение *n*

10106 variant
  d Variante *f*
  f variante *f*
  r вариант *m*

10107 variation
  d Variation *f*
  f variation *f*
  r вариация *f*

10108 variation of ornament
  d Ornamentvariation *f*
  f variation *f* d'ornement
  r вариация *f* орнамента

* **variety** → 5774

* **VDU** → 10322

* **VE** → 10274

* **vector** → 10122

10109 vector
  d Vektor *m*
  f vecteur *m*
  r вектор *m*

10110 vector[-based] image; vector pattern
  d vektorisiertes Bild *n*; Vektorbild *n*
  f image *f* vectorielle
  r векторное изображение *n*

10111 vector calculus
   d Vektorrechnung *f*
   f calcul *m* vectoriel
   r векторное исчисление *n*

   * **vector depth** → 10126

10112 vector diagram
   d Vektordiagramm *n*
   f diagramme *m* vectoriel
   r векторная диаграмма *f*

10113 vector direction
   d Vektor-Richtung *f*
   f direction *f* de vecteur
   r направление *n* вектора

10114 vector drawing
   d Vektor-Zeichnung *f*
   f dessin *m* vectoriel
   r векторный рисунок *m*; векторный
      чертеж *m*

10115 vector expression
   d Vektorausdruck *m*
   f expression *f* vectorielle
   r векторное выражение *n*

10116 vector file
   d Vektor-Datei *f*
   f fichier *m* vectoriel
   r векторный файл *m*

10117 vector file format
   d Vektor-Dateiformat *n*
   f format *m* de fichier vectoriel
   r формат *m* векторного файла

10118 vector filter
   d Vektorfilter *m*
   f filtre *m* vectoriel
   r векторный фильтр *m*

   * **vector font** → 8278

10119 vector format
   d Vektorformat *n*
   f format *m* vectoriel
   r векторный формат *m*

10120 vector generator
   d Vektorgenerator *m*
   f générateur *m* de vecteurs
   r генератор *m* векторов

10121 vector graphics; scalable graphics
   d Vektorgrafik *f*
   f graphique *m* vectoriel
   r векторная графика *f*

10122 vector[ial]
   d vektoriell; Vektor-
   f vectoriel
   r векторный

10123 vectorial color space
   d Vektorraum *m* der Farben; Vektorraum der
      Farbvalenzen
   f espace *m* chromatique vectoriel
   r векторное цветовое пространство *n*

   * **vector image** → 10110

10124 vector irradiance
   d Vektor-Beleuchtungsdichte *f*
   f irradiance *f* vectorielle
   r векторная облученность *f*

10125 vectorization
   d Vektorisierung *f*
   f vectorisation *f*
   r векторизация *f*

10126 vector length; vector depth
   d Vektorlänge *f*
   f longueur *f* de vecteur
   r размерность *f* вектора; длина *f* вектора

10127 vector line
   d Vektorlinie *f*
   f ligne *f* de vecteur
   r векторная линия *f*

10128 vector memory
   d Vektorspeicher *m*
   f mémoire *f* vectorielle
   r векторная память *f*

10129 vector model
   d Vektormodell *n*
   f modèle *m* vectoriel
   r векторная модель *f*

10130 vector normal
   d Vektornormale *f*
   f normale *f* au vecteur
   r векторная нормаль *f*

   * **vector pattern** → 10110

10131 vector pattern fill
   d Vektormusterfüllung *f*
   f remplissage *m* d'image vectorielle
   r закрашивание *n* векторного изображения

10132 vector plotting
   d Vektorplotten *n*; grafische
      Vektordarstellung *f*
   f traçage *m* vectoriel
   r векторное вычерчивание *n* (графиков)

10133 vector processor
 d Vektorprozessor *m*
 f processeur *m* vecteur
 r векторный процессор *m*

10134 vector product
 d Vektorprodukt *n*
 f produit *m* vectoriel
 r векторное произведение *n*

10135 vector product format
 d Format *n* des Vektorprodukts
 f format *m* de produit vectoriel
 r формат *m* векторного произведения

10136 vector quantization
 d Vektor-Quantisierung *f*
 f quantification *f* de vecteur
 r векторная квантизация *f*; векторное
    квантование *n*

10137 vector representation
 d Vektordarstellung *f*
 f représentation *f* vectorielle
 r векторное представление *n*

 * **vector rotating in a circular motion →**
   8199

 * **vector rotation → 2341**

 * **vector space → 5605**

10138 vector to raster conversion
 d Vektor-Raster-Konvertierung *f*
 f conversion *f* de vecteur en rastre
 r векторно-растровое преобразование *n*

 * **velocity → 9029**

10139 velocity direction
 d Geschwindigkeitsrichtung *f*
 f direction *f* de la vélocité
 r направление *n* скорости

10140 velocity graph
 d Graph *m* der Geschwindigkeit
 f graphe *m* de vélocité
 r граф *m* скорости

10141 VE network
 d Netzwerk *n* der Virtualumgebung
 f réseau *m* d'environnement virtuel
 r сеть *f* виртуального окружения

 * **verb → 1890**

 * **verify *v* → 1450**

10142 version; release

 d Ausgabe *f*; Version *f*
 f version *f*; livraison *f*
 r выпуск *m*; версия *f*; редакция *f*

10143 version number
 d Versionsnummer *f*
 f numéro *m* de version
 r номер *m* версии

 * **vertex → 6220**

10144 vertex
    (of a solid angle)
 d Ecke *f*; Eckpunkt *m*
 f sommet *m*
 r вершина *f*

10145 vertex; apex
    (of a solid or a curve)
 d Spitze *f*
 f sommet *m*; apex *m*
 r вершина *f*

 * **vertex angles → 10156**

10146 vertex color
 d Knotenfarbe *f*
 f couleur *f* de sommet
 r цвет *m* вершины

10147 vertex deletion
 d Knoten[punkt]beseitigung *f*
 f suppression *f* de sommet
 r удаление *n* вершины

10148 vertex normal
 d Knotennormale *f*
 f normale *f* au sommet
 r нормаль *f* к вершине

 * **vertex of a bundle of planes → 1358**

10149 vertex of a cone; apex of a cone
 d Kegelspitze *f*
 f sommet *m* d'un cône
 r вершина *f* конуса

10150 vertex of a curve; apex of a curve
 d Scheitelpunkt *m* einer Kurve
 f sommet *m* d'une courbe
 r вершина *f* кривой

 * **vertex of a graph → 6224**

10151 vertex of an angle; angle vertex
 d Eckpunkt *m* eines Winkels; Winkelspitze *f*;
    Winkelecke *f*
 f sommet *m* d'un angle
 r вершина *f* угла

10152 vertex of a polygon
   d Ecke *f* eines Polygons
   f sommet *m* d'un polygone
   r вершина *f* многоугольника

   * **vertex of a sheaf of lines** → 1357

10153 vertical
   d Lotlinie *f*; Lot *n*; Senkrechte *f*; senkrechte
      Gerade *f*
   f verticale *f*
   r вертикаль *f*

10154 vertical *adj*
   d vertikal; senkrecht
   f vertical
   r вертикальный

10155 vertical aberration; vertical deflection
   d Vertikalablenkung *f*; vertikale Ablenkung *f*
   f aberration *f* verticale; déflexion *f* verticale
   r вертикальное отклонение *n*

   * **vertical alignment** → 10174

10156 vertical angles; vertex angles; apex angles;
   [vertically] opposite angles
   d Scheitelwinkel *mpl*; Spitzenwinkel *mpl*
   f angles *mpl* opposés par le sommet; angles au
      sommet
   r вертикальные углы *mpl*; углы при вершине

10157 vertical asymptote
   d vertikale Asymptote *f*
   f asymptote *f* verticale
   r вертикальная асимптота *f*

10158 vertical axis
   d vertikale Achse *f*; senkrechte Achse
   f axe *m* vertical
   r вертикальная ось *f*

10159 vertical bar
   (|)
   d vertikaler Strich *m*
   f barre *f* verticale
   r вертикальная черта *f*

   * **vertical-bar chart** → 10160

10160 vertical-bar diagram; vertical-bar chart;
   vertical-bar graph
   d vertikales Balkendiagramm *n*; senkrechtes
      Balkendiagramm
   f diagramme *m* à barres verticaux; graphique *m*
      à barres verticaux
   r вертикальная столбиковая диаграмма *f*

   * **vertical-bar graph** → 10160

10161 vertical collimation
   d Vertikalkollimation *f*
   f collimation *f* verticale
   r вертикальная коллимация *f*

10162 vertical constraint
   (in plotter)
   d vertikale Begrenzung *f*
   f contrainte *f* verticale
   r вертикальная ограничительная линия *f*

10163 vertical cylinder
   d Vertikalzylinder *m*
   f cylindre *m* vertical
   r вертикальный цилиндр *m*

10164 vertical datum
   d Vertikaldatum *n*
   f datum *m* vertical; repère *m* vertical
   r вертикальное начало *n* отсчета

   * **vertical deflection** → 10155

10165 vertical dimension
   d Vertikaldimension *f*
   f cotation *f* verticale; cote *f* verticale
   r вертикальное оразмерение *n*

10166 vertical dimension line
   d vertikale Dimensionslinie *f*
   f trait *m* de cote verticale
   r вертикальная размерная линия *f*

10167 vertical displacement; vertical shift[ing]
   d vertikale Verschiebung *f*
   f déplacement *m* vertical
   r вертикальное смещение *n*

10168 vertical flyback time
   d Vertikal-Rücklaufzeit *f*
   f temps *m* de retrait vertical
   r время *n* обратного вертикального хода

   * **vertical format** → 7335

10169 vertical frequency
   (of a screen)
   d vertikale Frequenz *f*
   f fréquence *f* verticale
   r вертикальная частота *f*

10170 vertical guideline
   d vertikale Richtlinie *f*
   f ligne *f* directrice verticale; ligne de conduite
      verticale
   r вертикальная направляющая *f*

10171 vertical interpolation
   d vertikale Interpolation *f*

f interpolation *f* verticale
r вертикальная интерполяция *f*

10172 vertical interpolation processor
  d Vertikal-Interpolation-Prozessor *m*
  f processeur *m* d'interpolation verticale
  r процессор *m* вертикальной интерполяции

10173 vertical interpolator
  d vertikaler Interpolator *m*
  f interpolateur *m* vertical
  r вертикальный интерполятор *m*

10174 vertical justification; vertical alignment
  d vertikale Ausrichtung *f*
  f alignement *m* vertical; justification *f* verticale
  r вертикальное выравнивание *n*

10175 vertical line
  d vertikale Linie *f*
  f ligne *f* verticale
  r вертикальная линия *f*

  * **vertical line spacing → 5205**

10176 vertical list box
  d vertikales Listenfeld *n*
  f zone *f* de liste déroulante verticale
  r вертикальное поле *n* списка

  * **vertically opposite angles → 10156**

10177 vertical plane
  d senkrechte Ebene *f*
  f plan *m* vertical
  r вертикальная плоскость *f*

10178 vertical point
  d vertikaler Zeiger *m*
  f pointeur *m* vertical
  r вертикальный указатель *m*

10179 vertical profile
  d Höhenprofil *n*
  f profil *m* vertical
  r высотный профиль *m*

10180 vertical projection; second projection
  d Vertikalprojektion *f*; Aufriss *m*; zweite Projektion *f*
  f projection *f* verticale; seconde projection; coupe *f* verticale
  r вертикальная проекция *f*; вторая проекция; вертикальный разрез *m*

10181 vertical projection plane; second plane of projection
  d Vertikalebene *f*; Aufrissebene *f*; Aufrisstafel *f*; zweite Projektionsebene *f*
  f plan *m* de projection vertical

r плоскость *f* вертикальной проекции

10182 vertical resolution
  d Vertikalauflösungsvermögen *n*
  f résolution *f* verticale
  r вертикальная разрешающая способность *f*

10183 vertical retrace
  d vertikaler Rücklauf *m*
  f retour *m* du spot vertical
  r обратный ход *m* кадровой развертки; обратный ход по кадру; вертикальный обратный ход

10184 vertical ruler
  d vertikales Lineal *n*
  f règle *f* verticale
  r вертикальная измерительная линейка *f*

  * **vertical scale → 8297**

10185 vertical scanning
  d vertikale Abtastung *f*
  f balayage *m* vertical; base *f* de temps d'image
  r вертикальная развертка *f*; кадровая развертка

  * **vertical screen partitioning → 10186**

10186 vertical screen split; vertical screen partitioning
  d vertikale Teilung *f* des Bildschirms
  f splittage *m* d'écran vertical
  r вертикальное расщепление *n* экрана

  * **vertical scroll → 10188**

10187 vertical scroll bar; vertical scroll line
  d vertikale Bildlaufleiste *f*; vertikaler Rollbalken *m*; vertikaler Verschiebenbalken *m*
  f barre *f* de défilement verticale; barre de déplacement verticale
  r вертикальная линейка *f* просмотра

10188 vertical scroll[ing]
  (of screen image)
  d vertikale Bild[schirmzeilen]verschiebung *f*
  f défilement *m* vertical; déroulement *m* vertical
  r вертикальная прокрутка *f*; вертикальное прокручивание *n*

  * **vertical scroll line → 10187**

10189 vertical shading
  d vertikale Schattierung *f*
  f ombrage *m* vertical
  r вертикальное затенение *n*

  * **vertical shift → 10167**

* **vertical shifting** → 10167

10190 vertical spacing
d vertikaler Abstand *m*
f espacement *m* vertical
r вертикальное расстояние *n*

10191 vertical split bar
d vertikaler Fensterteiler *m*
f barre *f* de fractionnement verticale
r вертикальная линейка *f* разбиения;
вертикальная разделительная линейка

* **vertical tab** → 10192

10192 vertical tab[ulation character]
d Vertikaleinstellungszeichen *n*; vertikaler
Tabulator *m*
f caractère *m* de tabulation verticale
r знак *m* вертикальной табуляции

10193 vertical toolbar
d vertikaler Werkzeugstreifen *m*
f barre *f* d'outils verticale
r вертикальная панель *f* инструментов

10194 vertical trace line; second trace line
(of a plane)
d vertikale Spurlinie *f*, zweite Spurlinie
f trace *f* verticale; deuxième trace
r вертикальный след *m* плоскости

10195 vertical visual selector
d vertikales visuelles Auswahlfeld *n*
f sélecteur *m* visuel vertical
r вертикальный визуальный селектор *m*

10196 vertices of polyline
d Knotenpunkte *mpl* der Polylinie
f sommets *mpl* de polyligne
r вершины *fpl* полилинии

10197 very fine grain
d Ultrafeinkorn *n*
f grain *m* ultra-fin
r ультрамелкозернистость *f*

* **VFD** → 10103

* **VGA output connector** → 3723

* **vicinity** → 7611

10198 video acceleration
d Videobeschleunigung *f*
f accélération *f* vidéo
r видеоускорение *n*

* **video accelerator** → 10199

10199 video accelerator [card]
d Videobeschleuniger *m*
f carte *f* vidéo accélérée; carte accélératrice;
accélérateur *m* vidéo
r видео-ускоритель *m*; видео-акселератор *m*;
плата *f* видео-ускорителя

* **video amplifier** → 4889

10200 video applications
d Videoanwendungen *fpl*
f vidéo-applications *fpl*
r видео-приложения *npl*

10201 video camera
d Videokamera *f*
f vidéocaméra *f*; caméra *f* vidéo
r видеокамера *f*

10202 video capture
d Videosammlung *f*
f vidéocapture *f*
r видеоулавливание *n*; видеозахват *m*

* **videocard** → 10208

* **videocasque** → 4552

10203 videoclip
d Videoclip *n*
f vidéoclip *m*; clip *m* vidéo
r видеоклип *m*

* **video coding** → 10209

* **videocommunication** → 10319

10204 video compatibility
d Videoverträglichkeit *f*
f vidéo-compatibilité *f*
r видеосовместимость *f*

10205 video conference
d Videokonferenz *f*
f vidéoconférence *f*
r видеоконференция *f*

10206 video digitizer
d Video-Digitalisierer *m*
f digitaliseur *m* vidéo
r устройство *n* оцифровки
видеоизображений

* **videodisk** → 6545

10207 video display
d Videobildschirm *m*
f vidéo-écran *m*
r видеодисплей *m*

* **video display board** → 10208

10208 video display card; video display board; display card; videocard; graphic[s] card
d Videokarte *f*; Grafikkarte *f*
f carte *f* vidéo; carte graphique
r видеокарта *f*; видеоплата *f*; графическая плата *f*; графическая карта *f*

10209 video [en]coding
d Videocodierung *f*
f vidéocodage *m*; codage *m* vidéo
r видеокодирование *n*

10210 video file
d Videodatei *f*
f fichier *m* vidéo
r видео-файл *m*

10211 videogame
d Videospiel *n*
f jeu *m* vidéo
r видеоигра *f*

* **videogram** → 665

10212 videographics
d Videografik *f*
f graphique *m* vidéo
r видеографика *f*

* **video hard copy unit** → 7027

* **video image** → 10219

10213 video input
d Videoeingang *m*
f entrée *f* vidéo
r вход *m* видеоданных

10214 video lines
d Videolinien *fpl*
f vidéo-lignes *fpl*
r видеолинии *fpl*

10215 video logic
d Videologik *f*
f logique *f* vidéo
r видео-логика *f*

10216 video memory
d Videospeicher *m*
f mémoire *f* vidéo
r видео-память *f*

10217 video on the Web
d Video *n* auf Web
f vidéo *m* sur le Web
r видео *n* в Web

10218 video output
d Videoausgang *m*
f sortie *f* vidéo
r выход *m* видеоданных

10219 video picture; video image
d Fernsehbild *n*; Videobild *n*
f image *f* vidéo
r видеоизображение *n*

10220 video printer
d Videodrucker *m*
f vidéo-imprimante *f*; imprimante *f* vidéo
r видеопринтер *m*

* **videoscan document reader** → 6546

10221 video scanner
d Bildscanner *m*
f scanner *m* vidéo
r видео-сканер *m*

10222 video signal
d Videosignal *n*
f signal *m* vidéo
r видеосигнал *m*

10223 videotexture
d Videotextur *f*
f vidéo-texture *f*
r видео-текстура *f*

10224 video wall
d Videowand *f*
f mur *m* vidéo
r видеостена *f*

10225 videoware
d Videosoftware *f*
f vidéociel *m*; logiciel *m* vidéo
r визуальное программное обеспечение *n*

10226 view
d Ansicht *f*; Ausblick *m*
f vue *f*; affichage *m*
r вид *m*; взгляд *m*

* **view** → 8076

10227 view adjustment
d Ansichteinstellung *f*
f ajustement *m* de vue
r настройка *f* представления

10228 view box
d Ansicht-Kasten *m*
f boîte *f* de vue
r ящик *m* представления

10229 view control
d Ansichtsteuerung *f*

f contrôle *m* de vue
r управление *n* представлением

10230 view correlation
  d Ansichtkorrelation *f*
  f corrélation *f* de vue
  r корреляция *f* представления

10231 view description
  d Ansicht-Beschreibung *f*
  f description *f* de vue
  r описание *n* представления

  * **viewer** → 1161, 6443

  * **viewing** → 10326

  * **viewing angle** → 389

10232 viewing direction
  d Visualisierungsrichtung *f*
  f direction *f* de visionnement
  r направление *n* выдавливания

10233 viewing distance
  d Augenabstand *m* der Visualisierung
  f distance *f* de visionnement
  r расстояние *n* визуализации

10234 viewing messages
  d Visualisierungsmeldungen *fpl*
  f messages *mpl* de visionnement
  r сообщения *npl* о выдавливании

10235 viewing mode
  d Visualisierungsmodus *m*
  f mode *m* de visionnement
  r режим *m* визуализации

10236 viewing options
  d Ansicht[s]optionen *fpl*
  f options *fpl* de visionnement
  r опции *fpl* визуализации

10237 viewing plane; viewplane
  d Ansicht[s]ebene *f*
  f plan *m* de visionnement; plan de vue
  r плоскость *f* представления

10238 viewing plane arrow
  d Pfeil *m* der Ansicht[s]ebene
  f flèche *f* de plan de vue
  r стрелка *f* к плоскости представления

  * **viewing transformation** → 10444

10239 view manager
  d Ansicht-Manager *m*
  f gestionnaire *m* de vues
  r менажер *m* представлений

10240 view menu items
  d Ansicht[s]menüelemente *npl*
  f éléments *mpl* de menu de représentation
  r элементы *mpl* меню представления

10241 view model
  d Ansicht[s]modell *n*
  f modèle *m* de vue
  r модель *f* представления

10242 view model database
  d Datenbasis *f* des Ansicht[s]modells
  f base *f* de données de modèles de vues
  r база *f* данных моделей представления

10243 view object
  d Ansicht[s]objekt *n*
  f objet *m* de vue
  r объект *m* представления

10244 view option
  d Darstellungsoption *f*; Anzeigeoption *f*
  f option *f* de vue
  r опция *f* представления

  * **viewplane** → 10237

10245 viewplane dependent drag
  d Ziehen *n* auf der Ansichtsebene
  f déplacement *m* [de l'image] en fonction du plan de vue
  r таскание *n* по плоскости представления

10246 viewplane direction
  d Ansicht[s]ebenenrichtung *f*
  f direction *f* de plan de vue
  r направление *n* плоскости представления

  * **viewpoint** → 7225

10247 viewpoint moving
  d Blickpunkt-Verschiebung *f*
  f mouvement *m* de point de vue
  r перемещение *n* точки зрения

10248 viewport; view window
  d Ansicht[s]fenster *n*; Darstellungsfeld *n*
  f clôture *f*; fenêtre *f* de vue
  r область *f* просмотра; окно *n* просмотра; видовой экран *m*

10249 viewport configuration
  d Ansicht[s]fenster-Konfiguration *f*
  f configuration *f* de clôture
  r конфигурация *f* области просмотра

10250 viewport identification number
  d Ansicht[s]fenster-Identifikationsnummer *f*
  f numéro *m* d'identification de clôture
  r идентификационный номер *m* видового экрана

10251 viewport layer
  d Ansicht[s]fensterebene *f*
  f plan *m* de clôture
  r слой *m* области просмотра; слой видового
      экрана

10252 viewport object
  d Ansicht[s]fensterobjekt *n*
  f objet *m* clôture
  r объект *m* типа области просмотра

10253 viewport scale factor
  d Ansicht[s]fenster-Skalenfaktor *m*
  f facteur *m* d'échelle de clôture
  r масштабный фактор *m* области просмотра;
      масштабный коэффициент *m* видового
      экрана

10254 viewports collection
  d Ansicht[s]fenstersammlung *f*
  f collection *f* de clôtures
  r коллекция *f* областей просмотра

10255 view property
  d Ansicht[s]eigenschaft *f*
  f caractéristique *f* de vue
  r признак *m* вида; свойство *n* представления

10256 view quality
  d Ansicht[s]qualität *f*
  f qualité *f* de vue
  r качество *n* представления

10257 view selection
  d Ansicht[s]auswahl *f*
  f sélection *f* de vue
  r выбор *n* представления

10258 view sphere
  d Ansicht[s]kugel *f*
  f sphère *f* de vue
  r сфера *f* представления

10259 view volume
  d Ansicht[s]volumen *n*
  f volume *m* de vue
  r объем *m* представления

  * **view window** → **10248**

10260 vignette
  d Vignette *f*
  f vignette *f*
  r виньетка *f*

10261 vignette effect
  d Vignetteneffekt *m*
  f effet *m* de vignette; effet de lucarne
  r эффект *m* виньетки

10262 vignetting
  d Vignettierung *f*
  f vignettage *m*
  r образование *n* виньеток

10263 violation
  d Verletzung *f*
  f violation *f*
  r повреждение *n*; нарушение *n*

10264 virtual
  d virtuell
  f virtuel
  r виртуальный

10265 virtual actor
  d virtueller Akteur *m*
  f acteur *m* virtuel
  r виртуальный актор *m*

10266 virtual agent
  d virtueller Agent *m*
  f agent *m* virtuel
  r виртуальный агент *m*

10267 virtual architecture
  d virtuelle Architektur *f*
  f architecture *f* virtuelle
  r виртуальная архитектура *f*

10268 virtual arm
  d virtueller Arm *m*
  f aiguille *f* virtuelle
  r виртуальная ручка *f*; виртуальный рычаг *m*

10269 virtual art
  d virtuelle Kunst *f*
  f art *m* virtuel
  r виртуальное искусство *n*

10270 virtual camera
  d virtuelle Kamera *f*
  f caméra *f* virtuelle
  r виртуальная камера *f*

10271 virtual community
  d virtuelle Gemeinschaft *f*
  f communauté *f* virtuelle
  r виртуальное общество *n*

10272 virtual creatures
  d virtuelle Schöpfungen *fpl*
  f créatures *fpl* virtuelles
  r виртуальные создания *npl*

10273 virtual 3D environment
  d virtuelle 3D-Umgebung *f*
  f environnement *m* virtuel 3D
  r виртуальное 3D пространство *n*

10274 virtual environment; VE
   d virtuelle Umgebung *f*
   f environnement *m* virtuel
   r виртуальная среда *f*

10275 virtual environment interface
   d Schnittstelle *f* der virtuellen Umgebung
   f interface *f* d'environnement virtuel
   r интерфейс *m* виртуального пространства

10276 virtual fashion
   d virtuelle Mode *f*; virtueller Schnitt *m*
   f mode *f* virtuelle
   r виртуальная мода *f*

10277 virtual hand
   d virtuelle Hand *f*
   f main *f* virtuelle
   r виртуальная рука *f*

10278 virtual human
   d virtueller Mensch *m*
   f homme *m* virtuel
   r виртуальный человек *m*

10279 virtual imagery
   d virtuelle Abbildung *f*
   f imagerie *f* virtuelle
   r виртуальные изображения *npl*

10280 virtualization
   d Virtualisierung *f*
   f virtualisation *f*
   r виртуализация *f*

10281 virtual line
   d virtuelle Linie *f*
   f droite *f* virtuelle
   r виртуальная линия *f*

10282 virtual mannequin
   d virtuelle Modellpuppe *f*
   f mannequin *m* virtuel
   r виртуальный манекен *m*

10283 virtual mark
   d virtuelle Marke *f*
   f marque *f* virtuelle
   r виртуальная метка *f*

10284 virtual memory
   d virtueller Speicher *m*
   f mémoire *f* virtuelle
   r виртуальная память *f*

10285 virtual model
   d virtuelles Modell *n*
   f modèle *m* virtuel
   r виртуальная модель *f*

10286 virtual pen
   d virtueller Stift *m*
   f crayon *m* virtuel
   r виртуальный карандаш *m*

10287 virtual prototype
   d virtueller Prototyp *m*
   f prototype *m* virtuel
   r виртуальный прототип *m*

* **virtual pushbutton** → 5536

10288 virtual reality; VR
   d virtuelle Realität *f*
   f réalité *f* virtuelle; RV
   r виртуальная реальность *f*

* **virtual reality language** → 10289

10289 virtual reality [modeling] language; VRML
   d Sprache *f* der Modellierung der virtuellen Realität
   f langage *m* de modélisation de la réalité virtuelle
   r язык *m* моделирования виртуальной реальности

10290 virtual representation
   d virtuelle Darstellung *f*
   f représentation *f* virtuelle
   r виртуальное представление *n*

10291 virtual space
   d virtueller Raum *m*
   f espace *m* virtuel
   r виртуальное пространство *n*

10292 virtual stereoscopic image
   d virtuelles stereoskopisches Bild *n*
   f image *f* stéréoscopique virtuelle
   r виртуальное стереоскопическое изображение *n*

10293 virtual studio
   d virtuelles Studio *n*
   f studio *m* virtuel
   r виртуальная студия *f*

10294 virtual surface
   d virtuelle Fläche *f*
   f surface *f* virtuelle
   r виртуальная поверхность *f*

10295 virtual trackball
   d virtuelle Rollkugel *f*
   f boule *f* de commande virtuelle
   r виртуальный шаровой указатель *m*

10296 virtual vision
   d virtuelle Vision *f*; virtuelles Sehen *n*

f vision *f* virtuelle
r виртуальное зрение *n*

10297 virtual world
   d virtuelle Welt *f*
   f monde *m* virtuel; univers *m* virtuel
   r виртуальный мир *m*

10298 visibility
   d Visibilität *f*; Sicht *f*; Sichtbarkeit *f*
   f visibilité *f*
   r видимость *f*

10299 visibility domain
   d Sichtgebiet *n*
   f domaine *m* de visibilité
   r область *f* видимости

10300 visibility loss
   d Sichtminderung *f*
   f perte *f* de visibilité
   r потеря *f* видимости; уменьшение *n* видимости

10301 visibility map
   d Sichtkarte *f*
   f carte *f* de visibilité
   r карта *f* видимости

10302 visible
   d sichtbar
   f visible
   r видимый

10303 visible cell
   d sichtbare Zelle *f*
   f cellule *f* visible
   r видимая клетка *f*

10304 visible elements
   d sichtbare Elemente *npl*
   f éléments *mpl* visibles
   r видимые элементы *mpl*

10305 visible light
   d sichtbares Licht *n*
   f lumière *f* visible
   r видимый свет *m*

10306 visible light beam
   d sichtbarer Lichtstrahl *m*
   f rayon *m* de lumière visible
   r видимый световой луч *m*

10307 visible point
   d sichtbarer Punkt *m*
   f point *m* visible
   r видимая точка *f*

10308 visible point sequence

   d sichtbare Punktfolge *f*
   f suite *f* de points visibles
   r последовательность *f* видимых точек

10309 visible range; visible region
   d sichtbarer Bereich *m*; sichtbares Gebiet *n*
   f domaine *m* visible
   r видимая область *f*

* **visible region → 10309**

* **visible signal → 6573**

10310 visible spectrum
   d sichtbares Spektrum *n*
   f spectre *m* visible
   r видимый спектр *m*

10311 vision
   d Vision *f*; Sehen *n*
   f vision *f*
   r [техническое] зрение *n*

10312 vision mixer
   d Vision[s]mixer *m*; Sichtmixer *m*
   f mélangeur *m* d'images
   r смеситель *m* изображений

10313 vision system
   d Sehsystem *n*
   f système *m* de vision
   r система *f* зрения

10314 vision test
   d Sehprüfung *f*
   f essai *m* de vision
   r проверка *f* машинного зрения

10315 visitor viewpoint
   d Besucher-Aug[en]punkt *m*
   f point *m* de vue du visiteur
   r точка *f* взгляда обследователя

10316 vista point
   d Blickpunkt *m*; Durchblickpunkt *m*
   f point *m* de perspective
   r точка *f* перспективы

10317 visual
   d visuell; anschaulich
   f visuel
   r визуальный; наглядный

10318 visual acuity
   d Sehschärfe *f*
   f acuité *f* visuelle
   r визуальная острота *f*

* **visual angle → 389**

10319 visual communication;
videocommunication
- *d* visuelle Kommunikation *f*;
  Videokommunikation *f*
- *f* communication *f* visuelle;
  vidéocommunication *f*
- *r* визуальная коммуникация *f*;
  видеокоммуникация *f*

10320 visual cue; cue
- *d* visueller Referenzpunkt *m*
- *f* point *m* de repère visuel
- *r* визуальный маркер *m*

10321 visual database
- *d* visuelle Datenbasis *f*
- *f* base *f* de données visuelles
- *r* база *f* визуальных данных;
  визуализационная база данных

10322 visual display unit; VDU
(dumb terminals and intelligent terminals)
- *d* visuelles Darstellungsgerät *n*
- *f* unité *f* d'affichage visuel
- *r* устройство *n* визуального представления

10323 visual element
- *d* visuelles Element *n*
- *f* élément *m* visuel
- *r* визуальный элемент *m*

10324 visual fidelity
- *d* visuelle Genauigkeit *f*
- *f* fidélité *f* visuelle
- *r* визуальная точность *f*

* **visual field** → 3737

* **visual forecast** → 10325

10325 visual forecast[ing]
- *d* visuelle Vorhersage *f*
- *f* prédiction *f* visuelle
- *r* визуальное прогнозирование *n*

10326 visualization; viewing
- *d* Visualisierung *f*; Sichtbarmachung *f*
- *f* visualisation *f*; visionnement *m*
- *r* визуализация *f*

10327 visualization algorithm
- *d* Visualisierungsalgorithmus *m*
- *f* algorithme *m* de visualisation
- *r* алгоритм *m* визуализации

10328 visualization application
- *d* Visualisierungsanwendung *f*
- *f* application *f* de visualisation
- *r* приложение *n* визуализации

10329 visualization clock
- *d* Anzeigetakt *m*
- *f* horloge *f* de visualisation
- *r* такт *m* визуализации

10330 visualization hardware
- *d* Visualisierungshardware *f*
- *f* matériel *m* de visualisation
- *r* аппаратное обеспечение *n* визуализации

10331 visualization of combined motion in
human joints
- *d* Darstellung *f* der kombinierten Bewegung der
  menschlichen Gelenke
- *f* visualisation *f* du mouvement combiné des
  articulations humaines
- *r* визуализация *f* комбинированного
  движения человеческих суставов

10332 visualization process sequence
- *d* Visualisierungsprozesskette *f*
- *f* séquence *f* de procédé de visualisation
- *r* последовательность *f* процесса
  визуализации

10333 visualization system
- *d* Visualisierungssystem *n*
- *f* système *m* de visualisation
- *r* визуализационная система *f*

10334 visualization task
- *d* Visualisierungsaufgabe *f*
- *f* tâche *f* de visualisation
- *r* задача *f* визуализации

10335 visualization toolkit; VTK
- *d* Visualisierung-Werkzeugsatz *m*
- *f* kit *m* d'instruments de visualisation
- *r* инструментальный набор *m* визуализации

10336 visual loss
- *d* visueller Verlust *m*
- *f* déperdition *f* visuelle; perte *f* visuelle
- *r* визуальные потери *fpl*

10337 visual perception
- *d* visuelle Wahrnehmung *f*
- *f* perception *f* visuelle
- *r* визуальное восприятие *n*

10338 visual realism
- *d* visueller Realismus *m*
- *f* réalisme *m* visuel
- *r* визуальный реализм *m*

10339 visual reality
- *d* visuelle Realität *f*
- *f* réalité *f* visuelle
- *r* визуальная реальность *f*

* **visual scanner** → 6570

10340 visual selector
   d visuelles Auswahlfeld *n*
   f sélecteur *m* visuel
   r визуальный селектор *m*

* **visual signal** → 6573

10341 visual simulation
   d visuelle Simulation *f*
   f simulation *f* visuelle
   r визуальная симуляция *f*

10342 visual simulation of natural phenomena
   d visuelle Simulation *f* der Naturerscheinungen
   f simulation *f* visuelle de phénomènes naturels
   r визуальная симуляция *f* естественных явлений

10343 visual system
   d visuelles System *n*
   f système *m* visuel
   r визуальная система *f*

* **void** → 990

10344 volume
   d Volumen *n*; Rauminhalt *m*
   f volume *m*
   r объем *m*

* **volume data** → 10350

* **volume element** → 3349

10345 volume hologram
   d Volumenhologramm *n*; dreidimensionales Hologramm *n*
   f hologramme *m* volumétrique
   r объемная голограмма *f*; трехмерная голограмма

10346 volume modeling; space modeling; spatial modeling
   d Volumen-Modellierung *f*; räumliche Modellierung
   f modélisation *f* volumique; modelage *m* spatial
   r объемное моделирование *n*; пространственное моделирование

10347 volume of a parallelepiped
   d Volumen *n* eines Parallelepipeds; Spatinhalt *m*
   f volume *m* d'un parallélépipède
   r объем *m* параллелепипеда

* **volume of computation** → 317

10348 volume of solids

d Körpervolumen *n*
f volume de solides
r объем *m* тел

* **volume pixel** → 3349

10349 volume primitives
   d räumliche Primitivelemente *npl*
   f primitives *fpl* volumétriques
   r объемные примитивы *mpl*; пространственные примитивы

* **volume rendering** → 10352

10350 volumetric data; volume data
   d räumliche Daten *npl*
   f données *fpl* volumétriques
   r объемные данные *npl*; пространственные данные

10351 volumetric light
   d räumliches Licht *n*
   f lumière *f* volumétrique
   r объемный свет *m*

10352 volumetric rendering; volume rendering
   d räumliches Rendering *n*
   f rendu *m* volumétrique
   r объемное тонирование *n*; объемный рендеринг *m*

10353 volumetric shadow
   d räumliches Schatten *n*
   f ombre *f* volumétrique
   r объемная тень *f*

10354 Voronoi diagram
   d Voronoi-Diagramm *n*
   f diagramme *m* de Voronoi
   r диаграмма *f* Вороного

10355 Voronoi edge
   d Voronoi-Kante *f*
   f arête *f* de Voronoi
   r ребро *n* Вороного

10356 Voronoi polygons
   d Voronoi-Polygone *npl*
   f polygones *mpl* de Voronoi
   r многоугольники *mpl* Вороного; полигоны *mpl* Вороного

* **vortex element** → 3350

* **vortex-free motion** → 5293

10357 vortex point; vortical point
   d Wirbelpunkt *m*
   f centre *m* de tourbillon
   r вихревая точка *f*; вихревой центр *m*

10358 vortex ring
 d Wirbelring *m*
 f anneau *m* de tourbillon
 r вихревое кольцо *n*

10359 vortex sheet; vorticity sheet
 d Wirbelschicht *f*; Wirbelband *n*
 f couche *f* tourbillonnaire
 r вихревая полоса *f*; вихревой слой *m*

10360 vortex surface; vorticity surface
 d Wirbelfläche *f*
 f surface *f* de tourbillon[s]; surface-tourbillon *f*
 r вихревая поверхность *f*

10361 vortical; rotational; turbulent
 d wirbelförmig
 f tourbillonnaire
 r вихревой

 * **vortical point** → **10357**

10362 vorticity
 d Wirbelbewegung *f*; Wirbelung *f*
 f tourbillonnement *m*
 r вихрение *n*; вихревое движение *n*

 * **vorticity sheet** → **10359**

 * **vorticity surface** → **10360**

 * **voxel** → **3349**

10363 voxel array
 d Voxel-Feld *n*
 f tableau *m* de pixels 3D
 r массив *m* элементов объема

10364 voxel detection
 d Voxel-Detektion *f*
 f détection *f* de pixel 3D
 r обнаруживание *n* элемента объема

10365 voxel-detection processor
 d Voxel-Detektion-Prozessor *m*
 f processeur *m* de détection de pixels 3D
 r процессор *m* обнаруживания элементов объема

10366 voxel memory
 d Voxel-Speicher *m*
 f mémoire *f* de pixels 3D
 r память *f* элементов объема

 * **VP** → **6210**

10367 VP locked to page
 d Fluchtpunkt *m* gesperrt an der Seite
 f point *m* de fuite verrouillé sur la page

 r нейтральная точка *f*, фиксированная к странице

 * **VR** → **10288**

10368 VR applications
 d Anwendungen *fpl* der virtuellen Realität
 f applications *fpl* de réalité virtuelle
 r приложения *npl* виртуальной реальности

10369 VR cockpit
 d virtuelle Pilotenkanzel *f*
 f poste *f* de pilotage virtuel
 r виртуальная кабина *f* (в самолете)

10370 VR design
 d Design *n* der virtuellen Realität
 f conception *f* de réalité virtuelle
 r проектирование *n* виртуальной реальности

10371 VR design system
 d Projektierungssystem *n* der virtuellen Realität
 f système *m* de conception de réalité virtuelle
 r система *f* проектирования виртуальной реальности

10372 VR dynamic simulator
 d dynamischer Simulator *m* der virtuellen Realität
 f simulateur *m* de réalité virtuelle dynamique
 r динамический симулятор *m* виртуальной реальности

 * **VRML** → **10289**

10373 VR model
 d Modell *n* der virtuellen Realität
 f modèle *m* de réalité virtuelle
 r модель *f* виртуальной реальности

 * **VR protocol** → **10376**

10374 VR system
 d System *n* der virtuellen Realität
 f système *m* à réalité virtuelle
 r система *f* виртуальной реальности

10375 VR technology
 d Technologie *f* der virtuellen Realität
 f technologie *f* de réalité virtuelle
 r технология *f* виртуальной реальности

10376 VR [transfer] protocol
 d Übertragungsprotokoll *n* der virtuellen Realität; Protokoll *n* der virtuellen Realität
 f protocole *m* de transfert de réalité virtuelle
 r протокол *m* [связи] виртуальной реальности

 * **VTK** → **10335**

W

* **waiting line** → 7685

* **walk** → 8540

* **walkthrough** → 9259

10377 wall
(in 3D chart)
d Wand *f*; Mauer *f*
f mur *m*
r стена *f*; граница *f*

10378 wallpaper
d Tapete *f*; Hintergrundmotiv *n*
f papier *m* peint; fond *m* d'écran
r [экранный] фон *m*; обои *pl*

10379 warm tints
d warme Farbtöne *mpl*
f teintes *fpl* chaudes
r теплые тона *mpl*

10380 warning color
d warnende Farbe *f*; Warnfarbe *f*
f couleur *f* d'avertissement
r предупредительный цвет *m*

10381 warp *v*
d verbiegen
f gondoler; gaucher
r искажать; деформировать

10382 warpage; warping
d Verbiegung *f*; Verkrümmung *f*
f gauchissement *m*; déformation *f* [non uniforme]
r деформирование *n*; [неоднородное] искажение *n*

10383 warped model
d verbogenes Modell *n*
f modèle *m* déformé
r деформированная модель *f*

10384 warped surface
d verbogene Fläche *f*; verzogene Fläche; verworfene Fläche
f surface *f* gauchie; surface ourdie
r искаженная поверхность *f*; деформированная поверхность

10385 warp filter
d Warp-Filter *m*

f filtre *m* de gauchissement
r фильтр *m* деформирования

* **warping** → 10382

10386 warping tools
d verwerfende Hilfsmittel *npl*
f outils *mpl* de déformation
r средства *npl* деформирования изображений

10387 water color; aquarelle
d Wasserfarbe *f*; Aquarellfarbe *f*
f aquarelle *f*
r акварель *f*

10388 water droplet model
d Modell *n* der Wassertröpfchen
f modèle *m* de gouttelettes d'eau
r модель *f* водных капелек

10389 watermark
d Wasserzeichen *n*
f filigrane *m*
r водяной знак *m*

10390 watermarked image
d Wasserzeichenbild *n*
f image *f* à filigrane
r изображение *n* с водяным знаком

* **watermark embedding** → 10394

10391 watermark extraction
d Wasserzeichen-Extraktion *f*
f extraction *f* de filigrane
r извлечение *n* водяного знака

10392 watermark generation
d Wasserzeichengenerierung *f*
f génération *f* de filigrane
r генерирование *n* водяного знака

10393 watermarking algorithm
d Wasserzeichenalgorithmus *m*
f algorithme *m* de création de filigrane
r алгоритм *m* изготовления водяного знака

10394 watermark insertion; watermark embedding
d Wasserzeichen-Einbetten *n*
f insertion *f* de filigrane
r вставка *f* водяного знака

10395 watermark intensity
d Wasserzeichen-Intensität *f*
f intensité *f* de filigrane
r интенсивность *f* водяного знака

10396 watermark personalizing
d Wasserzeichen-Personalisierung *f*

f personnification *f* de filigrane
r олицетворение *n* водяного знака

10397 wave
  d Welle *f*
  f onde *f*
  r волна *f*

  * wave → 9669

  * wavelet → 8176

10398 wave shape
  d Wellenform *f*
  f forme *f* d'onde
  r форма *f* волны

10399 wavy lines
  d Wellenlinien *fpl*
  f lignes *fpl* ondulées
  r волнистые линии *fpl*

  * way → 2862, 8228

10400 waypoint
  d Wegpunkt *m*; Wegmarke *f*
  f point *m* de route; point de cheminement
  r точка *f* маршрута

  * WCS → 10471

  * weak sheaf → 8333

10401 wearable computer
  (worn on the body)
  d tragbarer Computer *m*
  f ordinateur *m* vestimentaire; ordinateur corporel
  r переносимый компьютер *m*

10402 Web browser
  d Web-Browser *m*
  f butineur *m* Web
  r Web браузер *m*

10403 Web document
  d Web-Dokument *n*
  f document *m* Web
  r Web документ *m*

10404 Web graphics
  d Web-Grafik *f*
  f graphique *m* Web
  r Web графика *f*

10405 wedge
  d Keil *m*
  f biseau *m*; coin *m*
  r клин *m*

10406 weight
  d Gewicht *n*
  f poids *m*
  r вес *m*

10407 weighted graph
  d gewichteter Graph; bewerteter Graph *m*
  f graphe *m* pondéré
  r взвешенный граф *m*

10408 weight factor
  d Gewichtsfaktor *m*
  f coefficient *m* de pondération; facteur *m* de poids
  r весовой коэффициент *m*; множитель *m* веса

10409 weighting
  d Bewertung *f*
  f pondération *f*
  r взвешивание *n*

  * weld → 4086

10410 weld *v*
  d löten; verlöten; vereinigen
  f souder
  r спаивать; связывать

10411 weld *v* **all**
  d alles verschmelzen
  f tout souder
  r связывать все

  * welding → 4086

10412 wet ink
  d nasse Tinte *f*; nasse Farbe *f*
  f encre *f* humide
  r мокрая печатная краска *f*; влажные чернила *npl*

10413 wet paint effect
  d Nassfarbeneffekt *m*
  f effet *m* de mouillage; effet de peinture humide
  r эффект *m* непросохшей краски

10414 white balance
  d Weißbalance *f*; Weißabgleich *m*
  f balance *f* du blanc
  r баланс *m* белого

10415 white balance adjustment
  d Einstellung *f* der Weißbalance
  f correction *f* de balance du blanc
  r наладка *f* баланса белого

10416 white light
  d weißes Licht *n*; Weißlicht *n*

f lumière *f* blanche
r белый свет *m*

* **white noise** → 4115

10417 white point
d Weißpunkt *m*
f point *m* du blanc
r точка *f* белого

10418 white vector
d Weißvektor *m*
f vecteur *m* blanc
r белый вектор *m*

10419 wide band
d dicker Streifen *m*
f bande *f* large
r широкая лента *f*

10420 wide line; heavy line
d dicke Linie *f*; fette Linie
f ligne *f* large; ligne grasse
r толстая линия *f*; жирная линия

10421 wide polyline
d dicke Polylinie *f*
f polyligne *f* large
r толстая полилиния *f*

10422 widget
d Widget *n*; Trickfenster *n*
f widget *m*
r штучка *f*; штуковина *f*; элемент *m* управления окном

* **width** → 1128

* **wildcard** → 10423

10423 wildcard [character]
d Wildcardzeichen *n*; Stellvertreterzeichen *n*
f caractère *m* générique; caractère de remplacement; caractère de substitution
r подстановочный символ *m*

10424 wind *v*
d wickeln
f enrouler
r гнуться; извиваться; изгибаться; вертеть; поворачивать

* **winding** → 4556

10425 window
d Fenster *n*; Ausschnitt *m*
f fenêtre *f*
r окно *n*

10426 window border

d Fensterrand *m*
f bordure *f* de fenêtre
r граница *f* окна

10427 window commutation
d Fensterkommutierung *f*
f commutation *f* de fenêtres
r переключение *n* окон

10428 windowed environment
d Fensterumgebung *f*
f environnement *m* à fenêtres
r оконная среда *f*

10429 window elements
d Fensterelemente *npl*
f éléments *m* de fenêtre
r элементы *mpl* окна

10430 window frame
d Fensterrahmen *m*
f filet *m* de fenêtre
r рамка *f* окна

10431 window function
d Windowfunktion *f*
f fonction *f* fenêtre
r функция-окно *f*

10432 windowing; fenestration
d Fensterung *f*; Fenstertechnik *f*; Ausschnittsdarstellung *f*
f fenêtrage *m*
r кадрирование *n* [изображения]; организация *f* окон

10433 window list
d Fenstersliste *f*
f liste *f* de fenêtres
r список *m* окон

10434 window menu
d Fenstermenü *n*
f menu *m* fenêtre
r оконное меню *n*

10435 window object
d Fenster-Objekt *n*
f objet *m* fenêtre
r объект *m* типа окна

10436 window polygon
d Fensterpolygon *n*
f polygone *m* de fenêtre
r многоугольник *m* окна

10437 window selection
d Fensterauswahl *f*
f sélection *f* de fenêtre
r выбор *m* окна

10438 **window selection mode**
   d Fensterauswahlmodus *m*
   f mode *m* de sélection de fenêtre
   r режим *m* выбора в окне

10439 **window size**
   d Fenstergröße *f*
   f taille *f* de fenêtre
   r размер *m* окна

10440 **Windows metafile; WMF**
   d Windows-Metadatei *f*; WMF
   f métafichier *m* Windows; WMF
   r Windows метафайл *m*; WMF

10441 **windows programming**
   d Programmierung *f* der Fenster
   f programmation *f* de fenêtres
   r программирование *n* окон

10442 **windows system**
   d Fenstersystem *n*
   f système *m* de fenêtres
   r оконная система *f*

10443 **window tree**
   d Baum *m* der Fenster
   f arbre *m* de fenêtres
   r дерево *n* окон

10444 **window/viewport transformation; viewing transformation**
   d Fenster/Ansichtsfenster-Transformation *f*
   f transformation *f* fenêtre/clôture
   r преобразование *n* окна в область просмотра

   * **winged edge** → 3715

10445 **wire** *v*
   d verdrahten
   f enfiler
   r соединять проводами

10446 **wire**
   d Draht *m*; Leiter *m*
   f fil *m*
   r провод[ник] *m*; жила *f*; проволока *f*

   * **wired glove** → 2481

10447 **wireframe**
   d Drahtrahmen *m*; Wire-Frame *n*
   f fil *m* de fer
   r каркас *m*

   * **wireframe animation** → 8752

10448 **wireframe color**
   d Drahtrahmen-Farbe *f*

   f couleur *f* en fil de fer
   r цвет *m* каркаса

10449 **wireframe display mode**
   d Drahtrahmendarstellungsmodus *m*
   f mode *m* d'affichage fil de fer; mode d'affichage filaire
   r режим *m* каркасного изображения

10450 **wireframe lens**
   d Drahtrahmen-Linse *f*
   f lentille *f* filaire; lentille structurelle
   r каркасная линза *f*

10451 **wireframe line**
   d Drahtrahmenlinie *f*
   f ligne *f* fil de fer
   r каркасная линия *f*

10452 **wireframe model**
   d Drahtrahmenmodell *n*
   f modèle *m* filaire; modèle de type fil de fer; modèle structurel
   r каркасная модель *f*

10453 **wireframe representation**
   d Drahtrahmendarstellung *f*; Wire-Frame-Darstellung *f*
   f représentation *f* fil de fer; représentation filaire
   r каркасное представление *n*

10454 **wireframe view**
   d Drahtrahmen-Ansicht *f*
   f vue *f* fil de fer; vue filaire
   r каркасный вид *m*

10455 **wiring**
   d Verdrahtung *f*
   f câblage *m*
   r прокладка *f*; проводка *f*; межсоединения *npl*

10456 **wizard**
   d Assistent *m*
   f assistant *m*
   r советник *m*; советчик *m*; мастер *m*

   * **WMF** → 10440

10457 **WMF graphics**
   d WMF-Grafik *f*
   f graphique *m* WMF
   r графика *f* формата WMF

   * **word processing** → 9577

   * **word space** → 10458

10458 word spacing; spacing between words; word space
d Wortabstand *m*; Abstand *m* zwischen Wörtern; Wortraum *m*
f intervalle *m* entre les mots; espace *m* entre les mots
r пробел *m* между словами; расстояние *n* между словами

10459 word wrap
d Wortumbruch *m*
f habillage *m* de mot; retour *m* automatique de mot à la ligne
r завертывание *n* слова

10460 work area; workspace; scratch area
d Arbeitsbereich *m*; Arbeitsfeld *n*
f espace *m* de travail; zone *f* de travail; domaine *m* de travail
r рабочая область *f*; рабочая зона *f*

10461 workbook
d Arbeitsheft *n*
f livre *f* de travail
r рабочий журнал *m*

*   **working page → 2351**

10462 working plane
d Arbeitsebene *f*
f plan *m* de travail
r рабочая плоскость *f*

10463 working view
d Arbeitsansicht *f*
f vue *f* de travail
r рабочий вид *n*

*   **working window → 2353**

10464 work session
d Arbeitssitzung *f*
f session *f* de travail
r рабочая сессия *f*

10465 worksheet
d Arbeitsblatt *n*
f feuille *f* de travail
r рабочий лист *m*

10466 worksheet formatting
d Arbeitsblatt-Formatierung *f*
f formatage *m* de feuille de travail
r форматирование *n* рабочего листа

10467 worksheet orientation
d Arbeitsblatt-Orientierung *f*
f orientation *f* de feuille de travail
r ориентация *f* рабочего листа

10468 worksheet splitting
d Arbeitsblatt-Aufteilung *f*
f splittage *m* de feuille de travail
r разделение *n* рабочего листа

10469 worksheet switching
d Durchschaltung *f* der Arbeitsblätter
f commutation *f* de feuilles de travail
r переключение *n* рабочих листов

*   **workspace → 10460**

10470 world coordinate
d Weltkoordinate *f*
f coordonnée *f* universelle
r мировая координата *f*

10471 world coordinate system; WCS; global coordinate system
d Weltkoordinatensystem *n*; globales Koordinatensystem *n*
f système *m* de coordonnées mondial
r мировая координатная система *f*; глобальная система координат

10472 world direction
d Weltrichtung *f*
f direction *f* mondiale
r мировое направление *n*

10473 world map
d Weltkarte *f*
f carte *f* mondiale
r карта *f* мира

10474 world space
d Weltraum *m*
f espace *m* mondial
r мировое пространство *n*

10475 worst-case scenario
d Szenarium *n* der schlechtesten Grenzbedingungen
f scénario *m* en conditions limites
r сценарий *m* наихудших условий

*   **wound → 8837**

10476 wraparound
d Umlauf *m*
f bouclage *m*; retour *m* en boucle
r заворачивание *n*

10477 wrapped image
d Wickelbild *n*; gewickeltes Bild *n*; umhülltes Bild
f image *f* habillée; image vêtue; image entourée; image enveloppée; image enroulée
r окутанное изображение *n*; охваченное изображение

10478 wrapping
    d Umhüllung *f*; Umbruch *m*
    f habillage *m*; emballage *m*; enroulement *m*
    r окутывание *n*; завертывание *n*;
       охватывание *n*; обертка *f*

10479 wrinkle
    d Runzel *f*
    f ride *f*; pli *m*
    r морщина *f*; складка *f*

10480 write *v*; **record** *v*
    d schreiben; einschreiben
    f écrire; enregistrer
    r писать; записывать

10481 write; writing; registration; recording
    d Schreiben *n*; Registrierung *f*
    f écriture *f*; inscription *f*; enregistrement *m*
    r записывание *n*; запись *f*;
       регистрирование *n*

    * writing → **10481**

10482 writing tools
    d Schreibhilfsmittel *npl*
    f outils *mpl* d'enregistrement
    r инструменты *mpl* регистрирования

10483 wysiwyg
    d Was du siehst, bekommst du; Wysiwyg *n*
    f tel écran-tel écrit; tel-tel
    r что видишь, то и получишь (при печати)

10484 wysiwyg program
    d Wysiwyg-Programm *n*
    f programme *m* tel-tel
    r программа *f* wysiwyg

X

10485 X axis
 d X-Achse *f*
 f axe *m* de X; axe des abscisses
 r ось *f* X

10486 X coordinate
 d X-Koordinate *f*
 f coordonnée *f* X
 r X-координата *f*

 * **X-coordinate of a point → 9**

10487 X-cut
 d X-Schnitt *m*; Schnitt *m* auf der X-Achse
 f coupe *f* selon l'axe X
 r срез *m* по оси X

10488 xerocopy
 d Xerokopie *f*
 f xérocopie *f*
 r ксерокопия *f*

10489 xerography; xerox art; electrophotography
 d Xerografie *f*
 f xérographie *f*
 r ксерография *f*

 * **xerox art → 10489**

10490 X-intercept
 d Abschnitt *m* auf der X-Achse
 f segment *m* de l'axe X
 r отрезок *m* оси X

10491 X spacing
 d X-Abstand *m*
 f espacement *m* X
 r расстояние *n* по X

10492 XY chart
 d XY-Diagramm *n*
 f diagramme *m* XY
 r XY диаграмма *f*

10493 XY [coordinate] plotter
 d XY-Koordinatenplotter *m*; XY-Plotter *m*
 f traceur *m* XY; traceur à deux coordonnées; traceur sur axes X et Y
 r двухкоординатный графопостроитель *m*

 * **XY coordinates → 2500**

10494 XY plane
 d XY-Ebene *f*
 f plan *m* XY
 r плоскость *f* XY

 * **XY plotter → 10493**

10495 XYZ axes
 d XYZ-Achsen *fpl*
 f axes *mpl* de XYZ
 r оси *fpl* XYZ

 * **XYZ coordinates → 2501**

 * **XYZ filter → 10496**

10496 XYZ[-point] filter
 d XYZ-Punktfilter *m*; XYZ-Filter *m*
 f filtre *m* [de point] XYZ
 r фильтр *m* [точки] XYZ

10497 XYZ/RGB matrix
 d XYZ/RGB-Matrix *f*
 f matrice *f* XYZ/RGB
 r матрица *f* XYZ/RGB

Y

10498 yaw
 d Gieren *n*
 f lacet *m*; écart *m*
 r отклонение *n* от направления движения;
   рыскание *n*; зазор *m*

10499 yaw *v*
 d gieren
 f faire dévier; faire une embardée
 r отклоняться от курса

10500 Y axis
 d Y-Achse *f*
 f axe *m* de Y; axe des ordonnées
 r ось *f* Y

10501 Y coordinate
 d Y-Koordinate *f*
 f coordonnée *f* Y
 r Y-координата *f*

 * **Y coordinate of a point → 6610**

10502 Y-cut
 d Y-Schnitt *m*; Schnitt *m* auf der Y-Achse
 f coupe *f* selon l'axe Y
 r срез *m* по оси Y

10503 yellow filter
 d Gelbfilter *m*
 f filtre *m* jaune
 r желтый фильтр *m*

10504 Y spacing
 d Y-Abstand *m*
 f espacement *m* Y
 r расстояние *n* по Y

Z

10505 Z aliasing
   d Z-Aliasing *n*
   f Z-crénelage *m*; Z-repliement *m*
   r Z-неровность *f*; Z-ступенчатость *f*

10506 Z axis
   d Z-Achse *f*
   f axe *m* de Z
   r ось *f* Z

10507 Z axis rotate
   d Z-Achse-Drehung *f*
   f rotation *f* d'axe Z
   r ротация *f* оси Z

10508 Z axis vector
   d Z-Achse-Vektor *m*
   f vecteur *m* d'axe Z
   r вектор *m* оси Z

10509 Z buffer; depth buffer
   (of 3D graphics subsystem)
   d Z-Puffer *m*; Puffer *m* der Tiefe
   f mémoire *f* de la troisième dimension;
   Z-buffer *m*; buffer *m* de profondeur
   r Z-буфер *m*; буфер *m* глубины

10510 Z buffer algorithm
   d Z-Puffer-Algorithmus *m*
   f algorithme *m* de Z-buffer
   r алгоритм *m* Z-буфера

10511 Z coordinate
   d Z-Koordinate *f*
   f coordonnée *f* Z
   r Z-координата *f*

   * **zenithal orthomorphic projection** → 9199

10512 zero
   d Null *f*; Nullstelle *f*
   f zéro *m*
   r нуль *m*

10513 zero direction
   d Nullpunktrichtung *f*
   f direction *f* zéro
   r нулевое направление *n*

10514 zero-dispersion
   d Dispersionsnullstelle *f*; Nulldispersion *f*
   f dispersion *f* nulle
   r нулевая дисперсия *f*

10515 Z filter
   d Z-Filter *m*
   f filtre *m* Z
   r Z-фильтр *m*

10516 zigzag
   d Zickzack *n*
   f zigzag *m*
   r зигзаг *m*

10517 zigzag filter
   d Zickzack-Filter *m*
   f filtre *m* zigzag
   r зигзаг-фильтр *m*

10518 zone; area; range
   d Zone *f*; Bereich *m*; Gebiet *n*
   f zone *f*; domaine *m*
   r зона *f*; область *f*; участок *m*

10519 zone of influence; influence zone; area of influence
   d Einflussbereich *m*; Einflusszone *f*
   f zone *f* d'influence
   r зона *f* влияния

   * **zone of sharp focus** → 10520

10520 zone of sharpness; zone of sharp focus
   d Schärfezone *f*
   f zone *f* de netteté
   r зона *f* резкости

10521 zoning
   d Begrenzung *f*; Unterteilung *f* in Zonen
   f zonage *m*
   r зонирование *m*

   * **zoom** → 10529

   * **zoom all** → 4079

10522 zoom box
   d Zoomfeld *n*
   f boîte *f* de zoom
   r рамка *f* трансфокации

10523 zoom center
   d Zoom-Zentrum *n*
   f centre *m* de zoom
   r центр *m* динамического масштабирования

10524 zoom coefficient
   d Zoomkoeffizient *m*
   f coefficient *m* de zoom
   r коэффициент *m* динамического масштабирования

10525 zoom extent
   d Zoomextent *m*

f étendue f de zoom
r расширение n динамического масштабирования

10526 zoom function
d Zoom-Funktion f
f fonction f de zoom
r функция f динамического масштабирования

10527 zoom in
d Vergrößerung f
f zoom m [d'accompagnement] avant
r наезд m; приближение n (изображения)

10528 zoom v in
d Gummilinse zuziehen
f faire un zoom vers gros plan
r раскрывать; распахивать (окно); приближать (изображения); увеличить масштаб

10529 zoom[ing]
d Zoomen n; dynamisches Skalieren n
f variation f de focale; effet m de loupe; zooming m; zoom m
r изменение n масштаба изображения; трансфокация f; наводка f на резкость

10530 zoom-in limit
d Grenze f der Vergrößerung
f limite f de zoom avant
r граница f приближения

10531 zoom-lens
d Zoom-Objektiv n; Gummilinse f
f objectif m de zoom; objectif à focale variable
r объектив m с переменным фокусным расстоянием; трансфокатор m; панкратический объектив

10532 zoom out; unzoom
d Verkleinerung f
f zoom m [d'accompagnement] arrière
r отъезд m (от изображения)

10533 zoom v out; unzoom v
d Gummilinse aufziehen
f faire un zoom vers plan général
r отдалять (изображения); запахивать (окно); уменьшить масштаб

10534 zoom-out limit
d Grenze f der Verkleinerung
f limite f de zoom arrière
r граница f отъезда (от изображения)

10535 zoom previous
d vorhergehendes Zoomen n
f zoom m avant

r предыдущее динамическое масштабирование n

10536 zoom range
d Zoomumfang m
f domaine m de zoom
r охват m масштабирования

10537 zoom window
d Zoom-Fenster n
f fenêtre m de zoom
r окно n масштабирования

10538 zoom zone
(on toolbar)
d Zoom-Bereich m
f zone f de zoom
r зона f масштабирования

10539 ZX cutting plane
d ZX Schnittebene f
f plan m de coupe ZX
r ZX секущая плоскость f

10540 ZX plane
d ZX-Ebene f
f plan m ZX
r плоскость f ZX

Deutsch

Nordlicht 6310
Norm 9136
Normal- 6294
normal 6294
Normalansicht 6309
Normale 6304
normale Abweichung 6295
normale Ansicht 6309
Normalebene 6305
Normalenvektor 6308
normaler Einfall 6298
normaler Schraffurstil 6297
Normalfarbsystem 152
Normalform der Ebenengleichung 4124
Normalform der Geradengleichung 4126
Normalisierung 6299
Normalreflexion 9026
Normalverteilung 6296
Normfarben 7411
Normfarbraum 7412
normierte Gerätekoordinate 6300
normierte Projektionskoordinaten 6302
normierter Modus 9142
normierte Transformation 6303
Normierung 6299
Notation 6311
Note 8356
Nuance 9695
Nukleus 5360
Null 2489, 10512
Nulldispersion 10514
Nullebene 6314
Nullobjekt 6313
Nullpunkt 6315
Nullpunkt des Koordinatensystems 6633
Nullpunktrichtung 10513
Nullpunkttransformation 9832
Nullpunktverschiebung 9832
Nullstelle 10512
Nullstrahl 6316
Nullwert 6317
Numerierung 6320
numerisch 6329
numerische Berechnung 6332
numerische Datenbasis 6335
numerische Fotomontage 2786
numerische Funktion 6338
numerische Kettendaten 6333
numerischer Ausdruck 6336
numerischer Fotospeicher 2785
numerischer Kasten 6331
numerischer Kurvenschreiber 2787
numerisches Display 2770
numerisches Format 6337
numerisches Foto 2784

numerisches Modell 2783
numerisches Video 2795
Nummer 6318
Nutzenfunktion 10093
Nutzer 10081
Nutzfläche 3317
Nutzung 6451, 10080

Obelisk 6339
obere Fläche 9773
obere Grenze 10074
obere Halbebene 10072
obere Hülle 10071
oberer Index 9335
oberer Knoten 9732
oberer Nachbar 8543
Oberfläche 9348
Oberfläche eines Rotationskörpers 553
Oberflächenbehandlung 9385
Oberflächenelement 3345
Oberflächenrauheit 9379
Oberflächenschicht 9361
Oberflächenspannung 9383
Oberflächenstruktur 9381
Oberflächenstück 9374
Oberflächenstück-Anpassung 6887
Oberflächenstück-Normale 9375
Oberflächentextur 9384
Objekt 6340
Objektattribute 6341
Objektaufteilung 6402
Objekt-Auskellern 6388
Objektbehandlung 6362
Objektbreite 6407
Objektbrennebene 4035
Objektbrowser 6342
Objektdaten 6350
Objektdatenfeld 6351
Objekt der realen Welt 7835
Objekte
    sich schneidende ~ 5245
Objektebene 6387
Objekte beschleunigen 44
Objekteigenschaften 6390
Objekteinfügung 6364
Objekterstellung 6348
Objekt-Exportieren 6356
Objektfang 6398
    an anderen Objekten ~ 8847
    an dem Gitter ~ 8848
    an der Richtlinie ~ 8849
    an Objekten ~ 8847
Objektfang-Einrichtung 6675
Objektfang-Modus 6397
Objektfarbe 6345
Objektform 6396
Objektformat 6357
Objektgitter 6358

Objektgriff 6359
Objekt-Größenänderung 6393
Objektgruppierung 6361
Objekthauptebene 7431
Objekthauptpunkt 7432
Objekthöhe 6363
Objektiv 5497
Objektivlinse 6367
Objektivöffnung 467
Objekt-Kellerung 6403
Objektklasse 6343
Objektklassifikator 6344
Objektknotenpunkt 6380
Objektkonjugation 6346
Objekt-Koordinatensystem 6347
Objekt-Linientyp 6368
Objekt-Manager 6352
Objektmarkierung 6365
Objektmessung 6371
Objekt mit einer Textur 9602
Objektmodell 6373
Objekt-Modellierer 6374
Objektmodellierung 6375
Objektmodifizierung 6376
Objektname 6379
objektorientiert 6382
objektorientierte Grafik 6384
objektorientierte grafische Sprache 6383
objektorientierte Plattform 6385
objektorientiertes Rendering-System 6386
Objektorientierung 6381
Objektposition 6389
Objektrasterfang 8848
Objektraum 6401
Objektregenerierung 6391
Objektrotation 8207
Objektschicht 6366
Objektschicht isolieren 5307
Objektschnitt 6349
Objektselektion 6395
Objektskalierung 6394
Objektsortierung 6399
Objekt sperren 5686
Objektstapelung 6403
Objekt strecken 9234
Objekt-Textur 6404
Objekttiefe 6353
Objekttyp 6406
Objektumbenennung 6392
Objektveränderung 6405
Objekt-Vergrößern/Verkleinern 6393
Objektverschiebung 6377
Objektverschiebung 6354
Objektverschmelzung 6372
Objekt-Ziehen 6355
OCR-Schrift 6452
offen 6501

Français

abaissement 5722
aberration 3
aberration chromatique 1471
aberration chromatique
    transversale 9862
aberration horizontale 4681
aberration sphérique oblique 6430
aberration verticale 10155
abolir 6710
abondant 39
abrégé 1
abrègement 2
abréviation 2
abréviature 2
abroger 6710
abscisse 8
abscisse d'un point 9
absence 10
absence de corrélation 11
absolu 12
absorbabilité 33
absorbant 24
absorptance 31
absorption 28
absorption de la lumière 5531
absorption optique 5531
absorption sélective 8475
absorptivité 33
abstraction 37
abstraction de forme 8602
abstraire 35
abstrait 34
accélérateur 47
accélérateur 3D 2448
accélérateur graphique 4302
accélérateur vidéo 10199
accélération 45
accélération 2D 2446
accélération 3D 2447
accélération vidéo 10198
accélérer 40
accélérer des objets 44
accélérer des remplissages 43
accent 49
accent circonflexe 1289
accentuation des contrastes 2156
accentuer 50
acceptabilité 52
accepter 51
accepteur 53
accès 54
accès aléatoire 7729
accès aux données 2468
accès optique 6534
accès rapide 8648
accessibilité 55
accessibilité de point 7207
accessoire 61
accidentel 7728
accolades 2344

accolades indiquées 9294
accoler 3819
accoler du texte 3825
accoler du texte à l'encadré 3826
accoler du texte au tracé 3828
accoler du texte sur un objet 3827
accommodation 65
accommodation de lentille 66
accommoder 64
accouplement 4103
accrochage 353, 8846
accrochage à la grille 4443
accrochage à l'objet le plus
    proche 6173
accrochage à une tangente 9482
accrochage au nœud 6228
accrochage au perpendiculaire
    6978
accrochage au quadrant 7652
accrochage automatique 713
accrochage aux objets 6398
accrochage de décalage 6464
accrochage d'insertion 5124
accrochage d'objet vers d'autres
    objets 8847
accrochage d'objet vers la grille
    8848
accrochage d'objet vers ligne
    directrice 8849
accrochage d'objet vers objets
    8847
accrochage le plus proche 6173
accrochage rapide 7688
accrochage vers intersection 5253
accrocher 8839
accrocher à la grille 8856
accrocher à la ligne conduite
    8857
accrocher à la ligne directrice
    8857
accrocher aux objets 8858
accroissement 5017
accroître 5016
accumulation d'images 4813
accumuler 68
acheminement 8230
acheminement de papier 6779
acheminement heuristique 4585
acheminement par polylignes
    3045
acheminer 3724
acheteur 53
achèvement 9529
achever 1918
achromat 84
achromaticité 83
achromatique 81
achromatisme 87
achromatisme de grossissement
    88

acnode 89
acoustique 90
acousto-optique 92
acquisition de données 2469
acquisition de mouvement 6046
acquisition de scènes 3D 3195
acteur 9432
acteur virtuel 10265
actif 104
actinique 94
actinisme 97
action 98
action de retour 3725
actions d'annulation 9992
activation 103
activer 101
activité 130
actor 9432
actualisable 10061
actualisation 10067
actualisation de hachure 4539
actualiser 10063
actuel 2346
acuité 132
acuité visuelle 10318
acutangle 135
acyclique 138
adaptable 141
adaptateur graphique 4302
adaptatif 141
adaptation 142
adaptation de palette de couleurs
    1796
adaptation des caractères 1429
adapter 140
additif 150
addition 149
additionnel 150
additionner 146
additivité 160
additivité de luminance 161
adhérence 176
adhérent 173
adhérer 172
adhésion 176
adjacence 177
adjacent 178
adjoindre 191
adjoint 192
adjonction 194
admettre 9346
administration 199
admissibilité 200
admissible 201
adoucissement 1051
adressabilité 167
adressable en tous points 284
adressage de nœud 6222
adresse 165
adresse de nœud 6221

carroyage 4444
carte 5782
carte accélératrice 10199
carte couleur personnalisée 2392
carte cubique 2333
carte 2D 3008
carte 3D 3009
carte de base 843
carte de couleurs 1713
carte de couleurs d'arc-en-ciel
    7726
carte de disposition 5460
carte de plan cadastral 6611
carte dérivée 2619
carte de site 8749
carte des réflexions 7939
carte de visibilité 10301
carte en courbes 2133
carte en courbes de niveau 2133
carte en relief 8015
carte géographique 4164
carte graphique 10208
carte graphique 3D 2682
carte-image 1543
carte imagée 1543
carte mondiale 10473
carte schématique 8353
cartes de textures 9613
cartes disposées en mosaïque
    9672
carte sensible 1543
cartésien 1292
carte topographique 9736
carte topologique 5460
carte vidéo 10208
carte vidéo accélérée 10199
cartographe thématique 9632
cartographie 1297
cartographie automatisée 684
cartographie cadastrale 1210
cartographier 5780
cartométrie 1298
cascade 1299, 1300
case 1118, 1307
case à cocher 1451
case de commande 1201
case délimitée 1111
case de saisie multiple 8402
case de saisie simple 6474
case-dialogue 2695
case d'option 1451
case d'un tableau 9446
casque audio stéréo 660
casque de vision 3D 4552
casque de visualisation 4552
casque stéréoscopique 9203
casser 1261, 6710
casse-tête 7640
catalogue 2880
catalogue de bibliothèque 5524

catalogue de système 9436
catalogue d'images 1310
catégorie 1311
caténaire 1312
caténaire hyperbolique 4743
caténoïde 1313
cathète 5490
caustique 1314
cavité 1318
cavité extérieure 3614
cellule 1322, 1323
cellule ajustable 196
cellule bipolaire 942
cellule carrée 9122
cellule circulaire 1493
cellule de demi-teinte 4481
cellule de filtre 3786
cellule de grille 8106
cellule frontière 1092
cellule rectangulaire 7860
cellule topologique 9746
cellule vide 3404
cellule visible 10303
centigrade 1373
centrage 1347
central 1374
centre 1342
centré 1345
centre coloré 1711
centre d'aberration 4
centre de collinéation 1364
centre de courbure 1361
centre de courbure principale
    1366
centre de la gravité 1362
centre de la sphère exinscrite
    3560
centre de l'image 1365
centre de masse 1363
centre de perspective 1364
centre de point de vue 1369
centre de projection 1364
centre de répétition 8067
centre de rotation 1367
centre de symétrie 1368
centre de tourbillon 10357
centre de tourbillonnement 1370
centre de zoom 10523
centre d'homologie 1364
centre du cercle circonscrit 1513
centre du cercle exinscrit 3559
centre du cercle inscrit 4983
centre d'un cercle 1351
centre d'une boule 1350
centre d'une conique 1352
centre d'une ellipse 1354
centre d'une étoile 1360
centre d'une gerbe de plans 1358
centre d'une hyperbole 1353
centre d'un ellipsoïde 1355

centre d'un faisceau 1356
centre d'un faisceau de droites
    1357
centre d'un polygone régulier
    1359
centre géométrique 4169
centre optique 6538
centre perspectif 1364
centre radical 7708
centrer un dessin 1343
centricité 1387
centrode 1388
centroïde 1389
centroïde de groupe 4453
centroïde d'image 4823
cercle 1480
cercle anticrénelé 439
cercle-boussole 1904
cercle circonscrit 1514
cercle de contact 1483
cercle de courbure 1484
cercle de distance 2959
cercle dégénéré 2575
cercle de gorge d'une surface de
    révolution 4258
cercle d'option 7710
cercle exinscrit 3532
cercle exinscrit d'un triangle 3567
cercle focal 3894
cercle géodésique 4153
cercle inscrit 5108
cercle isométrique 5312
cercle oscillateur 1484
cercle rempli 8885
cercles concentriques 2011
cercles conjugués 2058
cercles de Bresenham 1134
cercles disjoints 2904
cercles isométriques
    concentriques 2013
cercles orthogonaux 6644
cercles sécants 8416
cercles tangents 9469
cercle topologique 9747
cercle unité 10023
chaînage 1392
chaînage de points de trame 3055
chaîne 1390, 7080, 9238
chaîne cinématique 5375
chaîne de bits 953
chaîne de caractères Unicode
    10002
chaîne de contrôle 2173
chaîne de côtes 8540
chaîne de direction 2867
chaîne de Markov 5814
chaîne de recherche 8415
chaîne de triangles 1393
chaînette 1312
chaînette hyperbolique 4743

courbe orientée 6622
courbe osculatrice 6670
courbe ouverte 6507
courbe parabolique 6791
courbe paramétrique 6841
courbe paramétrisée 6849
courbe plane 7136
courbe podaire 6920
courbe ponctuelle 7233
courbe projective 7551
courbe rectifiable 7873
courbe régulière 7986
courbe représentative 1439
courbe représentative d'une
    fonction 4390
courbes bitangentes 950
courbes de Bézier rationnelles
    7781
courbes discrètes 2896
courbe sécante 8417
courbes entrelacées 5199
courbe sigmoïde 8677
courbe simple 8702
courbe simple fermée 8701
courbe sinus 8746
courbe sinusoïdale 8746
courbe sinusoïdale ouverte 6515
courbe sinus ouverte 6515
courbes mutuellement entrelacées
    5199
courbes orthogonaux 6646
courbes parallèles 6817
courbe spatiale 8919
courbe spectrale 8992
courbe tangente 9472
courbe tautochrone 9503
courbe trace 9796
courbure 882
courbure constante 2087
courbure de seconde espèce 9778
courbure d'une courbe 2369
courbure externe 3617
courbure géodésique 4155
courbure intrinsèque 5258
courbure moyenne 5864
courbure principale 7422
courbure projective 7550
courbure relative 8008
courbure signé 8682
courbure spécifique 8980
courbure sphérique 9036
courbure tangentielle 4155
couronne 1505
couronne circulaire 1505
couronne circulaire ouverte 6504
couronne ouverte 6504
couronne sphérique 9043
couronne sphérique fermée 1594
couronne sphérique ouverte 6517
cours 8228, 8248

en ~ 2346
couverture 2281
covariance 2277
covariant 2279
CPN 6302
crayon 6925
crayon électronique 5554
crayon lumineux 5554
crayon virtuel 10286
créateur 2289
création 2288
création de demi-teintes 4487
création de grisé numérique 2776
création de modèle 6007
création de terrain 9533
création d'objet 6348
création d'une couleur 1726
créatures virtuelles 10272
créer 2284
créer un modèle 2286
créer un motif 2286
crénage 5362
créneau 8799
crénelage 259
crénelage de plage 7739
crête 6916
crêtes d'histogramme 4645
creux 4652
criblage 8674
critère de fidélité 3732
critère de lissage 8828
critère d'interrogation 7681
crochets 1122, 9120
crochets indiqués 9294
croisé 9860
croisée des fils 2305
croisement 2310, 2323
croiser 5242
croissance 669
croissant 595
croître 5016
croix 2297
    en forme de ~ 2325
croix fermé 1578
croquage 8846
croquis 1044, 8214, 9662
croquis détaillé 2649
croquis minuscule 9662
croustillance 2291
cruciforme 2325
cryptage 3416
cryptoopération 3416
cube 2328
cube à n dimensions 6169
cube couleur 1727
cubique 2329
culbute 9937
cumul 8186
curl 2341
curseur 2354, 8788

curseur adressable 168
curseur clignotant 1019
curseur d'actualisation 10064
curseur de défilement 8400
curseur de fractionnement 9084
curseur de la souris 6070
curseur de réglage 8788
curseur de sélection 8462
curseur matériel 4510
curseur RVB 8147
curviligne 2384
curvilinéaire 2384
cuspide 2388
cyan, magenta, jaune et noir 2419
cyan, magenta et jaune 2418
cyberart 2420
cyberespace 2421
cybermonde 2422
cycle 2423
    sans ~s 138
cycle de balayage 8322
cycle d'imagination 4943
cycle fermé 1586
cyclique 2424
cycloïde 2429
cycloïde allongée 7585
cycloïde elliptique 3374
cycloïde raccourcie 2365
cylindrage 8183
cylindre 2431
cylindre circonscrit 1519
cylindre circulaire 1496
cylindre circulaire oblique 6417
cylindre de projection 7531
cylindre de révolution 2432
cylindre droit 8160
cylindre elliptique 3375
cylindre généralisé 4130
cylindre horizontal 4688
cylindre hyperbolique 4745
cylindre incliné 6422
cylindre parabolique 6792
cylindre solide 8882
cylindre tronqué 9930
cylindre vertical 10163
cylindrique 2433
cylindroïde 2442

2D 9956
    en ~ 9956
3D 9649
    en ~ 9649
dallage 9681
dalle plane 3857
DAO 1972
datum 2484, 2489
datum à une dimension 6472
datum vertical 10164
déballer 10041
débit 9660

émoticône 8806
émouture 8632
empaqueter 6715
empilage automatique 702
empilage d'objet 6403
empilement 6718
empilement de sphères 6719
empirique 3402
emplacement 5679
employer 493
empoigner 1280
empreinte 8679
empreinte digitale 3804
émulateur 3406
émulation 3405
émulsion 3407
encadré de texte 9564
encadreur 3992
encapsulage 1275
encapsuler 3409
encastré 6186
encastrement 6189
encastrement d'image 4852
encastrement d'objets graphiques 4351
encastrer 6185
enchaînement 1392
enclore 3414
encombrement 6451
encrage 5086
encre 5082
encre humide 10412
encrier 5088
endécaèdre 4571
endécagonal 4570
endécagone 4569
endommager 2269
endroit 7120
enduire 8804
enfichable 7200
enfiler 10445
engagement 6451
engagement double 3092
engendrement 4140
engendrer 4136
énigme 7640
enlacement 5203
enlèvement 8028
ennéagone 6244
enregistrement 8232, 8356, 10481
enregistrement d'image 4898
enregistrement d'image simple 8705
enregistrement optique 6566
enregistrement trame 7777
enregistrer 5687, 10480
enregistreur d'images en couleurs 1763
enrichissement 3443
enrobage 1275

enroulement 10478
enroulement de ligne 5648
enrouler 10424
ensemble 8557
ensemble de frontières 1108
ensemble de frontières liées 2275
ensemble de générateurs 3702
ensemble de Mandelbrot 5773
ensemble de pixels 7115
ensemble de sections 2411
ensemble de sélection 7045
ensemble de sélection actif 118
ensemble de sélection de filtrage 3793
ensemble de sélection d'entités 3459
ensemble des images 4913
ensemble des paramètres de traçage 7174
ensemble d'opérations sur objets spatiaux 8965
ensemble non énumérable 6258
ensemble non vide 6257
ensemble projectif 7541
ensemble sélectionné 7045
en-tête 4550
en-tête de colonne 1864
en-tête de page 6731
en-tête de zone 4457
en-tête d'image 4868
entier 3450, 5137
entité 3452, 3453
entité à coter 2822
entité arc 522
entité bloc 1032
entité cercle 1481
entité corps 1056
entité géométrique 3453
entité ligne 5615
entités de base 836
entourage 9388
entourer 9387
entraîné 5069
entraînement 3126
entraînement d'objet 6355
entraînement dynamique 3256
entraîner 3724
entraxe 7082
entrée 3463, 5098
entrée de balayage 8323
entrée de données 2475
entrée de données géométriques 4177
entrée de données graphiques 4317
entrée de données par plume 6922
entrée géométrique 4177
entrée-sortie 5101
entrée vidéo 10213
entrelaçage 5203

entrelaçage de lignes 5621
entrelacement 5203
entrelacement d'audio et vidéo 661
entrelacer 5198
entreprise 3448
entrer 3446
entretien 5761
énumération 3465
enveloppante 3468
enveloppe 3468, 3474, 3467
enveloppe convexe 2200
enveloppe convexe 3D 2506
enveloppe convexe plane 2505
enveloppe de texte 9556
enveloppe d'une famille de courbes planes 3470
enveloppe d'une famille de droites 3469
enveloppe d'une famille de surfaces 3471
enveloppe inférieure 5720
envelopper 2211
enveloppe supérieure 10071
environnement 3475
environnement à fenêtres 10428
environnement de dessin 3142
environnement de développement intégré 5141
environnement de réseau 6195
environnement de système 9437
environnement mélangé 5991
environnement virtuel 10274
environnement virtuel 3D 10273
environnement virtuel à distance 2967
environnement virtuel à grande échelle 5413
environnement virtuel distribué 2984
environnement virtuel partagé 8624
envoyer 8523
envoyer en bas 8524
épaisseur 9640
épaisseur à la moitié 4488
épaisseur de contour 6687
épaisseur de trait 9249
épaisseur d'extrusion 3649
épaississement 9639
épicycloïde 3482
épicycloïde allongée 7587
épicycloïde raccourcie 2366
épine 9648
épitrochoïde 3483
épreuve 640
épurateur 1534
équateur 3493
équateur céleste 1320
équation 3490

lunettes 3D 2678
lunule 5739
lustre 1137
lutin 9111

machine 5740
macro 5742
macrostructure 5743
macrostructure 3D 3006
maculage 8833
maculage d'image 4922
maculature 4106
maculer 8834
magique 5745
magnétisme 8846
maillage par polygones 7278
maillage par polygones 3D 3111
maillage par polygones à formes
    libres 4005
maille 5920
maille 3D 3010
maille d'éléments finis 3808
maille du corps 1058
maille polyface 7273
maille polygonale 7278
maille polygonale torique 9777
maille rectangulaire 7864
maille superficielle 9362
maille surfacique 9362
maille surfacique à base d'arêtes
    3283
maille surfacique tabulée 9460
maille triangulaire 9889
main 4492
    à la ~ 5776
maintenance 5761
main virtuelle 10277
maître 5756
maître de diapositives 8787
majorité 5768
majuscule 10070
majuscules petites 8801
management 5770
management d'erreurs 3526
manche à balai 5350
manette 5350
maniement 4495
manipulation 4495
manipulation de modèle 3D 3018
manipuler 4494
mannequin virtuel 10282
manque 8770
manuel 5775, 5776
mappage 7529
mappage couleur 1781
mappage de couleurs régulier
    7985
mappage de forme 8611
mappage d'environnement
    cubique 2332

mappage de réflexions 7936
mappage de réflexion sphérique
    9057
mappage de texture 9611
mappage de vidéo-image en
    temps réel 7829
mappage d'ombre 8596
mappage photographique en
    couleurs 7015
mappage polaire sphérique 9050
mappage polyvalent transparent
    4075
mappage transparent 9842
mappe 7528
mappé 5792
mapper sur un objet 5803
mappe thématique 9631
mappeur thématique 9632
mapping 7529
maquettage 7609
maquette 9512
maquette de page 6739
maquette de texte 9585
maquette de traçage 7169
maquettes incorporées 1183
maquettes isométriques 5323
marbre 5804
marbrure 6059
marche 8248
marche de rayons 7796
marches d'escalier 5340
marge 5805
marge de référence 7914
marge de reliure 4470
marge d'orientation 6616
marge du bas 1080
marge du haut 10074
marge inférieure 1080
marquage 5811
marquage de point de rotation
    8209
marquage en trait 2466
marquage par éclairage 4635
marque 5809
    sans ~ 10038
marque centrale 1349
marque de fin 3425
marque de fin de paragraphe 6806
marque de guide 4469
marque de paragraphe 6810
marque de recherche 1021
marque d'imprimante 7463
marque-page 1069
marque ponctuelle 3051
marquer 5806
marquer d'accrochage
    automatique 714
marquer de taches 2445
marques de repérage 7980
marqueur 5809

marqueur de couleur pantone
    6774
marqueur de données de sous-
    classe 9276
marqueur de fin 3425
marqueur de point 7216
marqueur de point final 3429
marqueur de texture 9614
marqueur réfléchissant 7942
marque virtuelle 10283
masquage 4614, 5819
masquage de couche 5820
masquage de couleurs 1760
masqué 4596
masque 5816
masque additive 156
masque anti-buée 446
masque circulaire 1499
masque complexe 1933
masque couleur bitmap 958
masque d'aperture 466
masque de fente 8794
masque de grille 4436
masque de projection 7532
masque de texte 9570
masque d'image 4875
masque distincte 8628
masque d'ombrage 8580
masque d'ombre 8580
masque elliptique 3378
masque en couleurs 1782
masque en points 3063
masque non distincte 446
masque numérique 2792
masque photolithographique 7026
masquer 4610, 5817
masque sensible aux couleurs
    1828
masse 5828
masse apparente 3318
masse effective 3318
mat 3224
matage 5851
matériau procédural 7488
matériel 4508, 4509
matériel à texture 9600
matériel 3D 2683
matériel de mappage de texture
    9612
matériel de visualisation 10330
matériel graphique 4335
matériel texturé 9600
matrice 5847
matrice active 112
matrice cellulaire 1337
matrice de couleurs 1700
matrice de covariance 2278
matrice de juxtaposition 2991
matrice de niveau de gris 4411
matrice de pixels 7104

matrice de points 3064
matrice de réflectance 7925
matrice de rotation 8204
matrice des transformations 9821
matrice de Vandermonde
    généralisée 4131
matrice inverse 5266
matrice jacobienne 5339
matrice mosaïque 6039
matrice orthogonale 6651
matrice passive 6879
matrice RGB/XYZ 8148
matrice XYZ/RGB 10497
maximal 5852
maximaliser 5854
maximum 5857
maximum absolu 16
maximum d'intensité 5153
maximum global 16
mécanisme de balayage 8325
mécanisme d'encrage 5084
média 5881
médial 5882
médian 5862
médiane 5884
médiane de cercle 1348
médiane d'un triangle 5887
médiateur 5888
médiatrice 5889
médium 5862, 5894
mégabit 5896
méga-octet 5897
mégapixel 5898
mélange 5995, 8358
mélangé 5990
mélange alpha 288
mélange de couleurs 1787
mélange de couleurs additif 153
mélange de couleurs soustractif
    9315
mélange en temps réel 7816
mélanger 5989
mélangeur 5994
mélangeur de couleurs 1786
mélangeur d'images 10312
membre 5899
membre d'un groupe 5900
mémoire 5901
mémoire de carte graphique 4306
mémoire de la troisième
    dimension 10509
mémoire de pixels 3D 10366
mémoire de textures 9615
mémoire de textures anisotropes
    424
mémoire d'image 3982
mémoire d'images rastres 7764
mémoire vectorielle 10128
mémoire vidéo 10216
mémoire virtuelle 10284

mémorisation 9212
mémoriser 9213
menu 5903
menu à liste directe 7326
menu arborescent 9870
menu barre 829
menu cascade 1304
menu contextuel 2111
menu d'aide 4563
menu d'assistance 4563
menu de base 844
menu d'écran 8376
menu de curseur 2359
menu de dimension 2832
menu d'édition 3311
menu de navigation 6165
menu de racine 5759
menu déroulant 7633
menu de tablette 9452
menu de tracement 3171
menu en cascade 1304
menu en incrustation 7326
menu fenêtre 10434
menu flottant 3867
menu hiérarchique 4618
menu iconique 4785
menu personnalisé 2402
menu principal 5759
menu relevant 7326
menu superposable 7326
menu système 9439
méridien 5919
message 5925
message d'erreur 3527
messages de visionnement 10234
mesurage 5869
mesurage d'angles 4257
mesurage d'objets 6371
mesurage spectrale 9005
mesure 5867
mesure angulaire 5871
mesure approximative 506
mesure d'angle 5871
mesure d'asymétrie 5878
mesure de dispersion 5874
mesure de dissymétrie 5878
mesure de kurtosis 5875
mesure de longueur 5876
mesure de position 5877
mesure des angles 4257
mesure des coordonnées 2226
mesure des directions 2874
mesure d'un angle en degrés 5872
mesure d'un angle en radians
    5873
mesure en degrés 4270
mesure en radians 7701
mesure optique 6559
mesures d'arc 534
mesure spectrale 9004

métafichier 5926
métafichier d'infographie 1982
métafichier Windows 10440
métagraphe 5927
métalangage hypertexte 4769
méta-modèle 5929
métamorphose 5930
métaphore 5932
métaphore d'un visage 3662
méthode 5933
méthode analytique 339
méthode approximative 5934
méthode booléenne 1071
méthode cinématique 5377
méthode d'actualisation 10065
méthode d'approximation 5934
méthode de balayage 8328
méthode d'échantillonnage 8267
méthode d'échantillonnage par
    points 3067
méthode de correspondance de
    couleurs 1784
méthode de décalage 6462
méthode d'effaçage 1539
méthode de hachure 4535
méthode de mappage 5795
méthode de parallélogramme
    6827
méthode de Phong 7007
méthode de raytracing 7795
méthode de reproduction de
    couleurs 1817
méthode de rotation 8197
méthode des coordonnées 2227
méthode de sélection 5935
méthode des gradients 4280
méthode des moindres carrés
    5473
méthode des moyennes 735
méthode de splittage 9088
méthode d'exploration d'images
    7060
méthode d'illumination 5677
méthode d'importation 4967
méthode d'interpolation 5232
méthode d'interrogation 5103
méthode d'itération 5335
méthode du centrage 735
méthode du col 8255
méthode graphique 4347
méthode itérative 5335
méthodologie de simulation 8720
mètre de brillance 1141
mètre de luminance 5733
métrique angulaire 398
métrique euclidienne 3542
métrique projective 7564
mettre au point 263
mettre en évidence 4630
mettre en évidence de menu 4636

réfraction non linéaire 6271
réfractomètre 7961
réfrangibilité 7960
refuser 7996
regagner 7849
regard 8675
régénération 7971
régénération automatique 699
régénération d'image 4897
régénération d'objet 6391
régénérer 7968
régénérer une texture 7970
régime 6000
régime de couleurs RVB 8140
région 7972
région active 116
régionalisation 7973
région circulaire 1504
région 3D 3173
région de découpage 1565
région de la lumière 5560
région de mélange 1010
région de mise à jour 10066
région de spectre 9007
région en trait 2465
région fermée 1593
région hachurée 8570
régions composées 1947
régions coplanaires 2241
régions non coplanaires 6250
registre 1307, 7977
registre inférieur 5719
réglage 7989
réglage automatique du contraste
    691
réglage du blanc 1709
règle 8243, 8245
règle de calcul 1215
règle de la main droite 8164
règle de la section dorée 4255
règle de mouvement 6076
règle d'or 4252
règle du nombre d'or 4255
règle du tire-bouchon 8164
règle en incrustation 7328
règle flottante 3870
règle graduée 4286
règle horizontale 4706
régler 195
réglette 8788
règle verticale 10184
régression 7982
régression linéaire 5601
régularisation 7989
régularité 7988
régularité de motif 6907
régulation 7989
régulation de caméra 1235
régulier 7983
réinitialiser 8095

rejet 7997
rejet de cadre 3995
rejet d'image 4899
rejeter 1261, 7996
relâchement par bouton de la
    souris 6069
relatif 8002
relation 7999, 8001
relation affine 6984
relation de dualité 3221
relation d'homogénéité 4665
relation mutuelle 8001
relation mutuelle géométrique
    4196
relation perspective affine 6984
relaxation 8012
relaxation stochastique 9211
relevant 7323
reléveateur 5680
reléveateur de coordonnées 5680
relief 8014
relief apparent 478
relief en courbes de niveau 8077
relief en hachures 8078
relief par contraste de luminosité
    1143
reliure 5655
relocation 8022
relogeabilité 7331
relogeable 7332
relogement 8022
rémanence 6981
remappage 8023
remarque 8024
remédier 8062
remettre 7849
remettre en forme 8096
remise 8110
remise en état 8110
remplaçable 7200
remplacement 8071
remplacement de composant de
    gris 4404
remplacer 8068
remplacer de couleur 8069
remplacer de text 8073
remplacer un filtre de couleur
    8070
rempli 3759
rempli graduellement 4282
remplir 3756
remplissage 3767, 6720
remplissage conique 2050
remplissage de carré 9123
remplissage de cellule 1328
remplissage de l'intervalle de
    temps entre les trames 5184
remplissage de polygones 7287
remplissage de régions 7974
remplissage de solide

quadrilatéral 7661
remplissage de texture PostScript
    7363
remplissage de trace 9798
remplissage de zones 7974
remplissage d'image vectorielle
    10131
remplissage double 3233
remplissage favori 3714
remplissage graduel 4277
remplissage interactif 5165
remplissage interpolé 5230
remplissage linéaire 5589
remplissage non associatif 6245
remplissage par défaut 2549
remplissage par dégradé 3953
remplissage par dégradé prédéfini
    7396
remplissage par entraînement
    3770
remplissage par hachure 4532
remplissage par inondation 3874
remplissage par motif 6901
remplissage par motif bitmap à
    deux couleurs 9950
remplissage radial 7696
remplissages à plein couleur 4056
remplissages en drapeaux 3128
remplissage solide 8883
remplissage standard 2549
remplissage texturiel 9597
remplissage uni 10012
remplissage uniforme 10012
remuer 6074
rendement 9660
rendement en radiation 7702
rendre 8034
rendu 8046
rendu affin 226
rendu couleur 1813
rendu de polygones 7295
rendu de segment linéaire 5634
rendu de tonalité 9712
rendu d'image 4900
rendu d'objet dynamique 3261
rendu d'objets gazeux 4109
rendu du métal 5928
rendu en couleurs 1813
rendu en temps réel 7825
rendu lancé de rayons 7792
rendu photoréaliste 7031
rendu pixel 7113
rendu plat 3853
rendu triangulaire 9881
rendu volumétrique 10352
renflement 1187
renommer 8032
renommer une page 8033
renversant l'orientation 6618
renversé 8123

squelettique 8751
stabilité 9128
stabilité de la lumière 5569
stabilité d'image 4926
stable 9129
stade 9132
standard 2546, 9136
standard d'affichage 2945
standard de conception 3119
standard de dessin 9139
standards graphiques 4375
station de travail graphique 1983
stationnaire 9171
statique 9171
statistique 9179, 9183
statistique de couleurs 1845
statistique de texte 9583
statistique topologique 9770
statut 9169
stencil 9189
stencils de base 853
stéradian 9194
stéréo animé 6083
stéréo binoculaire 937
stéréocaméra 9195
stéréo en mouvement 6083
stéréogramme 9196
stéréographique 9197
stéréophoto 9201
stéréophotographie 9201
stéréoscopie 9206
stéréoscopique 9202
stéréovue 9208
stochastique 7728
stock 8065
stockage 9212
stocker 9213
stop 4491
strate 5517
stratégie 9223
stratégie de recherche 8410
stratégie de sélection des points
     de vue 9224
stratégies d'écartement 2340
stratégies de simplification 8714
stratification 9225
strict 9235
strophoïde 9251
strophoïde oblique 6433
structural 9252
structure 9255
structure abstraite fonctionnelle
     36
structure alvéolée 4678
structure arborescente 9871
structure d'arbre 9871
structure de base 854
structure de cellule régulière 7984
structure de document 3039
structure de données 5061

structure de la surface 9381
structure de liens et de nœuds
     5649
structure d'incidence 4987
structure d'information 5061
structure du menu 5912
structure en chaîne 1394
structure en grappes 1610
structure fermée 1596
structure filaire anticrénelée 443
structure inférieure 5973
structure latérale 5431
structure logique 5698
structure mineure 5973
structures infinies 5054
structure topologique 9760
studio 9261
studio de monde réel 7836
studio virtuel 10293
style 9264
style actif 122
style 3D 3213
style de bordure 1077
style de cotation 2835
style de cotation actif 105
style de cote 2835
style de cote actif 105
style de cote fils 1456
style de couleur 1846
style de hachure 4547
style de hachure normal 6297
style de jeu de caractères 9963
style de layout 5462
style de ligne 5638
style de multiligne 6109
style de point 7229
style de police graphique 4332
style de remplissage 3779
style des enveloppes 3472
style des étiquettes 5391
style de texte 9584
style de texte actif 123
style de tracement 3164
style de types 1417
style d'impression 7476
style externe de hachure 6678
style graphique 4380
style graphique par défaut 2550
stylo 3954, 6921
stylo magique 5747
subdivision 9278
subdivision de triangle à base
     d'arêtes 3281
subséquent 9299
substituer 8068
substitueur 8072
substitueur de couleur 1814
substitution 9305
substitution de couleur 1816
substrat 9306

successif 9324
succession 9323
suffixation 9327
suffixe 9326
suite 8539
suite de points 8541
suite de points visibles 10308
suivi 9804
suivre 9810
super-échantillonnage 9334
superposable 9330
superposer 6713, 9331
superposition 6704, 9333
superstructure 9336
supertrame 6093
supplément 9337
supplément par option 6591
support 1290, 1357, 1358
support de plume 6924
supporter 9340
supposer 9346
suppression 8028, 9347
suppression de sommet 10147
supprimer 1261
supprimer le bruit 8031
supprimer les lignes cachées 8030
supprimer une face 8029
supremum 5474
supremum essentiel 3535
surbrillance 1135
     en ~ 4631
surcharger 6705
suréchantillonnage 6712
sûreté 8443
surfaçage 3684
surface 9348
surface à courbure constante 9367
surface à haut 10076
surface analytique 341
surface annulaire 436
surface à symétrie de révolution
     9371
surface balayée 8311
surface bicubique 909
surface bilatérale 9959
surface B-spline 1174
surface B-spline rationnelle non
     uniforme 6293
surface cachée 4606
surface centrale 1385
surface complexe 1937
surface concave 2002
surface conique 2052
surface connexe 2071
surface convergente 2179
surface courbée 2374
surface cylindrique 2440
surface d'affichage 2946
surface d'arête 3298
surface de base 855

volume 10344
volume de calcul 317
volume de solides 10348
volume de vue 10259
volume d'irradiance 5281
volume d'un parallélépipède 10347
voûte 3048
voyant 247
vrai 9921
vraie forme 9926
vrillage 9946
vue 8675, 10226
vue abrégée 7
vue aérienne 214
vue améliorée 3442
vue arborescente 9872
vue arrière 7840
vue auxiliaire 728
vue à vol d'oiseau 944
vue 2D 3238
vue 3D 3239
vue 3D interactive 2848
vue d'arbre 9872
vue d'ébauche 3121
vue décomposée 3582
vue de côté droit 8172
vue de côté gauche 5486
vue d'écran 8389
vue de demi-section 4478
vue de derrière 3434
vue de hausse 10078
vue de la caméra 1257
vue de liste 5666
vue de plan rapprochée 1601
vue de pleine face 4060
vue de profil 7507
vue de scènes 8347
vue de travail 10463
vue diagonale 2693
vue du bas 1086
vue dynamique 3269
vue dynamique 3D 2521
vue éclatée 3582
vue en coupe 8433
vue fantôme 7003
vue filaire 10454
vue fil de fer 10454
vue frontale 4041
vue géographique 4165
vue isométrique 5325
vue latérale 8672
vue nommée 6148
vue normale 6309
vue orthogonale 6660
vue orthographique 6662
vue panoramique 6771
vue plane 7151
vue rapide 7689
vue rapprochée 1601

vue réduite 7899
vue renversée 10078
vues en correspondance 2268
vues en opposition 6531
vues multidimensionnelles 6092
vues partielles 6869
vues spéciaux 8976
vue synoptique 6714
vue topographique 9742
vue transversale 8433

widget 10422
WMF 10440

xérocopie 10488
xérographie 10489

Z-buffer 10509
Z-buffer à virgule flottante 3869
Z-buffer non linéaire 6273
Z-crénelage 10505
zéro 10512
zéro structurel 7121
zéro teneur de place 7121
zigzag 10516
zonage 10521
zone 10518
zone adressable en tous points 285
zone à main levée 4007
zone brusque 8626
zone claire 5533
zone cliquable 4718
zone d'accrochage 354
zone d'aperçu 7405
zone de couleur 1696
zone de coupage 2294
zone de Delaunay 2587
zone de diffraction 2736
zone de diffusion 2755
zone de forme libre 4003
zone de groupe 4452
zone de liste déroulante 1876, 5664
zone de liste déroulante fixe 3180
zone de liste déroulante horizontale 4700
zone de liste déroulante modifiable 3181
zone de liste déroulante verticale 10176
zone de mémoire d'image 3982
zone de menu de tablette 9453
zone de netteté 10520
zone d'entrée 2476
zone de prévisualisation 7405
zone de proximité 7612
zone de saisie 2476
zone de sauvegarde 8275
zone de sélection de couleur 1825

zone d'étendue 3601
zone détériorée 2450
zone de texte 6474
zone de texte multiligne 8402
zone de texte simple ligne 6474
zone de tolérance 9707
zone de tolérance projective 7519
zone de traçage 7189
zone de travail 10460
zone de zoom 10538
zone diffusée 2755
zone d'image 7054
zone d'influence 10519
zone d'objet courant 2349
zone d'ombre 8599
zone elliptique 3369
zone émissive 3401
zone fermée 1582
zone imprimable 7443
zone intérieure 5189
zone lisse 8813
zone lumineuse 5736
zone neutre 6205
zone rectangulaire 7856
zones chaotiques 1407
zones de Brillouin 1148
zone sensible 4718
zones marquées 5808
zone sombre 2459
zone sphérique 9062
zone tampon 1177
zoom 10529
zoom avant 10535
zoom axé sur la superficie 545
zoom continu 2127
zoom arrière 10532
zoom avant 10527
zoom d'accompagnement arrière 10532
zoom d'accompagnement avant 10527
zoom de caméra 1260
zoom d'image 4936
zoom dynamique 3271
zoom en temps réel 7833
zooming 10529
zoom numérique 2799
zoom panoramique 6772
zoom rapide 3712
zoom total 4079
Z-repliement 10505

Русский